MINOR HISTORICAL WRITINGS

MINOR
HISTORICAL WRITINGS
and Other Essays

By

HENRY CHARLES LEA

Edited by

ARTHUR C. HOWLAND

KENNIKAT PRESS
Port Washington, N. Y./London

MINOR HISTORICAL WRITINGS

Copyright 1942 by University of Pennsylvania Press
Reissued in 1971 by Kennikat Press by arrangement
Library of Congress Catalog Card No: 74-132087
ISBN 0-8046-1415-6

Manufactured by Taylor Publishing Company   Dallas, Texas

ESSAY AND GENERAL LITERATURE INDEX REPRINT SERIES

CONTENTS

	Page
Foreword by *Arthur C. Howland*	vii

HISTORICAL STUDIES: GENERAL

Witch Persecutions in Transalpine Europe, Sixteenth to Eighteenth Centuries	3
Ethical Values in History	56

HISTORICAL STUDIES: THE INQUISITION

Canonization of San Pedro Arbués	71
Die Inquisition von Toledo, 1575-1610	75
The Spanish Inquisition as an Alienist	83

HISTORICAL STUDIES: THE CHURCH

The Absolution Formula of the Templars	97
The Taxes of the Papal Penitentiary	113
The Ecclesiastical Treatment of Usury	129
The Dead Hand	152
Occult Compensation	169
Is There a Roman Catholic Church?	187

HISTORICAL STUDIES: SPANISH HISTORY

Spanish Experiments in Coinage	203
The Decadence of Spain	220
The Indian Policy of Spain	234

CONTEMPORARY (NINETEENTH CENTURY) CHURCH AFFAIRS

The Religious Reform Movement in Italy	267
Monks and Nuns in France	288
Key Notes from Rome	300
Catholicism and Politics	313
An Anti-Masonic Mystification	316

PUBLIC INTERESTS

Bible View of Polygamy	331
Municipal Government	337
International Copyright	344
The Policy of Insurance	352

Page

Fetichism in Politics   355
The Increase of Crime, and Positivist Criminology   360

BOOK REVIEWS
Du Cange: *Glossarium*   371
Güterbock: *Bracton and His Relation to the Roman Law*   374
Lagrèze: *Histoire du Droit dans les Pyrénées*   377
Schottmüller: *Der Untergang des Templer-Ordens*   381
Gmelin: *Schuld oder Unschuld des Templerordens*   387
Reusch: *Der Index der verbotenen Bücher*   391

YOUTHFUL SCIENTIFIC WRITINGS
Remarks Upon an Examination of the Peroxide of Manganese   401
Description of Some New Species of Marine Shells Inhabiting the
    Coast of the United States   407

LIST OF ARTICLES LATER INCORPORATED IN LEA'S
    HISTORICAL WORKS   413

FOREWORD

Mr. Lea's career as a productive scholar extended over a space of sixty-eight years, from 1841 to 1909. During the first forty years of this period he was also engaged in active business life whereby he greatly augmented the modest fortune inherited from his father. The results of his researches, at first in natural science and later and more extensively in history, are to be found in seven papers published in leading scientific journals; in thirty-four historical articles appearing in various learned reviews; in a chapter entitled "The Eve of the Reformation," contributed to the *Cambridge Modern History* (Vol. I, ch. 19); and in ten historical works comprising a total of seventeen volumes. At the time of his death he was engaged in researches preparatory to writing a history of witchcraft and the notes and material thus collected have since been published in three volumes (University of Pennsylvania Press, 1939).

Lea began to publish the results of original investigation at the age of sixteen, when there appeared in the pages of Silliman's *Journal* (*The American Journal of Science and Art*) for 1841 two articles, the first dealing with his analysis of the peroxide of manganese, and the second describing certain new species of fossil shells found in the eocene deposits of Alabama. The next seven years saw the publication of six other papers on mollusks, three relating to fossil shells and three describing still living forms. Other intellectual interests were at the same time attracting his attention. Between the ages of sixteen and twenty-three he found time to translate into English verse the odes of Anacreon and certain other short poems from the Greek; and to publish, mostly in the pages of *The Southern Literary Messenger*, eight critical essays on contemporary poets and six studies in literary history.

These scholarly pursuits, carried on at an age when most young students are content merely to absorb the learning of others, occupied but a portion of his time, for in 1843, at the age of eighteen, he began the business side of his career as clerk in the old publishing house of Lea and Blanchard, in which his father was senior partner. Here he spent the long working days of the period in learning the details of the business, leaving for research and writing only the evening and early morning hours. The demands of this double life on a naturally frail constitution led in 1847 to a physical breakdown threatening permanent invalidism. On his recovery his physician's orders forced him to choose between business and scholarship, and from a sense of family obligation he reluctantly chose the former. His scientific work was dropped, temporarily as he thought at the time, but permanently as it turned out; and during the next ten years he devoted his energies to the publishing business with such good effect that on the retirement of his father in 1851 he was admitted to the firm as junior partner and thereafter gradually assumed direction of its policy. In 1865 on the retirement of the other partner he became sole owner and director of the firm, by which time it had become, due largely to his management, the leading medical publishing house of the country. He remained head of the firm until 1880 when its active control was handed over to his son and he was thereafter free to devote his days, as well as his evenings, to the historical research which had meanwhile become his chief avocation.

The transfer of Lea's interest from science and literature to medieval history was the almost accidental result of the breakdown of his health in 1847. Forced to abandon scientific research in order to conserve his strength, he found relaxation from business cares and satisfaction of intellectual curiosity by a course of reading in the medieval French chronicles. To these he devoted his evenings and was soon faced with the problem of their reliability and the extent to which their statements could be trusted. To satisfy himself on these points he began the collection and study of other source material for the Middle Ages and thus laid the foundations of the great medieval library which at his death passed to the University of Pennsylvania. For some ten years Lea's leisure hours were devoted to historical research, the results of which began to appear between 1858 and 1861 in the pages of the *North American Review* as a series of book reviews which were, in reality, monographs on certain aspects of medieval history.

Then came the Civil War, which left little time for learned investigations. Outside of business hours his energies were devoted to the public service. He played an active part in the raising and equipping of volunteers, became an active member of various committees, commissions, and patriotic organizations and, as member of the Board of Publications of the Union League, wrote many pamphlets and broadsides to arouse and direct public opinion. After the close of the war Lea again turned to historical pursuits, publishing his first book, *Superstition and Force,* in 1866, his *History of Sacerdotal Celibacy* in 1867 and *Studies in Church History* in 1869. These three books appearing in such quick succession indicate not only the thorough scholarly researches of the preceding twenty years, but likewise the main fields of interest to which the author devoted himself for the remainder of his life—legal institutions and the medieval church, both finding expression in his *Inquisition of the Middle Ages,* which appeared in 1888.

Though his daytime hours were, until 1880, devoted to business affairs and most of his evenings to historical research, Lea took an active part in the public life of the day, as is attested by the list of 116 articles and pamphlets dealing with contemporary affairs which are listed in the bibliography appended to Dr. Bradley's life of Lea.[1] These items include discussions of state and national politics and illustrate his active participation in movements to secure civil service reform, to uncover and suppress the corruptions of city government, especially in Philadelphia, and to promote important legislation in the public interest. Lea is credited with the leading part in overthrowing the infamous "Gas Ring" which for many years dominated and mismanaged the government of his native city; and it was his judgment and leadership which finally secured the passage of the first international copyright law in this country, the Chace bill, which he drew up and which, after many years of agitation, he saw enacted into law in 1891.

The collection of essays and studies published in the present volume contains all of Lea's minor historical writings not later incorporated in his larger works, including an unpublished excursus on witch persecutions in transalpine Europe originally intended for inclusion in his *History of the Inquisition of Spain*, but omitted for lack of space (see Burr's Introduction to the excursus in the present volume). Following the historical studies come articles dealing with various aspects of the modern Catholic church—matters of interest at the time of their publication though of less importance at the present time. These are followed by discussions of social and political topics indicating the scholar's close contact with the life of the community. A few of his many book reviews have also been included as examples of the conscientious manner in which he responded to this demand upon his time. Finally, two of Lea's youthful scientific papers are here reprinted to suggest how promising a career in that field was abandoned in favor of historical research.

ARTHUR C. HOWLAND

Lea Library
University of Pennsylvania
January 9, 1942

[1] For a full list of Lea's writings see the excellent biography by E. S. Bradley: *Henry Charles Lea* (Philadelphia, 1931), pp. 365-81.

HISTORICAL STUDIES

General

THE WITCH PERSECUTIONS IN
TRANSALPINE EUROPE*

Sixteenth to Eighteenth Centuries

INTRODUCTION BY GEORGE L. BURR

THIS SKETCH of the history of witch persecutions in transalpine Europe from the sixteenth century to the eighteenth was prepared by Mr. Lea for insertion in his *History of the Inquisition of Spain*—its object being "to bring out the comparative tolerance of the Inquisition." "It is a very curious fact," he wrote me, "which I have nowhere seen recognized, that in both Spain and Italy the Holy Office took a decidedly sceptical attitude with regard to the Sabbat and the Cap. *Episcopi*, that preserved those lands from the madness prevailing elsewhere. I have a good many original documents that place this in a clear light and I think will prove a surprise to the demonologists."

These documents were duly cited,[1] but the *Inquisition of Spain* proved to have no room for the excursus on witch persecution in transalpine Europe. "I hope eventually," he wrote me (April 6, 1905), "to gather up a little volume of essays in which it can find a place." Such a place it now finds; and its readers should be reminded that the best introduction to it is to be found in Mr. Lea's chapter on "Witchcraft" in his *Inquisition of Spain*.[2] That chapter, however, tells us little about the Inquisition of Italy—"the Inquisition Roman and universal." To Mr. Lea, as to all other investigators—even the Catholic—the archives of the Roman Inquisition remained closed. But in 1912, three years after Mr. Lea's death, a Catholic scholar—Ludwig von Pastor, the historian of the papacy—who had knocked at those doors in vain despite the backing of Pope Leo XIII, gave himself the satisfaction of printing in the *Historisches Jahrbuch* of the Görres-Gesellschaft[3] such scraps of the sixteenth-century legislation of the Holy Office as he had nevertheless gleaned; and among these, else from manuscripts, he included passages from one old book which was, he said, "so rare as to be almost a manuscript." This was the folio volume, *De inconstantia in jure admittenda vel non,* published in his old age (1683) by Cardinal Francesco Albizzi (1593-1684), long guiding spirit of the Roman Inquisition. It was meant, Pastor tells us,

---

* An excursus originally intended for inclusion in the *History of the Inquisition of Spain*, following Chapter ix of Book VIII. Additional notes to this excursus are by Professor George L. Burr (signed ."B").

[1] *Inquisition of Spain*, IV, 206-47.

[2] Bk. VIII, ch. ix.

[3] Vol. XXXIII, 479-549.

3

only for the private use of the Inquisition itself; and Moroni, who had
been a papal chamberlain, tells us in his ecclesiastico-historical dictionary
how it was given out only to the cardinals and the consultors of the
Inquisition and was recalled at the death or retirement of each.[4] Reusch,
in his volumes on the Index,[5] thinks no copy ever crossed the Alps, and
with Moroni counts false the imprint "Amstelaedami," believing it
printed at Rome. Pastor could find a copy in but one Roman library
(the Casanatensian), and that an incomplete one, but was lent one by
the Roman antiquary Bocca.

Mr. Lea seems never to have had access to the work; but in 1919 I was
so happy as to secure Bocca's copy for the White Historical Library at
Cornell,[6] and so interesting is what it tells of the Roman Inquisition's
attitude toward the witch-sabbat that it deserves here a few lines. No
more, of course, than the Inquisition of Spain did the Roman Inquisition
question that the witch-sabbat or the flight to it *could* be real or *were*
often real. Both these it firmly maintained. But not less firmly it maintained that these could be, and often were, mere illusion, and that Satan
delighted in deluding his victims into falsely accusing their neighbors.
Albizzi tells us, too (in cap. xxxii of Tom. I of his *De Inconstantia in
Fide*, which makes up nearly all his volume):

What it is practical to know is that the deposition of a witch that she has
seen at the witch-sabbat women or men is not, in the courts of the Holy Inquisition in Italy, accorded attention to the effect of proceeding against them.
For, although it is perhaps the more common opinion that witches are transported bodily from place to place and to the nocturnal assemblies [and he
cites many authorities], and though Lessius [and others] pronounce the
contrary opinion to be false and pernicious to the commonweal. . . . Nevertheless, since often these are not transported to the witch-sabbat, save only
by illusion and in fancy, as the afore-cited Doctors admit, not only in the
Suprema is the opinion not observed that the testimony of two witches
creates an *indicium ad torturam*, as Martin del Rio maintains, who is refuted
by Farinacci [and others]; but this does not suffice for even an *indicium ad
inquirendum*.[7] . . . Also that, when witches assert that at the witch-sabbat

---

[4] Moroni, *Dizionario di Erudizione Storico-Ecclesiastica*, XVI, 228.

[5] Vol. I, 434 (Bonn, 1883).

[6] And later have even been so fortunate as to pick up two more copies, one of which I
have gladly given to the Lea Library at the University of Pennsylvania. As two of my three
bear evidence of having been in the significant custody of the Gregorian university at Rome,
it is possible that the book is now being granted a wider diffusion.

[7] "Quod spectat ad praxim sciendum est, quod depositio Sagae, se vidisse ad locum
ludi chorearum, vel sacrificii mulieres, vel homines, non attenditur in Tribunalibus Sanctae
Inquisitionis Italiae ad effectum procedendi contra illas. Licet enim fortasse sit communior
opinio, quod Striges corporaliter transferantur de loco ad locum, et ad conventus nocturnos.
. . . Et opinionem contrariam esse falsam et Reipublicae perniciosam dicit Lessius [et al.].
. . . Nihilominus cum saepe saepius corporaliter non ferantur ad Conventus, sed fiant

they have seen such and such persons, it is not to be given credence to any effect whatever against them, because these are held to be illusions as has several times been resolved by the Suprema, etc., but especially in a decision at Farrara, 12 November 1594, and in another at Fermi, 4 February 1595. And with these is ended the conflict of opinions among the Doctors.[8]

It is on this account [he adds], that was always disapproved the practice of the courts of Germany, whether ecclesiastical or lay, of proceeding against witches on the testimony of a single witch who deposed to seeing others at the witch-sabbat, and of convicting a witch on the testimony of two others —a procedure against which Father Tanner inveighs in his published commentary on this subject and the "incertus Auctor Theologus Romanus" [Spee] in his *Cautio criminalis. . . .* printed at Rinteln in 1631.[9]

Very interesting is the testimony of this passage to the influence of the eloquent protests of the Jesuits Tanner and Spee on the courts of the Roman Inquisition. Albizzi remembers, too, with what horror, when (in 1635) he accompanied Cardinal Ginetti, the papal legate, into Germany for the negotiation of a general peace, they all gazed on the horrid spectacle of the countless stakes outside the walls of towns and villages which marked where poor and wretched women had been consumed by flames as witches.

[And] even while I was transcribing these lines [he adds], the Inquisition of Besançon, according to the legal custom of those parts, was relaxing to the secular arm for execution several persons, both men and women. . . . I saw their trials later [he goes on] in the Suprema [at Rome], where they were adjudged null and unjust, wherefore the accused were absolved, the Inquisitor recalled, and a new Inquisitor appointed who should conduct these trials in accordance with the *Instructio Romana.*[10]

That episode at Besançon is else known well. It was then, in 1657, and because of this, that these well-known Roman Instructions[11] were

---

per illusiones in imagine et fantasia, ut notant *praecitati* Doctores, non solum in Suprema non servatur opinio, quod ex dicto duarum Sagarum oriatur indicium ad torturam, ut voluit Martin. del Rio, quem cum aliis refellit Farinaccius. . . . Sed nec faciunt indicium ad inquirendum." Albizzi, *op. cit.,* pp. 354-55.

[8] "Et quod, strigibus affirmantibus, se in ludis Diabolicis vidisse tales personas non credatur ad quemcunque effectum contra illas, quia habentur pro illusionibus, resoluit pluries Suprema etc. sed praesertim in una Ferrarien. 12 Novembris 1594, et in altera Firmana 4 Februarii 1595. Et ex hoc cessat conflictus opinionum Doctorum." *Ibid.*

[9] "Ideo semper improbata fuit Tribunalium sive Ecclesiasticorum, sive laicorum Germaniae praxis procedendi contra Sagas ex dicto unius Sagae, quae testatur, se vidisse alias ad Conventum, et ex dicto duarum convinci alias Sagas; adversus quam praxim invehit P. Tannerus *ea de re edito Commentario;* et incertus Auctor Theologus Romanus, eo quo inscribitur libro, *Cautio Criminalibus* [sic], seu *de Processibus contra Sagas liber ad Magistratus Germaniae hoc tempore necessarius impressus Renthelii* [sic] *anno 1631.*" Ibid.

[10] *Ibid.*

[11] In use since 1635 at least. See Paulus *Hexenwahn und Hexenprozess,* pp. 271, 272, and Lea, *Materials toward a History of Witchcraft,* pp. 950-66.

put by the Inquisition into print. Then, too, as this passage shows, Albizzi's book was being penned.

But let me further point out that already, when in 1602 the juristic faculty of the University of Bologna, replying to a question from the Archduke Maximilian of Bavaria, alleged that in all the courts of Italy, especially those of the Inquisition, both at Rome and at Bologna, the testimony of witches as to others seen at the witch-sabbat was disregarded, Maximilian's confessor, the Jesuit Buslidius, writing (May 2) on behalf of the Archduke to Martin del Rio, who also had been consulted, of this divergence from his own counsel, asked him

whether, since this is a matter for theologians to decide, and since the Pope has placed at the head of the Inquisition theologians who hold that the testimony of witches as to others seen at the witch-sabbat is no adequate basis for torture, we ought not to follow them, or at least advise the Archduke to make sure whether the jurists of Bologna are correct as to the Inquisition's position.

Whereupon in reply (May 21, 1603) Del Rio urges that to follow the Bologna advice would be fatal to witch-prosecution, and sends a new edition of his own book (Mainz, 1603), whose Appendix as to procedure seems to have convinced the Bavarians.[12]

But this growing incredulity of the Roman Inquisition must not be thought a doctrinal change. Albizzi is careful to tell us that, while the confessions of witches against others as present at the witch-sabbat were discredited, their testimony against themselves was still fully received "et quoad abjurationem et quoad poenam"—unless what they confessed was preposterous—so that, while this might and did, as Del Rio warned, hamper witch-trials, it could do little to check belief in witchcraft.

George L. Burr.

WITCH PERSECUTIONS IN TRANSALPINE EUROPE

Thus the two lands of Christendom in which the Inquisition was thoroughly organized [Spain and Italy] escaped the worst horrors of the witch-craze. It is true that in the earlier period the Inquisition was active and unsparing. Bartolommeo Spina tells us that in the diocese of Como alone the inquisitor and his eight or ten vicars every year examined over a thousand cases and burned more than a hundred, but

---

[12] As to all this see Duhr (Geschichte der Jesuiten in den Ländern deutscher Zunge, II, ii, pp. 506-08), who uses the mss in the Munich archives; and see also Paulus, op. cit., pp. 271-72, who points out further that on May 1, 1593, the Inquisitor of Milan was instructed from Rome to give no credence to the testimony of witches as to others seen at the witch-sabbat and that at the opening of the seventeenth century the Roman jurist Scaccia reports the punishment by the Roman Inquisition of a commissioner who dealt otherwise.

Paramo probably exaggerates when, in 1598, he boasts that during a century and a half his beloved institution had burned thirty thousand.[1] This severity, however, as we have seen, passed away, and to appreciate how great a service was thus rendered to humanity requires a brief examination of the· methods adopted throughout the rest of Europe, Protestant as well as Catholic, to resist the attacks of Satan acting through his human instruments.

While the Suprema was earnestly seeking to curb the intemperate zeal of the tribunals, Charles V in Germany was issuing in 1532 the criminal code known as the *Carolina*, which long remained there the basis of procedure. In this, popular repute sufficed to justify the use of torture in accusations of witchcraft. The instructions for examination assumed the truth of all the grotesque details ascribed to the Sabbat, and whenever any injury had been inflicted on persons or things the punishment was pitiless burning alive.[2] It mattered little that a clear practical intellect like that of Jerome Cardan treated witchcraft wholly as an illusion—not an illusion wrought by the demon, but by the drugs composing the witch-ointment which ·caused violent dreams filled with all sorts of wonders—while ligatures and the tales of incubi and succubi received equally rationalistic explanations.[3] Belief in the reality of all the horrors described in the *Malleus Maleficarum* spread through the population of Christendom; no measures were deemed too energetic or too cruel for their suppression and these inevitably intensified the evil. The reckless use of torture obtained from the victims confessions of whatever was desired and these confirmed the belief in the powers of the witch, her malignity and the extent of the ruin which she wrought, while the admission of her evidence against all whom she pretended to have seen in the Sabbat and the eager extortion of that evidence afforded convincing proof of the countless numbers of these slaves of Satan and their existence in all ranks of society. In a trial of a company of witches before the Parlement of Normandy, in 1670, Jean le Cousteur named a hundred and fifty whom he had seen in the Sabbat; Jacques le Gastelois, eighty-five; Marguerite Marguerie, ninety; Siméon, her son, seventy-eight; Jean le Marchand, forty-three; René le Marchand, fifteen; Charles Champel, thirty-five; Anne Noël, twenty, and Catherine Roberde, five;

---

[1] Bartolommeo Spina, *Quaest. de Strigibus* (Rome, 1576), c. xiii; Paramo, *De Origine et Progressu Officii S. Inquisitionis* (Madrid, 1598), p. 296. Spina says (*op. cit.,* c. ii) that the multitude of witches is innumerable and that every one of them is required every fortnight, or at least every month, to bewitch a child.

[2] Charles V, *Leges capitales,* cc. XLIV, LII, CIX, CXCII.

[3] Jerome Cardan, *De Subtilitate* (Paris, 1500), Lib. XVIII. The composition of the witch ointment he states to be the fat of children, juice of garlic, aconite, pentaphyllum, nightshade, and soot.

or, in all, five hundred and twenty-five, of whom more than a hundred were priests.[4] This accounts for the frequent prosecution of men and women of high official and social position and of irreproachable reputation. From such an accusation no one was safe and when once on trial the methods of procedure allowed few to escape. Many confessed at once, preferring to face the inevitable end and obtain the privilege of strangulation before burning rather than to reach it through an interminable course of unendurable torture.

There were those, of course, who objected to prosecution on such slender evidence and who pointed out that demons might personate in the Sabbat innocent persons, but they were met with the irrefragable answer that in so secret a crime there could scarce be had other proof. It was piously added that God impelled the witch to denounce her associates in spite of the demon; that this was the operation of God was clear because it was rarely found that the innocent were named and when they were God took care that their innocence should be proved—which was all a very self-evident proposition, although even Bishop Binsfeld admits that the severity of •torture often caused the innocent to confess themselves guilty and he objects to trying, torturing, and executing on the same day. It not infrequently happened that the convict on the way to the stake would ask for delay and would beg the prayers of the people for having wrongfully accused certain persons, or, when confronted with them, would revoke the testimony, but this revocation was held to be invalid and the prior accusation was adhered to.[5] All the ordinary rules of law were set aside and all doubts were to be cast against the accused, irrespective of what injustice might result. As the University of Ingolstadt unanimously replied, in 1590, to a question from Duke Wilhelm of Bavaria, the public benefit was more important than private injury: it was no matter if the innocent were sometimes condemned in

---

[4] Jules Baissac, *Les Grands Jours de la Sorcellerie* (Paris, 1890), p. 571. [Baissac's knowledge of this episode is drawn from the saucy *Lettres au sujet de la Magie, des Maléfices et des Sorciers* (Paris, 1725) of Dr. St.-André, who used some of the court records, and from the credulous *Recueil de Lettres au sujet des Maléfices et des Sortilèges* (Paris, 1731) written in reply by Dr. Boissier, who had studied them all; but Baissac is here careless. His slips as to names and figures ("Le Coustelier" for Le Cousteur, "150" for 154) I have corrected in Mr. Lea's text; but, as to the total of 525, it should be added (as Boissier on page 198 does) that "almost all those accused by Le Cousteur were likewise named by the others." For the statement, borrowed from Baissac, that of the accused "more than a hundred were priests" I can find no warrant. Boissier mentions but five. Strictly speaking, too, it was not in the trial of 1670 before the Parlement of Normandy, but in 1669 before a lower court, that this evidence was given. Such wholesale accusation was, however, nothing uncommon.—B.]

[5] Del Rio, *Disquisitiones Magicae* (Mainz, 1612), Lib. v, append. ii, q. 1, pp. 843-44; Binsfeld, *De Confessionibus Maleficorum et Sagarum* (Cologne, 1623), pp. 249-53, 276-85, 318-28, 560, 577-80. The first edition of this work appeared in 1589 and it was repeatedly reprinted.

accordance with the testimony: it was of more importance to the commonweal that sentences should be pronounced in accordance with what was alleged and proved than that the innocent should never be condemned: all theologians and jurists agreed that the judge should condemn him who was proved guilty, although he privately knew him to be innocent.[6] The assiduous enforcement of these principles brought about a condition of universal suspicion. Every person was a probable or at least a potential witch. As Bishop Binsfeld says, What man dare affirm his wife to be innocent, although he is with her day and night? Or what woman can assert her husband to be free from this crime?[7]

An occasional voice was raised in protest. William, duke of Cleves and Juliers, held that, misled by the devil, old women imagined that they caused the evils happening to those whom they desired to harm; and consequently in his dominions they were not put to death, although in cases of poisoning the law took its course after careful investigation. His physician, the Calvinist Johann Weyer, to whom he doubtless owed this rationalistic view, was one of the most learned and enlightened men of his time, and set forth this theory in a work published in 1563. In this he ascribes the popular belief to the influence of Satan for the injury of mankind; for even the religious quarrels of the age, he says, caused no such misery.

Daily experience shows what execrable alienation from God, what fellowship with the devil, what hatred between kinsmen, what strife between neighbors, what enmities among the peasantry, what differences between cities, what frequent slaughter of the innocent, are caused by that most fruitful mother of calamities, the belief in the sorcery of witches.

Certain temperaments, he held—melancholy persons and weak-minded old women—were especially liable to these diabolic illusions; these the devil led to enter into pacts with him and made them believe all that he suggested to their imaginations.[8]

The spread of belief in witchcraft and the suffering caused by it he attributed largely to ignorant and greedy priests and monks. For the pious ones he expresses great veneration; but for the most part, he says, when applied to in any distress of mind or body, instead of urging recourse to God they blamed it upon some poor old woman and sug-

---

[6] Binsfeld, *op. cit.*, pp. 255, 265; Del Rio, *op. cit.*, pp. 835-36.

[7] Binsfeld, *op. cit.*, p. 261.

[8] Weyer, *De Praestigiis Daemonum* (Basel, 1563), Dedicatio, Lib. III, c. v. [The citations are from the edition of 1568—the fourth—much enlarged and with an added book. It is Weyer himself who, in his dedicatory letter to his prince, tells us that prince's opinion. On Weyer see the two excellent studies by Eschbach (in the *Beiträge zur Geschichte des Niederrheins*, Düsseldorf, 1886, I) and by Binz (*Doctor Johann Weyer*, Bonn, 1885; 2d ed., 1896).—B.]

gested means of detecting her. Thus they replaced peace with discord, set neighbors and kindred to quarrelling and fighting, they filled the prisons with victims and the land with slaughter. In one small town where he once lived, a stranger priest who came to it at once pointed out three hundred witches. Out of this they made profit by their exorcisms and remedies, of which holy water was the chief, besides exorcised salt, scraps of wax from paschal candles or those lighted on Purification Day, herbs hung up before the church on St. John's Day or sprinkled with holy water on the feast of the Assumption, and other similar wares.[9]

Weyer's indignation, however, was especially kindled by the cruelty of the tribunals and their methods. He is aroused to eloquence in describing how, in contrast to the prescriptions of the law, on mere malicious accusation or the false suspicion of rude and ignorant peasants, old women, deluded or possessed of the devil, are thrown by judges into the terrible dens of robbers and caves of evil demons and then handed over to be butchered with the most exquisite torture, beyond the capacity of human endurance, which is continued until the innocent are compelled to confess themselves guilty. If, indeed, overcome by the severity of the torture they die in the hands of their butchers or if their strength, exhausted by suffering and confinement, gives way and they die when they are brought forth, lo the joyful cry goes up that they have made way with themselves or that the devil has killed them.

But when the Great Searcher of Hearts, from whom naught is hidden, shall appear, your deeds shall be made manifest, O cruel tyrants, blood-thirsty judges, butchers, torturers and truculent robbers who have cast off humanity and know no mercy! Thus I summon you to the tribunal of the Great Judge who shall decide between you and me, when the truth which you have trodden under foot shall arise and confound you, demanding vengeance for your robberies.[10]

The records of the courts, he tells us, will show thousands of cases like some specimen confessions which he gives to illustrate the futility of the evidence on which they were extorted by these methods. One of these relates how the fishermen of Rotterdam and Schiedam went to the herring fishery, when the former's nets were full of fish while those of the latter came up filled with stones. They at once suspected sorcery and on their return they seized a woman who in due course confessed that after their departure she had changed herself into a mussel-shell (*mosselcolp*) at the bottom of the sea, had gone to where the nets were

---

[9] Weyer, *op. cit.*, Lib. II, c. xvii; Lib. cc. ii, iii; Lib. VI, c. i.
[10] *Ibid.*, Lib. VI, cc. iv, vi.

and by spells had driven away the fish and replaced them with stones—for which she was duly executed.[11]

The call for repeated editions of Weyer's book shows that it excited attention and doubtless was not without temporary influence. Indeed, in his subsequent work, *De Lamiis,* he boasted that it had checked in many places the persecution of old women as witches and that some judges no longer condemned them to death.[12] To counteract this, Jean Bodin, who was second to none in France as a jurist and publicist, composed, in 1580, his *De la Démonomanie des Sorciers* which was translated into various languages and long continued to be reprinted. In this he could scarce express his indignation against Weyer, who had earned the title of Defender of Witches and had taught the world their arts and processes, thus alluring people to the nets of the devil. Such a work could proceed only from a most ignorant or a most wicked man; but Weyer was a physician, and therefore was not ignorant.[13] Bodin himself had been concerned in some trials and condemnations of witches and was not without personal interest in the controversy. He complains that under Charles IX (1561-74) in France the good work had slackened so that, assured of impunity, witches flocked thither from all sides, especially from Italy, until the kingdom was full of them. Prominent among them was one Trois-Échelles, or Triscalain, who appears to have been a skilful juggler—a dangerous calling when prestidigitation was apt to be ascribed to magic. He was condemned at Le Mans, but was pardoned on the promise of pointing out his fellows, the number of whom in France he asserted to be a hundred thousand—or three hundred thousand as Bodin states it in another passage. He was brought before Charles IX, whom he astounded by his jugglery and to whom he related all the details of the Sabbat. Admiral Coligny, who was present, confirmed his statement of the deadly character of the witches' powder by relating a case that had occurred in Poitou. Trois-Échelles was carried to places of popular resort and indicated those whom he had seen in the Sabbat or whom he recognized by marks, and the marks were duly found upon them. So many were thus accused, both rich and poor, that they assisted each other to escape; the judges were bribed and an irreparable mischief was inflicted on the community, not only

[11] *Ibid.,* Lib. VI, c. ix, The *De Praestigiis Daemonum* went through six editions, revised and enlarged, the last appearing in 1583. In addition he wrote on cognate subjects a *Liber Apologeticus, Pseudomonarchia Daemonum* and *De Lamiis Liber.* A collected edition of his works was issued in Amsterdam in 1660.

[12] *De Lamiis,* Præfat.

[13] Bodin, *De la Démonomanie des Sorciers* (Paris, 1580), pp. 54-55, 218-19; Latin ed., *De Magorum Daemonomania* (Basel, 1581), pp. 103-04, 417-18.

by their wickedness but by the troubles with which God afflicted France for disobeying the divine command to Moses.[14]

Notwithstanding Bodin's grief at this remissness, he speaks of a general prosecution of witches occurring in 1571 and of a number recently burnt at Le Mans who confessed all about the Sabbat, while his frequent allusions to special cases indicate that there was a tolerably active, if fitful, persecution generally on foot.[15] This did not satisfy his zeal, the savageness of which in a man of liberal culture and elevation of thought is the saddest proof of the intensity of the delusion. The punishment of burning alive does not last more than half an hour or an hour, he says, and this is insufficient, for roasting over a slow fire is an inadequate penalty for such offences, since the object is to appease the wrath of God impending over the people and to serve as a deterrent. Children are not to be spared, although, in consideration of their tender years, they may, if repentant, be strangled before burning.[16] If the strict processes of law were adhered to, he says, not one in a hundred thousand would be convicted. He therefore urges the establishment of what would virtually be a special Inquisition; the judges should not wait for accusations, but should make inquests. The people fear witches more than God or judges, and therefore informers should be shielded by secrecy and boxes should be placed in churches into which anyone could cast written denunciations with details. Although in ordinary crimes accusations by accomplices are not received, in this they should be encouraged by promises of diminished penalties or of impunity. The children of suspects should be seized, for, at their tender age, they can be persuaded or forced to denounce their parents. Deceit on the part of the judge is allowable, for lying for a good purpose is defensible. No rules of law are to be observed in so atrocious a crime, for now scarce one witch in a thousand is punished.[17] When these were the views of a specially enlightened man we may well cease to wonder at the blind ferocity of the vulgar. Bodin's efforts to stimulate persecution were not attended with success. Pierre de l'Estoile chronicles, February 27, 1586, the strangling and burning in Paris of Dominique Miraille and his wife as a matter which surprised the people, for these vermin had always been safe. Henry III himself was accused of magic practices and his loving subjects of Paris amused themselves by making figurines of him, placing them on the altars during mass and piercing them through the heart with some phrase of incantation at the end of the solemnities, as well as

---

[14] *Ibid.* (Basel ed.), Præfat., pp. 159, 255, 265, 288-89, 319, 406.

[15] *Ibid.*, pp. 163, 166, 177.

[16] *Ibid.*, pp. 315-16, 408.

[17] *Ibid.*, pp. 319-22, 326, 328, 341, 356, 415.

performing, in the religious procession, some cognate magic rites with torches and formulas taught to them by sorcerers.[18]

The next champion to enter the lists was an Englishman, Reginald Scot, styled by Glanvil "the Father of the modern Witch-Advocates," who, in 1584, published his *Discovery of Witchcraft*, reprinted in 1602, when it had the honor to be burnt and suppressed by the royal demonologist, James I.[19] It was translated into Dutch, however, at Leyden in 1609, and was repeatedly reprinted in the latter half of the seventeenth century. Its character is sufficiently expressed by the verbose title of the edition of 1665[20] and it has the honor of being the first of the controversial works which resolutely denied the reality of witchcraft and the power of the devil. From it we may gather that at the time witch-executions were by no means uncommon in England, and this naturally increased with the accession of James, whose convictions had been strengthened by his own experience of the storm raised by witchcraft to overwhelm him during his voyage from Denmark in 1590, and who then personally superintended the torture of the accused. He was induced, he tells us, to write his *Daemonologia*, in 1597, by the formidable multitude of witches in the kingdom and to confute the pestiferous opinions of Scot and Weyer. James fully accepted all the superstitious details of the Sabbat, disbelievers in which were Sadducees. To spare the death-penalty, even to children, was to share the guilt of Saul with Agag; it was impossible to secure conviction except on the testimony of accomplices and God would not permit the demon to personate the innocent.[21] It is not easy to imagine a philosophic mind like that of Lord Bacon accepting these beliefs but, if he entertained doubts, he was too good a courtier to betray them; he admitted the royal definition

---

[18] Pierre de l'Estoile, *Journal du Règne de Henry III* (ann. 1586, 1589).

[19] [A reprint of 1602 is now denied; but Nicholson in his well-edited reprint of 1886 still thinks Scot's book was burned.—B.]

[20] Scot, *The Discovery of Witchcraft: proving that the Compacts and Contracts of Witches with Devils and all infernal Spirits and Familiars are but Erroneous Novelties and Imaginary Conceptions. Also discovering, How far their Power extendeth in Killing, Tormenting, Consuming or Curing the bodies of Men, Women, Children or Animals by Charm, Philtres, Periapts, Pentacles, Curses and Conjurations. Wherein likewise The Unchristian Practices and Inhuman Dealings of Searchers and Witch-tryers upon Aged, Mellancholly and Superstitious people, in extorting Confessions by Terrors and Tortures, and in devising false Marks and Symptoms, are notably Detected. And the Knavery of Juglers, Conjurers, Charmers, Soothsayers, Figure-Casters, Dreamers, Alchemists and Philterers; with many other things that have long lain hidden, fully Opened and Deciphered. All which Are very necessary to be known for the Undeceiving of Judges, Justices, and Jurors, before they pass Sentence upon Poor Miserable and Ignorant People; who are frequently Arraigned, Condemned and Executed for Witches and Wizzards* (London, 1665).

[21] James I, *Daemonologia, sive Dialogus de Artibus Magicis*, Præfat.; Lib. II, c. vii; Lib. III, c. ii (*Jacobi Regis Opera*, Frankfurt am Main, 1689, pp. 44, 57, 61-62).

that witchcraft was the height of idolatry and, about 1611, in his charge
to the court of the Verge, he said,

For witchcraft by the former law it was not death except it were the actual
and gross invocation of evil spirits, or making covenant with them or taking
away life by witchcraft; but now, by an act in his majesty's times, charms
and sorceries in certain cases of procuring unlawful love or bodily hurt and
some others, are made felony the second offence; the first being imprisonment
and pillory.[22]

We shall see hereafter what this cost England.

On the Continent, meanwhile, the witch-craze was spreading. In the
province of Trier, deficient harvests in 1586 and 1587, which caused
much suffering, were attributed to witchcraft, leading to persecution
from 1586 to 1591. A partial list shows 306 victims burnt in some twenty
villages. This might have continued indefinitely had not Archbishop
Schönenberg in 1591 lessened the slaughter.[23] His suffragan bishop,
Peter Binsfeld, however, justified the persecution in his well-known
work, in which he tells us that many ask when the burnings are to
cease, to which the only answer is that the punishment must continue
as long as the crime. The chief cause of its prevalence he ascribes to the
ignorance of the priesthood, who are too idle and uncultured to cope
with the devil. Only advocates of sorcerers, he declares, deny the existence of incubi and succubi, and he takes the high ground that it is heresy
to dispute the reality of the details of witchcraft. In this, which marks
an advance by rendering the belief an article of faith, he was justified,
for in 1591 a Doctor of Theology, one Cornelius Loos, wrote a work
to prove that witchcraft was an illusion, but when it was partly printed
in Köln it was suppressed and the papal nuncio, Ottavio, bishop of
Tricarico, compelled the author to recant.[24]

In Protestant Germany, however, matters had not as yet developed
quite so rapidly. In 1591, Doctor Joh. Georg Godelmann, professor in
Rostock, published a work, repeatedly reprinted, in which, while admitting the power of witches to injure men and beasts, he denied their
ability to raise tempests, he ridiculed the belief in incubi and succubi and,
like Cardan, he ascribed the Sabbat to the inunction with ointment. He

---

[22] Bacon, *Advancement of Learning* (*Works*, Philadelphia, 1844), Book II, Vol. I, p. 244;
II, 291.

[23] J. Diefenbach in Wetzer und Welte *Kirchenlexikon*, V, 1998.

[24] Binsfeld, *De Confessionibus*, pp. 28-29 (ed. 1623). [The pages already printed may
still be seen in the City Library at Köln, and the MS of the first of the two books of
Loos's treatise (doubtless all he had yet completed) was in 1886 unearthed on the shelves
of the City Library (formerly those of the Jesuits) at Trier, where it still is. His recantation, embodied by Del Rio in an appendix to his Liber v, appears in all the editions of
his book.—B.]

earnestly argued in favor of the regular process of law in their trials
and pleaded that doubts should be construed in favor of the accused,
for it was better that many guilty should escape rather than a single
innocent should be condemned.[25]

In the same year, 1591, a Jesuit, Benoit Pereira, a man of immense and
varied erudition, issued a little work, *Adversus fallaces et superstitiosas
artes,* of which repeated editions appeared until 1612. In this he carefully avoided allusions to witchcraft, but his reasoning as to necromancy
and the powers of the demon was none the less destructive. All the
wonders of the magician were juggler's tricks or else illusions
wrought by the demon, and, although he admitted the power of the
latter to move human and other bodies, to excite tempests and to produce illusions, all this was strictly limited and could be exercised only
when God permitted it to test the good or to punish the wicked. Tried
by such tests, there was little left of the stories of the Sabbat.[26] Another
Jesuit, the learned Doctor Petrus Thyræus, turned this line of argument
the other way in 1594. He admitted the Cap. *Episcopi* in so far that
sometimes the presence of women in the Sabbat was only in dreams,
but it was beyond contradiction that they were carried thither bodily
by demons; there could be no doubt that demons had the power of
representing there the simulacra of innocent persons, but it was equally
unquestionable that a special providence of God prevented them from
doing so; "demons could only use their power in so far as God permits,
as is shown by the fact that they lose the power of conveying witches
away as soon as the latter fall into the hands of justice."[27] Judges could
thus be at ease when they burnt those against whom the only testimony
was that they had been seen in the Sabbat.

In 1595 there appeared a more formidable champion on the side of
severity. Nicholas Remy was a judge especially deputed for witchcraft
cases in Lorraine and he boasts on his title-page that his book is based
on about nine hundred cases of witches executed within fifteen years.
As he states that about as many more had saved their lives by flight or
by the endurance of torture, it will be seen that his work is drawn from

[25] Godelmann, *De Magis, Veneficis et Lamiis* (Frankfurt, 1591), Lib. II, cc. iv, v, vi; Lib.
III. Godelmann in 1584 had printed eighty propositions and publicly defended them in disputation, proving that the confessions of witches were dreams and illusions; magicians and
poisoners, he said, were worthy of death, but not witches, who were innocent before God
and man.—Michaelis, *Pneumalogie, ou Discours des Esprits, en tant qu'il est de besoin
pour entendre et resouldre la matière difficile des Sorciers, comprinse en la sentence contre
eux donné en Avignon l'an de grace 1582* (Paris, 1587), fols. 120-21 [See below, note 78].

[26] Pereira, *Adversus fallaces et superstitiosas artes, id est, De Magia, de observatione
Somnorum et de Divinatione Astrologica* (Lyons, 1602), Lib. I, cc. vi, vii, viii, ix, xi.

[27] Thyræus, *De Variis tam Spirituum quam Vivorum Hominum Prodigiosis Apparitioni-
bus* (Cologne, 1594), Lib. II, cc. xiii, xiv.

an exceptionally rich experience. It is, in fact, a complete manual of demonology as exhibited in witchcraft. Even the *Malleus Maleficarum* is not so varied and full of details drawn as were these from the actual trials of nearly a thousand culprits who satisfied the demands of their judges with all that imagination sharpened by torture could invent.[28] The dedication of the work to Cardinal Charles of Lorraine shows that it met the approbation of those high in Church and State, while its numerous editions, both in the original and a German translation, prove the popular favor which it enjoyed. It is said that Remy finally confessed himself to be a witchmaster and perished at the stake; if so, some of his victims must have testified to having seen him in the Sabbat and, in the application of his own principles of procedure, he was tried and proved unable to endure the torture.[29] More regular was the fate of another persecutor, B. Voss, who, in the territory of the abbey of Fulda, between 1603 and 1607, put to death some two hundred and fifty unfortunates. Prince-Abbot von Schwalbach stopped it in 1607 by imprisoning Voss, whom he put to death in 1618.[30]

Our information concerning these outbursts of fanaticism is fragmentary; many of them occurred in obscure places and all records of them have been lost, while in others the researches of scholars are constantly bringing to light new facts. There was an unending stream of more or less isolated cases everywhere, amounting to large numbers in the aggregate, and then, when some untimely frost or drought or flood or pestilence created distress, it would be attributed as a matter of course to witchcraft, popular fury would arise, accusations would pour in, every trial led to fresh denunciations, and a judicial massacre would follow. Thus in Würzburg, as the result of harvest failures, in about two years, from 1627 to the beginning of 1629, there were twenty-nine burnings with from two to nine victims in each, amounting altogether to 162. Some of these were nobles, professional men, and officials; others children, specified as being twelve years old—probably because that was regarded as the age of responsibility.[31] In Bamberg at about the same time some six hundred are said to have perished in the flames. In Nassau-Dillenburg

---

[28] N. Remy, *Daemonolatreiae Libri Tres* (Cologne, 1596). [The first ed. was of Lyons, 1595.—B.]

[29] J. Diefenbach in Wetzer und Welte, *loc. cit.* [Remy died in his bed, high in honor. See Pfister in *Revue Hist.*, XCIII, 239 n. 5.—B.]

[30] *Ibid.*, p. 1999. [On Voss, whose name seems rather to have been Ross—not Voss or Nuss—see Malkmus, *Fuldaer Anekdotenbüchlein* (Fulda, 1875); also *Mitteilungen des Vereins für Geschichte und Altertumskunde in Frankfurt am Main*, VI, 36.—B.]

[31] Soldan-Heppe, *Geschichte der Hexenprozesse* (Stuttgart, 1880), pp. 45-51. [And when this Würzburg list breaks off the burnings were in full swing. A later list, printed at Bamberg gives "over nine hundred" as the number burned by the Bishop of Würzburg in his diocese.—B.]

and Herborn, between 1628 and 1632, there were 226 executions; in Wolfenbüttel the stakes were compared to a pine forest; in Quedlinburg, 133 were burnt on a single day; in Osnabrück, 125 in a year; the great Saxon jurist, Benedikt Carpzov, who strenuously taught the reality of all the horrors of witchcraft, is said to have signed twenty thousand death-sentences.[32] Accurate statistics are impossible from such desultory material, but the estimate is probably moderate that in Germany during the seventeenth century there were no less than a hundred thousand victims of the witch-craze.[33]

We hear little of witchcraft in Sweden, although, in the middle of the sixteenth century, Olaus Magnus describes it as literally the seat of Satan, where demons have full power to injure man and where, on the mountain Jungfrun, in the island of Öland, the witches of the North assemble to report their doings.[34] Still there was a very curious witch-craft epidemic which illustrates the contagious nature of the craze and the auto-hypnotism which explains the self-accusation that sometimes forms a distinguishing feature in these psychological developments. On July 5, 1668, the pastor of Elfdalen in Dalecarlia reported to his bishop that Gertrude Svensen, a girl of eighteen, who was skilled in incantation, had stolen several children for the devil. She had been detected by Eric Ericsen, a boy of fifteen, who included others in his accusation, among them a woman of seventy, who confessed, while the rest denied. The king (Charles XI) rewarded the pastor's zeal with a better benefice and, on May 22, 1669, ordered the bishop to appoint a commission of twenty men who, with delegates from the royal council, should bring back the simple multitude to the way of salvation by mild measures, without imprisonment or cruel punishment. He was likewise to order public prayers throughout the diocese to avert the rage of the devil. This naturally increased popular excitement and when the commission met it did not confine itself to the merciful measures proposed. After a hasty examination, lasting from August 13 to 25, it condemned to death twenty-three persons, of whom fifteen, convicted on their own confessions, were beheaded and burnt the same day, while eight were reserved

[32] J. Diefenbach, in Wetzer und Welte, V, 1998, 1999. [On Carpzov and his twenty thousand death sentences see the study of Paulus, in his *Hexenwahn und Hexenprozess,* (1910). Stintzing, too, the historian of German law, finds the number credible. But these were not witches only, though the number of witches sentenced by him must have been enormous.—B.]

[33] G. Plitt (revising Henke's art. on *Hexen* in Herzog's *Realencyclopädie,* VI, 97). From first to last in Germany, Georg Längin assumes that the number of victims was over a million.—*Religion und Hexenprozess* (Leipzig, 1888), p. 268.

[34] Olaus Magnus, *Historia de Gentibus Septentrionalibus* (Rome, 1555), Lib. II, c. xxiii; Lib. III, cc. xv, xvii, xxii.

for further examination by the royal council. Thirty-six children, moreover, who had been seduced by the witches, were scourged with rods
and two hundred more were subjected to public penance.

So far was this wholesome severity from checking the evil that it
merely seemed to scatter its seeds far and wide. September 25, King
Charles ordered the bishop to assemble a new commisison, as the previous
one had accomplished nothing. December 19 a new form of prayer was
ordered for the whole kingdom, as witchcraft was said to have pene-
trated as far as Bohus. In 1670 several commissions were appointed for
Helsingen, Örbyhus and Upsala. What was the result of their activity we
do not know, but they probably did not spare the guilty. Their president
was Andreas Stjernbok, a member of the council of Dorpat, and one of
his colleagues was Charles Lund, professor of law in Upsala. A letter
of Stjernbok to Charles XI describes the horrible apparition of the devil
to himself and Lund, and the latter frequently referred to it in his lectures. Men under such influences were not likely to be merciful. It was
apparently about this time that the duke of Holstein made inquiry of
Charles as to the matter, to which the king replied that his judges and
commissioners had burnt divers men, women, and children, but whether
the acts brought against them and confessed by them were real or only
the effects of a strong imagination he was not as yet able to determine.[35]

In this epidemic of spiritual surexcitation a new development occurred
in 1672 in the parish of Nordingra in Angermanland. Two boys, one
sixteen and the other eighteen years of age, began to preach to their
fellows, leading to an epidemic of angelic visions among young and
old. A royal commission made inquisition throughout the parishes of
Thorsaker, Ytterlannas, and Dahl, in the course of which seventy-one
persons were beheaded and burnt during 1674 and 1675, besides many
others who suffered in Hernosand. In 1676 the witchcraft contagion
spread to Stockholm, invited by the measure taken to avert it in a day
set apart for public prayer. Under orders from the royal council the
consistory, on March 31, delivered an opinion which confirmed the
public infatuation. Accusations came pouring in, trials were held, six
women were promptly executed, the prisons were crowded, many accused themselves and persisted in it to the death, and the popular excitement was kept up by vigils, fasts, and prayers. In the case of a Finnish
woman named Magdalen Matsdotter, her two daughters joined others
in accusing her, swearing that they had seen the devil standing beside
her. She refused to confess and was burnt alive, her youngest daughter
accompanying her to the stake and imploring her to confess. Then it

[35] *Spottiswoode Miscellany*, II, 50.

was discovered that some of the accusers had acted from envy or revenge
or the hope of gain. They were executed, King Charles ordered all prosecutions for witchcraft to be discontinued and the hallucination ceased.[36]

For a long interval during this period there seems to have arisen no
one hardy enough to question the reality of witchcraft, although there
were some who ventured to protest against the reckless illegality of
procedure. There were three Jesuits who thus distinguished themselves.
The first of these was Father Adam Tanner, who took care to guard
himself by a preliminary objurgation of witches as the worst and most
destructive enemies of the human race, worthy of death in the most
cruel form and to be exterminated as far as possible. He sustained the
canon *Episcopi*, but admitted that bodily transportation to the Sabbat
sometimes occurred and that when it was illusory the witch, in believing
and consenting to its reality, committed apostasy. Still he argued that,
if a crime cannot be punished without danger to the innocent, it should
be left to the judgment of God rather than involve the innocent with
the guilty by intemperate and pernicious zeal. If one innocent is condemned among the guilty, it would be better to let the guilty escape,
especially as when once the process is commenced, the number to be
punished multiplies until there is no end; there is also the lasting infamy
inflicted on honorable families and the disgrace to the Catholic religion
when so many of the condemned, including priests, have been regarded
as exemplars of piety. He ascribes the deplorable results to the profuse
use of torture and the denial to the accused of all practical means of

---

[36] George Ph. Hallenberg, *De Inquisitione Sagarum in Suecia* (Upsala, 1787). An account of the first portion of this epidemic, translated from the German, is appended to
Glanvil's *Sadducismus Triumphatus* (London, 1681 and later eds.).

All this shedding of innocent blood would have been avoided had King Charles respected
the wise caution of his predecessor, for Queen Christina, February 16, 1649, in answer to
an inquiry from an official in the German provinces of Sweden about a current epidemic
of witchcraft, asserted that these persecutions, as shown by abundant examples, led to evil
consequences and that the deeper one plunged into them the more inextricable became
the labyrinth. Therefore to protect his district from the further extension of the epidemic
he is ordered to suspend all action and further inquisition and prosecution and to discharge
all prisoners; his powers and jurisdiction otherwise were not to be impaired, and the discharged prisoners were to have no grounds of action against him.—Hauber, *Bibliotheca
Magica*, III, 250.

This is understood to have been a general order embracing all the Germanic provinces of
Sweden (A. Rhamm, *Hexenglaube und Hexenprozesse*, p. 99) and is memorable as perhaps the earliest authoritative legislation curbing the witch-slaughter. [That this was a
general order is proved by Cardinal Albizzi's statement that after her abdication Christina
had often told him that when queen she had issued orders forbidding the death penalty
against witches and sorcerers unless it could be clearly proved that they were guilty of infanticide or homicide; for she was convinced that what these women confessed were only
illusions due either to female functional disorders or to diabolical suggestion.—Albizzi, *De
Inconstantia in Jure* (1683), p. 355.—H.]

defence, as well as to the large arbitrary discretion left to the judge. His suggestions, however, for an improved method of procedure were too halting to prove of much benefit to the accused, had they been put in practice.[37] Carefully as Father Tanner had expressed his profound detestation of witchcraft, these liberal views so displeased the clergy of his native Innsbruck that, when he died there, in 1632, they refused Christian burial to his remains;[38] and Spee tells us that two inquisitors, after reading his work, declared that if they could get hold of him they would torture him on the strength of it.[39]

The next Jesuit to condemn the treatment of witches was Paul Laymann, whose systematic work on Moral Theology, first published in 1625, had a success attested by innumerable editions issued during more than a century. He devotes a section to the subject, in which he accepts as true the details of the Sabbat and the evils wrought by witches. He manifests no disposition to spare them, for when the law decrees death by burning they are to be burnt alive, though he regards as laudable the custom that those who repent shall have a bag of gunpowder hung around the neck to shorten their sufferings. Still he argues forcibly against the abuses of procedure, which confound the innocent with the guilty to such a degree that, if the system is continued, whole districts, towns and cities will be depopulated, involving honorable persons high in office as well as priests and other ecclesiastics.[40] This section of his work was printed separately in repeated editions, both in Latin and in a German translation.

As, under the rigid organization of the Society of Jesus, no member could print a work without the approbation of his superiors, it may be inferred that that powerful order was at least neutral on the questions connected with witch-trials. If so, it seemed to learn caution, for the next member to deprecate the cruelty of procedure issued his work anonymously, which he could only have done with the express permission, if not at the command, of those who controlled the policy of the Order. This was Friedrich Spee's *Cautio criminalis,* appearing in 1631, a book

---

[37] "Tractatus theologicus de Processu adversus Veneficas," nn. 5-19, 80, 126-33; "De Translatione Sagarum" (q. 3 of tractate "De Potentia locomotiva Angelorum"), nn. 14, 15 (*Diversi Tractatus,* Cologne, 1629). These are extracted from Father Tanner's *Disputationes in omnes partes Summæ S. Th. Aquinat.* (Ingolstadt, 1618 [De Backer, II, 624]). —Rapp, *Die Hexenprozesse und ihre Gegner aus Tirol* (Innsbruck, 1874), pp. 59-61. [2d enlarged ed., Brixen, 1891.]

[38] Nicoladoni, *Christian Thomasius* (Berlin, 1888), p. 88. There is a different account, however, of Tanner's burial in unconsecrated ground by the Benedictine, Placidus Taller, in Hauber's *Bibliotheca Magica,* II, 63.

[39] Spee, *Cautio criminalis,* dub. ix.

[40] P. Laymann, *Theologia Moralis,* Lib. III, tract. vi, c. v, § 1. [But the *Processus Juridicus,* or *Rechtlicher Prozess,* which in 1629 appeared in German at Aschaffenburg and Köln under Laymann's name, was not his. See Lea, *Materials,* pp. 688-89.—B.]

to which has been attributed vastly more importance than it merits. Spee was deputed to serve as confessor to criminals condemned to death in Würzburg and Bamberg, where, after he had accompanied to the stake some two hundred witches, he could no longer endure the strain of witnessing the martyrdom of those whose dying words convinced him of their innocence, and he sought another post. His terrible experience convinced him of the injustice and cruelty of procedure, which he set forth vigorously in his little book. The secret of the authorship was so well preserved that it was not known [by the general public] until it was revealed in 1697 by Leibnitz, who had learned it from Joh. Philipp von Schönborn, archbishop of Mainz, a friend of Spee's; and, even in 1703, Christian Thomasius, who knew only the edition of 1696, conjectured that it was written by some one who wisely professed faith in witchcraft to escape the ordinary charge of atheism.[41] Spee casts no doubt upon the reality of witchcraft and its crimes, though he thinks that in many cases there is illusion, and he attributes its apparent frequency to the hideous injustice of the process used for its detection and punishment—out of fifty condemned to the stake, he says that scarce five or rather scarce two are really guilty, the rest, although innocent, being forced to confess by the unsparing use of torture. He rightly condemns the practice of the German princes, who, in appointing special judges for these offences, give them no regular salary, but pay them four of five thalers for every conviction, and he goes somewhat farther than Laymann when he says that whole districts are depopulated and that if this continues there will be no end to the burnings short of exhausting the whole region.[42]

These were *voces clamantes in eremo*. Their reasoning was unanswerable, but it produced no effect, and witch-burnings continued as numerous as ever. They admitted the reality of witchcraft with its devil-worship and evil-doings and so long as they did so it was merely a question of policy as to the efficient means of suppressing crimes the most monstrous that a Christian could commit. Hardier combatants were needed and these could scarce be Catholics, for the Church had so long and so repeatedly committed itself to belief in the existence of relations of the kind between human beings and demons that to deny them was virtual heresy and at once placed the disputant out of court. It was inevitable, therefore, that the radical cure of overthrowing the whole struc-

---

[41] Hauber, *Bibliotheca Magica*, III, p. 15, note; Christian Thomasius, *Kurze Lehrsätze von dem Laster der Zauberey* (1703), pp. 9-10. [As to Spee see also Mr. Lea's *Materials*, pp. 697 ff., especially p. 726. Father Duhr shows us how narrowly Spee escaped expulsion by the Jesuits.—B.]

[42] *Cautio criminalis, seu de Processibus contra Sagas*. Auctore incerto Theologo Romano (2d ed.; Frankfurt, 1632), dub. i, iii, viii, xxix.

ture built by the superstition of ages could only come from Protestants; and, with the gradual spread of enlightenment, some writers were found hardy enough to disregard the epithets of Sadducees and atheists that were freely hurled at them. After Reginald Scot, in the previous century, the first of these was John Webster, a retired physician, whose *Displaying of supposed Witchcraft* appeared in 1677. The purport of the work is sufficiently set forth in its descriptive title-page[43] and in it the author sought to show that popular belief was based on the mistranslation and misinterpretation of Scripture. Webster's work called forth vigorous defenders of the belief. Joseph Glanvil, a Fellow of the Royal Society, had already, in 1666, published *Some philosophical considerations touching the being of Witches and Witchcraft*, which was issued in 1681, after his death, by his friend Henry More, as *Sadducismus Triumphatus; Or, full and plain evidence concerning Witches and Apparitions*. This was several times reprinted and was translated into German. Still more successful was the well-known *Satan's Invisible World discovered*, issued in Edinburgh in 1685 by George Sinclar, a man of science, professor of philosophy and mathematics in the University of Glasgow, who, after being expelled, in 1666, for refusal to conform to episcopacy, turned his acquirements to account as a surveyor and mining engineer, but was recalled in 1688 and continued to serve until his death in 1696. His work was repeatedly reprinted and even until the nineteenth century, we are told, formed part of every cottage library in Scotland.[44]

More important in its enlightening influence was Balthasar Bekker's *De Betoverde Weereld*, which appeared in Amsterdam, from 1691 to 1693. Translated into French, with the author's assistance, under the title of *Le Monde enchanté* (Amsterdam, 1694) and rendered into German and many other languages, it had a wide circulation—four thousand copies are said to have been immediately taken.[45] Bekker struck at the foundation of the belief in witchcraft by maintaining that the activity of good and bad spirits in human affairs was a pagan belief infiltrated into Christianity and that the power ascribed to Satan was

---

[43] *The Displaying of supposed Witchcraft, wherein it is affirmed that there are many sorts of Deceivers and Imposters and divers persons under a passive delusion of Melancholy and Fancy. But that there is a corporeal league made between the Devil and the Witch or that he sucks the Witches Body, has carnal copulation or that Witches are turned into Cats, Dogs, raise Tempests or the like is utterly denied and disproved.* By John Webster, Practitioner in Physick, London, 1677.

A German translation was published, in 1719, under the auspices of Christian Thomasius.

[44] Prefatory Note to Edinburgh Edition of 1871, pp. xiv, xlvii, 1.

[45] To prevent unauthorized or mutilated editions, every copy of the Dutch and French issues is signed by Bekker himself. [Its first part only was translated into English as *The World Bewitched* (London, 1695), and this was so slow of sale that in 1700 it was brought out again under the changed title of *The World Turn'd Upside Down.*—B.]

derived from Manicheism. There can be no communication and mutual interaction between man and spirits and pacts with the demon are ridiculous and incredible. He concludes that neither reason nor revelation nor experience justifies the attribution to evil spirits of the effects commonly ascribed to the devil or to men confederated with him. Bekker sought to be wholly orthodox. He examined minutely all passages of Scripture, seeking to explain them away and arguing that current popular beliefs were wholly in opposition to the truths of the Bible.

As early as 1670, when in Franeker, Bekker had been denounced as a Cartesian on the strength of a catechism which he published. After he had been called to Amsterdam, a tract, issued in 1683, to allay popular fears as to the comets of 1680, 1681, and 1682 was looked upon askance by his orthodox brethren. He had excited many enmities, which eagerly availed themselves of his rationalistic treatment of witchcraft. An immense clamor arose, and controversial writings on both sides appeared in abundance. Medals in gold and silver were struck in his honor and others against him. He was a pastor and therefore subject to discipline, which was duly brought to bear. After fruitless endeavors to induce him to recant, he was deprived of his functions, excommunicated and expelled from the Church. Efforts were made without success to have his book burnt and suppressed. The magistracy of Amsterdam, however, stood by him; his stipend was continued and no one was allowed to take his place—those who preached in his stead had to do so without pay—but he had not been restored to the Church when he died, June 11, 1698.[46]

Germany was the stronghold of the belief in witchcraft and the protagonist in the conflict against it there was Christian Thomasius, who in so many ways broke up conservative habits of thought and opened the path to modern culture. He gave the first impulse to the abolition of torture, to the improvement of the law in other respects and to the undermining of the oppressive power of the clergy. He was the *enfant terrible* of the University of Leipzig in which he was a professor and, in February 1689, the theological faculty complained of him to the Oberconsistorium of Dresden as one who despised God and religion and

---

[46] W. H. Beckher, *Schediasma critico-litterarium de controversiis præcipuis Balthasari Bekkero motis* (Königsberg and Leipzig, 1721); Schwager, *Beytrag zur Geschichte der Intoleranz, oder Leben, Meynungen und Schicksale des . . . Doct. Balthazar Bekkers* (Leipzig, 1780), pp. 15, 32, 110-11, 154-55.

It was easy for Bekker's adversaries to point out that God would not have permitted his Church to be infected with such an error throughout its whole existence, so that even the Reformation was but a sewer to convey the corruption.—*Idée générale de la Théologie payenne, servant de réfutation au Système de Mr. Bekker. Par Mr. B. [Binet]* (Amsterdam, 1699).

ridiculed the preachers. To escape arrest, in June 1690, he fled to the
Elector Friedrich Wilhelm at Berlin, but his family were detained and
his property was sequestrated. He was warmly received and assigned a
position in the Ritteracademie of Halle, which was speedily developed
into a university, planned on a liberal and progressive basis; it was
immediately and largely successful and its establishment formed a
turning-point in the annals of German culture.

Thomasius had had his legal training under the influence of Carpzov
and in 1694, when a witch-case was brought before the University, he
carelessly voted against the accused, for which he was reproved by his
former teacher Stryck. This gave him pause; and, as similar cases came
for action, he gradually reached the conviction that there was no basis
for the belief. In 1701 he took this ground in a disputation *De Crimine
Magiæ,* which, in 1702, appeared also in German under the title of
Kurtze Lehr-Sätze von dem Laster der Zauberey. In this he argued that
belief in witchcraft was a papistical error, evidently with a view of enlist-
ing Protestant support and disarming the hostility of the pastors. Various
other works followed, controversial and argumentative, translations (in
1719) of Webster's *Displaying of Supposed Witchcraft* and (in 1721) of
Beaumont's *Treatise of Spirits, Apparitions, Witchcrafts and other
Magical Practices,* besides his labors for the abrogation of torture, on
which the conviction of witches depended. Until his death, in 1728, he
kept up the attack, which his immense reputation, his wide learning
and his vigorous sarcasm rendered more effective than any that had
preceded it. Up to his time credulity had been unbroken in Germany;
there were intelligent skeptics, of course, but they were for the most
part silent and the power of the clergy was too great to be resisted; the
mass of the people accepted the traditional view and the judicial slaughter was unchecked. It was Thomasius, as Frederic the Great said, who
vindicated the right of women to grow old in safety.[47]

Yet so deeply rooted an error could only be eradicated gradually with
the progress of enlightenment. It is true that, December 15, 1714, Friedrich Wilhelm I of Prussia issued a sharp edict against witch persecution,

[47] H. Luden, *Christian Thomasius, nach seinen Schicksalen und Schriften* (Berlin,
1805), pp. 270-75, 283; Alex. Nicoladoni, *Christian Thomasius: ein Beitrag zur Geschichte
der Aufklärung* (Berlin, 1888).

The action of Thomasius, of course, called forth a number of active allies and quite a
literature speedily developed. Some forgotten earlier assailants of witch-persecution were
also resuscitated by the Licentiate Johann Reiche in his *Unterschiedliche Schrifften von
Unfug des Hexen-Processes* (Halle, 1703), which includes a translation of the *Cautio
criminalis* and a curious selection of actual prosecutions of witches.

but other lands were not so fortunate.[48] In the *Criminalcodex* of Bavaria, drawn up in 1751 by an eminent jurist, the Freiherr von Kreittmayr, under the cultured Elector Maximilian Joseph, all the old beliefs in the Sabbat, the devil-worship, the incubi and succubi, are explained and are punished with fire, although injury to persons, cattle, and harvests wrought with the aid of the demon escape with beheading; while judges are warned not to trust too blindly the evidence of accomplices. That the penalty was not a mere threat is shown in the burning at Landshut, in 1754 and 1756, of Veronica Zerritschin, a child of thirteen, and of Marie Klossnerin.[49] Bavaria was not alone in this. The witch-craze records no greater atrocity than that displayed in a group of cases occurring in the Swiss Canton of Zug in 1737. Katherina Kalbacher, a girl of seventeen, who was a half-crazy demoniac, confessed to having been a witch since childhood and accused eight persons as accomplices. One of these, Katherina Gelli, entered the prison August 12, a strong hearty woman of forty. A succession of the severest tortures elicited no confession, until on January 29, 1738, she was found doubled up in a corner of her cell dead, with little semblance of a human being. As she wore a scapular and had a rosary around her neck she was adjudged to have purged herself by her sufferings in the torture and to have died in the faith, in consequence of which she was secretly buried with Christian rites. Mark Stadlin and his daughter Euphemia, a girl of eighteen, endured repeated and frightful torture without confession and were acquitted. Stadlin's wife, Anna Maria, had less endurance; six times she revoked confessions made under torture, but her powers of resistance finally were exhausted, she ratified her confession and was torn with red-hot pincers, strangled, and burnt. Similar vigorous proceedings produced similar results with the rest of the accused. Elizabeth Bossard was thrice torn with hot pincers in the right hand and both feet and was burnt alive. Margaretha Bossard was torn twice with hot pincers and was burnt alive. Theresia Bossard had her right hand hewed off, her tongue torn out with hot pincers, and was strangled and burnt. Anna Maria Bossard was torn with hot pincers and burnt alive. The accuser, Katherina Kalbacher, escaped with beheading. The five who were burnt were reduced to ashes and the ashes were buried so that no one might dread further infection from them. In the reduplication of agony thus provided, there is a strange gleam of humanity in the provision that those who were burnt alive had bags of powder hung around the neck

---

[48] Rhamm, *Hexenglaube und Hexenprocesse* (Wolfenbüttel, 1882), p. 101.

[49] Längin, *Religion und Hexenprozess* (Leipzig, 1888), pp. 303-04; Riezler, *Geschichte der Hexenprozesse in Bayern* (Stuttgart, 1896), pp. 274, 297.

in order to shorten their suffering. These, however, were not the only victims of the zeal against witchcraft at Zug. The record contains also the sentences to more or less frightful deaths as witches of Anna Maria Müller, Anna Bidermann, Katharina Eglin, Anna Bucher, Verena Wyss, Barbara Widmer and Katharina Mouss.[50]

This savage ferocity is a measure of the unreasoning terror which had grown upon the people during three centuries of persecution and the resultant accumulation of horrors confessed by hundreds of thousands of women in the agony of the torture chamber.

A similar instance was furnished in Rome, in 1742, where a band of nine malefactors, headed by Silvestro Orlando, aged seventy-eight, and his wife Anna, aged seventy, were convicted, not only of the murders, robberies, and arson which they had committed, but of killing four hundred children, whose blood they sucked, as an offering to the demon; of bringing on numerous tempests to ruin the harvests and of poisoning the pastures to the destruction of an infinite number of cattle. The apportionment of these various crimes between the culprits shows that it was derived from their confessions: thus one of them named Barnaba is said to have caused seventeen destructive storms and to have poisoned pastures sixteen times. On September 2, 1742, they were condemned to be torn with hot pincers and burnt alive, and the sentence was executed within two hours. The old woman was paraded in a cart while her breasts were torn off and the blood stanched with red-hot irons. The men were tied to the stakes and duly tortured, and all were burnt alive.[51]

The people might well believe in the marvels attributed to witchcraft when they were vouched for by those to whom they looked for guidance in temporal and spiritual things. This was seen in a celebrated case which occurred in Würzburg in 1749. Maria Renata, we are told, when but seven or eight years old, was inducted into all the foul mysteries of witchcraft. Her parents, unable to support her, obliged her, at the age of nineteen, to enter the convent of Unterzell, near Würzburg, where she

---

[50] *Der Hexen-Prozess und die Blutschwitzer-Prozedur* (Zug, 1849); Soldan-Heppe, *Geschichte der Hexenprozesse*, II, 315-22. [This grim episode, oft related and the theme of a novel or two, has been subjected to modern scientific analysis by Professor Otto Stoll, in his *Suggestion und Hypnotismus in der Völkerpsychologie* (2d ed., Leipzig, 1904), pp. 401-27.—B.]

Tearing with hot pincers was not wholly a novelty. July 14, 1581, Didier Finance was sentenced to this, prior to burning alive; his witchcraft, however, was complicated with parricide. He eluded the penalty by committing suicide with a knife carelessly left with his bread.—Remy, *Daemonolatreia*, p. 356.

In 1572 four witches were torn thrice with hot pincers before burning in the little town of Thann (Alsace), and in 1574 two more.—Reuss, *La Sorcellerie au XVe et XVIe Siècle, particulièrement en Alsace* (Paris, 1871), p. 192.

[51] *Nova vera e destinta Relazione della Gran tremenda Giustizia seguita in Roma adi 1 Settembre 1742 di nove scelerati Stregoni* (Rome and Milan, 1742, Con. Lic. de' Super.).

set an example of piety and good works. She was the first to enter the choir and the last to leave it, she was zealous in all religious exercises, her way of life was irreproachable and her talk spiritual, so that she was made sub-prioress. This continued for fifty years, but Satan was growing impatient; she had not won for him a single sister and he forced her to exercise her evil powers on the nuns. Some became possessed by demons and continued so in spite of exorcisms. Then others fell sick of maladies that baffled the physicians. There were nightly disturbances, moreover, for which no one could account. Evidently there was some malignant influence at work in the house, which at first was ascribed to the cats, of which there were many, especially in her cell, but driving them all out afforded no relief. A watchful Providence, however, would not allow half a century of hypocrisy and devil-worship to go unpunished. God's patience was exhausted and he caused one of the sick nuns to accuse to her confessor Maria Renata as a sorceress and the cause of all the evil. The good father reproved her and warned her not to die with such sin on her soul, but she solemnly declared that she would appear without fear before the judgment-seat of God. Then, compelled by exorcisms, the demons in the energumens admitted that Maria was a witch and the troubles were her work. The provost and the prelate of the order summoned her before them and exhorted her to seek a remedy for her soul. She persistently denied and was ordered to be taken to the castle of Marienberg, when she asked to be allowed to return once to her cell. This was refused and on searching it there were found her pot of ointment, some herbs used in sorcery, and the yellow robe in which she was wont to fly to the Sabbat. Some accounts say that she was tortured, others that she confessed at once and gave every sign of repentance, but the latter was doubtful, for the demons in the possessed women were forced to admit that she was feigning and that every night she went with them and renewed the pact. Moreover the nightly disturbances continued and among the evil spirits that came she was recognized. It seems not to have occurred to any one to ask why, if she could thus fly from her prison at night, she should return to it every morning.

The bishop humanely permitted her to be beheaded before burning, and at the scaffold, June 21, 1749, the Jesuit, Father Georg Gaar, preached a sermon in which he related all the details of her wickedness. He confessed that he was unable to explain the secret mystery of God in bringing to light this evil after it had been so long shrouded in darkness, but he suggested several reasons, the chief of which was that it was to convince the incredulous and the atheists that there are spiritual as well as corporeal beings and that man has a soul. He dilated at large on the foulness of witchcraft, which comprises almost all conceivable wicked-

ness, and he was uncompromising in demanding the penalty of death
for all witches. Sister Renata made a most edifying end, begging Father
Gaar to entreat the sisters of Unterzell and all present to forgive her for
the evil which she had wrought and to pray for her soul.[52] The good
father was so proud of his sermon that he printed it, but unfortunately
this did not result as he expected, for the whole hideous story produced
a revulsion of feeling and led to considerable discussion which was not
favorable to the conservatives.[53]

About the same time (1749) a similar tragedy was enacted at Mühldorf
(Salzburg). A *poltergeist* in a workshop made tools and other objects
fly around mysteriously. The inmates of the house were frightened except

---

[52] *Acta historico-ecclesiastica* (Weimar, 1749), Tom. XIII, 370-89. [Maria Renata belonged to the noble family of Singer von Mossau. As to the documents in her case, see
Memminger, *Das verhexte Kloster* (Würzburg, 1904; revised 1908), and Duhr, *Die Jesuiten
in den Ländern Deutscher Zunge*, IV. But others are still in MS, including some bought in
1899 from the estate of Dr. F. Leitschuh, the Bamberg librarian, for the White Library at
Cornell University, which leave no doubt that the nun was tortured.—B.]

[53] Father Gaar's sermon was promptly translated into Italian by Girolamo Tartarotti
(under the pseudonym of Dr. F. A. T.) and published in Verona, in 1749, with some
disparaging comments, to which Gaar replied at considerable length, roundly affirming
his belief in the Sabbat, incubi and succubi, and all the rest. Father Gaar was answered by
Tartarotti's student, Professor Joh. Bapt. Graser in his *Propugnatio adnotationum criticorum
in sermonem de Maria Renata, Saga, adversus responsa P. Georgii Gaar, S.J.* (Venice, 1742).
Both of these are printed at the end of *Animavversioni critiche sopra il Notturno Congresso delle Lammie* (Venice, 1751).

Meanwhile Tartarotti had developed his views in his *Notturno Congresso delle Lammie*,
published in Roveredo in 1749, elaborately disproving the Sabbat but admitting the existence of magic. This brought upon him attacks from both parties. The conservatives were
well represented by the learned P. Benedetto Bonelli in his *Animavversioni critiche sopra
il Notturno Congresso delle Lammie*, while on the other side the most important con-
troversialist was the Marquis Scipione Maffei, who denied the existence of magic in his
Arte magica dileguata (Verona, 1749), which aroused, it is said, fourteen opponents,
among them an anonymous writer calling himself an Oratorian priest, who printed in
the same year his *Osservazioni sopra l'Opuscolo che ha per titolo Arte magica dileguata*
(Venice, s.a.). Maffei then composed a more elaborate treatise, *Arte magica annichilata*
(Verona, 1754), which met with much applause. It was probably the same anonymous
writer who answered it in *Riflessioni sopra l'Arte magica annichilata* (Venice, 1755), when
the death of Maffei put an end to the discussion.

The writings of Maffei formed the basis of *Die Nichtigkeit der Hexerey und Zauber-
kunst* by Father Jordan Simon, an Augustinian who concealed his name under the ana-
gram of Ardoino Ubbidente dell'Osa (Frankfurt and Leipzig, 1766).

For an account of Tartarotti see Rapp, *Die Hexenprozesse und ihre Gegner aus Tirol*, p.
71. He and Maffei were personal friends.

Tartarotti in his early youth had the opportunity of seeing the effect of witch-persecution,
for, in 1716 and 1717, not far from Roveredo, his birthplace, Maria Bertoletti and Dome-
nica Pedrotti were beheaded and burnt as witches, and several others would have shared
the same fate had they not died in prison. In 1728, also in the neighborhood, Maddalena
Todeschi died in the prison to which she had been sentenced for life on the same charge.
—Rapp, *op. cit.*, p. 75.

Tartarotti's *Del Congresso* was delayed two years by the Venetian censorship's refusing
to grant license to print.—Rapp, *op. cit.*, p. 90.

a nursemaid named Anna Maria Bavarin, who laughed at it. It continued until she was dismissed, when it followed her to her new habitation. She was arrested and under threat of torture confessed that she had given herself to the devil, had attended the Sabbat and on one occasion had brought thence some sugar which she had thrown into a churn, when for six months the latter had turned out no butter. She accused a woman of Neuötting of having led her into this, whereupon the latter was arrested and confessed and both women were beheaded and burnt. They both made edifying Christian ends, protesting their innocence to the last.[54] Possibly torture may not have been used in these cases; but, if so, it was only because it was not needed. In 1752, three women tried in Croatia were suspended for four, six and even twenty hours; the record states that they were only removed when they fainted and it reports, as doubtless strangled by Satan, one who never recovered.[55]

Apparently Austria was the first German Catholic land to check these enormities. It is suggestive as to clerical influence in the matter that the Empress Maria Theresa, July 11, 1755, issued an edict addressed to all priests ordering them to take no action in cases of witchcraft, treasure-seeking, magic, or demoniacal possession, but to leave such matters strictly to the secular authorities. In 1756 a rescript concerning a man condemned to death in Bohemia ordered him, as ignorant but malicious, to be imprisoned and instructed, and this was followed by a general order that in all capital cases of magic, before sentences of torture or death were executed, the matter should be referred to her with details of the evidence.[56] Ten years later she was engaged in the preparation of a new criminal code, but, in anticipation of it, she issued in 1766 a *Landesverordnung* devoted to sorcery, to be observed until the new code should be published. In this she congratulated her people that, during the twenty-seven years of her reign, in all her empire no witch or magician had been found, but that all cases of punishment had been of impostors, or fools, or for other accompanying crimes, and she prescribed rules in such cases which rendered conviction virtually impossible.[57] This was not satisfactory to the conservative ecclesiastical element and was attacked by Father Angelus März, who was answered by Father Jordan Simon— the latter, however, prudently issuing his work anonymously.[58] Finally,

---

[54] *Ragguaglio sincero su la Sentenza di Morte in Salisburgo ultimamente seguita* (Venice, 1751), p. 168.

[55] Constantin Franz de Cauz, *De Cultibus Magicis* (Vienna, 1767), p. 287.

[56] *Ibid.*, pp. 196, 338, 339, 375. Cauz's object in this work is to disprove wholly witchcraft and magic. He assumes that this is the view of the empress, but that she sought to enforce it by rendering proof and punishment impossible, without arousing the superstitious fears and prejudices of her subjects by flat denial.

[57] *Ibid.*, pp. 339-46.

[58] Grässe, *Bibliotheca Magica* (Leipzig, 1843), p. 65.

December 26, 1768, was issued the *Theresiana*, the long-expected criminal code. This still admits the existence of witchcraft, but says that it has been greatly exaggerated by popular credulity and has been punished in disregard of all rules of law. Great care is therefore prescribed to discern the true from the false; torture is only to be used when injury has been inflicted on persons, cattle or harvests; impostors pretending to possess such powers are to receive the penalties due to whatever crimes they may have committed, and, when witchcraft really has been proved, such extraordinary cases are to be submitted to the empress, who will designate the punishment.[59] It is safe to assume that those who drafted the code were skeptics and only admitted the possibility of witchcraft from motives of policy and out of respect to the church.

Yet the belief in witchcraft was by no means eradicated, even in the imperial court. Anton von Haen, the empress' chief physician, in 1774 issued a work to check the progress of skepticism. He tells us that three women, condemned as witches in Croatia, had been sent to Vienna; the empress had them placed in the hospital for examination, when he and his colleague Van Swieten pronounced them innocent and the empress gave them money and sent them home. This led him to investigate the subject, and he wrote his book to correct the mistake of those who denied the existence of witchcraft. He ranges himself with Spee, admitting its existence but deploring the abuses through which so many innocent beings had been sacrificed. Spee wrote when everybody believed in witchcraft and the rigor of the courts had to be moderated. Now that the opinion of the majority had swung to the other extreme he writes in order to restore the true belief that there are witches, but they are not numerous and should have equitable trials, free from the cruelty and injustice caused by the fanaticism or greed of the judges, which had given occasion to so much misery.[60]

Although theoretically the belief might be upheld, practically the courts were abandoning it. The last execution on German soil is said to have been that of Anna Maria Schwägelin, beheaded in Kempten (Bavaria) April 11, 1775. In Switzerland there was one still later, for, in 1782, in Protestant Glarus, Anna Göldi was beheaded for bewitching her em-

---

[59] *Constitutio Criminalis Theresiana* (Vienna, 1769), Art. lviii, pp. 167-73.

[60] Ant. de Haen, *De Magia* (Leipzig, 1774), Præfat. The book had a large and immediate circulation. There was another Leipzig edition in 1775, one in Venice the same year, two in Vienna, 1775 and 1776, and one in Paris, 1777.

A *Dissertatio de Magia*, by Paul Josef Riegger, appeared in Vienna in 1773 (Grässe, *op. cit.*, p. 60). I have not met with it, but it was put on the Spanish Index by decree of February 1, 1793.—*Suplemento al Indice Expurgatorio* (Madrid, 1805), p. 46. [The booklet is a vigorous assault upon the whole body of witch-superstitions by an eminent canonist who was one of the foremost advisers of Maria Theresa. Its standpoint is that of Cauz, whose book it lauds.—B]

ployer's child, while her assumed accomplice, a respected citizen named Steinmüller, hanged himself in prison after undergoing severe torture. Poland was still more dilatory, for in 1793 two women were burnt as witches in Posen by the local magistracy. The Prussian authorities, as soon as they heard of the sentence, forbade its execution, but their commands arrived too late.[61]

Still discussion was kept up. In 1786 Professor Joseph Weber of Dilingen in his lectures taught that diseases of cattle were not caused by witchcraft and that cleanliness and care were the best preventives. This caused some talk, and in 1787 he defended his position in a little work which he boasts was the first one denying the existence of witchcraft that had passed episcopal censure.[62] This was answered by an anonymous writer styling himself a *Katholischer Weltmann*, whereupon another, under the name of a *Landpfarrer*, or country priest, took up the argument in defence of Weber. The *Weltmann* returned to the charge in 1791 in a work the spirit of which may be gathered from its using as a motto the terrible words of Exodus, XXII:18, "Thou shalt not suffer a witch to live." He admits the awful excesses of past ages as depicted in the *Cautio criminalis*, but he assumes that the current skepticism threatens equally dangerous consequences to morality and to personal safety. There is a grave earnestness in his style which shows how deeply he felt the importance of the question, and in a dispute between Catholics his reliance on Scripture, the Fathers, and the unbroken consistency of the Church throughout the centuries was difficult to answer.[63] Even he was not the last defender of the old belief. In 1792 there appeared in Venice a little tract arguing that the crimes ascribed to witches should not remain unpunished, although in general they should be sent to a physician rather than to the stake.[64]

[61] Soldan-Heppe, *op. cit.*, II, 322, 327.

[62] Joseph Weber, *Ungrund des Hexen-und Gespensterglaubens in ökonomischen Lehrstunden dargestellt* (Dilingen, 1787).

[63] *Und der Satz: Teuflische Magie existirt, bestehet noch: In einer Antwort des katholischen Weltmannes auf die von einem Herrn Landpfarrer herausgegebene Apologie der Professor Weber'schen Hexenreformation* (Augsburg, 1791). [His first pamphlet had called itself *Ueber die Hexenreformation des Herrn Professor Weber zu Dilingen* (Augsburg, 1787). The "Catholic Man of the World" was an Augsburg tobacconist, Franz Josef Schmid, who had received a Jesuit training. The "Country Priest" who came to Weber's defence was Friedrich Bauer of Mertingen. Weber, however, did not escape a penalty. In 1793 the bishop, who had long stood by him, yielded to clerical pressure and silenced his popular lectures. He might teach philosophy, but in Latin, and was soon restricted to physics. See Reusch's article on Weber in the *Allgemeine deutsche Biographie.*—B.]

[64] Renazzi, *De Sortilegio et Magia* (Venice, 1792). [This little treatise of the eminent Roman jurisconsult, Filippe Maria Renazzi, though as to some points it affects suspension of judgment, seems wholly rational in intent, quoting the arguments not only of Spee but of Weyer and Scot, Bekker and Thomasius, Tartarotti and Cauz. The printer claims that the MS has been lent him by a friend and that he takes the liberty to print it; but this, too, may be a ruse of the author.—B.]

In France the materials for the history of witchcraft are less abundant than in Germany and there would seem to have been fewer of the violent epidemics of persecution, but there was the constant succession of trials and convictions, which in the aggregate amounted to a deplorable number of victims. We have some suggestive details concerning the eastern provinces subsequently subjected to the French crown. In the small community of Thann (in southern Alsace) a collection of documents records 115 burnings for witchcraft in the forty-eight years from 1572 to 1620.[65] To the adjoining region of Franche-Comté, then in Spanish hands, we owe one of the most instructive manuals. Henry Boguet was chief judge of St.-Claude when Loyse Maillat, a sick child, eight years old, was assumed to be possessed. Under exorcism the demons were compelled to admit this and when Loyse was asked who had sent the demons into her she pointed out Françoise Secretain, who was among the bystanders. Françoise was arrested; she seemed to be a pious woman, assiduous in her devotions, and steadily denied the charge, but when she was shaved she trembled all over and confessed freely. Those whom she designated as her accomplices were seized and named others; how far the contagion extended we have no means of accurately knowing, but Boguet, in the systematic work based on his experiences, incidentally alludes to about forty, nearly all of whom seem to have been burnt. Apparently there had been previously no special legislation on the subject, for, when the persecution was well-nigh over, the Cardinal Archduke Albert and the Infanta Isabella issued an edict, February 19, 1604, reciting that in the County of Burgundy there are many sorcerers frequenting the Sabbat and committing execrable crimes, wherefore all such are to be punished with death and all judges exercising *haute justice*

---

[65] Reuss, *La Sorcellerie . . . en Alsace,* pp. 192-94. [The "collection of documents" mentioned by Mr. Lea is the chronicle of the Franciscans at Thann, compiled in the early eighteenth century by Brother Malachias Tschamser (and printed at Colmar in 1864). In Reuss's excerpts, used by Mr. Lea, I can count but 102 witches burned at Thann (Reuss himself counts but 101—see his *L'Alsace au XVIIe siècle,* II, 106), the other burnings belonging to neighbor towns; but another chronicle of Thann (the *Kleine Thanner-Chronik,* printed at Colmar in 1764 and at Mülhausen in 1855) narrates that the witches burned at Thann between 1572 and 1620 amounted to some 152—partly from the immediate neighborhood, partly from outlying districts. (See Stöber, "Die Hexenprozesse im Elsass," in *Alsatia* (1856-57), p. 307). And Tschamser himself tells us (II, p. 270) that in the vale of St. Amarin and its neighborhood more than two hundred had been burned by 1596, and yet the witches there were believed as many as ever. What can be learned as to the total of victims in Alsace has been gathered by Reuss (revising the earlier estimates of his *La Sorcellerie en Alsace* and his *La Justice Criminelle à Strasbourg*) in his *L'Alsace au XVIIe siècle* (Paris, 1897-98), c. ii, pp. 105-07. There were thousands, but he finds the evidence too fragmentary for a guess. Thann was at this time, like most of southern Alsace, in possession of the House of Hapsburg.—B.]

were granted cognizance in such cases, without prejudice to the jurisdiction of the Inquisition.[66]

Boguet evidently was not a cruel man and acted only on his honest
convictions. He shows human feeling in his account of the confrontation of Guillaume Vuillermoz with his son Pierre, a child of twelve who
persistently accused his father of taking him to the Sabbat. "It was a
thing no less strange than pitiful to be present at these confrontations;
the father was exhausted with imprisonment, he was chained hand and
foot, he lamented, he cried, he threw himself on the ground." The father
was burnt; the boy denied that he had given himself to the devil and
was not punished but was placed under instruction. Christofle l'Aran-
thon, a girl of fourteen, was merely banished after being made to see
four others burnt, as a deterrent, and Boguet says that a more severe
judge would have burnt her; she might have been scourged, he adds,
but it was thought that this would have hardened her, as in the case of
Jeanne Harvillier, scourged as a child at Verbery and burned alive,
thirty years after, at Ribemond. On the other hand, he remarks elsewhere that when the only charge is that of having been seen in the
Sabbat, some judges are so scrupulous that they hand the culprit over
to the Church, but the proper rule is to burn him.[67]

His stolid credulity accepts all the wonders that the imagination of
the accused, stimulated by torture, could invent for his satisfaction, even
when they are contradictory or incompatible. A new and original feature
of the Sabbat, which he gravely describes, is that at its conclusion the
presiding demon burns himself to ashes, which are divided among the
witches and form the powder that they use in their evil deeds. The
necessity for this is scarce apparent, for their powers are almost un-

---

[66] Boguet, *Discours des Sorciers* (Lyons, 1612), c. 73, p. 550 *ad calcem*. [The first edition of this work appeared in Lyons in 1602, followed by others—Paris, 1603; Rouen,
1603, 1606, and Lyons, 1605, 1607, 1608, 1610, and 1611. It evidently was a very popular
book and did its full share in stimulating the horror of witchcraft.—H.]

[As a result, witch-persecution throve in Franche-Comté till late in the century. The
edict of 1604 punished with death mere attendance at the Sabbat, and made it no longer
necessary to prove actual harm to man or beast, as under the code of Charles V. The Inquisition, indeed, claimed jurisdiction in such cases (see Lucien Febure, *Notes et Documents sur la Réforme et l'Inquisition en Franche-Comté* [Paris, 1912], p. 40), but the
lay judge had now concurrent jurisdiction and should proceed, even after the ecclesiastical court has punished, since that court can not adequately punish a crime so monstrous.
The edict restricts the penalty of death to witches of the "age of discretion"; but
Boguet would include even children below the age of puberty since the crime is so horrible and since those once in the power of Satan seldom escape, and he finds a Biblical
precedent in the children devoured by bears for mocking Elisha.—J. Des Loix, *Speculum
Inquisitionis Bisuntinae* (Dole, 1628); A. Déy, *Histoire de la Sorcellerie dans le Comté de
Bourgogne* (Vesoul, 1861); C. Joseph Tissot, "Notice sur l'Inquisition en Franche-Comté"
in his *L'imagination* (Paris, 1868).—B.]

[67] Boguet, *op. cit.*, cc. lv, lix, lxxiii.

limited; they can kill or sicken with their words, their breath, their looks, their touch, or with a wand, besides numerous other methods and devices.[68] In corroboration of all this he gravely cites as facts the myths of classical antiquity, the feats of Apollonius of Tyana, passages from the poets and even the stories told by Lucian and Apuleius, as well as random accounts of marvels related to him by his friends. Yet he draws the line at lycanthropy and denies that human beings can be changed to were-wolves, although he had the confessions of a number of his victims to that effect. He does not, however, disbelieve the stories which he tells, but argues that the demon acts as the wolf after throwing the witch into a stupor in which he imagines himself to be the actor.[69]

There would seem to have been no misplaced mercy in strangling or beheading before burning and the chief anxiety of the poor wretches was that their agony at the stake should not be prolonged. Clauda Janguillaume said to the executioner that he would do her an evil turn and make her burn slowly, and her fears were justified, for three times she managed to loosen herself and leaped from the flames, so that he was obliged to knock her on the head in order to burn her. Antoine Gandillon when sentenced begged repeatedly that she should not be made to languish, but she was longer in dying than any of the six who were burnt with her, among whom were her father and brother.[70] Custom, however, varied as to this. At Montbéliard, witches were mostly strangled or beheaded before burning; but in 1611, in the case of Jacque Jean Thiébaud, the savage wish of Bodin was fulfilled, for he was sentenced to be roasted over a slow fire.[71]

Southwestern France seems at the same time to have been plagued with witches for, in 1609, Henry IV issued a commission to Pierre de Lancre and to the president D'Espagnet to clear the Pays de Labour of them, a work which they performed energetically, although the six hundred burnings ascribed to them are doubtless exaggerated; and in

---

[68] *Ibid.*, cc. xxii, xxvi-xxx.

[69] *Ibid.*, c. liii. [Truth to tell, Boguet was on all sides of this question. "As for me," he says, "I think that sometimes Satan puts the witch to sleep behind a bush, and goes himself to carry out what the witch has willed"; "but," he adds a little later, "I hold that for the most part the witch carries it out in person, not actually transformed into a wolf, but fancying to be so." And a page or two later he is quite ready to admit their actual wolfhood, though this is a "controverted matter." In any case, he tells us, they are equally guilty, for the intent was theirs.—B.]

[70] *Ibid.*, c. li. [It was, however, as Boguet tells us ("Instruction," p. 27) only those guilty of lycanthropy who were burnt alive; but most of the cases reported by him involved lycanthropy. The strange confessions are analyzed by Calmail, *De la Folie* (Paris, 1845), I, 310-36.—B.]

[71] Alex. Tuetey, *La Sorcellerie dans le Pays de Montbéliard* (Dole, 1886), p. 4.

1610 the Parlement of Bordeaux executed four Spaniards for the same offence.[72]

I am inclined to think that during the rest of the seventeenth century there was considerably less activity of persecution in France than in Germany. When, in 1691, the Parlement of Paris was called upon to act in a case of witchcraft its records were searched for precedents and only twelve cases were alleged, of which only one, occurring in 1684, was later than 1604.[73] The Parlement of Paris, in fact, within the territories under its jurisdiction, exercised a repressive influence on the persecution of witches. It opposed, as far as it could, the revival of the water ordeal as evidence, which was largely practised in Germany and spread into France. At Dinteville (Champagne) June 15, 1594, a woman, after having been shaved all over to remove charms, and tied thumbs to toes, was thrice, by order of the local judge, cast into water seven or eight feet deep and each time she rose to the surface. After each immersion she was interrogated and persisted in denial, but the proof was deemed to justify torture which was applied so severely that she died, her body being subsequently burnt. The Parlement thereupon forbade the authorities of Dinteville to use the ordeal and repeated the prohibition on other occasions, until finally, on an appeal to it from such a sentence after an investigation of the subject, by an *Arrêt* of December 1, 1601, it formally prohibited the custom in all courts under its jurisdiction.[74] Moreover it ordered that all persons accused of sorcery should be delivered for confinement in the Conciergerie, thus assuming for itself cognizance of all such cases. It adopted the rule that when the only charge was that of attendance at the Sabbat, without infliction of injury, it would not prosecute or punish, but where such injury or sacrilege or impiety was proved, after a fair trial, the offence was capital. It was rigid as respects evidence and revoked or moderated many sentences of the lower courts and it even discharged some persons who had been condemned to the stake at Troyes.[75] This last assertion is confirmed by a statement of the celebrated surgeon Pierre Pigray, in his *Epitome Præceptorum Medicinæ chirurgicæ* (Paris, 1612), which shows how rationalistic was its treatment of these affairs. Fourteen persons condemned to death for

[72] Garinet, *Histoire de la Magie en France* (Paris, 1818), pp. 175-77, 303; Le Brun, *Histoire critique des Pratiques superstitieuses* (Rouen, 1702), pp. 514-15; *Factums et Arrest du Parlement de Paris, contre des Bergers Sorciers executez depuis peu dans la Province de Brie* (Paris, 1695), p. 63.

[73] *Factums et Arrest du Parlement de Paris*, pp. 32, 61. [This may be found in the work of Le Brun cited in note 72.—B.]

[74] Le Brun, *op. cit.*, pp. 502-06. [In the ed. of Amsterdam, 1733-36, I, 173-77, and II, 162-64.—B.]

[75] *Ibid.*, pp. 506-12.

sorcery were submitted by it to the examination of Pigray and three other physicians, who searched them all over unsuccessfully for the insensible witchmark and reported that they were in need of hellebore rather than of the stake, for they were victims of melancholia, some of them careless of life and the others wishing to die, whereupon the Parlement released them.[76]

Although its jurisdiction was territorially limited, this naturally exerted a repressive influence, not only on the other courts but on public opinion. We do not meet in France with that incessant stream of books on the subject which in Germany and England indicates how great was the popular preoccupation, and, as witchcraft was primarily a disease of the imagination, the absence of discussion in itself was not only a symptom of sanity but a cause of cure. Gabriel Naudé, who in 1625 published his *Apologie pour les grands Hommes*, turns with contempt from the vulgar stories of witchcraft; and, if he seems to admit the possibility of incubi and succubi, it is only to show that, even if it is accepted, generation is out of the question.[77]

It is perhaps not without significance that the most notable cases during the seventeenth century were connected with diabolical possession, like that of Maria Renata, and thus were in clerical hands. The almost incredible absurdities surrounding the exorcism of demoniacs and the acceptance of the utterances of knavish or hysterical girls as truths extorted from the possessing demons are conspicuously revealed in the case of Louis Gaufridy, parish priest of Nôtre Dame des Acoules, one of the four parishes of Marseilles. He was a man universally respected and beyond suspicion, regarded as perhaps the most eminent of the clergy of the city for his good qualities.[78] It chanced, however, that, in

---

[76] St.-André, *Lettres au sujet de la Magie* (Paris, 1725), p. 372.

[77] *Apologie pour les grands Hommes souçonnez de Magie* (Paris, 1623), cc. ii, xvi.

The work was reprinted in 1653, 1669, 1679, and 1712. In 1671 it was answered by the learned Capuchin, Jacques de Chevannes, under the pseudonym of Jacques d'Autun, in a work entitled *L'Incrédulité sçavante et la Crédulité ignorante*. This was dedicated to the Parlement of Dijon with great laudation of its severity toward these crimes. Cf. Hauber, *Bibliotheca Magica*, I, 637.

[78] . . . "Il n'y avoit rien de plus couvert ny de plus inimaginable que ledit Gaufridy fust Magicien, estant au contraire en la meilleure opinion des gens, de tous les hommes de sa qualité, le maling lui baillant un entregent admirable, en vertu duquel il estoit aimé et bien venu de tous. Mais Dieu ne permet pas que tels hypocrites demeurent impunis dans son Eglise."—Michaëlis, *Histoire admirable de la Possession et Conversion d'une Pénitente* (Paris, 1612), Pt. II, p. 124.

This work by the Dominican doctor, Frère Sébastien Michaëlis, the chief manager of the tragedy, is dedicated to the queen regent, Marie de Medici. Other editions appeared in 1613 and 1614 and an English translation by "W.B." was printed in London, 1613.

Michaëlis was an experienced hand in these matters. He had been present in Avignon, in 1582, when the Inquisition relaxed eighteen witches, which led him to write his *Pneumalogie, ou Discours des Esprits*. [Revised and enlarged by him, and with the words

November 1610, Father Michaëlis, as Prior of the convent of Ste. Magdalen at St.-Maximin, sent to Ste.-Baume two girls possessed by demons, Magdaleine de Demandouls, *dite* De la Palud, and Louyse Capeau, to be exorcised. Experienced exorcizers took them in hand and after considerable delay compelled the demons to talk, but to eject them was a more difficult matter and the process continued until the last of them, Belzebub, abandoned De la Palud, April 22, 1612, on seeing that an assembly of exorcists was gathered to proceed against him juridically. Much of the information imparted by the demons during this long struggle was difficult of belief, as that Solomon was damned and Nebuchadnezzar was saved or that the demons prayed to God for the conversion of Gaufridy and offered the merits of Christ and the Virgin in exchange, but when De la Palud declared that Gaufridy had led her to be a witch and had taken her to the Sabbat there could be no doubt of the truth of her assertion. Gaufridy was decoyed to Ste.-Baume under pretext of asking his aid in exorcism, and while he was there the demons gave full accounts of his evil doings. When asked why Gaufridy ate so little, Belzebub replied that he did not need the convent fare, for every day the flesh of young children was brought to him invisibly from the Sabbat. He was the prince of magicians and it would be easier to release from hell the souls of Cain, Pilate, Herod, and Judas than to reclaim him from his wickedness. In fact the two girls rivalled each other in denouncing Gaufridy to his face and the friars wrote it all down as evidence coming from demons compelled by exorcisms to tell the truth. There was talk of locking Gaufridy up in the convent prison, but the bishop of Marseilles sent four of his canons to Ste.-Baume, who rescued him, January 7, and carried him back to the city. Then Michaëlis laid before the Parlement of Aix all the incoherent gabble which had been so industriously collected; that body took the matter up, arrested Gaufridy, tried him, in conjunction with an episcopal delegate, obtained some kind of a confession from him by means which can readily be conjectured[79] and on April 30 sentenced him to be burnt alive and his

---

preceding "Discours" dropped from the title, it was republished as a supplement to his *Histoire admirable* (but with distinct title-page and pagination) in 1612 and the years following. This revision is often found detached.—B.]

[79] Gaufridy made a confession, recorded as "voluntary," on April 14 and 15, and then retracted it on the afternoon of April 15 (Michaëlis, *op. cit.*, Pt. II, p. 118). Michaëlis does not print it, but it was printed in the *Mercure François* of 1617 and is reprinted by Hauber (*Bibl. Magica*, I, 457-68). This does not assume to be complete, but is very long (in fifty-three articles) and has every appearance of being factitious. He is made to say that he sold himself to the devil in return for the power of seducing women by breathing in their faces and that in this way he had seduced a thousand (p. 459). In the description he gives of the Sabbat there is a long account of the mass celebrated there; there are twelve priests, who sit apart as special princes or dignitaries, and each one in his turn

property to be confiscated; but before execution he was to be submitted to the *question ordinaire et extraordinaire* to discover his accomplices. The torture was immediately applied, the bishop of Marseilles degraded him from his orders and by five o'clock the same afternoon the miserable man was duly consumed and his ashes thrown to the winds. De la Palud had a vision in which she saw his soul tormented in hell more severely than that of Judas, while Verrine, the persistent demon of Louyse Capeau, accused a poor blind girl, named Honorée, of witchcraft. She was arrested, the witch-mark was found on her and she was duly burnt.[80] De la Palud showed such earnest repentance that,

---

performs the ceremonies and distributes communion in the form of bread crusts (arts xxxiii-xlvii, pp. 467-69). Now, De la Palud in her confessions describes the Sabbat and says that Gaufridy invented this sacrilegious mass, saying that he offered the sacrifice to Lucifer and distributed the consecrated bread to the crowd, who trampled it underfoot and then gave it to the dogs (Michaëlis, Pt. ii, p. 30). Altogether the passage in Gaufridy's confession has every appearance of being an expansion of this talk of De la Palud. She also says that the Sabbat ends with intercourse with incubi and succubi; on Thursdays this is sodomy, on Saturdays bestiality and on other nights in the natural way. The Sabbats are held nightly. (Michaëlis, *loc. cit.*)

[Gaufridy's confession was not a judicial matter, and is not a part of the records. It purports to have been made "to two Capuchin Fathers for the Convent of Aix" and was printed at Aix, "with the permission of the Court of Parlement," in 1611, the year of the priest's death. Already by 1612, an English chapbook containing it, *The Life and Death of Lewis Gaufredy*, was printed in London. But one need not take it too seriously. It was, says Lorédan (in his book cited below, p. 272), "evidently imagined, dictated by these two monks, revised and corrected by the Grand Inquisitor himself"—i.e. Michaëlis; "it reproduced textually most of the wild allegations of the hysterical Magdaleine and sundry phrases of the *Histoire admirable*." Doubtless the broken victim, at most, gave only assent. Yet how bravely he could still refuse to name any accomplice appears from the heart-rending record of his torture, as narrated by Lorédan from the documents.

For this famous case there should also be studied the account of the Dominican, Dooms (Domptuis), who was one of the exorcists and had aided Michaëlis in editing the records for his *Histoire admirable*, but who later, after his return to Flanders (where in 1613 at Lille he again played a notable role as an exorcist) threw the story into narrative form. It was published along with the story of the bewitched Briggittines of Lille, in both French and Latin (Paris, 1623), under the editorship of J. Lenormant de Chiremont, forming a second volume of his *Histoire veritable et memorable*, etc., with the distinct title of *De la Vocation des Magiciens et Magiciennes*. There is, too, a little study by Dr. Jacques Fontaine, one of the medical examiners in the case, *Des Marques des Sorciers* (Lyons, 1611), which exists also in modern reprint (Arras, *cir.* 1850). In 1907 the documents were sifted in an excellent little book by the Provençal poet, Raoul Gineste (*Les grandes Victimes de l'Hysterie: Louis Gaufridi et Magdaleine et la Palud*; but in 1912 at Paris, appeared a much more thorough study, using all manuscript records, by Jean Lorédan (*Un grand Procès de Sorcellerie au XVIIᵉ siècle.*—B.]

[80] Michaëlis, *op. cit.*; Garinet, *Hist. de la Magie*, p. 189. Peiresc, one of the most learned and intelligent men of the time, was fully persuaded of the truth of the accusations, and though he subsequently came to doubt whether there might not be some imposture, he approved of the execution on the ground that the lustful Gaufridy had profaned the sacred mysteries of religion. He held that even if witches did not really frequent the Sabbat, their desire to do so subjected them to the penalty.—Bayle, *Réponse aux Questions d'un Provincial*, c. xxxv.

although she had frequented the Sabbat, she escaped punishment. On the death of her parents she inherited property. We hear of her keeping a servant and at a *bastide* belonging to her near Marseilles she founded a chapel. For more than forty years she passed her life in works of piety and charity, but the day of retribution came. A girl named Magdeleine Hodoul became possessed and under exorcism her demon Belzebub declared that De la Palud had sent him there. She was arrested and tried by the Parlement of Aix; she vainly protested her innocence and though she seems to have been spared the torture she was condemned, July 17, 1653, to imprisonment for life in a convent or hospital.[81]

There were probably other cases of the kind leading to the submission to the Sorbonne of the question as to the admissibility of the evidence of possessing demons under exorcism. To this it replied by an Act, February 16, 1620, declaring that demons should never be allowed to accuse any one and much less should exorcisms be employed to learn the faults of another, or whether he is a magician. Great as is the torture inflicted on the demon by the exorcism, he is so much the enemy of man that he would rather endure it than tell the truth. It was pointed out that the best of men would not be safe from such attacks and that Aquinas had said that the demon is not to be believed, even when he tells the truth.[82] This opinion from the highest theological authority in

---

[Lorédan, *op. cit.*, pp. 379-416, narrates in much detail the fate of De la Palud. She was kept in prison eighteen months, then allowed to take refuge near a noble kinswoman in an Alpine hamlet, where she died in 1670.—B.]

[81] *Condamnation d'une Fille accusée d'être Sorcière.*
There is no date to this fragment, but an allusion to the *Convulsionnaires* shows it to have been written about 1735. It gives some documents of the trial, textually.

In the Bibliothèque Nationale (Imprimés, Ll 37, Réserve, 5148) there is a tract entitled *Histoire prodigieuse et espouvantable de plus de deux cens 50 sorciers et sorcières emmenez pour leur estre fait, et parfait leur procez au Parlement de Tholoze: avec l'exécution exemplaire d'un grand nombre en divers lieux: ce qui a causé la cherté des bleds.* Its only importance lies in its illustrating the popular credulity that rendered such productions profitable. It professes to be based on a letter from Toulouse [and a modern reprint ascribes it to "Paris, 1649."—B.]

There is a bearing on this case of Gaufridy and on that of Grandier and others in the rule that it is illicit for an exorcist to inquire of the demon of an energumen as to the author of the *maléfice* which has caused the possession. The theologians decided that this was to ask a service of the demon, which involved pact and friendship with him, and moreover, as he is the father of lies and always seeking to deceive, there is no credence to be given to what he says.—Bordoni, *Sacrum Tribunal* (Rome, 1648), c. xvii, no. 42.

Carena says that the Roman Rota pronounced this to be a *pessima praxis.*—Carena, *De Officio SS. Inquisitionis,* p. ii, tit. xii, n. 199.

[82] *Histoire des Diables de Loudun,* pp. 195-97. [See below, note 85.]
I have not been able to verify this, but in 1623 the Sorbonne condemned a book to be burnt for containing certain errors, among which were the assertion that credence is to be placed in the utterances of demons under exorcism and that demons can be thus used as accusers.—D'Argentré, *Collectio Judiciorum de novis Erroribus,* II, 139-40.

the kingdom ought to have put an end to such judicial murders, but it was disregarded in the celebrated case of Urbain Grandier. Grandier was a man of talent and culture, but a scandalous libertine and somewhat passionate and vindictive. As parish priest of St.-Pierre-du-Marché in Loudun and prebendary in the church of Ste.-Croix he made many enemies and was prosecuted both in the secular and ecclesiastical courts. After a good deal of trouble he was acquitted in each and he began reprisals against his persecutors. To protect themselves they had recourse to the nuns of a little Ursuline convent, whose confessor, Mignon, was one of their allies. After considerable instruction some of the nuns were able to simulate diabolical possession, and their exorcisers procured from the demons statements that Grandier was the cause of their trouble, and that he was a master of witchcraft. The civil authorities were called in to draw up official statements as a basis for prosecution, but the affair was clumsily managed. Archbishop Sourdis of Bordeaux, the metropolitan, issued an order March 21, 1633, forbidding Mignon and Barré, his confederate, to exorcise the women further; the energumens became silent and the matter settled down.

Too many people of influence, however, had been drawn into the plot to allow it to be abandoned. It happened that a creature of Richelieu's named Laubardemont, a kinsman of Madame de Belcier, superior of the convent, was just then sent to Loudun with a commission to pull down the castle. He was told that Grandier was the author of the "Lettre de la Cordonnière de la Reine Mère à M. de Baradas"—the most scandalous attack that had appeared against Richelieu and one that he had felt deeply. There is no evidence that this was true, but the assertion was enough and the opportunity of punishment was not to be lost, especially as one of the nuns, Claire de Sazilly, was related to the cardinal. A commission was formed, selected by Laubardemont and with him at its head, with full powers to arrest, to try, and to punish Grandier as a sorcerer. Without waiting to take testimony, Grandier was promptly arrested and his papers were seized. New exorcisers were found, the most prominent of whom were two Capuchins, the Pères Lactance and Tranquille, and a Jesuit, Père Surin. The energumens resumed their revelations and fresh accusations rained on Grandier, with details even more absurd and incongruous than in the case of Gaufridy. Ample evidence as to his licentious life was accumulated in order further to prejudice his case. No effort seems to have been made to obtain other testimony except to ascertain whether Grandier had the insensible spot, or witch-mark, which was the conclusive evidence of pact with Satan, and this was readily done by thrusting into him the sharp end of an instrument and producing pain and then touching him lightly on the back with the blunt end, which he did not feel.[83] His contract, written with his blood, surrendering himself to the devil, body and soul, was also obligingly brought by Asmodeus from Lucifer's cabinet. Naturally, the opportunity of defence was limited in every way. When some of the women retracted their statements, this was assumed to be a shallow device of the demons to save their associate, even though the Mother Superior, after presenting herself before Laubardemont as a penitent with a halter around her neck to render satisfaction for her false witness, endeavored to hang herself in despair and would have succeeded had she not been cut down by some of the nuns. When Grandier's friends endeavored to act, revelations came which warned them that they too would be inculpated, or Laubardemont gave them to understand that they would incur the royal wrath. A certain Abbé Quillet,[84] who chanced to be present at one of the public exorcisms, offered to prove imposture, when Laubardemont made out a warrant of arrest and he saved himself by flight to Italy. Grandier's three brothers, two of whom were parish priests, also were obliged to fly to escape prosecution. When a meeting held in the hôtel de ville, with the Bailli at its head, resolved to write to the king, complaining of the proceedings, Laubardemont arbitrarily forbade it as an assault on the royal authority embodied in the commission.

Grandier stoutly maintained his innocence. The predetermined end was reached August 18, 1634, when sentence was rendered condemning him to be burnt alive, with preliminary *question ordinaire et extraordinaire* to reveal his accomplices. As a preparation for this, to remove all charms, he was shaved from head to foot and the surgeon was ordered to tear out his nails, but he refused to commit this atrocity. The torture was so severe that one of his legs was broken; but in spite of this he resolutely affirmed his innocence and that he had no accomplices. From the torture he was carried to the stake, the accompanying friars making a great display of exorcising air and water to prevent Satan from saving his servant. Grandier had been promised the opportunity of addressing the people and the favor of being strangled. The former the friars pre-

[83] [Opposite this statement Mr. Lea inserts in the margin of his MS a question-mark. It is from Aubin (see note 85) that the statement is derived. Dr. Legué (*Urbain Grandier* [Paris, 1884], p. 229) using the MSS of the Bibliothèque Nationale, asserts that Grandier was so far from insensible to pain that his cries could be heard in the street and that the surgeon found spots alleged insensible by prodding him with his thumb instead of the lancet. He adds that an indignant apothecary of Poitiers snatched the lancet, and found the spots sensitive enough to its pricks. Fourneau, the surgeon who later prepared him for the torture, certified that the only two suspicious spots he could find were fully sensible.—B.]

[84] [Claude Quillet was then not yet an abbé, but a physician practicing close by at Chinon. He later took orders, but is better known as poet and wit.—B.]

vented by deluging him with holy water when he attempted to open his mouth and striking him in the face with an iron crucifix under pretext of making him kiss it. The latter was also eluded by knotting the cord prepared for strangulation, when Père Lactance cut short debate by seizing a wisp of straw, lighting it and himself starting the pyre. Grandier is said with his last words to have summoned him to the judgment seat of God within a month, a story doubtless suggested by the fact that Lactance died insane on September 18. Père Tranquille died, also insane, some five years later. That there was trickery in the pricking for the insensible spots is rendered probable by the fact that the surgeon Mannouri, who was employed as pricker, was haunted by the specter of Grandier and died in delirium caused by it.

For some years the performances of the energumens were kept up and it seems to have made Loudun a fashionable place of resort for the curious. Gaston, duke of Orléans, visited it in May 1635, was duly edified and obligingly signed a certificate as to the wonders which he had witnessed. Lord Montagu, also, who came there, was so impressed that he was converted to Catholicism. A year or two later, however, the Duchess d'Aiguillon, Richelieu's niece, came with some skeptics in her train who readily convinced her of the imposture. On her return to Paris she communicated this to her uncle. Richelieu's interest in the affair had passed; he suppressed the pension of four thousand livres that had been granted to the performers, and the exorcisms and revelations ceased.[85]

---

[85] *Histoire des Diables de Loudun, ou de la Possession des Religieuses Ursulines et de la Condamnation et du Suplice d'Urbain Grandier* (Amsterdam, 1752).

This work was written by Aubin, a French refugee. The first edition appeared in Amsterdam in 1693 and it was reprinted in 1716, 1737, and 1752. It is of course in no sense an impartial narrative and one would hesitate to accept its statements if it were not for the attempted refutation by Père de la Ménardaye (*Examen et Discussion critique de l'Histoire des Diables de Loudun* [Paris, 1747]). In this the criticism is so minute and captious as to give assurance that statements not controverted are admitted as true, and the admissions are such as to justify Aubin as to all the main facts. It is true that we are told that at the execution the brutal use of an iron crucifix must be false because crucifixes are not made of iron, and that the knot in the cord prepared to strangle Grandier was the result of accident and not of design, which may be correct. We may, however, reasonably doubt the writer's reasoning powers when he seriously argues (pp. 220-31, 237) that the cases in which the possession was shown to be fraudulent, in reality, only prove its truth, as showing the astuteness of the demons; and also when he answers the objections urged against the appointment of a special commission by telling us that it does not become right-minded men to criticise the acts of their superiors (p. 62). He professes to have discovered Grandier's motive in bewitching the nuns by stating that, when a vacancy occurred in the confessorship of the convent, Grandier sought the position and vented his wrath on the successful candidate, Canon Mignon, by giving him the heavy burden of a houseful of demoniacs (pp. 447-48).

[Much has been written on the case of Grandier. See Yve-Plessis, *Bibliographie française de la Sorcellerie,* nos. 1284-1339. But there is much, too, in the histories of witchcraft (notably Garinet, important for documents; and Baissac, for fullness, pp. 455-521). So

The tragi-comedy of demoniacal possession was infectious and other cases followed, of which the most conspicuous was that of the Franciscan nunnery of Louviers, where twenty-three out of fifty-two sisters wére affected. The spiritual director of the house was Mathurin Picard, parish priest of Mesnil-Jourdain, a man of irreproachable piety, somewhat inclined to mysticism, who was occasionally replaced by his vicar, Thomas Boullé. Fortunately for himself Picard died in 1642 and was buried in the church near the altar. On a visitation by the bishop of Evreux, in 1643, the possessed sisters accused him and Boullé of causing their troubles, when the bishop ordered the corpse to be disinterred secretly and thrust into unconsecrated ground. This became known and the Parlement of Normandy took up the matter as an infringement of its jurisdiction. The trial lasted until 1647 and the character of the testimony may be inferred from that of one of the women, Madeleine Bavent, who swore that on a Holy Thursday in the Sabbat she had eaten part of a roasted child served whole, the other partakers at the table being Picard, Boullé, and a demon in the shape of David, the predecessor of Picard in the direction of the convent. On the strength of such evidence the Parlement, August 24, 1647, rendered a sentence under which, the same day, Boullé was burnt alive, chained to the remains of Picard. A person named Duval, whom Madeleine recognized as having seen in the Sabbat, was also burnt. Madeleine herself was imprisoned until death, a sister Simonne Gaguin was not released till after eight years, the other nuns were scattered and the house was razed.[86] The Parlement of Rouen, in 1670, had a case of greater importance, in an epidemic of witchcraft near Coutances, when it confirmed the death-sentence of the local authorities on twelve persons. Fortunately an appeal was made to Louis XIV, who, on the advice of Colbert, commuted the

---

lately as 1859 the Abbé Leriche published a book to prove the possessions genuine (*Études sur les Possessions*, etc. [Paris, 1859]; but the most important modern studies are those of Dr. Gabriel Legué, who in 1874 published *Documents pour servir à l'Histoire médicale des Possédées de Loudun*, in 1880, largely from unpublished records, his *Urbain Grandier et les Possédées de Loudun* (reprinted in 1884 less sumptuously, but with additions); and in 1886, with Dr. G. de La Tourette, edited for the first time the autobiography of Mme Belcier, the Ursuline Superior (*Sœur Jeanne des Anges* [Paris, 1886], in the *Bibliothèque diabolique*: "Collection Bourneville"). Of Aubin's book a racy English translation, ascribed to Daniel Defoe, was published at London in 1703 under the title *The Cheats and Illusions of Romish Priests and Exorcists discovered in the History of the Devils of Loudun.*—B.]

[86] Baissac, *Les Grands Jours de la Sorcellerie*, pp. 545-67. [The Louviers episode, too, gave rise to much literature. The titles may be found in Yve-Plessis, *op. cit.*, nos. 1340-79. The more important of the sources were in 1878-79 reprinted at Rouen in two rival editions. To these pieces should be added especially the thick quarto of the Capuchin, Esprit de Bosrogar (*La Piété affligée* [Rouen, 1652]), whose astounding credulity, as Michelet long ago pointed out, betrays the cause he thinks to help.—B.]

penalty to banishment from the province and ordered the discontinuance of the trials of the numerous accomplices inculpated. Against this the Parlement protested, insisting on the reality of the Sabbat and the evils, material and spiritual, attending it, but in vain.[87]

A royal edict against poisoners, July 1682, treats as impostors all diviners and practitioners of magic.[88] This has been regarded as putting an end to witchcraft and sorcery prosecutions in France, but it was not so, for not long afterwards a case which excited wide interest occupied the courts from 1688 to 1691. Some shepherds of Brie who quarrelled with their masters were accused of destroying cattle and sheep to the value of over a hundred thousand crowns, causing intense excitement throughout the province; the peasant farmers felt themselves to be at the mercy of their men and the Archbishop of Sens was besieged with letters from the parish priests. On the arrest of one of the accused, known as Bras-de-fer, large quantities of arsenic, verdigris, corrosive-sublimate and cantharides were found in his possession, which would have explained the trouble to those not predetermined to attribute it to witchcraft; but this was too simple a solution, especially as a book of conjurations and imprecations was also found, and the accused were condemned to be hanged and burnt by the local authorities. Appeal was made to the parlement and, as some of the judges thought that it might have been simple poisoning of cattle which was not subject to the death-penalty, the sentence was commuted to the galleys. Further developments, however, led to a revision of this decision; one of the accused named Hocque died suddenly in prison at the moment when one of his accomplices destroyed the charm that had wrought the damage; confessions of sorcery were obtained and Pierre Biaule and Medard Lavaux were condemned to be hanged and burnt, while some others were banished for nine years.[89] The authorities were more merciful in a case occurring at Montigny le

[87] Baissac, op. cit., pp. 568-76; Garinet, Hist. de la Magie, p. 337; De la Ménardaye, op. cit., p. 404. For the absurd character of the testimony on which this was based, see the analysis of it by St. André, Lettres, pp. 374-430.

Belief in witchcraft as the inciting cause of demoniacal possession is still cherished. In the epidemic at Morzine, in the Cottian Alps, which lasted from 1857 to 1862 and involved 120 persons in the sparse population of the valley, the local authorities were convinced that it would not cease until Jean Berger was beheaded and two or three other persons were publicly burnt. The government finally interfered by prohibiting all exorcisms and placing a guard at the door of every house where there was a sufferer, after which they all recovered. So in Verzegnis, a valley in the Carnic Alps, in 1878, witchcraft was assigned as the cause of an epidemic of possession. In this there were but nineteen cases, for the authorities took up the matter speedily and cut short the trouble by the same measures that had proved efficacious at Morzine.—Franzolini, L'Epidemia di Istero—Demonopatie in Verzegnis (Reggio nell' Emilia, 1879).

[88] Isambert, Anciennes Lois Françaises, XX, 396.

[89] Factums et Arrest du Parlement de Paris (in Le Brun, op. cit., pp. 506, 516-25; IV, 92-139 of enlarged ed.).

Roi, near Auxerre, in 1696. Three men and three women, tired of being reputed as sorcerers, offered to undergo the cold-water ordeal. As we learn from a formal notarial act, the trial took place June 5, in the river Senin, near the abbey of Pontigny. The parties were duly tied, wrists to ankles, and thrown in. Three sank—a man and two women—while two men and a woman floated like corks for half an hour in spite of all devices to obtain submersion. The officials wisely declined to prosecute and the poor wretches exiled themselves.[90] About the same time the learned Jean Baptiste Thiers gives full credence to the powers of malignant sorcery, but he utters the caution that accusations of the kind should be investigated with the utmost care, for they are apt to be the result of calumny.[91]

After this we hear little of sorcery in France. The celebrated case of La Cadière and Père Girard, S.J., scarce comes within its scope. She was an ecstatic with visions and the stigmata; he was her father confessor and seduced her. Recognizing that he had led her into sin, she changed her confessor and brought a formal accusation against him in 1730. The affair attracted wide attention and was decided by the Parlement of Aix, which restored La Cadière to her mother, but did not condemn Girard; to escape the vengeance of the mob he had to be conveyed away secretly and died two years afterwards in the odor of sanctity according to his Jesuit brethren.[92] That the belief in sorcery, however, still lingered even among the intelligent and educated is shown by the little work of St.-André, consulting physician to the king, in 1725, in which he takes the ground that the powers attributed to demons are an insult to Divinity; he treats the Sabbat as a fable and while he does not deny the evils wrought by so-called sorcerers he ascribes them to emanations and sympathy. His book was not allowed to appear without corrections, omissions, and additions by a doctor of the Sorbonne, but even thus it was denounced to the next assembly of the French clergy, where several prelates of high rank deemed it worthy of censure. Still more significant was the answer which it called forth in 1731 from the Sieur Boissier, who treats St.-André as an advocate of the devil. He argues for the reality of the Sabbat and tells us that to regard it as imaginary is greatly to the advantage of the devil and his subjects who are already reaping the benefit of incredulity in the peaceable enjoyment of their privileges.[93] Boissier had no difficulty in alleging ample orthodox theol-

---

[90] Ibid., pp. 529-34 of orig. ed.

[91] J. B. Thiers, Traité des Superstitions, Liv. II, cc. iv, v (Paris, 1697).

[92] Factum pour Marie Catherine Cadière, contre le Père J. B. Girard; Mémoire instructif pour le père J. B. Girard; Suite des Procedures de Cath. Cadière contre le père Girard (La Haye, 1731); Michelet, La Sorcière, cc. x, xi, xii.

[93] St.-André, Lettres, etc.; Boissier, Recueil, etc., pp. 34, 132, 138, 149, 156, 161, etc.

ogy in support of his conservatism, but it was ineffectual; incredulity was becoming permanent, and, in 1738, D'Argens alludes to the parlements which used to burn those accused of magic but now treat them as impostors or insane.[94] There were some cases of possession, in 1735 and 1746, in which an attempt was made to hold parties responsible, as Maria Renata was soon afterwards in Würzburg, but they were failures. Popular enlightenment, however, developed more slowly and on April 28, 1770, the Parlement of Paris condemned Jean Lacombe to be broken on the wheel and burnt because he and some others on May 22, 1768, had burnt alive in the parish of Genneton (Saumur) a laborer named Jauneau as a sorcerer.[95]

In Great Britain the witch-craze seems to have been somewhat later in development than on the Continent. The earliest legal enactment on the subject is that of Henry VIII, in 1542, which made it felony to practise or cause to be practised conjuration, witchcraft, enchantment, or sorcery to get money or to consume any person in his body, members or goods or to provoke any person to unlawful love.[96] This was repealed under Edward VI, in 1547,[97] and again under Mary in 1553,[98] but in 1562, under Elizabeth, it was revived in somewhat milder form, a first offence being punishable only with the pillory.[99] The demonological King James naturally made it his early care to give his English subjects the benefit of the Scottish law which had been passed in 1563, and his first parliament adopted, in 1604, a statute inflicting death without benefit of clergy or sanctuary for sorcery and witchcraft, which continued in force until the 18th century.[100]

In this legislation there was a cardinal difference from that of the rest of Europe. England had never known the blessings of the inquisitorial process and its attendant torture—except surreptitiously for political prisoners under the Tudors and early Stuarts. All criminal trials were conducted before a jury; the statutes merely defined sorcery and witchcraft, if resulting in injury, to be a felony; they were not excepted or reserved

[94] Argens, Jean Baptiste de Boyer, Marquis d', Lettres Cabalistiques (La Haye, 1738), lett. lxxxix.

[95] Abbé de la Chapelle, Le Ventriloque (Paris, 1772), p. 507.

[96] Leges, 33 Henry VIII, c. viii.

[97] Ibid., 1 Edward VI, c. xii, § 4.

[98] Ibid., 1 Mary, Sess. 1, c. i, § 5.

[99] Ibid., 6 Elizabeth, c. xvi.

[100] Ibid., 1 James I, c. xii. See Gentleman's Magazine Library, Vol. III: Popular Superstitions, (London, 1884), p. 234. In 1560 eight men were tried in London for conjuration and sorcery; all confessed and were sent to the pillory after taking an oath to abstain in future from such unlawful practices.—Hutchinson, Historical Essay concerning Witchcraft (London, 1720), pp. 3, 4, 216 ff. [1st ed., 1718.]

crimes; they were tried like any others and the penalty for conviction was hanging, as in other capital offences. In practice, however, it must be admitted that these safeguards against injustice were largely eluded. If formal torture was not used by the courts, yet in the preliminary proceedings before country magistrates or in the unlawful violence of the people there was its equivalent. As recently as 1715 a writer on the subject tells us that

The surest way to discover such as practice this odious Craft, besides their evil Lives and Conversations, is, first by their Mark, which is insensible, and, secondly, by their swimming upon the Water, God having ordained, that such as had cast off the Water of Baptism, should not be received into Water, but swim upon it.[101]

The water ordeal conducted by a howling mob with every species of ill usage and prolonged to excess was a torture eminently adapted to bring all but the strongest minds into compliance with the demand for confession. The search for the witch-mark consisted of thrusting long pins into all parts of the body until insensibility supervened and the "witch-pricker" triumphantly proclaimed that he had found the insensible spot, or until the victim's power of endurance was exhausted and she made some kind of confession. There was also the torture of sleeplessness—keeping her awake by pricks and beatings until the mind and will lost their capacity of resistance—and this was sometimes enhanced by making her sit cross-legged on a stool. A minor infliction, but one sufficiently discomposing, arose from a belief that the sufferer from witchcraft could obtain relief by scratching the witch till the blood came, so that the accused when brought before a magistrate would be assailed by those who believed themselves bewitched, who would tear her face with their nails. As the accused were usually decrepit old women, we can thus understand the confessions which so frequently figure in the trials.

When confessions had been thus obtained it is difficult for us to enter into the depth of prejudice that could ascribe weight to them from women whose attitude at the gallows was such as that of three who were hanged at Exeter in 1682 after trial before Chief-Justice North. As she mounted the ladder Susanna Edwards simply said, "The Lord Jesus speed me; though my sins be red as scarlet the Lord Jesus can make them white as snow; the Lord help my soul." Mary Trembles said, "Lord Jesus receive my soul; Lord Jesus speed me." Temperance Lloyd said, "Jesus Christ speed me well; Lord forgive all my sins; Lord Jesus Christ be merciful to my poor soul."[102] This is not the language of women

[101] Boulton, *Compleat History of Magick, Sorcery, and Witchcraft* (London, 1715), I, 23.
[102] Boulton, *op. cit.*, I, 250-54.

who had sold their souls to Satan for the poor privilege of working evil
on their neighbors.

When confessions were not obtained in this manner, the universal
prejudice against witches rendered the trial almost as great a mockery of
justice as the inquisitorial process. Counsel as yet were not allowed to
the defendant in criminal cases and the poor ignorant wretches were
utterly incapable of defending themselves. In the celebrated case of Rose
Cullender and Amy Duny, tried March 10, 1664, before so upright a
judge as Sir Matthew Hale, all kinds of evidence were admitted against
them, there was no cross-examination and no defence. When they were
asked what they had to say for themselves, they could only reply
"Nothing material to anything that was proved against them." Then
the case was given to the jury, Hale charging them that he had no doubt
that there were such things as witches. The verdict of twelve good and
true men of the vicinage, already convinced in advance, could only be
in one way, and in half an hour they rendered one of guilty. The two
old women accordingly were hanged on March 16, protesting their innocence to the last.[103]

Yet, with all these imperfections of procedure, prosecution in England
lacked the systematic completeness that characterized Germany and the
number of victims was comparatively few—far less than the estimates
commonly current. In Middlesex county, comprising London, from 1550
to 1666, there were only eight executions for witchcraft and numerous
acquittals.[104] There was an undercurrent of wholesome skepticism which
occasionally made itself manifest and checked the development of the
epidemic. Dr. Francis Hutchinson, in 1718, collected all the cases of which
his industry could find mention, and they are mostly scattering—one,
two, or three at a time. Larger groups are rare. In 1612 there were fifteen
indicted and twelve convicted at Lancaster, but this is the only group
of any size prior to the Great Rebellion.[105] In 1634, there were seventeen
of Pendle Forest condemned in Lancashire, but they were reprieved by
the judge; the king ordered a bishop to examine them, when it was
found that they had all been convicted on the evidence of a boy of ten
or eleven who pretended to be able to recognize them; on being separated from his father he acknowledged the imposture and they were
discharged.[106]

From 1644 to 1646 there was a sudden explosion of witch-hunting

---

[103] A Tryal of Witches at the Assizes held at Bury St. Edmunds, March 10, 1664 (London, 1682).

[104] Inderwick, Side-lights on the Stuarts (London, 1888), p. 169.

[105] Hutchinson, op. cit., p. 47.

[106] Ibid., pp. 50, 270-71; Webster, Displaying of Supposed Witchcraft, pp. 277-78.

which may be compared to similar outbreaks in Germany. This was due to the industry of a certain Matthew Hopkins, who styled himself Witch-finder General, and was stimulated by the Long Parliament which, in 1645, appointed a commission for the detection of witches. Hopkins, with an assistant named John Sterne, drove a thriving trade, going from town to town and being well paid for cleansing them of witchcraft. Deprivation of sleep and food or the water ordeal seems to have been his usual formula for detection, and he traversed the counties of Essex, Suffolk, Norfolk, and Huntingdon, leaving a track of blood behind him. What was the aggregate of his victims it would be impossible now to estimate, but we hear, in 1644, of thirty-seven executed in Manningtree, his own town, and of sixteen in Yarmouth; in 1645, of fifteen in Chelmsford and twenty in Norfolk; in 1645 and 1646, of about forty in Bury St. Edmunds and in 1646, of many in Huntingdon. Fortunately his devastating career was cut short by some unbelievers who tied him, thumbs to toes, and cast him into the water, when he floated, which destroyed his reputation. The impulse still continued, however, and, in 1647, we hear of a number convicted at Newcastle by pricking.[107]

Under the Restoration, skepticism increased. In 1664, there were a number accused in Somersetshire where Robert Hunt, justice of the peace, busied himself energetically in collecting evidence; "and had not his Discoveries and Endeavours met with great Opposition and Discouragement from some then in Authority, the whole Clan of those Hellish Confederates in these parts had been justly exposed and punished."[108] Judges were becoming less credulous and convictions were rare. In 1686, three women were tried in Wiltshire before Chief Justice Raynsford, of whom two were convicted and one acquitted, but pricking and sleeplessness had been prohibited and eleven suspects were discharged.[109] In fact, in the Western Circuit, from 1670 to 1712, there were fifty-two trials for witchcraft with only seven convictions, and one of the latter was reprieved.[110] Between 1694 and 1696 there were four trials before Chief Justice Holt, with the same kind of testimony as that which convicted Rose Cullender and Amy Duny, but he so charged the juries that they

---

[107] Hutchinson, *op. cit.*, pp. 50-51, 79-87; Inderwick, *op. cit.*, p. 161. See also *The Witches of Huntingdon, their Examinations and Confessions* (London, 1646). [The career of Hopkins has since been studied in the books of Notestein, Kittredge, and Ewen. That he was ever "swum" is now more than doubtful. That he died in his bed of consumption is what we are told by his assistant, Sterne. It is Butler who in his *Hudibras* tells the story of his swimming.—B.]

[108] Glanvil, *Sadducismus Triumphatus*, Pt. II, pp. 67-89.

[109] *Gentleman's Magazine Library*, III, 287; Inderwick, *op. cit.*, p. 171.

[110] *Ibid.*, p. 174.

were all acquitted and it was the same with eleven more cases up to 1701.[111]

Juries were not always thus amenable to the wisdom of the bench, as was seen in a case that attracted much attention in 1712. Jane Wenham was an elderly woman who for some fifteen years had been regarded with suspicion. A lying young wench, named Anne Thorne, accused her of having bewitched her. When brought before Mr. Chauncey, the committing magistrate, Anne flew at her and scratched and tore her face, while Chauncey thrust pins into her and counseled her to confess as the safest course for her. The bewildered old woman confessed that she was a witch and on the ensuing trial such evidence was gravely admitted as that of Anne's that she had seen cats with faces like the defendant's and that down pillows had been found with feathers caked together in them. Two local clergymen produced much impression on the jury by their attestations of belief and, in spite of the efforts of the judge, Sir John Powell, they brought in a verdict of guilty. Powell exerted himself to save her and procured a pardon from Queen Anne, for which good work he ran some risk of his life in country districts. The case excited much discussion and produced a shower of pamphlets on both sides; the excited people would still have killed her, but Colonel Plummer of Gilston protected her, taking her into his service, and Hutchinson, in 1718, informs us that she was still living, performing her religious duties regularly and universally recognized as innocent.[112] Yet in that same year, 1712, five witches were hanged at Northampton; on the other hand, at Brentwood, Essex, when a popular application of the water ordeal had resulted in the death of the patient and the chief actors were tried, the jury desired to bring in a verdict of manslaughter, but Chief Justice Parker made it murder, so that presumably they were hanged. Witchcraft, as a recognized crime, was now nearing its end; the last case is said to have occurred in 1716, when Mary Hickes and her daughter, a child but nine years old, were executed, July 28, at Huntingdon.[113] Still, the statute of James I remained in force until 1736, when it was abrogated, as well as the Scottish law, to take effect June 24; but, to discourage pretenders to sorcery, they were to be imprisoned for a year without bail and to be exposed four times in the pillory.[114]

---

[111] Hutchinson, op. cit., pp. 59-61, 63.

[112] The Case of the Hertfordshire Witchcraft considered (London, 1712); Hutchinson, op. cit., pp. 164-65; Inderwick, op. cit., pp. 175-76.

[113] Inderwick, op. cit., pp. 177, 178; Hutchinson, op. cit., pp. 175-76. [Notestein, Witchcraft in England (1911), and Ewen, Witchcraft and Demonianism (1933), reject the story of Mrs. Hickes and her daughter and know nothing of the five at Northampton.—B.]

[114] Leges, 9 George II, c. v.

It was easier to remove laws from the statute-book than to eradicate beliefs so long entertained and by many regarded as a necessary part of religion. In 1751, at Tring in Hertfordshire, a publican named Butterfield accused an old couple, Osborne and his wife, of bewitching him. With a view to profits from attracting a crowd, it was cried in several market towns that on April 22 they would be ducked at Longmarston. This brought together an immense mob; to save the victims they were conveyed from the workhouse to the church, but the mob broke into the workhouse, seized the governor and threatened to drown him and to burn the town. They attained their object; stripped the poor wretches, tied them thumbs to toes, dragged them some miles to a stream and cast them in with abundant beating and kicking. The man was left for dead, but recovered; the woman died on the spot. A number of the participants were indicted, but only one, the chief actor, named Colley, was hanged. At his execution he had the entire sympathy of the assembled crowd.[115]

This is not to be wondered at when men of the highest character for learning and piety still cherished the belief in witchcraft. Sir Matthew Hale, a fortnight after sending to the gallows the two poor women mentioned above, composed a discourse on the power of evil spirits in which he says, "it is also confirmed to us by daily experience of the power and energy of these evil spirits in witches and by them."[116] Meric Casaubon, who enjoyed the dignity of the doctorate of Divinity, tells us that those who oppose the belief in witchcraft are either notorious atheists, such as Pomponazzi, Vanini, and the like, or "confident illiterate wretches, as one of this country, Reginald Scot."[117] The dictum of John Wesley is well-known that "the giving up witchcraft is, in effect, giving up the Bible."[118] William Robertson, the historian, accepts the reality of witchcraft when, in speaking of King James, he says, "But though James connived at real crimes, witchcraft, which is commonly an imaginary one, engrossed his attention."[119] Even so enlightened a lawyer as Sir William Blackstone does not hesitate to say that "To deny the possibility, nay, actual existence of witchcraft and sorcery, is at once flatly to contradict the revealed word of God . . . and the thing itself is a truth to which every nation in the world hath in its turn borne testimony."[120]

[115] Gentleman's Magazine Library, III, 268-70, 320.

[116] A Collection of Modern Relations concerning Witches, to which is prefixed a Meditation by the late Lord Chief Justice Hale (London, 1693).

[117] A Treatise proving Spirits, Witches and Supernatural Operations with the Imprimatur of the Archbishop of Canterbury (London, 1672), pp. 40, 42, 47.

[118] Wesley, Journal, 1768.

[119] Robertson, History of Scotland, Book VIII.

[120] Blackstone's Commentaries (Oxford, 1775), IV, 60.

The Spanish Inquisition, therefore, is scarce to be judged harshly if it maintained to the last its belief in pact with Satan.

The predilection of extreme Protestantism for the Old Testament may perhaps explain in part why Scotland suffered so much more than England from the witch-craze, and when to this is added the free use of torture the reason becomes clear. It was not, however, until 1563 that the Act was passed which punished with death not only all who used witchcraft, sorcery, or necromancy, or pretended skill therein, but also all who consulted them.[121] It is true that the accused had trial by jury, but this gave small promise of escape, for a jury that "assoilzied" a witch were themselves liable to prosecution on the charge of wilful error and to be condemned to fine and imprisonment. On such an occasion, in 1591, King James himself occupied the bench; the jurors humbled themselves and pleaded ignorant error and the monarch graciously pardoned them.[122] Under such circumstances it can be imagined that acquittals were not numerous.

The presbyteries took an active part in these affairs. In 1640 the General Assembly ordered "all ministers carefully to take notice of charmers, witches and all such abusers of the people and to urge the Acts of Parliament to be executed against them."[123] It would seem that the usual routine, when any one complained of being bewitched, was for the local presbytery to apply to the lords of the Privy Council, who thereupon issued a commission appointing certain parties to "take precognition" of the matter. When evidence was thus collected and put into shape, another commission was issued to try the accused; the presbytery then appointed some of its members to supervise the trial and urge forward the proceedings, and it also named days of fasting and prayer to God to restrain the rage of Satan.[124] After the Restoration, we are told, the

---

[121] Erskine's *Law of Scotland*, p. 488.

[122] Rogers, *Scotland, Social and Domestic* (London, 1869), p. 280.

[123] *Ibid.*, p. 288.

[124] *A History of the Witches of Renfrewshire* (Paisley, 1877), Introd., pp. xxvii-xxxi. This is a reprint, with additions of documents, of *True Narrative of the Sufferings and Relief of a Young Girl* (Edinburgh, 1698). There are also editions of 1775 and 1809.

[In his *Studies in Church History* (ed. of 1883, p. 500), Mr. Lea has this further to say: "The kirk-sessions, moreover, were the principal promoters of the fearful prosecutions for witchcraft, which perhaps were worse in Scotland than in any other country. They paid the 'prickers' who tortured miserable old women to obtain proof, and they voted supplies of firewood for the resultant auto-da-fé. While they vigorously prohibited funerals and marriages on the Sabbath as a profanation of the sacredness of the day, witch-burnings were deemed a good work allowable on the Lord's day, and committees of ministers attended them officially. Zealous ministers, indeed, sometimes did not content themselves with simply directing these proceedings. In 1650, Mr. John Aird, minister of Stow, reported to his kirk-session his success in personally convicting a witch by pricking her, having

records of the Privy Council consist chiefly of the issuing of these commissions to try witches, and in the session of November 7, 1661, there were no less than fourteen of them.

While the water ordeal was admitted as evidence, it was not so much in favor as the insensible witch-mark discovered by pricking. This was employed to such an extent that witch-pricking became a recognized profession, liberally paid. The accused was stripped and tied hand and foot and pins were thrust in everywhere until the insensible spot was discovered; and few there were in whom the experienced pricker failed to identify it. George Cathie was an expert practitioner of the art in the West of Scotland and did not forfeit his reputation even after he had pronounced to be witches twelve parishioners of Crawford-Douglas whose accuser, on their trial, was proved to be a lunatic. John Kincaid was a still more prominent witch-pricker, who enjoyed the office of "common pricker" to the Court of Judiciary. He never failed to discover the witch-mark, but when he undertook to practise his art on his own account and without authority the Court of Judiciary threw him into prison and he was liberated only after he had pledged himself not to act without judicial warrant. The slaughter caused by these brutes was not small. One who was hanged confessed at the gallows that he had illegally caused the death of 120 women. When confession was deemed necessary during a trial, tortures of increasing severity were unsparingly applied, without limitation, to an extent far exceeding those habitual in the Inquisition and far more revolting in their ingenuity, so that death was not an uncommon result. When these failed the inhuman device was sometimes resorted to of bringing into the prison the parents or children of the accused and torturing them in her presence. The stern uncompromising Calvinistic spirit shrank from nothing when engaged in a personal conflict with Satan. The punishment, as on the Continent, was the stake but, as there, for those who confessed it was mitigated by preliminary strangulation. Even as late as 1722, a demented old woman, condemned to the stake in the county of Sutherland, warmed her stiffened hands as the flames approached her and chattered her gratification at the unaccustomed comfort. It is satisfactory to know that the sheriff responsible for this superfluous zeal was reprimanded.[125]

Yet in one respect Scottish procedure was more equitable than English, for the accused was allowed defence by counsel. We have an example of this by Sir George McKenzie, in a case occurring between 1660 and 1670, in which it is interesting to see the advocate citing the Cap. *Episcopi*

---

triumphantly thrust into her shoulder a pin up to the head." And he cites for this Rogers, *op. cit.*, pp. 29, 270, 328.—B.]

[125] Rogers, *op. cit.*, pp. 265-66, 268-69, 301.

and Ponzinibio to prove that the Sabbat is an illusion. He does not venture to deny the existence of witchcraft, but argues that it should be clearly proved, "since the crime is so improbable and the conclusion so severe." The final summary of his argument describes so accurately the situation existing in Scotland that it is worth transcribing.

Consider how much fancy does influence ordinar Judges in the trial of this crime, for none now labour under any extraordinar Disease but it is instantly said to come by Witch-craft and then the next old deform'd or envyed woman is presently charged with it; from this ariseth a confused noise of her guilt, called *diffamatio* by Lawyers, who make it a ground for seizure, upon which she being apprehended is imprisoned, starved, kept from sleep and oft times tortured: To free themselves from which they must confess and, having confest, imagine they dare not thereafter retreat. And then Judges allow themselves too much liberty in condemning such as are accused of this crime, because they conclude they cannot be severe enough to the enemies of God and Assisers are affraid to suffer such to escape as are re-mitted to them, lest they let loose an enraged Wizard in their neighbor-hood. And thus the poor Innocents die in multitudes by an unworthy Martyredom and Burning comes in fashion.[126]

In an appeal to the superior court, Sir George felt at liberty to speak freely as to the lower tribunals in which the vast majority of cases were definitely decided, for the poor old crones who were the usual victims had neither the knowledge nor the means to employ skilled advocates and the privilege to do so was, for the most part, as illusory as the crimes with which they were charged.

Nowhere perhaps more thoroughly than in Scotland was the popula-tion interpenetrated with unquestioning belief in witchcraft or with the resolute determination to extirpate it, which formed so large a factor in its development and growth. Therefore, we may safely assume, I think, that during the existence of the witch-craze Scotland stands at the head of the melancholy list in the proportion of executions to the number of inhabitants. Statistics are, of course, inaccessible, but Mr. Rogers is probably not far from the mark in his estimate that, from first to last, there were in Great Britain about thirty thousand victims, of which a fourth may be assigned to Scotland.[127]

---

[126] Sir George McKenzie, *Pleadings in some remarkable Cases before the Supreme Courts of Scotland, since the Year 1661* (Edinburgh, 1672), pp. 188, 194, 196.

[127] Rogers, *op. cit.*, p. 302. [This estimate, by a Scot, may still be credible for Scotland, though Mr. Rogers does not tell us whose is the count nor on what it is based; but it is no longer so for England, where attempts at a census have now been made by Notestein (*History of Witchcraft in England, 1558-1718* [1911] and Ewen (*Witch Hunting and Witch-Trials,* 1929; *Witchcraft and Demonianism,* 1932). Mr. Ewen thinks (p. 112 of his *Witch-Hunting)* "the number of executions for witchcraft in England from 1542 to 1786

The act of Parliament of 1736 abolished not only the English statute of 1604, but the Scottish one of 1563, and defined the punishment in future as that for imposture. This was not submitted to without a protest by the Presbyterian clergy. In 1743 the associate Presbytery of Edinburgh issued a pastoral in which the act was denounced as a great national sin,[128] and in 1785 we are told that in the annual confession of sin read from the pulpits there was still included the repeal of the statutes against witches, contrary to the express law of God. This was rather an academic concession to belief than an anticipation of a change in practice, for the courts had ceased to execute the statute, and the case of 1722, above alluded to, is supposed to have been the last in Scotland.[129]

Still, popular faith was unalterable by Acts of Parliament. So recently as 1815 a learned minister felt it necessary to write a book to defend religion and the Scriptures from the charge that belief in the Bible necessarily involves belief in the existence of witchcraft. Brought by his pastoral duties into the most intimate relations with people of all classes, his experience is condensed in the assertion,

Nor is it possible to converse concerning witchcraft with those in the lower walks of life, or even with a majority of those who have received a better education and whose opinions are more consonant with reason, without observing the rooted conviction of its existence which obtains in their minds.[130]

This long and dismal history of a hallucination through which pious and well-meaning men, for centuries, inflicted incalculable misery on their fellow beings under the belief that they were serving God in combating Satan, has seemed to be necessary in order to measure the service performed by the Inquisition in Spain and Italy. It could not reject the belief so long inculcated by the Church, but at least it restricted to the narrowest limits the evil consequences of that belief.

---

may be guessed at less than 1000," though he admits the sad inadequacy of our evidence. For Scotland, Dr. George F. Black, who undertakes in the *Bulletin* of the New York Public Library (Nov., Dec. 1937, Jan. 1938) the first careful list, would guess the executions there, between 1590 and 1680, at 4,400; and there were earlier and later ones.—B.]

[128] Rogers, *op. cit.,* p. 302; *The Witches of Renfrewshire,* p. 214.

[129] [Mr. Lea, like Mr. Lecky, dates back to 1722 the witch-burning reported by Captain Burt (in his *Letters from the North of Scotland,* I, 227-34, 271-77) as of 1727.—B.]

[130] *A Belief in Witchcraft unsupported by Scripture:* An Essay by James Paterson, A.M., Minister of the Associated Congregation, Midmar (Aberdeen, 1815).

ETHICAL VALUES IN HISTORY*

CIRCUMSTANCES deprive me of the honor of presiding over this meeting of the American Historical Association to which your kindly appreciation has called me, but at least I can fulfil the pleasant duty of addressing to you a few words on a topic which is of interest to all of us, whether students or writers of history. In this I do not pretend to instruct those whose opinions are, to say the least, fully as mature and worthy of consideration as my own, but merely to contribute to a discussion which will probably continue as long as men shall strive to bring the annals of the past to the knowledge of the present.

One whose loss we all deplore and whose memory we honor as perhaps the most learned and thoughtful scholar in the English-speaking world—the late Lord Acton—in his well-known Cambridge lecture, has formally placed on record his opinion on ethical values in history when saying,

I exhort you never to debase the moral currency or to lower the standard of rectitude, but to try others by the final maxim that governs your own lives and to suffer no man and no cause to escape the undying penalty which history has the power to inflict on wrong. The plea in extenuation of guilt and mitigation of punishment is perpetual. At every step we are met by arguments which go to confuse, to palliate, to confound right and wrong, and to reduce the just man to the level of the reprobate. The men who plot to baffle and resist us are, first of all, those who made history what it has become. They set up the principle that only a foolish Conservative judges the present time with the ideas of the past; that only a foolish Liberal judges the past with the ideas of the present.

The argument with which Lord Acton justifies this exhortation to his students presupposes a fixed and unalterable standard of morality, together with the comfortable assurance that we have attained to that absolute knowledge of right and wrong which enables us to pass final judgment on the men of the past, secure that we make no mistake when we measure them by our own moral yardstick. Every foregone age has similarly flattered itself, and presumably every succeeding one will continue to cherish the same illusion.

I must confess that to me all this seems to be based on false premises and to lead to unfortunate conclusions as to the objects and purposes of history, however much it may serve to give point and piquancy to a narrative, to stimulate the interest of the casual reader by heightening

* Presidential address, read before the annual meeting of the American Historical Association at New Orleans, December 29, 1903. Printed in the *American Historical Review*, IX (1903-4), 233-46.

lights and deepening shadows, and to subserve the purpose of propagating the opinions of the writer.

As regards the inferred premiss that there is an absolute and invariable moral code by which the men of all ages and of all degrees of civilization are to be tried and convicted or acquitted, a very slender acquaintance with the history of ethics would appear sufficient to establish its fallacy. It would be overbold to suggest that morals are purely conventional and arbitrary, yet anthropological research has shown that there is scarce a sin condemned in the Decalogue which has not been or may not now be regarded rather as a virtue, or at least as an allowable practice, at some time or place among a portion of mankind, and no one would be so hardy as to judge with the severity of the Hebrew lawgiver those who merely follow the habits and customs in which they have been trained. We regard the gallows as the rightful portion of him who slays his fellow creature for gain, yet who among you would inflict the death penalty on the head-hunter of Borneo? You would condemn the superstition which leads him to glory in the deed, but your conscience would acquit him of personal guilt, for he but follows the tradition of his race, and he may in all other human relations lead an exemplary life. The actor in a Corsican vendetta is not to be judged as a common murderer, although his life may rightly pay to society the forfeit arising from his being the survival of an older and ruder civilization.

Race, civilization, environment, all influence the moral perceptions, which vary from age to age, while the standards of right and wrong are modified and adapted to what at the moment are regarded as the objects most beneficial to the individual or to the social organization. At one time these may concern the purity or advancement of religion; at another, self-preservation or the welfare of the clan or the nation; at another, personal well-being and the development of industry as a means to that end. Whatever stands foremost in any given period will be apt to receive special recognition from both the ethical teacher and the lawgiver. It is to legislation that we must look if we desire to understand the modes of thought and the moral standards of past ages; and a comparison of these with those now current will show how unstable and fluctuating are ethical conceptions. We are unable to conceive of vicarious punishment as justifiable, yet Hammurabi in some cases slays the innocent son and lets the guilty father go scathless. To us the idea of levirate marriage is abhorrent, but it has been regarded as legally a duty by races so far removed from each other in origin and distance as the Hebrew and the Hindu. Among the Hebrews the severest of all penalties was lapidation, which was reserved for the most atrocious crimes. Of these, omitting sexual aberrations which we need not consider here, Thonissen enumerates eight—idol worship, consecration of children to Moloch, magic and divination, blasphemy, Sabbath breaking, cursing a parent, and disobedience to parents. Examine our modern codes, in which these have either disappeared or are treated as comparatively trivial offenses, and you will be constrained to admit that crime is largely conventional, dependent not on an eternal and imprescriptible moral law, but on the environment in which a portion of mankind happens at the time to be placed. To the Hebrew priest the preservation of his religion was the one essential thing, and no penalty was too severe for aught that threatened its supremacy.

So it was in the Middle Ages, when the priest erected a similar standard of morals, claimed for it the sanction of divine law, and compelled its insertion in statute law. No character in medieval history stands forth with greater luster than the good St. Louis of France, yet, if his faithful biographer, De Joinville, is to be believed, he held that the only argument which a layman should use with a heretic was to thrust a sword into him; and we know by authentic documents that he fostered the nascent Inquisition and had no scruple in enriching his treasury with the confiscations resulting from the burning of heretics. We of to-day are not lacking in religious convictions, though we are learning the lesson of toleration; lapidation and the stake for opinion's sake are abhorrent to us, but who among us would feel justified in applying Lord Acton's formula and condemning the Hebrew or St. Louis when we feel that they acted on profound conviction? No English jurist has left a fairer record than Chief Justice Hale, yet he calmly sent to the gallows poor old women for witchcraft, such being the law of the land to which he gave his. hearty concurrence. Would you condemn him as you would a modern judge? Voltaire has sufficiently shown the use that may be made of thus trying one age by the standards of another in his mocking sketch of David, the man after God's own heart.

It may perhaps be urged that in thus asserting the temporary and variable character of morals we are destroying the foundations of morality in general and the eternal distinction between right and wrong. This is begging the question, for it presupposes that there is a universal and inflexible standard of morals. Such there may be, like the so-called law of nature of the Scholastic theologians, but the history of mankind fails to reveal it, and the truest test of any period is the standard which it made or accepted, for this shows better than aught else whether it was a period of progress or one of retrogression. Speculations enough there have been among philosophers, ancient and modern, as to the origin of the conception of what we call sin and righteousness, which would lead us too far from our subject to discuss here. Suffice it to say that what we find current around us is merely the result of the finite wisdom of our ancestors adapting themselves to the exigencies of their surroundings. We have fortunately inherited the noble ideals of the school of Hillel, broadened and deepened and rendered applicable to all mankind by the teachings of Christ. We have accepted them in theory for well-nigh two thousand years, yet only within a century or two has there been any serious effort to reduce them to practice, and that effort thus far has been more significant in its failures than in its successes. There is ample work before us in laboring for their embodiment in our daily lives, and we can well afford to cast the mantle of charity over those who, in fact, have been only one or two steps behind us in the application of the Sermon on the Mount.

Meanwhile, as connected with our subject, we may reflect that there is some truth in the distinction drawn by the casuists between material and formal sin—the sin which a man commits in ignorance being venial, while that which he does knowingly is mortal. This doctrine is not without its dangers, and Pascal has exposed the unmoral results to which it may lead in skilful hands, but for our purpose it may be borne in mind when we feel called upon to pass judgment on historical characters. It makes the human conscience the standard of conduct. If a man does wrong, conscientiously believing it to be right, he is justified before God; if he does right believing it to be wrong, he is condemned. Roughly speaking, in a region so full of pitfalls for unwary feet, the theory of invincible ignorance though liable to abuse is not to be overlooked.

Thus far I have sought briefly to show that Lord Acton's dictum is defective in principle. As regards its practical application, I presume that you will agree with me that history is not to be written as a Sunday-school tale for children of larger growth. It is, or should be, a serious attempt to ascertain the severest truth as to the past and to set it forth without fear or favor. It may and it generally will, convey a moral, but that moral should educe itself from the facts. Characters historically prominent are usually so because they are men of their time, the representatives of its beliefs and aspirations; and they should be judged accordingly. If those beliefs and aspirations lead to evil the historian should seek to trace out their origin and development, and he can, if he so chooses, point out their results; but he should not hold responsible the men who obeyed their consciences, even if this led them into what we conceive to be wrongdoing. It is otherwise with those who have sinned against the light vouchsafed to them, for to condemn them is simply to judge them by the standards of their time.

In other words, this is merely to apply the truism that the historian should so familiarize himself with the period under treatment that, for the time, he is living in it, feeling with the men whose actions he describes, and viewing events from their standpoint. Thus alone can he give us an accurate picture of the past, making us realize its emotions and understand the evolution of its successive stages. This is the true philosophy of history, and from this the reader can gather for himself the lessons which it teaches.

To depart from this and to inject modern ethical theories into the judgment of men and things of bygone times is to introduce subjectivity into what should be purely objective. We all of us have our convictions—perchance our prejudices—and nothing for the historian is more vital than to be on his guard against their affecting his judgment and coloring his narrative. Above all things he should cultivate the detachment which enables him soberly and impartially to search for and to set forth the truth. He may often feel righteous indignation—or what he conceives to be righteous—but he should strenuously repress it as a luxury to be left to his reader. Moreover, he should beware of theories; for when a theory once takes possession of a writer it renders him an unsafe guide and inspires reasonable distrust. The historian who becomes an advocate or a prosecutor instead of a judge forfeits his title to confidence, and, if he aspires to be a judge, he should not try a case by a code unknown to the defendant.

Perhaps this somewhat dry disquisition can be rendered more interesting by a concrete example; and for this I know of none fitter than Philip II of Spain, whose character has exercised so many brilliant pens. Our eloquent Motley, who represents him as a monster with scarce a redeeming trait, says that

To judge him, or any man in his position, simply from his own point of view, is weak and illogical. History judges the man from its point of view. It condemns or applauds the point of view itself. The point of view of a malefactor is not to excuse robbery and murder. Nor is the spirit of the age to be pleaded in favor of the evil doer at a time when mortals were divided into almost equal troops.[1]

This is the language of a partisan and not of an historian; and the writer is blind to the inference to be drawn from another remark, "That monarch considered himself born to suppress heresy and he had certainly been carrying out the work during his whole lifetime."[2]

Now, Philip II, as an abstract object of contemplation, is in no sense an attractive figure. In all that awful sixteenth century there was, perhaps, no one who wrought, directly or indirectly, so much of human

[1] *History of the United Netherlands* (New York, 1861), I, 6.
[2] *Ibid.*, I, 257.

misery, no one who was more ready to supplement open force with secret guile, no one who hesitated less to resort to corruption or, if needs be, to murder. To the historian who is content with the surface of things, it is easy to condemn him offhand and to adduce ample evidence in support of the verdict—the execution of Montigny, the assassination of William the Silent and of Escobedo, the terrors of the Tribunal of Blood, the horrors of the rebellion of Granada, the stimulation of the wars of the League, the systematic bribery by which he bought the secrets of every court in Europe, to say nothing of the satisfaction which he derived from the spectacle of his own subjects in an auto-da-fé. All this is true, and to the superficial observer it may seem idle to say a word in extenuation of so black a catalogue of misdeeds. Yet the student in earnest quest of truth may reasonably pause and ask himself whether Philip is to be held morally responsible for all these crimes; whether he was a mere bloodthirsty tyrant who rejoiced in the infliction of suffering on his fellow-creatures and revelled, like the Emperor Claudius, in witnessing human agony; or whether he was the misguided agent of a false standard of duty, and conscientiously believed himself to be rendering the highest service to God and to man. If the latter be the case, we must acquit Philip of conscious guilt, and reserve our censure for the spirit of the age which misled him. If Elijah is praised for slaying in one night 450 priests of Baal, how is Philip to be condemned for merely utilizing larger opportunities in the same spirit? Does not, in truth, the difference lie only in the question, Whose ox is gored? Even in the assassinations which he ordered he had the assurance of his confessor, Fray Diego de Chaves, that a prince was fully authorized to take the lives of his subjects without process of law.

When, in fact, we analyze his reign, we find that the enforcement of religious unity was the primary motive of his public career, and that it was the object of almost all the acts for which we are asked to condemn him. For three hundred years it had been the uncontested rule in both Church and State that the obstinate dissident, or heretic, was to be put to death by fire. Even men of the largest Christian charity accepted this as one of the eternal verities, and he who ventured to question it became himself a heretic who must either recant or share the same fate. Heresy was not only a sin, subject to spiritual animadversion, but a crime visited with capital punishment by all the secular codes of Europe. Pity were better invoked for the murderer or the highwayman than for the heretic; for the heretic was the slayer of souls, while the ordinary criminal affected only the body or the purse. With the outbreak of the Reformation, the threatened disruption of the unity of faith inflamed to the highest pitch the zeal for its preservation, though we need not pause to inquire how much the lust of worldly power and wealth disguised itself under the striving for the salvation of souls. When dynasties depended on dogmas, religion became of necessity the most absorbing of public questions, and the self-deception was easy which clothed secular ambitions in spiritual garments. In the passions of the tremendous struggle each side was equally sure that it alone possessed the true faith, which was to be vindicated with fire and sword. If the canon law required sovereigns to put heretics to death, Luther in 1528 subscribed to a declaration of the Wittenberg theologians prescribing the same fate for those whom they classed as such. If Paul IV in 1555 decreed that all who denied the Trinity should be pitilessly burned, even though they recanted and professed conversion, he but followed the example which Calvin had set, two years before, in the case of Miguel Servet. If France had her feast of St. Bartholomew, Germany had led the way in the slaughter of the Anabaptists. If Spain had her Inquisition, England in 1550 under the reforming Edward VI created a similar organization, with Cranmer at its head, and Ridley, Miles Coverdale, and other eminent Protestants as inquisitors, to seek out, try, and punish dissidents, and to abandon to the secular arm those who proved to be obstinate. Motley fell into grievous error when he asserted that in the sixteenth century "mortals were divided into almost equal troops" concerning the "spirit of the age." Those whom he represents as struggling for freedom of conscience only wanted freedom to coerce the consciences of others, as was shown in 1566 by the Fury of Antwerp, and in 1618 when the synod of Dort sat in judgment on the Remonstrants. How the Calvinists shared the "spirit of the age" is well expressed in John Knox's exulting declaration that in 1561, before the arrival in Scotland of Queen Mary, "the Papistis war so confounded that none within the Realme durst more avow the hearing or saying of Messe then the theavis of Lyddesdaill durst avow their stowth [stealing] in the presence of aney upryght judge."[3] The Massachusetts law of October 19, 1658, under which Quakers were put to death on Boston Common, suffices in itself to show that this conception of public duty was not confined to one race or to one confession of faith.

This was the inevitable result of the deplorable doctrine of exclusive salvation, which rendered the extinction of heresy a duty to God and man. To its abandonment by Protestantism is attributable the gradual spread of toleration. To its retention by the Latin Church is ascribable the Ordonnance of May 14, 1724, under which, so late as 1762, Rochette, a pastor of the desert, was executed, merely for performing the rites of

---

[3] [Knox, *History of the Reformation in Scotland* (Edinburgh, 1848), Bk. III, p. 265.—H.]

his religion. It is, moreover, the inspiration of the encyclical of 1864 in which the kind-hearted Pius IX ordered every Catholic to condemn the error that a man is free to follow the religion which his reason dictates.

The embers which thus are not yet extinct were burning fiercely in the sixteenth century, and into its superheated fanaticism Philip II was born in 1527. The very air which he breathed in childhood and youth was surcharged with all the elements that made persecution a supreme duty and toleration a denial of God. His tutor was a narrow-minded bigot, Martinez Siliceo, rewarded in 1541 with the see of Murcia, and in 1546 with the primatial dignity of Toledo, where he distinguished himself by forcibly introducing the rule that no cathedral preferment should ever be conferred on one who had the slightest trace of Jewish or Moorish blood. Under such guidance, in such environment, and with the example before him of his father as the champion of Catholicism, it was impossible for a youth of Philip's sickly frame, limitations of thought, sluggishness of intellect, habitual suspicion, and obstinate tenacity of purpose to be other than what he was. When he succeeded to the great Spanish monarchy and found himself the most powerful sovereign in the civilized world, with authority stretching from the North Sea to the Mediterranean and from the farthest Atlantic to the Indian Ocean, he could scarce fail to regard himself as the instrument selected by Providence to defend the true religion and to overcome the powers of evil which had risen to supplant the Kingdom of God. He could not but feel that this enormous power had been intrusted to him for a purpose, and that it carried with it a correlative obligation to employ it for that purpose. To borrow the happy phrase of Major Hume, he felt himself to be the junior partner of God, and in carrying out with unswerving resolution the plans of God he was answerable to no human judgment.

If, in the performance of this supreme duty, he found or deemed it necessary to employ craft and cruelty, treachery and corruption, he was but combating the adversaries of God with their own weapons—weapons, indeed, which the statecraft of the age had rendered familiar to all, and which were sanctified by the cause to which they were devoted. The maxims which Machiavelli had formulated with such cynical clearness were utilized by others to gratify the lust of vulgar ambition; should he be debarred from using them when interests were at stake superior to all worldly possessions? Nor, indeed, is the present age entitled to cast the first stone at the sixteenth century, when we consider the duplicity and the contempt for human rights which have continued to mark the career of statesmen from that time to this, save perhaps in the matter of assassination, which has been abandoned to anarchism.

Apart from religious convictions, moreover, Philip as a statesman might well feel it to be his supreme allotted task to preserve in his own dominions the unity of faith which at the time was, reasonably enough, regarded as the absolute condition precedent of internal peace. Religious differences were not mere academic questions to be debated in the schools with more or less acrimony. We need not pause to ask against whom the responsibility for this is to be charged, and we may be content to accept the fact that in the passionate zeal of the time there was nothing which so deeply stirred popular feeling or lent more bitterness to civil broils than the theological issues which to-day arouse an interest comparatively so faint. Philip might well look upon the internal wars of Germany and France as a warning to keep his own territories free from the pestilent innovators whose claim to exercise freedom of conscience included the right of resistance to any authority that denied the claim. To him they were perturbators of the public peace, potential rebels who at all and every cost must be prevented from gaining a foothold if the prosperity of the state and the divine right of kings were to be maintained. In the earlier years of his reign the growing disquiet of the Netherlands emphasized the importance of this precaution and, in the latter part, the fierce struggle which exhausted his resources demonstrated the necessity of strangling heresy in the cradle.

Human motives, as a rule, are complex: pride and ambition doubtless had their share in those which urged him on his course, especially when he nourished vain hopes of establishing a daughter on the throne of France; but religious conviction and the welfare, temporal and eternal, as it was then regarded, of his subjects were ample to impel him along the course which he had inherited with his crown and for which he had been carefully trained. Philip at least was no hypocrite, using religion merely as a pretext. The sincerity of his faith can not be called into question and, if his favorite vice was licentiousness, the dissociation of religion and morals is too common an anomaly to excite special incredulity. The keen-witted Venetian envoys concur in admitting his piety, although their experiences at his court were not such as to propitiate their favor, and they were by no means blind to his defects. Perhaps the severest characterization of him is that of Gianfrancesco Morosini in 1581:

His temper is cruel, although he covers it with zeal for justice. He was never known to pardon a criminal, even his own son. He shows no affection for his children and no sign of regret at the death of his nearest kin. He is a great observer of religion, but is very vindictive. Yet he manifests no signs of it, and there is a proverb in Spain that between the king's smile and a knife there is little to choose.[4]

---

[4] [*Relazione degli Ambasciatori Veneti al Senato*, Ser. I, v, 324 (condensed).—H.]

A portion of this unflattering characterization is justified by Philip's treatment of his erstwhile favorite, Antonio Pérez, who had abused his master's confidence and had misled him into ordering the murder of Escobedo; but in other respects the habitual Spanish self-control, the studied repression of all exhibition of feeling under an exterior of kindly courtesy, deceived the Venetian, for Philip was in reality a most affectionate father. No one can read his familiar letters to his daughters, girls of fourteen and fifteen, written during the cares of his conquest of Portugal in 1581 and 1582, without recognizing a most unexpected side of his character, while his allusions to their letters to him show that the family intercourse was delightfully intimate and unreserved. His solicitude as to their welfare is extreme. He relates whatever is passing around him that he thinks will amuse or interest them. There is no sermonizing, but only the unaffected expression of a love that is sure of reciprocation. When he commences a long letter, June 26, 1581, by saying that he had been unable to write on the previous Monday, and now, in order to prevent a similar omission, he begins before taking up the business that will probably occupy him until late, we recognize that he did not allow the cares of state to choke up the fountains of mutual affection. Even more unlooked for are the references to Madalena, an old serving-woman who scolds him and threatens to leave him when he does not please her. On one occasion she had promised to write to the girls but had not shown herself; perhaps wine was the cause of this, but if she knew of his suggesting such a thing she would make him smart for it. Altogether this revelation of the *vie intime* of Philip and his family gives us a more human conception of the gloomy monarch whom we are accustomed to picture to ourselves as ensconced in the Escurial, toiling through the midnight hours in scrawling notes on ever accumulating despatches and interminable consultas.

The unaffected tenderness of the relations between Philip and his daughters throws some light on the tragedy of Don Carlos, which has been used so effectually to blacken Philip's memory. Nothing but a sense of the most absolute necessity would have led him to deprive his son of the succession which would have relieved him of the burden of royalty. Sickly and suffering, indolent by nature, and fond of country life, if he had had sons fit to govern, Sigismondo Cavalli tells us, in 1570, that he would have abandoned to them all affairs of state and have retired to the Escurial. Unfortunately, Carlos by his wayward excesses had long forfeited the affection and confidence of his father when in 1568 he was confined. From his early years he had been an object of dread to all who looked forward to his future reign. At the age of twelve Federigo Badoero describes him as bright and quick, but fierce, passionate, and obstinate. When small animals, such as rabbits, were brought in from the chase he took delight in roasting them alive and watching their agonies. At a still earlier age, when he learned that the marriage treaty between his father and Mary of England provided that the Netherlands should descend to their issue, he declared that he would not submit to it, but would fight his future half-brother, and he wrote to Charles V, then in Brussels, and asked to have a suit of armor made for him. As he reached manhood the curse of insanity which he inherited from his great-grandmother, Queen Juana la loca, developed into actions manifesting his dangerous unfitness for the throne. At the age of twenty-two he one day shut himself up in his stables for five hours, and when he came out he left twenty horses maimed with the most brutal cruelty. The slightest cause of displeasure provoked threats, or attempts to poniard, or to throw out of window, irrespective of the dignity of the offender. In one of his midnight sallies through the streets of Madrid a little water chanced to fall upon him, when he ordered the house from which it came to be burned and its occupants to be put to death, and his servants only evaded his commands by pretending that when they went there for the purpose they were prevented by finding that the holy sacrament was being carried in. When to these evidences of a disordered brain we add the unpardonable indiscretions manifested in the conduct of public business in which Philip was endeavoring to train him, we may imagine how the father might well shudder at the prospect of his vast monarchy, the bulwark of the Catholic faith, falling into such hands at a time when all constitutional barriers had been broken down and no check existed to curb the impulses of the sovereign. He might well fear also for his own life for Carlos had avowed mortal hatred of him, and in a nature so violent and ungovernable that hatred might at any moment express itself in acts. Yet what to do with a successor to whom the estates of Castile had already sworn allegiance was a problem to tax to the utmost the wisdom of the king and his advisers. Simply to declare him incapable of succession, to ask the cortes to revoke their oaths, and to await the birth and maturity of some more promising heir would merely be to invite insubordination and civil war with the prospect that Carlos, if left at liberty, would execute the design which was the immediate cause of his arrest—of flying from Spain and raising Italy or Flanders in open revolt. The only practicable solution seemed to be to treat him as Queen Juana had been treated— to place him in confinement where in the course of six months despair led him to commit such excesses of alternate gluttony and abstinence that his fragile and enfeebled frame sank under them. The cold impassiveness with which Philip watched the extinction of a young life that had opened under such brilliant promise invites criticism, but what was passing under that exterior trained to repress all manifestations of emotion none may guess. Paternal affection, it is true, had been chilled by the strained relations which had long existed, but the complications in his plans caused by the catastrophe must have been the severest of trials, and he doubtless sought consolation in imagining himself to be repeating the sacrifice of Abraham. Prescott, it seems to me, shows a curious blindness to the situation when he asks the question, "Can those who reject the imputation of murder acquit that father of inexorable rigor toward his child in the measures which he employed or of the dreadful responsibility which attaches to the consequences of them?"[5]

It has been no part of my purpose to attempt the rehabilitation of Philip. I have simply sought to represent him as an ordinary man fashioned by influences which one may hope will wholly pass away in the course of human progress, although the *affaire Dreyfus* and the massacre of Kitcheneff show how the fires of the persecuting spirit are still occasionally rekindled in their ashes. To judge of Philip in this manner is not to approve, tacitly or overtly, the influences which made him what he was—what, in fact, he could not help being. These influences we may condemn all the more heartily when we see that they made of a man, slow of intellect but obstinate in the performance of what he was taught to regard as his duty, the scourge of his fellow-creatures in place of being their benefactor. We can, moreover, enforce this lesson by the fact that this perverted sense of duty proved a curse not only to those on whom he trampled, but to his native land which he fondly imagined that he was guiding to the height of glory and prosperity. It had already been dangerously crippled by his father whose striving for the universal monarchy was disguised by zeal for the faith. Philip's ardor in the extirpation of heresy not only wasted the millions which he drew from the mines of the New World, but exhausted Spain to a point that left for his successors a land of indescribable misery, of which the outward decadence but faintly reflected the internal wretchedness. Yet the principles which misled him survived him, and to the Spaniard of the seventeenth century Philip the Prudent remained the incarnate ideal of a Catholic prince.

It is not to be assumed that history loses, in the colorless treatment which I advocate, its claims as a teacher of the higher morality—if I may be allowed thus to designate some system of practical ethics superior to that in which we of to-day are groping somewhat blindly. To depict a man like Philip as a monster of iniquity, delighting in human misery,

[5] [*The Reign of Philip II* (London, 1855), II, 450.—H.]

may gratify prejudice and may lend superficial life and vigor to narrative, but it teaches in reality no lesson. To represent him truthfully as the inevitable product of a distorted ethical conception is to trace effects to causes and to point out the way to improvement. This is not only the scientific method applied to history, but it ennobles the historian's labors by rendering them contributory to that progress which adds to the sum of human happiness and fits mankind for a higher standard of existence. The study of the past in this spirit may perhaps render us more impatient of the present, and yet more hopeful of the future.

As one of the last survivors of a past generation, whose career is rapidly nearing its end, in bidding you farewell I may perhaps be permitted to express the gratification with which, during nearly half a century, I have watched the development of historical work among us in the adoption of scientific methods. Year after year I have marked with growing pleasure the evidence of thorough and earnest research on the part of a constantly increasing circle of well-trained scholars who have no cause to shun comparison with those of the older hemisphere. In such hands the future of the American school of history is safe and we can look forward with assurance to the honored position which it will assume in the literature of the world.

HISTORICAL STUDIES

The Inquisition

CANONIZATION OF SAN PEDRO ARBUÉS*

[This account of Pedro Arbués' canonization constitutes the last four pages of a paper entitled "The Martyrdom of San Pedro Arbués," read before the American Historical Association in December 1888. The monograph described the establishment of the Inquisition in the Kingdom of Aragon against widespread opposition, the activity of its first inquisitor, his murder as the result of a plot among the Jewish *Conversos* who were the chief objects of his attacks, and the dire vengeance taken by the Inquisition on all implicated in the crime. The entire paper with almost no changes was later incorporated by Mr. Lea in his *History of the Inquisition of Spain,* I, 243-60, except the account of Arbués' long-delayed canonization, which formed no part of the earlier episode. It is here reprinted from the original article.—H.]

* * * * *

THE CANONIZATION of San Pedro Arbués offers a significant contrast to that of St. Peter Martyr, who was enrolled in the catalogue of saints in less than a year after his assassination.[1] In spite of the miracles which accompanied the death of Arbués,[2] and of innumerable subsequent ones which attested his sanctity, the papacy was by no means disposed to recognize him as a saint. The Holy See was at the time involved in contests with the Spanish Inquisition over questions of appeals, and it was gradually excluded from all supervision and control, which presumably may account for its indisposition to bear testimony to the merits of the martyr. There must have been some jealousy at work to enable the kindred of the assassins to obtain from the curia an order for the removal from the cathedral of the *insignias y mantetas* of the guilty— the scrolls bearing their names, their crimes, and their punishment, the exposure of which to public view in the churches was part of the routine of the Inquisition, and an infliction keenly felt by the families of the convicts. It required strenuous efforts to obtain permission to let them remain.[3] So strong was the feeling excited that Martín García, bishop of

* From *Papers of the American Historical Association,* III (1889), 206-09.

[1] [See *History of the Inquisition of the Middle Ages,* II, 207-17; I, 460-61.—H.]

[2] [His death occurred September 17, 1485, two days after the attack of the assassins in the cathedral of Saragossa.—H.]

[3] Libro Verde (*Revista de España,* CVI, 288). They are still to be seen in the cathedral, after three centuries have passed away (*Amador de los Rios,* III, p. 266), and the swords of the assassins still hang on the pillars near the entrance of the chancel (Vincente de la Fuente, in Oviedo's *Quinquagenas,* I, p. 73). Oviedo himself states that he had seen the withered hands of the murderers still attached to the door of the Diputacion, and he tells the story of a lady of his acquaintance whose father and mother had been burned as accomplices in the murder. She accompanied Catharine of Aragon to England as maid of honor, and one day while flirting with a gentleman of the court she several times called

Barcelona and inquisitor of Saragossa, who had participated actively in
the trials, pronounced the papal bull to be obreptitious, and inflicted on
it the indignity of placing it on the tomb with the *sanbenitos* of the
assassins.[4]

This was not calculated to placate the Holy See, and the effort to obtain the canonization of Arbués was endless. In 1537, at the request of
the all-powerful Charles V, Paul III at last ordered informations to be
taken, when many miracles were put on record, but nothing was concluded. In 1604 another attempt was made, with no result, except to swell
the list of authentic marvels wrought by his intercession. At the instance
of Philip III, in 1615, Paul V had another investigation commenced, and
yet another in 1618. Again, in 1622, Gregory XV yielded to the united
requests of Philip IV, of the Inquisition, of the city and church of Saragossa, and of the Cofradia de San Pedro Martyr for another inquest. In
1652 the matter was again agitated by renewed demands from the same
sources; the case dragged on, until, in 1663, the Congregation of Rites
announced that, after mature discussion, the martyrdom and miracles
were approved, and that in due time the canonization might be safely
proceeded with. Alexander VII, however, without awaiting this due
time, issued a brief of beatification April 17, 1668, which permitted
Arbués to be represented with the nimbus of sanctity, his relics to be
exposed for veneration, but not to be carried in processions, and his office
to be celebrated on September 17 in the cathedral of Saragossa, the church
of Epila, and the chapels of the inquisitor-general and of the Aragonese
Inquisition.[5] Arbués was thus admitted into the inferior order of the
Blessed; this step in the process of canonization seems to have satisfied
Spain for the time, and the declaration of the dignity of saintship was
postponed for a couple of centuries.

To the Spaniards, however, his sanctity was unquestionable, and he
was commonly called San Pedro Arbués, in spite of the fact that the
Holy See had thus halted half-way. It was not until the Spanish Inquisition had long been merely a matter of history that he was declared to
be on a level with those kindred spirits, St. Peter Martyr and St. Giovanni

---

him "un frio." Losing patience he retorted that at least she could not sing the song "dese
mal murio mi madre." At this brutal reminder of the horrors through which she had
passed she burst into tears, and was obliged abruptly to leave the royal circle (*Quinquagenas*, I, pp. 72-73).

[4] Paramo, *De Orig. Officii S. Inquis.*, p. 184.

[5] Trasmiera, *Vida de Pedro Arbués*, pp. 98, 99, 133, 137, 139.—Benedict XIV, *De Ser-
vorum Dei Beatificatione*, Lib. I, c. xxx, no. 4.—*Mag. Bull. Roman.* (ed. Luxemb.), VI,
195. For the distinction between beatification and canonization the reader can consult
Ferraris, *Prompta Bibliotheca, s. v.* "Veneratio Sanctorum," nn. 11ff.

Capistrano.[6] In the efforts of Pius IX to restore to the Church its mediæval luster, the function of adding to the calendar of saints was not lost sight of. Archbishop Josaphat of Polocz had been beatified in 1642, and the nineteen martyrs of Gorcum in 1675. Their cases, and that of Arbués, were taken up in 1864, together with four others. García ·Gil, archbishop of Saragossa, and his canons promptly presented the necessary supplication for the canonization of Arbués, pointing out that the storm which threatened the Church could best be met by the blood and triumph of the martyrs; and it is perhaps significant that two days before the issue of the syllabus of 1864, on December 6, the relator of the cause, Cardinal Carlo Sacconi, in consistory, put the question whether the canonization of Arbués could be safely proceeded with, and the cardinals unanimously voted in the affirmative. Pius, however, postponed rendering his supreme judgment, and asked those present to pray for God's help to enlighten him. It was not until February 23, 1865, that Pius announced that the canonization could be safely carried out, and Cardinal Patrizi in publishing the decree called attention to the infinite wisdom of God which had delayed the matter until these times when the Jews were furnishing money and brains to the enemies of the Church in their ceaseless assaults. Then a long interval occurred, attributable doubtless to the rapid development of Victor Emmanuel's kingdom, until May 11, 1866, when, in a secret consistory, Pius announced that in these perilous times, when the bonds of society seem to be dissolved, he had been led to carry to the end the canonization of the two martyrs, Josaphat Kunciewicz and Pedro Arbués, and on the question being put the cardinals unanimously answered: "Placet." The struggle of Austria with Italy and Prussia during the summer of 1866 was not conducive to the furtherance of the matter, and it was not until November that Pietro Giannelli, archbishop of Sardinia, and secretary of the Congregation of the Council, was instructed to notify, on December 8, all the bishops throughout the world, that on June 29, 1867, the eighteenth centenary of the martyrdom of Peter and Paul, the canonization would be celebrated of Josaphat, Arbués, and the rest. The prelates were summoned to be in Rome at least one month in advance, in order to be present in the consistories in which they were to vote.[7]

From all the four quarters of the globe covered by the wonderful organization of the Catholic Church, the prelates assembled to the number of about 230. As they arrived, printed statements of the claims of the several nominees for saintship were handed to them, that they might be

---

[6] [See *Inquisition of the Middle Ages,* II, 555, n.—H.]

[7] Domenico Bartolini, *Commentarium Actorum Omnium Canonizationis,* etc. (Rome, 1868), I, 17, 23, 31, 32, 62, 67, 71, 91-94.

able to act understandingly, and in that relating to Arbués the Freemasons were enumerated with the Jews as persecutors of the Church,
and it was pointed out that the inscrutable divine wisdom had resolved
that, from his seat among the Blessed, Arbués should rush to commence
the contest with the Jews. Consistories were held on the third, sixth, and
twelfth of June, in which the merits of the saints were recited, and in
the last one a vote was taken, in addition to which everyone present was
required to hand in a written opinion. The result was of course unanimous, and on the twenty-ninth, in St. Peter's, magnificently decorated for
the occasion, the formal canonization was celebrated with the solemn
and impressive ceremonies which the Church so well knows how to
organize. The venerable pontiff pronounced the sentence of canonization: "We decree and define them to be saints, and we add them to the
catalogue of saints, ordering their memory to be commemorated with
pious devotion every year by the Church universal."[8]

Thus, after a struggle which had lasted for nearly three centuries, the
merits of the martyr of Saragossa at last received their due acknowledgment.

[8] *Ibid.,* I, 133-39, 226-65, 491; II, 275 ff., 318.

DIE INQUISITION VON TOLEDO
1575-1610[*]

[Before the third volume of his *Inquisition of the Middle Ages* had left the press in 1888, Mr. Lea was already pursuing his researches among the archives of the Spanish Inquistion and was arranging for the copying of the manuscript material needed for a history of that institution. He had but recently taught himself to read German, and among the works in that language purchased in 1888 was Böhmer's *Franziska Hernandez und Frai Franzisco Ortiz*. On p. 188 of this book he found mention of a manuscript in the library of the University of Halle embodying the report of the Inquisition of Toledo to the Suprema, or central authority, covering all the actions of the local tribunal from 1575 to 1610. Realizing the importance of such a record, he wrote to Professor Böhmer asking for further information and for advice as to the proper procedure to follow in order to secure the loan of the manuscript for use in his own home. As an assurance of his reliability and the seriousness of his interest he informs Böhmer that in preparing his recent work on the *Inquisition of the Middle Ages* he had been favored with loans of manuscripts from the royal libraries of Copenhagen and Munich and from the Bodleian and the University of Dublin libraries. "I may as well mention," he adds, "that I am not a professor—only a retired man of business who am able to devote myself to the studies which were the relaxation of my previous active life."

On the recommendation of Böhmer, Lea procured through the American Minister at Berlin the consent of the Prussian Ministry of Education to the loan of the desired material, which was forwarded to him in sections through the Smithsonian Institution as intermediary, each section being returned before the next was sent.

The statistics drawn from the Halle manuscript formed the basis of a paper submitted in 1891 to the Real Academia de la Historia of Madrid for publication in its *Boletín*. No action was taken by its editors and after waiting for two years Mr. Lea wrote asking for a return of the article, which was then submitted to the *Zeitschrift für Kirchengeschichte* and at once published in its issue of Oct. 1893.

The statistics given in the following article, together with figures from other sources, are summarized in *Inquisition of Spain*, III, pp. 551-54.—H.]

* * * * *

Eine hervorragend wichtige Quelle für die Geschichte des heiligen Officiums bietet Bd. Y, c. 20, Tl. I der Königlichen Universitätsbibliothek zu Halle.[1] Er bildet einen Teil der Abschriftensammlung, die vor etwa

---

[*] From Brieger's *Zeitschrift für Kirchengeschichte*, XIV (1893), pp. 192-201.

[1] Der Verwaltung der Hallischen Universitätsbibliothek, die in so liberaler Weise mir die Sammlung zur Benutzung überliefs, sage ich auch an dieser Stelle meinen wärmsten Dank.

vierzig Jahren Gotthold Heine aus Spanien heimgebracht hat. — Um die ayuda de costa zu erlangen, mufsten die Provinzialtribunale dem Consejo de la Suprema in mehr oder minder regelmässigen Zwischenräumen über alle ihre Massnahmen Bericht erstatten. Der erwähnte Band nun besteht aus den Duplikaten der Berichte von 1575-1610, die bei der Inquisition von Toledo aufbewahrt wurden. Das Dokument ist nicht ganz vollständig, denn das auto de la fé von 1595 ist ausgelassen, und leider bricht auch das Manuskript im Anfang des auto von 1610 ab, so dass davon nur zehn Prozesse mitgeteilt werden. Mit diesen Ausnahmen, sowie auch mit Ausnahme der Verhöre von Familiaren, geben uns die Berichte eine vollständige Übersicht des ganzen während fünfunddreissig Jahren von dem bedeutendsten Tribunal Spaniens vollbrachten Werkes, denn der Bezirk von Toledo schloss zu jener Zeit die Corte ein. Im ganzen werden 1172 Prozesse aufgeführt, und dies ergiebt, wenn wir die fehlenden autos mit in Anrechnung bringen, eine Durchschnittszahl von ungefähr 35 Prozessen im Jahre.

Ein solches Schriftstück dient zu umfassender Aufklärung über die Wirksamkeit der Inquisition und deren Einfluss auf die populären Stimmungen. Ich hoffe, künftig Gelegenheit zu haben, diese Dinge im einzelnen zu erörtern; an dieser Stelle beschränke ich mich darauf, die Statistik mitzuteilen, welche ich durch sorgfältige Analyse des umfangreichen Dokumentes gewonnen habe. Das augenfälligste Ergebnis dieser Statistik ist die Widerlegung der so ungenauen und übertriebenen Zahlenangaben Llorente's, die ja bisher allgemein für glaubwürdig angesehen wurden. Seiner Schätzung nach kamen für den früheren Teil der genannten Periode auf jedes der sechzehn Tribunale in Spanien jährlich acht in Person und vier in effigie verbrannte Opfer; für den späteren Teil fünf in Person und zwei in effigie verbrannte.[2] Im folgenden wird der Nachweis geliefert werden, dass das Tribunal von Toledo während dieser fünfunddreissig Jahre im ganzen nur elf Individuen in Person und fünfzehn in effigie zum Verbrennen verurteilte. Wenn wir nun das fehlende auto von 1595 und das unvollständige von 1610 in Anrechnung bringen, so ergiebt sich, dass in Toledo alle drei Jahre nur eine lebende Person zum Feuertod und alle zwei Jahre eine zur Verbrennung in effigie verurteilt wurde. Hinsichtlich der Zahl der mit Bussen belegten Personen irrt Llorente nicht so weit von der Wahrheit ab. Er schätzt 36 bis 40 jährlich auf jedes Tribunal. Wie ich bereits erwähnt, verhandelte die Inquisition von Toledo durchschnittlich etwa 35 Prozesse im Jahr; ein Teil derselben endigte jedoch, wie wir sehen werden, mit Freisprechung oder Einstellung des Verfahrens, und bei

---

[2] Llorente, *Historia Critica* (Madrid, 1822), IX, 219—220.

vielen handelte es sich um geringfügige Vergehen, die mit leichten Strafen belegt wurden.

Diese geringfügigen Fälle liefern die interessantesten und belehrendsten Züge im ganzen dieser Berichte. Der feierliche Charakter der autos publicos de la fé hat die fast ungeteilte Aufmerksamkeit der Forscher auf sie gelenkt, während sie in Wahrheit nur einen untergeordneten Teil des Wirkens der Inquisition bildeten. So gehören von den in diesen Berichten aufgeführten 1172 Prozessen nur 386 den in Toledo abgehaltenen zwölf autos an, und von diesen wurden 47, mit Einschlufs von vier in Person und drei in effigie Verbrannten, von anderen Tribunalen überwiesen, um das Interesse an den autos von 1591 und 1600 zu erhöhen, da bei ihnen Philipp II. und Philipp III. zugegen waren. So spielte also weniger als ein Drittel der von dem Tribunal abgeurteilten Prozesse bei den autos eine Rolle.

Mit einigen wenigen Ausnahmen waren die von den autos ausgeschlossenen Fälle individuell von geringer Bedeutung, im ganzen aber übten sie eine grosse Wirkung aus, indem sie das Denken und Reden des Volkes im Zaume hielten. Dieser Seite der Thätigkeit des heiligen Officiums ist bisher nur wenig Beachtung zuteil geworden, da es an dem zu seiner Prüfung erforderlichen Materiale mangelte; es leuchtet aber von selbst ein, dass auf diesem Wege auf die Entwickelung des Nationalcharakters ein gewaltiger Einfluss ausgeübt worden ist. Jedes unbedachte, zornige oder im Scherze geäusserte Wort, das sich als Missachtung der Kirche oder des Glaubens deuten liess, konnte der Inquisition gemeldet werden und alle Anfechtungen und Sorgen eines langwierigen Prozesses im Gefolge haben. Ein derartiger Fall konnte mit einer geringen Strafe enden, oder er konnte suspendiert oder eingestellt werden, und doch war der Angeklagte der Schande eines Verhörs vor dem heiligen Officium mit der damit verbundenen langen, bangen Ungewissheit ausgesetzt; denn wie gering auch das Vergehen sein mochte, so wurden gleichwohl die umständlichen Formen der Voruntersuchung, der Mahnungen, der Anklage, des Zeugenaufgebotes und der Ernennung eines letrado für die Verteidigung streng beobachtet. So fühlte sich jeder Einzelne einer beständigen Gefahr ausgesetzt. Die Zahl der Fälle, in denen Frauen oder Kinder, Gatten oder Eltern oder Dienstboten der Angeklagten als Kläger auftraten, zeigt, dass die heiligsten Familienbande nicht gegen Denunziation schützten, und dass niemand sich im Schosse seiner Familie sicher fühlen konnte. Wie weitverbreitet dieses Gefühl der Unsicherheit war, erkennen wir daraus, dass in zahlreichen Fällen die Schuldigen aus freien Stücken erschienen, um sich selbst wegen irgendeines in einem unbewachten Augenblicke gesprochenen Wortes anzuklagen. In diesen Berichten beziffert die Zahl solcher Selbstanklagen sich auf nicht weniger als 170, das heisst auf etwas mehr als einen unter je sieben Fällen.

Nachstehende Tabelle der bei den Prozessen verhandelten Fälle ist nach verschiedenen Richtungen hin interessant. Sie zeigt, wie ausgedehnt die von dem heiligen Officium ausgeübte Jurisdiktion war und wie wenig es mit eigentlicher Ketzerei zu thun hatte. Desgleichen ergiebt sich eine verhältnismässig grosse Zahl gewisser Arten von Vergehen, während die Menge der Anklagen wegen proposiciones unmittelbar den repressiven Einfluss des heiligen Officiums auf das volkstümliche Denken, seine heilsame Funktion als custos morum, sowie die zu jener Zeit von irrtümlicher Spekulation eingeschlagenen Richtungen erkennen lässt.

Mauren	190	Fälle
Juden	174	”
Lutheraner (sämtliche protest. Sekten)	47	”
Solicitantes in actu confessionis	52	”
Bigamisten	53	”
Gotteslästerung	46	”
Zauberei	18	”
Falsche Zeugen	8	”
Illuminati	12	”
Messelesen ohne Ordination	25	”
Vergehen wider die Inquisition	22	”
Vergehen von Beamten der Inquisition[3]	10	Fälle
Unberechtigtes Auftreten als Beamter d. Inqu.	13	”
Falsche Angaben über Limpieza	57	”
Griechische Christen	3	”
Unehrerbietigkeit	2	”
Verleumdung	1	”
Zwitter	1	”
Streit über eine irische Pfründe	1	”
Schwindler	1	”
Ausfuhr von Pferden	1	”
Abtrünnige Mönche	2	”
Sakrileg gegen Bilder	3	”
Parteinahme für Vandoma (Heinrich IV. von Frankreich)	1	”
Unregelmässigkeiten	1	”
Irrlehren:		
Dass einfache Unzucht keine Todsünde sei	264	”
Dass der Ehestand besser sei als d. Priestertum	30	”
Scholastische Diskussion zu Alcalá	7	”
Verhöhnung frommer Gebräuche	3	”

[3] Vergehen der Familiaren sind nicht einbegriffen. Diese wurden offenbar nicht für wichtig genug gehalten, um dem Consejo de la Suprema berichtet zu werden.

Unanständige Geschichte von Christus und Petrus . . . 4 Fälle
Entschuldigung der Gotteslästerung . . . . 1 "
Über Gott . . . . 9 "
   " Christus . . . . 5 "
   " die Jungfrau Maria . . . . 4 "
   " Magdalena . . . . 4 "
   " den Glauben an die heil. Jungfrau und d. Heiligen . 1 "
   " die Gnade Gottes . . . . 1 "
   " die Erlösung . . . . 12 "
   " die Auferstehung . . . . 6 "
   " das künftige Leben . . . . 4 "
   " Ablass . . . . 9 "
   " Bilder . . . . 6 "
   " die Notwendigkeit der Messe . . . . 6 "
   " die Beichte . . . . 5 "
   " Fürbitten . . . . 1 "
   " Opfer für die Toten . . . . 3 "
   " das heilige Abendmahl . . . . 3 "
   " die Sakramente . . . . 1 "
   " Kanonisierung und Heilige . . . . 3 "
   " die Autorität der heil. Schrift . . . . 1 "
   " des Wunder von d. Broten u. Fischen . . . . 7 "
   " die Stigmata des St. Franciscus . . . . 1 "
   " Exkommunikation . . . . 1 "
   " Ehe und Ehebruch . . . . 9 "
   " Eide . . . . 1 "
   " den geistlichen Stand . . . . 1 "
   " die Mauren . . . . 1 "
   " Selbstverdammung . . . . 1 "
   " Ungläubigkeit . . . . 1 "
   " Sündlosigkeit . . . . 1 "
   " unvermeidliche Sünde . . . . 1 "
   " die päpstliche Gewalt . . . . 2 "
   " Weiber . . . . 1 "
   " Tötung . . . . 1 "
   " das heilige Officium . . . . 3 "
   " die königliche Gewalt . . . . 3 "
   " Blutschande . . . . 1 "
   " die Niederlage der Armada . . . . 1 "
Vermischte Lehren . . . . 9 "

1172 Fälle

Ein anderer interessanter Zug dieser Berichte besteht in dem Einblick, den sie uns in das Ergebnis der Prozesse und in die Natur der gewöhnlich verhängten Strafen gewähren. So finden wir, dass von den 1172 Angeklagten 57 freigesprochen wurden, worunter zwei wegen Irrsinns; 98 Prozesse wurden suspendiert, darunter sechs wegen Irrsinns; 30 Prozesse wurden eingestellt (sobreseydas). Sieben Todesfälle ereigneten sich während der Kerkerhaft, desgleichen ein Selbstmord. Hinsichtlich der Strafen finden wir eine sehr grosse Mannigfaltigkeit. Das heilige Officium in Spanien war nicht auf geistliche Bussen beschränkt und wendete dieselben in der That nur selten an, es sei denn, dass man das Anhören der Messe en forma de penitente als eine solche betrachte. Die von der Inquisition verhängten weltlichen Strafen waren sehr verschiedenartig, denn das Verfahren des Tribunals war ein willkürliches, und es konnte fast jede Strafe verhängen, die ihm für das Vergehen angemessen dünkte. Die Urteile waren überdies in der Regel kompliziert, indem sie mehrere verschiedenartige Strafen umfassten. Abgesehen von den schwersten Fällen finden sich zwei Züge bei fast allen, nämlich die abjuracion de levi und der Verweis; letzterer wurde gewöhnlich im Gerichtssaale erteilt, und nach etlichen mir anderweitig zu Gesichte gekommenen Proben muss er höchst demütigender Natur gewesen sein.

Nachfolgende Tabelle zeigt die in den Berichten vermerkten Strafen mit Weglassung der Verweise und der abjuraciones de levi.

Überlieferung an den weltlichen Arm in Person[4]	15
” ” ” ” ” in effigie	18
Konfiskation[5]	185
Aussöhnung	207
Aussöhnung in effigie	1
Sanbenito	186
Einkerkerung	87
” lebenslänglich	60
” ” unerlassbar	6
Verbannung	167
Auspeitschung	133
Galeerenstrafe	91
Verbot, ins Ausland zu gehen	6
Öffentliche Demütigung	26
Einsperrung in ein Kloster	87
Knebelung	20

[4] Wie bereits erwähnt, wurden von anderen Tribunalen vier Verurteilte zum Verbrennen in Person und drei zum Verbrennen in effigie eingeliefert.

[5] Hierzu kommen noch etwa 24 durch ein Versehen des Schreibers weggelassene Konfiskationen in Fällen von Auslieferung an den weltlichen Arm und Aussöhnung, die stets Konfiskation im Gefolge hatten.

Verbot des Beichthörens 42
Disziplinarstrafen 11
Mönche verurteilt, die letzten im Chor und Refektorium zu sein. 26
Entziehung des Anrechts auf Priesterweihe 10
Als Büsser eine Messe zu hören, im Gerichtssaal 150
„ „ „ „ „ „ in einer Kirche 66
Abschwörung de vehementi 21
Geistliche Bussen 17
Geldbussen 141

Hierzu kommen noch Fälle, die nur mit den leichten Strafen eines Verweises und der Abschwörung abgethan wurden. Diese können wie folgt klassifiziert werden:

Einfacher Verweis 40
Einfache Abschwörung de levi 19
Einfache Verwarnung 1
Verweis und Abschwörung de levi 27
Verweis und Verwarnung 15
Verweis, Verwarnung und Abschwörung de levi 3

Ausser diesen gab es gelegentlich spezielle Strafen, wie z. B. das Verbot, Bücher zu schreiben, Suspendierung vom Predigen und Messelesen, öffentliche Widerrufung von Irrlehren, Unterweisung im Glauben auf eine bestimmte Zeit u. s. w. Die Geldstrafen wurden „para los gastos extraordinarios del Santo Oficio" auferlegt und waren in der Regel von geringem Betrage — zuweilen nur zwei oder drei Dukaten oder 1000 maravedís—, denn die Gefangenen der Inquisition gehörten grösstenteils den ärmeren und niederen Klassen der Tagelöhner, Bauern, Handwerker und Kleinhändler an. Die einzige bedeutende Geldbusse, die in den Berichten angeführt wird, betrug 3000 Dukaten; dieselbe wurde 1604 einem in Madrid lebenden Deutschen, Namens Giraldo Paris, auferlegt, der ein Alchemist gewesen zu sein scheint und der sich verschiedener ketzerischer Lehren schuldig machte, unter anderem der Behauptung, dass „Hiob ein Alchemist gewesen sei". Die Gesammtsumme der 141 Geldstrafen belief sich nur auf 4535 Dukaten und 886 000 maravedís, oder auf 2 586 625 maravedís im ganzen, was durchschnittlich weniger als 75 000 maravedís im Jahre ausmacht.

Die Anwendung der Folter in den Inquisitionsprozessen hat zu viel Aufmerksamkeit erregt und zu viele Hypothesen hervorgerufen, als dass nicht jede erreichbare Statistik von Interesse wäre. Die einzigen in diesen Berichten erwähnten Formen sind der cordel und der garrote auf dem potro. Die Folter nahm stets mit dem cordel ihren Anfang; blieb der Angeklagte hartnäckig beim Leugnen, so wurde dieselbe mit dem garrote fortgesetzt. Unter den 1172 Prozessen wurde sie in 109 Prozessen einmal und in acht Prozessen zweimal angewendet; in zwei Prozessen musste sie eingestellt werden, weil die Opfer in Ohnmacht fielen. In fünf Prozessen lautete das Urteil, dass der Angeklagte mit der Folter bedroht werden sollte. In sieben weiteren wurde ein Geständnis erlangt, ehe mit der Folterung begonnen wurde.

Es wäre natürlich verfehlt, aus den Verhandlungen eines einzigen Tribunals während einer Periode von wenig mehr als einem Dritteljahrhundert absolute Schlüsse zu ziehen; indessen dürfte diese statistische Zusammenstellung die grösste sein, die bis jetzt über die Einzelheiten der Wirksamkeit des heiligen Officiums authentisch mitgeteilt wurde, und sie scheint geeignet, manche falsche Vorstellungen zu beseitigen.

THE SPANISH INQUISITION AS AN ALIENIST*

THE degree of responsibility attaching to insane criminals has in all ages been a difficult problem for the dispenser of justice. I am not aware that the contributions made to its elucidation by the Spanish Inquisition have ever received attention, and the history of a few cases which throw light upon this phase of the subject may not be without interest.[1]

On September 20, 1621, Madrid was startled by the report of a shocking sacrilege committed in the chapel of the archiepiscopal prison. A vagrant Catalan, named Benito Ferrer, had been arrested as an impostor for begging in clerical garments without being in orders. The offense was not serious, and after a month's detention he was about to be discharged, when, at the morning mass, as the bell tinkled to announce the elevation of the Host, Benito, who was praying with a rosary in an upper chamber, rushed down like a madman to the chapel, seized the Host, which had been deposited on the communion cloth, broke it, flung the fragments on the floor and trampled on them, exclaiming, "O traitor God of darkness, now you shall pay me!" He was promptly seized and carried to the courtyard, where he was stripped of his cassock, and when some fragments which had lodged in it fell to the ground he endeavored to stamp on them with similar ejaculations. The first care of those present was to gather reverently the pieces of the body of the Lord; the soles of Benito's shoes were carefully scraped, and the dust and sand of the courtyard were swept up into a white cloth. He was chained hand and foot, maintaining a sullen silence and refusing to answer questions.

The affair, of course, excited the utmost horror. The young king, Philip IV, then only five months on the throne, sent his favorite, Count Olivares, to ascertain for him the facts, and the papal nuncio eagerly sought the details to report them to Rome. The archiepiscopal vicar, Diego Vela, was at first disposed to take a rationalistic view of the matter: he asserted the insanity of his prisoner, and proposed to discharge him, doubtless thinking it wiser to assume that no Spaniard in his senses could be capable of an offence so heinous. He was soon, however, made to understand that this would not be allowed, and it came near bringing him into trouble. The Holy Office asserted its jurisdiction over a case of heresy so flagrant; on the twenty-third, Vela surrendered Benito to the supreme council of the Inquisition, and he was sent to the tribunal of Toledo (for as yet there was none in Madrid), with orders that his trial should be pushed with all expedition—an urgency that was soon

* From the *Popular Science Monthly*, xliii (1893), 289-300.
[1] I am indebted to the custodians of the Königliche Bibliothek of the University of Halle for the opportunity of consulting the records of these cases. [A discussion of insanity as a plea in defense will be found in *Inquisition of Spain*, III, 8-9, 58-63.—H.]

after twice repeated, with the significant addition that the king took special interest in the matter and desired to know its progress.

The Toledan inquisitors were prompt and zealous. The dilatory and cumbersome forms of procedure were hurried as rapidly as the traditions of the tribunal would permit, and in exactly two months, on November 23, they were ready to pronounce sentence. Yet the end was still far off. In his examinations Benito had been made to give the details of his life. He was forty-three years old, born at Camprodon of an Old Christian father and a mother who had Jewish blood in her veins —a fact which told heavily against him. His father, who was a clothshearer, took him, at the age of thirteen, to Montserrat and placed him with an uncle, a chaplain in the monastery, who in six months sent him back to his father in Barcelona. For some time he served as page to persons of quality, and finally Don Bernardo Terres took him to Flanders, when the Cardinal Archduke, Albert of Austria, went thither in 1595. There he had a succession of masters, with one of whom he returned through France to Catalonia. Filled with desire for a religious life, in 1603 he entered the Barefooted Carmelite convent of Mataron as a novice, but was expelled in about six months. After vainly seeking to join the Carthusians of Monte Alegre and the Jeronymites of Murta, at last the Observantine Franciscans of Barcelona gave him the habit, but deprived him of it in about eight months. Then two years were spent in study at Tarragona, which he left in 1606, and since then he had led a wandering life in pious pilgrimages. He had offered his devotions at the shrine of his namesake, San Vicente Ferrer, at Vannes; twice he had been to Rome and once to Monte Cassino and Sicily, besides traversing Spain and Portugal in all directions. About 1609 came the shadow which darkened his subsequent life. Fray Francisco de la Virgen, the master of the novices at Mataron, was Antichrist, and had bewitched him, since when all men whom he met were demons. He had ceased to attend mass or to confess and take communion, for he could find no priest who was not a demon. When, in the upper room of the prison, he was praying and heard the bell that told of the elevation of the host, it was revealed to him that the officiating priest was a demon and the Host was another. In doing what he did he performed a service to God, and he would repeat it fifty millions of times if the occasion required. This Carmelite Antichrist, moreover, had in 1606 killed Philip III and his three children, and their places had since then been filled by demons. There was also some wild talk about Toledo being no longer Toledo, nor Madrid, Madrid, for Saint Joseph had changed them all. Barcelona is now La Imperial de Santa Ana, and is on the Straits of Gibraltar, for Catalonia has grown so that it is now larger than all

Spain was formerly. The emperor of La Imperial is Don Dalman de Queralt, who daily sends him food in prison, so that he has not to accept it from the demon alcaide and his attendants. The inquisitors have no power to burn him, for they are all demons and he is in the hands of God. With all this he was strictly orthodox in his replies to the searching questions of the inquisitors as to his belief in transubstantiation and other points, except that he attributed five persons to the Godhead—Michael and Gabriel being added to the Trinity. Throughout the course of his prolonged trial nothing could make him swerve from these hallucinations or modify his story. He defied the inquisitors, for he had a revelation in prison that they were demons and had no power to harm him.

Anxious as were the inquisitors to push the trial to a conclusion, they felt that evidence of his sanity was necessary. For this they examined the alcaide of the prison and his assistant and three fellow-prisoners confined in the same cell. All testified to Benito's soundness of mind as evinced in his daily actions, though he was silent and reserved and spent most of his time in prayer or in reading his breviary. Then three physicians were made to visit him several times, who reported that he talked sanely on most subjects but wildly on others; the insanity seemed feigned, and according to the rules of the medical art he was sane. Thus fortified, on November 23 the inquisitors called together the regular consulta, an assembly of experts, to decide on the case. There were nine of them in all—the three inquisitors, the vicar general as representative of the archbishop of Toledo, and five *consultores* or assessors. Opinions were not harmonious. Four voted to put Benito to the torture to verify his sanity, and if this failed then to make inquiry into his antecedents. Three voted to relax him to the secular arm for burning, first employing learned theologians to convince him of his heresy. Two were in favor of the common-sense plan of endeavoring to ascertain his sanity without torturing him.

When, in the customary routine, these diverse views were submitted to the inquisitor general and supreme council, that body considered the case maturely. Statements of the leading points involved were laid before three skilled theologians, two of whom pronounced Benito to be a sacrilegious heretic whose delusions were feigned. The third opined that he might be subject to demoniacal possession, for which he should be exorcised and subsequently tortured to ascertain the truth. On January 12, 1622, the council sent these *calcificaciones* or opinions to Toledo, with instructions to get similar ones from learned men there; also, to examine more carefully into Benito's sanity and to investigate the causes of his expulsion from the convents which he had sought to enter. Accordingly, on January 15, the Toledo tribunal assembled four Dominican masters of theology, who unanimously pronounced Benito a heretic and an impostor. To ascertain details about an insignificant novice who some twenty years before had passed a few months in a convent might seem impossible, but the perfected organization of the Inquisition was equal to it. The tribunals of Barcelona and Valencia were called upon; the frailes who had been novices in Benito's time were hunted up in the convents to which they had scattered, and four were found who entertained some recollection of him. Three of these described him as mentally deficient, and one of these remembered his having revelations; the fourth spoke of him as "melancholy" and like one possessed by the devil.

May was drawing to an end when the result of these investigations reached Toledo, and the summer was spent in fresh examinations of those in the prison who had access to Benito, and in getting opinions from theologians and physicians. That he showed signs of insanity was evident, but the experts held that the proof of soundness of mind was infallible and the madness feigned. So when, on September 10, another consulta was held, the vote to burn him was unanimous—the two assessors who had previously advocated simple investigation having been discreetly omitted from the meeting. On this decision being submitted to the supreme council, it met with no greater acceptance than the former one, and it was sent back September 17, with orders to torture Benito to ascertain his intention in the sacrilege and the fiction of his insanity.

In the proceedings of the Inquisition torture was so universal a resource in cases of doubt that its use for the diagnosis of insanity need not be a matter of surprise. On October 13 it was duly applied. Benito was brought in and told that if he would not confess the truth he would be tortured, to which he replied quietly and earnestly that he had told the truth and was not mad; he had acted only as a faithful Christian and at the command of the Eternal Father. In the administration of torture the nerve of the patient was tested at every step with adjurations to tell the truth and with promises of mercy—lying promises, for confession would only secure the boon of being garroted before burning. So in this case, at the making out of the sentence of torture, its formal signing, the adjournment to the torture chamber, the stripping of the prisoner, the tying him to the banquillo or trestle, the adjusting of the cordeles or sharp cords around each thigh and each upper arm—at every stage he was entreated affectionately (*con mucho amor*) to tell the truth and save his soul. Benito's resolution was immovable; to every adjuration his reply was the same—he had told the truth, and the inquisitors were demons. Then the torture began, scientifically graduated, and at every interval came the adjuration and the response. First a single cord around each member was successfully tightened and twisted into the flesh, then another and another, until there were six on each limb and the blood was dripping from them all—in spite of the universal rule that torture was never to be carried so far as to cause effusion of blood. The official report of the examination minutely records his shrieks and groans and writhings, his fruitless prayer for water, his despairing appeals to Jesus, Mary, and Joseph, his cries that he is dying, and through it all his unvarying response that he had told the truth and that the inquisitors were demons—an assertion which he once offered to prove if they would give him a Bible. When the capacity of the cordeles to inflict increased torment was exhausted he was threatened with the rack, but to no purpose. It was made ready and he was stretched on it, but this augmentation of agony was fruitless. His resolution was unconquerable, and at last his wearied judges ordered him to be untied, still threatening him with a continuation of the infliction if he would not tell the truth. Exhausted nature could do no more; with a final ejaculation that he had told the truth, for they were demons, he sank motionless and remained silent.

For three unbroken hours the torture had lasted, and the inquisitors said that it was too late for more that day, so they suspended it, warning him that they were not satisfied, and that it would be resumed if he did not tell the truth. He was carried back to his cell, and two days later was brought before the tribunal again. Even in the pitiless secular criminal legislation of the period the endurance of torture without confession was held to purge away the evidence against the accused and to entitle him to an acquittal, but it was otherwise in the Inquisition. The torure had been merely to gratify the curiosity of the judges and to justify the foregone conclusion of his burning. Therefore, when they now examined him and adjured him to tell the truth, and he answered by referring to his previous statements as the truth, they had him carried back to his cell and coolly assembled their *consultores* to pronounce on him a second sentence of relaxation to the secular arm for burning. This was duly submitted to the supreme council, which postponed its answer until November 24. Then it said that it held him to be insufficiently tortured, but that for the present he should be kept in prison and carefully watched to determine his sanity. He was to be confined with persons who could be relied upon and sworn to secrecy, who should observe him and report.

Another cell was accordingly selected for him, in which were two friars and a physician awaiting trial, who were duly sworn and instructed.

So matters continued for a year, with occasional examinations of his fellow-prisoners. The friars pronounced him a heretic and an impostor; the physician, a sane man subject to delusions. Finally, in November, 1623, another consultation was held to vote upon his case, and he was unanimously sentenced to burning. To this at last the Supreme Council assented, but desired the execution to take place in Madrid, where the sacrilege had been committed. He was to be sedulously kept in ignorance, and to be secretly conveyed to the capital. There, on the Plaza Mayor, January 21, 1624, there was a solemn *auto da fé* celebrated, and he was burned alive as an *impenitente negativo*.[2]

If this was expected to strike salutary terror into the hearts of sacrilegious heretics and to instill respect for the venerable sacrament, it signally failed of its purpose. In less than six months, on Friday, July 5, 1624, Madrid was again thrown into excitement by a double sacrilege that had every appearance of organized premeditation. During the celebration of morning mass in the church of San Felipe, a man named René Perrault, who was kneeling near the altar, suddenly leaped forward at the elevation of the Host, and crying out, "Why do you elevate this idol of Christ, so that the people commit idolatry and offend God?" he snatched it from the hand of the priest and scattered it in fragments on the floor, while with a sweep of his arm he overturned the cup that was standing on the altar. At the same moment a similar scene was enacted at the church of Santa Barbara, by a man named Gabriel de Guevara. It was with difficulty that the offenders were rescued from the summary vengeance of the worshipers, and they were forthwith brought before the inquisitor general, Andrés Pacheco. Apparently his experience of the Toledo Inquisition in the previous affair had not been satisfactory, for he at once himself undertook the preliminaries of the case, and hastily organized for its trial in Madrid a tribunal which sat in extemporized quarters in the convent of the Barefooted Carmelites. The documents concerning Guevara are not accessible, but those of the trial of Perrault present to us another aspect of the dealings of the Inquisition with insanity.

Friday was busily occupied with the examination of witnesses, and at 10 P. M. Perrault was brought before the inquisitor. He was still defiant, and told his story without hesitation or concealment. He was about forty years old, born at Angers, of Catholic parents. Brought up in strict orthodoxy, he had, until within a fortnight, always been a good Catholic, regular in his attendance on confession, communion, and mass. For

[2] [Reference to this case will be found in *Inquisition of Spain*, III, 47, 60-61.—H.]

twelve years he had wandered around Spain as a peddler of needles, thimbles, and such small wares, till a fortnight before at Talavera, while in the street seeking customers, a sudden revelation from God showed him that there was only one God, the Creator; that Christ was an impostor, who had properly expiated on the cross the blasphemy of calling himself the Son of God, and that what the people adored was idolatry and an offence to the Almighty. From that time this idea was ever present to him, on the road and in the house. God impelled him to do what he had done, and to come to Madrid for the purpose, so that the act should be more conspicuous. He had left his saddle-bags at Getafé, a village a few leagues distant, on Tuesday, July 2, and had come with his mule to Madrid. There he first looked up a French paper and fruit seller named Domingo Diaz, of whom he inquired the address of his brother, Pierre Perrault, an embroiderer living in Madrid. He found him, and told him of the revelation and his consequent intention, when Pierre earnestly reasoned with him, telling him that it was a suggestion of the devil, and that he would denounce him to the Inquisition if he were not his brother. The next morning Pierre came to him with an Italian, a tailor; they bought some food, crossed the bridge of Toledo, breakfasted by the roadside, and René agreed to return to Getafé. After parting he traveled half a league on his mule; he chanced to overtake a man going thither, by whom he sent word to his host to forward his saddle-bags to Madrid, and he turned back to the city. To render his act more symbolical, he resolved to postpone it until Friday, so he had a day and a half on his hands. These he spent in seeing the sights of the capital, and he mentioned his disappointment on going to the theater and finding there was no performance. On Friday morning, at breakfast, he abstained from his customary flask of wine, in order that it might not be said that he was drunk. He went to San Felipe and committed the sacrilege.

The next day, when brought again before the tribunal, his enthusiasm had evaporated. Excitement had been followed by reaction; he realized the terrible fate in store for him, and was eager to avert it in any way he could. He had been drunk, he said, the day before, and had stumbled against the priest; he was crazy; people had given him food which rendered him insane, and the ill-treatment to which he had been exposed habitually on the road had driven him mad. At Consuegra he had been beaten; at Medellin, beaten, imprisoned, and his goods confiscated; he was a good Catholic, and believed all that the Church believed, and he remembered nothing of the confession of yesterday; or, if he had said such things, he must have been out of his senses. When, later in the day, his formal defense was drawn up and presented by his advocate, it was that he had been drunk, and he now supplicated mercy and penance.

Probably no trial before the Inquisition, since the abounding harvest of its early days, was ever conducted so speedily. Though all the formalities were observed, on Sunday, July 7, the consultation was held to determine the sentence. The opinion was unanimous that he should be relaxed to the secular arm for burning, but on the question of preliminary torture a difference arose. The Inquisition was naturally desirous to know whether he had accomplices; the simultaneous crime of Gabriel de Guevara pointed to concerted action; besides, one of the witnesses had testified that René entered San Felipe with two men clad in the French fashion, who departed at the commencement of the mass. René had consistently denied this, asserting his independence of action and sole responsibility; but heretic plots were always floating before the inquisitorial imagination, and it was manifestly impolitic to burn René without utilizing him for the conviction of his possible confederates. While, therefore, all the consulters agreed that he should be subjected to unlimited torture, some held that it should be *in caput alienum,* to discover his associates; while others, in view of his varying confessions, humanely urged that it should be employed for the benefit of his soul, and to confirm him in the faith. The next day the supreme council, in approving the sentence, decided that the torture should be *in caput alienum.*

At ten o'clock that night René was brought before his judges and questioned as to accomplices, but he only repeated his story, with a few additional details. In the torture which followed he manifested a curious mingling of strength and weakness. Before it commenced he flung himself on his knees and begged piteously for mercy, but refused to forfeit his soul by perjury, for he had no associates, and no Frenchmen entered San Felipe with him. During all the stages of graduated torment he screamed and struggled desperately, but he adhered resolutely to this, and refused to incriminate any one; he had never breathed his intention to any save his brother, who threatened to denounce him to the Inquisition. This continued till half past one o'clock, when the inquisitors, finding the torture fruitless, announced its discontinuance; but next morning they commenced proceedings against Pierre Perrault and Domingo Diaz. What was the result of these we do not know; but had anything been extracted from them further compromising René, it would have appeared in the records of his trial.

If the torture thus was useless *in caput alienum,* it at all events served the more humane purpose of confirming the sufferer in the faith. On July 12 word was brought to the inquisitor Chacon that René desired to return to the Church: he hastened to the temporary prison where the culprit was confined and found this to be the case. Now that he had nothing further to hope, René said that his first statement was true. He had been misled and tempted by Satan for fifteen days before the crime, and had believed that he was rendering a service to God; but now God had enlightened him, and he reverted to his former belief in the Trinity, in the passion of Christ, and the transubstantiation of the sacrament, and he desired to be reconciled to the Church.

On the following Sunday, July 14, Madrid enjoyed the religious spectacle of an *auto da fé* in which René Perrault was burned, but doubtless his recantation obtained for him the privilege of being garroted before the pile was lighted. Thus, if Spain furnished to Geneva the Unitarian, Miguel Servet, France returned the favor with René Perrault.

Another case, less tragic in its issue, illustrates a different phase of the subject. At Cobeña, a village not far from Alcalá de Henares a poor carpenter of plows named Benito Peñas, or de Valdepeñas, created scandal by denying that Christ had died on the cross. He was wholly illiterate but devout, and once, when visiting Madrid with a load of corn, he had heard in the church of San Felipe a sermon by a fraile, who spoke of the passion and resurrection as metaphorical.[3] The idea took possession of his brain and played havoc with the anthropomorphic conceptions of orthodox theology, including the humanity of Christ. This had been going on for several years when early in 1640 the attention of the archiepiscopal visitor, Bernardo Garcia de San Pedro, was called to it on his reaching Cobeña. He promptly threw Benito into the village jail, where many priests and friars visited him and labored fruitlessly to convince him of his error. Then, in July, Dr. Buendia, the physician of Cobeña, denounced him to the nearest commissioner of the Inquisition, Juan Burgalez Diaz, at Fuente el Saz. The affair was now fully in train. Diaz hastened to Cobeña, took testimony of some of the chief inhabitants, and forwarded the papers to the tribunal of Toledo. The inquisitors submitted to *calificadores* the propositions contained in the reports of Benito's talk and they were duly condemned as heretical and Manichæan. The Inqui-

[3] The Spanish preachers of the period allowed themselves the largest license in the effort to attract attention, and shrank from no grotesqueness of irreverence. In the trial in 1592, of Fray Joseph de Sigüenza, a distinguished Jeronymite friar and favorite of Philip II, there is a description of a sermon preached before the king by Fray Cristóbal de Lafra, another Jeronymite, on the feast of the Nativity of the Virgin. He said the Minotaur was Christ and the Labyrinth the gospel *liber generationis*; Ariadne was Our Lady, and the child she bore to Theseus was Faith; and that if any one desired to enter the Labyrinth he must pray to the Virgin for her child. He also said that God was the heifer Io, who converted Jews; that wherever God trod he left his footprints, which are his works; asking who made these admirable works of the sun, the moon, etc., the answer, Yo Yo, gave the name, which is God—the name impressed by the steps of the heifer. It is therefore by no means improbable that Benito Peñas may have heard a sermon which conveyed to him the impression he described and led to his misfortunes.

sition, however, appears to have thought little of the matter, and it would probably have gone no farther, had not a zealous cleric of Cobeña, toward the end of the year, written that the people were scandalized at the delay in acting in an affair so notorious. Thus stimulated, on January 25, 1641, the inquisitors issued an order to bring Benito to Toledo, and to sequestrate his property—the latter being the customary precaution for the event of a sentence of confiscation.

It was the invariable practice of the Inquisition, whenever possible, to make the accused, whether innocent or guilty, pay all the expenses attending his trial. The familiar to whom the order was sent was therefore required, in sequestrating Benito's property and placing it in the hands of a receiver, to keep thirty ducats for expenses; if there was no money or grain, then he was to sell at auction enough to realize this amount, and he was also to reserve a bed and bring it with him for Benito's use in prison. These customary instructions were rigidly carried out as far as practicable. A reversionary interest in some money left by a dead brother was garnisheed, and security taken to await the result of the trial. The only ready money in Benito's possession amounted to nineteen copper coins or quartos, worth in all about two reales and a half; so on Sunday, February 10, his pitiful store of furniture, tools, and clothing was sold by auction in the public square after high mass, reserving only the garments on his back and one of two old shirts for him to wear; even the rosary in his hands was taken and sold. The total proceeds amounted to only two hundred and forty and a half reales, or less than twenty-two ducats, and, after deducting costs, the commissioner handed over to the familiar twenty ducats. The expenses of guards and the journey to Toledo consumed more than half of this; and when Benito was delivered on February 16 at the *carceles secretas*, there were but one hundred and five and a half reales left, which were duly entered on the prison books. The timid suggestion of the familiar of some remuneration for his time was left unnoticed.

When on February 18 Benito was examined, he willingly repeated all the articles of the creed except "suffered under Pontius Pilate, was crucified, dead, and buried, and on the third day arose from the dead," which he obstinately refused to utter. It was easy to entangle him in a theological discussion in which he was led to deny the incarnation and conception by virtue of the Holy Ghost, the birth and death, and the second advent. The efforts made to convince him of his error of course only hardened him in his belief, and he resolutely accepted the inferences drawn from it until he came virtually to deny the Trinity—the three names were but three different designations for the one God. He was ready, he declared, to die in defense of his belief, and all the theologians in France and Spain could not convert him. When the counsel assigned to him by the Inquisition found him immovable, he formally withdrew from the defense in order not to incur the penalties decreed against advocates who undertook to defend heretics.

In March the inquisitors began to entertain doubts as to Benito's sanity, and sent to Cobeña to obtain testimony respecting it. The evidence was emphatic as to his soundness of mind. The *cura* had known him for forty years, and had never entertained a doubt of it; the alcalde and others who knew him said the same. It was true that for a year or more prior to his arrest he had grown very devout, praying much and frequenting the church; moreover, on one occasion he had remained shut up in his house for some days, until the alcalde and *cura* broke in and found him lying with a rosary in his hand in a trance, from which they aroused him with a rope's end, and he had repeated this in a hermitage near the town, but in all the relations of life he had shown himself in full possession of his faculties.

Thus the case went on with the deliberation customary in the Inquisition, until in July it was resolved to make a more thorough investigation as to his sanity. Two learned theologians were deputed to examine him, who reported him to be crazy: his answers bore no relation to the questions put to him; he talked of the omnipotent God and the sweet name of Jesus; the Virgin was created without father and mother, and was anterior to Eve; when we die our bodies are not converted into dust; in fine, he was not a case for the Inquisition, but for a madhouse. Then two more theologians were called in, and their opinions were the same. Evidently under the paternal care of the Inquisition his insanity was developing rapidly.

In August the three physicians of the Holy Office were summoned to examine him. Two of them questioned and cross-questioned him, and were prepared to pronounce him sane when the third arrived, and in the course of examination chanced to ask him what signs he had of his own salvation, to which he replied that when he commended himself to God he saw lights like stars descend from heaven to him. This convinced them, and they reported that he was insane or was subject to diabolic illusions. The alcaide of the prison and his assistant were then interrogated; they had no doubt of his insanity from his disordered talk and from the fact that they always found him kneeling in prayer. Then as a last effort two more distinguished theologians were deputed to convince him of his errors, but they found their labors hopeless, and declared that he was crazy.

It was impossible to resist this cumulative evidence, and when, on August 29, the customary consultation was held to decide upon his fate, the opinion was unanimous that he was irresponsible. It was agreed to write to the authorities of Cobeña to that effect; his relatives must send for him and take care of him; he was never to be allowed to leave the town, and must henceforth wear a doublet half gray and half green. To this the response was that he had no kindred, but Juan de San Pedro was sent to bring him home, while a plaintive allusion to the expense of the journey and the absence of all property from which to defray it received no attention.

Thus the poor wretch was beggared, deprived of all means of livelihood, and condemned to the disgrace of exhibiting his shame in a parti-colored garment at a time when such insignia had a peculiarly sinister significance. According to the convictions of the period, it was all for the greater glory of God; but as an alienist, the Inquisition was clearly not a success.[4]

[4] [For brief reference to this case see *Inquisition of Spain*, II, 494-95.—H.]

HISTORICAL STUDIES

The Church

THE ABSOLUTION FORMULA OF THE TEMPLARS*

[The complete Rule of the Knights Templars was printed for the first time by H. de Curzon in the Publications of the Société de l'Histoire de France in 1886 (Volume I of that year). The work came into Mr. Lea's hands in 1888, too late to be utilized in his account of the Templars in the third volume of his *Inquisition of the Middle Ages*. A résumé of the following paper was, however, incorporated in the French translation of the book (Paris, 1900-02), III, 325-29, and in the German translation (Bonn, 1905-13), III, 307-11. A brief reference to the subject appears, also, in his *History of Auricular Confession and Indulgences*, I, 204.—H.]

* * * * *

AMONG THE accusations brought against the Templars by Pope Clement V in 1308, there was one to the effect that the officers of the order—the master, the visitors, and the preceptors—absolved the brethren from their sins. It is further asserted that De Molay admitted this in the presence of high personages before his arrest.[1] That the accusation was an afterthought is shown by the fact that it is not contained in the preliminary list of charges sent in September 1307, by the Inquisitor Guillaume de Paris to his subordinates as a guide for them in the expected trials of the Templars.[2] Yet Clement was not the first to take note of this assumption of sacerdotal prerogatives which, in fact, was well known to all who busied themselves with canon law, and public attention had already been called to it. In a diatribe on the disorders of the Church, written by a mendicant friar apparently towards the end of the thirteenth century, all the three great military orders—the Hospital, the Temple, and the Teutonic Knights—are reproved for this usurpation of the power of the keys, although it is ascribed rather to ignorance than to wilful intrusion on priestly functions.[3] The truth or the falsity of the accusation has never,

---

* From *Papers of the American Church History Society*, V (1892), 37-58.

[1] As formally expressed in the bull *Faciens misericordiam*, August 12, 1308, the charge is: "Item quod credebant, et sic dicebatur eis quod magnus magister a peccatis poterit eos absolvere. Item quod visitator. Item quod preceptores quorum multi erant layci.

"Item quod hæc faciebant de facto. Item quod aliqui eorum.

"Item quod magnus magister ordinis predicti hoc fuit de se confessus in presencia magnarum personarum antequam esset captus."—Michelet, *Procès des Templiers*, I, 91. Cf. *Mag. Bullar. Roman.* (ed. Luxemb.), IX, 129.

[2] Pissot, *Procès et Condamnation des Templiers* (Paris, 1805), p. 39.

[3] In treating of the three Military Orders the writer says: "Usurpant laici sacerdotum officia, pœnitentiam pro excessibus injungentes et eandem pro libito relaxantes, cum non sint eis claves commissæ, nec ligandi et solvendi uti debeant potestate. Remedium, ut magistri domorum mittant fratres literatos ad studendum circa theologicas lectiones, nec circa scientias sæculares, ut habeant literatos priores et sacerdotes."—*Collectio de Scandalis Ecclesiæ* (Döllinger, *Beiträge zur politischen, kirchlichen u. Cultur-geschichte*, III, 196).

I believe, been investigated, and though the question is a subordinate
one, yet everything connected with the catastrophe of the Temple possesses interest, and this derives adventitious importance from its relation
to the development of Catholic doctrine in the thirteenth century.

To understand it rightly, we must bear in mind that the members of
the military orders were monks, subject to all the rules and entitled to all
the privileges of monachism. To appreciate their relations to the great
subject of the sacrament of penitence, we must, therefore, consider what,
at the date of their foundation, were the customs of the religious orders,
as well as what were the teachings of the Church with regard to confession and absolution, and we can then estimate how far Clement V
was justified in including this among the charges for which the order
was destroyed.

The Templar Rule was based on the Cistercian, which in turn was a
reform of the Benedictine. In the original Rule of Benedict there are no
defined regulations on the subject. The sinner is counseled to confess to
his abbot or to one of the older monks and to seek his advice, but, of
course, there is nothing said as to absolution which, in its sacramental
character, was the creation of the Schoolmen of the twelfth and thirteenth centuries. Public confession in the daily assemblage or chapter was
ordered for any external fault committed in the prescribed routine of daily
labor[4]—an exercise which had already, prior to Benedict, become customary in the monachism of the time.[5] In the Cistercian reform this
was insisted upon and developed. Every day, after mass, the brethren
assembled in chapter. Any one conscious of sin was expected to confess
it and ask for pardon. If he did not do so, any one cognizant of it was
required to accuse him; he could defend himself, and judgment was
pronounced by a majority of those present. If he was condemned to the
discipline, he promptly stripped himself to the waist and was scourged
till the abbot commanded it to cease, and the proceedings terminated
by the prior listening to private confessions of such things as nocturnal
illusions for which he granted absolution and penance.[6] In all this there
is evidently nothing of the formal sacrament of penitence, and no other
form of confession is prescribed. Even on the death-bed the dying monk
only said "Confiteor" or "Mea culpa, de omnibus peccatis meis precor vos
orate pro me."[7]

---

[4] *Regul. S. Benedict.*, cc. vii, xlvi (Migne's *Patrologia*, LXVI, 373, 694). *Cf.* Smaragdus,
Comment. (Migne, *op. cit.*, CII, 885); *Reg. S. Chrodegangi*, c. xviii; Jonas Aurelianens., *De
Instit. Laicali*, Lib. I, c. xvi.

[5] S. Eucherius, *Homil.* VIII.

[6] *Usus antiquiores Ordinis Cisterciensis*, cc. lxx, lxxv (Migne, *op. cit.*, CLXVI, 1443-46).

[7] *Ibid.*, c. xciv, 1471. By the time of St. Bernard, however, there seems to be a custom
springing up of annual confession at Easter.—S. Bernardus, *Serm. in Die Paschæ*, § 15
(Migne, *op. cit.*, CLXXXIII, 281).

Here we have the prototype of the chapters of the Templars as described in their Rule. Wherever four or more of the brethren were together they were commanded to hold a chapter on the vigils of Christmas, Easter, and Pentecost, and on every Sunday of the year, excepting those of the three feasts. These were religious assemblies: each one on entering crossed himself in the name of the Father, Son, and Holy Ghost, and recited a paternoster before taking his seat. The preceptor or presiding officer preached a sermon, after which every one conscious of sin was expected to confess it. If he did not do so, any one acquainted with it called upon him to confess; if he denied it, witnesses were summoned and the case was debated. The culprit withdrew; the chapter determined what penance to prescribe, and he was recalled. If this was scourging, it was performed on the spot by the presiding officer, but there were many degrees of penance, culminating in expulsion, and a long catalogue of offences is detailed, classified according to the penances due to them.[8] In very light cases the chapter sometimes referred the offender to the chaplain who prescribed the penance.[9] The proceedings of the chapter closed with a prayer by the presiding officer, prior to which he absolved all those present and warned them that those who did not confess their sins had no share in the spiritual merits and benefits of the order.[10] The object for which the chapters were instituted was the confession and penancing of sins;[11] in fact, the chapter was a confessional, and each brother was instructed before entering it to search his conscience and reflect whether he had any transgression to confess and render satisfaction for.[12]

The Rule in the elaborate form in which we have it dates from about the middle of the thirteenth century, and contains certain sacerdotal elements which I will consider hereafter. In its early simplicity, as granted by the council of Troyes in 1127, the whole matter of hearing confessions and imposing penance is entrusted to the master. There is nothing said as to absolution, but the expressions used show that the performance of the penance imposed by him is expected to obtain salvation for the sinner.[13] At that time the Schoolmen had not fairly commenced their

---

[8] *La Règle du Temple*, publiée pour la Société de l'Histoire de France, par Henri de Curzon (Paris, 1886), Artt., 385-502.

[9] *Ibid.*, Art. 526.

[10] "Quar le Maistre ou cil qui tient le chapistre les assols dou pooir que il ait devant que il comence sa proiere."—*Ibid.*, Art. 503. See also Art. 538.

[11] "Et sachiés que nostre chapistre furent etabli por ce que li frere se confessassent de lor fautes et les amendassent."—*Ibid.*, Art. 389.

[12] *Ibid.*, Art. 394.

[13] "Si aliquis frater loquendo vel militando aut aliter aliquid leve deliquerit, ipse ultro delictum suum satisfaciendo magistro ostendat. De levibus si consuetudinem non habeant, levem pœnitentiam habeat. Si vero eo tacente per aliquem alium culpa cognita fuerit,

work; nothing was known of penitence as a sacrament, and even the power of the keys was as yet a vague conception. Naturally, therefore, in this original Rule there are no commands as to confession to priests or the seeking of absolution from them. Whatever power to bind or to loose was exercised in the order lay in the hands of the master, and the penalties which he inflicted were not punishment, but penance. The distinction between the *forum internum* and the *forum externum*, between reconciliation to the Church and reconciliation to God, had not as yet been clearly defined by the Schoolmen; it was virtually unknown in practice and all offences were on the same plane.

In the completed Rule we can trace these same characteristics. The proceedings in the chapter were not simply to enforce the discipline of the order, but to save the soul of the sinner.[14] The penitential character of the inflictions is seen in the injunction that the culprit is to endure them cheerfully and willingly—he should feel shame for the sin, but not for the penance;[15] and when this is scourging, administered on the spot, all those present are enjoined to pray God to pardon him, whereupon the brethren all recite a paternoster, and if there is a chaplain present he offers a special prayer.[16] When the penance is a prolonged one, the chapter must determine when it shall cease, and then before the penitent is introduced all the brethren kneel and pray God to give him grace to preserve him from sin hereafter.[17] The religious character of the penance is still further seen in the regulation that if it is not administered on the spot by the presiding officer, it is subsequently to be inflicted by the chaplain; as sacerdotalism advanced, indeed, some even argued that it ought always to be done by a priest and not by the master or commander.[18]

At the time when the order was organized there was nothing strange

---

majori et evidentiori subjaceat disciplinæ et emendationi. Si autem grave erit delictum retrahetur a familiaritate fratrum, nec cum illis simul in eadem mensa edat sed solus refectionem sumat. Dispensationi et judicio Magistri totum incumbat, ut salvus in judicii die permaneat."—Harduin, *Concil.*, VI, ii, 1144.

[14] "Nul frere ne doit reprendre autre frere fors par charité et par entention de faire li sauver s'arme."—*Règle*, Art. 412.

[15] "Chaucun frere doit bien et volentiers faire la penance qui li est enchargée par chapistre."—*Ibid.*, Art. 415. "Et nul frere ne doit avoir honte de penance en maniere que il l'en laisse a faire; mais chascun doit avoir bien honte de faire le pechié, et la penance doit chascun faire volenterement."—*Ibid.*, Art. 494. "Mais bien sachiés que mult est bele chose de faire penance."—*Ibid.*, Art. 533. When the penance comprised weekly public scourging in church "et doit venir a sa discipline o grant devocion et recevre le en patience devant tout le peuple qui sera au mostier." *Ibid.*, Art. 468. See also Artt. 469-73.

[16] "Biau seignors freres, veés ci vostre frere qui vient a la discipline, priés notre Seignor qu'i li pardoint ses defautes."—*Ibid.*, Art. 502.

[17] *Ibid.*, Art. 520.

[18] *Ibid.*, Artt. 523, 525.

in thus entrusting to the master or preceptor the administration of the rites of confession, absolution, and satisfaction. The monk, though not in holy orders, by his vows and his dedication to the service of God, was invested with a quasi-sacerdotal character. Even at the end of the twelfth century we learn from Peter Cantor that in some convents a monk could confess to any of his brethren and accept penance from him, though by this time absolution was becoming recognized as a sacerdotal function and was administered by the abbot, the sacrament being thus split in two.[19] But even apart from this monastic character laymen had not as yet been excluded from the hearing of confessions. It was not long before the founding of the order that the Blessed Lanfranc taught that confession of secret sins could be made to any ecclesiastic, from priest to ostiarius, or in their absence to a righteous layman who could cleanse the soul from sin.[20] No work of the twelfth century exercised so controlling an influence on the development of the sacramental conception of penitence as the forgery which passed current under the authoritative name of St. Augustine, yet in this it is asserted that, in the absence of a priest, confession to a layman is equally efficacious[21]—a principle which was adopted by Gratian and Peter Lombard.[22] In the thirteenth century, even after the Lateran canon which prescribed annual confession to the parish priest, the stories related by Cæsarius of Heisterbach to allure the people to the confessional show that the prevailing conception still was that the virtue of confession lay in the act, irrespective of the character of the person to whom it was made.[23] If by this time the theologians refused to go thus far they at least still admitted the validity of confession to laymen in case of necessity,[24] of which we have an example in the narrative of the Sire de Joinville, who relates how he heard the confession of Gui d'Ebelin, constable of Cyprus, and granted him absolution, when both were expecting instant death from the Moslem.[25] As the sacramental theory became perfected, Aquinas explained that in such cases God supplies the place of the priest; the absolution of the layman is quasi-

[19] Jo. Morinus, *De Administr. Sacram. Pœnitent.*, Liv. VIII, c. ix, n. 23.—Martène, *De antiq. Ritibus Ecclesiæ*, Lib. I, c. vi, Art. 6, n. 5. This division of the sacrament was not long afterwards forbidden. See S. Raimundus, *Summa*, Postill. ad § 4, Tit. xxxiv, Lib. III.

[20] Lanfranc, *Lib. de Celanda Confessione* (Migne, *op. cit.*, CL, 629-30).

[21] "Tanta itaque vis confessionis est ut si deest sacerdos confiteatur proximo."—Pseudo-August., *Lib. de vera et falsa Pœnitentia*, c. x.

[22] Gratian, *Decr.*, c. i, Caus. xxxiii, q. iii, Dist. 6.—P. Lombard, *Sententt.*, Lib. IV, Dist. 17, § 5.

[23] Cæsar. Heisterb., *Dial.*, Dist. 3, cc. ii, xxi.

[24] S. Raymundus, *op. cit.*, Lib. III, Tit. xxxiv, § 4.—*Gloss. sup. Decr.*, Caus. xxxiii, q. iii, Dist. 5.

[25] "En couste de moy se agenoilla Messire Guy d'Ebelin, Connestable de Chippre; et se confessa a moy; et je luy donnay telle absolucion comme Dieu m'en donnait le povoir."—*Mémoires du Sire de Joinville* (ed. 1785), II, 20.

sacramental; it secures pardon from God, and the penitent is thus absolved in the *forum internum*, but he is as yet unreconciled to the Church
and should therefore, when opportunity offers, confess again to a priest
and obtain the full sacrament of penitence.[26] Nor is the lack of a priest
confined to such desperate occasions as that related by Joinville; if a
man knows his parish priest to be unfit and cannot obtain his license
to confess to another he is released from the obligation to employ a priest
and can lawfully confess to a layman.[27] It is quite probable that the discussion of the matter provoked by the Templar trials led to a change in
the attitude of the Church. Astesanus de Asti, writing in 1317, examines
the subject with a minuteness which shows that it had been attracting
fresh attention. While he quotes the authorities in its favor, he concludes
that such confession is in no way sacramental and does not obtain absolution.[28] Still the question would not settle itself, for the more the Church
inculcated the necessity of the sacrament of penitence for salvation, the
more the faithful sought for it in whatever form it could be obtained.
Early in the fifteenth century Prierias returned to the opinion of Aquinas,
and even held that a layman could absolve from excommunication on
the death-bed.[29] It was in vain that the council of Trent in 1551 defined
absolutely that no one except bishops and priests had power to hear
sacramental confession and grant absolution.[30] Not long afterwards
Azpilcueta argues that it is not a sin—at least a mortal sin—to believe,
as many do, that any layman can hear confessions and grant absolution
to the dying.[31] In the seventeenth century, however, Diana condemns
the practice as utterly useless, though he admits that it is common among
sailors in fear of shipwreck.[32]

Another point indispensable to a clear appreciation of the functions
of the master or preceptor of the chapter of the Templars is the nature
of the absolution granted to sinners in the twelfth century. The power
of the keys had not at that time been defined with precision, and much
debate in the Schools was still requisite before a practical working theory
could be evolved and accepted. It would lead me too far from our
subject to enter into the details of these forgotten wrangles and it will

---

[26] Aquinas, *Summa*, Suppl. q. viii, Art. 2; cf. Hostiensis, *Aurea Summa*, Lib. V, *De Pœn. et Remiss.* § 7.

[27] Aquinas, *op. cit.*, Suppl. q. viii, Art. 4.

[28] Astesanus, *Summa de Casibus*, Lib. V, Tit. XIII, q. ii. "Unde male sensit Ber. extra de offi. ord. pastoralis dicens quod laicus absolvere potest in necessitate et hoc non tantum a peccatis sed etiam ab excommunicatione."

[29] *Summa Sylvestrina*, s. v. "Confessor," 1, §§ 1, 6.

[30] C. Trident., sess. xiv, *De Pœnit.*, c. vi.

[31] Azpilcueta, *Comment. in VII. Distinct. de Pœnit.*, Dist. 6, c. i, nn. 81, 83.

[32] *Summa Diana*, s. vv. "Confessarius" n. 2, "Confessionis necessitas" nn. 13, 14.

suffice for our present purposes to state that as yet the priest was held to have scarce more than an intercessory power with God. His intercession was more efficacious than that of a layman, but although the rapid development of sacerdotalism was constantly tending to confer on him augmented power, he as yet did not pretend of himself to grant absolution. Fathers Morin and Martène have abundantly shown that prior to the thirteenth century the formulas of absolution were universally deprecatory, or at most of a transitional character, in which the priest speaks in doubtful terms as to his own powers.[33] To the Church of the twelfth century, therefore, there was nothing offensive or shocking in a man clothed with the quasi-sacerdotal character of a monk offering the prayer and granting the conditional absolution which were customary at the period.[34] It was not until about 1240 that the absolute indicative form, *Ego te absolvo*, was introduced, giving rise to so much objection and animadversion that some thirty years afterwards Aquinas was required by the Dominican general to write an elaborate defence of it, in which he tells us that the University of Paris had decided that without these words there was no absolution.[35] Various formulas, however, continued to be used and towards the close of the century Duns Scotus argues that while *Ego te absolvo* is well fitted for its purpose, the priest should not be restricted in his form of expression, which is indifferent so long as the purport is conveyed.[36] It was not till 1439, at the council of Florence,

[33] Even as late as the eleventh century the *Corrector Burchardi* knows nothing of absolution. The most that the priest can do is to offer a prayer, such as: "Deus omnipotens sit adjutor et protector tuus et præstet indulgentiam de peccatis tuis præteritis, præsentibus et futuris."—Wasserschleben, *Bussordnungen*, p. 667.

In a typical later transitional formula, the priest assumes somewhat more power, but is careful not to define its extent. "Ipse te absolvat ab omnibus peccatis et de istis peccatis quæ modo mihi coram Deo confessus es . . . cum ista pœnitentia quam modo accepisti sis absolutus a Deo Patre et Filio et Spiritu sancto et ab omnibus sanctis ejus et a me misero peccatore, ut dimittat tibi Dominus omnia delicta tua et perducat te Christus ad vitam æternam . . . absolvat te sanctus Petrus et beatus Michael archangelus et nos, in quantum data est nobis potestas ligandi et solvendi, absolutionem damus, adjuvante Domino nostro Jesu Christo."—*Ordo ad dandam Pœnitentiam ex insigni Rituali Codice membranaceo* xi. *Sæculi Bibl. Canonicorum Reg. S. Salvatoris Bononiæ* (ed. Garofali, Rome, 1791), p. 15. It will be seen how closely this compares with the essential part of the Templar absolution.

[34] The formula of absolution as set forth in the *Règle* is: "Mais cil qui se confessent bien de lor defautes et ne laissent a dire ne a confesser lor failles por honte de la char ne por paor de la justise de la maison, et qui sont bien repentant des choses que il ont mau faites, cil prennent bone partie au pardon de nostre chapistre et as autres biens qui se font en nostre maison; et a ceaus fais je autel pardon come je puis de par Dieu et de par nostre Dame et de par mon seignor saint Pierre et mon seignor saint Pol apostres et de par nostre pere l'apostoille, et de par vos meismes qui m'avés doné le pooir; et prie a Dieu que il par sa misericorde et por l'amor de la soe doce mere et por les merites de lui et de tous les sains vos deet pardoner vos fautes ensi come il pardona a la gloriose sainte Marie Magdalaine."—*Règle*, Art. 539.

[35] Aquinas, *Opusc.* xxii, c. ii.

[36] J. Scotus, *Super Libb. Sententt.* (ed. Venet. c. 1470), fol. 285 *a*.

in the decree of union with the Armenians, that the Church formally adopted this formula,[37] and the council of Trent, in 1551, pronounced it to be the sole essential part of the sacrament and that all else is unnecessary.[38]

Evidently the error of the Templars consisted in not moving with the world, in not adapting themselves properly to the development of the sacramental theory in the Church, and in this they were pardonable, seeing that they were ostensibly warriors and not theologians or canon lawyers. For a long while, indeed, after the foundation of the order the delimitation of sacerdotal functions was still vague and undefined. John of Salisbury, who died in 1180, complains of monks in general that they sought to obtain a share in the harvest created by the constantly enlarging power of the keys and did not hesitate to hear confessions and exercise a stolen authority to bind and to loose.[39] As for the Templars, it was doubtless because their sacerdotal functions were confined to their own members that he finds no fault with them for this, though his indignation is excited by their increasing patronage of church livings, through which indirectly they furnished sacraments to the faithful.[40] That the Templar custom of capitular absolution was well known to the Holy See, through both the twelfth and thirteenth centuries, and that it had full papal approval, is easily demonstrated. When, in 1199, Innocent III approved the founding of the Teutonic Order, he instructed it to follow the Johannite Rule as to hospitals and the care of the sick, and the Templar Rule as to the knights and priests. In 1209 he confirmed the Teutonic *consuetudines*, and they are repeatedly alluded to in bulls of Honorius III. In 1244 Alexander IV authorized a revision of the Rule, so that in the shape in which it has reached us it cannot be earlier than the middle of the thirteenth century, while the age of the various MS copies shows that it remained unaltered during the fourteenth and fifteenth centuries.[41] Max Perlbach's careful labors have recently rendered it accessible to scholars in its various versions, and its intimate dependence on the Templar Rule renders it an undoubted authority on the question before us. We find in it the same provisions for weekly chapters which are religious assemblages where the sins of the

---

[37] Decr. Union. in C. Florent., ann. 1439 (Harduin. *Concil.*, IX, 440).

[38] C. Trident., sess. xiv, *De Pœnitent.*, c. iii.

[39] "Confessiones excipiunt et claves Ecclesiæ usurpantes aut subripientes Petro ligare præsumunt et solvere, et, Domino prohibente, falcem mittunt in messem alienam."—J. Saresburiens., *Polycrat.*, VII, xxi.

[40] "Milites namque Templi sui [papæ] favore ecclesiarum dispositionem vindicant, occupant personatus et quodammodo sanguinem Christi fidelibus ministrare præsumunt quorum fere professio est humanam sanguinem fundere."—*Ibid.*

[41] Perlbach, *Die Statuten des deutschen Ordens* (Halle a. S., 1890), pp. xliv, xlvi, li, lii, lix.

brethren are confessed or denounced. There is the same elaborate classification of offences with their appropriate penances, and this penance, which is administered by the chapter, is not only valid in the *forum externum*, but is sacramental, inasmuch as its performance releases the sinner from the pains of purgatory.[42] From this it follows that the absolution administered by the master, after the performance of the penance, or in his absence by a preceptor, was likewise sacramental absolution, and not merely readmission to the society and privileges and duties of the brethren.[43] In estimating the force of these provisions we must bear in mind that they were not the work of rude and ignorant knights, but that all the rules and statutes of the order required the approval of the Holy See.

If further confirmation of all this were needed, it is to be found in the gradual change of theory as to the sacramental character of the proceedings in monastic chapters, as the doctrine of the sacrament of penitence and power of the keys was elaborated. To the good Cistercian, Cæsarius of Heisterbach, the monastic chapter covered the whole field of the *forum internum* as well as *externum*.[44] By the time of Aquinas there had arisen doubts as to the principle involved, though the fact was still admitted in practice—the chapter was a judicial more than a penitential forum; it could be held by one who was not a priest, but the absolution granted in it was good in the forum of penitence.[45] This covers completely the Templar case, and even in 1317, after the destruction of the order, it was still quoted as good canon law by Astesanus,[46] but subsequent theologians had no difficulty in declaring that chapters were wholly unsacramental, and even cited Aquinas to this effect.[47] In addi-

---

[42] *Fratrum Teutonicor. Institt.*, c. xxxiii (Perlbach, p. 77): "Statuimus ut culpe, licet leves videantur, occulte quidem per confessionem expientur, manifeste vero in capitulo proclamate, competentem accipiant satisfactionem . . . ut sic religionem pro purgatorio habentes in capituli judicio cremabilia ignis purgatorii abstergant, et in morte demon quid eis obiciat non valeat invenire." Or, as more clearly expressed in the French version, "et que il espurgent en jugement dou chapistre les choses qui devroient estres brulees en purgatoire." See also the *Rule* c. xxxvi (Perlbach, p. 55), providing in general terms for the prescription of penance by the chapter "ut salvus in die judicii permaneat."

[43] "Quando frater aliquis a magistro vel ejus vicem gerente penitenciam susceperit non possunt eum perceptor, marschalchus vel alius inferior absolvere sine licencia magistri si fuerit tam vicinus ut adiri valeat de hoc negocio consulendus. At si magister ad remota loca recederet fratrisque penitencia bene peracta non possit haberi, licebit preceptori cum aliis fratribus in capitulo congregatis sepedictam penitenciam relaxare."—*Ibid.*, c. iii (Perlbach, p. 64).

[44] Cæsar. Heisterb., *Dial.*, Dist. 3, c. xlix.

[45] "Quia in capitulo agitur quasi forum judiciale magis quam pœnitentiale, unde etiam non sacerdotes capitulum tenent, sed absolvetur a pœna injuncta vel debita pro peccato in foro pœnitentiali."—Aquinas, *Summa*, Supplem. q. xxvii, Art. 2 ad 2.

[46] Astesanus, *Summa de Casibus*, Lib. V, Tit. XL, Art. 5, q. ii.

[47] Caietanus, *Opusc.*, Tract. xvi, c. ii; *Summa Sylvestrina, s. v.* "Indulgentia," § 21.

tion to this I may observe that the special question as to the power of
the masters and preceptors of the military orders to grant valid absolution was debated at least as early as the time of St. Ramon de Pennafort
(*ca.* 1235), who replies to it hesitatingly; he does not think that a layman
can absolve unless he has special delegated powers from the Holy See—
and we have seen from the Templar formula that the pope was included
among those in whose behalf the absolution was given. No adverse decision was rendered against the practice, for this state of doubt in the
minds of theologians seems to have continued until the downfall of the
order, since John of Freiburg quotes Ramon without adducing any later
authority or adding any opinion of his own.[48]

From all this it is fairly deducible that if the Templars had persevered
to the last in their original custom of confessing exclusively in the
chapter and receiving absolution only from the presiding officer, the
Church would have had no real ground of complaint against them. They
did not do this, however, for to their early simple forms they superadded regular sacramental confession and absolution when that had
grown to be the rule of the Church. At first they had no special chaplains
of their own; in the earliest Rule their religious needs of communion,
masses for the dead, etc., are directed to be supplied by priests whom
they might engage for stated periods, and who were paid by whatever
oblations or alms might be given to them.[49] In 1163, however, Alexander III, by the bull *Omne datum optimum*, granted to them the right
to receive into the order clerics and priests, so that they might more
conveniently enjoy the sacraments and divine offices.[50] It is a convincing

---

[48] "Quis possit absolvere Templarios, Hospitalarios et alios religiosos non habentes præla-
tum sacerdotem? Respondeo secundum Raym. § xviii. *Item quod Templarii.* Credo quod
non possint absolvi a talibus prelatis cum non habeant ordinem clericalem nisi habeant hoc
de speciali privilegio sedis apostolicæ."—Joh. Friburgens., *Summa Confessorum,* Lib. III,
Tit. xxxiii, q. xlvii. Jothn of Freiburg adds that the question had settled itself as to the
Hospitallers by requiring their priors to be in priest's orders: "Hodie autem expressum est
de fratribus Hospitalis Jerosolymitani quod possunt a suis prioribus, qui presbyteri debent
esse, absolvi sicut regulares alii a suis prælatis." If we may believe the confession of Ber-
trand de Villiers, Preceptor of Roche St. Pol, March 29, 1311, the question as to the validity
of the absolution granted in the chapters had begun to be discussed in the Order itself.—
Michelet, *Procès des Templiers,* II, 124.

[49] *Regulæ,* Arts. 3, 4. (Harduin, VI, ii, 1134): "capellanis ac clericis vobiscum ad ter-
minum caritative summo sacerdoti servientibus." The retention of this in the completed *Rule*
(Arts. 62, 64) shows how the latter is an accretion and accumulation of statutes. The interpolations not infrequently conflict with the original text, rendering it difficult to determine what was the precise usage at the time of compilation.

[50] "Ut autem ad plenitudinem salutis et curam animarum vestrarum nichil vobis desit et
ecclesiastica sacramenta et divina officia vestro sacro collegio commodius exhibeantur." At
the same time he took care to provide that they should not be restricted to their own chaplains in the emergencies of their warlike lives, when at any moment they might need the
consolations of religion. "Decernimus insuper auctoritate apostolica ut ad quemcunque locum
vos venire contigerit, ab honestis atque catholicis sacerdotibus pœnitentiam, unctiones seu alia

evidence of the quasi-sacerdotal character of the order that the priests thus admitted into it were entitled within it to none of the immunities and exemptions for which the Church was then so earnestly battling with the secular power. It was in 1170 that Thomas Becket fell a martyr to the unflinching resolution of Rome to enforce its claim of the exemption of all ecclesiastics from secular jurisdiction, yet the Templar priests, by the terms of the bull, were held in strict subjection to the laymen who ruled the order. On admission they were to place on the altar a writing in which they promised implicit obedience—"seque militaturos Domino diebus vitæ suæ sub obedientia Magistri Templi"—they could be dismissed at pleasure, and, what is especially significant, they were not to take any part in the chapters beyond what might be enjoined on them, nor to take any care of the souls of the brethren unless called upon to do so.[51] This subordination was strictly construed and enforced. The priest was subject to the jurisdiction of the chapter and was punished like other brethren. He could even be placed in irons or in perpetual prison.[52] One single privilege was allowed him. Among the heavier penances was that of being degraded for a longer or shorter period, usually for a year and a day, during which time the offender was deprived of intercourse with his fellows, he ate on the ground, and performed the vilest services with the slaves, such as leading asses, scullion's work, etc., with the addition in certain cases of a weekly scourging in church on Sundays.[53] In such penance, for the honor of the cloth, a priestly penitent was spared labor with the slaves, in lieu of which he was required to recite his psalter.[54] A further tribute to his position was that at table he

---

quælibet sacramenta ecclesiastica vobis suscipere liceat, ne forte ad perceptionem spiritualium bonorum vobis quippiam deesse valeat." In this the word "catholicis" suggests that the object of the clause was inferentially to interdict the ministrations of Greek priests, who doubtless in Palestine were often more accessible than Catholic ones. Professor Prutz, in his admirable *Entwicklung und Untergang des Tempelherrenordens*, gives the date of this bull (on page 33) as June 18, 1163, and (on page 260) as Tours, January 7, 1162. This latter can scarce be correct, as Alexander at that time was traveling through Italy on his way to France (Jaffé, *Regesta*, p. 84). Rymer (*Fœdera*, I, 30, 54) gives two copies of it, one issued in 1172 by Alexander to the Grand Master Eudes de S. Amand, and the other by Lucius III in 1181 to Amand de Torroge. The latter of these Jaffé dates April 28, 1183.

[51] "Sed nec ipsis liceat de capitulo aut cura domus vestræ se temere intromittere nisi quantum a vobis fuerit injunctum. Curam quoque animarum tantum habeant quantum a vobis fuerint requisiti."—Bull *Omne datum optimum*.

[52] *Règle*, Art. 271. In the Teutonic Order there was some limitation on the punishment to be inflicted by the chapter on clerics, but enough was permitted to destroy the principle of clerical immunity.—*Fratrum Teuton. Institt.*, 40, 44 (Perlbach, pp. 87-89).

[53] *Règle*, Arts. 468-73, 493, 495.—Segregation and eating on the ground were customary features of monastic penance. See *Statuta Ordinis Cisterciens.*, ann. 1186, c. vi (Martène, *Thesaur. Anecd.*, IV, 1260); Gousset, *Actes de la Province ecclésiastique de Reims*, II, 345-48.

[54] *Règle*, Art. 270.

was placed next to the master and that both he and the master had special cups.[55]

The order being thus provided with priests of its own, when the necessity of sacramental confession and absolution became more strongly urged by the Church and was prescribed by the Lateran decree of 1216, the practice of the Templars became complicated with a curious and illogical admixture of the old system and the new. The new was superadded to the old, without much care to reconcile their incompatibility, and the result, as recorded in the contradictory prescriptions of the later Rule, is not easy to analyze and define with accuracy. Probably this may in part be attributed to a deficiency in the number of priests admitted to the order, together with the minute subdivision of its members scattered among its numerous and widely separated possessions throughout Europe and Syria. The proportion of priests among the Templars whose confessions have reached us is exceedingly small. Out of sixty members arrested at Beaucaire in 1307 but one was a priest; of thirty-three imprisoned in the Chateau d'Alais in June 1310, there was but one priest.[56] The leaders of the Order seem to have desired to limit the number of unproductive members who could neither work nor fight, and possibly there was a jealousy of allowing undue sacerdotal influence. For a lay member to take holy orders was classed with the gravest offences and was visited with the heaviest punishment, that of expulsion.[57] When it is remembered that the holding of weekly chapters was required in all places where four members could assemble, it is evident that in most of them no priest of their own could be present, and that confession and absolution must be performed according to the original Rule, unless the temporary services of some neighboring chaplain could be secured. This doubtless explains some of the apparent discrepancies of the later Rule, and in fact it is provided for in one article, showing that the presence of the chaplain was in no sense indispensable.[58]

Some confusion, moreover, has arisen as to the functions of the chaplain in the chapters from the double meaning of the word "confession," which signifies either a formal ritualistic general confession of a vague and comprehensive character, or a special sacramental confession of sins actually committed. After the introduction of priests into the order, when they were present in chapters, the services were assimilated to the regular church ritual by the chaplain causing all present to recite after him this general confession, after which he granted them the customary general

[55] Ibid., Art. 188.

[56] Vaissette, Hist. de Languedoc, IV, 141.

[57] Règle, Art. 450. Thus the Templars had not the resource of the Hospitallers, whose priors were required to be in priest's orders.

[58] Ibid., Art. 542: "Mais se le frere chapelain n'i estoit, chascun frere doit dire après la priere une pater nostre et le salu de nostre Dame une fois."

absolution[59]—an absolution which was held by the theologians to secure pardon for venial and forgotten sins.[60] There was no sacramental confession to the chaplain in the chapters, but gradually the custom of auricular confession to priests virtually supplanted the original capitular confession and penance. It is easy to understand why this change should occur, for not only was it in conformity with the general tendency of the Church and its prescriptions, but it was in every way attractive to the sinner. The confession of derelictions in the chapter was of itself a humiliation hard to endure, and yet harder were the penances provided in the Rule for offences of every grade. Almost the least of these was scourging on the spot, and Raoul Gisi tells us that many brethren concealed their sins rather than submit to the shame of being stripped to the waist and undergoing the flagellation.[61] On the other hand, confession to the priest was secret; by this time the old penitential canons were obsolete, and the confessor had arbitrary discretion to impose as little penance as he saw fit. Besides, the penitent had to be consulted about it, for the essence of sacramental penance was its voluntary character, and if he thought

[59] The prescriptions of the Rule are well calculated to lead astray any one who does not bear in mind the distinction between general and auricular confession. Thus Art. 504 says: "Et après la proiere de celui qui a tenu le chapistre, chascun frere doit dire sa confession, et li frere chapelains, après que li frere ont dite lor confession doit faire l'asolution autele come bien li semblera." Art. 542 is even more misleading. The chaplain addresses the brethren: "Biaus seignors freres dites vos confessions après moi . . . et quant tuit auront dit lor confession, le frere chapelain doit dire l'asolution et assoudre tous les freres ensi come li semblera que bon soit, et ensi come il est acostumé a nostre maison. Quar sachiés que li frere chapelain a grant pooir de par nostre pere le pape de assoudre les freres toutes fois selon la qualité et la quantité de la faute." This has every appearance of sacramental confession and absolution, except that the ceremony was performed in common in the assemblage which was never authorized with the sacrament, except in extreme necessity, such as battle or shipwreck; to do so otherwise was a mortal sin (Angeli de Clavasio, *Summa Angelica, s. v.* "Confessio," 1, § 29). Moreover, Templars could confess sacramentally only to their own priests, while they had no hesitation in inviting Franciscans, Dominicans, and Carmelites to officiate in their chapters.—*Processus Cypricus* (Schottmüller, II, 317).

What really was the ceremony in the chapters is clearly described in the confession of Giraud de Caux, January 11, 1311. After the final prayer of the preceptor all knelt "et frater presbyter dicebat eis: Dicatis ista verba quæ ego dicam: Confiteor omnipotenti Deo etc., sicut confessio generaliter fit in ecclesia; et ipsi in secreto dicebant et faciebant dictam confessionem, tundendo pectora sua; et facta confessione dictus presbyter, secundum quod fit in ecclesia, dicebat: Misereatur vestri etc. et absolucionem et remissionem omnium peccatorum vestrorum tribuat vobis omnipotens et misericors Deus, et recedebant" (Michelet, *Procès,* I, 390-91). See also the confessions of Raoul Gisi and Gui Dauphin (*ibid.,* pp. 398, 419).

I have dwelt on this point because Professor Prutz has confounded this general confession with sacramental confession, leading him to state that the Templars confessed to the priest in the chapters (*Entwicklung und Untergang,* etc., pp. 47-8). In his subsequent remarks on the faculties of the Templar priests he has been somewhat misled through lack of familiarity with the rather intricate canon law respecting reserved cases.

[60] Hostiensis, *Aurea Summa,* Lib. V, *De Pœn. et Remiss.,* § 8.

[61] Michelet, *Procès,* I, 398.

that what was suggested to him was too hard to bear, he could refuse to accept it; he could elect to make good the deficiency in purgatory, and it became a commonplace among the doctors that the confessor should grant absolution if he could induce the sinner to say a single Paternoster by way of penance.[62] As zeal diminished in the order and demoralization grew, the habit of capitular confession seems to have been wellnigh abandoned, and the formula of absolution by the preceptor was altered to a pardon for the sins which the brethren concealed through shame or fear of penance.[63] This deplorable laxity did not suit the older and more rigid members of the order. We hear of Giraud de Villiers, visitor of France, about the year 1300, reproving the priest, Jean de Calmota, for the ease with which he and the other Templar priests absolved its guilty members. The privileges of the order, he said, were such that the preceptors could absolve the brethren in the chapters, and if that custom had been preserved, they would be more cautious in stealing the property of the order and committing other wickedness, but now the priests absolved them for gain and shared with them the goods pilfered from the Temple.[64]

Thus practically the distinction was established between the *forum internum* and *externum*, and the control of the latter passed virtually into the hands of the priests. Under the new system the brethren were required to confess exclusively to the chaplains of the order.[65] This was essential, for many of the offences to be confessed were necessarily violations of the Rule, which would not be appreciable by other priests, and the revelation of which would be an infraction of the inviolable secrecy enjoined on all brethren of the Temple. Three confessions a year were prescribed, and these presumably were coincident with the three communions required—at Christmas, Easter, and Pentecost.[66]

There is an evident contradiction in the Rule in regard to the special

---

[62] S. Raymundus, *Summa*, Lib. III, Tit. xxxiv, § 4.—Hostiensis, *op. cit.*, Lib. V, *De Pœn. et Remiss.*, § 58.—Bonaventura, *Confessionale*, cap. iv, partic. iii.—Synodus Nemausensis, ann. 1284 (Harduin, VII, 910-11).—Caietanus, *Opusc.*, Tract. v, *De Confessione*, q. iii.—Zerola, *Praxis Sacr. Pœnitent.*, c. xxv, q. ix, xxxvi. Alexander Hales, however *Summa*, Pt. IV, q. xviii., membr. 2, Art. 1), argues against the current theory that the penitent can elect between accepting adequate penance and taking his chances in purgatory.

[63] "Attamen de omnibus illis que obmitteretis nobis dicere ob verecundiam carnis vel ob metum justicie ordinis, nos facimus vobis indulgenciam quam possimus et debemus." —Confession of Giraud de Caux (Michelet, *Procès*, I, 390). See also those of Raoul Gisi (*ibid.*, p. 398), of Renaud de Tremblaye (*ibid.*, p. 425), of Pierre de Blois (*ibid.*, p. 517), and of Guillem de Masayas (*ibid.*, II, 126).

[64] Confession of Robert le Brioys (*ibid.*, I, 448).

[65] "Les freres chapelains doivent oyr les confessions des freres; ne nul frere ne se doit confesser a autre part fors que a lui, par que il puisse avoir le frere chapelain sans congié."—*Règle*, Art. 269, cf. Art. 354. This was also the rule in the Teutonic Order.— *Fratrum Teutonicor. Institt.*, c. iii, xxi (Perlbach, pp. 63, 72).

[66] Confession of Raoul Gisi (Michelet, *Procès*, I, 398); of Ramon Sa Guardia (*ibid.*, II, 458).

faculties of the chaplains, which seems only explicable by incongruous interpolations of customs varying at different periods. One passage boasts that they have greater power to absolve than that possessed by an archbishop.[67] This would seem to refer to a privilege granted by Honorius III in 1223. Violence offered to a cleric or monk had been made a papal reserved case by Innocent II at the council of Lateran in 1139—that is, absolution for the excommunication incurred by it was reserved to the Holy See—and this had been carried into the canon law.[68] In the frequent bickerings between inmates of the same monastery this had been found to lead to much unprofitable wandering to Rome of those who should be strictly confined to their religious duties, and an exception had been made by which abbots were empowered to absolve for such cases occurring between their monks. The Templars asked to have this privilege extended to them, and Honorius granted that the chaplain of the principal house in each province should have this power—a faculty which in 1265 was extended for ten years by Clement IV to all the chaplains of the order.[69] In this limited sense the chaplains had greater power than bishops or archbishops, but even this is contradicted by a subsequent article of the Rule which asserts that a chaplain cannot absolve a brother for the homicide of a Christian, for striking a brother and drawing blood, for violence to an ecclesiastic, and for entering the Order by simony or by denying the possession of holy orders—for all these the culprit must go for absolution to the bishop, archbishop, or patriarch of the country.[70] Apparently the temporary privilege granted by Clement IV was not renewed, and this is confirmed by the statement of John of Freiburg, that if a Templar of one diocese strikes a Templar of another, the two bishops must meet together to absolve him, or one must delegate his power to the other.[71] In practice it would seem, however, that the chaplain had no hesitation in exerting the powers granted by the bull of Honorius III for the Rule recites a precedent, in point, which likewise shows that the distinction between the *forum pœnitentiæ* and the *forum judiciale* had become fully recognized. When the convent was at Jaca, two of the brethren quarrelled and one threw the other from his horse. The marshal, Hugo de Monllo, assembled a chapter; the culprit begged for pardon, and was sent out of the chapter with the chaplain who absolved him "quar il avoit bien le pooir." Then they returned to the chapter where the chaplain reported the absolution. The penitent was made to beg for pardon again, and was sent out again, and finally the sentence was to deprive him of the vestments of the order and imprison

[67] "Car il en ont greignor pooir de l'apostoile d'eaus assudre que un arceveque."—*Règle*, Art. 269.

[68] Gratian, *Decr.*, c. xxix, Caus. xvii, q. iv.

[69] Prutz, *Entwicklung*, etc., pp. 282, 289.

[70] *Règle*, Art. 272-73.

[71] Joh. Friburgens., *loc. cit.* [n. 48].

him in chains, and he was duly sent to Château-Pelerin.[72] Another case would seem to show that the chaplains even presumed to absolve for violence to clerics in general, in spite of the Lateran canon. When brother Hermant was "comandour de la boverie" at Acre, two clerics robbed the dovecote; he warned them to desist, but they persisted; he set a watch, caught them in the act, and had them beaten soundly, one being wounded in the head. For this violation of clerical immunity they appealed to the papal legate, and the legate complained to the master. He at once had the assailants absolved and then made them beg pardon in the chapter, which condemned them to lose the vestments and be sent in irons to Cyprus "por ce que la bateure estoit trop laide."[73]

From all this it would appear that the accusation in the bull *Faciens misericordiam* was true of the Temple during the first century of its existence, and that, relying upon its privileges and the papal favor, it was less prompt than other monastic bodies in modifying its primitive customs to suit the progressive changes in the doctrine and practice of the Church. Towards the close of its career, with increasing corruption, the laxity of the sacramental confessional was found greatly more attractive than the rigor of the Rule as enforced in the chapters, and peccant brethren no longer confessed their sins to their associates, but discharged their consciences in the three auricular confessions yearly which had become a matter of prescription. Complaints and accusations were still made in the chapters, and when they could be proved they were punished according to the Rule, but this was the *forum externum* and not as of old the *forum internum*. Then the formula of absolution granted by the master underwent a fundamental alteration: in place of being an absolution for sins confessed, it became a pardon for sins not confessed. Such a pardon could be in no sense sacramental; it only affected the relations between the culprit and the order, and not between him and God. What may have been the admissions which Clement V states that De Molay made prior to his arrest we have no means of knowing, but we may conjecture that he asserted the original power of absolution as expressed in the Rule, and that it might be employed, at least in preceptories where there were no chaplains. It is impossible that the curia could be ignorant of the practice of the Templars and of the Teutonic Knights, which we have seen was the subject of discussion among canonists, and the embodiment of the charge as we see it in the bull *Faciens misericordiam* betrays a consciousness of the flimsiness of the graver accusations in the eagerness with which one was brought forward based upon theological subtilties that at the time were still under debate by the Schoolmen.

[72] *Règle*, Art. 593.
[73] *Ibid.*, Art. 591.

THE TAXES OF THE PAPAL PENITENTIARY*

[In 1891 Mr. Lea purchased from a Berlin bookseller a manuscript which, on examination, proved to include the earliest known formulary of the papal Penitentiary, dating from the second quarter of the thirteenth century. No other copy of the document is known and it was published by Lea with a full introduction in 1892. This early formulary makes no mention of the fees or taxes charged by the Penitentiary to those seeking papal absolution, but this aspect of the subject had long since attracted his interest, and his investigations resulted in the following paper, published the next year in the *English Historical Review*. The same topic is more briefly discussed in his *History of Auricular Confession and Indulgences,* II, 160-68.—H.]

* * * * *

THE GENUINENESS of the so-called "Taxes of the Penitentiary" was long a subject of dispute. Protestants eagerly reprinted them in the two recensions which were accessible, and a series of commentators—Du Pinet, Banck, Du Mont, Collin de Plancy, Mendham, Gibbings, Saint-André —accompanied them with more or less exasperating elucidations. The Roman Index prohibited them to the faithful in a cautious manner which left their genuineness undetermined.[1] Up to within a recent period Catholic writers have been accustomed to throw doubts upon their very existence, but the evidence to this was finally recognised as incontrovertible, and in 1872 Father Green admitted it, shifting the ground of the debate to the nature of the implied transaction, and arguing that the absolutions offered were merely in the *forum externum,* from ecclesiastical censures, and that the sums set forth in the tax-lists were simply payments for clerical services.[2] It is natural that an honorable Catholic should repel with indignation the assertion that the Holy See for centuries advertised the pardon of the foulest sins for a few *gros tournois,* and this with an inexplicable indifference as to the relation between the degree of guilt and the price of remission.[3] The question has thus long been a vexed

---

* From the *English Historical Review*, VIII (1893), 424-28.

[1] The earliest prohibition occurs in the Appendix to the *Antwerp Index* of 1570, p. 69— "Praxis et Taxa officianae poenitentiariae Papae." This is copied literally in the suppressed *Index of Sixtus V* in 1590 (Mendham's edition, p. 51). Clement VIII in 1596 added the cautious phrase "ab haereticis depravata" (*Index Clementis VIII* [Urbino, 1596], fol. 43 b). Benedict XIV in 1758 adopted the more doubtful formula "cum ab haereticis sit depravata," and attributed the prohibition to the Appendix of the Tridentine Index (*Index Benedicti XIV* [Rome, 1758], p. 216), which phrase has been retained to the present time (*Index Leonis XIII* [Turin, 1890], p. 320).

[2] Green, *Indulgences, Sacramental Absolutions and the Tax-Tables of the Roman Chancery and Penitentiary* (London, 1872), p. 165.

[3] Two or three items from the oldest of the Protestant editions of the *Taxae* will show how little relation the price affixed bears to the sin remitted:

one, but recent researches of scholars have brought to light many documents elucidating the practice of the Roman Chancery and Penitentiary, and the subject can now be understood, if not completely, at all events with an approximation to the truth. In 1888 the learned Father Denifle printed what he regards as the oldest tax-table of the penitentiary, issued by Benedict XII in 1338,[4] and in 1892 Herr Tangl gave us the taxes of the chancery of the Avignonese popes, illustrated by an exhaustive investigation of contemporaneous documents, edited and inedited.[5] The Chancery and the Penitentiary were so closely connected, and their functions overlapped in so wide a range of subjects, that the practice of the one can safely be used where it serves to supply deficiencies in our information as to the other.[6]

To appreciate the matter properly we must bear in mind that the use of money in expiation of sin by no means excited in pre-Reformation times the general abhorrence with which we moderns are trained to regard it. The barter of pardon for pence disguised itself in many ways till it became so habitual that only an occasional moralist or publicist ventured to utter an indignant remonstrance. "Almsgiving" was a convenient euphemism which relieved such transactions of all impropriety. "Water quencheth a flaming fire and alms resisteth sins," and "Redeem thou thy sins with alms," were texts perpetually quoted and applied.[7] As early as the close of the sixth century, Gregory the Great reminds his bishops that they live on the sins of their flocks, that they eat the sins of their people.[8] To the end of the Middle Ages the lesson was sedulously taught that, of all forms of penance, almsgiving was the one universally most efficacious.[9] It was habitually prescribed in the confessional and is

---

"Pro laico a lapsu carnis super quocunque actu libidinoso, in foro conscientiae, turon. 6, ducat. 2.

"Ab incestu pro laico, in foro conscientiae tantum, turon. 4.

"Ab adulterio cum incestu, pro una persona tantum, turon. 6."—*Taxes des Parties casuelles de la Boutique du Pape,* avec annotations, etc., par A. D. P. (Antoine du Pinet), (Lyons, 1564), pp. 81, 82.

[4] *Archiv für Literatur- und Kirchengeschichte des Mittelalters,* IV, 201.

[5] *Mittheilungen des Instituts für österreichische Geschichtsforschung,* XIII, 1.

[6] See the *Formulary of the Papal Penitentiary in the Thirteenth Century* (ed. Lea, [Philadelphia, 1892]), in which most of the formulas are on subjects equally under the jurisdiction of the Chancery. The same is visible by a comparison of the tax-tables printed by Denifle and Tangl. It was not until the reformation of the Penitentiary by Pius IV and Pius V in 1562 and 1569, that it was restricted to the *forum conscientiae* except in respect to the religious orders.

[7] Ecclus. iii:33; Daniel iv:24. See also Tobias xii:9.

[8] Gregory I, *Homil. XVIII in Evangel.,* nn. 8, 18.

[9] "Elimosina completius habet vim satisfactionis quam oratio, oratio quam ieiunia. . . . Et propter hoc elimosina magis indicitur ut universalis medicina pro peccatis quam alia." —Joh. Friburgens., *Summa confessorum,* Lib. III, Tit. xxiv, q. cxxiii. Cf. S. Antoninus, *Summa,* Pt. III, Tit. xiv, c. xx, § 3; *Summa Sylvestrina, s.v.* "Satisfactio."

still retained in the Roman ritual, with the single restriction that the priest must not keep the money himself.[10] In practice, almsgiving meant payments or gifts to the Church. It was always technically "the poor" on whom charity could be most worthily and advantageously bestowed, and the success of its teachings is seen in the immense growth of its possessions, granted, for the most part, as the charters bear witness, *pro remissione peccatorum*.[11] Even so high-minded a pontiff as Alexander II, in a case of involuntary fratricide, had no hesitation in imposing as penance the confiscation to "the poor" of the whole of the penitent's property, allowing him, however, the usufruct of one half of it during life.[12]

In addition to this, the Church, in its efforts to win over its barbarian converts, adapted itself to their customs, and the practice arose of permitting all penances canonically imposed to be redeemed with money. Tables of commutations are given in nearly all the penitentials and in the collections of penitential canons, regulating the amounts to be paid in lieu of fasts of a day, or a week, or a month, or a year, and a perfect equivalency was recognised between the payment of money and other works of penitence.[13] So completely was this system established, that in the eleventh century St. Peter Damiani indignantly complains that no layman would endure a fast of three days in the week, and that the penitential canons must be cast aside as obsolete if the redemptions are not abolished.[14] Damiani's prediction was verified, but it was the redemption system that triumphed. In the thirteenth century, with the introduction of enforced sacramental confession, the canons became practically obsolete. The assignment of penance grew to be wholly at the discretion of the confessor, and its acceptance became voluntary with the penitent, except in the rapidly diminishing cases of public penance, which need not detain us here, while the alternative of redemption remained in force;[15] indeed, as a factor in the theory of indulgences, it took a new and most important development. Of course, repentance was taught as a condition precedent to absolution, but the schoolmen so diluted it with their definitions of sufficing servile attrition that in ordinary everyday practice it became scarce more than a formality.

While, therefore, absolution was not openly and unblushingly sold,

---

[10] *Rituale Romanum*, Tit. III, c. i.

[11] For ample details see Muratori, *Antiq. Ital.*, Dist. 48.

[12] Alexander II, *Epist.* 100 (Migne's *Patrologia*, CXLVI, 1386).

[13] Pseudo-Beda, *Poenitent.*, c. xli; Pseudo-Egbertus, *Poenitent.*, Lib. III, cc. lx, lxi; Cummeanus, *Poenitent.*, "De modis poenitentiae" (Wasserschleben, *Bussordnungen*, pp. 276, 340, 462); Regino, *De Eccles. Discipl.*, Lib. II, cc. cdxxxviii-xlvi; Burchard, *Decreta*, Lib. XIX, cc. xi-xxv; Ivo Carnotens., *Decr.*, Pt. XV, c. ccv.

[14] S. Petrus Damiani, *Epistt.*, Lib. I, Epist. 15.

[15] C. 8, Extra, v. 38; Joh. Friburgens., *op. cit.*, Tit. xxxiv, q. cxxxv.

the nice distinctions between this and the current practice were not easily apprehensible by the common mind, and in the existing condition of imperfect moral development among the people, the belief was not unnatural that absolution was purchasable—not merely the pardon in the *forum externum*, but the absolute forgiveness of sin in the *forum conscientiae*, through the power of the keys and the application of the treasure of the merits of Christ and the saints. To the trained scholastic theologian, the distinction was sufficient to enable John XXII, when he wished to discipline his penitentiaries in Rome for removing the excommunication of Louis of Bavaria and his adherents, to impute it to them as a crime that they claimed to control the keys of heaven and hell, and sold to sinners absolutions *a poena et a culpa* for the most serious sins. Twenty-five years later Clement VI, in winding up the business of the jubilee of 1350, dismissed a number of penitentiaries who had bought their offices from him, and had naturally made what they could out of the investment by trading in absolutions for money.[16] We need not, at the moment, ask whether the papal indignation was excited by the sale of pardons or by the diversion of the proceeds from the camera to the individual penitentiaries; it suffices to point out that such commerce could not flourish unless sinners had been trained to believe that pardons were purchasable for cash. Clement himself contributed to this belief when he granted to John, archbishop of Brindisi, his nuncio at Naples, faculty to grant the jubilee indulgence to thirty persons, legitimately impeded from performing the pilgrimage to Rome, on their paying what the pilgrimage would cost.[17] That such was the general estimate of the transactions of the Penitentiary is seen in the protest which the German nation, at the council of Constance, presented, in 1418, against the election of a pope before the necessary work of reformation was accomplished. It describes the sale of pardons for sin in the penitential forum, under the color of fees for letters, in the most forcible terms as an abuse more

---

[16] *Bullarium Vaticanum*, I, 273, 343. We shall see presently that the offence of Clement's penitentiaries probably was merely the retention of some of the pecuniary penances inflicted. As to the purchase of the office, doubtless illegal bribes were given to persons of influence with the curia, for, prior to Boniface IX, offices were not openly sold, but the recognised cost of obtaining the position was not trifling. The letter commissioning a penitentiary for the jubilee of 1350, according to the Avignonese tax-table printed by Tangl (*op. cit.*, p. 89), is rated at sixteen *gros tournois*, and this was only about a fourth of the fees required, bringing the total to something more than one pound sterling in the English money of the period. Of course the curia could not expect a priest to make this outlay simply through zeal for saving souls; he could only regard it as an investment which through some means or other must bring in satisfactory returns, and his official oath to the contrary was merely a decent pretext to save appearances.

[17] Raynaldus, *Annal.*, ann. 1350, n. 2. It is scarce supposable that this was the only similar grant.

horrible than ordinary simony.[18] Pius II, before his accession to the papacy, had no hesitation in making a similar assertion.[19] When the Lutheran revolt loosened the tongues of the laity, the diet of Nürnberg, in 1523, in drawing up the celebrated list of grievances to be presented to the emperor, complains that spiritual penances are changed to pecuniary, and that the cases reserved to pope and bishops are merely used as means of extortion, for absolution can never be obtained without payment.[20] About 1536 Pius III sought advice from his counsellors as to the demands for reformation of the curia. A report presented to him admits that the taxes of the chancery are a scandal to many pious souls, but argues that the money is not demanded for the absolution but in satisfaction of the sin, and is properly expended in the pious uses of the Holy See.[21] This scholastic distinction, which had served through so many centuries, did not satisfy the cardinals who, in 1538, drew up the well-known *Consilium de emendanda Ecclesia*. They boldly declared that the Penitentiary and the Datary were the refuge of the wicked, who there found impunity in return for money, to the notorious scandal of Christendom; the Church assumed the right to maintain abuses so monstrous that they would destroy any purely human society.[22] These references, which could readily be multiplied, show that, during the period before us, it was universally understood in all the lands of the Roman obedience that pardon for sin in the forum of conscience was to be had in Rome for money. It remains for us to reconcile this with the apparently trivial and illogical fees prescribed in the tax-table of Benedict XII.

From what has been stated above it is evident that the penitentiary

---

[18] "In foroque poenitentiali, quod horrendius est quam simoniacae pravitatis vitium, ubi non in remedium animarum sed sub colore appretiandarum chartarum crimina delinquentium aut gratiae dispensationum praecise secundum qualitatem suam ut res profanae taxantur, abusiones manifeste nefandas committendo."—*Protestatio Nationis Germanicae* (Von der Hardt, *Concil. Constant.*, IV, 1422).

[19] "Nihil est quod absque argento Romana curia dedat. Nam et ipsae manus impositiones et Spiritus sancti dona venduntur. Nec peccatorum venia nisi nummatis impenditur."—Æneas Sylvius, Epist. 66 (*Opp.* [Basel, 1571], p. 549).

After he had become a member of the curia he sought to defend it, but his defence is merely of the *tu quoque* kind—all men crave money; where the concourse is greatest the craving is strongest; Rome is not worse than the courts of the German prelates.—*De Moribus Germaniae* (*ibid.* pp. 1049-50).

[20] *Gravamina Germanicae Nationis*, nn. 5, 67 (*Fascic. Rer. Expetend.* [ed. 1690], I, 355, 369).

[21] "Neque pro absolutione sed pro peccati satisfactione possit imponi mulcta pecuniaria expendenda in pias expensas quas plurimas facit Sanctitas vestra in operibus piis innumeris."—Döllinger, *Beiträge zur politischen, kirchlichen und Culturgeschichte*, III, 210.

[22] Le Plat, *Monument. Concil. Trident.*, II, 601.

had two sources of profit—one peculiar to itself in the absolution of sin, the other common to it and to the chancery in their dealings with all who came before them as suppliants for favors.

The first source was based on the system of pecuniary penance. Under the Avignonese papacy the Penitentiary consisted of a cardinal *Major Poenitentiarius*, with a staff of assistants and scriveners; connected with the office were two minor penitentiaries, or confessors with special faculties, stationed in St. Peter's, to whom Clement VI, on his accession in 1342, added a third, stationed in St. John Lateran.[23] When the curia was absent from Rome, similar provision was made in the principal church of its place of residence.[24] To these minor penitentiaries the penitent seeking pardon for his sins made confession, accepted penance, and received from them letters of absolution. They were prohibited from asking or receiving anything for the performance of their duties, but they evidently were expected to impose pecuniary penances for the benefit of the camera, for there is a special clause in Benedict's bull of 1338 forbidding them to divert such pecuniary penance to themselves, or to their order or to any special person,[25] and this was considered so important that they were required to swear to it in the oath of office administered to them with their commissions.[26] Evidently, only one recipient of the proceeds was allowed, and although this is not specifically named its identity with the camera cannot be mistaken. As the penances were arbitrary we may presume that their pecuniary features were proportioned to the degree of sin and the ability of the penitent, and further that the payment was secured by requiring its deposit in a chest provided for the purpose in the church, for we have an indication of a similar arrangement in the preparations for the jubilee of 1500. On this occasion Alexander VI commissioned eleven special penitentiaries for St. Peter's, empowered to absolve in all reserved cases except four, and he suspended the special faculties of all the other confessors in Rome, while the pilgrims were exhorted to satisfy God by repentance and "almsgiving." The amount of the "alms" is evidently left to the discretion of the penitentiaries in each individual case, but when release from purgatory for the dead was concerned there was a fixed sum prescribed, and as the intervention of the penitentiaries was not required for souls in purgatory the pilgrims were informed that the amount was to be de-

---

[23] *Bullar. Vatican.*, I, 343.

[24] Benedict XII, Bull *In agro dominico* (Denifle, p. 212).

[25] *Ibid.*, pp. 212, 213.

[26] The oath was a formal feudal oath of allegiance to the pope, with special clauses added, among which is "Et quod non injungam poenitentias pecuniarias expresse mihi vel personae certae [vel ordini meo vel] alteri applicandas." *Bullar. Vatican.*, I, 338.

posited in the chest provided for the purpose in the Church.[27] From all this it would appear reasonable to conclude that absolution from sin by the papal Penitentiary was productive in a manner not hinted at in the tax-tables and not hitherto suggested in the controversy over them.

This serves, moreover, to explain the figures set forth in the taxes which have appeared so mysterious. In the somewhat crude and archaic form drawn up by Benedict XII in 1338, there are 214 separate items, of which by far the greater portion are dispensations for irregularities and disabilities. The individual sins which have subtended so large an angle in the eyes of controversialists are bunched together for the most part and despatched with a curtness which shows that the penitents had already settled with the penitentiaries, and that the heinousness of their guilt had nothing to do with the price of the letters of absolution—in fact, when the penitent is absolutely poor, Benedict directs that the letters shall be written gratuitously, and that such cases shall have priority of expedition, for it is better to serve God for the poor than men for gain.[28] Thus a few items dispose of a large portion of the sins for which absolution was commonly sought:—

Item, pro littera uxoricidii, non ultra . . . . III Turon.
    "   "   patricidii aut matricidii aut fratricidii, non ultra IIII "
    "   "   laicalis homicidii, periurii, incendii, incestus,
              spolii, rapine et sacrilegii, non ultra . .   V " 29

[27] Alexander VI, Constit. *Pastoris aeterni*, December 20, 1499; *Inter curas multiplices*, December 20, 1499 (Stephanus ex Nottis, *Opus Remissionis* [Milan, 1500], fols. 159, 160).

[28] Bull *In agro dominico* (Denifle, *op. cit.*, p. 216). This would seem to be a well-meant effort to reform an inveterate abuse of the curia. A few years earlier, in 1335, Bishop Alvaro Pelayo, who had himself served as papal penitentiary, describes it forcibly and shows how little John XXII's tax-list had checked the greed which rendered all spiritual graces a matter of profit. "Mundet igitur Dei vicarius curiam suam consuetudinibus simoniacis . . . Nullus quasi pauper hodie ad papam entrare potest. Clamat et non auditur, quia non habet quid solvat. Vix aliqua petitio expeditur per eum nisi mediantibus interventoribus corruptis pecunia . . . Sed caveat Dominus noster de ignorantia crassa quae non excusat ipsum apud Deum. Corrigat precia immoderata quae accipiuntur pro bulla, pro scriptura litterarum. Hodie sic immoderata salaria pro litteris et aliis accipiuntur in curia quod per indirectum gratiae spirituales et beneficiales venduntur et omnes officiales quasi calumniatores et concussores sunt, ultra etiam constitutum precium extorquentes."—*De Planctu Ecclesiae*, Lib. II, Art. 15 (ed. 1517, fol. 118 *a*). As early as 1316, long before the issue of his tax-list, John had taxed all letters *in forma pauperum* at eight *gros tournois*, and ordered this to be inviolably observed as a special benevolence to the poor.—Bull *Cum ad sacrosanctae* (Extrav. Johann. XXII. Tit. XIII).

[29] Taxae Benedicti XII. (Denifle, *op. cit.*, p. 216). According to the penitential canons collected by Astesanus de Asti and nominally in force at this period, the penance for incest was at least seven years, for voluntary homicide seven, for accidental homicide five, for matricide ten, and for uxoricide something more, for perjury from seven to twelve, for sacrilege seven, for arson three. *Canones Poenitentiales*, §§ 6, 8, 15, 16, 18, 21, 29, 43, 48 (Astesanus, *Summa de Casibus*, Lib. V, Tit. XXXII). Presumably the pecuniary fines inflicted by the penitentiaries were graduated as redemptions of these terms.

No more grievous sin could be imagined in that age than for a monk to have himself circumcised; the letter given in such a case describes it as a matter not to be spoken of through shame, and requiring the offender to be shut up till his satisfaction washes out his guilt, yet the charge for the letter is only four *gros tournois*.[30] Almost equally heinous is the offence of a monk adhering to the Saracens, and for this a letter of absolution is taxed at only six *gros*.[31] Manifestly, such payments were in themselves no condonation of the sins, and the charge bore no proportion to the degree of guilt.

Yet at the same time there evidently were factors affecting the charges which were not simply the length of the document and the labor of the scrivener. The latter undoubtedly had its influence in letters of the same class. In 1316, John XXII specified for letters of appointment to benefices the price or fee of ten *gros tournois,* and twelve for the executive letters, provided they were of the ordinary form; if additional clauses were inserted these were charged at one *gros* for every four lines. This rate of four lines for one *gros* was his established rule, and to prevent frauds by the scriveners he specified that every line must contain twenty-five words or one hundred and fifty letters.[32] It did not, however, take long for the scriveners to secure an increased rate. At the end of John's tax-list for the chancery there is a general regulation, that for letters not specified in it the tax is to be one *gros* for three lines, up to thirty lines; beyond that limit, owing to the greater risk and loss arising from errors requiring re-copying, the price is to be one *gros* for every two lines, while twenty-five words are still reckoned as a line.[33] In the tax-list itself, which has evidently undergone considerable modification, there is a prescription that for all letters not specifically rated the charge is to be two lines for one *gros*, up to thirty lines, and beyond that one *gros* per line.[34] Yet even this rule is not followed in such items of the list as

---

[30] Denifle, *op. cit.*, p. 224. "Dum reatum advertimus in religionis professore maiorem et verba pudor intercipit et factum litterarum vestrarum vix admittit proloqui" (*Formulary of the Papal Penitentiary*, p. 64). In such a case as this the culprit as a monk doubtless had not funds wherewith to redeem the penance.

[31] Denifle, *op. cit.*, p. 233.

[32] John XXII, Bull *Cum ad sacrosanctae* (Extrav. Johann. XXII, Tit. xiii). Like so many other restrictions promulgated by the popes, this proved a feeble restraint on the greed of the officials. Æneas Sylvius complains of the devices adopted by the scriveners to spread out the writing. "Quibus cum salarium per lineas sit institutum, ex duobus verbis lineam conficiunt et verba trahunt quantum possunt, nec utuntur abbreviationibus aut titellis."—*De Moribus Germaniae* (p. 1049).

[33] Tangl. *op. cit.*, p. 103.

[34] *Ibid.*, p. 79.

happen to allude to the length of the letter; thus a license to an abbot to exchange certain revenues with the king is described as about sixteen lines and yet it is charged at twenty-four *gros*, and the exemption of a benefice from impetration is mentioned as fifteen lines and is rated at twenty *gros*.[35] We will consider presently the slender relation borne by these prices to the actual cost of the letters, and meanwhile it suffices to say that in 1418 Martin V restored the rates to those current under John XXII, Benedict XII, and Gregory XI, and that in 1445 Eugenius IV, in revising the tax-list, ordered that of John to continue in force with some alterations and additions.[36] Through the fifteenth century therefore the regulations of John may be considered to have remained the official standard, at least nominally.

These, as we have seen, assigned one hundred words to the *gros*, and it may be not without interest to compare this rate with some of the prices contained in Benedict's "Taxes of the Penitentiary," where we can identify them with letters contained in the *Formulary*. Of these the longest is the absolution for the murder of a bishop, which contains 368 words, with a formal clause not given in full, possibly extending it to four hundred. This would make the price four *gros*, while in the tax-list it is rated at six.[37] Another is *De occultis et gravibus excessis*, containing 181 words, which, at the utmost, would cost two *gros*, but in the tax-list the price is five.[38] The letter for the circumcised monk, which we have seen rated at four *gros*, has only 179 words, and therefore, at the utmost, should be but two.[39] Simony committed in the reception of a monk is also rated at four *gros*; the corresponding letter has 232 words, bringing it only to two and a half.[40] Absolution and dispensation for a concubinary priest is taxed at four *gros*; of this there are a number of formulas, the longest not exceeding 175 words, thus implying only a *gros* and three-quarters.[41] It is true that in the tax-list the price is always specified as the maximum—"non ultra"—but the constant excess of the tax over the rating by words would seem to indicate that the latter was rather theoretical than practical. It certainly was not observed in many cases in which the business of the Penitentiary concerned exclusively the *forum externum*, and the higher range of rates generally observable in these latter would seem to strengthen the hypothesis that when the

---

[35] *Ibid.*, pp. 94, 95.

[36] Martin V, Bull *In apostolicae dignitatis*, §§ 1, 2, 12, 26 (*Bullar. Roman.* [ed. Luxemb.], I, 295); Eugenius IV, Bull *Romani Pontificis* (Tangl, *op. cit.*, p. 45).

[37] *Formulary of the Penitentiary*, p. 20; Denifle, *op. cit.*, p. 222.

[38] *Ibid.*, p. 61; Denifle, *op. cit.*, p. 224.

[39] *Ibid.*, p. 64; Denifle, *op. cit.*, p. 224.

[40] *Ibid.*, p. 18; Denifle, *op. cit.*, p. 221.

[41] *Ibid.*, pp. 95-99; Denifle, *op. cit.*, p. 227.

forum conscientiae was involved the substantive tax was determined and collected by the minor penitentiaries before they issued their letters of absolution or dispensation, leaving only the formal charges of the letters to be settled.

There is further a class of cases in which the amount of tax is evidently dependent not on the length of the letter, but on the character of the applicant. A letter of absolution for an individual who has adhered to rebels against the Church is taxed at six *gros*, but if issued to a city it is twenty, and if it includes a whole diocese it is forty, an increase which cannot be explained by the addition of a few words. So a general absolution and dispensation for the whole Cluniac order is taxed at seventy *gros*, while a similar letter for one of the mendicant orders is only forty, and for a single province, twenty. Absolution and dispensation for the clergy of a city who have celebrated mass during an interdict are rated at thirty *gros*, while for a province the charge is forty, and for a single priest only four. Simple clericide is rated at four, but if the people of a town have been concerned in the death of a monk, the tax is twenty.[42]

It is evident from this that the sums set forth in the tax-list comprehended something more than the mere scrivener's fee—that there was a margin of profit for someone, and that this profit demanded that a body or community of offenders should not be let off as cheaply as an individual. Nor was this all, for it would be a grave mistake to imagine that the tax as set forth in the tables measured the profit to the curia or the cost to the suppliant for absolution or dispensation or other favor. The passage quoted above from Bishop Pelayo shows how the applicant was required to soothe innumerable itching palms before he could obtain the grace for which he sued. There are no accessible details to illustrate this as regards the penitentiary, but the industry of Herr Tangl has accumulated much instructive material respecting the chancery, which is safely applicable to the penitentiary, though, when the minor penitentiaries alone were concerned, allowance should probably be made for simpler forms in their letters of absolution. The tax in the tables represents only the charge made for one stage in the process, whereas there were several, each of which had to be paid for. First a rough draft or minute had to be made of the letter, then it had to be engrossed without correction or erasure, carefully compared and signed, bullated or sealed, and finally entered on the papal registers. All this kept busy a large

[42] Denifle, *op. cit.*, pp. 222, 223, 226, 227, 233. During the struggle with Louis of Bavaria there were numerous cases of non-observance of papal interdicts. For absolution in such cases John of Winterthur informs us the cost to an individual priest was one florin, equivalent to ten *gros.*—J. Vitoduranus, *Chron.*, ann. 1345 (Eccard, *Corp. Hist.*, I, 1910).

number of officials, who had to be paid in addition to providing the profits accruing from the business to the Holy See. Thus on August 12, 1381, the letter of investiture granted to Charles of Durazzo for the kingdom of Naples is taxed at the enormous sum of ten thousand *gros* or one thousand florins, and a like sum was assessed on the similar letter issued to his son Ladislas, while in the obligation given by the latter to the camera for the expenses incurred in the two investitures, these letters are set down at 3,100 florins apiece, which Tangl explains by one thousand each for the writing, the sealing, and the registry, and a hundred florins for the extra work on the finished copy, the scrivener receiving ten per cent on the single tax.[43]

When the great schism came, the receipts were necessarily divided between the rival popes; there were two treasuries to be replenished, and the demoralisation of the period aided the stimulus thus given to the acquisitiveness of the curia. Under the greedy and shameless Boniface IX, this resulted in a saturnalia of rapacious simony, when dispensations were in the market for all applicants, drafted in any form the purchaser desired, provided he paid enough for them; when expectatives were sold to one person after another, and the earlier buyers were defrauded without mercy. The second letters would have in them the clause *anteferri*, giving them priority over the first, and then ingenuity invented the clause *antelationis praerogativa*, which cut out the second, letters with *anteferri* costing twenty-five florins, while those with the *antelatio* were reckoned at fifty. Boniface appears also to have been the first to introduce the worst of abuses—the sale of the offices of the curia—and the appointees were obliged to commit perjury in taking the accustomed oath that they had given nothing, and knew of nothing being given for the position.[44]

Under such a régime the revenue derived from the letters of the chancery naturally increased. In 1403 the approbation-bull of Ruprecht, king of the Romans, was taxed like those of Charles of Durazzo and Ladislas at one thousand florins, but its cost to the king was four thousand.[45] A transaction of the city of Cologne in 1393 shows even more forcibly how little relation the regular tax bore to the real expenditure. A *rotulus* of seven briefs was obtained (including a jubilee indulgence, for which one thousand florins was paid to the camera), the cost for which, according to the tables, was 115 *gros*, or eleven and a half florins. The

[43] Tangl, *op. cit.*, pp. 63-64. The obligation given by Ladislas to Boniface IX, March 3, 1390, admits an indebtedness of 8,587 florins incurred as fees in these transactions.

[44] Dietrich von Nieheim, *De Schismate* (Strassburg, 1609), Lib. I, c. viii-xi, pp. 82-87.

[45] Tangl, *op. cit.*, p. 64.

detailed account of Dr. John von Neuenstein, the envoy sent by the city
to negotiate the matter, shows that he expended—

For drafting and correction	20 florins
For two clean copies	2 "
For the preparation of the draft	45 "
For revision	20 "
For the clean copies	17 "
For the bullation	15 "
For the registry	20 "
For the camera and *minuta servitia*	1,050 "
Propina to the procurator	20 "
To the bishop of Aix, to whom the matter was referred .	57 "
	1,266 "

or 12,660 *gros*. In addition to this, on reaching Rome, he had paid twenty
florins to the patriarch of Grado, the protector of Cologne, a girdle and
a purse of twenty florins to the bishop of Aix, thirty florins to the advocate of Cologne, and twenty to its procurator, fifteen to the papal janitor,
and six for drawing up the supplications.[46] Rome evidently flourished
on the tribute exacted from the barbarians.

The council of Constance was the protest of Christendom against this
burdensome system, and Martin V was elected to reform the Church
in its head and its members. We have seen how, immediately after his
accession, he ordered the Avignonese tax-tables to be observed, under
strenuous injunctions against overcharges. To what extent these injunctions were obeyed may be gathered from a transaction of the abbey of
St. Albans. In 1423 Abbot John of Whethamstede was called to Italy to
attend the council of Siena. He made thence a pilgrimage to Rome to

[46] Tangl, *op. cit.*, pp. 65-67. The camera at first asked eight thousand florins for the
jubilee indulgence, but finally accepted one thousand. Dietrich von Nieheim can scarce
be accused of much exaggeration in his description of the camera. "Quia superius tangitur
Camera Apostolica, restat etiam pauca de ea explicare, quae assimilatur mari in quod
intrant omnia flumina et non inundat. Sic enim in istam portantur quotidie de diversis
mundi partibus auri pondo multa, attamen non impletur; in qua est generatio quae pro
dentibus gladios commutat, ut comedat inopes de terra et pauperes ex hominibus, et in qua
sunt multae sanguisugae dicentes Affer, affer. . . . Sic ut ab eadem camera liberatus ea
vice recte dicere possit, Cantabit vacuus coram latrone viator. Omnis enim abinde pietas,
misericordia et clementia longissime avolarunt."—*Nemus Unionis*, tract. VI, c. xxxvii, p.
504. Boniface only exaggerated what had been for ages the object of ceaseless complaint.
Even in the much more limited sphere of action of the Holy See in the twelfth century,
Hildebert archbishop of Tours sang of it—

Roma nocens, manifeste docens exempla nocendi,
Scylla rapax, puteusque capax, avidusque tenendi.
Hildebertus Cenoman., *Opp.* (Migne, *op. cit.*, CLXII, 1441).

obtain the jubilee indulgence proclaimed by Martin V in that year, and he utilised the opportunity to procure three bulls desired by the abbey. They were simple enough: one was a dispensation to eat meat in Lent, the tax for which in the Avignonese lists was ten *gros*; another was a privilege to have portable altars in the houses of the abbey at the university and in London, which is similarly taxed at ten *gros*; the third was for some financial arrangement concerning the abbey revenues, which does not seem to be specially provided for in the tables. The first of these bulls as granted contains 433 words, the second 397, and the third 509, which, according to the Avignonese rate of fifty words per *gros*, would bring them respectively to nine, eight, and eleven *gros*. Their cost, as figured in the abbey accounts, is instructive. On his second interview with Pope Martin, Abbot John, in presenting his supplications, felt it necessary to offer the pontiff a *propina*, consisting of some pieces of silver gilt, costing 16*l*. 3*s*. 4*d*., which was graciously accepted.[47] The record of the subsequent outlay is as follows:

Pro bulla de jejunio.

Imprimis pro charta	iij bol.
Item, pro minuta	viij flor.
Item, pro scriptore	viij flor.
Item, in bullaria	xxij flor.
Item, in registro	viij flor.
Item, clerico registranti	ij grossi.
Summa in moneta Anglicana, vij li. xiiij s.	

Bulla altaris portabilis.

Item, pro minuta	x flor.
Item, pro charta	iij bol.
Item, pro scriptore	x flor.
Item, pro bulla	xj flor.
Item, pro registro.	x flor.
Item, pro clerico registranti	ij grossi.
Item, clericis domini secretarii pro scriptura dictarum minutarum	vj grossi.
Summa de moneta Anglicana vj li. xviij s. x d.	

Bulla de perinde valere pro Firmis.

Item, pro minuta	viij flor.
Item, pro charta	iij bol.

---

[47] The custom of thus propitiating the pope by those asking favors was by no means new. The biographer of Innocent III finds it a subject of special praise that he refused all *propinae*, and he gained similar repute while a cardinal by never accepting gifts until he had accomplished the work which earned them.—*Gesta Innocent. III*, nn. 4, 41.

Item, pro scriptore .   .   .   .   .   .   viij flor.

Item, pro bulla .   .   .   .   . viij flor. viij grossi.

Item, pro registro .   .   .   .   .   viij flor.

Item, pro clerico registranti .   .   .   .   .   ij grossi.

Summa in moneta Anglicana, v li. xv s. iiij d.[48]

Thus the first two of these, which are nominally taxed at ten *gros* each, cost respectively about 462 and 418 *gros*, amounts not to be explained either by the increased rate charged to communities or the reduplication of fees at each successive stage of the process of issuing. There was evidently ample ground for the complaints of overcharging uttered at the council of Basle which Eugenius IV proposed to meet by ordering the taxes of John XXII to be exposed in public, so that they could not be exceeded, a perfectly futile device, even if it was ever carried into effect.[49]

It is evident from these examples that by far the largest portion of these so-called expenses were in reality the profits of the camera—profits in addition to what it might get as the price of its favours in granting the supplications of the applicants.[50] What this portion may have been it would be impossible now to define with accuracy, but it is suggestive to observe in the above that the payment to the registering clerk is two *gros*, while the fee for registering is eighty or a hundred. Some light on this point, moreover, is afforded by the act of Parliament in 1533, when the whole business of issuing dispensations, licenses, faculties, etc., was

---

[48] Amundesham, *Annal. Monast. S. Albani* (ed. Riley), I, 143, 152 ff.; II, 271.

[49] Tangl, *op. cit.*, p. 50. Tangl tells us that towards the end of. the fifteenth century the chief center of abuse appears to be the *Bullaria*, and that in 1486 Innocent VIII adopted the characteristic measure of reform of creating a college of seventy-one *collectores plumbi*, each of whom had to pay fifty florins for his office (*ibid.*, p. 71). He took a further step in the same direction in the following year, 1487. In order to redeem his tiara and other jewels, pawned for a loan of one hundred thousand ducats, he increased the number of secretaries from six to twenty-four and required each one to pay the sum of 2,600 florins towards the redemption of the pledges. In return for this they were allowed to sell their offices and were given the taxes on the rough drafts of letters for notaries, portable altars, celebrating in interdicted places, perpetual *confessionalia*, indulgences in life and *in mortis articulo*; also one-fifth of the taxes on all letters issued by the *camera secreta*, and other emoluments. They were formed into a college and all receipts were divided between them equally every month, so that the pay was wholly irrespective of any labor performed.—Innocent VIII, Bull *Non debet*, 1487 (*Mag. Bullar. Roman.*, I, 441).

[50] Thus a letter of provision for a benefice, with or without cure of souls, is taxed at ten *gros* (Tangl, *op. cit.*, p. 77), but this, however much it may have been increased by the successive charges of the officials through whose hands it passed, had nothing whatever to do with the price of the benefice itself. We learn from the *Regulae Cancellariae* of John XXIII in 1410 and of Martin V in 1418 that the price of a benefice in Germany, England, and Scotland was twenty-five marks with cure of souls and eighteen without cure; in Italy, sixty and forty florins respectively; in France and Spain sixty and forty *livres tournois* (H. von der Hardt, *Concil. Constant.*, I, 958, 970). The *Regulae* of Sixtus IV, of which a copy printed in 1476 in Rome is before me, specifies no definite prices. As benefices continued to be sold, it probably had been found more advantageous to have no uniform rate.

cut off from Rome, not with the object, as the act declares, "to decline or vary from the congregation of Christ's church in any things concerning the very articles of the Catholick Faith of Christendom," but to put an end to the frauds and extortions and excessive payments and delays of Rome "to the great impoverishment of this Realm." It was a simple transfer from Rome to Canterbury, and the Roman prices, or rather their equivalents in sterling, were maintained. Where the Roman cost was under four pounds, "which be matters of no great importance," the seal of the archbishop suffices; for larger transactions the confirmation of the lord chancellor with the great seal is required. Each of these dignitaries is to have a clerk for the purpose, who is to provide, without charge from his stipend, the necessary parchment, wax, and silken laces. The proceeds of the documents issued above four pounds are divided, one-half to the king, one-ninth to the chancellor, and one-eighteenth to his clerk, two-ninths to the archbishop, and one-ninth to his clerk. Below the four-pound limit the archbishop takes two-thirds, his clerk one-sixth, and his commissary one-sixth for sealing. Thus five-sixths are clear profit, and one-sixth suffices for the actual clerical work.[51]

We may not unreasonably assume that the profits accruing to the camera from the Chancery and the Penitentiary were not less than this percentage, and possibly more. The business was a large one and the income proportionate. Tangl has laboriously summed up the receipts recorded in the rubrics of the register of the sixth year of Innocent VI (1358), and finds them to be 42,865 gros, in addition to many of which the tax is not registered, and the cost to the applicants was fourfold this amount, for the rough draft, the clean copy, the sealing, and the registering. In this year the clear revenue to the camera from its commerce in letters was over five thousand florins, which may be compared with the total revenue in 1353 of something over 260,000 florins.[52] Yet this is

---

[51] 25 Henr. VIII, c. xxi. We see from this that a papal letter costing four pounds, is assumed to concern only trivial matters. What was the import of this sum at the period may be gathered from a provision of the act of 1529, one of Wolsey's measures of reform. Its object is to repress the abuse of pluralities, and it provides that, with the exception of some favoured classes, no one possessing a cure "being of the yearly value of viij. pound" or above, shall obtain another (21 Henr. VIII, c. xiii). Thus eight pounds per annum was considered sufficient support for a parson. In thus transferring to England the business of the Roman Chancery there is no provision for absolutions from sin; the dispensations alluded to are for defects of birth, pluralities, marriage within the prohibited degrees, etc. The taxes of the Penitentiary appear to drop out of sight, and it is expressly declared that the dispensations are to be "in no manner wise . . . for any cause or matter repugnant to the law of Almighty God."

[52] Tangl, op. cit., pp. 38, 39. According to Sismondi (Répub. Ital., c. xxxvi) the revenue of Florence at this period was three hundred thousand florins, while Villani (Chron., c. xi, p. 92) states that France, Florence, and Naples were the three richest states in Europe, ranking in the order named.

moderate compared with the growth in the succeeding century. Under John XXIII the clear revenue from papal letters amounted to 45,000 florins in forty months, or over 1,100 florins per month, while under Sixtus IV, out of an income of from 250,000 to 260,000 florins, 36,000 were derived from letters.[53] Of course it would be impossible to apportion this between the Chancery and the Penitentiary, though the larger portion was doubtless derived from the former, and it would be fruitless to conjecture what were the additional receipts accruing from the pecuniary penances imposed by the minor penitentiaries.

[53] Tangl, *op. cit.*, pp. 40, 44.

THE ECCLESIASTICAL TREATMENT OF USURY*

[In March 1893, Professor George P. Fisher, one of the Board of Editors of the *Yale Review*, wrote Mr. Lea inviting him to contribute an article on some subject of his own choosing "to enrich the pages" of that periodical, then in its second year. Mr. Lea accordingly prepared the following essay on the Church's attitude toward usury, which was submitted in October of the same year and appeared in the *Review* the following February. He had earlier referred to the same subject in his *Inquisition of the Middle Ages*, I, 359 note, and later embodied some of his conclusions in the *History of Auricular Confession and Indulgences*, II, 385-86 and in the *Inquisition of Spain*, IV, 371-74.—H.]

* * * * *

IN CONSIDERING the history of usury, it is necessary to bear in mind that the word in its ecclesiastical sense does not mean exorbitant usance for the forbearance of money, but any charge or profit whatsoever arising from the loan of money or other article of value, however moderate may be such charge or profit.

There is ample scriptural warrant for the prohibition of all such gains. The Hebrew lawgivers strictly commanded that all loans should be made without the exaction of increase. In the New Law there is less insistence on this, evidently because it was accepted as a matter of course in the precepts which inculcated the brotherhood of mankind and the principles of universal kindliness.[1] Naturally the early Fathers condemned it with a unanimity which renders special reference superfluous, while it is significant as showing how ineradicable was the practice, and how fruitless the efforts of repression. The earliest codes of discipline tell the same story. The so-called Apostolic Canons decree deposition for bishop, priest, or deacon who will not abandon it.[2] The council of Elvira permits a single warning to a layman, when, if he repeats the offence, he is to be expelled from the Church.[3] The council of Nicæa deplores the fact that many clerics lend money at one per cent a month, and corn to be returned with fifty per cent increase, wherefore all who seek such gains are to be deposed from their grades.[4] Of course the usurer was deemed ineligible to ordination, but Basil the Great tells us that if he will abandon his avarice, and give all his gains to the poor, he may be admitted to

---

* From the *Yale Review*, II (1894), 356-65.
[1] Exod. XXII:25; Levit. XXV:35-37; Deut. XXIII:19-20; Ps. XIV:5; Prov. XXVIII:8; II Esdras V:11; Matt. V:42; Luke VI:35.

[2] *Canon. Apostolor.*, xliii.

[3] *Concil. Eliberitan.*, ann. 313, c. xx.

[4] *Concil. Nicæn.*, I, ann. 325, c. xxvii. Cf. *C. Laodicensa.*, c. ann. 350, c. iv; *C. Carthag.*, III, ann. 397, c. xvi.

the priesthood.[5] Successive popes and councils of the following centuries repeat these and similar injunctions with an iteration which shows how steadfastly the Church carried on the endless and fruitless struggle. Their utterances were embodied in the collections of disciplinary canons and in the penitentials, and furnished ample material to guide the priest in dealing with his penitents.[6]

When in the twelfth century canon law began to take a definite shape, Gratian collected a store of extracts from the Fathers and councils to show how impious is usury, that the profits of usurers are not to be accepted as alms, and that usurers are not to be received to penance without making restitution of their gains.[7] Alexander III was unremitting in his efforts to suppress the evil, and in 1179, under his impulsion, the third council of Lateran deplored that it was increasing everywhere, and that men devoted themselves to it exclusively, as though it were lawful; wherefore all such offenders are to be deprived of communion and of Christian burial, and their money is not to be accepted in oblations, while priests not enforcing these rules are to be suspended until they repay what they may have received, and render satisfaction at the discretion of the bishop.[8] As this council was œcumenic, its utterances were accepted as the direct inspiration of the Holy Ghost, but they accomplished little. Towards the close of the century Bernard of Pavia, in his commentary on Gratian, affords us a view of the current legal state of the questions involved. Usury was purely an ecclesiastical offence; the secular laws had no provisions prohibiting usurious contracts; if the borrower had sworn, as was customary, to pay interest, he must do so,

[5] S. Basil, *Epist. Canon.*, I, can. xiv.

[6] Regino, De *Discipl. Eccles.*, Lib. I, cc. ccxxi-xxv; Lib. II, c. clxxxv; Burchard, *Decret.*, Lib. II, cc. cxix-xxvii; Ivo, *Decret.*, P. VI, cc. lxv-lxvi. The penance for usury was of three years duration, the first of which comprised fasting on bread and water.— *Pœnitentiale Pseudo-Bedæ*, c. xxxix, § 2; *Pœnit. Pseudo-Roman.*, c. vii, § 3.

[7] Gratian, *Decret.*, Caus. xiv, q. iii-vi.

[8] *Concil. Lateran.*, III, ann. 1179, c. xxv. However ineffective may have been the efforts to suppress usury, the prohibition of sepulture was at least sometimes enforced. A case referred to the papal Penitentiary in the first half of the thirteenth century shows that the archbishop of Genoa forbade burial to the corpse of a usurer. The Benedictines of the abbey of St. Syrus, however, secretly interred it, and then, becoming frightened, removed it from their cemetery. Disregarding the suspension thus incurred under the Lateran canon, they continued to perform divine service until the abbot applied to the Penitentiary for relief, and was told in reply that, if the matter was public, it should be referred to the archbishop to inflict the punishment due to the offence. If it was secret, the Dominican prior of Genoa was ordered to prescribe for them a salutary penance, and, when they should restore to the victims of the usurer whatever money they might have received for the burial, the suspension could be removed. In another case, the abbot of St. Alban's applied for permission to bury the body of a usurer who on his death-bed promised to make restitution. His widow and heirs have now engaged to do so, and the Penitentiary permits the rites to be performed, provided he had given security before he died, and the survivors have fulfilled their promises.—*Formulary of the Papal Penitentiary* (ed. Lea, Philadelphia, 1892), pp. 172, 174.

and then bring suit to recover in a spiritual court, for the lay courts had no jurisdiction.[9] If the borrower chose freely to give something over and above the principal, it could be accepted without sin; if no interest was specified in the contract, and yet the lender exacted or extorted something, this was not usury legally, but it was spiritually a sin for which he must answer in the confessional and be subjected to penance[10]—which of course would imply restitution as a condition precedent. *Superabundantia*—a term borrowed from St. Jerome—was usury; it meant obtaining some profit in addition to the principal, as when a field was hypothecated as security, and the lender enjoyed its fruits during the existence of the loan; all such fruits were to be computed as partial payments, though already there had commenced exceptions in favor of the Church, for, if a layman held a piece of Church property, clerics lending money on it could enjoy the fruits, which Bernard says seems strange, but that it is not for gain, but to enable them to redeem the property from the layman.[11] Usury could lawfully be exacted from an enemy, one whom you might slay, like a Saracen, nor was it usurious to obtain hire for a horse or rent for a house.[12] A penalty for default in payment at the appointed time was not usury if it was appraised by a judge, or if it was a definite sum named in the contract to enforce the obligation, but it was usury if otherwise exacted; such contracts, he tells us, were customarily required at Bologna of students from beyond the Alps, and bore the penalty of an ounce in every mark (ten per cent) if settlements were not made at the customary periods of fairtime or the vintage.[13] Usurers were to be deprived of communion while living, and of Christian sepulture when dead, nor was their money to be accepted in oblations, though some greedy priests were accustomed to say that the coin had committed no sin; clerics were to be suspended and, if persistent, to be deposed. Restitution of usurious gains could be enforced, even from the heirs of the usurer.[14] Already the device was known and prohibited of accompanying a loan with the sale of some object at a price above its value. Selling on credit at a higher rate than for cash was usury; whether this was the case in buying for future delivery at less than the market rate—as in purchasing and paying for grain in advance of the harvest—depended

[9] Cum hoc crimen sit ecclesiasticum semper est in hujusmodi ad ecclesiasticum judicem recurrendum.—Bernardus Papiensis, *Summa*, Lib. V, Tit. xv, §§ 13, 14.

[10] *Ibid.*, §§ 2, 8.

[11] *Ibid.*, §§ 3, 5, 12.

[12] *Ibid.*, §§ 4, 5.

[13] *Ibid.*, § 9. A later authority, of the date of 1338, declares that it is not decent to exact the penalty and not lawful when the debtor, without fault of his own, is unable to make payment at the designated term.—In *Summa Pisanella*, *s. v.* "Usura," I, § xxii.

[14] *Ibid.*, §§ 10, 11.

on whether the price paid was too low.[15] We can see from all this what fatal restrictions were laid on trade and credit, and what abundant material the subject afforded for nice distinctions and obscure cases of conscience.

When, at the command of Gregory IX, St. Ramon de Pennafort in 1234 codified the new canon law in the official compilation known as the *Decretals* of Gregory IX, the collection of decrees on the subject of usury which he embodied shows how earnestly the popes had been endeavoring to suppress it, and how ineradicable it proved. Clerics and laymen were alike engaged in it, monasteries and pious organizations had to be reproved and forbidden to seek its unhallowed gains, and the various ingenious subterfuges of what came to be known in the schools as indirect or covert usury were largely practiced in the endeavor to escape the unreasoning prohibition. Even the secular power was required to lend its aid in enforcing restitution. At the same time an exception as to enjoying the fruits of hypothecated lands was made in favor of a husband who took them as security for a deferred dowry, in view of the expense of maintaining his wife. Gregory IX, moreover, gave a further illustration of the impossibility of determining the questions involved on logical principles when he forbade the lender to charge for the risk of a loan made to a merchant about to start on a journey or a voyage, while he admitted that selling higher on credit or buying lower for future delivery, might be justified by uncertainty as to the value of the goods at the time of settlement.[16] With the constantly increasing strictness of practice the first portion of this decree was enforced, while the second was subsequently argued away.

So the interminable contest with human nature was carried on, the Church constantly endeavoring to redeem its failure by ever exaggerated severity. Under Gregory X the œcumenic council of Lyons in 1273, in order, as it declares, to repress the whirlpool of usury which devours souls and exhausts property, ordered the Lateran canon to be inviolably observed, and added to it that no college or community or person should permit strangers publicly engaged in usury to rent or occupy houses, but should expel them from their lands and never allow them entrance. Obedience to this was to be enforced on laymen and clerics with excommunication by their bishops, on prelates with suspension, on colleges and communities with interdict. Even if dying usurers should order resti-

---

[15] *Ibid.*, § 7. The *Summa* of Master Roland (afterwards Alexander III) is much less in detail, but in the same spirit (Caus. xiv, q. iv, v). Stephen of Tournay (*Summa*, Caus. xiv, q. iv, v) copies Roland. The form of contract known as Mohatra, in which the lender sold some article at a high price and immediately repurchased it at a lower continued to be in vogue until the eighteenth century in spite of perpetual condemnation by the Church.

[16] C. 16, 18, 19, Extra, Lib. V, Tit. xix; C. 4, Extra, Lib. III, Tit. xxi.

tution, Christian sepulture was to be withheld until the restitution was made to those to whom it was due, or if the latter were absent, until security was given to the bishop or priest for its due performance, and all, whether monks or priests, who should bury a usurer in contravention of this, were subjected to the penalties provided for usurers by the Lateran canon. No confessor, moreover, was to admit a manifest usurer to confession, until he should make restitution or give security to do so. All this was duly embodied in the canon law by Boniface VIII.[17] The latter is even said by a contemporary to have excepted usury from the benefit of the indulgence of the jubilee of 1300, and, although this is questionable, the assertion illustrates the feeling of the churchmen of the period.[18]

All this was not enough. It would seem that no œcumenical council could assemble without devising more rigorous measures for the suppression of usury, and that of Vienne in 1312, under the presidency of Clement V, went far beyond its predecessors. It declared its grief on learning that some communities favored usurers by laws enforcing the payment of usurious contracts, wherefore it ordered that all such laws should be erased from the statute books within three months, under pain of excommunication of all rulers and magistrates guilty of disobedience. As ingenious devices were employed to conceal the true nature of such transactions, all books of account were directed to be produced and submitted to examination. Any one so hardy as to assert that the taking of interest is not a sin was declared to be a heretic and, as such, the Inquisition was ordered to prosecute him. All this was likewise embodied in the canon law to be taught in all schools and be enforced in all courts.[19]

Thus the infallible Church had exhausted all its resources. To make gain of any kind by the loan of money or of money's worth was a mortal sin; to deny this was a heresy, punishable by burning alive if persisted in. The usurer was a presumptive heretic, a "suspect," and the Inquisition was formally let loose upon him to find out whether he sinned knowingly and would make restitution, or whether he believed

---

[17] C. 1, 2 in Sexto, Lib. V, Tit. v. The severity of the prohibition of sepulture was modified in time by the facility with which absolutions for all infractions of the canons could be purchased. In a copy of the Taxes of the Penitentiary issued towards the close of the fifteenth century, the price of absolution for burying a public usurer is set at eight *gros tournois*, equivalent at that period to one florin, and, though this was only a portion of the total cost, it was much cheaper than restitution by the heirs.—*Libellus Taxarum Cancellariæ Apostolicæ* (White Historical Library, Cornell University, A. 6124).

[18] Zaccaria, *Dell' Anno Santo*, II, 88.

[19] C. 1, Clement., Lib. V, Tit. v. For the prolonged struggle between the civil and the canon lawyers over the question of the validity of laws permitting the payment of interest, see Niccolò da Osimo, *In Summa Pisanella, s. v.* "Usura," I, § 27.

himself to be innocent, in which case, unless he recanted, he was fit
only for the stake. No one, we may be assured, ever was reckless enough
to persist and endure such a fate, but the Inquisition found in usury a
profitable subject of exploitation when, about this time, the suppression
of Catharism deprived it of its main occupation. Usurers for the most
part were a timid folk, and in a rich commercial city like Florence, where
bankers flourished and the payment of interest was habitual, it was easy
to extort large sums as the price of immunity. In two years, from 1344
to 1346, the inquisitor of Florence, Fra Piero d'Aquila, thus accumulated
more than seven thousand florins, though there were no real heretics
in Florence, and the offences on which he speculated were usury and
blasphemy.[20] There was assuredly no lack of offenders, for about this
period Bishop Pelayo informs us that the bishops of Tuscany habitually
employed the funds of their churches in this manner.[21]

While the Church, through its official organization, was thus sharpening its laws against usury, its theologians were not idle in defining the
sin in all its ramifications. The questions to be discussed were not confined to the *forum externum*, but were of the utmost importance also in
the *forum internum*. The fourth council of Lateran in 1216 had made
annual confession compulsory on all Christians, under pain of exclusion
from the Church and deprivation of Christian burial. Restitution of
usurious gains was a condition precedent to absolution; thus all dealings liable to suspicion had to be made manifest in the confessional, and
the confessor had to determine whether or not they were usurious and
what restitution and penance were required. In the simpler transactions
of rural communities as well as in the more complicated ones of commercial marts, there were innumerable doubtful questions submitted
to his judgment, and it was necessary for the Schoolmen to define the
principles involved in the nature of usury and for the compilers of the
Summæ, or manuals, to apply these principles to details, and to instruct
the priest how to discharge the duties thrust upon him in the constantly
increasing development of commercial and industrial interests. Thus
Aquinas explained that usury may consist not only in receiving money

---

[20] Villani, *Cronica*, XII, 58. Already in 1258 Alexander IV had given the Inquisition
jurisdiction over usury by the bull *Quod super nonnullis*, which was repeatedly reissued
(Raynaldus, *Annal.*, ann. 1258, n. 23; Potthast, *Regesta*, nn. 17745, 18396). In 1285 we
find Simon, archbishop of Bourges, employing his episcopal jurisdiction over it as a
heresy, and forcing a number of usurers to abjure at Gourdon, each one being obliged
to state what his gains had been, and to swear to make restitution (Harduin, *Concil.*,
VII, 1017-19). In 1317 the great canonist, Astesanus de Asti ⟨*Summa de Casibus Conscientiæ*, Lib. III, Tit. LVIII, Art. 8), says that inquisitors are not to concern themselves
with questions of usury, but he doubtless had not seen the canons of Vienne, the publication of which had been delayed, and which were only issued in that year by John XXII.

[21] Alvar. Pelagius, *De Planctu Ecclesiæ*, Lib. II, Art. 7.

or other tangible things, but in service of every kind, whether of the hand or tongue, and any contract by which a loan is to be rewarded in this way, whether expressly or tacitly, is usurious, for all such service is worth money. The borrower, however, was elaborately proved to be innocent; he felt no pleasure in paying for a loan, but only in getting it; he did not give the usurer the opportunity of making unjust gains, but only of making a loan, when the latter, from the wickedness of his heart, seized the chance of committing sin.[22] On the other hand, Duns Scotus, the *Doctor Subtilissimus*, whose keen intelligence led him to run counter to the teachings of his contemporaries in so many things, argues that what the usurer gains he gains by his own industry; it is his and he can retain it. If he were to restore it to the borrower, the latter would be guilty of usury in making profits from the labor of another.[23]

This was a mere exercise of dialectic ingenuity, and had no influence in practice. The confessor was instructed that the test of usury was intention. If the object in making the loan was gain, even though no conditions were imposed, anything that the borrower might spontaneously give was usurious, whether money or money's worth, in things or service; the most that was conceded was that if the chief motive in making the loan was kindness, belief that some benefit might follow did not render it sinful, and a man might assist a neighbor, believing that the latter might in turn be naturally prompted to do him the same favor.[24] If one lent an article for consumption, and received in return by agreement, tacit or expressed, something else of greater value, whether money or otherwise, the transaction was usurious, and he was bound to make restitution.[25] Tacit compacts were rigidly construed to mean any word or sign by which the borrower was given to understand that something was expected. If there was such an understanding that the borrower would return the favor, it was usurious. The theory of *superabundantia* required that if a pledge were a house, or a coat, or a bed, an agreement that the lender could use it while in his possession was usurious, and of course a house could not be occupied.[26] The principle that no countervailing service was to be rendered required that there should be no condition, even by implication, that the borrower should have his corn

[22] Aquinas, *Summa*, Sec. Sec., q. lxxviii, Art 3, ad 3; Art. 4. ad 1, 2.—Post-Tridentine theologians drew nicer distinctions as to the guilt of paying interest. Manuel Sa tells us that to borrow on interest in case of necessity is no sin, but, if there is no necessity or advantage, it is sin (Em. Sa, *Aphorismi Confessarior., s. v.* "Usura," n. 5). Diana says (*Summa Diana s. v.* "Usura," nn. 4, 5) that there is no sin in paying interest, but it is a sin to offer interest with a view of inducing the lender to commit sin.

[23] Jo. Scotus, *In IV. Sententt.*, Dist. 15, q. ii, *de Quarto*.

[24] *Summa Pisanella, s. v.* "Usura," I, § 1.

[25] *Ibid.*, § 2.

[26] *Summa Pacifica*, c. x.

ground at the lender's mill, or bread baked in his oven, or make purchases at his shop, or attend his school; if just prices were received for
these things, the lender's profits must be given to the poor; if undue
charges were made, he was bound in addition to make restitution of
the excess. The admission by Gregory IX that selling on credit at a
higher price, or buying for future delivery at a lower, might perhaps not
be usurious had become obsolete, and both were strictly prohibited.
Intricate questions arose as to a wife's dower derived from an usurious
father, but the received conclusion was that after his death it must be
restored to his victims, as otherwise both husband and wife would live
in a state of damnation, though there were some laxists who argued that
if at the time of the receipt of the dower the father was rich enough to
make restitution himself, they could retain it even though he had become impoverished at death.[27] It was a disputed question whether, in
making a loan to a merchant about to sail, the lender could insure the
goods at the current rate of premium,[28] but it was generally admitted
that the testament of a usurer was invalid, unless before death he had
made provision for the restitution of his unlawful gains.[29]

Details such as these might be multiplied almost indefinitely, for the
ingenuity which devised means of evasion was inexhaustible, and, with
the growth of commerce, the questions which arose out of the dealings in
exchange were in themselves intricate and numerous enough to tax to
the utmost the keenness of the canonists. The space devoted to the subject in the manuals compiled towards the end of the fifteenth century,
such as the *Summa Angelica* of Angelo da Chivasso, and the *Summa
Rosella* of Baptista Tornamala, show how important and arduous a
portion of the duties of the confessional consisted in the adjudication
of matters connected with usury, direct or indirect, for these were not
mere closet speculations of the theologian, but practical instructions for
the priest in his dealings with his penitents. How strictly the canons
were construed in practice may be gathered from some cases submitted to the papal Penitentiary in the thirteenth century. The abbot
of St.-Michel au peril de la Mer had lent to a crusader, named Foulques
Paganel, a sum of money under a contract by which the borrower agreed
to indemnify the abbey for losses and expenses. The abbot pleads ignorance of the illegality of this transaction as an extenuation of his continuing to perform his functions, in spite of the *ipso facto* excommunication incurred, and he is ordered to be absolved with salutary penance
and temporary suspension. So the abbot of St. Josaphat of Chartres
confesses that he had lent money to some nobles on their promising to

[27] Bart. de Chaimis, *Interrogatorium* (Venice, 1486), fol. 35*a*, 37*b*.
[28] *Summa Pisanella, s. v.* "Usura," I, § xxiv.
[29] *Ibid., s. v.* "Confessor," II, in *corp.*

protect the abbey, and, in ignorance of the censure incurred, had continued to act as abbot; in his case the decision was the same as in the previous one.[30]

It is scarce necessary to point out how deplorable was the influence exercised by all this on the development of commerce and peaceful industry, and it largely explains the success of those communities, like Florence, Venice, and Genoa, in which the necessities of trade established a custom overruling the prescriptions of the Church. Freed from these shackles, they easily outstripped competitors less independent of ecclesiastical guidance. Moreover, the greatest sufferers were of course those whom the precepts were designed to favor. When throughout Christendom usury was heresy and its gains were robbery, to be rigidly restored under penalty of eternal perdition, the only lenders were those whose greed overcame all scruple, or Jews who were not subject to ecclesiastical law. Under such conditions, there could be little competition of capital, and the risk and odium had to be paid for in exaggerated profits. There could be no credit when credit could not be charged for. Under such a system, productive industries and the interchange of commodities were hampered in every way, and while borrowers and lenders both suffered, the borrower as the weaker party suffered the most. It is thus easy to understand the scarcity of money in the middle ages and the fearful rates of interest current.

In France an ordinance of Philip Augustus in 1206, regulating the usury of the Jews, forbids a charge of more than two deniers per livre per week, thus authorizing interest at the rate of forty-three and a third per cent per annum.[31] In England the Caoursins, Italian merchants protected by the Holy See, and popularly believed to share with it their gains, claimed even larger profits. In 1235, Matthew Paris gives the form of bond used by them in lending money to abbeys, under which, if the debt was not paid at maturity, it carried interest at the rate of ten per cent per month, besides all expenses of collection, including a *per diem* for a merchant with a horse and servant. In 1253, Bishop Robert Grosseteste states that a bond for a year would be drawn in pounds, when only marcs (half-pounds) were advanced.[32] In Spain the Jews were more numerous and wealthy, and their business was protected by the law, so that the rates were lower. In Aragon they were permitted to charge twenty per cent per annum, in Castile, thirty-three and a third.[33]

[30] *Formulary of the Papal Penitentiary*, pp. 102, 103.

[31] Isambert, *Anciennes Loix Françaises*, I, 200.

[32] Matt. Paris, *Hist. Angl.*, ann. 1235, 1253.

[33] *Marca Hispanica*, pp. 1415, 1426, 1431.—*Constitutions de Cathalunya superfluas*, (Barcelona, 1589), Lib. I, Tit. v, c. ii, p. 7.—Villanueva, *Viage Literario*, XXII, 301.—*El Fuero Real*, Lib. IV, Tit. ii, ley 6.

Yet sometimes even this was exceeded, for we read that in 1326 the *Aljama*, or Jewish community of Cuenca, declared the legal rate of thirty-three and a third per cent too low, and refused to lend either money or corn, causing great distress till the town-council persuaded them to accept forty per cent.[34] In Italy the bankers of Florence had no hesitation in exacting forty per cent between interest and penalties.[35]

With all its rigidity, the Holy See could wink at infractions of the canons, when its own interests were involved. The income of the curia was largely derived from the sums levied upon those who came to Rome for favors—to procure benefices, or the confirmation of elections to abbacies or bishoprics, or favorable judgments in litigation. The prices charged for these, together with the enormous attendant expenses, were commonly far beyond the ability of the applicants to settle on the spot; they were compelled to borrow largely of the Roman bankers, and there was a popular belief that in many cases the ostensible bankers were in reality only the secret agents of the popes.[36] It is self-evident that these loans to strangers were not made out of pure Christian charity, and the popes, who enforced on distant abbots the minute provisions respecting indirect usury, and the refusal of sepulture to usurers, were ever ready with their censures to compel the payment of principal and interest to the bankers, on whose business the gains of the curia so largely depended. The chancellor of the archbishop of Canterbury, when attending the council of the Lateran in 1179, thus was obliged to contract debts with Bolognese money lenders. On his return home there was delay in payment, so Lucius III wrote to the archbishop to employ censures to enforce a settlement of the debt and its accretions—the accretions being evidently interest, probably disguised in the form of penalties—and the embodiment of this letter in the canon law shows that it was to serve as a precedent in a settled policy.[37] In the course of time all reserve was thrown off. In the fifteenth century the agents of the Teutonic Order in Rome report that the interest charged by the Roman bankers ranged from ten to sixteen per cent.[38]

As the Church gradually acquired a disproportionate share of the wealth of Europe, not only in lands but in money, it became much

[34] Amador de los Rios, *Judíos de España*, II, p. 139.

[35] Villari, *I primi due Secoli della Storia di Firenze*, I, 288.

[36] *De Recuperatione Terræ Sanctæ*, c. xvii (Bongars, *Gesta Dei per Francos*, II, 325). For the enormous sums which applicants for papal favors had to borrow in Rome, see Faucon et Thomas, *Registres de Boniface VIII*, nn. 2451, 2506-07, 2520, 2533, 2598-99, 2802, 2805-6, etc. In 1430 the agent of the Teutonic Order in Rome reports that, in a suit between the order and the clergy of Riga, the latter had spent fourteen thousand ducats, and that it would still cost the order six thousand ducats more to bring it to a conclusion.—Johannes Voight (see Raumer's *Historisches Taschenbuch*, 1833, p. 150).

[37] C. 3, Extra, Lib. III, Tit. xxII. Cf. Innocent III, *Regest.*, VII, 215.

[38] Johannes Voight (see Raumer's *Historisches Taschenbuch*, p. 168).

oftener a lender than a borrower and it had little difficulty in evading the prohibition of usury in the profitable employment of its spare capital. It would make loans to a needy noble on the security of his lands, taking a so-called *census* or ground-rent of one mark for every ten or twelve or fourteen paid down, the borrower being at any time entitled to pay off the debt, while the lender renounced the right to call it in. These arrangements were especially common in Germany, whence they acquired the name of *contractus Germanici*. They were plainly usurious according to all the definitions of usury, but when, about 1425, some nobles of Silesia endeavored to repudiate their obligations on that score, the clergy of Breslau appealed to Martin V, representing that such contracts had been customary for a time beyond the memory of man, and that the funds of the churches and canonries were largely invested in them, more than two thousand altars being thus endowed. Pope Martin lent a favorable ear to the appeal, and pronounced such contracts lawful and liable to enforcement if contested. In 1455 a similar appeal from the bishop of Merseburg came to Calixtus III, and met the same favorable response.[39] It is true that in 1490 the University of Paris condemned as usurious a contract of this nature, which had been running for twenty-six years, and decided that all the rent paid must be computed as partial payments on the principal, which left the lender in debt to the borrower,[40] but this did not affect the continuance of the custom. In this case the lender had a right to call in the loan after two months' notice, but this was not irregular, for such contracts were made subject to every variety of conditions. The rents were sometimes secured on real estate, and were sometimes personal, the seller (or borrower) pledging his own security which covered all his property. They were drawn in perpetuity, or for a term of years, or dependent on one or more lives, and were payable in money, or in the productions of the hypothecated property. They were sometimes redeemable at the pleasure of the borrower, and sometimes at that of the lender; when irredeemable, the property could not be sold without the assent of the holder of the ground-rent, who was entitled to five or ten per cent of the purchase money—a payment known as *laudemium*. When the rent fell into arrears, it became subject to compound interest.[41] In 1569 Pius V introduced a sweeping reform. Personal rents were abolished, together with the *laudemium* and compound interest. The borrower had the privilege of redemption after giving two months' notice, while the lender could only call in the loan in case the borrower had given such notice and had

[39] C. 1, 2, Extrav. Commun., Lib. III, Tit. III.

[40] Du Plessis d'Argentré, *Collect. Judic. de novis Erroribus*, I, II, 323.

[41] Razzi, *Cento Casi di Coscienza* (Venice, 1585), pp. 331-67.—Laymann, *Theol. Moral.*, Lib. III, Tract, IV, c. xviii.—Gobat, *Alphab. Confessarior.*, n. 567.

failed to make the payment, when for a year he had the right to enforce payment. Any other form of rent Pius declared to be usurious.[42] This was drawing a nice distinction, but the argument of the theologians to prove that money could be invested in these rents without committing the sin of usury affords an instructive example of the ingenious casuistry which could demonstrate dialectically any required theorem in morals or religion. The ordinary rate of interest on these investments, though lower than that on precarious loans, was not moderate. Father Razzi in 1584 informs us that in the kingdom of Naples it was ten per cent per annum; not long before he had been prior of a Dominican convent in the Abruzzi, and desired to place at interest a sum of money given to the convent; the bishop of the town told him that if he took less than ten per cent, he would be doing injustice to the Church and to the convent, but he thought the friars should set a good example, and contented himself with eight. In Perugia he tells us the current rate was seven or eight.[43]

Another concession to the inevitable came with the establishment of the *Montes Pietatis, monts de piété*, or public pawn-broking institutions. If restrictions on the rate of interest are in any way justifiable, it is for the protection of the necessitous poor; no lenders are so heartlessly grasping as those who supply the wants of poverty, and none pay so ruinous a rate of interest as their victims. If this is the case to-day, it was worse when all interest was under the ban; the poor had perforce to be borrowers, and their creditors were merciless. To relieve them a movement was set on foot in the fifteenth century in Italy to establish in all cities places where money could be raised on the humble pledges which poverty could offer; this was naturally opposed by the moneyed classes, and Fra Bernardino da Feltre devoted himself to the mission of founding them. In Florence the money lenders were strong enough to drive him from the city, but in Mantua, where in 1494 an inquisitor undertook to prosecute as heretics all engaged in establishing one, Fra Bernardino succeeded in compelling a cessation of persecution.[44] Nominally no interest was charged in the *Montes*, but it was not easy to obtain from

[42] Pius V, Bull *Cum onus*, 1569 (*Bullar. Roman.* [ed. Luxemb.], II, 295).

The *Laudemium* was a fine paid to the feudal lord on the alienation of property held as a fief; see Du Cange, *s. v.* "Laudare," 4. The bull of Pope Pius was not accepted everywhere, and in places where it was not received the local customs continued to regulate these transactions.—Bonacina, *Compend., s. v.* "Census," n. 3.

Even contracts so aleatory as annuities were lawful—annual payments dependent on the life of either seller or purchaser, the principal being forfeited. The expectation of life was roughly determined by halving the years remaining from the commencement of the contract up to the extreme period of probable life.—Bonacina, *loc. cit.*, n. 11.

[43] Razzi, *op. cit.*, p. 376.

[44] Burlamacchi, *Vita di Savonarola* (in Baluze et Mansi, I, 557).—Wadding, *Annal. Ord. Minor.*, ann. 1494, n. 6.

the charitable money to carry them on, so a small monthly charge, amounting at first to two or three per cent per annum was made for the purpose of defraying the unavoidable expenses. If the pledge was not redeemed at a fixed time, it was sold, and the proceeds were returned to the borrower after deducting the loan and the expenses. This brought the plan within the purview of the time-honored definitions of usury, and there was much division of theological opinion as to its permissibility. At the fifth Lateran council in 1515, Leo X endeavored to suppress the opposition by declaring the system lawful and approved by his predecessors; he threatened excommunication for all who should teach or write against it, but notwithstanding this, such high authorities as Cardinal Caietano and Domingo Soto continued audaciously to denounce it.[45]

In the earlier *Montes* the capital to be loaned out was supplied by contributions from the charitable and pious bequests, which were stimulated by the offer of indulgences, but when the enthusiasm was exhausted which provided these means gratuitously, another form of *Mons* was organized to receive deposits, on which five per cent per annum was paid, and this was added to the charge for expenses, bringing the rate to the borrower up to eight or ten per cent. We happen to be told that in 1636 the *Mons* at Brussels charged twelve per cent. This was of course a flagrant violation of the canons against usury, but the theologians discovered that to hold money subject to loan was a service which could be paid for without usury, and it even received papal sanction, for in 1549 Paul III, by the bull *Charitatis opera*, authorized the payment of five per cent per annum to all who would deposit money with the institution at Ferrara, and there were similar ones under papal auspices at Bologna and Modena.[46] There can be little doubt that these institutions contributed to diminish the odium attaching to usury, for, however the theologians might argue, there could be no doubt that the charges for expenses were interest payments; from those expenses the officials of the *Montes* derived their living, and this is what the usurer likewise did.

A further exception to the canons came in public loans; rulers were

[45] S. Antoninus, *Summa*, Pt. III, Tit. xvii, c. xvi, § 2.—*C. Lateranens.* V, Sess. x (Harduin, *Concil.*, IX, 1773).—Card. Toletus, *Instruct. Sacred.*, Lib. V, c. xxxviii.—Em. Sa, *Aphorismi Confessarior.*, s. v. "Usura," n. 16.

Fra Giovanni da Taggia, writing in 1518, gives a full summary of the arguments brought against the *Montes*, but appends the Lateran decree, to which he humbly submits and revokes whatever he may have written to the contrary.—*Summa Tabiena, s. v.* "Usura," I, §7.

The council of Trent (Sess. xxi, De Reform., c. viii) enumerates the *Montes Pietatis* among the *pia loca* over which bishops have supervision.

[46] Caramuel, *Theol. Fundamentalis*, n. 1797.—Felix Potesta, *Examen Ecclesiasticum*, I, n. 24, q. ii-xvi.—The authenticity of the bull *Charitatis opera* has been questioned, but other similar ones were issued by Paul III, Julius III, and Pius IV.—S. Alphonso Liguori, *Theol. Moral.*, Lib. III, n. 765.

obliged to borrow, and bankers could scarce be expected to furnish money out of simple charity. Florentine transactions of this kind were enormous. That republic itself was frequently in the market for funds wherewith to carry on its enterprises; its loans were aggregated into a *Monte*, and its most recent historian tells us that the dealers in these securities had nothing to learn of the arts of the modern stock exchange.[47] In 1343 a financial panic bankrupted nearly all the merchants of Florence in consequence of their inability to collect from Edward III of England and Robert the Good of Naples the immense sums loaned to those monarchs, which certainly had not been done without compacts promising profit.[48] About the middle of the fifteenth century St. Antonino classes the Venetian loans with the *monts de piété* as the subject of discussion among the doctors as to the legality of their usurious transactions.[49] Whatever doubt there was, gradually disappeared. Even so rigid a moralist as Caietano admits that a State can sell an annual rent secured by its revenues and can redeem it, which, like the private *census*, was a transparent cover for borrowing on interest. Whatever may have been the case, he says, they are now so common that to dispute over them would be idle. He even admits that obligations of the *Monte* of Genoa, due in three years, can be sold without recourse at seventy per cent, and this he argues is not lending and borrowing, but buying and selling, which is lawful.[50] In the latter half of the sixteenth century Cardinal Toletus, tells us that many of these governmental *rentes* were redeemable at ten years purchase; the obligations could be sold at a premium without committing usury, in fact the only usury would consist in the State putting forth more of them than its revenues would suffice to meet.[51]

The popes, who had been accustomed, when in want of money, to pledge the tiara or jewels, or corn-duties for temporary loans, saw the advantage of this funding of debts, and had no hesitation in adopting it. Clement VII raised a loan called the *Mons Fidei*, in which the rate of interest was seven per cent, to be paid in perpetuity to the holder, the obligations being transferable. Pius IV issued what were virtually annuities, in what was known as the *Mons Redemptionis*—obligations bearing twelve per cent, and terminating at the death of the purchaser, though interest was guaranteed for the first three years. There was another kind of joint-stock operation peculiar to the Holy See and favored by the curia, as it rendered offices more marketable. All offices since the

---

[47] Villari, *I primi due Secoli della Storia di Firenze*, I, 288.

[48] Villani, *Cronica*, XI, 138; XII, 55, 58.

[49] S. Antoninus, *Summa*, Pt. III, Tit. xvii, c. xvi, § 2.

[50] Caietanus, *Summula, s. v.* "Usura."

[51] Toletus, *Instruct. Sacerd.*, Lib. V, c. xxxix, nn. 2-5. We see from this how the French word *rentes* for public funds is derived from the old *census*. The term *Monte* by which they were known in Italy seems to have survived only in the sense of a public pawnshop.

time of Boniface IX were bought and sold; the new *Societates Officiorum* enabled a man to purchase who could not raise sufficient cash, by selling shares on which he paid twelve per cent per annum out of the revenue of the office, giving security for the repayment of the principal, even in case of his death when the office would lapse—and it is significant of the state of society in Rome that there was an exception in case his death should be by violence, so as to remove from his associates the temptation of assassinating him to get their money returned. How the popes played fast and loose with usury is exhibited in a bull of Paul IV prohibiting such societies for the purchase of any office save those of the curia, any attempt to do so being punishable as usury.[52]

Yet with this progressive laxity in public matters, where the interests of rulers were concerned, there was no yielding of the strict construction of the ancient canons in private transactions; in fact, it would seem as though the sin were compounded for by increased rigidity. The theologians of the sixteenth and seventeenth centuries are as unwavering as those of the thirteenth in defining the unlawful nature of all usurious gains, however disguised, and in insisting upon the inviolable duty of restitution and the necessity of the confessor enforcing it before granting absolution. Even mental usury was defined to be a mortal sin—the hope, when making a loan, that the borrower would give something or render some service in recognition of the favor, although no word was spoken to induce him, and although the service might consist merely in some act for the benefit of others, such as almsgiving to the poor or contributing to the fund for the redemption of captives.[53] So heinous was usury considered that it was classed among the sins for which *parvitas materiæ* was not admitted in extenuation. In many sins, such for instance as theft, the trifling character of an offence suffices to remove it from the category of mortal sins— to steal a few coins is venial—but usury was held to be worse than theft, and the smallest gain by its means was mortal.[54] On the other hand, there grew a tendency to give more consideration to what are known as *lucrum cessans* and *damnum emergens* as justifying the receipt of some profit from a loan. If a man could buy a house bringing him in rent, and if in place of doing so he should lend the money to a poor neighbor, or if, in consequence of the loan, he suffered material injury, it seemed reasonable that he should in some way have compensation. These questions had been mooted since the thirteenth century, and now there was a greater willingness to admit their justice, though ex-

---

[52] Toletus, *Instruct. Sacerd.*, Lib. v, cc. xxxix, xl.

[53] Caietanus, *loc. cit.*—Toletus, *loc. cit.*, cc. xxviii-xxxi.—Em. Sa, *loc. cit.*—Busenbaum, *Medull. Theol. Moral.*, Lib. III, tract. v, c. iii, dub. 7.—Gobat, *Alphab. Confessar.*, n. 568.—Laymann, *Theol. Moral.*, Lib. III, tract. iv, c. xvi.

[54] Alphonsus de Leone, *De Offic. et Potestate Confessar.* (Rimini, 1630), Recoll. VII, n. 37.

treme jealousy was shown in guarding them with restrictions and limiting them to cases in which the loss or damage actually occurred.[55]

In spite of the theologians, human intelligence was making progress and was striving to throw off the shackles of medievalism, but the Church was too firmly committed on the subject of usury to be moved. Moralists of the laxer school, like Caramuel, argued that the only pure loan is one made on call with adequate security, and in such the taking of interest is theft, but when a definite period of forbearance is agreed upon, it becomes a contract in which risk and time are factors which may reasonably be paid for;[56] but in 1666 Alexander VII, after mature deliberation, condemned this as scandalous, and forbade it to be taught under pain of excommunication removable only by the Holy See.[57] Thirteen years later his successor, Innocent XI, found himself called upon similarly to condemn two other propositions then current, which show how the casuists were endeavoring to undermine the old foundations. One of these held that, as money in hand is worth more than money in the future, the lender can without usury demand from the borrower something more than the principal. The other asserted that to demand something additional is only usury when claimed as a right and not as an expression of gratitude and kindness.[58] Mildly tentative as were these propositions, they were sternly condemned; the Holy See was evidently determined to stand in the ancient ways, and to yield nothing to modern enlightenment and necessities. In fact, these decisions of Alexander and Innocent have never been revoked and they are still the law of the Church.[59] These papal utterances checked whatever tendency existed to-

[55] *Summa Pisanella, s.v.* "Usura," I, §§ 23, 25.—Caietanus, *loc. cit.*—Toletus, *loc. cit.*, c. xxxii, xxxiii.—Busenbaum, *loc. cit.*, n. 10.—Laymann, *loc. cit.*, n. 8.

[56] Caramuel, *Theol. Fundamentalis*, n. 1782-3. Writing in 1656, he describes how, in the disturbed state of Europe, and with the devices of debtors to resist or evade payment, it was almost impossible for lenders to recover their money. His argument (*ibid.*, n. 1796) for the justice of payment for time loans would seem to be irrefragable on the ground of morality.

The question as to the lawfulness of payment for stipulated forbearance was a subject of considerable discussion at the time. Diana (*Summa, s. v.* "Mutuum," n. 16) cites doctors on both sides and expresses no opinion of his own.

Some verses current in the schools enumerate fifteen reasons justifying payment for loans. It is observable that they include neither risk nor time—

> Feuda, fideijussor, pro dote, stipendia cleri,
> Venditio fructus, cui velles jure nocere,
> Vendens sub dubio, pretium post tempora solvens,
> Pœna nec in fraudem, lex commissoria, gratis
> Dans sociis, pompa, plus sorte modis datur istis.
>
> Reginald, *Praxis Fori Pœnitentialis*, Lib. xxv, n. 213.

[57] Alexander VII, Decr. *Sanctissimus*, 1666, Prop. 42.

[58] Innocent XI, Decr. *Sanctissimus*, 1679, Prop. 41, 42.

[59] Miguel Sanchez, *Prontuario de Teología Moral.*, Trat. xx, Punto v, n. 5 (Madrid, 1878). —Gab. de Varceno, *Compend. Theol. Moral.* (Turin, 1889), Trat. xii, pt. 2, c. i, Art. 6, § 1.

wards a more liberal construction of the canons. The Jesuit, Viva, belonged to the laxer school of Probabilists, but in his *Theology*, printed in 1722, he declared that usury is forbidden not only by the divine and canon laws, but by the natural law, as much as theft; in all doubtful cases the doubt must be construed in favor of the borrower, and even gifts from him should be refused, lest they be the offering of fear rather than of gratitude.[60]

The eighteenth century was a period of rapid commercial development, the benefits of which were largely grasped by England and Holland—Protestant nations whose trade was not embarrassed by scruples of conscience on the subject of usury, which contented themselves with protecting the poor and defenceless from extortion, and did not require the merchant and banker to submit annually or oftener the details of their transactions to their confessors, and make whatever restitution of their profits the ghostly father might require under pain of eternal damnation. While this of course cannot be alleged as the main cause of Protestant commercial prosperity, it undoubtedly was a contributing factor, and as the industrial spirit gradually grew more powerful than the military, it was inevitable that Catholics should grow restive under the bonds which crippled their energies and handicapped them in the race for wealth. It was natural that the cry for relief should come from Belgium, where in 1743 Broedersen started the discussion by a work entitled *De Usuris licitis et illicitis,* in which with much learning he sought to prove that money is not, as the schoolmen held, unproductive, and that interest can justly be charged on loans made, not to the poor for their support, but to those who can employ them at a profit in their ventures. The discussion aroused by this led Benedict XIV in 1745 to have the matter maturely debated in the Sacred College, and the result of the deliberations was promulgated in a bull which declared that any charge whatever for the use of money is unlawful and usurious, even if loans are made at moderate rates to rich men to be used in their business. It is true that there are circumstances under which moderate profits can be lawfully secured, but these are by no means universal, and everyone should closely scrutinize his conscience to determine whether what he proposes to do is free from sin.[61] Subsequently, when not speaking *ex cathedra*, he repeated the condemnation of the distinction between

---

As I shall have occasion to cite this latter work I may mention that Gabriele da Guarceno was formerly professor of theology in the Capuchin convent in Rome and is a consultor of the propaganda and theologian of the datary. His *Compendium* has reached its ninth edition since its first appearance in 1871 and presumably may be regarded as representing the opinions officially current in Rome.

[60] Viva, *Cursus Theol. Moralis*, Pt. IV, q. iii, Art. 2, nn. 6, 7.

[61] Benedict XIV, Bull *Vix pervenit*, 1745 (*Bullar. Bened. XIV*, T. I, p. 259.)

loans made to the rich and to the poor, which he stigmatized as an
impious doctrine invented by heretics such as John Calvin, Charles
Dumoulin, and Claude Saumaise.[62] The rigorist Dominican, Father
Concina, plunged into the fray with his *Commentarius in Epistolam
Encyclicam contra Usuram*, in which he defended vigorously the ancient
doctrine of the Church.[63] In 1746 another advocate of the new views,
Scipione Maffei, came forward with a treatise *Sull' impiego del danaro*,
dedicated to Benedict XIV, which produced a great effect. He argued
that interest is illegal only when excessive; the usury which is forbidden is that which injures, not that which benefits, and that Scripture and the Fathers only condemn extortion on the poor. In spite
of the condemnation of this doctrine so emphatically uttered by Benedict XIV, it was accepted and defended by theologians of undoubted
authority and orthodoxy—Bolgeni, Cardinal de la Lucerna, Rolando, and
Mastrofini, while the conservative side had champions no less eminent.
St. Alphonso Liguori, whose work was destined to become of paramount authority, makes a fair presentation of the traditional teaching
of the Church, and gives no countenance to a distinction between the rich
and poor as borrowers.[64] In the confessional, however, where all such
questions were practically decided, he taught the lax doctrine which for
more than a century had been gaining ground, that the confessor is to
be guided solely by what seems to him to promise best, and that when
no result appears likely to accrue from warning a penitent that he
must make restitution of illegal gains, he can omit to do so.[65] Practically
this relegated the matter to the conscience of the usurer, which was daily
becoming more hardened with the spreading popular conviction that
the taking of interest is not a sin, though the prolonged discussion of
the subject shows how difficult the problem had become. Thus Scipione
de'Ricci, the Jansenist bishop of Pistoja, classed notorious usurers with
robbers and actors to whom the Eucharist is to be denied.[66] Father de
Charmes is very strict in his definition of the *lucrum cessans* and *damnum emergens*, which he holds to be the only justification of receiving
profit from a loan.[67]

[62] *Id., De Synodo Diocesana*, Lib. x, c. iv, nn. 1-4.

[63] I have not access to this work, but presumably it is only an expansion of the position
assumed by Concina in his *Theologia Christiana* (Lib. IX, Dist. 4, c. ii), where he says
that the common people ascribe the crime of usury only to excessive charges. This has
been adopted by modern heretics and by one or two ignorant Catholics, but there is no
difference between loans made to the poor for their support and to merchants to enable
them to increase their gains; all are equally forbidden. Of course he has no trouble in
proving this from Scripture, from the Fathers, from the canons, and from the older
theologians.

[64] Liguori, *Theol. Moral.*, Lib. III, nn. 758-92.

[65] *Op. cit.*, Lib. VI, n. 616.

[66] Ad Casus Conscientiae anno 1784 in *Civ. Pistoriensi discussos Resolutiones*, p. 81.

[67] Th. de Charmes, *Compend. Theol. Univers.*, Tract. xv, Dist. 2, c. iii, § 3.

The whole subject was thus involved in uncertainty which was discreditable to the Church and most embarrassing to confessors. In strictness, their only authorized rule of action was furnished by the canons of the œcumenic councils of the Lateran, Lyons, and Vienne, and the unbroken tradition of the Church from the beginning. These demanded of them a close inquisition into every business transaction of their penitents, with the refusal of absolution to those who would not make restitution of any gains tainted in ever so light a degree with usury. Yet the enforcement of this would require a large portion of the faithful to surrender their incomes, for the world had moved on, and left the Church behind, and there were few who scrupled about employing their capital in any way that promised the best returns. Confessors inclined to rigor would be involved in perpetual antagonism with their penitents, and would find their confessionals deserted for those of laxer views. There was no authoritative decision under which a conscientious priest or penitent could seek escape from the strict construction of the absolute rules so long enunciated and enforced, while yet in daily life every one treated those rules as obsolete. The situation was unendurable, and yet the Holy See held out, as it did in the matter of the Copernican theory, with a pertinacity which showed how much it cost to make acknowledgment of its fallibility, and that for centuries it had been teaching false doctrine in its œcumenic councils and papal decrees. At length the pressure grew too strong, and it gave way, but it did so in a manner so awkward as to emphasize the admission of defeat, for it made no concession of principle and merely sanctioned a laxity of practice which is a prostitution of the sacrament so long as there is no revocation of the doctrine that usury is a sin and its defence a heresy. It was not until 1822 that any recorded action was taken, and this consisted merely in shuffling off a decision in a way which manifested how unwelcome was the question. A woman of Lyons appealed to the Congregation of the Inquisition, complaining that she had placed her capital out at interest, and that her confessor refused to grant her absolution unless she would make restitution of her income to her debtors. In response to this the Holy Office decreed, July 3, 1822, that an answer would be given to her at an opportune time, and that meanwhile her confessor could absolve her without requiring restitution, provided she was ready to obey all future mandates.[68]

[68] "Eminentissimi decreverunt: Oratrici pro nunc dicatur quod responsa ad propositos casus ipsi opportuno tempore dabuntur. Interim vero, licet non peracta ulla illarum restitutionum de quarum obligatione S. Sedem consuluit, a proprio confessore absolvi sacramentaliter posse, dummodo vere parata sit stare mandatis."

This decision of 1822 is not commonly given in the books. It occurs in a collection officially issued by Archbishop Fransoni of Turin under the title *Sanctae Apostolicae Sedis Responsa circa Lucrum ex Mutuo.* (Pesaro, 1834), from which I also draw the succeeding decisions, some of which are likewise not alluded to by the systematic writers.

Doubtless applications such as this were constantly pouring in upon the Holy See from all quarters, but the next response recorded does not appear until 1830, when the Bishop of Rennes made an earnest appeal to the Holy Office for some decision that should set the question at rest. The confessors of his diocese, he said, were not unanimous; there was a sharp dispute over the meaning of Benedict XIV's Encyclical *Vix pervenit*; there were quarrels and dissensions, the denial of the sacrament to many merchants who put out money at interest, and damage to innumerable souls. Many confessors adopted a middle course; if consulted, they endeavored to persuade from seeking such gains; if the penitent persisted, they would absolve him on his promise of obedience to the future judgment of the Holy See when it should be rendered; if the penitent did not allude to such gains in his confession, they made no inquiry but granted absolution, fearing that he would refuse to make restitution and to abstain for the future. The bishop, therefore, asked whether he should approve the course of these confessors, and exhort the more rigid to adopt it. To this the cardinals of the Congregation replied briefly, August 18, 1830, that such confessors were not to be disturbed, and that his second question was answered in the response to the first.

In the same year, 1830, Professor Denavit of the seminary of Lyons raised the question in a different shape before the papal Penitentiary. He stated that the Penitentiary was accustomed to answer all inquiries on the subject by referring the inquirers to the encyclical of Benedict XIV. Notwithstanding this, there were priests who argued that it is licit to receive five per cent interest, without reference to *lucrum cessans* or *damnum emergens*, simply on the ground of the national law prescribing that rate, and that this secular law annihilated the divine and ecclesiastical laws prohibiting usury. He therefore had been accustomed to refuse absolution to priests holding this opinion, and he asked whether he was justified in doing so. The inquiry was shrewdly framed, for the question of the preponderance of the civil or of the ecclesiastical law was well calculated to arouse the susceptibility of the curia, but the Penitentiary contented itself with replying, September 16, 1830, that such priests were not to be disturbed if they were prepared to obey the decision of the Holy See when it should be rendered. In 1831 the same question, together with those of

---

In his Preface the archbishop dwells on the importance and the unsettled state of the question, and the uncertainty which beset the consciences of the faithful, even after the Holy See had said substantially all that it has thus far seen fit to utter—"In universa rei Moralis scientia non erit questionem magis agitatam, jactatam et hinc inde oppugnatam, quam argumentum de Lucro ex Mutuo: immensæ quæstionis est pro qua parte magis pugnet ratio controversiæ, de qua in utramque partem potest disputare, quum adhuc desideretur supremum judicium disputationibus finem imponens, ac propterea intra contrarias partes decertantes hærent Fidelium conscientiæ."

the bishop of Rennes in a more developed shape, was submitted by the bishop of Verona to the Penitentiary. It referred them to the Holy Office and transmitted the reply, August 14, 1831, which was as usual the evasive one, *"non esse inquietandos"* until the appearance of that papal decision which was always implicitly promised and never forthcoming. About the same time, the bishop of Viviers applied for the solution of some doubts connected with the authority of the secular law, not resolved in the response to the bishop of Rennes, in reply to which the Holy Office sent to him, September 24, 1831, its answers to the bishops of Rennes and Verona. Contemporaneously, the matter was presented in the most practical shape by the chapter of Locarno, in the Swiss territory of the diocese of Como. The tithes on which the prebends had been supported were suppressed, and the amount of their capitalization paid over in money: that money must bring in an income, or the canons would shortly consume it and then starve; the *census*, or ground-rent, was prohibited by municipal law; if they invested in real estate it would bring them in only 2 and one-half per cent, and, besides, the lands of the district were mostly in the hands of large proprietors; they were in despair, and begged to know whether they could not put out their capital on interest, and thus be enabled to continue their religious duties. To this the response of the imperturbable Holy Office, August 21, 1831, was as usual that they were not to be disturbed, provided they were prepared to obey the mandates of the Holy See. Simultaneously, the irrepressible Professor Denavit retorted on the Penitentiary that in France the universal teaching was that the civil law could not override the canon law; he therefore was accustomed to refuse absolution to all who justified themselves by it in receiving interest and who refused to make restitution, and he asked whether in this he was too harsh. The answer to this September 24, 1831, was as usual—he was too harsh, and his penitents "non esse inquietandos." Then in January, 1832, Dr. Giuseppe Antonio Avvaro, professor at Pignerol, and pro-vicar of the diocese, addressed the Penitentiary, stating that the subject was creating great dissension, in which both sides appealed to the encyclical of Benedict XIV; his position required him to give answers to those consulting him, and he desired some definite instructions for his guidance. To this reply was made, February 16, 1832, by sending to him the responses to Professor Denavit and the bishop of Verona. Then later in 1832 the bishop of Aix asked for some rule by which the consciences of confessors and penitents could be quieted, when he received the same answer. These are doubtless only a few examples of innumerable appeals for light on the vexed question, to which the Holy See had but one answer—temporizing and evasion. It could resist no longer the advance of intelligence and civilization, it

could not own itself vanquished, or that for centuries it had been teaching false doctrines, and it took refuge in tacitly accepting the situation,
while it vainly asserted its supremacy by holding out the promise of a
decision which has never come. The Vatican council afforded the opportunity of revoking the utterances of the council of Vienne, but it was not
utilized, and thus all who justify the taking of interest are heretics, yet
they are admitted to the sacraments, and are allowed to cherish their
heresy. Nay more, in the second response to Professor Denavit, November 11, 1831, there was a clause that penitents who had accepted interest
in good faith were not to be disturbed. This raised the question whether
the decisions applied to those who were doubtful as to the legality of
usury, and a conscientious penitent consulting a rigid confessor might
be told that the very inquiry was sufficient to deprive him of the privilege.[69] To meet this, a subsequent decision was issued January 17, 1838,
in which the Penitentiary ordered that absolution without requiring
restitution must be given to the penitent, even if he himself believes the
taking of interest to be unlawful.[70] The latest utterance is one by the
Holy Office, December 18, 1872, in response to an inquiry by the bishop
of Ariano, by which it was ordered that those who take eight per cent
per annum "non esse inquietandos."[71]

Of course, to the systematic theologians, dealing with an interminable
line of contrary opinions in the invariable traditions of centuries, this
changed attitude of the Holy See, carefully guarded and evasive though
it be, is a troublesome matter to explain. Doctrinally, the old definitions
have never been revoked; the difficulty is to reconcile them with the
modern instructions as to practice. Father Gury's argument to prove by
the *lucrum cessans* and the *damnum emergens*, by the supreme power
of the state and by the rules of Probabilism, that it is lawful to take the
legal rate of interest is a model of ingenious and graceful retreat from
a position which had become untenable. Besides, there are the assurances
of the responses of the Holy See that the faithful are not to be disturbed
until a decision is rendered, which surely shows that it is probable that
such gains are lawful, for if this were not probable, they would have to
be disturbed.[72]

There are still conservatives, however, who cannot persuade themselves
that the church taught false doctrines up to within a couple of generations, and who, without disputing the authority of the modern decisions,
take advantage of their evasiveness to maintain the old rules. Miguel
Sanchez, for instance, denounces usury as a thing in itself intrinsically

---

[69] Gury, *Casus Conscientiæ*, I, 892.
[70] Miguel Sanchez, *Prontuario de la Teología Moral*, tract. xx, Punto v, n. 5.
[71] Varceno, *Compend. Theol. Moral.*, tract. xii, Pt. ii, c. i, Art. 6, § 2, punct. 4.
[72] Gury, *Compend. Theol. Moral.*, I, 857-64.

and essentially evil, causing incalculable injury to agriculture, commerce, and industry, besides being a violation of the divine law, which entangles more consciences and gives more anxiety to confessors than any other, although it is true that some theologians hold that under certain conditions and in great moderation it is not intolerable. But as a guide in the confessional, where complicated and difficult cases are apt to present themselves, he still prescribes only the old exceptions of delay in the payment of dower, *the lucrum cessans,* the *damnum emergens,* and the expenses of the *monts de piété.*[73]

It must be admitted that honest, obstinate consistency such as this is more to be respected than the casuistic dexterity which makes pretence of reconciling the irreconcilable. The theological student may well be pardoned some perplexity on finding in his text book all the old authorities leading to the absolute assertion that the smallest gain from lending money is unjust and unlawful, that the lender acquires no property in it, and must make restitution, or his heirs must do so after his death, and then, after turning a few pages, to read that all this is merely doctrine, that in practice the exaction of eight per cent per annum is legitimate, that interest payment is of the utmost service to society in stimulating commerce and industry, and that if a confessor enforces restitution he is bound to make it good to his penitent.[74]

[73] Sanchez, *loc. cit.,* n. 2, 3, 6.

[74] Varceno, *loc. cit.,* Art. 6, §1; §2, punct. 4. "Ex dictis patet esse omnino illicitum ac injustum lucrum, etiam minimum, exigere vi mutui." To escape from this conclusion Guarceno relies for justification wholly on the local law, conveniently ignoring the fact that, as we have seen, the council of Vienne under Clement V pronounced all such laws invalid and ordered them removed from the statute books.

THE DEAD HAND*

[The annexation of the Philippines at the close of the war with Spain forced the government of the United States to consider the problems arising from the extensive landholdings of the Friars in those islands. As a background for the consideration of the question Mr. Lea wrote the following sketch showing how the governments of Catholic states had in the past dealt with the landed wealth of the Church in their respective territories. The essay was first submitted to the *International Monthly* but was declined by its editor on the ground that it would be too heavy for its readers unless put in briefer and more popular form. Mr. Lea accordingly printed the essay privately and distributed it to those he thought interested in the subject. In sending a copy to his friend, Professor Charles Molinier, he wrote: "Je vous envoie un bien petit essai sur les secularizations que l'Église a dû subir pendant le siècle passé—un étude qui m'a été suggeré par les problèmes que nous avons hérité de l'Espagne dans les Isles Philippines."

The Dead Hand was at once translated into French by M. Salomon Reinach under the title *Esquisse d'une Histoire de la Main Morte* (Paris, 1901) with the following introductory note:

M. Henry-Charles Lea, l'illustre auteur de *l'Histoire de l'inquisition au moyen âge*, vient de publier en Amérique un essai sur l'histoire de la Main Morte et les efforts tentés par les gouvernements, depuis de longs siècles, pour la supprimer ou en restreindre les progrès. Il nous a paru que ce résumé, traité de main de maître, pouvait être mis avec avantage à la portée du public français.

The same year a Dutch translation appeared at Amsterdam under the title *De Doode Hand.*—H.]

* * * * *

IMPORTANT QUESTIONS will soon arise as to the destiny of the large bodies of ecclesiastical property in the Philippines and of the religious orders which form a disturbing element in the social organization of the islands. It, therefore, is not without interest to examine how similar problems have been dealt with by Catholic powers.

The control which the Church exercises over the hopes and fears of the sinner, especially on the deathbed, and the teaching, amply warranted by Scripture, that well-directed almsgiving is the best antidote for sin, has given it in all ages an unequalled opportunity for acquisition. Moreover, whatever it acquired it retained. It held in mortmain —in the dead hand—and its possessions were inalienable: Pope Symmachus declared that even the pope could not sell the property of the Church. The danger of this to the State was recognized at an early

* Privately printed, Philadelphia, 1900.

period, and laws of the Christian emperors in 370, 372, and 390 prohibited legacies to churches and clerics and pronounced them invalid —provisions which St. Ambrose and St. Jerome approved, while deploring their necessity and the artifices employed by clerics to nullify them. When Charlemagne endeavored to reconstruct society after the barbarian invasions he too sought to diminish the evil, and, in 811, he asked his assembled bishops whether renunciation of the world is exhibited by those who were constantly seeking to augment their possessions by exploiting the hope of heaven and the fear of hell and inducing men to disinherit their heirs. His rebuke was unheeded, and in 816 his son, Louis the Pious, decreed that no cleric should receive donations from those whose children would thus be disinherited; anyone so doing should be punished and the property be restored to the heirs.

During the succeeding centuries the process continued with increasing momentum. The exemption from public burdens claimed for church lands stimulated their acquisition, for it enabled churchmen to lay up surplus revenues for fresh investments, and for these they could afford to pay more—estimated at one-third—than lay purchasers, as land being untaxable in their hands brought them in larger returns. To the State this was a distinct disadvantage—if the lands were noble, it lost the military service; if *roturier*, either its revenues were diminished or the burden on the remaining population was increased.

It was Spain which earliest sought a remedy for this. In the tenth and eleventh centuries it became customary to regard bequests to the Church as limited to three years, after which they were revendicated by the heirs. Against this the councils of Leon, in 1020, and of Coyanza, in 1050, protested and decreed that such gifts were perpetual. In this they doubtless succeeded, but it only led to prohibitive legislation, in 1106 under Alfonso VI, forbidding, under pain of forfeiture, all gifts or bequests of lands to the Church, except to that of Toledo, then recently recovered from the Saracens; and this, we are told, remained in force in spite of the strenuous efforts of Gregory IX with San Fernando III to procure its abrogation in the thirteenth century. About 1125 the cortes of Najera extended the prohibition to purchases, so that no lands subject to royal jurisdiction should fall into mortmain, adding significantly that no tricks or devices should protect the purchaser from confiscation. It was one thing, however, to frame such laws and quite another to enforce them. Popular piety on the one hand and ecclesiastical greed on the other conspired to render them nugatory. From this time until the middle of the sixteenth century, with occasional intermissions, almost every assembly of the cortes of Castile petitioned the monarchs for their enforcement or adopted some plan to mitigate the evil, and every code of Spanish mediæval law has provisions on the subject. It would occupy too much space to present these in detail, their chief importance being to show by their perpetual iteration how impotent were the authorities to devise or enforce a remedy.

When, in the seventeenth century, the decadence of tne monarchy became apparent, publicists had no hesitation in attributing it largely to the overgrown numbers and wealth of the clergy. Fray Angel Manrique, although himself a friar, in 1624 deplores their increase. There is not a town, he says, in which the convents had not trebled within fifty years while the population was decreasing in even greater ratio, for Burgos, which formerly had seven thousand hearths now has but nine hundred; Leon, which had five thousand, now has but five hundred, while the small towns are depopulated and the middle-sized ones are becoming so; moreover, the wealth of the Church is correspondingly swollen to the great detriment of the Republic. Doctor Pedro de Salazar y Mendoza, a dignitary of the cathedral of Toledo, about the same time expresses similar opinions: the main cause of the depopulation of Spain is the excessive number of clerics and religious, for which some remedy is necessary. In 1670 the attention of the court was called to the subject by a petition from the town of Camarma de Esteruelas representing that the purchase of lands by convents had reduced the population from three hundred families to seventy, of whom thirty were *labradores* or peasants compelled to endure the whole burden of taxation formerly divided among the three hundred, and the council of finance, to which the petition was referred, told the queen-regent that the condition of Camarma was shared by many other towns. There was some talk of a statute of mortmain, but it ended in nothing. The same fate attended an attempt of Carlos II in 1677, who applied to the pope for the necessary preliminary powers. The churches and religious orders were too strong for the enfeebled and bigoted Hapsburgs; action was postponed until there should seem to be a better prospect of success, and the increase of clerical wealth and numbers went on unchecked.

With the advent of the Bourbons, at the commencement of the eighteenth century, there came a change in the subservience of the state to the Church, slight at first but destined in its development to give a new life to Spain. In 1713 Philip V characterized with severity the frauds of confessors who persuade dying penitents to impoverish their heirs; he wishes that he could without papal assent or a concordat give the needed relief to his subjects, but, while awaiting this, he annuls as invalid all legacies by penitents in mortal sickness to confessors, their kindred, convents, or orders, for in such cases the testator is not to be considered as possessed of free will—a law which Carlos III reissued in 1770, saying that it had fallen into complete oblivion. It was not until

1737 that Philip succeeded in negotiating a concordat, and then he had to content himself with a trifling concession. Article eight recites that, in view of the insupportable burden thrown upon the laity by the increase of lands held in mortmain, the king had asked that all such acquisitions made since the commencement of his reign should be subject to taxation. Clement XII, however, denied this moderate request and would concede only that lands acquired subsequently to the date of the concordat should be taxable. Even this was largely evaded by frauds and devices to escape its operation. A royal *cédula* of 1745 says that the ecclesiastics had up to that time prevented the execution of the concordat, wherefore instructions are framed for its enforcement. To accomplish this seemed impossible. In 1756 Ferdinand VI issued fresh commands; in 1760 Carlos III complained that the concordat had never been obeyed, and he ordered a perquisition into all lands acquired since 1737, while in 1795 Carlos IV was obliged to reissue the *cédula* of 1745. Carlos III further endeavored to check the continued absorption of lands in mortmain. In 1763 he referred to the repeated instructions given not to issue licences for such transfers, and he ordered that they should not be granted even for objects of the greatest piety and necessity in view of the intolerable injury to the public occasioned by them. Yet it was impossible to dam the flood, and, in 1795, Carlos IV endeavored to save something by imposing a tax of fifteen per cent on all such transactions.

I have dwelt thus at length on the example of Spain because the preponderance of the Church there gave it fairer opportunity for the development of its acquisitiveness, but the same struggle was going on in almost every land of Europe. Frederic II, in 1232, when legislating for his kingdom of the Two Sicilies, revived a forgotten law forbidding the alienation of land to clerics or clerical corporations by gift or sale; if land is so devised by will the legatee must, within a year, under pain of confiscation, sell it to the heirs or to some other layman. In England, Edward I, in 1279, issued the statute of mortmain, which forfeited to the lord of the fee, or in default of action by him to the king, all lands conveyed to the dead hand, although the Church succeeded largely in evading it until the more comprehensive act of 1391. In Germany, the Saxon law, which ruled the northeastern provinces, allowed for thirty years and a day the heirs to reclaim a property sold to the Church. The *Schwabenspiegel*, which was in force in the southern and western regions, shows much greater trace of clerical influence as might be expected in the land of the great prince-bishops. It imposes no restrictions on mortmain and stimulates liberality to the Church. The result of this was that at the outbreak of the Reformation one-half of the land in Germany is estimated to have belonged to the Church. The rulers, however, were beginning to recognize the impolicy of this, and Maximilian I, by an edict of January 6, 1518, forbade alienations to religious bodies without the assent of the sovereign and the diet, in default of which the nearest relative or the sovereign or any layman could take the land at a reasonable price. This was repeated by Ferdinand I in 1564, and Leopold I in 1669 added that all such alienations were void. In 1716, at the request of the diet, Charles VI issued a decree reciting that the evasions and devices of ecclesiastics neutralized these laws which he therefore reissued and confirmed. This he repeated in 1720, and instituted an investigation into all acquisitions since 1669, which he annulled, ordering the holders to sell them to laymen within three months. Bavaria adopted the same policy. In 1672 the Elector Ferdinand I required a licence from the sovereign for the acquisition by the Church of all lands of nobles, which, in 1764, was extended to all real estate by Maximilian Joseph, who further ordered that the number of inmates in all convents should be reduced to what it had been at their foundation, so as to deprive them of excuse for acquisition, and no novices were to be admitted without the consent of the sovereign.

The Italian States were similarly averse to mortmain. In 1432, Amadeo VIII, of Savoy and Piedmont, required all ecclesiastical bodies to surrender the feudal lands which they had acquired and prohibited future acquisitions, which was only enforced after considerable opposition. In 1584, Emmanuele I subjected ecclesiastical property to taxation and resisted the repeated efforts of the Holy See to restore the exemption and, in 1863, Cavour suppressed all the monastic houses, applying their possessions to the improvement of the clergy. In Venice a law of 1329 restricted the bequest or donation of land for pious uses to the term of ten years, after which it had to be sold, and in 1536 this term was reduced to two years. In 1605 this law was extended over all the Venetian territories on the mainland, and no alienation by sale or otherwise to the Church was permitted without the assent of the council of Pregadi. This measure, together with a law of 1603 forbidding the erection of churches without licence from the senate, was one of the leading causes of the bitter quarrel between Paul V and the Republic in 1606 and 1607, but the Signoria was immovable in spite of interdicts, and the laws remained unaltered. In Tuscany the Florentine code of 1415 permitted the bequest of land but prohibited all sales and donations to the Church, and although Martin V, in 1427, procured the revocation of this regulation it was renewed in 1457. It was disregarded, however, by the ecclesiastical bodies and a compromise was reached with Leo X, in the concordat of 1515, whereby all acquisitions of land during the past fifty years were subject to the public burdens. This again was disregarded, and when Duke Ferdinando I endeavored to collect imposts the ecclesiastics cited him before the curia and carried their point. The House of Lorraine was more independent than the Medici. In 1751 the Grand Duke Francesco I forbade the transfer to mortmain of all land and of more than a hundred sequins of personal property without licence from the prince, and this was enforced in spite of the protests of Benedict XIV. In 1769 the Grand Duke Leopold I increased the rigidity of these limitations on the lines of a decree issued not long before for Lombardy by his mother Maria Theresa, and he further assumed the right to licence alienations of Church property. He had thoughts of abolishing all the monastic orders, but felt himself not strong enough for this, and was forced to be content with suppressing some of the houses.

In Portugal Affonso II (died 1223) while permitting gifts and legacies forbade the purchase of land by the Church without royal permission. Early in the fifteenth century João I added that gifts and legacies must be sold to laymen within a year and a day, and in 1500, King Manoel subjected to the public burdens lands purchased under royal licence. These laws continue in force, although in 1635, the papal nuncio and collector, Alessandro Cavalcanti, had the audacity, on Palm Sunday, to publish an edict abrogating them. Despite his subservience to the Church, Philip IV of Spain, then also king of Portugal, could not submit to this; June 4, 1636, he issued an *auto* declaring that Cavalcanti had no authority for his act; Urban VIII yielded, and on April 5, 1637, the nuncio publicly withdrew his edict.

In Flanders, Count Guy de Dampierre, in 1293, forbade the alienation of land to the dead hand. In Brabant, in the fifteenth century, Philippe le Bon subjected such sales to the right of redemption by the vendor or his heirs. These laws were not observed, and in 1515 an edict of Charles V pronounced invalid all gifts and legacies, while all sales to the Church required the assent of the prince and of the magistrates of the provincial capital—a law which was confirmed in 1520 in spite of the opposition of the Church. Clerical ingenuity, however, evaded it by various devices—frauds which Charles endeavored to suppress, in 1538, by a *pragmática* requiring all parties to every conveyance of land to swear that the transfer was not intended to make it fall into mortmain.

In France the earliest record of such rules is found in the collection known as the *Établissemens* of St. Louis, which state the law to be that devises of land to the Church are subject to seizure by the seigneur, though it was customary before doing so to give the legatee a year and a day in which to sell it. This was based on the feudal rule that no vassal can diminish his fief, and, as each one in the feudal hierarchy was responsible to the next lord above him, it carried the ultimate control to the king as the supreme lord. Thus grew up the *droit d'amortissement* under which all transfers of land to mortmain had to pay a tax to the crown. There was much and varying legislation under which this tax at different times was reckoned at from four to six years' fruits of the land or a sixth to a third of its value—in fact, Philip V in 1320 put it in cases of purchase at the price paid for the land, but this was subsequently reduced. The clergy, as a rule, evaded these payments, and inquests were made from time to time throughout the kingdom to trace these transactions and collect the royal dues. How frequently this was done we have no means of knowing, but we happen to hear of it in 1326, 1370, 1388, 1470, 1547, 1680, 1695, and 1700.

It was impossible to check these acquisitions or to prevent the multiplication of religious houses. Louis XIV, in 1666, revived the old laws which forbade new establishments without special royal licence, and he subjected the granting of licences to rigorous preliminary investigation and obstructive formalities, for through neglect of these laws, he said, the religious communities had so increased that in many places they possessed the larger half of the lands and revenues. Even the autocracy of Louis, however, was powerless to secure obedience, and the evil continued to grow. Finally, in 1749, an elaborate edict, drawn up by Chancellor d'Aguesseau, declared the constant increase of these communities to be one of the matters most immediately requiring remedy, wherefore the prohibition to found new ones without royal letters-patent was renewed; all which had been established in disregard of this were declared illegal and all so founded since the edict of 1666 and for thirty years prior were suppressed. No real estate in any form could be acquired without special royal letters for each transaction, and all legacies of such property were declared invalid, even if made under condition of obtaining such letters, and the issuing of these letters was surrounded with rigid precautions requiring the necessity or utility of the transaction to be clearly demonstrated.

This various legislation to a common end throughout the lands of the Roman obedience is of interest rather as showing the unanimous conviction of European statesmen during five or six centuries as to the evils of accumulation in mortmain than as exhibiting their power to curb the acquisitiveness of the Church. The constant iteration of legislation demonstrates its ineffectiveness. By one means or another the Church baffled the lawgivers, heedless of the temptations which it was offering and of the risk which it might run whenever circumstances should weaken its awful authority over the minds of princes and peoples. It did not anticipate that the time would come when those who might shrink from spoliation would reconcile their consciences to the euphemism of "secularization."

Yet there was a wholesome warning in the Reformation when it narrowly escaped much greater losses than those which it suffered. The violent measures of Henry VIII and his Court of Augmentations, and the progressive absorptions by the Protestant princes of Germany are foreign to our subject, for they were the work of schismatics and heretics. More to the purpose is the fact that some of the Catholic princes were scarcely more scrupulous than the Lutherans in seizing the property of the religious orders, and that in the reichstag of Augsburg, in 1524, it was seriously proposed by both parties to secularize the whole church property of Germany. The prelates were to receive a fitting income; the noble canons were to be paid as heretofore until they died off without successors; one or two nunneries were to be maintained in each circle of the empire as retreats for noble ladies; priests and preachers were to be decently supported, and the rest of the revenues was to be devoted to public uses, especially to the maintenance of a standing army for the defense of the empire.

This danger was eluded, and, reckless of the warning, the process of accumulation continued until the mocking philosophy of the eighteenth century had destroyed among the ruling classes all real respect for Latin Christianity. There was talk in 1743 of arranging terms between Maria Theresa and Charles VIII by secularizing for the benefit of the latter the great sees of Salzburg, Passau, Freisingen, Regensburg, Eichstätt, and Augsburg, but it was divulged prematurely and its authors disowned it, while Benedict XIV declared that he would shed his blood to prevent such spoliation. A somewhat similar project, in 1758, brought forth letters of remonstrance from Clement XIII to the Catholic powers. Secularization evidently was in the air, but the first blow was on a more moderate scale, although in principle it shattered the claims of the special sanctity of ecclesiastical ownership. The Society of Jesus had become a vast trading corporation with extensive colonial possessions which it exploited under the advantage of exemption from taxation. It invited attack in many ways, and Portugal took the initiative with a decree of expulsion, September 5, 1759, followed, after eighteen months' delay, by incorporating its property with the royal fisc. France suppressed the society in 1762, and devoted its funds to the payment of its indebtedness, the support of its members, and the maintenance of its former colleges. In Spain, the *pragmática* of Carlos III, April 2, 1767, expelling the Order, confiscated its property to pious uses and to pensioning the members, but in 1798 Carlos IV incorporated in the royal treasury what remained. When, in 1773, Clement XIV abolished the society, he formed a congregation of five cardinals and two prelates to administer its property for pious uses; the congregation sent to the German bishops orders to take possession of the temporalities for such purposes, but Joseph II refused to recognize the papal claims to control all church property, in consequence of which the princes confiscated all that lay within their dominions.

The next assault was made by the Emperor Joseph II, which has significance as showing the repugnance felt by enlightened rulers for the religious orders, especially those subject to foreign domination. As early as 1772 he forbade admissions to the Franciscan Tertiaries, and in 1784 he abolished them altogether. In March, 1781, he almost wholly sundered the relations of the orders with their superiors in Rome, and all exceptions to this were removed eighteen months later. More destructive was his decree of October 30, 1781, ordering the suppression of all the contemplative orders, in the execution of which about seven hundred religious houses (nearly two-fifths of all in his dominions) were abolished and their possessions were converted into a so-called *Religionsfond*, devoted mostly to education and the improvement of benefices with cure of souls. Finally, on November 30, 1784, the reception of novices was forbidden for twelve years, except by permission of the secular power, which was rarely given.

These were but the fitful gusts which heralded the tempest. It came inevitably with the outburst of the French Revolution, and its early date shows how ripe were men's minds for the secularization of ecclesiastical accumulations. Already, by November 2, 1789, the National Assembly voted the proposition of Talleyrand, then bishop of Autun, that all church property was at the disposition of the nation, and that the clergy should be supported with competent salaries. This was followed by the decree of February 13, 1790, suppressing the religious orders and absorbing their temporalities. It was natural that Pius VI should protest against these acts, as he did, March 10, 1791, in the brief *Quod aliquantum*, asserting the inviolability of ecclesiastical possessions and threatening with the fate of Heliodorus all who laid unhallowed hands upon it, while he stigmatized as an insufferable indignity the allotment of salaries to bishops and priests. Yet his successor, Pius VII, was obliged, in the concordat of 1801, to accept accomplished facts and to promise, for himself and his successors, not to disturb the purchasers in the enjoyment of their acquisitions. The organic articles attached to the concordat confirmed the suppression of the religious orders; an attempt to reintroduce them was defeated in 1804, and those which gradually crept in after the Restoration were still subject to the laws forbidding irrevocable vows. The objection to them still continues, and the government is understood to be now preparing a bill regulating associations which is to be directed primarily against the religious congregations.

Pius VII soon had a bitterer experience when orthodox and heretic Germany united together in a yet more gigantic seizure of temporalities.

A *Reichsrecess* of February 25, 1803, secularized the four great princely archbishoprics of Mayence, Trèves, Cologne, and Salzburg, and eighteen bishoprics, from Brixen to Lübeck, including the religious houses and involving possessions reckoned at four hundred and twenty million Rhenish gulden. It is estimated that by this measure the Church was stripped of territories containing 3,161,776 inhabitants, and of revenues amounting to twenty-one million florins. The whole was declared to be at the free disposition of the secular rulers, to be employed for the relief of their finances as well as for the maintenance of divine service and education, subject to the condition that the cathedrals were to be supported and the ejected clerics pensioned. It was in vain that Pius VII exhaled his indignation in a brief of February 12, 1803, to the Elector Maximilian of Bavaria, expatiating on the injustice and sacrilege of the measure. No attention was paid to this, nor was the nuncio Consalvi more successful when, at the congress of Vienna, he demanded the return of all church property, and on this being refused, he presented, June 14, 1815, in the name of the pope, a solemn protest against all that had been done in Germany since 1803 without the papal assent. Pius VII, in his allocution *Mirati*, September 4, 1815, confirmed this protest but expressed the hope that another assembly shortly to be held would be more regardful of the rights of the Church—a hope which remained unfulfilled.

Equally regardless of the claims of the Church has been the action of Italy. The laws of June 28 and July 7, 1866, and August 15, 1867, suppressed the religious houses and secularized their property, five per cent interest on the proceeds being devoted to the *fondo di culto*, with small pensions to those ejected. The process was unceremoniously rapid, for, in 1866, the number of houses suppressed was already 1,986, with 31,024 inmates and a revenue of 13,722,995 lire. Pius IX of course denounced, in the allocution *Universus Catholicus*, September 20, 1867, this legislation as in violation of all divine, human, and natural law, declared it invalid, and that its authors and supporters were involved in the excommunication provided for all who despoil the Church. His protests exercised no deterrent influence, and the occupation of Rome, in 1870, was followed by the law of June 19, 1873, disposing of the property of the houses suppressed there. When this was in preparation Pius declared that it would be invalid and that its supporters would incur *ipso facto* excommunication, and after its adoption, in his allocution *Prænunciavimus*, July 15, 1873, he asserted that all concerned were under major excommunication, especially purchasers of the property, and that all sales were void. Equally fruitless was the protest to foreign powers when, January 29, 1884, a decision of the Court of Cassation brought under the confiscating laws the property of the Congregation *De Propaganda Fide*.

In Spain the inevitable process was more prolonged and underwent several vicissitudes. The first attack was a feature of the Napoleonic invasion. Scarcely had Joseph been seated on his transitory throne when, by successive decrees of December 4, 1808, and April 27 and August 18, 1809, all the religious orders were declared to be suppressed and their property confiscated. Joseph's authority extended only as far as the swords of the French marshals reached, but these decrees served as an excuse for pillage, and, in the devastating war which ravaged nearly every corner of the Peninsula, few convents were left intact. The cortes of Cadiz, in June 1812, decreed that the property of those destroyed or of which the inmates were dispersed, should enure to the State, subject to return in case the communities were reorganized. The restoration of the bigoted Fernando VII, in 1814, of course rendered this legislation nugatory, but the violence of the reaction provoked the revolution of 1820, when the cortes, by decree of October 1st, suppressed the convents of nearly all the orders and consolidated those permitted to remain, prohibiting moreover the foundation of new houses and the admission of novices. The property of those suppressed was applied to the public debt, and a considerable amount was sold, but, in the reaction of 1823, under the ægis of the French invasion, by decrees of June 11 and 21, the monks and friars were reinstated, and the purchasers of the secularized property were ejected without compensation and with as little ceremony as the former holders had been.

The death of Fernando VII, in 1833, and the succession of the infant Isabella under the regency of her mother Maria Cristina, wrought a change. There were two pretenders—Don Carlos, who was supported by the irreconcilable clergy, secular and regular, and Ferdinando II, of Naples. The claims of the latter were countenanced by Austria and Gregory XVI, in his capacity of temporal prince, did not dare to offend the dominant power of northern Italy. He, therefore, refused to recognize Isabella, and even declined to confirm the nominations to Spanish bishoprics in the ordinary form because it implied her recognition. The relations between Madrid and the Quirinal thus became strained until they were broken off in 1836, not to be formally resumed until 1848, by which time more than half the Spanish sees were vacant.

All this necessarily threw the regency into the hands of the liberals and indisposed it to the clericals. It was imperative to weaken the latter; their temporalities offered a welcome resource to an exhausted treasury and secularization became only a question of time. The process, however, was more gradual than in other lands. It commenced, in 1834, by seizing the property of the Carlist clergy, regular and secular, who were aiding the insurrection; then the admission of novices was forbidden, and a *junta eclesiástica* was appointed to report on the condition of the Church so as to bring about a thorough reform. The result of this was the presentation to the cortes, February 19, 1835, of a project of a law applying to the public credit all the property of religious corporations, which drew from Pope Gregory, April 10, a vigorous protest asserting the inviolability of the temporalities. The only reply of the Spanish government to this was suppression, in July, first of the Jesuits and then of some nine hundred convents containing each less than twelve professed inmates. On this the revolutionary juntas in the provinces rose against the religious houses, which in many places were sacked and their inmates dispersed, some of the latter, it is said, being slain. Against this Pope Gregory again protested, deploring the atrocities perpetrated on so many peaceful religious, but to no purpose, for in October there was further anticlerical legislation in which nearly all the remaining convents were suppressed. It is no wonder that Gregory pronounced, February 1, 1836, the allocution *Sextus*, in which he complained that his repeated expostulations had been fruitless; there was no cessation in these most wicked attacks on the Church nor in the contempt for the papal authority; as all reclamations had been unavailing he now declares the whole series of legislation to be null and void. The reply to this was an edict of March 8, 1836, suppressing the remaining convents, except those of three minor charitable congregations. Then in September were confiscated the temporalities of all prelates not living in residence, and sundry measures were adopted to reduce the excessive numbers of the clergy, followed in July 1837, by others suppressing the tithes and first fruits while the property of the secular ecclesiastics was declared to belong to the nation.

In 1838 the *progresistas* were replaced by the *moderados*. The Carlist insurrection was nearing its end, and in 1840 peace was restored. By a law of July 16, 1840, the *moderados* assured the secular clergy in the enjoyment of their property, but, in twenty-four hours after this was proclaimed in Barcelona, the populace rose in rebellion, the movement spread throughout Spain, the reactionaries were driven from power, and in December the *progresistas* issued sundry decrees secularizing the convents in the recovered Carlist territories and putting up at auction the conventual churches not actually required for divine service. Against all this Pope Gregory protested, calling heaven and earth a thousand times to witness against the Spanish violations of the rights of the Church, annulled the decrees and declared them invalid. Printed copies of this were secretly introduced into Spain, and were publicly read from the pulpits. To this, of course, no government could submit, and the laws of the old monarchy were revived subjecting to prosecution all who circulated papal letters that had not received the royal exequatur. A law followed, September 2, revoking that of July 16, 1840, and providing for the sale of the temporalities which it declared to belong to the nation.

The ministry then presented to the cortes the project of a law virtually cutting the Spanish Church loose from the papacy which it described as actuated wholly by greed and ambition. This was a somewhat clumsy attempt at intimidation; it was privately sent to an agent in Rome with instructions to say that if the Spanish bishops were confirmed it would be dropped, otherwise the Spanish Church must provide for itself. Pope Gregory met this assault with consummate shrewdness in an encyclical address, February 22, 1842, to all the churches, repeating his annullation of all the anticlerical laws, including this one if it should pass. He deplored the afflictions of the pious Spanish nation for whose relief he had vainly prayed day and night. All the faithful were instructed to join with their bishops in public prayer to shorten for Spain these days of trial, and to stimulate their ardor he granted a jubilee indulgence to all who would thrice assist at these solemnities. These were weapons against which the government was powerless, and the threatened law was quietly dropped.

Early in 1844 the *moderados* returned to power under Narvaez. Anxious to resume relations with the papacy, they ventured to suspend the sale of church property as an indisputable preliminary, but they instructed Castillo y Ayensa, the agent whom they sent to Rome, that the restoration of unsold property must be accompanied with a recognition of the validity of previous sales, as in the French concordat. Castillo negotiated a convention and signed it, April 27, 1845, but the government refused to ratify it; it was the object of general denunciation, and he was driven from public life, although on April 3 the cortes had adopted a law restoring the unsold lands to the clergy.

At last, in 1851, a concordat was agreed upon which, as in France, recognized accomplished facts. It reëstablished the religious orders devoted to education and works of charity; it specified the salaries to be paid to prelates and clergy and the provision for divine service; it ordered the sale by auction of the remaining conventual property, the proceeds to be invested in government bonds and the interest to be applied to the restored convents; it secured to the Church the right to hold property and the inviolability of what it still possessed, never to be disturbed without the authority of the Holy See, which on its side guaranteed that the holders of what had been sold should not be interfered with. The promises of a state in so unstable an equilibrium as Spain, however, were worthless. In four years the law of May 1, 1855, placed on sale all the remaining ecclesiastical property and prohibited all acquisitions in mortmain. It was natural that Pius IX, in his allocution *Nemo vestrum*, of July 26th, should complain bitterly of this breach of faith; it released him and his successors from the pledge not to interfere with purchasers, and he endeavored to make this public in Spain so as to prevent further sales. In spite of this they continued until the convention of April 4, 1860, under which the government repealed the law of May 1, 1855, and promised that in future there should be no alienations of any kind without the authority of the Holy See, and that freedom of acquisition should be permitted, in return for which the pope confirmed the recent sales. This convention was as fragile as the concordat. The revolutionary government of 1868 proceeded to sell the remaining church property, which had twice been guaranteed, and Pius could only deplore this action in his allocution *Novam*, June 25, 1869. A further infraction involving the stipends of the clergy was made in 1872, against which Pius protested, December 22, in his allocution *Justus et misericors*. Under Alfonso XII, however, in 1876, decrees were issued restoring the scanty remains of the property and ordering the observance of the compacts with the Holy See.

Portugal was somewhat more prompt than Spain in this matter. By a decree of August 15, 1833, the Emperor Pedro I, as regent for his daughter Maria da Gloria, suppressed the convents and the military orders and incorporated their property with the fisc. The government neglected to pay the promised pensions and the ejected inmates suffered extreme misery. There have been efforts within the last few years to reintroduce the regular orders, but they have failed.

The former colonies of Spain form too important a portion of the Catholic world to be omitted from consideration. Early in their organization it was determined to protect them from the evils of accumulations in mortmain, and a law of Charles V, October 27, 1535, in ordering the distribution of land among discoverers and settlers, positively prohibited its sale to any church or ecclesiastic under pain of forfeiture, and the inclusion of this law in the *Recopilación de las Indias*, compiled in 1661, shows that it was considered to be still in force. Ample provision, in fact, for the building and maintenance of churches was made from other sources. The procuring, by the mission priests, of bequests to the Church from their dying Indian converts was prohibited by repeated decrees from 1580 to 1800, the iteration of which shows how ineradicable was the abuse. The religious orders, moreover, were a source of constant anxiety as manifested by the numerous provisions to restrict their number and restrain their disorders, and their acquisition of land was positively prohibited by Philip II, October 24, 1570. This was renewed by Philip IV, in 1631; in 1705 its observance was vainly demanded by the council of Indies, and under Fernando VI an attempt was again ineffectually made to enforce it.

Thus, as far as legislation could effect it, the colonies were protected against the curse of the dead hand; no land could legally be held by churches or convents, and yet, in defiance of law, ecclesiastical acquisitions were constantly on the increase. In 1644 the authorities of Mexico appealed to Philip IV to check this unwholesome growth; the greater portion of the land, they said, was already held by the Church, which, if not arrested, would soon own it all; there were too many convents of both sexes and too many clerics who multiplied faster than their means of support. Although something was gained, in 1767, by the expulsion of the Jesuits, yet in that same year the royal fiscal, or prosecuting officer in Mexico, in a legal argument declared that if the accumulations of the Inquisition were not checked the king would soon have little territory left to his jurisdiction, and Bancroft estimates that, before the revolution, fully one-half the real estate in Mexico was held in mortmain.

Yet after the war of independence Mexico was tardy in following the example of the mother country. It was not until 1856 that some laws curtailing ecclesiastical privilege led to disturbances which caused the government to declare that it would not submit its acts to the authority of the Holy See, and it followed this by a decree secularizing all church property and permitting the regulars to abandon the monastic life, leading Pius IX in his allocution *Nunquam fore*, December 15, 1856, to protest against these measures and declare them to be null and void. The clergy were naturally embittered and joined the disaffected army, leading to a sanguinary civil war, during which President Juarez, from his retreat in Vera Cruz, issued July 12 and 13, 1859, decrees confiscating all church property and suppressing all male convents; and, though nunneries were allowed to remain, women quitting them were to have their dowers returned or were to be paid five hundred dollars. When the defeat of Miramon, January 1861, and the triumph of the constitutionalists promised to render these measures effective, Pius IX interposed another protest in his allocution *Meminit unusquisque*, September 30, of the same year.

With the French intervention, in 1862, the clergy confidently expected to regain their possessions, but when Bazaine was installed in the capital and an attempt was made to interfere with the circulation of the securities issued by Juarez on the basis of the confiscated property, and also to prevent purchasers from building, it was found that such large interests in these holdings had already been created among foreigners, especially Frenchmen (Bazaine himself was said to be concerned), that the provisional government was forced to recognize their validity and to postpone final decision until the arrival of Maximilian. He is said to have promised at Miramar the restoration of the religious orders, but when, in 1864, a papal nuncio arrived with instructions to reëstablish them, to reclaim church property, and to procure the revocation of all anticlerical legislation, Maximilian declared his policy to be that the Church should abandon all claim to the secularizations, whereupon the nuncio returned to Rome. Decrees were soon issued confirming all sales legally made and providing for the execution of the laws of 1856 and 1859, whereupon Pius IX, in his allocution *Omnium ecclesiarum*, March 27, 1865, bitterly deplored this betrayal of his pledges by Maximilian, but expressed the hope that on maturer consideration he would restore the Mexican Church from its ruins. A few days later there arrived in Rome a commission empowered to arrange matters, but the papal demands were so extravagant that negotiations were broken off. At the last moment, when Bazaine was preparing to depart, Maximilian was misled into remaining by false hopes held out of a concordat and a promise of clerical support in return for a restoration of church property.

In 1873 the additions to the constitution declared the Church and the State to be independent of each other, promised free toleration, prohibited religious institutions from holding real estate or mortgages, and forbade the establishment of monastic orders of any kind. All public officials were required to make formal declaration to enforce these provisions, whereupon Pius IX fulminated excommunication on all who should do so, causing in some places violent riots, almost amounting to insurrection, but they were suppressed. The bishops continued to struggle, and March 6, 1876, Pius came to their assistance with his epistle *Nunquam hactenus*, granting a monthly plenary indulgence to all who should aid them, but it was in vain.

The details which the research of Mr. Bancroft has thus furnished us for Mexico are not easy to obtain for the multitudinous republics of Latin America, but a series of fiery invectives by Pius IX enables us to trace the course of affairs in New Granada. The allocution *Acerbissimum*, September 27, 1852, declares null and void various laws recently adopted, prohibiting religious orders which professed passive obedience, putting parish priests on a stipend to be fixed by parochial assemblies, and practically secularizing half the ecclesiastical revenues. This did not deter New Granada from further aggressions, deplored in the allocution *Meminit unusquisque*, September 30, 1861, whereby the Church was prohibited from using its power without consent of the state, the Jesuits were banished, and the papal nuncio was given three days in which to leave the country. The climax seems to have been reached in 1863, as described, September 17, in the allocution *Incredibili*, in which Pius says that he can scarce find words to express the enormity of the anticlerical legislation which he revokes and declares to be absolutely invalid. All the property of the Church, he says, has been seized and sold, and it is deprived of the power to acquire and possess; all the religious orders of both sexes have been totally suppressed, and the clergy are forced, under pain of exile, to swear to support these measures and all others that may be adopted. New Granada evidently was resolved that the state should be supreme.

Ecuador was more dilatory. Papal utterances in 1877, 1889, and 1893 seem to manifest a perfect understanding between the Republic and the Holy See, and its devotion was manifested until lately by sending a tithe of its revenues to Rome. Revolutions since then have wrought a change, and the journals inform us that a few months since, on the recommendation of President Alfaro, a law was adopted secularizing all ecclesiastical property and applying it to the schools. The religious orders, it is said, were endeavoring to elude this by fictitious conveyances to laymen which the government does not propose to recognize. As for other Latin American states some scattered notices show that, in 1824, Paraguay suppressed all monasteries, in 1829 Brazil prohibited the reception of novices so as to provide for the gradual extinction of the religious orders, and, in 1874, Venezuela summarily abolished them. The next movement will probably be in Nicaragua, where half the church revenues have been claimed by the state, and the clerical party is said to be preparing to resist by the customary method of a revolution.

It may perhaps be asked why the Spanish secularization decrees, from 1835 to 1868, were not enforced in the Philippines, where the large accumulations of the religious orders were especially vulnerable as being illegally acquired under the repeated prohibitions of Charles V and his successors, and where their exactions have been one of the prolific causes of popular discontent. The explanation is simple. The Spanish power in that distant colony was too weak to risk a struggle with the Friars who had long virtually controlled the islands, and had of old an awkward way of assassinating or imprisoning a governor whom they could not drive away. This preponderance has continued up to the Tagal insurrection. In 1850 they boasted that the conquest had really been effected by them and that no local laws could be executed in the villages without the confirmation of the parish priest.

In the long struggle between Church and State which we have thus followed the impressive fact is the unanimous conviction of Catholic statesmen that the dead hand is an evil to be strenuously repressed, and that the religious orders are an undesirable factor in the body politic. Not less noteworthy is their contemptuous disregard in modern times of the protests and fulminations of the Holy See.

OCCULT COMPENSATION*

[A brief résumé of this article will be found in the *History of Auricular Confession and Indulgences,* II, 394-96.—H.]

*　　*　　*　　*　　*

THE PROCESS known to moral theologians as Occult Compensation furnishes an interesting chapter to the history of ethics. It signifies that when a man has a valid claim which he is unable or unwilling to substantiate by legal process he can without sin compensate himself by stealing an equivalent from the debtor. It is thus a survival from the primitive stage of barbarism, before society had advanced to settled laws and machinery for their enforcement, when the safety of each individual's life and possessions depended upon the force or cunning with which he could protect them. With the advance of civilization it has been the earnest effort of all lawgivers to suppress this natural instinct; the preservation of social order depends on its renunciation and on the readiness of the citizen to submit even to an occasional injustice rather than to take the law into his own hands, to be judge in his own case, and to vindicate his rights, real or supposed, by violence or fraud. Human nature is too frail to be trusted with the power of determining, under the pressure of self-interest, when the eternal law prohibiting rapine and theft shall cease to operate.

In this both the ecclesiastical and the civil authority agreed during the earlier ages of Christianity. The spoiling of the Egyptians by the Hebrews to compensate themselves for their hard and unpaid labors— a favorite precedent for the theologians—was explained by St. Augustine as justified only by the special command of God: the chosen people would have sinned if they had done it of their own will or simply by command of Moses, and perhaps they sinned if they desired to do it.[1] The imperial jurisprudence was equally emphatic. A law of Gratian in 376 forbids any one from acting as judge in his own cause.[2] One of Valentinian II in 389 declares that he who attempts to right himself, in place of awaiting judicial action, shall forfeit the value of the thing for which he ought to have litigated,[3] and in the Justinian jurisprudence this assumed the shape of a rule that if any one attempted to seize a thing which he believed to be his own in the possession of another, he lost the ownership, if it proved to be his, and if not he was obliged to restore it and forfeit in addition its value.[4] So careful were the limitations imposed

---

* From the *International Journal of Ethics,* IV (1894), 285-308.

[1] S. Augustine, *Contra Faustum,* Lib. XXII, c. lxxii. See also his *Quæstt. in Heptateuch,* Lib. II, c. xxxix, which is carried into the collections of canons (Regino, *De Discip. Eccles.,* Lib. II, c. cclxxiii; Burchard, *Decret.,* Lib. XI, c. liii).

[2] L. I *Cod. Theod.,* Lib. II, Tit. II.—*Const.* I, Cod. III, v.

[3] L. 3 *Cod. Theod.,* Lib. IV, Tit. XXII.

[4] *Institt. Justin.,* Lib. IV, Tit. II, §1. Cf. *Const.* 7 Cod. VIII, iv.

on individual action that if a thief sold a stolen article the owner could not take from him by force the money received for it without being liable to an action for theft: the sum realized from a theft is not the thing stolen and is not itself stolen.[5] The utmost latitude allowed was that a man could secretly remove an object which he had lent, without being subject to prosecution for theft, provided the borrower had no claim for expenses incurred on it.[6] All private vindication of right, real or supposititious, was thus condemned equally in the *forum internum* and the *forum externum*.

As social order reconstituted itself after the barbarian conquests, these principles held good in the *forum externum*. The early codes show throughout the earnest effort of the legislators to bring the turbulent races to settled methods of procedure, and the only indication I have found in them recognizing any right to retake property is a provision in the Longobard law allowing a man to clear himself by oath when he has seized a horse or other animal belonging to another, believing it to be his own.[7] We shall see hereafter that the secular courts throughout the Middle Ages recognized no justification for theft in the fact that the thief was only endeavoring to make good a claim.

As for the *forum internum*, the Penitentials, in their prescriptions for theft, make no allusion to any extenuation arising from compensation. On the contrary, many of them seek to enforce the command of the Sermon on the Mount (Matt. v:39-42, Luke vi:29, 30) by ordering that if a man recovers from a thief that which has been stolen he shall give it to the poor.[8] The same absence of allusion to compensation is observable in the collections of canons which served as guides in the courts of conscience from the tenth to the twelfth century; and when, in the second half of the latter, the canon law became interpenetrated with the civil law, the *Summa* of Bernard of Pavia, in its elaborate definition of all species of theft, observes the same silence.[9] Gregory IX indeed positively prohibited a creditor from compensating himself out of a deposit made with him by a debtor;[10] whence, oddly enough, when subsequently occult compensation came into vogue, deposits with the creditor were excepted from among the things on which it could be exercised.

The first indication of a tendency to recognize such a principle is manifested in a passage of St. Ramon de Peñaforte, in which he quotes the

[5] Fr. 48, Dig. xlvii, ii.
[6] Fr. 15, 59, Dig. xlvii, ii.
[7] L. Langobard. Rotharis, 347.
[8] *Pœnitent. Bigotian.*, III, ii, § 2 (Wasserschleben, *Bussordnungen*, p. 452).—*Pœnit. Cummeani*, c. viii, § 4 (*ibid.*, p. 483).—*Pœnit. XXXV Capit.*, c. xxii (*ibid.*, p. 518).— *Pœnit. Pseudo-Theodori*, c. x, § 5 (*ibid.*, p. 594).
[9] Bernardus Papiens., *Summa Decretalium*, Lib. v, Tit. xxvi.
[10] C. 2 Extra, iii, xvi.

section of the Institutes referred to above, and says that if a man believes
a thing to be his and that he has a right to take it, he does not commit
theft, but is to be .punished otherwise.[11] A few years after this, Alexander
Hales treats the subject more at length. It was a question which, in
those ages of turbulence, must have frequently arisen, and the efforts of
legislators continued to be directed to the repression of the ever-recurring
tendency to obtain satisfaction by violence or fraud. Thus Hales tells us
that, if a man loses a thing by rapine or theft, he can, while his blood is
hot, retake it by force or theft; but if an interval occurs, and there is time
for passion to cool, he is guilty of theft, and is liable to punishment by
the secular courts; by the divine law, however, he is not held to restitution if without scandal he recovers his property or its equivalent, whether
openly or secretly.[12] He adds a remark which is of interest, as the first
utterance on a question which has remained a subject of debate to the
present time, and also as showing how thus far the matter was confined
to the recovery of some definite object taken, and how little the schoolmen imagined that the claim could be expanded to cover demands of
other kinds. Servants, he says, whose wages are not paid cannot steal
from their employers, for the master's property is not, and never has
been, the servant's; the debt cannot make it so, but only that it ought
to be so.[13] A few years later Cardinal Henry of Susa, in treating at much
length on all related questions, makes no allusion directly to this except
to say that a man cannot compensate himself out of a deposit; he seems
to know only the legal methods of obtaining restitution, save when in
hot blood a man regains possession by force.[14]

That the alleged principle, however, was commencing to attract attention is shown in its condemnation by Aquinas, who says that he who
secretly retakes an article unjustly detained by another commits sin; he
does not injure the detainer, and therefore is not required to make restitution, but he sins against common justice in usurping judgment to
himself and pretermitting the settled order of law.[15] Soon afterwards a
forward step in the evolution of occult compensation occurs in the remark
of Henry of Ghent that if a steward or factor is a creditor of his principal, and if something belonging to the latter comes secretly into his pos-

[11] S. Raymundus, *Summa*, Lib. III, Tit. VI, § 1. "Si aliquis credebat rem esse suam et
sibi licere rem suam surripere, non committit furtum liceat alias teneatur."

[12] Alex. de Ales, *Summa*, Pt. IV, q. XXIV, Membr. 5, Art. 3. The ecclesiastical definition of "scandal" is that which gives occasion to sin in others.

[13] *Ibid.* "De serviendo vero patet dici quod nec in tempore negatæ mercedis nec
post, licitum est ei spoliare dominum suum: quia nihil quod dominus habet est vel fuit
servientis, neque ipse serviendo et jam completo servitio effecit quod suum esset, sed
quod suum debeat esse."

[14] Hostiens., *Aurea Summa*, Lib. II, *De Causa Proprietatis*, § 7; *De Restitutione Spolia-
torum*, § 1.—Cf. Lib. V, *De Furto*, §§ 1, 2.

[15] Aquinas, *Summa, Sec. Sec.*, q. lxvi, Arts. 5 ad 3.

session, although as a rule a man cannot take the law into his own hands, still in this case it is conceded to him to do so as a minister of the law and special judge.[16] Here at length we find introduced the conception of compensation for a debt, and not the mere reclaiming of an object unjustly detained; and this is the only importance of the dictum, for we hear nothing more of the special case on which it is based.

For a while the decretal of Gregory IX and the views of Aquinas continued to be the rule. John of Freiburg about 1300 and Astesanus de Asti in 1317 are virtually at one in saying that no compensation can be taken from a deposit in the hands of a creditor, and that anyone who steals a thing belonging to him and unjustly withheld by another commits sin; he is not obliged to restore it, but he must render satisfaction to God, and must labor to remove any scandal which he may have caused to his neighbors. Astesanus, moreover, quotes Richard Middleton as assenting to this.[17] It was not long after this that Pierre de la Palu was the first to suggest the modern teaching, in opposition to his fellow-Dominican, Aquinas. Incidentally he asserts that a man can retake by stealing anything that has been stolen from him; that a subject, as well as a judge, has a right of vindication, for otherwise Hebrews sinned in spoiling the Egyptians and all wars would be unjust.[18] This new view did not commend itself to immediate acceptance. In 1338, Bartolommeo da St. Concordio copies the Institutes in saying that he who takes what he believes to be his does not commit theft, but is to be otherwise punished; and a century later his commentator Niccolò da Osimo explains that he thus loses the right he possessed in the article, and that if it proves not to be his he must restore it and forfeit as much again in penalty of seeking to make law for himself.[19]

While Niccolò thus held fast to the ancient lines, his contemporary, the Dominican St. Antonino of Florence, cut loose from Aquinas and formulated the principle of occult compensation in nearly the shape in which it has continued to the present day. It is true that he copies Bartolommeo, but he adds that a man has a right to compensate himself by recovering, secretly or otherwise, anything withheld from him unjustly through theft or rapine, usury or fraud. This right, however, is subject to seven conditions, which are worth enumerating, as they form the basis of all subsequent rules and were doubtless only the expression

[16] Henricus Gandavens., Quodl. VI, q. xxvii. I quote this at second hand, not having access to the works of the *Doctor Solennis*. I find it cited in the *Somma Pacifica*, c. x, and in Zuccherius, *Decisiones Patavina*, Mart. 1709, q. ii, n. 7.

[17] Jo. Friburgens., *Summa Confessorum*, Lib. II, Tit. VI, § 7.—Astesanus, *Summa de Casibus*, Pt. I, Lib. I, Tit. xxxiii, Art. 3, q. iii; Lib. v, Tit. xxix, Art. 2, q. iv.

[18] P. de Palude, *In IV. Sententt.*, Dis. 35, q. ii, Art. 4, Concl. 3.

[19] *Summa Pisanella*, s. v. "Furtum," *in corp.*

of what was gradually taking shape in the schools. The first condition is when the creditor cannot obtain his dues by personal application or through the courts. The second, that it must be a matter subject to the ordinary and common law, for no one can be a judge in his own cause. The third, that it must not be a doubtful claim. The fourth, that there must be no likelihood of scandal or injury to others, who may be accused of the theft. The fifth, that the creditor shall not run the risk of being reputed a thief through inability to prove the debt. The sixth, that he shall not imperil life or limb by being accused of the theft. The seventh, that he does not act against his own conscience, but believes that he has a right to do so, and is not prepared to commit perjury in case he is prosecuted for it.[20] An important feature of this is that the permission to steal is no longer confined to recovering an object unjustly detained, but is extended to ordinary claims, including those arising from the payment of interest on loans, which was always recoverable in the ecclesiastical courts; this alone opened a wide sphere of action, for usury, though under the ban of the canon law, was the commonest of offences.

Not long afterwards Pacifico da Novara follows St. Antonino and develops the subject still further. The claim may arise from any cause, including injuries suffered, thus enabling men to estimate their wrongs and redress themselves; the claimant is warned that if he is detected he will be punished as a thief, and he may be induced to commit perjury in the effort to escape; if the crime is imputed to another he must secretly return the article stolen and not attempt again to compensate himself; if the debtor should ignorantly pay him subsequently he must secretly return the amount, and in any case he must provide for such contingency by warning his heirs not to receive it after his death; he must also be conscientious in valuing his claim and not take more than will strictly settle it. Still, with all this, occult compensation is a sin to be confessed—a very grave sin if the debt could be collected by legal process, but the perpetrator is not required to make restitution. If, as was customary, the loser should cause an excommunication of the unknown thief to be published, he can confess to the priest or bishop, if they can be trusted to maintain secrecy, and can ask to be excepted from the intention of the excommunication; but if this is attended with risk he can rest in peace and disregard it.[21]

From all this we can see how gradual and how tentative was the development of the practice, and how, even in the permission, there still lurked a consciousness that it was wrong. Nor was it as yet universally admitted. Few authorities at the end of the fifteenth century had wider

[20] St. Antonino, *Summa,* Pt. II, Tit. I, c. xv, § I.
[21] *Somma Pacifica,* c. x.

or more enduring reputation than Angiolo da Chivasso, who gives the law as laid down in the Institutes and contents himself with the remark that this is the secular law, but that the divine law is different.[22] Baptista Tornamala briefly repeats Bartolommeo da St. Concordio.[23] Bartolommeo de Chaimis only says that if property of a debtor who will not pay falls into the hands of a creditor he can retain it if no evil or scandal is caused.[24] Still the practice made progress, though slowly and irregularly. Cardinal Caietano justifies it by natural law which has been impeded by civil law.[25] Prierias is evidently somewhat puzzled; he agrees with Aquinas and Richard Middleton that it is a sin, but that the property stolen need not be restored, and he adds that the doctors hold that there is no sin if six conditions are observed—conditions similar to those already mentioned.[26] Giovanni da Taggia is even more reserved; theft is not committed on one's own property, but an assertion that the thief believes it to be his own is not to be received, for thus everyone would readily escape, and his definition of *compensatio indirecta* is merely that if a debtor's property happens to come without fraud into the hands of a creditor he can detain it until the claim is settled.[27] Rosemond adheres more closely to Aquinas: a man sins who retakes his property, forcibly or secretly, but he is not required to make restitution.[28] Pope Adrian VI, who was a learned theologian before Charles V made him a cardinal, is quoted as teaching that although in the interest of public peace the law prohibits a man from thus righting himself, yet in the forum of conscience he cannot be required to make restitution, and he even extends the privilege to the loser at dice, who can thus recover his losses from the winner.[29] Towards the middle of the sixteenth century Bartolommeo Fumo holds that there is no sin in a man retaking furtively what is his own, provided he can get it in no other way and avoids the risk of scandal; he is not making a law unto himself, but is following the natural law, of which the civil law deprives him.[30]

The second half of the century saw the rise of the school of able and acute men who built up the new science of Moral Theology, who explored with exhaustless subtilty every possible aspect in which sin can be viewed, and whose refined distinctions sometimes argued away the existence of sin itself. Though not identified with this school, and though

---

[22] *Summa Angelica, s. v.* "Furtum," §§ 3, 6.

[23] *Summa Rosella, s. v.* "Furtum," *in corp.*

[24] Bart. de Chaimis, *Interrogatorium* (Venice, 1480), fol. 33*b*.

[25] Caietano, *Summula, s. v.* "Furtum."

[26] *Summa Sylvestrina, s. v.* "Furtum," §§ 16, 17.

[27] *Summa Tabiena, s. vv.* "Furtum, Compensatio," § 1.

[28] Rosemondus, *Confessionale* (Antwerp, 1519), fol. 83.

[29] Alfonso de Castro, *De Potest. Legis pœnal.,* Lib. 1, c. x, Arg. 4.

[30] *Armilla Aurea, s. v.* "Furtum," n. 5.

at times complaining of their endless disputations and audacious argumentation, Azpilcueta, the renowned *Doctor Navarrus*, shows their influence in the detailed investigation which he devotes to occult compensation. It is a mortal sin if the claim can readily be enforced at law, or if the claimant exposes himself to risk of life or limb through condemnation for the theft, or if he believes it to be a sin, or if he foresees that it will cause much scandal. It is no sin, however, if legal recovery is impeded by partiality of a judge, or if the expense is disproportionate to the value, or if legal action will lead to quarrels and loss of friendship, while restitution is due to any third party who may be exposed to corporal or spiritual damage. The claimant must steal no more than will satisfy his claim; the debtor must not be allowed to pay it over again, and the claim must be just and indubitable—a point on which he says that many deceive themselves. Under these circumstances the claimant can disregard any excommunication published against the thief, even if it includes those who may have committed the theft in compensation. Even articles pledged or deposited with the debtor can be taken, provided it does not expose him to too great injury; although this is denied by some authorities. If the claimant is prosecuted he will not commit perjury in swearing that he does not know the thief, for he can use the mental reservation that it is not a theft. If there is a doubt as to his ownership of the article taken he sins in stealing it, though he is not required to make restitution.[31]

Cardinal Toletus gives the same general rules, the only important modification being that if grave injury is caused to innocent third parties the thief must confess and restore the article stolen.[32] This feature of the matter is important, for such injury to others is an almost invariable accompaniment of occult compensation, and we shall see that later moralists were less nice. Bishop Angles adds another condition—that the article stolen be not specially necessary to the debtor, for in such case it is a sin to rob him.[33] This perpetual variation of limitations, which we shall find continue, indicates how difficult the theologians found it to justify the practice to themselves. There was no recognized standard. On the one hand, a contemporary authority suggests usury as a substitute for theft, though usury was a sin much graver than stealing; a man unable to collect a debt or to enforce a claim arising from injury endured can compensate himself by lending on interest until the gain satisfies the wrong.[34] On the other hand, Pelbartus de Temesvar, one of the last of the scholastic theologians, strictly follows Aquinas, and refuses to recog-

---

[31] Azpilcueta, *Manualis Confessarior.*, c. xvii, nn. 112-17.

[32] Fr. Toletus, *Instruct. Sacerd.*, Lib. v, c. xv, nn. 3-5.

[33] Jos. Angles, *Flores Theol. Quæstt.*, (Venice, 1584), Pt. ii, fol. 95-96.

[34] Agost. Montalcino, *Lucerna dell' Anima* (Venice, 1590), c. xiv, § 10, nn. 4, 5.

nize that there is no sin in such an act.[35] Henriquez assumes a some-what self-contradictory attitude; it is a mortal sin, and yet the thief and his accomplices are not bound by an excommunication uttered against them, even though its terms specially include such acts.[36]

Thus far, occult compensation was purely the creation of the theologians, without any authoritative definition by the Church. This latter came with the issue in 1607 of the only expurgatory Index attempted by the Holy See. Manuel Sa's *Aphorismi Confessariorum*, issued in 1595, was one of the books subjected to its censorship, which disapproved of his paragraph on this subject, and ordered it erased and the following substituted, which may therefore be accepted as embodying the official opinion of the Church:

If you cannot conveniently otherwise collect a debt, you can take it secretly, provided you are careful that the debtor shall not pay it a second time, and that it is done without scandal or danger of reputation or life to you or to others; nor are you held to reveal it even if a prelate orders this under pain of excommunication, if it is probable that on revealing it you will be forced to make restitution, nor are others obliged to reveal it, if they know for certain that you have received it justly.

A subsequent passage authorizing the retention of what is stolen, even if there is doubt as to your ownership, passed the censorship without alteration.[37]

The first half of the seventeenth century witnessed the marvellously rapid growth of Probabilism and casuistry, leading in many cases to conclusions deplorably lax. Occult compensation did not escape the scrutiny of the theologians of the new school; it was universally accepted as justifiable, and, while some still held to the old limitations, others extended its sphere of action. Forcible seizure was generally recognized as not permissible, though burglary could be committed; false swearing with mental reservation was recommended to those unlucky enough to be suspected and prosecuted; it was not necessary to await the maturity of a debt if the creditor feared that the debtor would not pay when due; an uncollectible claim against a prince could be recovered by cheating the revenue, even though this were farmed out, and Juan Sanchez goes so far as to assert that claims not recoverable at law, such as gambling and outlawed debts, can thus be made good. There was still sufficient reminiscence of the origin of the practice in the retaking of a certain object, for some authorities to insist on stealing being confined to articles

[35] Pelbartus de Temesvar, *Sacræ Theologiæ Rosarium, s. v.* "Furtum," § 7.

[36] Henriquez, *Summa Theol. Moral.* (Venice, 1600), Lib. XIII, c. xxi, n. 1.

[37] "Debitum tibi, si non potes aliter commode recuperare, potes clam tollere, modo cures ni creditor [*potius debitor*] iterum solvat, et id fiat sine scandalo et sine periculo tuæ vel alienæ famæ aut vitæ, neque teneris revelare etiam si prælatus præcipiat sub pœnam

of the same general nature as those from which the claim had arisen, although this of course could not be made to apply when a recompense was sought for insults, blows, or defamation.[38]

The teaching of the period is summed up by Tamburini, who says it is universally accepted by all doctors that occult compensation is permissible, even from a deposit made with a creditor by his debtor, in spite of the prohibition by Gregory IX, although anything lent to or pledged with the debtor must not be taken; the claim must be a valid one, but it need not have matured if there is a moral certainty that it will not be paid, while if the debtor will suffer loss by the anticipation allowance must be made for it; with regard to the question of a prior appeal to the courts, it may be assumed in practice that collection by legal process is always difficult; as for protecting the debtor against paying a second time, if this can easily be done by a fictitious release it is well; if not, to omit it is only a sin against charity and not against justice and does not entail restitution; if he pays you a second time you are only the cause of it *per accidens*; in the same spirit you are required to protect innocent third parties from falling under suspicion only if it can readily be done, for this also is an obligation merely of charity and not of justice, and therefore if through your negligence an innocent man is condemned to the galleys or to other severe punishment you sin gravely against charity but not against justice and are not required to make reparation; in these matters you should weigh your own advantage against your neighbor's danger, for charity requires that you should not, for a trifling consideration, bring upon him the gravest injury. If suspected, you can swear to ignorance and you can disregard excommunication. As respects the nature of the thing to be stolen, it should if possible be of the same class as that for which it is compensation, but if this is impossible you can steal anything else, and if it inflicts special damage on the debtor he has only himself to thank

---

excommunicationis, si est probabile quod revelans cogeris restituere, imo neque tenentur alii quicunque sint si certo sciant te hoc modo juste recipisse."—*Index Brasichellensis* (Bergomo, 1608) p. 351; Sa, *Aphorismi Confessar.* (Venice, 1617), s. v. "Debitum."

"Si accepisti quod dubitas an tuum esset, debere te restituere quidem aiunt, alii negant, quod in dubio melior est conditio possidentis: quæ opinio locum non habet quando res jam erat in alterius possessione."—Sa, s. v. "Furtum," n. 5. Whatever doubt there may be as to the meaning of this last passage is removed by a reference to Azpilcueta as cited above.

[38] Sayre, *Clavis Regia Sacerdot., Lib.* IX, c. xiv, nn. 5-15.—Reginaldus, *Praxis Fori Pœnitent.,* Lib. XXIII, nn. 7, 8.—Laymann, *Theol. Moral.,* Lib. III, Tract. III, Pt. I, c. i, nn. 9, 10.—Escobar, *Theol. Moral.,* Tract I, n. 83.—Alphonso de Leone, *De Officio et Potest. Confessarii,* Recollect. XI, nn. 618-32.—Mendo, *Epitome Opinionum Moralium, s. v.* "Furtum," n. 16.—Berteau, *Director Confessar.* (ed. XXI, Venice, 1684), p. 342.—*Summa Diana, s. v.* "Compensare," n. 2.—Gobat, *Alphabetum Confessar.,* n. 222.—Busenbaum, *Medullæ Theol. Moral.,* Lib. III, Tract. v, c. i, dub. I, n. 3.—J. Sanchez, *Selecta de Sacramentis,* Disp. XLIII, n. 56.

for it, though in this case also you should weigh your own gain against his loss.[39]

Naturally the class most addicted to taking advantage of this license to steal was that of employees, especially domestic servants, whose opportunities for pilfering were constant, who were accustomed to regard their wages as unjustly inadequate to their services, and who, when the principle was extended to compensation for personal injuries, were rarely without excuse arising from ill treatment, real or fancied. We have seen above how early this question arose, and how emphatically it was negatived by Alexander Hales. Prierias quotes approvingly Richard Middleton as holding that even when wages are unpaid a servant sins in compensating himself, though, in the forum of conscience, he cannot be required to make restitution.[40] Azpilcueta does not except servants from the benefits of occult compensation, but he says that many deceive themselves in thinking that they are justified in having recourse to it, as it is applicable only to legal claims and not to those arising from gratitude or as a recompense for zeal.[41] Cardinal Toletus endeavors to define the rights of servants as limited to stealing the equivalent of an amount actually due, when there has been an agreement as to wages, even if the wage is too low, provided that extra service has not been exacted; when no agreement has been made, then the current rate of wages is the standard.[42] It was easy to formulate rules, but difficult to restrain the cupidity of servants when once the way was opened to honest stealing; and Sayre repeats the complaint that many deceive themselves in thefts to which they have no right.[43] The tendency to laxism showed itself in this as in other departments of the subject, and the opinion became current, especially among the Jesuit confessors, that insufficient wages justify occult compensation,[44] and, as the servant necessarily was the sole judge of the value of his labors and of the adequacy of his pay, it can readily be conceived what encouragement was given to the art of domestic pilfering. The first protest against this abuse naturally arose in France, where the austere virtue concentrated in Port Royal, and afterwards stigmatized as Jansenism, was becoming scandalized at the growing laxity of casuistry and Probabilism. In 1639 the Sorbonne condemned a number of propositions contained in the *Somme des Pechez* of Père Estienne Bauny, S.J., among which was one asserting that servants who

[39] Tamburini, *Explic. Decalogi*, Lib. VIII, Tract. II, c. v, §§ 1-3. For the numerous editions of this authoritative work between 1654 and 1755 see De Backer, *Bibliothèque des Écrivains de la Compagnie de Jésus*, II, 617.

[40] *Summa Sylvestrina, s. v.* "Furtum," § 16.

[41] Azpilcueta, *loc. cit.*, n. 113.

[42] Fr. Toletus, *loc. cit.*, n. 5.

[43] Sayre, *loc. cit.*, n. 6.

[44] Laymann, *loc. cit.*, n. 10.—Busenbaum, *loc. cit.*

have been obliged to agree to inadequate wages can steal to make up what they consider to be the deficiency.[45] Pascal, of course, in his cruel satire, did not neglect the opportunity which this teaching afforded, and he made merry over a case, occurring in 1647, in which a certain Jean d'Alba, a servant in the Jesuit Collège de Clermont, was detected in stealing, and, on his trial at the Châtelet of Paris, claimed that thirty crowns were due him, and alleged this doctrine in his defence, much to the disgust of the good fathers, who hastened to disavow it. The court apparently admitted the truth of his allegations, for it discharged him with a reprimand and restored to him all his personal effects, merely enjoining him to return to his home.[46] When, in 1656, the parish priests of Paris and Rouen presented for condemnation, to the assembly of the Gallican clergy, a series of propositions drawn from Père Bauny's book, this was not omitted; and when the Jesuit, Pirot, in his unfortunate *Apologie des Casuistes*, was so ill advised as to assert "que les valets qui ne sont pas contents de leurs gages peuvent se payer de leurs mains," this was included among the errors extracted from that work and condemned by various French bishops in 1658 and 1659.[47] In 1657, moreover, at the instance of the bishop of Ghent, the University of Louvain condemned a series of propositions including this.[48]

The pressure on the Holy See to impose a check on the audacious and alarming progress of laxity among the moralists at last met with a measure of success. In 1665 and 1666, Alexander VII condemned a series of forty-five propositions, and, in 1679, Innocent XI followed this with a list of sixty-five more. Among the latter was included the assertion that household servants can steal from their employers what they consider sufficient to equalize their wages with their services.[49] As this was the only condemned proposition connected with occult compensation, by implication the equally demoralizing practices taught by Tamburini and others were tacitly approved, although Innocent, in the exordium of his decree, disclaimed responsibility for all propositions not explicitly condemned. Although excommunication, removable only by the pope, was imposed on all who should teach or defend the forbidden doctrines, the casuists were not accustomed to pay more respect to papal decrees than might be shown by their ingenuity in evading or arguing

---

[45] Antoine Arnauld, *Morale des Jésuites* (Cologne, 1667), p. 186.

[46] *Provinciales*, Lettre vi.—*Extraits des Assertions dangereuses*, etc. (Paris, 1762), T. III, 287. It is observable that Père Daniel in his elaborate rejoinder to Pascal (*Entretiens d'Eudoxe et de Cléandre*) discreetly avoids all allusion to this subject.

[47] Arnauld, *op. cit.*, pp. 288, 379, 614, 704, 737.

[48] D'Argentré, *Collect. Judic. de novis Erroribus*, III, ii, 286.

[49] "Famuli et famulæ domesticæ possunt occulte heris suis surripere ad compensandam operam suam quam majorem judicant salario quod recipiunt."—Innocent XI, Decr. *Sanctissimus*, 2 Mart. 1679, Prop. 37.

them away. It was held that Innocent only forbade the servant from compensating himself at his own estimation; he continued therefore to be told that he could steal without sin if his wages were unpaid, or if, pressed by necessity, he had hired himself at too low a rate, and, with a singular lack of humor, he was advised to consult his confessor or some "prudent man" as to the amount that he should pilfer. This has continued, up to the present time, to be the doctrine of the predominant laxer school of moral theologians.[50]

[50] Viva, *Comment. in Prop. 37 Innoc. XI.,* nn. 12, 13; *idem., Cursus Theol. Moral.,* Pt. III, q. vi, Art. 3, n. 8.—Zuccherius, *Decisiones Patavinæ,* Mart. 1708, q. ii, nn. 36-48.— Arsdekin, *Theol. Tripart.,* Pt. III, P. ii, tract. v, c. vii.—Sporer, *Theol. Moral.,* tract. v, c. v, nn. 83-84.—La Croix, *Theol. Moral.,* Lib. III, Pt. I, nn. 971-74.—Kresslinger, *Declaratio Propos. Damnat.,* n. 96.—Felix Potesta, *Examen Ecclesiast.,* T. I, nn. 2643-48.—Salmanticens. Collegius, *Cursus Theol. Moral.,* tract. xiii, c. i, nn. 315-17.—S. Alph. de Liguori, *Theol. Moral.,* Lib. III, n. 522; *idem., Istruzione Pratica per i Confessori,* c. vii, nn. 10-11.— Manzo, *Epitome Theol. Moral.* (Naples, 1836), tract. *de Restitutione,* nn. 154-56.—Gury, *Compend. Theol. Moral.,* I, n. 623.—Varceno, *Compend. Theol. Moral.* (Turin, 1889), tract. xiii, Pt. II, c. iii, Art. I, § 2.

Bonal, however, restricts it to cases where the servant has performed extra work at the desire, expressed or implied, of the employer.—*Institt. Theol. Moral.,* tract. *de Justitia,* (Toulouse, 1882), n. 180.

The rigorist school, which has become nearly extinct under the predominant influence of Liguori and his followers, naturally claims that the condemnation by Innocent XI applies to all domestic pilfering. See *Summa Alexandrina,* Pt. IV, n. 733.—Antoine, *Theo. Moral.,* tract. *de Justitia,* c. v, q. ix.—Th. à Charmes, *Comp. Theol. Univ.,* Pt. I, tract. xv, c. iv, § 3, q. viii.—Alasia, *Theol. Moral., De Restitutione* (Turin, 1834), Dist. I, n. 22.— Zenner, *Instructio Practica Confessarii* (Vienna, 1857), § 333.

Pontas, though strongly inclined to rigorism and hedging around occult compensation with almost impracticable conditions, is disposed to make exceptions in favor of servants. He holds the opinion, which is not universal even among the laxists, that a son who serves his father without pay can compensate himself (Pontas, *Dict. de Cas de Conscience, s. v.* "Compensation," c. v. Cf. Viva, *Cursus Theol. Moral.,* Pt. III, q. vi, Art. 3, n. 10).

Pontas *(loc. cit.,* c. x) gives the details of a case submitted to him for decision in 1697 which reads like a chapter from Le Sage and throws so curious a sidelight upon fashionable life in Paris that it may be worth repeating. A man entered the service of a woman of quality as a lackey and served for eleven years without wages or reward. He was then promoted to valetship, with a promise of one hundred livres a year, but when she died five years later he had received only one hundred and fifty livres. To compensate himself he managed at her death to steal a bag containing sixteen hundred livres, and was retained as valet by her married daughter, with the promise of one hundred and fifty livres a year. He served her for eight years without payment, as she habitually lost at cards the money given to her by her husband for the servants' wages; moreover he lent her three hundred livres, which she never returned, and two thousand to her brother, who died insolvent, besides spending two hundred in repairs to her countryseat. She kept a *table ouverte pour le jeu,* where the winners were expected to give to the attendant a gratification to pay for the cards and candles; according to custom this was a perquisite of the valet, but she made him account to her for it, and he had thus paid over to her four thousand livres, managing, however, to retain one thousand for himself, and he had in addition pilfered to the amount of six hundred livres. He still remained in her service without expectation of better pay in the future, but he desired a settlement with his conscience. Pontas decided that he ought to refund the one thousand livres retained from the gratifications, less the cost to him of the cards and candles, also the six hundred livres of stealings and the sixteen hundred taken at the death of his first mistress, less the loan of

With regard to occult compensation in general, the absence of any further allusions to it among the propositions condemned by Alexander VII, Innocent XI, and Alexander VIII during the last half of the seventeenth century, left the subject open to the speculations of the theologians. The Jansenist movement was the expression of the opposition of the more rigorous party, shocked at the prevailing fashionable laxity of the casuists, and two schools formed themselves, which maintained an active contest for more than a century. As a rule, the laxer teachers, known as probabilists, favored the extension of occult compensation, while the more rigid probabiliorists endeavored to restrict or suppress it. Occasionally, it is true, we find a Probabilist like Arsdekin who looks on it askance and urges that the cases are very rare in which it can be employed,[51] or a Probabiliorist like Wigandt who admits it, subject to the strict observance of the established conditions.[52] As a rule, however, the probabilists inclined to the largest liberty. Zuccheri argues away all the limitations with which the earlier moralists had sought to guard it against abuse, and the most eminent theologians of the laxer school adopted the views of Tamburini; it could even be used for debts not yet due if there were risk of their non-payment at maturity, and also when claims were not certain but only probable. In spite of the condemnation by Innocent XI of perjured oaths with mental restrictions, the thief, if suspected, could swear to ignorance, and the practice was even extended to priests who had been compelled to accept an inadequate fee for celebrating mass, or who had not been paid for what they celebrated.[53] When the moral teachers were thus liberal it was not likely that the people would be overnice in

three hundred, the two hundred spent on the countryseat, and the arrears of wages due on his first and second terms of service as valet. He was also entitled to wages for the first eleven years of unpaid service, which should be settled in court or by the judgment of a prudent man. The loan of two thousand livres to the deceased brother was not to be taken into consideration.

The natural deduction from all this is that the system of occult compensation was tacitly accepted by all parties. Employers were careless as to paying wages, knowing that the servants stole, and servants continued to serve without pay, satisfied with their stealings.

It is perhaps worth noting that a recent *Kathedersocialist* (Morrison I. Swift, *A League of Justice*, Boston, 1893), teaches the same doctrine: "people who are meagrely paid for their services to the rich would be quite justified in stealing from them."

[51] Arsdekin, *Theol. Tripartita*, Pt. II, P. ii, c. vii. At the same time he says that if a thing is detained unjustly, it can be recovered either secretly or by force (*ibid.*, Pt. iii, P. ii, tract. v, c. vii). This, as we have seen, was the original starting-point of the system. It is now, however, properly distinguished as *recuperatio*, in contradistinction to *compensatio* (Bonal, *op. cit.*, tract. *de Justitia*, n. 179).

[52] Wigandt, *Tribunal Confessar.*, tract. vii, Exam. vi, n. 129. See also Antoine, *Theol. Moral.*, tract. *de Justitia*, c. v, q. viii.

[53] Zuccherius, *Decisiones Patavinæ, Mart. 1708*, q. ii, nn. 8-26, 30.—Salmanticens. Collegius, *Cursus Theol. Moral.*, tract. xiii, c. i, nn. 318-24.—Viva, *Comment. in Prop. 37 Innoc. XI*, n. 13; *idem.*, *Cursus Theol. Moral.*, Pt. III, q. vi, Art. 3, nn. 1-12.—Sporer, *Theol. Moral.*, tract. v, c. 5, nn. 69-79.—La Croix, *Theol. Moral.*, Lib. III, P. i, nn. 962-8.

the exercise of the privileges accorded to them. Corella was no rigorist; he limits the conditions to only two—that the debt shall be certain and be overdue—and we therefore may well believe him when he tells us that the confessor will find many irregularities committed in this matter. Some, he says, when they think that an injury has been done to them, without taking the trouble to verify it, will steal something; others, when the debt is certain, will steal in excess of it; others again, when they lose anything, will compensate themselves by stealing from any one whom they suspect of having taken it.[54] Roncaglia, a moderate probabilist, adds his testimony to the caution which the confessor should exercise in admitting the justice of the compensations which servants and peasants are accustomed to allow themselves, for they are wont to do so on grounds not defensible.[55] The whole subject was a matter well fitted to arouse public indignation, and when, in 1762, the Parlement of Paris desired popular support in its movement for the suppression of the Jesuits, and caused to be compiled a collection of the lax doctrines taught by the theologians of the Society, occult compensation and theft furnished material for a section of formidable length.[56]

The rigorist school evidently were not without justification in endeavoring to abolish, or at least to limit strictly, the whole theory of occult compensation. Apparently the earliest to place himself on record against it was the Jesuit, Elizalde, whose treatise *De recta Doctrina Morum* appeared from 1670 to 1684 under a pseudonym and without the knowledge of his superiors.[57] Noël Alexandre abstains from all reference to it, except with regard to servants; apparently he was willing to allude only to that on which he could quote a papal condemnation.[58] Matteucci asserts that he who compensates himself commits mortal sin, though he is not obliged to make restitution if he has strictly observed all the conditions, but confessors are directed to inquire of the thief whether in the act he did not feel some doubt that suspicion might fall on an innocent third party, in which case he must restore the article stolen, for, though he had a right to take it, he had no right in taking

---

[54] Corella, *Pratica del Confessionario* (Parma, 1707), tract. vii, c. iv, p. 7, nn. 67-78. This work was one of the most popular of the eighteenth century. Besides more than twenty editions in the original Spanish, there were repeated issues of Italian and Latin translations. The latest I have met with is of Vienna, 1757. It was twice placed on the Index, in 1710 and 1712 (*Index Benedicti XIV*, 1758, p. 67), without interfering with its popularity.

[55] Roncaglia, *Universa Moralis Theol.*, tract. xiii, c. ix, ad calcem.

[56] *Extraits des Assertions dangereuses et pernicieuses que les soi-disans Jésuites ont soutenues*, etc. (Paris, 1762), T. III, 252-396.

[57] Concina, *Theol. Christiana contracta*, Lib. vi, Dist. i, c. v, n. 10.—De Backer, *op. cit.*, I, 283.

[58] *Summa Alexandrina*, Pt. iv, n. 733.

it to expose another to risk.[59] The rigorists, in fact, had a narrow path to tread. In the bitter controversy between the rival schools they were accused of Jansenism and of throwing unnecessary obstacles in the path to salvation; they could not utterly deny a custom which had the sanction of centuries, and they were reduced to nullifying it as far as they could in practice. Thus Habert fairly states the common opinion justifying occult compensation under the customary conditions, but he adds that these can rarely occur, for there scarce can be absence of danger of scandal or defamation; the confessor should never advise it, for there would be a shocking scandal if the thief should be caught and condemned to death and should plead that he only acted under the counsel of his priest; if consulted, the confessor should say that it is commonly affirmed under the requisite conditions, but that it is full of danger and is to be avoided.[60] Reiffenstuel contents himself with stating the conditions fully and pointing out the attendant risks, for judges are wont to punish such compensation as theft.[61] Reuter advises the confessor to discourage servants from compensating themselves, for the conditions can rarely be clearly fulfilled.[62]

As the general discussion waxed hotter between the contending schools, the rigorists took a bolder position. The Dominican, Daniele Concina, who devoted his life to the vain endeavor to stay the triumphant advance of probabilism, gives the customary list of conditions, which, he says, are rarely enforced in practice, for the moderns have so relaxed them that they are reduced to nothing; he laughs at the evasions with which Viva and La Croix nullify Innocent XI's condemnation of pilfering by servants. He admits that he cannot absolutely reject the opinions of so many eminent theologians in favor of occult compensation, but he argues forcibly against it as subversive of law and justice, as overriding the laws of the land, constituting a man a secret judge in his own cause, and opening the way to the violation of all law, human and divine, giving occasion to frauds and thefts and disturbing the social order; it is condemned, he says, in the secular courts, and why should it be permitted in the courts of conscience?[63] Concina's fellow Dominican and ally, Gianvincenzo Patuzzi, is equally outspoken. He devotes much space to this subject, and points out in full detail the results of the teaching of the casuists in authorizing theft and destroying confidence between man and man, especially in the relations between employer and employed.[64]

[59] Matteucci, *Cautela Confessarii* (Venice, 1710), Lib. II, c. xxi, nn. 31-33.
[60] Habert, *Theol. Dogmat. et Moral., De Injustitia*, c. ix, § 5, q. viii, ix.
[61] Reiffenstuel, *Theol. Moral.*, tract. ix, Dist. 5, nn. 117-18.
[62] Reuter, *Neoconfessarius instructus*, Pt. II, c. vi, q. ii, n. 4.
[63] Concina, *Theol. Christ. contracta* (Bologna, 1760), Lib. VI, Dist. I, c. 5.
[64] *Lettere di Eusebio Eraniste* (Venice, 1761), Lett. v, vi, T. I, 183-219.

Another systematic theologian of the same school treats the subject briefly, stating the usual conditions, and warning the confessor that he is never to advise it and rarely to permit it.[65]

These efforts were fruitless against the overshadowing authority of St. Alphonso Liguori, who, though he professed to be not strictly a Probabilist, nevertheless inclined almost invariably to the laxer side. He fully admits the principle of occult compensation; he cites Tamburini and La Croix, and quotes without dissent the opinion of the Salamanca theologians and other weighty authorities in favor of its application when the claim is only probable, though in his instructions to confessors he imposes three conditions,—that the debtor be not injured, that the debt be certain, and that satisfaction cannot be obtained otherwise.[66] This enlarged greatly the opportunities for exercising the privilege, for it ignored the factor of danger to the thief or to innocent third parties, on which the rigorists relied to prove that it could rarely be employed; but in fact it is necessary to eliminate these considerations if servants are to be allowed to compensate themselves, as Liguori emphatically states that they can. His beatification in 1816 and canonization in 1839, after exhaustive examination of all his writings to detect any possible errors or imperfections, and his final exaltation in 1870 to the dignity of a Doctor of the Church, the decision of the papal Penitentiary in 1831 that all confessors can safely follow blindly whatever they find in his works, without troubling themselves to investigate his reasons, and the laudations of successive popes who place him among the foremost of those whom God has raised up for the illumination and adornment of the Church, give him irrefragable authority, against which opposition is vain.[67] The rigorists, moreover, were discredited by stigmatizing them with the hated name of Jansenists, and it was officially declared that one of the chief merits of his great work on *Moral Theology* was that its appearance terrified the Jansenists like a stroke of lightning and inflicted on them a mortal wound.[68] Since then rigorism and Probabiliorism, discountenanced by the ruling influences in the Church, have steadily declined. Some sixty years ago Alasia, who was a Probabiliorist, sought to limit occult compensation as much as possible; it is, he says, inimical to the public good, for it opens a wide path for thefts, scandals, and duplicate payments, and he insists, as an additional condition, that it must never be practised without the advice of a learned and pious man.[69] Similarly,

[65] Jos. Anton of Kaysersberg, *Theol. Moral.* (Venice, 1772), tract. vi, Quæst. vii, Quær. xv.

[66] Liguori, *Theol. Moral.*, Lib. iii, n. 521.— *Idem., Istruzione Pratica,* c. x, n. 21.

[67] *Concessio Tituli Doctoris,* i, 23-24; iv, 6 (Rome, 1870).—*Vindiciæ Alphonsianæ* (Rome, 1873), pp. x ff.

[68] *Concessio Tituli Doctoris,* i, 10.

[69] Alasia, *Theol. Moral.* (Turin, 1834), *De Restitutione,* Dist. i, nn. 19-22.

Bishop Zenner, who about forty years ago was vicar-general of Vienna, insists on all the old conditions, and points out that their coexistence is exceedingly rare, wherefore the confessor is never to advise it, for it can scarce ever be without danger of scandal or defamation; when a penitent, however, has thus compensated himself, he is not required to make restitution.[70]

On the other hand, the modern textbooks of Moral Theology which are almost universally used in the seminaries are based upon Liguori and teach his doctrines. Cardinal Gousset defines occult compensation to be lawful when through lack of evidence a debt cannot be proved and yet is certain, when the debtor refuses a settlement, or when the object stolen belongs to the thief and he does not take too much.[71] Archbishop Kenrick only says that it is a venial sin to have recourse to it when other means are available, unless judicial proceedings are expensive or tardy, or there is some other weighty reason.[72] Subsequent authorities are not wholly in accord with each other as to the conditions, though they are all much less rigid than those prescribed by the older theologians, and the slight differences between them are important only as indicating the substratum of uncertainty in the minds of the writers. An opening is even made for claims of doubtful validity. Gury and Guarceno require only what is called "moral certainty," which in the mind of a claimant is a term of elastic capabilities, while Bonal states that if there is doubt the theft should be reduced proportionately— though he admits that this is a procedure full of peril. Marc is more rigid, and requires the debt to be certain, though there is no necessity of claiming it at law if this should entail expense. A very wide extension is further given to occult compensation in the general assent to the proposition that it is permissible in cases where a man is condemned by court to pay a debt which he has not incurred or which he feels certain that he has already paid.[73] In the complication of human transactions there are few defeated defendants who will not range themselves with this class, while defeated plaintiffs can assign judicial partiality as a similar justification.

The practical application of occult compensation can perhaps best be understood through a few examples furnished by recent casuists.

[70] Zenner, *Instructio Practica Confessarii* (Vienna, 1857), § 333.

[71] Gousset, *Théologie Morale* (Paris, 1850), I, n. 777.

[72] Kenrick, *Theol. Moral.*, tract. iii, n. 167.

[73] Gury, *Compend. Theol. Moral.*, I, nn. 622-25.—Bonal, *Institt. Theologicæ*, tract. *de Justitia*, nn. 180-81.—Varceno, *Comp. Theol. Moral.*, tract. xiii, P. ii, c. 3, Art. i, § 2.— Miguel Sanchez, *Prontuario de la Teología Moral.*, tract. xx, Punto vi, n. 1.—Marc, *Institutiones Morales Alphonsianæ* (Rome, 1893), nn. 916-18.—Pruner, *Lehrbuch der katholischen Moraltheologie* (Freiburg i. B. 1883), p. 680.

A man's ass is stolen; it escapes from the thief and commits damages for which the owner is forced to pay. This is unjust, and he can compensate himself secretly.

A man who is treated unjustly but legally in the division of an estate with his sisters compensates himself in the distribution of the assets. He is within his rights in so doing, but we are told that it is dangerous unless he first consults some honest man as to the amount to be secreted. After it is done, however, the confessor had better let it pass without requiring him to make restitution.

A servant breaks a valuable piece of glassware, and his employer deducts the value from his wages; if the breakage was unintentional he can compensate himself by stealing.

A borrows a hundred napoleons from *B*, and meeting him promises to send the amount to him the next day, whereupon *B* confidingly gives him a receipt. Now, *B*'s father had died owing a similar sum to *A*'s father, wherefore *A* refuses to fulfil his promise, and when sued exhibits the receipt and swears that he has paid the debt. *B* is defeated and cast in the costs. *A*'s conduct is perfectly justifiable throughout.[74]

A peasant woman confesses to stealing her neighbors' chickens, and alleges four reasons—1. that her chickens are lost and she takes her neighbors'; 2. that she knows her neighbors steal hers; 3. that the chickens which she stole consorted with her own when young and ate her food; 4. that the neighboring chickens damage her garden. Of these the first and third are pronounced insufficient, while the second and fourth justify her.[75]

[74] Gury, *Casus Conscientiæ* (Ratisbon, 1865), I, 106, 499, 500, 573, 575, 576-78.
[75] Bertolotti, *Sylloge Casuum* (Rome, 1893), I, 147.

IS THERE A ROMAN CATHOLIC CHURCH?*

An Excursus in Scholastic Theology

THE WHOLE structure of the Latin Church and the salvation of its members depend upon the sacraments and their due administration. Without the sacrament of orders there is no priesthood, and no gift of supernatural powers; without that of baptism there is no membership in the Church Militant, and no admission to the Church Triumphant; without that of confirmation there is no perfected Christian; without that of penitence, sins, save in rare cases of perfect contrition, are unforgiven; without that of the Eucharist the most efficient means of grace are lost; without that of matrimony marriage is but concubinage.[1] If, therefore, anything in the whole range of Catholic doctrine and practice should be unquestioned and unquestionable, it is the validity of the administration of the sacraments on which the very existence of the Church is founded. Yet it is a curious result of the labors of the schoolmen and theologians who have built up the vast and intricate structure of modern Catholic belief, that no priest or prelate can be certain that he enjoys the power of the keys, or even that he is capable of holding his position, and no member of the laity can feel assured that any sacrament which he receives is validly administered, even if the officiating priest is canonically capable of his functions.

This has arisen from the necessity which the Church has experienced of formulating the doctrine that, in addition to the material and form of a sacrament, the "intention" of the ministrant to perfect it is requisite to its supernatural efficacy. This sprang indirectly from the development of another great question which agitated the Church in its earlier period —the validity of sacraments administered by polluted hands. It was one of the Donatist heresies that baptism was invalid when administered by those who had lapsed, and St. Augustine, in combating the heretics, declared that it made no difference whether the ministrant was good or evil, drunk or sober; it was Christ who baptized, not the priest.[2] As yet the question of intention had not been broached, but several passages show that he considered the intention of the ministrant to be as unimportant as his character.[3] That this, in fact, was the opinion of the Church of the time, is shown by a story which has greatly exercised modern orthodox theologians. Rufinus, and after him Sozomen, relates that St. Athanasius, when a boy, with his playfellows once parodied the services

* From *The Independent*, XLII (1890), 1623-24, 1666-67. Privately reprinted, Philadelphia, 1891.

[1] Nascitur Baptismate homo, Confirmatione adolescit, Eucharistia nutritur, Pœnitentia ab ægritudinibus liberatur, Unctione extrema a criminum expiatur reliquiis, Ordine ad Sacra peragenda instituitur, Matrimonio humana species propagata cujus congregatione Ecclesia resultat.—Escobar, *Moral. Theol.*, tract. vii, c. i.

of the Church; he acted as bishop, and in that capacity performed the
rite of baptism on some of his comrades. Alexander, the bishop of Alex-
andria, chanced to witness the sport from a window, and thinking that
the boys were going too far had them brought before him. On investigating the details of what Athanasius had done, he pronounced the baptisms to be valid, and ordered those who had undergone the rite not to
be re-baptized.[4] Whether the story be true or not, it is evident that at the
time of the historians there was no question as to the validity of a sacrament, administered even in jest, and the labored arguments of post-
Tridentine theologians as to details are idle.[5]

With the disappearance of the Donatists the question as to the validity
of the sacraments in polluted hands slumbered for ages. It emerged
partially toward the close of the eleventh century, when Gregory VII,
in his war against priestly marriage, forbade attendance on the masses
of married priests; but the age was not a critical one, and the Church
managed to tide over the inconsistency without difficulty. It was different
when, in the following century, heretics arose, especially the Waldenses,
who denied that a wicked priest could perform the awful sacrifice of the
altar or could wash away the sins of others with the waters of baptism.
The development of sacerdotalism was largely increasing the powers
claimed and exercised by the ministers of religion, while the flagitious
lives of a majority of them were notorious. The Church could not abandon the position that their sins had no influence on their ministrations.
The mysteries of the sacraments were accomplished *ex opere operato*—
by the work itself—and not *ex opere operantis*—by the worker.

This degraded the minister into a mere mechanical functionary—a
puppet invested with certain attributes and performing certain ceremonies or reciting certain magic formulas which, like the conjurations
of the sorcerer, wrought their own results. It was impossible that this
should escape the attention of the schoolmen who in the twelfth century commenced the labors which were to result in constructing modern
Catholic theology, and in furnishing justification for the growing claims
of sacerdotalism. Evidently the priest must be declared entitled to some
share in the supernatural effects of the sacraments administered by him,
but it was not easy to reconcile this with the position taken by the Church
in the third century, and maintained against the Donatists. Hugh of St.
Victor (died 1141), one of the earliest and most efficient contributors to
the development of the theory of the sacraments, shows the confusion

---

[2] St. August., *In Joannem*, tract. v. n. 18; *De Unitate Ecclesiæ*, c. xxii.
[3] St. August., Epist. 98, § 2 ad. Bonif.; *Contra Cresconium*, Lib. III, c. viii.
[4] Rufin., *Hist. Eccl.*, I, 24.—Sozomen, *Eccl. Hist.*, II, 27.
[5] Busenbaum, *Medulla Theol.*, Lib. VI, tract. i, c. ii, dub. i.—Liguori, *Theol. Moral.*, Lib.
VI, n. 25.—Benedict XIV, *De Synodo Diœcesana*, Lib. VII, c. iv, n. 5.

of ideas existing in this formative period. He admits fully the orthodox view that baptism is valid, whether bestowed by Catholic or heretic, believer or infidel,[6] but he contradicts this by arguing at much length that explicit belief in the Trinity is essential on the part of the ministrant —if this is present, the formula employed is comparatively unimportant; if it is lacking the sacrament is void.[7] This introduced the question of the mental condition of the ministrant, and Hugh took a further step when he considered the much vexed question of the validity of baptism performed in jest; if there was an intention to baptize, the lack of reverence did not neutralize it, and the sacrament was valid.[8] Thus the idea of intention as influencing validity in the sacraments was fairly suggested, yet how little the writer imagined its importance is seen in his definition of a sacrament as consisting of things, acts, and words[9]—the modern definition, adopted from Aquinas, which makes intention an integral part, was evidently unthought of.

For some time we hear nothing more as to the virtue of intention. Gratian, who about 1150 compiled the authoritative body of the canon law, has no allusion to the necessity of the ministrant's volition to the perfection of a sacrament. Peter Lombard, whose *Sentences*, written about the same time, remained for centuries the foundation of all theological teaching, is equally silent, save an allusion to the old question, whether a baptism performed in jest is a valid baptism—a question to which he prudently evades an answer.[10] Toward the close of the century, however, Magister Bandinus refers incidentally to the intention of the priest as an element in the consecration of the host.[11] Yet this was evi-

---

[6] Nulla ratione illud iterato accipiat, sive in Ecclesia, sive extra Ecclesiam, hoc est a Catholico sive ab hæretico, sive denique a fideli sive ab infidele, cujuscunque conditionis, ætatis aut sexus persona illud acceperit.—Hugo de S. Victore, *De Sacramentis*, Lib. II, Pt. VI, c. viii. Cf. *idem, Summa Sententt.*, tract. v, c. viii.—Gratian, *Decret.*, Pt. III. Dist. 4, cc. xxiv, li.—Alexander Hales even seems to consider it necessary to point out that the devil is an exception, and that he cannot baptize (Reschinger, *Repertorium Alexandri de Hales* [Basel, 1502], *s. v.* "Baptisare")."

[7] Vides ergo qualiter in fide Trinitatis solo Patre vel Filio vel Spiritu sancto nuncupato plenum sit baptismatis sacramentum, et quemadmodum sine fide Trinitatis etiam tribus simul-nominatis imperfectum.—Hugo de S. Victore, *De Sacramentis*, Lib. ii, *loc. cit.*, c. ii.

[8] Ubi ergo intentio baptizandi est, etiamsi reverentia debita in agendo non est, sacramentum quidem est, quia omnino agitur et hoc intenditur.—*Ibid.*, c. xiii.

In both this work of Hugh's (tract. v, c. ix) and the *Sentences* of Peter Lombard (Lib. IV, Dist. 6, n. 5), there is inserted an impudent forgery attributed to St. Augustine, affirming the necessity of intention. This is probably of comparatively modern date, as it does not seem to be referred to by the commentators.

[9] Hugo de S. Victore, *Summa Sententt.*, tract. iv, c. i.—"In tribus constitit sacramentum; rebus, factis, dictis. Rebus, ut sunt aqua, oleum et similia. Factis, ut sunt submersio, insufflatio. Dictis, ut est invocatio Trinitatis."

[10] Solet etiam quæri de illo qui jocans, sicut mimus, commemoratione tamen Trinitatis, immergitur, utrum baptizatus est.—P. Lombard, *loc. cit.*

[11] Conficitur autem hoc sacramentum a quolibet secundum ritum et intentionem conficiendi, utique si in unitate Ecclesiæ est.—Bandinus, *Sententt.*, Lib. IV, Dist. 13.

dently regarded as a theological speculation of no practical moment. St. Ramon of Pennafort, the greatest canonist of his day, in his *Summa*, written about 1235, makes no allusion to it, though treating of the sacraments in a manner which would have required its introduction had he accepted it.[12] The Schoolmen, however, were now rapidly developing their system in all directions, and about this time we find the Irrefragable Doctor, Alexander Hales, adopting the doctrine of intention as a factor in the sacraments, but arguing that when it is lacking God confers the grace on the recipient without the real sacrament[13]—a position nearly akin to that which was afterward condemned in Luther, and virtually denying that intention is a necessity. St. Bonaventura practically took the same ground. He tells us that there were two opinions current; one that, in the absence of intention, God considers the baptism valid, though the Church does not; the other, that there is no sacrament. He inclines to the latter but adds, like Luther, that in the adult, faith supplies the defect and that in the infant it is pious to believe that God may take the place of the priest.[14] The gradual advance of opinion, in this transition period, is seen in the treatment of the question by Henry of Susa, cardinal of Ostia, who asserts that if the priest intends not to baptize there is no baptism, but that if he has no intention either way, as when drunk, the sacrament is valid.[15]

In this, as in so much else, St. Thomas Aquinas gave the final direction to the doctrines of the Church. Yet Aquinas himself found it by no means easy to grope his way through so doubtful and intricate a subject. In his *Commentary upon the Sentences*, he contents himself with stating the two conflicting opinions current at the time—the one being that just quoted from St. Bonaventura, the other being that intention is unnecessary because it is sufficiently implied by the employment of the customary formula—and he ventures to express no decision of his own.[16] In his *Opusculum* on the Sacraments, he asserts positively that without intention there is no sacrament.[17] Yet in his last and crowning

[12] *Summa S. Raymundi*, Lib. iii, Tit. xxiv, § 5.

[13] Viva, *Damnatorum Thesium Theologica Trutina*, Prop. 28, Alexandri VIII.

[14] S. Bonavent., *In Quartum Lib. Sententt.*, Dist. 7, q. i.—"Utrum autem sit baptizatus vel non hic est duplex opinio. Una est quod Deus reputat illum baptizatum non tamen ecclesia . . . et ideo dictunt alii quod non est sacramentum quamvis ibi sunt verba. . . . Si quæras an aliter salvetur. Dicendum quod si adultus baptizatur ut debet, fides interior supplet. Si parvulus, pium est credere quod summus sacerdos suppleat."

[15] Consideratur etiam intentio baptizantis, qui si intendat non baptizare nihil agitur, quidquid Gra. et alii dicant, sed si intendit baptizare vel non habeat intentionem baptizato contrarium, valet, unde ebrius baptizat.—Hostiensis, *Aurea Summa,* Lib. iii, De Baptismo, n. 8.

[16] Aquinas, *Super Libb. Sententt.*, Lib. iv, Dist. 6, Art. 2.

[17] Si aliquid deest, id est si non sit debita forma verborum, et si non sit debita materia, et si minister sacramenti non intendit sacramentum conficere non perficitur sacramentum.—*Opusc.* v, De Art. Fidei et Ecclesiæ Sacramentis.

work, unfortunately left unfinished at his death, the secondary questions which speedily suggested themselves made him waver and speak with an inconsistency that has caused him to be cited as authority by theologians of opposite schools. In one passage the priest is relegated to the position of a puppet by the ingenious suggestion of a kind of intention, designated as "habitual" or "virtual," the existence of which is sufficiently proved by his repeating the prescribed formula; this expresses the intention of the Church and suffices for the perfection of the sacraments, unless the contrary is publicly declared at the time. As Aquinas expresses it, he is simply an *instrumentum animatum,* whose only function is to perform mechanically a certain ceremony and to abstain from openly declaring it void. But this he modifies in another passage, in which he says that any perverse intention, such as jocularity or contempt, destroys the validity of the sacrament, especially if manifested externally.[18]

Under the supreme authority of Aquinas, the doctrine of intention, which had been so long struggling for recognition, found a secure lodgment in the theological structure. Durand de Saint-Pourçain, who wrote about a half century later, treats it as an accepted fact that without intention the words of the sacrament are an empty formula.[19] He illustrates the absolute necessity of specific intention by a celebrated proposition, which has been authenticated by its adoption in the rubrics of the Roman missal. If, he says, a priest has eleven wafers before him to consecrate, and thinks that there are only ten, but intends to consecrate them all, they will all be consecrated; if he intends to consecrate only ten, and fixes his mind on one to be excluded while he repeats the formula, then only that one remains unconsecrated; but if he does not exclude one, then none are consecrated, for the intention with regard to each one is imperfect.[20] The necessity of this is proved by another celebrated proposition of the doctors, that if the magic power resided in the words of the formula alone, then a priest at meals, reading aloud the Gospels, and coming to the words *"Hoc est corpus meum; hic est sanguis meus,"* would consecrate all the bread and wine on the table.[21]

Thus far the question had developed itself in the schools, and had won its place as an accepted dogma without papal recognition. There were still some doubters, and Pierre de la Palu, one of the most eminent

[18] *Summa,* Pt. III, q. 64, Artt. 8, 10: "Intentio ministri perversa et mala respectu sacramenti tollit veritatem sacramenti . . . puta cum aliquis non intendit sacramentum conferre, sed derisorie aliquid agere; et talis perversitas tollit veritatem sacramenti præcipue quando suam intentionem exterius manifestat."

[19] Durandus de S. Portiano, *Comment. super Sententias,* Lib. IV, Dist. vi, q. 2, §§ 8-10.

[20] *Ibid.,* Dist. 11, p. 7: "Probatio, quia illa intentio non sufficit ad consecrationem alicujus hostiæ sub qua æqualiter quælibet hostia includitur et excluditur." Cf. Ferraris, *s. v.* "Intentio," § 24.

[21] Ferraris, *loc. cit.,* § 25.

theologians of the early fourteenth century, although a Dominican, adhered to the transition opinions of Alexander Hales and Bonaventura.[22] At last, however, the seal of papal acceptance of the doctrine was given incidentally by Martin V, at the council of Constance in 1417, in the instructions to the inquisitors for the suppression of Wickliffitism and Hussitism.[23] This virtual admission was rendered absolute by Eugenius IV, November 22, 1439, at the council of Florence, in the decree of union with the Armenians, where the definition of the sacrament was based upon the *Opusculum* of Aquinas and the absence of intention on the part of the ministrant was declared to render the sacrament imperfect.[24] Thenceforth there could be no question as to the authority of the doctrine as an article of Catholic faith. Savonarola, in his directions to confessors, instructs them to inquire of priestly penitents whether in baptizing they have performed the rites with the proper intention.[25]

Occasion soon came to define the doctrine still more formally. Luther's object was to eliminate sacerdotalism, to exalt as much as possible the effects of faith in the believer, and to diminish the functions of the priest as the channel of grace from God to man. It is true that in his first mutterings of revolt, one of the articles nailed to the church door at Wittenburg, in 1517, invoked eternal perdition on those who had faith in the promises of pardon conveyed in indulgences;[26] but he soon after uttered the celebrated proposition that even if a priest granted absolution in jest, if the penitent believed himself absolved he was absolved, so great was the power of faith and of the words of Christ.[27] This, which was virtually the opinion of Alexander Hales, Bonaventura, and Pierre de la Palu, was included by Leo X among the Lutheran errors denounced in the bull of condemnation in 1520.[28] When the council of Trent undertook to define the position of the Church in the face of advancing heresy, it spoke in no uncertain terms on this question, and asserted it to be a point of faith that intention is indispensable in the administration of the sacraments.[29] After such a definition there can no longer be reasonable

[22] Viva, *Theologica Trutina*, ubi sup.—Pallavicini, *Historia Conc. Trident.*, IX, vi, 2.

[23] Item, utrum credat quod malus sacerdos cum debita materia et forma et cum intentione faciendi quod facit ecclesia, vere conficiat, vere absolvat, vere baptizet et vere conferat alia sacramenta.—Concil. Constant., sess. ult. (Harduin, *Collect. Concil.*, VIII, 915).

[24] Hæc omnia sacramenta tribus perficiuntur, videlicet rebus tanquam materia, verbis tanquam forma, et persona ministri conferentis sacramentum cum intentione faciendi quod facit ecclesia; quorum si aliquod desit non perficitur sacramentum.—Concil. Florent. (*Ibid.*, IX, 438).

[25] Savonarola, *Confessionale* (ed. 1578), fol. 32*b*.

[26] Luther, *Theses*, Art. 32.

[27] Luther, *Concio de Pœnitentia* (*Opp.*, Jena, 1564, T. I, fol. 15*a*).

[28] Leo X, bull *Exsurge Domine*, Prop. 12 (*Mag. Bullar. Roman.*, [ed. Luxemb.], I,. 611).

[29] Si quis dixerit: in ministris dum sacramenta conficiunt et conferunt non requiri intentionem saltem faciendi quod facit ecclesia, anathema sit.—C. Trident., sess. VII, *De Sacramentis in genere*, c. xi.

doubt that it is *de fide* that the intention of the priest forms an integral and indispensable part of a valid sacrament. In a catechism drawn up in 1578, by order of the bishop of Pavia, for the examination of candidates for ordination, the question as to the constituent parts of a sacrament is answered, "the matter, the form, and the intention of the minister."[30]

It is true that a doctrine of origin so recent and fraught with consequences so tremendous could not be injected into the faith without some protests and some efforts to mitigate its dangers. As the validity of all the ministrations of the Church, involving the future life of all its members, depended on the secret mental processes of the ministrant, casuists busied themselves with defining the undefinable and infinite varieties of intention which a priest might have in performing his functions. The simplest classification is into four species—actual, virtual, habitual, and interpretative. Actual intention is held to be desirable, but not essential; it exists when the priest has his attention fixed on his acts and wishes to perform them. Virtual intention is when he does what he otherwise would not do in virtue of an intention previously held and not revoked, as when he puts on the vestments to celebrate mass and performs the ceremony without further thought. Habitual intention is volition previously entertained and not revoked, but so interrupted that it cannot be regarded as efficacious. Interpretative intention is what one has not but would have if he happened to think about the matter. Then there are explicit and implicit attention, direct and indirect, absolute and conditioned. In practice the line is drawn between virtual and habitual intention: the former suffices for the validity of sacraments, the latter does not. Neither will indirect attention; if a priest intends to administer a sacrament and gets drunk he cannot be considered to have more than habitual intention, which is insufficient, though we have seen that St. Augustine considered him capable, and that this opinion was entertained as lately as the time of Cardinal Henry of Ostia. Nor does it suffice that the priest has a mere material intention of employing the matter and form materially; there must be a formal intention of using them sacramentally and of doing what the Church does; the Church does not perform a profane and material ceremony, but a holy and supernatural one, which requires the participation of the volition of the performer.[31]

[30] "Ex materia, forma et intentione ministri."—Dr. Alex. Saulius, *Addit. ad Savonarolæ Confessionale*, fol. 66b. (Cf. Fr. Toletus, *Summa Casuum Conscientiæ*, Lib. II, c. xvi; Caramuelis, *Theol. Fundamentalis*, n. 1915; Estius, *In Lib. IV. Sententt.*, Dist. I, § 23; Reiffenstuel, *Theol. Moralis*, tract. xiv, Dist. I, n. 36; Escobar, *Moral. Theol.*, tract. vii, c. iii).

[31] Ferraris, *Prompta Biblioth.*, s. v. "Intentio," nn. 1-23.—(Cf. Busenbaum, *Medulla Theol.*, Lib. VI, tract. I, c. ii, dub. I.— Liguori, *Theol. Moral.*, Lib. VI, nn. 16, 17, 18, 25.—Escobar, *ubi sup.*).

In 1506 there was an attempt to explain the spread of witchcraft in the Tyrol by the

This, however, by no means exhausted the boundless field of speculation as to the infinite varieties of mental processes which still further complicated the already hopelessly tangled question. As a rule, all theologians agreed that virtual intention suffices, but the definition of virtual intention was no easy matter in practice. Scotus, Suarez, and Vasquez frame one formula, Coninch another, Lugo and Dicastillo another; all these are authorities of the first rank, and the shrewd Jesuit, Viva, who reports them wisely declines to decide between them.[32] Then the fact that the priest may have two intentions gives rise to many nice distinctions; the more powerful of the two is held to be the determining one; but if they are successive the later, unless the earlier had rendered void all subsequent ones; in any case, if there is doubt concerning them the validity of the sacrament is doubtful.[33] An explicit intention of making the sacrament is not essential, for if a man intends to do what the Church does this is sufficient, even if he does not believe in the sacrament; thus the heretic can baptize even if he laughs at the doctrine that baptism is a sacrament and does not wish to do what the Roman Church does; for he wishes to do what Christ commanded, and this prevails over his error in thinking his own Church the true one. But if the celebrant believes that an explicit intention is necessary and he has not such explicit intention, then he does not administer a valid sacrament.[34] These examples will suffice to show how dangerous was the question which involved such subtle metaphysical distinctions, and only became more complicated and doubtful the more it was elucidated.

There were a few theologians sufficiently alive to the uncertainty thus cast on all the ministrations of the Church to seek for some mitigation of the Tridentine canon. The learned Dominican, Ambrogio Caterino, was a member of the Council and vigorously opposed its decision, pointing out the desolation which a wicked or infidel priest might spread among the faithful by withholding his intention and thus rendering invalid the baptism of those who might afterward rise to high places in the Church, all of whose ordinations and other acts would be nugatory; it was no answer to say that such cases were rare, for in that corrupt age they were frequent. In spite of his protests the canon was adopted; but his sense of impending evils was so strong that he soon afterward, in

drunkenness of the priests, who were unable to baptize children properly, or to absolve penitents, so that the people were easily betrayed to Satan.—Rapp, *Die Hexenprocesse und ihre Gegner aus Tyrol*, p. 148.

[32] Viva, *Theologica Trutina, ubi sup.*

[33] Liguori, *Theol. Moral.*, Lib. v, n. 24.

[34] *Ibid.*, nn. 22, 25. For the curious process of reasoning by which it is proved that baptism can be validly performed by an infidel who does not even know what baptism is, see *Summa Sylvestrina, s. v.* "Baptismus," III, 2.

1552, wrote a tract *"De Intentione Ministri,"* to prove that the only intention requisite was that of performing the external rite without reference to the internal mental operation.[35] Though Caterino was eventually promoted to the archbishopric of Conza, his argument reduced the Tridentine definition to so absurd a nullity that it found no favor and was speedily forgotten. In the next century, however, it was revived by Joseph Maria Scribonius, a Frenchman, who labored to show that it had not been condemned at Trent, and he was followed by several others, mostly of the same nationality, such as Salmeron, Contenson, Bossuet, Serry, and Juenin.[36] At length the Holy See felt it necessary to put an end to these speculations, and in a list of errors condemned by Alexander VIII, December 7, 1690, was the one of maintaining that baptism is valid, even if the ministrant declares internally that it is not his intention to do what the Church does. Under pain of *ipso facto* excommunication, removable only by the Pope, even the discussion of this proposition was forbidden except to attack it.[37] Since this emphatic warning there has been little dissidence of opinion. The learned Benedict XIV, it is true, unofficially stated that there had been no express definition by the Holy See as to the manner in which God regards the question; but as the common opinion of theologians requires actual or virtual intention, that opinion is always to be followed in practice, yet bishops ought not to condemn the other side.[38] The leading modern authorities, however, are unequivocal in their assertion of the necessity of intention. La Croix even holds that not only intention but attention is requisite, and that distraction on the part of the priest invalidates the sacrament, but he stands alone in this.[39]

Yet one kindly exception has been made in deference to the needs of human society. As the social organization is built upon the family, and as matrimony is a sacrament, it would be too great a demand upon the obedience of the faithful to inflict upon all married persons the torturing doubt as to whether they are living in concubinage and whether their children are illegitimate, in consequence of the unknown and

[35] Sarpi, *Hist. del Conc. Trident.*, Lib. II (ed. Helmstadt, 1, 224).—Benedict XIV, *De Synodo Diœces.*, Lib. VII, c. iv, n. 6.—Though Caterino won renown in his controversies with Luther he was regarded as an erratic theologian and some of his works came into the Index. From a single one of them Spina, the master of the sacred palace, drew up a list of fifty errors. See Reusch, *Der Index der verbotenen Bücher*, I, 569.

[36] Viva, *Theologica Trutina, ubi sup.*—Benedict XIV, *loc cit.*—Liguori, *Theol. Moral.*, Lib. VI, n. 23.—Addis and Arnold, *Catholic Dictionary, s. v.* "Sacraments of the Gospel," § 5.

[37] Alexander VIII, Constit. *Pro pastorali cura*, Prop. 28 (*Bullar. Rom.*, T. XII, 67).

[38] Benedict XIV, *loc. cit.*, n. 9.

[39] Ferraris, *s. v.* "Intentio," n. 23.—Liguori, *op. cit.*, Lib. VI, nn. 1, 13, 14.—Sanchez, *Prontuario de la Theologia Moral.*, trat. i, Punto iv, §§ 2, 5, 6.

impenetrable mental condition of the minister officiating at their nuptials. The theologians, therefore, for the most part, have mercifully discovered that in matrimony the real ministers of the sacrament are the contracting parties themselves and not the priest. It is true that some great authorities, including Melchior Cano, deny this; but the mass of Catholic doctors, represented by the° supreme name of Alphonso Liguori, decide in favor of the sacramental character of the action of the bride and groom, so that the uncertainty which hangs over the administration of all other sacraments need not cast a shadow over the households of the faithful.[40] Yet, after all, this only transfers the doubt from the priest to the contracting parties, for their intention thus becomes necessary to the validity of the sacrament, and this gives rise to a further endless series of questions on which the authorities are by no means agreed. The common opinion is that intention is sufficiently to be inferred if the man expresses consent and the woman holds out her hand to him.[41] This, however, is far from settling the matter, for the consent may have been given under misapprehension or through deceit, rendering the contract a virtually conditional one in which the condition is not fulfilled, and there is thus no real intention. It would be useless to follow the theologians through their interminable debates as to the precise degree of error necessary to invalidate a marriage, or to review the nice distinctions drawn and the conflict of authorities which perplex the matter until the attempt to lay down rules for guidance only renders it more difficult of solution.[42] The practical import of all this was illustrated a few weeks since, in a Philadelphia tribunal, where there was an effort to break a consummated marriage between a Catholic girl and a Jew. Father Dressmann brought his authorities into court and argued that the bride had been deceived as to the religion of the groom and therefore there had been no marriage. "It was not the intention," he said, "of Anna Eichert to be married to a Jew; it was not her intention to be married to the son of the old Steins; the mutual consent on her part was wanting."[43] If his facts were true he

---

[40] Melchior Cano, *De Locis Theolog.*, Lib. VIII, c. v.—Liguori, *op. cit.*, Lib. VI, n. 897.— Sanchez, *loc. cit.*, § 1, n. 2.

[41] Liguori, *loc. cit.*, n. 889.

[42] Liguori, *loc. cit.*, nn. 1012-23.

[43] In this case the learned judge refused to accept the Catholic view and informed the bride: "By the law of God your marriage was not null and void. . . . By the law of the land you are irrevocably bound to him"; and on his instructing her that she was free to go with her husband she joyfully did so.

The case attracted some attention in Catholic circles and, on the Sunday following, Father McDermott made it the subject of a sermon. So far as reported in the daily press he seems not to have followed Father Dressmann in insisting on the question of intention, but to have based his argument on the invalidity of marriage between Catholic and Jew, and on the assertion that the marriage laws of Pennsylvania are not in harmony with the law of God and are not binding on the conscience.

was perfectly correct, according to the doctrines of the theologians; but it would be a misfortune for society if every disillusioned husband and wife were able thus to prove the nullity of an ill-assorted marriage.

Having thus established the necessity of the intention of the ministrant to the validity of the sacraments, the Church must accept the results, even if they lead to its self-extinction. It would be difficult indeed to limit the consequences of the position to which it has been driven in its contests with the heretics. As the doctrine of intention is a matter of faith, it is part of the economy of the universe, and has existed from the time of the Apostles, and not merely since the thirteenth century, when it was discovered. There are, therefore, twelve centuries during which the ignorance of it must have led to innumerable baptisms and ordinations which were invalid and void. Even after its recognition no one cognizant of the weakness of human nature or familiar with the perpetually recurring denunciations of clerical corruption, can doubt that, at least until recent times, the Church has been full of reckless, careless, and perverse priests, whose ministrations have been void through ignorance or indolence, if not through malice or infidelity, and of bishops whose worldliness rendered the performance of their office a mere perfunctory duty. Since the outbreak of the Reformation, moreover, there have been thousands of apostates, who before openly leaving the Church may have desired to harm it as much as possible. The effect of all this has been twofold. As regards the faithful themselves, it would be impossible to compute the millions who have been consigned to the eternal torments of hell, either through failure to enjoy valid baptism, and thus to become Christians, or through failure to obtain valid absolution, on which they have relied for the pardon of their sins. This has not only resulted from lack of due intention on the part of the ministrants of the sacraments, but from the fact that there has been a steadily increasing number of ecclesiastics whose defective ordination has precluded them from administering any valid sacraments save baptism.

This latter is, perhaps, the most serious aspect of the doctrine, as it may vitiate the whole organization of the Church. Of the myriads whose baptism has been invalid great numbers have unquestionably entered the Church, although in reality incapacitated from ordination,[44] and to these are to be added those whose ordination by careless bishops has been defective. Besides this, as though to make it still more perplexing, the necessity of intention has been extended to the recipient of orders, thus rendering void the ordination of anyone who had not at the moment

[44] Lib. III, Extra, Tit. XLII, c. iii.

the proper degree of intention.[45] Any of those thus imperfectly ordained
who have reached the episcopal rank have been incapable of conferring
valid ordination; and those to whom they have administered the sacrament of orders have not been really priests. Such a source of infection
spreads incomputably, for every unbaptized or imperfectly ordained
priest who becomes a bishop becomes also a new center whence the
impalpable and invisible virus extends on all sides. It is, therefore, uncertain to-day whether any priest is really a priest; and it is among the
possibilities that from the pope down there is not one who is actually
in orders and in possession of the supernatural powers which he claims
to exercise. Thus take the venerable Leo XIII. If in the interminable line
of his spiritual ancestry there has been a single one whose ordination
was thus vitiated, Leo is not really in orders, and all his acts are invalid.
Or if this has happened to any former pope, his creations of cardinals
have been void, and subsequent popes have been elected by a hopelessly
unlawful body. No man can tell whether the whole organization of the
Church may not be fatally "irregular," and whether there has been for
centuries a real successor to St. Peter. It is, therefore, a fair subject for
speculation whether by this time the Church has not extinguished itself.

There have not been wanting those who from time to time have called
attention to some of these consequences of the dogma, and the attempts
made to answer them show their arguments to be unanswerable. While
the doctrine was establishing itself, St. Bonaventura, as we have seen,
argued that the faith of the recipient or the mercy of God might perhaps supply the defect, but he adds that, if it does not, God desires us to
be uncertain of our salvation as a reproof to our pride.[46] When it had
become established in the schools its opponents pointed out that no one
could tell whether a priest was really a priest. All that Durand de Saint-
Pourçain can advance in reply to this is to dismiss it as frivolous, because
you cannot expect to have certainty in everything.[47] When Caterino
urged the same argument fruitlessly on the Fathers of Trent, Cardinal
Pallavicino makes a labored effort to refute him by pointing out that
lack of intention is not the only danger which we incur in the sacraments, for a wicked priest can nullify them by omitting necessary words
—thus admitting the danger and multiplying it—and that we must rely
on Providence to guide the hearts of men or avert the evil in some unknown manner; besides, men cannot complain if they fail of salvation,

[45] Ut Ordo sit validus requirit præter materiam et formam intentionem tam ministri quam
suscipientis.—*Summa Diana, s. v.* "Ordinis subjectum"; cf. Corella, *Praxis Confessionalis*
(Laubach, 1713), tract. xii, c. i.

[46] Si tamen non facit juste facit, et nos esse voluit incertos de salute ad deponendam su-
perbiam et excitandam diligentiam.—Bonaventura, *In Quart. Lib. Sententt.,* Dist. 6, q. 1.

[47] Durandus de S.-Portiano, *Comment. super Sententt.,* Lib. IV, Dist. 19, q. ii, § 7.

for they are unworthy of it, and perhaps God may supply what is lacking in the act of the priest—all of which confesses that the only way to escape the consequences of the doctrine is to abandon it.[48] Willem van Est, one of the soundest and sanest theologians of the seventeenth century, satisfies himself with assuring the faithful that they must be content with what he assumes to be moral certainty and not trouble themselves about possibilities.[49] Ferraris meets the argument that it is contrary to the goodness of God that infants or contrite sinners should be damned through the malice of a priest by coolly remarking that they are damned for their sins, original or actual; there is no defect in God's goodness, who has provided the means of salvation, and he is not bound, even if he could, to impede the malice of the minister.[50] All this shows that the Church admits the consequences of the position taken at Trent, but is unable to devise a remedy.

Yet I do not for a moment suppose that Leo XIII entertains the slightest doubt as to the validity of his claim to act as the Vicegerent of Christ, or that the faithful in general allow their equanimity to be disturbed as to the efficacy of the sacraments administered to them, save in the rare cases when a priest abandons the Church and his recent penitents feel it incumbent on them to repeat their confessions and obtain absolution *ad cautelam*. Nevertheless, the subject is not without interest as an illustration of the imbecility of man when he attempts to control the infinite and arrogates to himself a portion of God's power without sharing God's omniscience.

[48] Pallavicini, *Hist. C. Trident.*, IX, vi, 4-6.
[49] Estius, *In Lib.* IV, *Sententt.*, Dist. I, § 24.
[50] Ferraris, *Prompta Bibl.*, *s. v.* "Intentio," n. 30.

HISTORICAL STUDIES

Spanish History

SPANISH EXPERIMENTS IN COINAGE*

[At the end of the nineteenth century two matters of absorbing interest occupied the public mind—the currency issue and the war with Spain. These gave Lea the opportunity of demonstrating his belief that history, while offering no specific answers to contemporary problems, furnishes an indispensable background for an understanding and solution of these problems. The publication of the three volumes of his *History of Auricular Confession and Indulgences* in 1896 had left him free to turn again to the study of the Spanish Inquisition, which had occupied much of his time since the appearance of his *Inquisition of the Middle Ages* in 1888. In the history of Spain he found much that seemed to him useful in solving our own problems. Consequently, he published the three following essays, *Spanish Experiments in Coinage, The Indian Policy of Spain,* and *The Decadence of Spain,* in periodicals which would secure them a wide audience. Shortly thereafter, when the question of the Friars' lands in the Philippines arose, he printed privately, and circulated, his study of *The Dead Hand.*

A brief survey of the history of Spanish coinage will also be found in the *Inquisition of Spain,* I, 560-66 and IV, 482-83.—H.]

*   *   *   *   *

MUCH INSTRUCTIVE research has of late years been devoted to the history and inevitable results of paper inflation. The French assignats, our own Continental money, colonial overissues, and the practically irredeemable currency of the banks of some of the states prior to the Civil War have furnished subjects for elaborate discussion and have yielded their appropriate warnings; but I am not aware that the most remarkable and significant of all attempts to create and sustain fiat money has ever received the attention which is its due. I term it the most remarkable because it was made with coin and not with paper and the vitiated currency was comparatively small in amount, because it was carried on for more than two centuries with true Spanish persistency, and because it permanently and disastrously affected the destinies of a great nation. Many causes contributed to the decadence of Spain, but, after the expulsion of the Jews and Moors, none perhaps did more to destroy its industry and commerce than its vicious currency legislation. The story is a long one, and I can here touch only on its more salient points. If some of the measures adopted should seem incredibly violent, it must be borne in mind that they were the devices, not of rude and unlettered savages, but of the best trained and most experienced statesmen of the land vainly seeking to escape the consequences of the first fatal step in the wrong

* From *Popular Science Monthly,* LI (1897), 577-93.

direction. The lesson taught is the more impressive from the fact that, in the sixteenth century, Spain was by far the richest and most powerful state in Europe, practically owning Italy through her hold on Naples, Milan, Sicily, Sardinia, and Corsica, and mistress of the wealthy provinces of the Netherlands. She, moreover enjoyed the monopoly of commerce with the New World and its stores of precious metals; and this enormous power, military and financial, was wielded by an absolute monarch who combined the legislative and executive functions unhampered and unrestrained. If ever a successful attempt could be made to overcome the self-acting laws which govern trade it could be made by Philip II and his successors.

Like all other mediæval kingdoms, Castile had had ample experience of the evils of an uncertain standard of value. In the latter half of the fifteenth century the feeble Henry IV, among other devices to secure the allegiance of faithless magnates, parted freely with the right to coin money, until there were about 150 private mints scattering their issues throughout the land. The crown itself reduced the standard of gold coin to 7 carats, while the irresponsible private coiners debased it to whatever their cupidity dictated. When Ferdinand and Isabella came to the throne their resolute sagacity speedily put an end to this deplorable condition. In their final legislation the gold standard was fixed at 23¾ carats; that of silver at the one traditional in Spain known as 11 *dineros* and 4 grains, equivalent to 0.925 fine. The marc, or half pound, of gold, containing 4,608 grains, was worked into 65⅓ *excelentes* or ducats, also known as *escudos* or crowns. The marc of silver was worked into 67 *reales* or ryals. The monetary unit was the *maravedí*, of which there were 34 to the ryal and 374 to the crown, there being thus 11 ryals to the crown. For convenience in small transactions there was an alloy known as *vellon*, consisting of 7 grains of silver to the marc of copper, the marc being worked into 192 *blancas*, the blanca being half a maravedí, and the value f the marc of alloy and the cost of coinage being reckoned at 96 maravedís.[1]

In 1537 Charles V reduced the standard of the gold crown to 22 carats

---

[1] It will perhaps facilitate the comprehension of the Spanish coinage to remind the reader that the *peso* or *real de á ocho*, the "piece of eight," containing 8 ryals, is the Spanish dollar, adopted as our monetary unit by act of Congress in 1786. The ryal is thus one eighth of a dollar, or 12½ cents, well known to the older generation, when our silver currency was almost exclusively Spanish or Mexican, as the "ninepence" of New England and Virginia, the "shilling" of New York, and the "elevenpenny bit" shortened to "levy" in Pennsylvania, or to "bit" in the West and Southwest. Our "quarter" was the two-ryal piece or *peseta*, and the "pistareen," which rated at 20 cents, was the similar coin of an inferior currency, which, as we shall see hereafter, was known as "provincial."

The maravedí, as the thirty-fourth part of the silver ryal, was equivalent to nearly three-eighths of a cent.

and its weight to 68 to the marc, diminishing its value to 330 maravedís, which he says brought it to an equality with the best coinage of France and Italy. In 1552, moreover, he reduced the silver alloy in the marc of vellon from 7 to 5½ grains, giving as a reason that there had been a profit in the exportation of the blancas, rendering them scarce at home. Thus far there had been no serious tampering with the currency, but not long after this, in 1566, the necessities of Philip II led him to seek relief in debasing the minor coinage. It is true that he was the richest monarch in the civilized world; that, besides his revenues from his European dominions, the crown claimed twenty per cent of all the precious metals mined in the Indies and ten per cent seigniorage for minting the rest; but the Venetian envoy, Paolo Tiepolo, tells us in 1565 that his expenditure for interest alone was 5,050,000 ducats per annum, which, when capitalized at eight per cent, amounted to 63,000,000 ducats of indebtedness—a sum incredible even to the Italian financiers of the period. He had little scruple as to the means of alleviating the burden. In 1559 he had experimented with methods suggested to him of issuing money falsified with a certain powder combined with quicksilver, which when rubbed over copper gave it the semblance of silver, and was proof, as we are told, against the touchstone and the hammer, but not against fire. One inventor of this promising scheme, named Tiberio della Rocca, lost Philip's favor through a quarrel with the royal confessor; another one, a German named Peter Sternberg, was more fortunate, and secured payments amounting to 2,000 ducats for his discovery; but, although every effort was made to keep the matter secret, the Cortes got wind of it, and their remonstrances forced the abandonment of the scheme.

Compared with this wholesale fraud, an enlargement of the token coinage of base metal might well seem harmless, and it is a striking proof of the dangers attendant on any vitiation of the currency that consequences so deplorable and so lasting should have sprung from a source apparently so trivial. In 1566 Philip ordered the coinage of a new alloy, to be known as *moneda de vellon rica*, with a larger proportion of silver—98 grains to the marc of copper, or about 1/47. The coins were all small: *quartillos*, 80 to the marc, to be current for a quarter of a ryal (about three cents); *quartos*, 170 to the marc, worth four maravedís (about a cent and a half); and *medios quartos*, 340 to the marc, worth two maravedís. At the same time the old blancas, two to the maravedí, were retained, but the silver alloy was reduced to four grains in the marc; and the number to be worked from the marc was increased to 240, augmenting the profit on every marc by a ryal and a quarter. What amount of this new vellon coinage was poured forth from the mint we have no means of ascertaining, but there can be little doubt that it was as great as the rude mechanical facilities of the age were capable of producing, for Philip's necessities were ever growing, what with the construction of the Escurial, the perpetual drain of the Flemish revolt, the maintenance of the religious wars in France, the conquest of Portugal, the crusade which brought the triumph of Lepanto, the collapse of the Armada, and other ceaseless efforts, prompted by zeal for the faith and thirst of aggrandizement. Yet the infiltration of the currency with these little debased coins was a slow process, and its effects were correspondingly deferred, but they manifested themselves at last, and the *calderilla*—as this coinage came to be popularly designated—grew to be a load which the ablest statesmen of Spain for a century vainly endeavored to shake off. Apparently the process of manufacture became too slow to supply the increasing wants of the treasury, for we hear in 1602 of a restamping of the vellon coinage, doubtless to give it an increased fictitious value. At the same time Philip III made a new issue of pure copper, to the amount of 2,448,000 ducats, working 280 maravedís to the marc, the cost of metal and coinage being only 80 maravedís. Prices rose, and there was general discontent, voiced by the learned historian Mariana in a tract on the coinage written with so much vigor that it cost him an imprisonment by the Inquisition. Thus the reservoir became filled to overflowing, and the inevitable depreciation commenced. To arrest it Philip III, in 1619, solemnly decreed that there should be no more vellon money coined for twenty years; but financial promises of this nature are made to be broken, as is witnessed by Philip IV, in 1632, renewing the pledge conditionally for another twenty years. In spite of these promises, the vellon fell to a discount. There was no formal suspension of gold and silver payments; the silver fleet from Mexico and the galleons from Tierra Firma yearly poured into Spain the treasure won from the mines of the New World; but all the power of an autocratic sovereign could not maintain the parity of the currency. The inequality became so firmly established that it had to be recognized, and Philip IV, in 1625, endeavored to regulate it by a decree permitting a difference of ten per cent. Beyond this any transaction entailed on the receiver, for a first offense, the forfeiture of the principal with a fourfold fine, applicable in thirds to the informer, the judge, and the fisc; for a second offense, the same, with the addition of six years' exile. At the same time it was enacted that no one could demand gold or silver who had not given them, and no obligation to pay in gold or silver was lawful unless gold or silver was lent. These provisions show that already the vellon coinage had risen from its function as a token currency in petty dealings, and was rapidly becoming the standard medium of exchange in all com-

mercial transactions. It is as such that we shall have henceforth to consider it, and it is to this that it owes its importance.

The situation was growing insupportable. Commerce and industry
were equally stagnant. No land in Europe had greater resources than
Spain in the fine wools of Castile, Aragon, and La Mancha; the flax
and hemp of Asturias, Catalonia, Galicia, and Leon; the excellent silk
of Murcia and Valencia; the iron, steel, and timber of Navarre, Guipuscoa,
and Biscay; the wines and fruits of Andalusia; but these were all exported as raw materials, and, though the trade of the Indies was a
jealous monopoly, half the goods sent thither in the fleets were the
property of Hollanders, under the names of Spaniards, although Spain
was at war with Holland. Partly this was attributable to the disordered
currency, and the communities throughout the Peninsula supplicated the
crown for relief. There was but one way to obtain this—by retracing
the vicious course of the last half century, and the attempt was heroically
made. By a *pragmática* of August 7, 1628, it was decreed that after the
day of publication all the vellon money should be reduced one half in
value. To diminish the loss to the holders a complicated arrangement
was ordered, by which one half of the depreciation should be made good
to them by their towns and villages, and in view of the sacrifice thus
imposed on the nation the royal faith was solemnly pledged by Philip
IV, for himself and his successors, with all the force of a compact between the crown and the people, that the value of the vellon coinage
should never again be tampered with, either to raise or to depress it.
After this, any transaction disturbing the parity of the various coinages
was declared an offense subject to the severest punishment and to render
the measure effective the sternest penalties were directed against the
introduction into the kingdom of foreign vellon money. The profits on
this had already called forth the most vigorous efforts of repression,
and these were now sharpened by declaring it to be a matter of lèse
majesté, and subjecting it to the pains of heresy—death by fire, confiscation of all property, and disabilities inflicted on descendants to the second
generation. Any vessel bringing it, even without the knowledge of the
master, was forfeited; an unsuccessful attempt to import it was punished
with death, and knowledge of such attempt without denouncing it
incurred the galleys and confiscation. For a while, in fact, the crime
was made justiciable by the Inquisition, which was a tribunal inspiring
far greater popular dread than the ordinary courts. Evidently the law-
making power in Spain had few scruples, and no constitutional limitations in its control over the currency.

Yet with all its power it might as well have attempted to control the
tides or the winds, and the solemn pledges of the throne were not worth

the paper on which they were printed. Richelieu was pressing Spain
hard, and the condition of Spanish finance was becoming more and more
desperate. Recourse was again had to a forced loan under the device of
another inflation of the currency. A royal *cédula* of March 12, 1636,
called in all the restamped vellon; from the day of publication of the
edict no one was to pass it, or spend it, or pay it out, but was to convey
it to the nearest mint, where he would receive its current value; and
whoever, after eighty days, was found in possession of any of it incurred the severe penalties decreed against the holders of unlawful money.
Having thus provided for obtaining possession of all the coinage, the
mints were set to work restamping it with a valuation threefold that
which it had borne: the quarto, thus far current for four maravedís,
was raised to twelve, and the other coins in proportion, while death and
confiscation were threatened for any violation of the coinage laws. The
result of this arbitrary creation of value is seen in the edict of April 30
of the same year, permitting a premium on gold and silver of twenty-
five per cent until the arrival of the galleons, after which it was to be
reduced to twenty; and that this was below the ruling market rate is
assumable from a sharpening of the penalties provided for those who
should demand or accept a higher premium. Six months later an effort
was made to bring the precious metals to par by suspending the permission to exchange them at a premium, but the distress caused by this
suspension was so severe that a decree of March 20, 1637, renewed the
recognition of twenty-five per cent premium, and added that in the larger
cities *casas de diputación*, or exchanges, could be established, where
transactions could be negotiated at twenty-eight per cent, with a broker-
age of one quarter or one half. The extreme importance attached to
regulating the premium is visible in the punitive clauses of the edict. Any
deviation from the established rate was classed with treason, irrevocably
punishable with confiscation, disability for office, and personal infamy.
In prosecutions all reasonable means of defense were withdrawn from
the accused; the names of witnesses were kept secret, and judicial forms
were not to be observed. Even ambassadorial immunity was set aside;
the foreign ministers resident in Madrid were liable to accusation, when
the king would determine as to their imprisonment and punishment.

This was speedily followed by a reaction. Of course, there were two
parties in Spain, as elsewhere—inflationists and contractionists—and the
policy of the state fluctuated as one or the other obtained preponderance
with the king, or rather with his all-powerful minister, the Count-Duke
Olivares. The contractionists now had control, and their views were expressed in a *pragmática* of January 29, 1638, which lamented the misfortunes brought upon the land by the superabundance of vellon money

which had injured commerce, had raised extravagantly the prices of the necessaries of life, and had driven silver out of circulation, depriving it of its natural function as money and converting it into a commodity to be bought and sold, while the only currency was the debased coinage, fabricated for the most part by the enemies of Spain, eager to gain the enormous profits accruing from its manufacture. As this, if unchecked, may work the ruin of the kingdom, the king declares that he has had the matter repeatedly discussed by his ministers, and as the result he orders that all the unstamped vellon money shall be melted down into bullion and be sold for silver, the proceeds being used to purchase more of the precious metal. It is expected that the vacuum thus created will bring silver into circulation, and to aid in this all the bullion brought by the galleons shall be coined; moreover, the savage edict of 1628 against the introduction of vellon is repeated; even the importation of copper is prohibited, and the laws forbidding the export of the precious metals are ordered to be enforced with the utmost rigor.

Had this policy been steadily pursued, perhaps it would in time have restored health to the currency, but it was neutralized by the financial exigencies of the state, which kept the mints busy in turning out debased coinage. It was impossible under the circumstances for the contractionists to win more than a temporary ascendency, and with the progressive dilution of the currency the premium on the precious metals obstinately kept advancing, in spite of the laws which punished such traffic as a crime. A decree of January 21, 1640, declares that this has become more inexcusable in view of the large amount of silver brought by the galleons in 1639 and the activity of the mints in coining vellon. To render its chastisement more certain, the rate of twenty-eight per cent is permitted in open market, but only for four months, after which it will be lowered; special judges are provided whose sole business shall be to try infractions of this law; every case that is heard of shall be prosecuted, and negligent judges shall be severely punished. The laws forbidding the export of the precious metals shall be still more vigorously enforced, especially those which require merchants bringing foreign goods into the country to take away an equivalent amount in merchandise.

The revolt of Portugal and Catalonia brought fresh financial complications, and recourse was again had to the ruinous expedient of a further debasement of the currency. A *cédula* of February 11, 1641, orders all the four-maravedí vellon pieces to be surrendered to the mints, where they will be paid for at their current value; this is to be done within thirty days, after which they can not be paid out or otherwise used. They are then to be restamped and issued at the valuation of eight maravedís; all other restamped vellon is to be surrendered by May 15, after which it is to be no longer current, and disobedience of these orders is visited with death and confiscation. The natural result of this measure is seen in a decree of September 5 of the same year, limiting the premium on specie to fifty per cent until the arrival of the silver fleets. That this was below the market rate is shown in the prohibition of all indirect ways of evasion and of dealing in futures. How this condition affected all transactions, large and small, and how business was conducted under the double stand-ard, are illustrated in some statements now before me of the expenses of the Supreme Council of the Inquisition about this time. After sum-ming up the aggregate of the salaries and other items, in one case twenty-eight per cent and in another fifty per cent is added to show the total amount to be provided in vellon. When governmental outlays were thus increased we cannot wonder at the struggle to keep down the premium on the one hand while stimulating it on the other by constant dilutions of the currency. The situation affords a singularly forcible illus-tration of the power possessed by an inferior money to force a superior one out of circulation. The largest of the debased coinage was only a piece of a quarter of a ryal, equivalent in our modern American system to three cents, yet it had completely demonetized silver and gold, and had become the practical standard of value. The Spanish possessions were the chief source from which the civilized world obtained its supply of the precious metals, yet Spain, in spite of the most arbitrary measures, could retain none of them within her borders. So scarce had they be-come that for twenty years, from 1623 to 1642, there had been repeated decrees forbidding the use of gold and silver in the arts—their melting and fashioning by artisans, even their employment for plating and gilding and in embroidery. In 1642 these laws were supplemented by others prohibiting the sale of silver plate except to be broken up for coinage, and owners were tempted to bring it to the mints with the promise of a bonus of five per cent in vellon, in addition to the coin that it would yield. At the same time the laws against exportation were rendered still more rigorous, suspending even licenses to carry silver away for the royal service in Flanders and Italy.

The contractionist policy was now granted another trial, and a com-prehensive scheme was evolved to get rid of the intolerable burden and bring all the various kinds of coinage to a parity. The partial attempt of 1628 had proved a failure; but if all the base money in the land could be controlled, there was reasonable prospect that another effort might be successful. To accomplish this a *pragmática* was signed August 31, 1642, and sent under seal to the local authorities everywhere with instructions to open it on September 15. At the same hour throughout Spain they were to go to the shops of all bankers, brokers, agents, traders, etc., seize whatever vellon money they should find, weigh it, register it, and convey it to a secure place, where it was to be kept under three pad-locks, the keys being held by as many officials. When this was done they were to proclaim that the value of all vellon money was reduced to one sixth: the piece that had been circulating for twelve maravedís was in future to be worth but two, and so forth. All discount or premium between the metals was prohibited for the future, under the customary severe penalties, and it was hoped that the general benefit thus derived by the community at large would compensate for the losses inflicted on individuals, but to lessen these there were vague promises held out of satisfaction to be adjusted by the registry of the amount of vellon seized; and it was suggested that the king would consider any propositions made by those who should prefer honors or privileges or some other ad-vantages in lieu of satisfaction.

Apparently it was soon found that something more was needed to bring the refractory metals closer together, and a *cédula* of December 23 endeavored to accomplish this by diluting the silver coinage. The marc of silver, in place of furnishing sixty-seven ryals, was ordered to be worked into eighty-three and one quartillo, thus diminishing the value of the ryal by twenty-five per cent; and in accordance with this, the existing *pesos*, or pieces of eight, were declared to be worth ten ryals, the profit on those in private hands being generously left to the holders. Gold was more simply treated by marking up the crown from 440 to 550 maravedís, and by a subsequent decree of January 12, 1643, to 612. The effect of this on the specie premium was, however, neutralized by dimin-ishing from 98 grains to 75.3, the amount of silver to the marc of copper in the *moneda de vellon rica*, and holders of the white metal were tempted to have it thus employed by offering to coin it for them in vellon without charge of seigniorage.

Taken as a whole, these decrees formed but a halting measure of con-traction; but, even as it was, it brought a strain too sudden and severe to be endured, and the effort was soon abandoned. A *pragmática* of March 12, 1643, announced that the vellon coinage (except some recent issue by the mint of Segovia) should in future be current at a fourfold increase of value, the piece of two maravedís being raised to eight and the rest in proportion. The dilution of the silver coinage was similarly revoked, or at least suspended until the arrival of the fleet; the pieces of eight were to be current for eight ryals and no more, while the gold crown was reduced to 510 maravedís. As usual, the royal word and faith were pledged that there should be no further variation in the value of the vellon coinage, and that it should remain forever on the basis then assigned to it. Of course, the premium on the precious metals reappeared, and efforts to repress it by law were vain. It had to be recognized, and in 1647 a decree permitted it to the extent of twenty-five per cent, with stern punishment for those who should exceed the limit.

There could be no prosperous trade subject to such fluctuations in the standard of value, and the royal revenues must have suffered accordingly, for the next change was distinctly a method of raising money. The old calderilla coinage of Philip II had remained thus far undisturbed, and now by a *cédula* of November 11, 1651, all the rest of the base coin was restored to the value which it had borne prior to the reduction of 1642. The profit of this increase was reserved to the crown by requiring all holders of vellon to bring it to the mints within thirty days, after which it was demonetized and could no longer be used as currency. They were to receive its present value in the restamped issue at the new rate, and anyone hoarding or passing the old money after the expiration of the limit incurred death and confiscation. The premium on specie, in spite of the law of 1647, had already reached fifty per cent, and the sternest penalties were decreed to prevent its rising above that figure—for a first offense, confiscation and six years of *presidio* (service in the African forts) for nobles, confiscation and six years of galleys for plebeians; for a second offense, death without distinction of rank. If absolute power could regulate values, Spanish thoroughness would have accomplished it.

Kings may propose, but in matters like this it is the people that dispose. The natural result of this measure was to drive not only the precious metals but even the calderilla out of circulation. It required only six months to demonstrate the error committed, and a heroic effort to bring some sort of order into the medium of exchange was made in a *pragmática* of June 25, 1652. Under this the old calderilla remained unchanged, but the *vellon grueso*, or large coinage, which had been advanced in value six months before, was reduced to one fourth, at which it was to be current until the end of the year, and on January 1, 1653, it was to be demonetized and its use prohibited under the severe penalties for passing false money. The plan of seizing it all and sequestrating it at a given hour throughout Spain was adopted, but the crown proposed to assume the loss, not only on about seven millions of the restamped coin in the treasury, but by giving to those who surrendered it assignations on the tobacco tax, bearing five per cent interest. All arrears of taxes were also receivable in it for two months, and various other methods were offered of relieving the community. All the *vellon grueso* thus received was to be melted down, and to make a market for the copper the laws prohibiting its importation, even in the shape of manufactured articles, were to be strictly enforced. It was argued that when this, which through its superabundance had caused so much trouble, was out of the way, there would remain only the calderilla, which would all be needed for petty traffic, so that for larger transactions the precious metals would come forth and circulate abundantly at par, compensating the nation for the losses and sacrifices entailed by the measure.

This was a bold attempt in the right direction, but it was too sudden and too severe to be successful. It must have caused abundant ruin and distress, and the clamor for relief must have become irresistible, for in less than five months another edict was issued (November 14), announcing a complete reversal of the means proposed for attaining the end in view. This time the *vellon grueso* was retained as money and the calderilla was proscribed and demonetized on the spot. Those who should register what they held within fifteen days and surrender it within two months were promised the same satisfaction as that offered in the previous decree to the holders of vellon, and any one in whose hands it should be found after sixty days was liable to the penalties for circulating forbidden money. This reduction in the base currency, together with the large amount of the precious metals in the country and the yearly accessions by the fleet, it was argued, deprived any difference in value of all excuse. As this measure was the ultimate remedy whereby to obtain absolute parity between them, any deviation from such equality was declared a species of treason. Any premium or discount, however small, exposed all participating in it, whether as principals or brokers, to confiscation and deprivation of office and of citizenship. A special court was established for the prosecution of such cases, in which the trial was to be secret and the names of the witnesses withheld from the accused. Judges everywhere were ordered to see that prices were reduced by one third, and all outstanding debts and obligations were required to be settled at the same reduction.

This fresh disturbance of all business relations was as fruitless as its predecessors. The calderilla thus called in was not melted down but was restamped, and by a decree of October 22, 1654, was received at its old valuation. Large amounts had apparently been retained by the people in spite of the threatened penalties, and this they were told would be receivable for dues to the fisc at one half its nominal value, or might be taken to the mints and be exchanged for half the amount in the restamped coin. Forty days were allowed for this, after which its possession involved confiscation and six years of *presidio*, or galleys.

After this there was a pause in legislation until September 24, 1658, when an attempt was made to unify the minor coinage by withdrawing the vellon grueso and substituting a new copper issue of the same weight and nominal value as the calderilla, so that there should be but one kind of currency. To check the temptation to import imitations of this, the same savage penalties as before were reënacted—confiscation and the stake, with the forfeiture of any vessel bringing it. The vellon grueso, however, refused to be withdrawn, and on May 6, 1659, a compromise was attempted by reducing it in value one half. Moderate as was this contraction of the currency, it served merely as a prelude for further inflation. Although the Peace of the Pyrenees, in 1659, might be expected to lighten the financial necessities of the state, a *pragmática* of September 11, 1660, under pretext of providing a currency lighter, easier of transport, and more convenient for use, ordered all the vellon grueso to be called in and reworked, so that the marc of copper in place of producing 34 pieces of 2 maravedís should furnish 51 pieces of 4, thus trebling its nominal value. This must have called forth energetic expressions of dissatisfaction, for in less than two months—on October 29—a new project was announced. The coinage of pure copper was stopped, and in its place a new alloy was ordered containing 20 grains of silver to the marc (1/230), to be worked into 51 pieces of 16 maravedís, and smaller coins in proportion. The existing calderilla and vellon grueso were allowed to remain in circulation, to be gradually worked over into the new coinage as they should reach the treasury. The new issue was styled *moneda de molino de vellon ligado*—mill money alloyed—shortened into *moneda de molino*,[2] and added to the confusion by furnishing a third debased coinage, for of course the two older ones remained in circulation. The country speedily was flooded with the new currency, and prices began to rise still higher. Some relief was necessary, and, as usual, it was applied in a violent and summary manner. A *pragmática* of 1664 reduced the value of the new moneda de molino by one half—the 16-maravedí piece was to pass for only 8; for thirty days it would be received at the old rate by the treasury in settlement of overdue debts and taxes up to the end of 1662; after thirty days it would be accepted only at fifty per cent of its face, and the Royal Council was vaguely ordered to adopt such measures as it should deem wise to prevent injustice between buyers and sellers, debtors and creditors. As there ought to be only one base-metal currency, moreover, the edict prohibited the further use of the calderilla and vellon grueso—those coinages which had undergone so many vicissitudes, and which, in spite of prohibitions, persistently continued in circulation. They were a shirt of Nessus, clinging to the victim and impossible to discard.

Again the load became too onerous to be endured, and relief was im-

---

[2] It seems to have been not long before this that the mill or machine for stamping was introduced, enabling coins to have a raised and milled edge, to check clipping. In the Indies the primitive *labor de martillo,* or hammering process, was maintained until 1728, when mills were ordered to be erected. Where practicable, these were run with water power; when this was not available, by mules.

perative. The mints were pouring forth the molino money; there were quantities of it in circulation of pure copper illegitimately issued, and the land was filled with imitations brought from abroad. To remedy this, a decree of February 10, 1680, orders the simultaneous registration and sequestration of the whole, carefully distinguishing the three varieties. The first, or legitimate alloyed coin, was reduced to one fourth of its existing value—that is, the piece which had been originally issued for 16 maravedís, and had in 1664 been cut down to 8, was now still further diminished to 2; the same was done with the native counterfeits, while the foreign ones were accepted at one eighth of their current value. To soften the blow to the holders the legitimate molino was redeemable at the treasury in gold or silver at fifty per cent premium, and was receivable for sixty days for all overdue debts to the fisc up to the end of 1677, while, as a further act of grace, arrearages due up to the end of 1673, amounting to over 12,000,000 ducats, were forgiven.

This measure appears to have been designed as a preliminary to the total extinction of the molino money, for it was followed, May 23, by an elaborate *pragmática* demonetizing this wholly and forbidding its use, only twenty-four hours being allowed during which it could be spent for the purchase of bread, meat, and wine, and for nothing else. In all these efforts at contraction it was expected that the inflated prices, which were a standing grievance, would collapse with the diminution in the circulating medium, and when this result did not follow with sufficient rapidity, there was no hesitation in fixing a scale of *máxima*, for the transgression of which heavy penalties were threatened. Thus on the present occasion a most elaborate edict was issued, November 27, 1680, consisting of over a hundred folio pages, regulating all dealings. All rents in Madrid are to be reduced to what they had been in 1670, and for buildings of later construction or enlargement the rates are to be determined by the magistrates. Then follows a most extensive list of maximum prices, embracing nearly three thousand items, from raw materials by wholesale to finished products by retail, from wool by the *arroba* to rhubarb by the drachm, and including what a tailor should receive for making a coat and a washerwoman for washing a shirt. Such supervision by the state becomes endless, and a supplementary edict was requisite, May 2, 1681, supplying omissions and making changes. If currency and values were capable of governmental regulation, it would have been accomplished by Spain.

All this time the prohibited calderilla and vellon grueso were in circulation, the latter running 74 maravedís to the marc, or about 56 cents of our money to the pound, while copper was worth about 29. The legalized premium on gold and silver was still fifty per cent. Even copper was now becoming scarce under the ceaseless labor of the mints. A proclamation of May 14, 1683, sets forth that it is for the common benefit to have abundance of copper money; and, in order that all the metal in the kingdom may be thus utilized, all pieces of copper brought to the mints will be paid for at the rate of 3½ ryals of vellon for the pound. To prevent its being wasted by consumption in the arts, all coppersmiths are forbidden to manufacture articles of it, or to repair old ones that may be brought to them to be mended. Their shops are to be visited, and their stocks of metal seized and paid for at the above price; inventories of their finished work are to be drawn up, and sixty days allowed for the sale of the articles. Anything concealed is declared to be forfeited, and severe penalties of fine, confiscation, and exile are decreed for evasions or infractions of the order. A false financial system had brought Spain to such a pass that, with the wealth of the Indies pouring into her lap, gold and silver had been driven from circulation, and she was ransacking the shops for scraps of copper to keep her mints busy.

These resources proved insufficient to supply the ever-growing demands of a depreciated currency, and resort was had to remonetizing the molino alloyed coinage which had been prohibited in 1680. By an edict of October 9, 1684, it was restored to circulation at a valuation double that which it had borne prior to its demonetization, which would seem to render superfluous an accompanying threat of penalties for its exportation, the same as for gold and silver.

Having thus apparently exhausted the possibilities of copper inflation, attention was turned to gold and silver which had hitherto been but little tampered with. A *pragmática* of October 14, 1686, ordered a reduction of weight of twenty-five per cent in the silver ryal by working 84 to the marc in place of 67. The existing pesos or pieces of eight were rechristened crowns, and were ordered to pass for ten ryals, and the smaller coins in proportion. This was purely an inflation measure without any view of reducing the discount on vellon, for the fifty per cent premium was ordered to be applicable to the new light-weight silver coins, of which the piece of eight was declared equivalent to twelve ryals vellon, and the old one, now called a crown, to fifteen. No change was made in the weight of the gold coinage, but the value was raised to correspond, the single doubloon, or gold crown, being declared worth nineteen silver ryals in place of fifteen, and a month later it was further raised to twenty. In this reduction of the standard the interests of the debtor class were tenderly guarded by decreeing that outstanding obligations in gold or silver could be settled on the new basis. Some concession, however, was made on this point where suits arose as to specie lying on deposit or bills of exchange drawn in silver or gold prior to depreciation, for these were ordered to be paid at the old standard.

The War of Succession, which broke out in 1701, naturally brought large quantities of French silver into Spain. The *quart d'écu* was held for a time to be equivalent to the two-ryal piece, and came to be known as the *peseta* or little peso, but it was pronounced to be inferior in value, and in 1709 its further introduction was prohibited. At the same time the silver standard was reduced to 11 dineros or .91667 fine in place of the .925 at which it had stood for centuries. This did not arrest the progressive depreciation of the vellon currency, which in 1718 we find legally recognized in the equivalence of a silver ryal to nearly two ryals vellon, and not long afterward the regular exchange was as one to two. This was allowed by law, and it doubtless was frequently exceeded, for dealers kept the copper coin in bags representing fixed amounts, and those who preferred gold or silver were charged extra for it. This would have worked comparatively little evil if the inferior currency had been confined to the petty traffic for which it was originally designed, but for more than a century it had become the standard of value and the precious metals had been rendered merely a commodity. Thus in the regulations of the mints the salaries are all defined in reales de vellon or escudos de vellon, and the treasurer has to give security in 20,000 *ducados* de vellon on unincumbered real estate. It was always necessary, when mentioning a sum, to specify whether it was in reales de vellon or reales *de plata*, and with the complexities which crept into the silver coinage we even sometimes find a further definition required, as in such expressions as *"un real de plata provincial, valor de 16 quartos de vellon."* The evils entailed by the system were freely admitted, but the country had been plunged so long into this financial debauchery that recovery seemed impossible. In 1718 Philip V acknowledged the grave injuries which it inflicted on trade and commerce, but the remedy which he proposed was futile. In 1743 he again deplored the manner in which greed and malice had used the increase of copper money to drive silver from circulation and reduce it to the condition of merchandise. To remedy this he ordered that payments in vellon should not exceed 300 ryals, and he forbade any charge for exchanging the metals under the same penalties enjoined by the law of November 14, 1652—confiscation and loss of citizenship. It was in vain; the distinction between the coinages was too firmly established, and the tendency was even to increase the premium on the precious metals. In 1772 Charles III, in issuing a new gold coinage, prescribes that the gold crown shall be worth 37½ vellon ryals, and as it was equal only to 16 silver ryals, this shows a premium of over one hundred per cent.

The question of the premium on silver was further complicated by tampering with the silver coinage. In 1726 it was ordered that the peso should be counted for 9.5 ryals; the small silver coins of two ryals and less were worked 77 ryals to the marc, in place of the old weight of 67, and only 10 dineros fine in place of 11, thus lowering them to twenty per cent below the standard; and in 1728 the fineness was further reduced to 9 dineros (22 grains), or 0.798, increasing the deficiency to twenty-five per cent. The mintage of the Indies, principally in the larger pieces, was not reduced, and thus there came to be two kinds of silver coinage, known as the *nacional* or heavier, and the *provincial* or lighter. Between these there was a recognized difference of twenty per cent, the *real de plata nacional* being worth 2.5 vellon ryals, or 20 quartos, while the *real de plata provincial* was only worth 2 vellon ryals, or 16 quartos. There were thus three established currencies of different values, two of silver and one of copper, and for awhile there was a fourth, for we hear, in 1728, of a new coinage popularly known as *Marias*, which is ordered to be demonetized by July 1 next ensuing. The order, as usual was disregarded, for in 1736 it was repeated, with a prohibition to draw bills of exchange in the forbidden currency.

The depreciation of the ryal has survived, to modern times, the revolution in the currency, which has become decimal, and is modeled on that of France. The peseta is the equivalent of the franc, worth approximately twenty cents in our money, and when ryals are quoted they are a fourth of the peseta, or five cents, thus being only two fifths of their nominal value in silver. Whether the vellon ryal has ceased to be the standard money of account I can not say, but I happen to have before me a draft drawn through the Bank of Spain, December 17, 1858, in Madrid on Jaen for *"la suma de tres mil reales de vellon en plata ú oro,"* showing that accounts were still kept in vellon and that every transaction involved a conversion of this into specie.[3]

There can be no exaggeration in attributing to these perpetual fluctuations in the standard of value a leading part in the industrial and commercial decadence of Spain. During the period we have traversed, Spain was the chief source through which Europe derived the precious metals, yet it could never retain them, in spite of savage laws prohibiting their export; its people were forced to content themselves with a debased coinage, and at times it could scarce procure enough copper to supply

[3] For further details on the coinage of the fifteenth century, see. Saez, *Demostración del Valor de las Monedas que corrian durante el Reinado de Don Enrique IV*, Madrid, 1805; for laws and decrees of later periods, see *Nueva Recopilación de las Leyes de España*, Lib. v, Tit. xxi; *Autos Acordados*, Lib. v, Tit. xxii, *Novíssima Recopilación*, Lib. ix, Tit. xvii.

even this. Commercial and industrial enterprise was impossible when no one could know from day to day what was to be the value of the money which was due to him, or in which he was to meet his obligations, and consequently the magnificent resources of the land remained undeveloped, while the rest of western Europe was entering on the modern era of industrialism. Once embarked on such a vicious course, return to a permanent standard was too painful a process to be endured, and the efforts made toward it from time to time only aggravated the trouble by increasing the uncertainty, for the distress which they caused was too acute for even Spanish endurance. Thus it dragged on from century to century, while the wealth of the Indies enriched the nations whose commercial instincts taught them the essential necessity of an unvarying standard of value. This was no new discovery, for the long-enduring prosperity of Florentine manufactures and commerce was largely attributable to the jealous care with which the republic preserved the purity and weight of its coinage, so that the florin became a recognized standard throughout Europe, the honesty of which no one ever questioned. Florence had learned the lesson from the Byzantine Empire, whose historian, Mr. Finlay, asserts that its prolonged duration was greatly owing to the wisdom which preserved its coinage unaltered for eight centuries, so that "the concave gold byzants of Isaac II (1185-1203) are precisely the same weight and value as the solidus of Constantine the Great." With the Latin conquest in 1204, barbaric recklessness was introduced from the West, and successive debasements of the coinage accompanied the decay and extinction of the empire of the Cæsars. Spain affords an exceedingly instructive example of the opposite, inasmuch as its trouble arose from a token currency of small denominations which was incautiously allowed to expand until it dominated the whole financial system, to the exclusion of the precious metals.

THE DECADENCE OF SPAIN*

[This subject is discussed by Mr. Lea, from a somewhat different point of view, in the concluding chapter of his *Inquisition of Spain*, Bk. IX, c. 11 (IV, 472-534).—H.]

* * * * *

WHEN Charles V was obliged to renounce the dream of a universal monarchy, and to abandon the Holy Roman Empire to his brother Ferdinand, he was still able to make over to his son Philip II territories which rendered Spain the preponderating power in the civilized world. Besides his ancestral dominions in the Peninsula, to which, in 1580, he added Portugal, Philip was master of the wealthy Netherlands, of Milan and Naples, of the Mediterranean islands, and of the New World. His revenues far exceeded those of any other monarch, his armies were admitted to be the most formidable in Europe, and his command of the sea was disputed only by the Turk, whose navy he crushed at Lepanto, until the disasters of the Armada gave warning that the old methods of maritime warfare were becoming obsolete. In every way the supremacy of Spain was the dread of the nations, and its destruction was the cherished object of statesmen for a century. It was not by their efforts, however, that the result was accomplished. Olivares, it is true, was overmatched by Richelieu, but Spain had a vantage ground enabling her to hold her own against external assault. The causes of her decadence were internal; they were numerous, but may be roughly defined as springing from pride, conservatism, and clericalism.

There is a pride which spurs nations on to great achievements, which reckons nothing done while aught remains to do, and which wisely adapts means to ends. Such was not the pride of Spain: it was proud of what it had done, and imagined that its superiority to the rest of the world left it nothing more to do; it could learn nothing and forget nothing; it had varied the centuries of the Reconquest with endless civil broils, while it left the arts of peace to subject Moors and Jews, until honest labor was regarded with disdain, and trade and commerce were treated in a barbarous fashion that choked all the springs of national prosperity. Derived from this blind and impenetrable pride was the spirit of conservatism which rejected all innovation in a world of incessant change, a world which had been sent by the Reformation spinning on a new track, a world in which modern industrialism was rapidly superseding the obsolescent militarism of Spain. The phrase current throughout Europe in the last century was not without foundation, that Africa

* From *The Atlantic Monthly*, LXXXII (1898), 119-55.

220

began at the Pyrenees. Last, but by no means least, was the clericalism which developed in Spain the ferocious spirit of intolerance; which in 1492 drove out the unhappy Jews, and in 1610 the Moriscos, thus striking at the root of the commercial prosperity and industry of the land; and which surrendered the nation to the Inquisition, paralyzing all intellectual movement, crippling trade, and keeping the people so completely in leading strings that the three generations since the Napoleonic upheaval have not sufficed for their training in the arts of self-government.

Yet the Spaniard has qualities which, if not thus counterbalanced, ought to have assured him a maintenance of the commanding position which he held in the sixteenth century. His intellect is strong and quick, his imagination is vivid, and, before the censorship of the Inquisition had curbed its expression, his literature' was the most promising in Europe. When fully aroused his perseverance is indefatigable. His courage is undoubted—not a merely evanescent valor, flaming up on occasion at the promise of success, but a persistent, obstinate, dogged quality, to be dreaded as much in defeat as in victory, and sustained by the pride of race which leads him to think all other races his inferiors. The unyielding steadfastness of the Spanish *tercios* on the disastrous field of Rocroy was paralleled in the defense of Saragossa. The exploits of the Conquistadores in the New World display a tenacity of daring amid unknown dangers which has rarely been equaled, and perhaps never surpassed. The practical efficiency of this determined valor is heightened, moreover, by a remarkable, callous indifference as to the means to be employed in accomplishing a given purpose. Spanish legislation is full of the sternest laws, enacted in utter disregard of their contingent and ulterior consequences provided the immediate object in view can be effected. Alva's reign of blood in the Netherlands is typical of this fierce and cold-blooded determination to achieve a result at whatever cost of life and suffering, and the reconcentrado policy of Weyler is only a modern exhibition of this inherited characteristic.

Effective as this disregard of consequences may often have proved, it was one of the elements which contributed to the decadence of Spain; for when directed, as it often was, without foresight or judgment, it wrought havoc with interests of greater moment than those it served. The expulsions of the Jews and of the Moriscos are conspicuous instances of this and, in a minor degree, the industries and commerce of the nation were perpetually wrecked by regulations, absurdly exaggerated, to serve some purpose that chanced at the moment to be uppermost in the minds of the rulers. When, to remedy the scarcity of the precious metals, repeated edicts, from 1623 to 1642, prohibited all manufactures of gold and silver, even to embroideries and gilding or plating, a flourishing branch of trade was destroyed for a time; and another was prostrated in 1683, when, to procure copper for the debased coinage of the mints, all of that metal in the hands of coppersmiths was practically sequestrated, and they were forbidden even to repair old utensils. Internal industry and external commerce were thus at the mercy of an infinity of fluctuating regulations which embarrassed transactions, and deprived manufacturers and merchants of all sense of security and all ability to forecast the future. During the period when the commerce of the world was developing into vast proportions, that commerce, with its resultant wealth and the power of offense and defense derived from wealth, fell into the hands of Spain's especial enemies, England and Holland. The Spaniard, who despised industry and commerce, thrust from him the inheritance of Venice and Florence, which the discovery of the New World and the Cape route to India had offered to him: and while his rivals waxed mightily, he grew poorer and poorer, in spite of the wealth of the Indies poured into his lap.

Labor, in fact, to Spanish pride, was the badge of inferiority, to be escaped in every possible way. It is the general complaint of the publicists of the seventeenth century that every one sought to gain a livelihood in the public service or in the Church, and no one to earn it by honest work. The immense number of useless consumers thus supported was constantly alleged as one of the leading causes of the general poverty, from which the most crushing and injudicious taxation could raise only insufficient revenues. Public offices were multiplied recklessly, and the steady increase in the ranks of the clergy, regular and secular, was a constant subject of remonstrance. In 1626, Navarette tells us that there were thirty-two universities and more than four thousand grammar schools crowded with sons of artisans and peasants striving to fit themselves for public office or holy orders; most of them failed in this through inaptitude, and drifted into the swarms of tramps and beggars who were a standing curse to the community, while the fields lay untilled for lack of labor, and the industrial arts were slowly perishing, so that Spain was forced to import the finished products which she could so easily have made for herself.[1] This national aversion to labor, moreover, manifested itself in an indolence which, except in Catalonia, rendered the pretense of working almost illusory. Dormer tells us of his compatriots that they did not work as in other lands; a few hours a day, and this intermittently, were expected to provide for them as much as

---

[1] [Navarette, *Discorsos Políticos* (Madrid, 1626), p. 299.—H.]

the incessant activity of the foreigner.[2] To these drawbacks on productive industry is to be added the multitude of feast days, which Navarette estimates at about one third of the working days, rising to one half at the critical season of the harvests[3]—feast days which, according to Archbishop Carranza, were spent in a debauchery rendering them especially welcome to the devil.[4] Under such conditions it was impossible for Spain to withstand the competition of the foreigner. How rapidly its industry declined is shown by the fact that in 1644 the shipments by the fleet to the West Indies from four cities of Castile—Toledo, Segovia, Ampudia, and Pastrana—amounted to $3,864,750, while in 1684 the total value of all Spanish goods carried by the fleet was only $800,000. It is true that in 1691 Carlos II proposed legislation to check the overgrown numbers of the clergy and the immoderate absorption of lands by the Church, but his feeble projects were abandoned.

Thus the nation possessed little recuperative power to make good the perpetual losses of its almost continuous foreign wars. Already, in the apogee of its greatness under Charles V, symptoms of exhaustion were not lacking. His election to the Empire, in 1520, was an unmitigated misfortune for Spain. Involved thenceforth in the entanglements of his Continental policy, the land was drained of its blood and treasure for quarrels in which it had no concern, and of which it bore the brunt without sharing the advantages. So heavy was the load of indebtedness incurred that, on his accession, Philip II seriously counseled with his ministers as to the advisability of repudiation. Under the latter monarch downward progress was accelerated. Imagining himself to be specially called of Heaven to uphold the threatened Catholic faith, he regarded no sacrifices as too great when heresy was to be repressed. For this he provoked the Low Countries to revolt, leading to a war of forty years, with uncounted expenditure of men and money. For this he incurred the crowning disaster of the Armada, and for this he stimulated and supported the wars of the League of France. Despite the unrivaled resources of the monarchy his finances were reduced to hopeless confusion; he was a constant borrower on usurious terms, and already in 1565 the Venetian envoy reported his annual interest payments at 5,050,000 ducats, which at eight per cent represented an indebtedness of 63,000,000 ducats—a sum, at that period, almost incredible. When the reins slipped from his grasp, in 1598, his successor was the feeble and bigoted Philip III, and the seventeenth century witnessed the fortunes of Spain

[2] [Dormer, *Discursos históricos políticos* (1684), Disc. i (cited by Colmeiro, *Cortes de Leon y de Castilla*, ii, 223).—H.]

[3] [Navarette, *op. cit.*, p. 79.—H.]

[4] [Carranza, *Comentarios sobre el Catechismo* (1558), fols. 209, 210.—H.]

in the hands of a succession of court favorites—Lerma, Olivares, Haro, Nithard, Oropesa, and their tribe—mostly worthless and grossly incompetent. Financial distress grew more and more acute, aggravated by senseless tampering with the currency, which drove to other lands the precious metals of the New World, until the whole active circulation of the country consisted of a token copper coinage, the value of which the government endeavored to regulate by a succession of edicts of the most contradictory character, producing inextricable perplexity and uncertainty, fatally crippling what productive industry had survived the temper of the people and the unwisdom of legislation.

Clericalism contributed its full share to this downward progress. The intensity of the Spanish character, which can do nothing by halves, lent an enormous power for evil to the exaggerated religious ardor of the people. In the earlier Middle Ages no other European nation had been so tolerant as Spain in its dealings with the Jew and the infidel, but, under the careful stimulation of the Church, this tolerant spirit had passed away with the fourteenth century, and in its place there had gradually arisen a fierce and implacable hatred of all faiths outside of Catholicism. This fanaticism gave to the priesthood preponderating power, which it utilized for its own behoof, in disregard of the public welfare, and all doubtful questions were apt to be decided in favor of the faith. The royal confessor was *ex officio* a member of the Council of State, and under a weak monarch his influence was almost unbounded. Fray Gaspar de Toledo, the confessor of Philip II, boasted that when he ordered his royal penitent to do or to leave undone anything, under penalty of mortal sin, he was obeyed; and the fate of a kingdom thus virtually subjected to the caprices of a narrow-minded friar can readily be divined. The royal confessorship was frequently a steppingstone to the supreme office of inquisitor-general, which controlled the conscience of the nation; and as under such a régime the delimitation between spiritual and temporal affairs was most uncertain, the wrangling between the religious and secular departments of the state was incessant, to the serious detriment of united and sagacious action. When, in the minority of Carlos II, the regent mother, Maria Anna of Austria, made her German Jesuit confessor, Nithard, inquisitor-general, it required a popular uprising to get rid of him and relegate him to Rome, for he was speedily becoming the real ruler of Spain.

This unreasoning religious ardor culminated in the Inquisition, established for the purpose of securing the supreme good of unblemished purity and uniformity of belief. Nothing was allowed to stand in the way of this, and no sacrifice was deemed too great for its accomplishment. All officials, from the king downward, were sworn to its support,

and the sinister influence which it exercised was proportioned to the
enormous power which it wielded. The tragic spectacles of the *autos-
da-fé* were abhorrent, but they were of little more importance than the
closely related bullfights in determining the fate of the nation, save in
so far as they stimulated the ruthless characteristics of the people. The
real significance of the Inquisition lay in the isolation to which it condemned the land, and its benumbing influence on the intellectual development of the people. It created a fresh source of pride, which led the
Spaniard to plume himself on the unsullied purity of his faith, and to
despise all other nations as given over, more or less, to the errors of
heresy. It obstructed his commercial relations by imposing absurd and
costly regulations at the ports to prevent the slightest chance of the introduction of heretical opinions. It organized a strict censorship to guard
against the intrusion of foreign ideas or the evolution of innovations at
home.[5] It paralyzed the national intelligence, and resolutely undertook
to keep the national mind in the grooves of the sixteenth century. While
the rest of the civilized world was bounding forward in a career of progress, while science and the useful arts were daily adding to the conquests
of man over the forces of Nature, and rival nations were growing in
wealth and power, the Inquisition condemned Spain to stagnation; invention and discovery were unknown at home, and their admission from
abroad was regarded with jealousy. Recuperative power was thus wholly
lacking to offset the destructive effects of misgovernment, the national
conservatism was intensified, and a habit of mind was engendered which
has kept Spain to this day a virtual survival of the Renaissance.

All these causes of retrogression were rendered more effective by the
autocratic absolutism of the form of government, which deprived the
people of all initiative, and subjected everything to the will of the monarch. The old Castilian liberties were lost in the uprising of the Comuni-
dades in 1520, and those of Valencia about the same time in the kindred
tumults of the Germania, while those which survived in Aragon and
Catalonia were swept away in 1707, when the War of Succession gave
Philip V the excuse for treating them as conquered provinces. Nowhere
in Europe, west of Russia, had the maxim of the imperial jurisprudence,
"Quod placuit principi legis habet vigorem," more absolute sway. The
legislative and executive functions were combined in the sovereign; there
were no national political life, no training in citizenship, no forces to
counterbalance the follies or prejudices of the king and his favorites.
Under a series of exceptionally able rulers, this form of government might
have maintained Spanish prosperity and power, while repressing en-

[5] [For a full treatment of censorship of the press in Spain and its effects, see Lea's
Chapters from the Religious History of Spain, pp. 15-211.—H.]

lightenment, but it was the peculiar curse of Spain that the last three Hapsburg princes, whose reigns filled the whole of the sixteenth century, were weak, and their choice of favorites, ghostly and secular, was unwise. Especially the latest one, Carlos II, brought Spain to the nadir of decadence. At his death, in 1700, the Spanish population is estimated to have shrunk within a century from ten to five millions. The prolonged War of Succession which followed partook so much of the nature of civil strife as to be peculiarly exhausting to the scanty resources left by the misgovernment of the preceding two centuries, but with the accession of the Bourbons there was a promise of improvement. Philip V was weak, but he was not as bigoted and obscurantist as his predecessors, and his sons, Ferdinand VI and Carlos III, were men of more liberal ideals. Especially was Carlos an enlightened monarch, who curbed to some extent the Inquisition, relaxed somewhat the rigid censorship of the press, and earnestly strove to promote the industrial development of his kingdom. Under his rule prosperity began to revive, and there seemed a prospect that Spain might assert her place among progressive nations.

The outbreak of the French Revolution, however, was the deathblow of liberalism. Dynastic considerations outweighed all others, and the rulers of Spain were especially sensitive to the dangers apprehended from the introduction of theories as to the rights of man and universal equality. Carlos III had died in 1788, and his son, Carlos IV, was weak, bigoted, reactionary, and wholly under the influence of his favorite, Godoy, the so-called Prince of Peace. His son and successor, Ferdinand VII, was trained in the same school. After the Napoleonic invasion and the Peninsular War, his restoration, in 1814, was the signal for the sternest repressive and reactionary measures; the monarch claimed absolute power, the Constitution of 1812 was set aside, censorship was revived in the most despotic fashion, the Inquisition was reëstablished, and nothing was left undone to bring back the conditions of the sixteenth century. These conditions were upset by the revolution of 1820, but restored by the intervention of the Holy Alliance in 1823, when the Duc d'Angoulême, at the head of a French army, executed the mandate of the Congress of Verona. The history of Spain since then, with its succession of civil wars, revolutions, and experiments in government, holds out little promise of settled and orderly progress. The national characteristic of indomitable pride which disdains to learn from the experience of other nations, the tendency to resort to violent and exaggerated methods, the dense political ignorance of the masses, so sedulously deprived through long generations of all means of political enlightenment and all training in political action, combine to render the nation incapable of conducting wisely the liberal institutions which are foreign importations, and not the outgrowth of native aspirations and experience. In many respects the Spaniard is still living in the sixteenth century, unable to assimilate the ideas of the nineteenth, or to realize that his country is no longer the mistress of the sea and the dominating power of the land.

There is still another cause which has contributed largely to Spanish decadence. All governments are more or less corrupt—absolute honesty would appear to be impossible in the conduct of public affairs—but the corruption and venality of Spanish administration have been peculiarly all-pervading and continuous. From the time of the youthful Charles V and his worthless horde of Flemish favorites, this has been a corroding cancer, sapping the vitality of Spanish resources. It was in vain that the most onerous and disabling imposts were laid on wealth and industry; the results were always insufficient, and the national finances were always in disorder, crippling all efforts at aggression or defense. Already in 1551 the cortes of Castile gave a deplorable account of the corruption in every branch of official life, the destruction of industry, and the misery of the people under their crushing burdens. In 1656, when Philip IV, under a complication of misfortunes, was struggling to avert bankruptcy, Cardinal Moscoso, the Archbishop of Toledo, bluntly told him that not more than ten per cent of the revenues collected reached the royal treasury. While income was thus fatally diminished, expenditure was similarly augmented through collusion, fraud, and bribery. It raises a curious psychological question, how pride and punctilious sensitiveness as to honor can coexist with eager rapacity for iniquitous gains, how undoubted patriotism can accommodate itself to a system which deprives the fatherland of the resources necessary to its existence; but human nature is often only consistent in inconsistency. To what extent this prevails at the present day must of course be only a matter of conjecture, but recent events would seem to indicate that supplies and munitions paid for are not on hand when urgently needed, and that troops in the field bear but a slender proportion to those on the payroll. When, the other day, Don Carlos alluded to "generously voted millions diverted from the fulfillment of their patriotic purpose to the pockets of fraudulent contractors and dishonest state employees, and disorder, peculation, and mendacity in every department of the public service," he merely described conditions which in Spain have been chronic for centuries.

If the above is a truthful outline of the causes of Spanish decadence, it can arouse no wonder that Spanish colonial policy has been a failure. All the defects of character and administration which produced such disastrous results at home had naturally fuller scope for development in the colonies. The discoveries of Columbus did not open up a new continent to be settled by industrious immigrants coming to found states and develop their resources in peaceful industry. The marvelous exploits of the Conquistadores were performed in the craziest thirst for gold, and those who succeeded them came in the hope of speedy enrichment and return, to accomplish which they exploited to the utmost the unhappy natives, and when these were no longer available replaced them with African slaves. The mother country similarly looked upon her new possessions simply as a source of revenue, to be drained to the utmost, either for herself or for the benefit of those whom she sent out to govern them. Colonists who finally settled and cast their lot in the New World were consequently exposed to every limitation and discrimination that perverse ingenuity could suggest, and were sacrificed to the advantage, real or imaginary, of Spain. The shortsighted financial and commercial policy at home would in itself have sufficed to condemn the colonies to stagnation and misery, but in addition they were subjected to special restrictions and burdens. It was not until 1788 that trade with them was permitted through any port but Cadiz, whose merchants made use of their monopoly to exact a profit of from one hundred to two hundred per cent. Export and import duties were multiplied, till the producer was deprived of all incentive to exertion, and the populations were taxed to their utmost capacity, the taxes being exacted with merciless severity.

As if this were not enough, the all-pervading influence of clericalism rendered good government well-nigh impossible. Under its influence the colonial organizations consisted of sundry independent jurisdictions, incompatible with the preservation of order in any community, and especially unfitted for the administration of a colony, separated by a thousand leagues from the supreme authority which alone could compose their differences. There was the royal representative, the viceroy or governor, responsible for the defense of the province and the maintenance of order. There was the church establishment with its bishop or archbishop, in no way subordinate to the civil power. There were the various regular orders—Franciscans, Dominicans, Augustinians, Jesuits, etc.— bitterly jealous of one another and prompt to quarrel, exempt from episcopal jurisdiction, and subject only to their respective superiors or to the Pope, except when suspicion of heresy might render individual members answerable to the Inquisition. Finally, there was the Inquisition itself, which owned obedience only to the Supreme Council of the Holy Office in Madrid, and held itself superior to all other jurisdictions; for under its delegated papal power it could at will paralyze the authority of any one, from the highest to the lowest, by its excommunication, while no priest or prelate could excommunicate its ministers. It was impossible that so irrational a scheme of social order should work smoothly. Causes of dissension, trivial or serious, between these rival and jealous jurisdictions were rarely lacking, and the internal history of the colonies consists in great part of their quarrels, which disturbed the peace of the communities and hindered prosperity and growth.

In *The Atlantic Monthly* for August, 1891, I described at some length a complicated quarrel between the Franciscans and the Bishop of Cartagena de las Indias, in which both the Inquisition and the royal governor intervened, keeping the community in an uproar from 1683 to 1688. This was followed, in 1693, by an outbreak between the governor, Ceballos, and the Inquisition. In the public meat-market a butcher refused to give precedence to a negro slave of the inquisitor, who thereupon had the indiscreet butcher arrested and confined in chains in the *carceles secretas* of the Inquisition. This in itself was a most serious punishment, for such imprisonment left an ineffaceable stigma on the sufferer and on his descendants for two generations. The governor pleaded in vain with the inquisitor, and then endeavored secretly to obtain testimony to send to Madrid, but without success, for no one dared to give evidence. The fact of his attempt leaked out, however, and the secretary of the Inquisition led a mob to the palace, and forced the governor, under threat of excommunication, to sign a declaration that he abandoned the case to the Inquisition, that all reference to it should be expunged from the records of the municipality and all papers relating to it should be delivered to the inquisitor. He submitted, and his only recourse was to write a piteous letter to the Council of the Indies.[6] Such appeal to the home authorities was of uncertain outcome, for the inquisitors were by no means ready to submit to an adverse decision. In a complicated quarrel between the Cruzada, the episcopal court, the Inquisition, and the viceroy of Peru, in 1729, the inquisitors of Lima formally and repeatedly refused obedience to a royal order sent through the viceroy, alleging that they were subject only to the Supreme Council of the Holy Office. In 1751 they took the same ground in a case in which the king decided against them, and they held out until 1760, when a more peremptory command was received, accompanied by a dispatch from the Council which they could not disregard.[7]

Thus, to a greater or less degree, all Spanish colonies were fields in which clericalism rioted at will. Paraguay, where the Jesuits succeeded in building up an independent theocracy, offers the most perfect illustration of the result, and a somewhat less conspicuous instance is found in the Philippines. There the missions of the Augustinian Recollects

[6] See *Inquisition in the Spanish Dependencies*, pp. 491-99.
[7] *Ibid.*, pp. 385-88.

acquired such power that the annals of that colony seem rather to be the records of the Augustinian province of San Nicolás than those of a royal dependency. This Augustinian supremacy was unsuccessfully disputed by the Dominicans, in the early years of the eighteenth century, but the Jesuits proved to be more dangerous rivals, who did not scruple, in 1736, to induce their native subjects to make war on those of the Augustinians. The banishment in 1767 of the Society of Jesus from the Spanish dominions left the field to the Augustinians who have since held it, apparently without making effort to secure the good will of their flocks. They had their own internal troubles, however, for in 1712 the hostility between the Aragonese and Castilians led to a schism which had to be referred to Spain for settlement, when the Castilians, who were·the losing party, refused to submit until the acting governor, Torralba, employed the persuasive influence of artillery. The character of their relations with the secular authority can be estimated from an occurrence in 1643, when the governor, Sebastian Hurtado de Corcuera, in preparing to resist an expected attack by the Dutch, undertook to fortify Manila. An Augustinian convent and church occupied a site required for a demilune. Corcuera offered the friars another church and four thousand pesos; but they refused to move, and obstinately remained in the convent until the progress of the works rendered it uninhabitable, when it was torn down and the materials were used in the lines. They raised a great clamor, which probably was the cause of the removal of Corcuera in 1644, when they prosecuted their grievance in court, and obtained a decree reinstating them and casting him in damages to the amount of twenty-five thousand pesos. They tore down the fortifications, rebuilt the church, and threw Corcuera into prison, where he languished under cruel treatment for five years. He had been an excellent administrator, and on his liberation Philip IV appointed him governor of the Canaries.

In such a community the position of governor had few attractions for an honest man. In 1719, a new one, Bustamente Bustillo, found on his arrival that all the royal officials had been busily embezzling and pilfering, leaving the treasury nearly empty. After ascertaining the facts he set to work energetically to recover the funds and to punish the guilty, who thereupon, as seems to have been customary in such cases, sought asylum in the churches. One of them had carried with him certain official records necessary for the verification of the accounts, and these Bustillo requested the archbishop to make him surrender. The archbishop replied with a learned argument, drawn up for him by a Jesuit, proving that the governor's request was illegal. Bustillo lost his temper at this, and arrested the archbishop, who forthwith cast an interdict over the city. Then the monks and friars turned out in organized bands, marching through the streets with crucifixes, and shouting, "Viva la fe! Viva la Iglesia!" They speedily collected a mob which they led to the palace; the doors were broken in, the governor and his son murdered, and when the archbishop was released he assumed the governorship, under the advice of an assembly consisting exclusively of ecclesiastical dignitaries.

In these perpetually recurring troubles between the secular and the clerical authorities the Inquisition was not behindhand, although there was no organized tribunal in Manila. The Philippines were an appendage to the viceroyalty of New Spain or Mexico, and the Holy Office of Mexico merely delegated a commissioner at Manila to execute its orders and make reports to it. Subordinate as was this position, those who held it deemed themselves superior to the royal authorities. About 1650 the padre commissioner received an order to arrest and send to Acapulco a person who was governor of one of the islands and commandant of a fortified town. The commissioner was also an officer of the government, and knew the risk he ran of offending the governor of the colony in not advising him of what was impending; but the obligation of secrecy in inquisitorial matters was superior to all other considerations. He quietly summoned his alcaide mayor and a sufficient number of familiars, sailed for the island, surprised the governor in his bed, carried him off, and imprisoned him in a convent until there should be an opportunity of shipping him to Mexico. The governor of the colony was Don Diego Fajardo, a violent and irascible soldier, whose term of service was a perpetual embroilment with the unruly jurisdictions under his charge, and who knew the danger of leaving a fortified post without a commander when there was almost constant war, either with the Dutch or with the natives. A rude explosion of wrath was to be expected at this contemptuous disregard of the respect due to his office and of the safety of the land, yet Don Diego so thoroughly recognized the supremacy of the Inquisition that when apprised of the affair he only chided the padre gently for not having given him a chance of winning the graces and indulgences promised for so pious a work, seeing that he would have regarded as the utmost good fortunte the opportunity of serving as an alguazil in making the arrest.

Twenty years later, the Augustinian Fray Joseph de Paternina Samaniego, then commissioner of the Inquisition, was even bolder. He was ordered from Mexico to take secret testimony against the governor of the colony, Don Diego de Salcedo, and forward it to Mexico for examination by the tribunal there. This was all that a commissioner was empowered to do, and he was especially instructed to go no farther; but the Augustinians had had quarrels with the governor, and the whole affair was probably a plot for his removal. Fray Paternina therefore proceeded to act on the testimony, although the judge, Don Francisco de Monte-mayor, warned him of his lack of authority, and that such a personage as·the governor could not be arrested without a special *cédula* from the king, passed upon by the council of the Inquisition. He drew up a war-rant of arrest, went at midnight to the palace with some friars and familiars, seized Salcedo in his bed, handcuffed him, and carried him off to the Augustinian convent, where the bells were rung in honor of the event. He then gave notice to the royal court that the governorship was vacant, and might be filled, which was done by the appointment of his ally, Don Juan Manuel de la Peña. He further issued an edict forbid-ding any one, under pain of excommunication, to speak about the arrest or about his other proceedings; and to inspire fear he brought charges against various persons, under pretext that they were inimical to the Holy Office. Salcedo's property was sequestrated, to the profit of those concerned in the affair, and he was shipped by the first vessel to Acapulco, but he died on the voyage. When the news of this outrage reached Madrid by way of Flanders, the council of the Indies complained bitterly, and asked that steps be taken to prevent a repetition of acts so dangerous to the safety of the colonies. The council of the Inquisition calmly replied that no new instructions were needed, for there were ample provisions for filling a sudden vacancy; as for Fray Paternina, if he had gone too far he would be duly corrected. The council of the Indies insisted, and was supported by the queen regent. Meanwhile, the council of the Inqui-sition had examined the testimony taken against Salcedo, pronounced it frivolous, declared his arrest void, and ordered his property to be restored to his heirs, while Fray Paternina was to be sent to Spain for trial. On the journey he died at Acapulco, and the matter was dropped.[8]

Successful colonization under such a system was a manifest impossi-bility, and it is no wonder that the Spanish dependencies languished, in spite of their infinite potentialities of wealth and prosperity. The narrow and selfish policy of the mother country deprived the colonists of all incentives to exertion; the officials sent from Spain enriched themselves, the tax-gatherers seized all superfluous earnings; there was no accu-mulation of capital and no advancement. In 1736, the viceroy of the vast kingdom of Peru, Don José Armendaris, Marquis of Castel-Fuerte, in the report which, according to custom, he drew up for the instruction of his successor, described the condition of the colony as deplorable. The Spanish population was mostly concentrated in Lima; the nobles and the wealthy oppressed the poor; the corregidores and priests oppressed the Indians; the priests paid little attention to their religious duties, for they were not compelled to residence by their bishops, and were abandoned to

[8] *Ibid.*, pp. 310-17.

sloth and licentiousness; the judges were venal; and the population was diminishing. The religious orders, he said, ought to be checked, and not encouraged, for in Lima there were thirty-four convents, each of them, on an average, equal to four in Spain, which was the most ecclesiastical of all lands. This monastic hypertrophy he attributed to the fact that the men had no other career open to them, and the women consequently could not find husbands. This gloomy utterance was reëchoed, twenty years later, by a subsequent viceroy, Don José Antonio Manto de Velasco.

Still more desponding is a report made in 1772 by Francisco Antonio Moreno y Escandon as to the condition of the "New Kingdom of Granada," embracing the northern coast from Panama to Venezuela, a region abounding in natural wealth. The local officials everywhere, he says, were indifferent and careless as to their duty; the people were steeped in poverty; trade was almost extinct; capital was lacking, and there were no opportunities for its investment; the only source of support was the cultivation of small patches of ground. Everyone sought to subsist on the government by procuring some little office. The mining of the precious metals was the sole source of trade, of procuring necessities from abroad, and of meeting the expenses of the government; but although the mines were as rich as ever, their product had greatly decreased. Commerce with Spain employed only one or two ships, with registered cargoes, a year from Cadiz to Cartagena, whence the goods were distributed through the interior, but so burdened with duties and expenses that no profit could be made on them. If freedom of export could be had for the rich productions of the country—cocoa, tobacco, precious woods, etc.—the colony would flourish; but there were no manufactures, and no money could be kept in the land. The missions had made no progress for a hundred years in Christianizing the Indians, for the missionaries undertook the duty only for the purpose of securing a life of ease and sloth.

Such was the result of three hundred years of colonization under Spanish methods; and we can scarce wonder that, after such a training, the nations which emancipated themselves have found self-government so difficult. Under the warning given by their loss, some improvement has been made in the insular possessions which were unable to throw off the yoke, but not enough to prevent chronic disaffection and constantly recurring efforts at revolt. Spain has made of her colonies the buried talent, and the fulfillment of the parable must come to pass.

THE INDIAN POLICY OF SPAIN*

[In sending this essay to the *Review* Mr. Lea wrote to Professor George P. Fisher, one of its editors:

"The subject is not novel, but I am not aware that anyone has utilized the material that has come to light in recent times. Ellis' chapter in Winsor's *History of America* might have been written fifty years ago, and no one seems to have taken the trouble to look up the Spanish colonial legislation.

"I was investigating the origins of the Mexican Inquisition and wandered off to considering the condition of the natives, which I found full of interest and not without some lessons which might be profitably pondered by our people just now if we are to inherit the Spanish colonies."—H.]

*   *   *   *   *

THE STORY of the relations between Spain and the natives of her western colonies is full of interest and instruction. Like our own dealings with our Indians, it shows how the kindly intentions of governments, expressed in beneficent legislation, may be rendered nugatory when administration is intrusted to unworthy hands or when sufficient influence is brought to bear by those who profit from abuses. In view of the responsibilities which the United States are assuming in the remnant of Spain's colonial empire, a brief review of early Spanish experiences may perhaps be not without wholesome warning.

It is to Bartolomé de las Casas that we owe most of our knowledge of the seamy side of Spanish conquest and colonization. Born, in 1474, of a good family in Seville, he had a university training and acquired the grade of licentiate in laws. His interest in the New World was inherited, for his father was one of the companions of Columbus and returned to Spain in 1497. In 1502, when Ovando was sent to Hispañola to replace Bobadilla, Bartolomé accompanied him, and his career thenceforth was irrevocably determined. At first, like his compatriots, he seems to have taken little thought as to the unhappy fate of the natives, but when, after entering the Church and taking orders, he accompanied, in 1511, Diego Velazquez in the conquest of Cuba, the ferocious cruelty of the invaders made such an impression on him that, after a short period of hesitation, he devoted the rest of his prolonged life to the relief of the oppressed. For this he was admirably fitted by nature and training. Though hot-tempered, he was gifted with perseverance which no rebuff or disappointment could outwear. Learned, eloquent, and fearless, his sacred character gave him an influence all-important in the Spanish

* From the *Yale Review*, VIII (1899), 119-55.

courts of the period, which was enhanced by his recognized disinterested-
ness. Singlehanded, he time and again overthrew the combinations organized by the powerful influences which he antagonized, but the evils
of corrupt administration were ineradicable and his triumphs in Spain
were persistently neutralized by defeats in the Caribbean. Nevertheless
he struggled unweariedly to the last, and, when advancing age rendered
active work impossible, his tireless pen was still employed in the good
cause. He died in 1566, at the ripe age of ninety-two, leaving unfinished
MSS on which he was laboring to the end. His voluminous writings
are the source of most of our knowledge of the subject; some of his
shorter tracts he gathered together and printed in a small volume at
Seville in 1552; the rest he left to the care of posterity, and it is only of
recent years that those which have been preserved have seen the light,
in the *Colección de Documentos inéditos para la Historia de España*,
accompanied with illustrative documents, and a detailed biography by
Señor Fabié. The life of Las Casas was so intimately bound up with the
fate of the Indians that a clear understanding of the influences which
controlled their treatment by the Spaniards can best be obtained by following his career.

In the little Seville volume the most noteworthy portion is the *Brevísima
Relación de la Destruyción de las Yndias*, written in 1542, for the instruction of Charles V and his advisers who were engaged in framing a new
body of legislation for the Indies. A more terrible story never shocked
humanity. Horrors are piled upon horrors until the sense becomes blunted
and one scarce realizes the savagery which had continued uninterruptedly
in one region after another for half a century. Doubtless there is eloquent
exaggeration in the recital; Las Casas was not a coldly scientific historian,
but an advocate and a preacher, who gathered hearsay evidence from all
sources and heightened the pathos of his narrative with his own warm
sympathies; but the general facts are corroborated by too many contemporary authorities to justify the attempts at exculpation which have
been fashionable of late years. We may reasonably doubt his accuracy
when he says that since the Discovery the Spanish had destroyed, by
cruelty and oppression, more than twelve millions of Indians, including
men, women, and children, and he verily thinks the number is more
than fifteen millions; nor is our confidence heightened when, in 1550,
he asserts that up to that time the destruction had increased to thirty
millions and in 1560 he puts the figure at forty millions,[1] but there can
be no question that the mortality by the sword and by the inhuman
slavery to which the Indians were reduced was frightful. In 1517 a cooler

---

[1] *Brevísima Relación* (Venice, 1643), p. 11; Las Casas, *Historia de las Indias*, Lib. III, cc.
cxxxvii, clv (*Colección de Documentos*, XLVI, 75, 164).

statement by the Dominicans of Hispañola informs us that when the first count of the inhabitants of the island was made they were found to number 1,100,000; some years later a census reduced the figures to sixteen thousand, and at the time of writing there were but ten thousand left.[2] This is virtually confirmed by Alonso de Zuazo, who had been sent out by Cardinal Ximenes with full powers of investigation, and who, in an official report to Chièvres, January 22, 1519, states that at the discovery the population was 1,130,000, which had been reduced to eleven thousand, and that these would disappear in three or four years if no remedy was applied.[3] It was much the same in Mexico, although the more warlike character of the natives and the features of the country rendered the process slower. About 1595, Padre Mendieta compares the crowded towns and populous country which he had seen in the earlier days with the deserted cities and rural solitudes that now everywhere met the eye, and Bancroft informs us that at the close of the century it was estimated that the Indians numbered only one fourth of what they had been at the time of the conquest.[4]

The rapidity of the Spanish conquest is partially explained by this ruthless extermination, for, as labor became scarce, slave-hunting expeditions, attended with fearful loss of life, were organized from Hispañola. Thus Puerto Rico fell a victim, then Jamaica, and then Cuba. By 1510 the Bahamas were virtually depopulated, and the discovery of Florida was due to disappointed slave hunters, who found no one to carry off from the Bahamas, and who pushed on to the mainland.[5] The Windward Islands were raided in the same way, although the fierce Carib cannibals were harder to capture. The coasts of Tierra Firme were harried, and from Cuba to Yucatan the transit was easy. All around the Caribbean the slave hunter opened the way to the conquistador. Zuazo tells us that Ferdinand the Catholic authorized this hideous traffic to remedy the lack of labor, which was so scarce that an Indian duly branded as a slave was known to have fetched the enormous price of eighty ducats.[6] Indian slavery, in fact, was subsequently rendered unlawful, except for crime, and the slave was designated by branding in the face, though Las Casas told Philip II that the royal branding iron was promiscuously applied and that all slaves thus marked ought to be

[2] *Hist. de las Indias*, Lib. III, c. xciv (*Col. de Doc.*, LXV, 338). Las Casas assumes the original population of Hispañola to have been three or four millions.—*Ibid.*, c. xix (*Col. de Doc.*, LXIV, 452).

[3] *Col. de Doc.*, II, 353.

[4] Mendieta, *Hist. Eclesiástica Indiana* (Mexico, 1870), p. 561.—Bancroft, *Hist. of Mexico*, II, 767.

[5] *Hist. de las Indias*, Lib. III, c. xx (*Col. de Doc.*, LXIV, 457).

[6] *Col. de Doc.*, II, 355.

adjudged free by the courts.[7] During the conquest of Central America and Mexico he says that they were captured in numbers far beyond the capacity of vessels to carry them away, and when brought down to the coast an Indian would be exchanged for a cheese or a hundred for a horse.[8]

There were two causes at work in this extermination—a temporary one in the callous cruelty of the conquerors, and a permanent one in the brutal oppression which worked the unhappy natives to death in the mines and fields and on the roads. The Spaniards who sought the New World were largely of the vilest class, either criminals escaping from justice or punished by transportation. By the returning fleet of 1498, Columbus begged the sovereigns to send out some good *frailes*, rather, as he says, to reform the faith of the Christians than to spread it among the Indians, and in their formal memorial of 1517 the Dominicans of Hispaniola described the colonists as the most infamous race of men that ever was known.[9] The secular clergy who sought their fortunes in the New World were scarce better, and could exercise no restraining influence. Even in 1551, the Mexican viceroy, Antonio de Mendoza, in the instructions drawn up for his successor, Luis de Velasco, says that the clergy who come out are infamous, and if it were not for the orders of the king and for baptism the Indians would be better without them.[10] Colonists of this character, when brought into contact with weak and submissive fellow creatures, were not likely to restrain their worst instincts, and they treated the Indians with less compassion than if they were beasts of the field. The merciless slaughter of war was followed by torture to discover hidden treasure and with purposeless cruelty to gratify pure bloodthirstiness. The edge of weapons was tested on defenceless wretches and we hear of killing fat Indians to make of their fat an ointment supposed to have peculiar virtues. We might hope that these

[7] *Recopilación de Leyes de las Indias*, Ley 1, Tit. ii, Lib. VI.—Fabié, *Vida* (*Col. de Doc.*, LXX, 165).

[8] *Brevísima Relación*, p. 70.

[9] *Hist. de las Indias*, Lib. I, c. clv (*Col. de Doc.*, LXIII, 341); Lib. III, c. xciv (*Col. de Doc.*, LXV, 341).

[10] *Col. de Doc.*, XXVI, 286. Oviedo (*Quinquagenas de la Nobleza da España*, I, 383) speaks of the licentiousness of the colonial clergy as inviting the destruction of the colonies; even as the marriage of the Greek priests had been punished by their subjugation under the Turks. Cortés, who had at first asked to have bishoprics erected, speedily changed his mind and requested Charles V to send out only friars, for he said the priests of the Indians were held to such rigid rules of modesty and chastity that if they should see the pomp and disorderly lives of the Spanish hierarchy they would regard the Christian religion as a farce and their conversion would be impracticable. Charles saw the wisdom of this and during the rest of his reign the bishops appointed belonged to the religious orders and secular clergy were sparingly permitted to go to the colonies.—Torquemada, *De la Monarquia Indiana* (ed. 1723), III, 2, 3.

were fables, but the reckless disregard of human life and suffering has
left an imperishable linguistic trace in the terrible word *aperrear*—to
throw to the dogs, not metaphorically, but literally, like the *ad bestias
mittere* of the Romans. The *perros bravos* or ferocious dogs, which were
brought by the colonists to aid them in hunting down Indians, were the
·objects of the utmost terror to the natives, who were frequently thrown
to them to be torn to pieces, and children were sometimes cut up and
fed to them.[11] This denial of the rights of humanity does not rest upon
the assertions of those who strove to protect the sufferers. Towards the
close of the sixteenth century, Bernardo de Vargas Machuca, governor
of Margarita, a valiant captain, who had served for thirty years in the
New World, wrote a work in defence of his fellow colonists against the
accusations of Las Casas, the whole texture of which reveals profound
unconsciousness that the Indian had any claim to consideration as a
human being. He sees nothing to reprove in the good missionary who,
after preaching on the pains of purgatory, offered to exhibit them to
any who were curious. Two Indians presented themselves, whom he
bound to a stake, built a circle of wood around them, set it on fire and
roasted them to death. For this freak he was tried by his archbishop, but
on protesting that it was by mistake that he had neglected to rake away
the fire in time, he was sent back to the mission to resume his pious
labors. Still more significant is a hideous story which he tells to illustrate his thesis that the sufferings of the Indians were mostly attributable
to the mistaken tenderness shown to them by the *chapetones*—a derisive
name applied to newly arrived officials from Spain who had not had
time enough to become hardened. In an Indian village named Hontibon,.
near Santafé de Bogotá, a Spanish soldier quarrelled with a native and
struck him repeatedly in the face. The villagers collected at the cries of
the sufferer and their aspect was so threatening that the soldier surrendered and was bound and carried somewhat roughly before the judge
in Santafé. The latter, in place of scolding the Indians for their audacity,
actually reproved the soldier, fined him and imprisoned him for a few
days. Burning to avenge himself, he bought a cross-bow and fifty arrows;
on a night of full moon he stationed himself at a bridge on the highroad
near Hontibon and when an Indian passed he asked him whence he
came. If the answer was "from Hontibon" he was forthwith despatched
and his corpse flung into the river. When the fifty arrows had each its
victim the soldier used his sword, and at sunrise, his vengeance being
glutted, he mounted his horse and escaped to Peru. Now all this slaugh-

---

[11] See a letter of the Dominicans of Hispañola to Chièvres (*Col. de Doc.*, LXX, 423),
also one of Las Casas, January 20, 1535, to the council of the Indies (*Ibid.*, p. 464).

ter, Machuca argues, would have been avoided if the judge had only done his duty in punishing the Indians.[12]

Destructive as was this supreme contempt for the lives of the subject race, the leading source of misery and extermination was the system of enforced labor. The Spaniard who went to the colonies did not go to support himself, but to be supported by the labor of others. As Machuca candidly says, in his argument to prove that the Indians were not wantonly destroyed, the Spaniards will not settle in an unoccupied land, no matter how healthy or how rich in gold and silver, but they go where there are Indians, although the land may be poor and unhealthy, for if they have not Indians to work for them they cannot enjoy what the land produces and to take possession of it would be of no benefit.[13] Now the alleged object, steadily asserted throughout the Spanish conquest, was the propagation of the faith. In the momentous bull *Inter cætera* of Alexander VI, May 4, 1493, bestowing on the sovereigns of Castile all lands discovered in the Western world, the sole motive alluded to is the spread of the Gospel and the bringing of the heathen into the fold of Christ.[14] In the codicil executed by Queen Isabella, November 23, 1504, three days before her death, she declares that her intention in obtaining the papal bull was to propagate the faith, and she charges her husband and children to regard this as the main object and to take the utmost care that the Indians be treated justly and sustain no wrong.[15] So on all occasions the moral and spiritual elevation of the natives was asserted to be the motive of the extension of Spanish domination. It was not easy to reconcile this with the system of *repartimientos* or *encomiendas*—allotting Indians to Spaniards to work the mines and cultivate the fields of their masters, which commenced even under Columbus in 1496, and spread in its development like a upas tree over all the Spanish colonies.[16] The theologians, however, were as usual equal to the occasion and their dialectics sufficed to quiet all scruples of conscience. Isabella was firmly resolved that her new vassals should be freemen; when, in 1498, the returning fleet brought six hundred Indians as slaves, of whom two hundred were given to the shipmasters to pay the freight on the rest, she was justly indignant; she ordered them all to be surrendered, under pain of death, and she gathered them together and sent them home—one of them, by a curious coincidence, being a boy given to Bartolomé de Las Casas by his father.[17] Yet even Isabella's scruples gave way to the

---

[12] Machuca, *Discorsos Apolóxicos* (*Col. de Doc.*, LXXI, 228, 301).

[13] *Ibid.*, p. 220.

[14] *Mag. Bullar. Roman.* (ed. Luxemb.), I, 454.

[15] Mariana, *Hist. de España* (ed. 1796), IX, App. xxvi.

[16] Fabié, *Vida* (*Col. de Doc.*, LXX, 377).

[17] *Hist. de las Indias*, Lib. I, c. clv (*Col. de Doc.*, LXIII, 340).—Fabié, *Vida* (*ubi sup.*, p. 11).

arguments that the Indians were perversely idle; idleness was a sin, and to eradicate it by the gentle enforcement of industry brought progress in the path of Christian virtue. Moreover, conversion was impossible unless the Indians associated with Christians; this they would not do willingly and some coercion was imperative. When, therefore, in 1502, Isabella sent Ovando to the West Indies to replace Bobadilla, while her instructions were emphatic that the freedom of the Indians should be maintained and that they should be protected from all wrong like her vassals of Castile, she followed these with a letter, December 20, 1503, empowering him to order the caciques each to supply a given number of men who were to be made to work, as freemen and not as slaves, at such reasonable wages as he might designate; they were to receive instruction on Sundays and feast days; they were to be well treated and any one wronging them was to be fined ten thousand maravedís. Ovando availed himself of this to assign to each of his Spaniards a cacique with his subjects, so that all, men, women and children, were practically reduced to slavery, and although there was an admonition to instruct them in the faith, this was purely formal.[18] The system was legalized by Ferdinand in *cédulas* of August 14, and November 12, 1509, ordering that as soon as natives are reduced to obedience the governor shall allot them among the settlers, each of whom shall have charge of those assigned to him, protecting them, providing a priest to instruct and administer the sacraments to them and training them in civilization.[19] Thus was inaugurated the system of repartimientos or encomiendas, which remained as the organization of the Spanish colonies. It mattered little what humane regulations might be prescribed by the sovereigns; the colonies were distant; the colonists were eager in the pursuit of wealth and utterly unscrupulous as to the means of gaining it; the Indians were slaves in all but name, without the protection afforded by ownership; under the lash they were worked beyond their strength with insufficient food, nor was there decent consideration for women big with child or exhausted by childbirth, and it is not surprising that they melted away like hoarfrost in the sun. The mining of the precious metals cost its millions, but perhaps even more deadly were the tasks imposed on them as carriers, for the islands afforded no native beasts of burden, imported horses were too valuable to be employed in such work, and all transportation was performed by Indians, who were overloaded and goaded till they perished. There is doubtless exaggeration in one of the accusations brought against Fernando Pizarro during his trial in Madrid— that he had slain more than twenty thousand infants torn from the

---

[18] *Hist. de las Indias*, Lib. II, c. xiii, xiv (*Col. de Doc.*, LXIV, 71, 81).
[19] *Recopilación*, Leyes 1, 2, Tit. viii, Lib. VI.

breasts of their mothers in order to use the latter in carrying supplies for his troops, but the formulation of such a charge in a legal prosecution shows that it was not considered at the time to be an improbability.[20] When Machuca reproaches the Indians with their proneness to suicide and infanticide, he merely exhibits to us their hopeless despair for themselves and their offspring.[21]

The civilizing intercourse with Christians, whereby Isabella hoped to spread the faith, was evidently a failure; in the frenzied pursuit of wealth the *encomendero* gave his wretched bondsmen no leisure for religious instruction, and the hatred which he excited naturally extended to his religion. As Juan Fernando de Angelo, bishop of Santa Marta, wrote to Charles V about 1540,

In these parts there are no Christians, but only demons . . . as for the Indians, nothing is more abhorrent to them than the name of Christians, whom they call in their language *yares*, which means demons, and they are right, for the works which are wrought here are not of Christians, nor of men endowed with reason, but of demons.[22]

It mattered little that the sovereigns were careful, in the commissions and instructions issued to the conquistadores, to keep ever before them that their first duty was to evangelize the heathen; few missionaries at first went over seas and these found the conditions too adverse for success. It is true that in the voyage of 1500, two Franciscans sailed, who boasted that they baptized three thousand Indians in the first port of Hispañola at which they touched;[23] other Franciscans accompanied Ovando in 1502, but they did nothing to convert the Indians or to alleviate their miseries.[24] It was not until 1510, when Fray Pedro de Córdova arrived with two fellow Dominicans, to be joined shortly afterwards by ten or twelve more, that any sustained attempt was made to give religious instruction, and we are told that on the afternoons of Sundays and feast days multitudes flocked to hear the good frailes, who had won general regard by their austere simplicity. Filled with profound compassion for the sufferings of the helpless creatures whom they had come to convert, they felt, after a residence of about a year, that it was their duty to utter the first protest against the abominations existing around them. After anxious prayer and discussion they drew up a sermon which Pedro de

---

[20] Fabié, *Vida* (*Col. de Doc.*, LXX, 236). This employment as carriers was recognized as one of the most cruel hardships inflicted on the Indians. Las Casas recurs to it frequently and the sovereigns in vain endeavored to suppress or to limit it. See *Recopilación*, leyes 6-18, Tit. xii, Lib. VI.

[21] *Col. de Doc.*, LXXI, 227.

[22] *Brevísima Relación*, p. 81.

[23] *Chron. Fr. Glassberger*, ann. 1500 (*Analecta Franciscana*, II, 525).

[24] *Hist. de las Indias*, Lib. III, cc. v, xiv (*Col. de Doc.*, LXIV, 372, 423).

Córdova ordered Anton Montesino, a fervid and fearless preacher, to deliver on the fourth Sunday in Advent, 1511, and to it they invited the admiral, Diego Colon, and all the royal officials and jurists. The sermon was a terrifying one, exposing the wickedness of the Spaniards and assuring them that they had no more chance of salvation than so many Turks. It created great excitement; in the afternoon the officials assembled in the residence of the admiral, who accompanied them to the humble Dominican house, where the frailes were required, under threat of expulsion from the island, to preach a sermon of recantation. They professed readiness to go at any moment, but finally promised that Montesino should endeavor to satisfy them on the next Sunday. Word of the expected revocation was passed around and the whole population crowded into the church; Montesino mounted the pulpit and delivered a denunciation more fiery than before, telling them that the brethren would no more receive them to confession and absolution than so many highway robbers, and that they might write home what they pleased to whom they pleased.[25]

The fury of the colonists found vent in letters to the court describing the fearful scandal caused by the Dominicans, who consigned them all to hell because they employed the Indians in the mines as the king had ordered—a doctrine destructive of the royal power and revenues, for twenty per cent of the product went to the crown. This caused great disturbance at home where powerful officials were interested in the abuses in the colony. Conchillos, the royal secretary, was one of these, and so was Fonseca, bishop of Burgos, who enjoyed Ferdinand's confidence and had the control of Indian affairs. Ferdinand summoned the Dominican provincial of Castile and ordered him to repair the scandals caused by his frailes or he would see to it himself.[26]

A still more effective measure of the colonial government was the sending to Spain of the Franciscan superior, Alonso del Espinal, whose principal convent was supported by an allotment of Indians. When the Dominicans heard of this they resolved to send Montesino to plead the cause of the natives; with no little difficulty they begged enough provisions for his voyage and the two frailes sailed in different ships. Espinal hurried to the court, where he was received as an angel of light and Ferdinand ordered that he should be admitted to audience at all times. Montesino first reported to his provincial and when he reached the court he found every avenue closed. The usher persistently refused him admittance to the king, till one day, when the door was opened to let someone out, he forced his way in and read to Ferdinand a long memorial

[25] *Ibid.*, Lib. II, c. liv; Lib. III, cc. iii, iv, v (*Col. de Doc.*, LXIV, 273, 361 ff.).
[26] *Ibid.* (LXIV, 370).

recounting the slaughters and cruelties and miseries inflicted on his subjects. Ferdinand was astonished and moved and willingly granted the request of Montesino to apply a remedy.[27]

The time had evidently arrived to frame a systematic body of laws regulating the relations between colonists and natives in the widening sphere of Spanish domination. To accomplish this Ferdinand summoned to Burgos, where the court was then residing, a conference of learned doctors and masters of law and theology. They were for the most part well-meaning men, but at their head was Bishop Fonseca and they were surrounded by courtiers interested in the preservation of abuses, while the Indians had no advocate but Montesino until near the close of the proceedings, when he was joined by Pedro de Córdova, who had hurried to Spain on receiving the letters written by his provincial at Ferdinand's order. The result was a foregone conclusion, but there is instruction in the theological arguments by which the royal conscience was soothed. Fray Bernardo de Mesa, one of the king's preachers, presented a thesis in which he proved dialectically that although the Indians were free, yet idleness was one of the greatest evils under which they suffered and it was the duty of the king to relieve them of it, and, as they were prone to it, absolute liberty was injurious to them. Besides, they were naturally inconstant, being islanders, and the moon is the mistress of the waters surrounding them. He therefore concluded that it was necessary to hold them in some kind of servitude to cure their vicious inclinations and constrain them to industry, and this was in conformity with the goodness of God. Another royal preacher, the licentiate Gregòrio, reached the same result with learned citations from Aristotle, Aquinas, Duns Scotus, St. Antonino of Florence, and Agostino da Ancona, and the fate of helpless millions was made to turn on scholastic word-spinning such as this. The conference resulted in seven propositions which, while recognizing the freedom of the Indians and their right to humane treatment, concluded that they must be subjected to coercion and be kept in communication with the Spaniards in order to promote their conversion—and when these points were once admitted everything depended on the administration of greedy officials at a distance of fifteen hundred leagues.[28]

On the basis thus laid down a council was assembled which proceeded to frame thirty-two laws—known as the Laws of Burgos, promulgated December 27, 1512—for the regulation of the existing and all future colonies. They embodied the principle that the Indians must be rescued from idleness by enforced labor, to be paid for at the rate of a ducat a year, and

[27] *Ibid.*, c. vi (LXIV, pp. 376 ff.).
[28] *Ibid.*, cc. viii, ix, xii (LXIV, pp. 386, 392, 410).

even the caciques were to be made to work at light tasks. The failure
of their conversion was attributed to their having been allowed to live
in their homes and villages, so they were required to be brought to the
residence of their masters, but at least one third were to be drafted
to the mines. There were various humanitarian regulations introduced
but, as there was no adequate machinery provided for their enforcement,
they were of course nugatory. Just as the code was being completed
Pedro de Córdova arrived; he saw that it meant the destruction of the
Indians and so informed Ferdinand, who empowered him to modify
the laws at his pleasure and promised that he would see them obeyed,
but Pedro shrank from the responsibility and the Indians lost their only
chance. Ferdinand, however, ordered a revision by a junta with Bishop
Fonseca at its head and the royal confessor, Tomás de Matienza, as one of
its members. Before this body Pedro de Córdova appeared and argued, but
to no effect; it reported to the king, under God and conscience, that he
was fully justified in making the Indians work and in granting their
services to whom he pleased. Thus the project was adopted, with a few
trifling additions, so that the whole, as Las Casas tells us, was iniquitous
and cruel, with some laws that were impossible and others that were
worse than barbarous.[29]

As the keepers of the royal conscience had decided that it was for the
service of God that the king should partition out the Indians, the
courtiers at once applied for grants. Bishop Fonseca obtained two hundred serfs in each of the four islands, Secretary Conchillos secured
eleven hundred in all and numerous others two hundred apiece. Moreover, all the royal officials in the islands, and the judges of appeal, who
were sent there in 1511 and 1512, received allotments in addition to their
salaries, so that the system was buttressed in the court, while in the
colonies those who should have restrained its abuses profited by them.
The courtiers sent out agents to work their Indians, which they did
inexorably and pitilessly; as the wretches died off they claimed that the
number should be made up; as there were not enough to go around
a new deal would be made and those who had not influence were
stripped; these, seeing that they were liable at any time to lose their
serfs, thought it better to work them to death, and in this frenzied
covetousness no laws protecting the natives were observed.[30] Zuazo, writing in 1519, attributes their destruction to the allotments, aggravated by
the successive distributions which greedy courtiers succeeded in having
made. Under these they were shifted from one master to another and from

---

[29] *Ibid.*, cc. xiii, xv, xvi, xvii (LXIV, pp. 417 ff.).
[30] *Ibid.*, c. xix (LXIV, p. 450).

the mountains to the lowlands and vice versa, resulting in their perishing by thousands through disease.[31]

Such was the state of affairs when Las Casas undertook what was to prove his lifework. He had returned from Cuba deeply impressed with the cruelty of the conquest, and when Pedro de Córdova came back from Spain they consulted together as to the remedy. Pedro told him that nothing could be done so long as Ferdinand lived, for he placed entire confidence in Fonseca and Conchillos, and they as well as other members of the royal council held too many Indians to consent to any reform. The ardor of Las Casas, however, was not to be balked; he sailed in September, 1515, and in Seville Archbishop Deza gave him a letter to Ferdinand with which in December he went to Plasencia. December 23 he had an audience in which he dwelt eloquently on the atrocities inflicted on the Indians; the king promised redress; he was about starting for Seville, and when there he would consider the matter thoroughly. At Seville Las Casas awaited his coming, only to receive the news of his death, January 23, 1516. It is a tribute to Ferdinand's character that Las Casas regards this as a great misfortune for the Indians, for he felt confident that the king would have put an end to their wrongs.[32]

This was the first of a long series of disappointments, which would have disheartened a man of less tenacity of purpose, but Las Casas forthwith resolved to go to Flanders and win over to his views the young sovereign, Charles. His first move, however, was to Madrid, where he presented a memorial in Spanish to Cardinal Ximenes, and one in Latin to Cardinal Adrian—the governors of Spain in the absence of the new king. Adrian was horrified at what he read and asked Ximenes if it could be true. Ximenes confirmed it and then advised Las Casas not to go to Flanders, for they would settle the matter to his satisfaction in Spain. Bishop Fonseca was deprived of authority and the two cardinals discussed the question with Las Casas, resulting in his being commissioned to draw up a plan for the relief of the Indians, which he did on the basis of abolishing the repartimientos and making provision to enable the Spaniards to live by honest labor. This was accepted by Ximenes, who asked Las Casas to undertake the task of finding persons suited to carry it into effect. This he was unable to do, and the cardinal concluded to intrust the matter to monks of the Geronimite order, so as to avoid the attrition inevitable between Dominicans and Franciscans. Twelve were selected, out of whom Las Casas chose three, but while the necessary papers and despatches were being drawn up, the enemy got hold of them; they held aloof from Las Casas, and when they reached Hispañola they fell completely under the

[31] Col. de Doc., II, 351.
[32] Hist. de las Indias, c. 84 (LXV, 277).

influence of the colonists. They made no attempt to execute the plan which, if it could have been carried out in good faith, would have resulted in a flourishing and industrious community where settler and native could live together in amity. There was an unfortunate clause, however, added by the royal council, providing for the continuance of the repartimientos in case it should be found that the Indians could not be settled in agricultural villages. This was decided against them in advance; the plan was never even tried, and when the kinsmen of the Geronimites followed them and were shrewdly given good allotments of Indians in Cuba by Diego Velazquez, there was no further hope of improvement.[33] It was not the first nor the last practical application of a formula, dear to the colonists when unpopular decrees reached them from over sea—*obedézcase pero no se cumpla*—let it be obeyed, but not enforced.

Ximenes had sent Las Casas at the same time to Hispañola with a kind of supervisory power which proved ineffective. His letters to the cardinal were intercepted and, finding himself unable to accomplish anything, he resolved to return to Spain. In May, 1517, he sailed and in fifty days he reached Aranda de Duero, where he found Ximenes breathing his last. The youthful Charles, however, had just arrived to take possession of his kingdom and Las Casas lost no time in making his way to the Court. He speedily recognized that everything was in the hands of the Flemish counselors and favorites, and he attached himself to the chancellor, Jean Le Sauvage, who took him into favor and soon relied upon him for everything connected with the Indies. An incident, at this time, which might have exercised a controlling influence on the destinies of the New World, illustrates perfectly the government of the young monarch. News came of the discovery of Yucatan, or Mexico. The admiral of Flanders, Adolf of Burgundy, promptly asked Charles to bestow it on him as a fief, with Cuba as a base from which to colonize it; the favorite Chièvres had charge of royal grants and favors and, as neither he nor his master knew anything about the Indies, the request was granted as readily as if it were a piece of meadow land. The admiral sent to Flanders and in due time there arrived at San Lucar five vessels loaded with Flemings to colonize the new territory. Meanwhile Las Casas had informed Diego Colon of this infringement on his rights; Colon made reclamation and the chancellor informed the admiral that the grant could not be confirmed until the suit was decided which Colon had brought to enforce the claims derived from his father to all lands discovered and to be discovered. Most of the Flemings brought to San Lucar died, and the rest returned home;

[33] *Ibid.*, cc. 85-95 (LXV, 281 ff.).

but had Mexico, Central America, and Cuba been settled from Flanders and Holland the history of America might have been vastly different.[34]

Le Sauvage brought Las Casas to the favorable notice of Charles, who ordered them to draw up a plan of reform. This Las Casas eagerly undertook and reproduced his previous project with some amendments. One of these was to carry to the colonies numbers of industrious peasants and start them there with a view to building up a self-supporting population. This came to nothing, as we shall see; but a more fateful one was the suggestion of permitting the importation of a few negroes. Cardinal Adrian and the chancellor approved his plan and all seemed to promise fair, although Bishop Fonseca had regained his position, it was supposed by bribing Chièvres. The court moved to Saragossa and Las Casas followed it, but fell sick by the way; on his recovery Fonseca was disabled for five weeks, causing further postponement, and then the chancellor Le Sauvage died, early in July 1518, after which Fonseca regained his former influence. Again Penelope's web was unraveled and the work had to be commenced anew.[35]

The suggestion as to negro slaves, however, had taken root and grown like other evil weeds. It had come to Las Casas from colonists who had told him that if they could get license to import ten or a dozen negroes they would willingly release their Indians. The idea apparently was floating in the air of Hispañola, for Zuazo, in his letter of January 22, 1519, to Chièvres, says that the importation of negroes is a necessity, and he asks, if it cannot be made general, that at least he should have authority to issue licenses for bringing in a hundred from Spain; they should be from fifteen to twenty years of age, of both sexes, and should be allowed to choose their masters for a term of not over one year, the masters being married settlers. By this time, moreover, after an abortive attempt in 1505-6, the sugar industry was beginning to establish itself, and the want of more athletic labor about the mills than that of Indians was making itself felt. On its face there was nothing about the project to alarm the most sensitive conscience. Under the treaty of Tordesillas the trade with Africa was reserved to the Portuguese; they were in the habit of bringing negroes to Spain as slaves, and there would seem to be nothing cruel in transferring a few of these to the West Indies, where the climate more nearly approached that of their native land. The suggestion of Las Casas was that licenses each for the importation of a dozen negroes should be issued, but when asked how many in all would be wanted, he replied that he could not tell. The question was then put to the Casa de Contratacion of Seville, which

[34] *Ibid.*, cc. xcv, xcix-ci (LXV, 343, 364 ff.).
[35] *Ibid.*, cc. cii, ciii (LXV, 380 ff.).

regulated the colonial trade, and it estimated the number at four thousand·for the four islands. The chance afforded for jobbery was seized at once, and a Flemish favorite, the governor of Bresse, begged and obtained from Charles the right to issue these licenses. This he promptly sold for twenty-five thousand ducats to some Genoese speculators, who made it a condition that no more licenses should be sold for eight years. Las Casas says that they cleared nearly three hundred thousand ducats by the operation, but this is manifestly an exaggerated estimate, for he elsewhere tells us that they sold them at about eight ducats a head. It was long before Las Casas recognized his mistake: as late as 1535, in a letter to the council of the Indies, he suggested that five or six hundred negroes be sent to each of the islands and be parcelled out, a few to each settler, or that free licenses be issued to import them. Towards the close of his life, however, he bitterly repented his error and recognized that he had only perpetuated the slavery which he had labored to abolish. He would not for the world, he says, have made so grievous a mistake; he had supposed that the negroes in Spain had been justly enslaved, but he doubts whether his ignorance and carelessness will excuse him before the divine judgment. The trade grew rapidly and, writing about 1560, he says that there had been some forty thousand carried to Hispañola and one hundred thousand to the Indies, for the sugar mills required them in increasing numbers, and from the profits derived from licenses and dues the king had built the alcázares of Madrid and Toledo. The Portuguese, who had long been stealing negroes in Guinea, were stimulated to greater activity in their nefarious traffic, and the natives made war with each other to capture slaves for sale. In Hispañola they died rapidly from overwork, and from the liquor which they made from the cane juice, while many escaped to the mountains, after killing their masters, and became *Cimarrones* or Maroons, so that the people lived in constant dread.[36]

For a moment after the death of Le Sauvage, Las Casas was in despair, but hope revived when La Mure, a nephew of Charles's favorite chamberlain La Chaulx, manifested an interest in the Indians which strengthened rapidly under Las Casas' eloquence. La Chaulx was induced to listen to him and became his warm supporter—in fact, the Flemings as a rule favored him, possibly as a part of their antagonism to the Spaniards. With their assistance the plan of inducing industrious peasants to emigrate was taken up and ample powers were conferred on Las Casas to carry it out. He set about it with his accustomed vigor and it promised well, but again his hopes were dashed. He was induced to appoint as his assistant a gentleman named Berrio, to whom a com-

[36] *Ibid.*, cc. cii, cxxix (LXV, 379; LXVI, 28); LXX, p. 484; II, pp. 370, 374.

mission was given placing him under the orders of Las Casas, but after it was signed by the king Bishop Fonseca secretly altered it, rendering him independent. After working together for a short time Berrio cut loose, went to Andalusia and collected some two hundred tramps and vagabonds, whom he took to Seville and handed over to the Contratacion. Las Casas had not yet given it instructions, but it shipped these choice colonists to Hispañola, where no preparations had been made for them; most of them perished and the rest took to evil courses. After such a beginning there was small hope of success and Las Casas abandoned the scheme when he learned that the Geronimites had sold the royal plantations out of which the immigrants were to receive allotments and when he found that Bishop Fonseca and the council refused to make the promised provision for their temporary support.[37]

Still indefatigable in spite of these repeated disappointments, he found favor in the eyes of the new chancellor Gattinara, with whom he speedily evolved a more daring scheme. Abandoning the islands, he resolved to try whether the peaceful colonization of new territory might not solve the problems which had thus far baffled Spanish statesmanship. Tierra Firme—the north coast of the Southern continent—had been scarcely touched, although Pedro de Córdova with his Dominicans and some Franciscans had established a few missionary stations there. He asked for the control of this land, to be settled under his direction, according to an elaborate and somewhat fantastic plan, which he worked out in the minutest detail, and in return for this he promised that in three years the king should derive from it a revenue of fifteen thousand ducats, growing to thirty thousand in six years, and to sixty thousand in ten years. It shows the confidence which he had inspired that he obtained this grant, consisting of three hundred leagues of the northern coast, from the Gulf of Paria to Santa Marta, and extending inland to the southern sea, comprising in fact, well-nigh half of South America. The "capitulation" was signed by Charles, May 19, 1520, at Coruña, two days before he sailed to assume the title of "King of the Romans." Las Casas owed this to the favor of Cardinal Adrian and the Flemings, for Bishop Fonseca and the council of the Indies had fought the project bitterly and he had only been successful at the last moment.[38]

On the strength of such a grant as this he had no trouble in raising the money requisite for the enterprise; the necessary papers were made out for him, friends contributed an ample store of beads, bells, and other trinkets for trading with the Indians, he gathered a sufficient number of industrious laborers, and on November 11, 1520, he set sail from

[37] *Ibid.*, Lib. III, cc. civ, cxxx (LXV, 391; LXVI, 33).
[38] *Ibid.*, cc. cxxxi-cxli, clv (LXVI, pp. 37 ff., 164).

San Lucar, full of hope, for he had at his disposal a vast territory on which no Spaniard could set foot without his permission and where he would have free scope to realize his convictions that the Indians could be converted and civilized by peaceful means. On his arrival at Puerto Rico, however, disastrous news awaited him. Spaniards engaged in the pearl fishery on Cubagna, one of the Leeward Isles near the coast, being in want of Indians to carry on that peculiarly deadly trade, had made a raid on the mainland for slaves; the exasperated natives had retaliated by massacring the Dominicans at Chiribichi and Maracapana, on whom he had relied for the commencement of his work, and, moreover, the authorities of Hispañola, under pretext of avenging this, were organizing a great slave raid in five vessels with three hundred men. There was thus little chance for the peaceful colonizing on which his scheme depended, but he waited in Puerto Rico to intercept and if possible arrest the expedition. When it came, however, the captain refused to obey the royal power delegated to Las Casas and proceeded on his errand of destruction. Las Casas went on to Hispañola, where the authorities threw every obstacle in the way of his plans, although they could not refuse to issue the required proclamation forbidding, under pain of death and confiscation, anyone to go to his territory without his license. He was finally obliged to come to a compromise, under which, in July 1521, he set out for the coast in two vessels laden with provisions and articles of barter. He landed in the river Cumana, where Gonzalo de Ocampo was endeavoring to found a Spanish settlement near a Franciscan mission, but his people were starving, for the Spaniards on Cubagna kept the whole coast in a state of alarm and the natives everywhere were hostile. Ocampo's men gladly seized the opportunity to escape and those whom Las Casas had brought refused to remain. There was nothing to do but to land the goods, to the value of fifty thousand castellanos, and to let the people go.[39]

It was evident that the peaceful conversion of the Indians was impossible unless the raids on the coast could be stopped, and for this it was necessary to invoke the royal authority. After long and prayerful consideration Las Casas concluded to appeal personally for this and he sailed for Hispañola; an ignorant pilot carried him to leeward of Cape Beata and two months were wasted in vainly beating against wind and current to get back. Finally he abandoned the attempt and landed at Yaquimo (Jacmel?) and made his way across the country to San Domingo, where he learned that his colony had been destroyed by the Indians, though most of his people had made their escape. The blow was crushing; the lofty hopes which he had cherished when leaving

[39] *Ibid.*, cc. clvi-clviii (LXVI, pp. 165 ff.).

Spain, with half a continent at his disposal, were irretrievably shattered, and it is no wonder that even his iron tenacity of purpose gave way for a time. He wrote to the king and while awaiting a reply, in 1523, he yielded to the solicitations of the Dominicans and entered their order. During his noviciate letters came from Cardinal Adrian and the Flemings of the court telling him that if he would return he should be received with greater favor than ever, but the superiors of the convent withheld them and he took the irrevocable vows.[40]

After the agitations and disappointments of the last eight years the peaceful existence of the convent was grateful and Las Casas found repose in the study of theology and in writing his *Historia Apologetica*. It shows that the kindly intentions of the Spanish rulers towards their Indian subjects were not dependent upon his exhortations, that during this period Charles V issued a decree, June 26, 1523, to the effect that no one should injure the Indians in person or property; anyone striking of killing them or taking from them anything against their will, except the legal tribute, or laying hands upon them or seizing their wives or children, should be punished according to the laws of Castile, and all royal officials were ordered to use the most watchful care in ascertaining and punishing wrongs committed upon them.[41] In 1523 also, he repeated to Cortés an injunction which he had given to Diego Velazquez in 1518, forbidding him from making repartimientos of the Indians.[42] They were thus fully recognized as free vassals of the Crown, like native Castilians, and the decree of 1523 was reissued in 1543, 1582, and 1620. Another decree of November 9, 1526, repeated in 1530, 1532, 1540, 1542, and 1548, forbade the enslaving of any Indian, even if captured in a just war; all permissions to that effect, issued by local authorities, were revoked; anyone holding, buying, selling, or exchanging an Indian slave was punishable with forfeiture of all his property, while the Indian was to be set free, and officials neglecting to enforce this with all rigor were deprived of their offices and mulcted in ten thousand maravedís.[43] Moreover, Charles caused a collection of the laws relating to the Indies to be made, to which were prefixed declarations of December 4, 1528 and August 24, 1529, stating that the object of the compilation was the conversion and good treatment of the Indians, wherefore he ordered the inviolable

---

[40] *Ibid.*, cc. clviii-clx (LXVI, 180 ff.).

[41] *Recopilación*, ley 4, Tit. x, Lib. vi. A practical commentary on this legislation is the torture administered to Guatemozin and his chiefs at the demand of the royal treasurer Julian de Alderete, to discover the treasure lost in the *Noche Triste*. Alderete was a creature of Bishop Fonseca.—Torquemada, *Monarquia Indiana* (ed. 1723), I, 574. Cf. Obregón, *México Viejo*, 2. Série, p. 9.

[42] Solorzano, *De Indiarum Jure* (Madrid, 1639), II, 266.

[43] *Recopilación*, ley 1, Tit. ii, Lib. vi.

observance of the laws, especially those in their favor, in spite of all supplications and appeals, and all viceroys, governors, judges, etc., were threatened with confiscation, suspension from office and punishment at the royal pleasure for disobedience.[44] If the Indians were oppressed it evidently was not through any lack of good intentions on the part of the monarch, especially as Bishop Fonseca had died in 1524.

Yet was there no abatement of cruelty and oppression. Cortés was trampling on Mexico, and Pizarro and Almagro were on the point of starting for Peru, where they were to earn an infamous immortality. The rumor of their project is said to have roused Las Casas from his retirement, leading him to visit Spain again, whence he returned with the decree of 1530, which he carried in 1532 to Peru, where Pizarro and Almagro received it obediently, promised to have it solemnly proclaimed with additional penalties, and coolly went on with their infernal work.[45] Thus restored to activity, Las Casas speedily regained his former ardor. We hear of him, in 1533, in Hispañola as prior of the convent of Puerto de Plata, where he created scandal by propagating, in his sermons and otherwise, scruples of conscience as to the treatment of the Indians and forcing a moribund to execute a will manumitting those whom he held, for which the judges complained bitterly of him to the emperor.[46] In 1535 he was aroused to fresh zeal by a report that in return for a loan of three or four hundred thousand ducats, some three or four hundred leagues of the coast of Tierra Firme had been leased to the Germans for four years. This brought from him a fiery letter to the council of the Indies on their responsibility for the destruction of the bodies and souls of the Indians, to remedy which he proposed, in full detail, a plan for ejecting all the conquistadores and placing the colonies in the hands of bishops and friars with troops under their orders.[47]

In 1536 we find him in Mexico, where, in derision of his peaceful theories, the Spaniards proposed his trying them on the province of Tuzulutlan, which from its rugged features and excessive rainfall had resisted all attempts at invasion. He accepted the challenge and entered into a formal agreement with the president, Alonso Maldonado, who promised that if the Indians should submit and pay such moderate tribute as the land could afford in gold, cotton, or maize, they should never be subjected to repartimientos and encomiendas, and that for five years no Spaniard should be allowed to enter the territory, so that his missionary labors should be undisturbed. Las Casas, with two frailes, succeeded in

---

[44] *Recopilación*, ley 5, Tit. I, Lib. VI.
[45] Fabié, *Vida* (*Col. de Doc.*, LXX, 136-38).
[46] *Col. de Doc.*, LXXX, 346.
[47] *Ibid.*, pp. 464-86.

converting the cacique and his people, but his work was cut short by a summons to Guatemala in 1538, for, as a Dominican, he was now subject to the orders of his superiors. Maldonado, who was by no means an admirer of Las Casas's theories, in a letter to the king, October 16, 1539, freely described the success of the effort and his regret that Las Casas should have been called off. In 1540 the agreement was confirmed by Charles, and May 1, 1543, he issued a *cédula* promising that neither he nor his successors would ever alienate the Indians of Tuzulutlan from the crown. In 1545 Las Casas, then bishop of Chiapa, had the satisfaction of visiting the province, when the Christian Indians and their caciques received him joyfully in crowds. In honor of this peaceful victory the name of Tuzulutlan, in 1547, was changed to Vera Paz; in 1560 it became the seat of a bishopric, which in 1605 was merged into that of Guatemala.[48] This was the one success of Las Casas in his long and active career, but it is of supreme importance as showing the truth of his postulate that men of apostolic spirit could have peacefully spread Christianity and civilization through the New World.

While in Guatemala, in 1539, Las Casas received instructions from Charles to continue his good work in pacifying the Indians, but he was anxious to interview the emperor and he procured a mission to go to Spain and bring out more members of his order. On his arrival he found that Charles was in Germany and to him wrote, December 15, 1540, that he had matters of importance to communicate, wherefore he solicited instructions to the Provincial of Castile to let him remain until the emperor's return.[49] The conjuncture was favorable, for Garcia de Loyasa, archbishop of Seville, who was then president of the council of the Indies, regarded Las Casas with much favor. It was resolved to reconsider the whole legislation regarding the Indians, and during 1541 and 1542 numerous conferences were held for the purpose of drafting new laws. As a contribution to the discussion Las Casas wrote several tracts, not printed until 1552, chief among which was his celebrated *Brevísima Relación de la Destruyción de las Yndias*, which has been translated into almost every European language and has formed the text of the discourses on the subject since then. Another of the tracts consists of the eighth of a series of remedies which, by order of the emperor, he laid before a conference held at Valladolid in 1542. This, he says, is the principal remedy, without which all the rest would be useless, viz. that the emperor shall cause an inviolable law to be passed by the cortes and be sworn to in the most solemn manner by the sovereign for himself and

---

[48] Fabié, *Vida* (*Col. de Doc.*, LXX, 144-53, 182-86, 487).—Gams, *Series Episcoporum*, p. 151.

[49] *Col. de Doc.*, VIII, 555.

his successors, incorporating as free vassals of the crown of Castile and Leon all Indians now or hereafter subjected, who are never to be alienated or granted in encomiendas to Spaniards.[50]

There can be little doubt that Las Casas exerted efficient influence on the character of the "New Laws," which were finally signed by Charles at Barcelona, November 20, 1542, and were sent not only to the viceroys and governors, but to the superiors of the convents, so that their execution should be supervised. While not all that he had asked for, they reflected his views too faithfully to retain their place in permanent legislation, for few traces of them are to be found in the final *Recopilación*, collected and promulgated in 1680. They prohibited all slavery of Indians, whom they required to be treated as what they were—vassals of the crown of Castile; all existing slaves were to be set free if the owners could not show legitimate title, and the courts were ordered to appoint proper persons to conduct their cases and to be paid out of the fines. The repartimientos and encomiendas were not abolished, but all new ones were prohibited and existing ones were to lapse on the death of the possessors, provision being made to compensate widows and children out of the Indian tribute.[51]

To appreciate the opposition excited by this project for the extinction of the encomiendas, we must consider the peculiar character of the Spanish conquests. They were not made by the royal fleets and armies, at the expense and under the direction of the crown, but by filibustering expeditions of adventurers who put at risk their money and their lives in the hope of profit, while the crown obtained the suzerainty of the conquered territories, with one-fifth of the precious metals discovered and a tribute from the Indians subdued. Ponce de Leon, Vasco Nuñez, Cortés, Pizarro, Alvarado, Hernando de Soto, were adventurers of this type, with at most a royal license granting them certain rights over what territory they might acquire. When the conquest was made it was organized by giving to each soldier, according to his merits and services, an encomienda, or tract of land, with so many Indians, to be held for two lives, after which it would lapse to the crown. The indignation not unnaturally excited among those threatened with the shortening of their tenures, is expressed with more vigor than courtliness in a letter to the emperor from the authorities of the city of Guatemala, September 10, 1543. They had heard of the New Laws, but had not yet received them, and they made haste to complain bitterly that their services are to be rewarded by depriving them of the grants solemnly assured to them. They had conquered the land at their own expense without cost to the

[50] *La Libertà pretesa dal supplice Indiano* (Venice, 1640), p. 7.
[51] *Brevísima Relación*, p. 135.—Fabié, *Vida (Col. de Doc.*, LXX, 159-61).

crown; they had been urged and ordered to marry and are now encumbered with families, while their children are to be left to starve by depriving them of the succession to the repartimientos, and all this to gratify the whims of an ignorant and scandalous friar, whose vanity will not allow him to be quiet and who had been driven from every place and every convent that had been afflicted by his presence.[52]

The crown was evidently in a false position. It had reaped where it had not sown and now it was seeking to deprive the laborers of all share in the harvest earned by their sweat and blood. The original vice in the methods of conquest rendered humanity to the Indians impossible. So lately as May 13, 1538, Charles had authorized the "commendation," for two lives, of Indian towns and villages to those who had deserved the reward,[53] and it could not be expected that they would submit quietly to this sudden change of policy, which meant ruin to their families, while aggrandizing the crown. When Blasco Nuñez Vela endeavored to enforce the new laws in Peru, it led to the revolt under Gonzalo Pizarro, and the same would have been the result in Mexico had not Francisco Tello de Sandoval prudently suspended them after publication. The loss of all the colonies on the mainland was imminent and Charles yielded. He was in Flanders, far removed from the influence of Las Casas, and at Mechlin, October 20, 1545, he issued a *cédula* revoking the provisions of 1542 on this subject.[54] The encomiendas thus were firmly established, and for a hundred years they continued to be the subject of perpetual legislation, mostly in the direction of protecting the Indians from the abuses inherent in the system. Theoretically, as described by Machuca, this was simply that all the Indians in an encomienda should pay to the lord a tribute fixed by law, in return for which he was required to establish and maintain a *doctrina*, or mission with a priest, to defend them in their suits, to cure them in their maladies, to pursue and seize all fugitives and to perform some other minor duties.[55] The statutes for their protection, in the constant reiteration of

[52] *Col. de Doc.*, LXX, 529.

[53] *Recopilación*, ley 3, Tit. VIII, Lib. VI.

[54] Solorzano, *De Indiarum Jure*, II, 598.—Garcilaso Inca, *Hist. Gen. del Perù*, Lib. IV, c. vii.—*Recopilación, ubi sup.*

[55] *Discursos Apolóxicos*, (*Col. de Doc.*, LXXI, 260). The encomiendas had originally been granted for two lives and there was naturally a constant pressure for extending or perpetuating the benefice. In 1555 Antonio de Ribera was sent to the emperor in Germany with an offer of six or seven millions of ducats if he would render them perpetual in Peru. Las Casas protested vigorously but Charles yielded, and by a *cédula* from Ghent, September 5, 1556, he conceded the request; the transaction, however, fell through owing to the impossibility of raising so enormous a sum (Solorzano, *loc. cit.*). Yet it was recognized as a hardship that the grandchildren of the conquerors should be disinherited and sundry laws of 1555, 1559, 1576, 1588 and 1607 recite that in this way the descendants of the original discoverers and settlers became impoverished, wherefore it was ordered that a third life

prohibitions of oppression, are eloquent of the wrongs to which the defenseless serfs were subjected, incurable by legislation, however beneficent. That repeated decrees forbade all officials and churches to hold encomiendas was evidently for the purpose of preventing them from being interested in the violation of laws which they were bound to enforce, but the necessity for reënunciating these decrees shows how little they were obeyed.[56] At the close of the century Mendieta describes the encomiendas as the most cruel infliction which threatens the destruction of the Indians, who were compelled to forced labor with unsparing rigor. His description of their condition is deplorable, for their tasks were exacted of them with merciless severity and they were treated far worse than the negro slaves, whose cost was some protection. It was a serious obstacle to their conversion, for the hatred thus aroused was especially directed to the ministers of God as the accomplices of their ruthless oppressors.[57] In the first quarter of the seventeenth century Fray Juan de Torquemada describes the system as the total destruction of the Indians through the forced labor imposed on them in the mines and elsewhere, though he deems it more prudent not to enter into details.[58] The saintly Palafox, who, in the discharge of his duties as bishop of Puebla, protector of the Indians and inspector-general of the tribunals, had traversed Mexico from shore to shore and thus had special knowledge of the situation, in 1650 addressed to Philip IV a touching appeal to enforce the laws for their protection; they were still subject to intolerable abuses, including enforced labor, but their long-suffering was such that they endured all in silence and rarely sought redress for the most flagrant wrongs unless stimulated to it by some Spaniard.[59]

In the New Laws of 1542, Las Casas had again apparently accomplished nearly all that he had sought, and in that year he was offered the bishopric of Cuzco, which he refused. Then the see of Chiapa fell vacant,

---

might be tolerated and then a fourth. Finally the rule of four lives was adopted for all grants made up to 1607. Those who subsequently obtained encomiendas endeavored to claim the benefit of this, but Philip IV, in 1637, decreed that unless a longer term was specified in the grant it should be deemed for two lives only (*Recopilación,* leyes 14, 15, Tit. XI, Lib. VI). They were in some sense military fiefs; the *encomiendero* was held to military service and was bound to keep horse and arms; the holding passed to the eldest son if there was one, and could never be sold or exchanged or alienated and one-third of the revenue was paid to the Crown (*Ibid.,* leyes 1-4, 8, 13, Tit. XI; leyes 38, 39, 44, Tit. VIII; leyes 4, 8, Tit. IX, Lib. VI). The Indians when gathered in pueblos or villages under this system were in some sense predial serfs, for they could not leave the spot; but there were also large numbers of them *de mita,* who were employed in forced labor at the mines and in transportation, in which their sufferings continued with little abatement· (leyes 16, 17, 22, 25, Tit. IX; Tit. XII, Lib. VI).

[56] *Recopilación,* ley 12, Tit. VIII, Lib. VI.

[57] Mendieta, *Hist. Ecles.,* pp. 519 ff.

[58] Torquemada, *Monarquia Indiana,* I, 647.

[59] Palafox, *De la Naturaliza del Indio* (Madrid, 1762), X, 451.

which he accepted. The year 1543 was passed in getting his bulls from Rome and in selecting a chosen band of forty-six Dominicans to accompany him, for he was resolved to make full use of the power inherent in the episcopal office to enforce the reforms which had been promised in the new legislation. He was consecrated in Seville, March 30, 1544, and on July 10 he sailed from San Lucar, reaching San Domingo, September 9. He found that the New Laws had not received the slightest attention; procurators had been sent to Spain to labor for their repeal, and it was with great difficulty that he obtained their publication without thereby securing their observance.[60] It was the same when he reached Campeachy, early in January 1545, and so great was the antagonism towards him that the people refused to receive him as their bishop or to pay his salary and tithes, so that he had no little trouble in raising money to defray a portion of the charter of the vessels that brought him and his frailes. After tribulations and losses he reached his episcopal city of Cuidad Real de Chiapa, where in his modest cathedral he found but two priests—the dean, Gil Quintana and canon, Juan Perera. His sermons and exhortations as to the Indians were uttered to deaf ears, but as Easter drew near he felt himself master of the situation. Paschal communion was a matter of obligation, which no Spaniard of that day could possibly omit, while sacramental confession and absolution were a condition precedent to communion. As bishop he had complete control of the confessional; he could determine who should hear confessions and what sins he should reserve for absolution by himself exclusively. He commenced by withdrawing all licenses to hear confessions, except those of Quintana and Perera, and to them he gave a list of cases reserved to himself, including not only the servitude and ill-treatment of the Indians, but the wealth acquired from them, which he classed as ill-gotten gains requiring restitution before the sinner could hope for absolution. This practical denial of the Easter sacrament produced a tumultuous agitation in which his life was threatened; Quintana favored the slaveholders and ventured to absolve four of them under his faculties as commissioner of the Santa Cruzada, for which Las Casas excommunicated him; but the people so boycotted the bishop and his Dominicans that they were in danger of starvation and took refuge with the Indians of Chiapa, who received them with rejoicing and earnestly sought conversion and baptism.[61]

Las Casas had summoned Marroquin, bishop of Guatemala, and Valdevieso of Nicaragua to meet him at Gracias á Dios, the capital of the province, for the purpose of demanding of the Audiencia, or royal

[60] Fabié, *Vida* (*Col. de Doc.*, LXX, pp. 161-71).
[61] *Ibid.*, pp. 172-86, 531-33.

court, the enforcement of the New Laws. To keep this engagement he left his retreat among the Indians and went to the capital, where the president Maldonado and the judges treated him with contempt and called him a fool and a madman. Nothing daunted, on October 22, 1545, he presented a formal demand that he should be supported by the civil power in his episcopal authority and that the New Laws should be enforced; if this was not done within three months, he pronounced on them a sentence of excommunication *ipso jure*. They replied that they would issue orders to enforce his jurisdiction and that they would obey the royal laws, but they appealed from his sentence to the pope; they denied his power to excommunicate them and threatened to report his excesses to the king in order that he might be properly punished. Both sides, in fact, wrote to Spain accusing the other. Las Casas and Valdevieso stated that the condition of the Indians was growing worse, that Maldonado and his kindred held allotments of sixty thousand of them and of course he would not enforce the New Laws; that the Bishop of Guatemala also held allotments, and that they would resign their sees unless there were prospects of improvement. Then news reached him that the people of Cuidad Real had organized to seize his temporalities and prevent his return. In spite of warnings that his life was at stake, he set out and entered the town at night. There were stormy and tumultuous proceedings, but his firmness triumphed, and by Christmas he was carried in procession to a house that had been prepared for him.[62]

His stay was short. In 1544 Francisco Tello de Sandoval had come to New Spain as *visitador*, or inspector-general, with instructions to promulgate the New Laws, which he did, March 28, 1545. They were not enforced, however, owing to the general opposition, and it was probably on this account that he summoned all the bishops and superiors of convents to meet him in Mexico. Towards the end of February 1546, Las Casas set out, secretly resolving never to return. There was a notable gathering of prelates and men of learning, who after many public conferences laid down eight principles, which are noteworthy as expressing the attitude of the Church on the policy of the conquest. These state that the only object of the Holy See in conceding the sovereignty of the Indies to Spain was the propagation of the faith; that the heathen justly possess what they hold, including their kingdoms, states, lordships, and jurisdictions; that conversion can only be accomplished by persuasion; that the Holy See, in granting the supreme overlordship to Spain, did not intend to deprive the natives of their estates and dignities and jurisdictions, or to concede anything that would interfere with the evangeliza-

[62] *Ibid.*, pp. 182-201, 535-41.

tion of the land, and that the kings of Castile, in volunteering to provide for the diffusion of the faith, were under obligation to defray all expenses necessary for that purpose. Moreover on this basis was framed a formulary for confessors in absolving Spaniards, and a memorial was drawn up to the king and the council of the Indies so that its principles might be embodied in legislation. In all this the slavery of the Indians was not alluded to, at the express desire of the viceroy, Antonio de Mendoza, but a sermon of Las Casas on the subject so moved him that he permitted it to be discussed in meetings held privately and offered to forward to the king their conclusions, which were that Indian slavery was unlawful, except of those captured in the second war of Jalisco, and that the enforced labor imposed on the natives was condemned.[63]

Las Casas was determined to return to Spain. In preparation for his absence he appointed, in November 1546, a provisor and confessors to whom he sent the instructions to confessors agreed upon in the conference of Mexico. These were so rigorous that, when they became known, appeal was made to Prince Philip, who, in November 1547, ordered them to be sent to Spain for examination. The uncompromising and unpractical character of these instructions renders easily intelligible the fierce hatred which Las Casas excited among the colonists. He had already, in 1543, expressed his views in a letter to Charles V, in which he argued that all the wealth acquired by the conquistadores and their successors was robbery. From this it followed that they should be stripped of it, except enough to sustain life; half of this should be restored to those from whom it had been taken or to their heirs, and the other half be used to send out and establish industrious settlers who would render the colonies flourishing.[64] Even this, however, was a compromise which he outgrew and in the instructions to confessors he assumed that not one of the conquistadores possessed rightfully a single maravedí—if he were rich as the duke of Medina Sidonia he could not with all his wealth make satisfactory restitution, and his heirs were in the same condition. As a preliminary to absolution, therefore, the penitent was required to make a valid legal conveyance before a notary of all his property, to be distributed at the discretion of the confessor, who might allow as alms to the heirs enough for a bare subsistence. Extravagant as may seem this violent transfer of all the wealth, real and personal, of the colonies through the hands of the confessors, it was so rigidly deducible from the conclusions of scholastic theology that all the doctors and theologians to whom the instructions were submitted

[63] Ibid., pp. 203-8.
[64] Col. de Doc., LXXI, 422.

approved of them, as they were bound to do.[65] In his zeal for the Indians, however, Las Casas cast aside the system of composition for ill-gotten gains of which the owner cannot be found, whereby the Church has prudently in practice left an outlet for the more or less repentant sinner, in order not to render confession "odious," and we have seen that he excommunicated his dean Quintana for exercising his power as commissioner of the Santa Cruzada, in which this faculty of prescribing compositions in such cases had been a source of abundant revenue. In his letter of 1543 to Charles V, Las Casas had admitted this principle of composition by advising that, in cases where the original owner or his heirs could not be found, authority be obtained from the pope to compound for one-half or one-fifth or one-sixth, according to the degree of criminality involved, and that the immense sums thus acquired be expended in spreading the faith and in establishing peaceful and industrious settlers, after having expelled the leaders of the conquistadores, such as Almagro. The synod of Santafé de Bogotá, in 1556, proposed a more thrifty solution of the problem by deciding that the holders of encomiendas, who had established missions in their lands and had paid their full dues to the Church, could conscientiously retain all that they had taken from the Indians, while those who had neglected to do so ought to make restitution, because the reason for the conquest was the spread of the faith.[66]

It argues well for the Spanish monarchs that Las Casas never lost their favor while maintaining and endeavoring to enforce doctrines so revolutionary and so disturbing to the state, for he applied them to the sovereign as well as to the subject. His theories, imperfectly expressed in the Declaration of Mexico in 1546, were that the king of Spain was merely overlord of the Indies, as the emperor was of Germany, and that even the papal grant required free confirmation by the native rulers to render it effective. The Indians were to be left to their own institutions, under their caciques, while the Spanish king was to be at the expense of maintaining and protecting the friars sent for their conversion. Even for this service he was debarred from exacting any tribute. In a letter of August 1555, to Carranza, the subsequent archbishop of Toledo, then in England with Philip II, he asks whether there is no one who will undeceive the sovereigns and make them understand that they cannot levy a real of tribute from the Indians with a good conscience. To reach these conclusions he did not hesitate, in an age of

[65] Fabié, Vida (Col. de Doc., LXX, 307).

[66] Groot, Hist. eclesiástica y civil de Nueva Granada, I, App. ii, p. 492. This is stated to be derived from the first Mexican council, held in 1556, but there is no such provision in the proceedings of the latter.

absolute monarchy, to affirm the broad principle that rulers are made for the people, not the people for the rulers.[67]

In 1547 Las Casas left the Indies for the last time. On his arrival in Spain he was almost at once involved in his celebrated contest with Gines de Sepúlveda, one of the leading theologians of the time, which occupied him until 1550. Sepúlveda had been retained by the adverse interests and had written a work entitled *Democrites alter*, to justify the subjugation of the Indians. The controversy was a bitter one, in which Sepúlveda endeavored to convict Las Casas of treason and heresy, but it is only of interest to us here as furnishing evidence that the conscience of the learned classes in Spain was more sensitive on the subject than has generally been thought, for, although Sepúlveda stood forward as the defender of the royal power and prerogative, his book was condemned by the universities of Alcalá and Salamanca, permission to print it was refused by both the councils of State and of the Indies, and when he sent it to Rome to be published its introduction into Spain was prohibited.[68] Moreover, by command of the council of the Indies, Las Casas, in 1552, wrote a tract enumerating the sufferings of the virtually enslaved Indians, and proving that Spaniards so holding them were in mortal sin and incapable of absolution until they should release all who were not legally in bondage.[69] To Las Casas may chiefly be attributed this enormous ethical advance, since Ferdinand's theologians justified the Laws of Burgos.

In 1550 Las Casas resigned his bishopric. Advancing years rendered him less able to perform active work in the cause to which he had dedicated himself, but, until his death in 1566, at the age of 92, he continued indefatigably with pen and tongue to defend the defenseless Indians. He was in constant correspondence with friends in the Indies, who kept him advised of their sufferings, his indignation remained as hot as ever and his zeal for their relief was unabated. Yet he was forced sorrowfully to admit, in a letter to the Dominicans of Guatemala, in 1562, that in the sixty-one years during which he had been a witness of Spanish tyranny, the oppression of the Indians had gone on constantly increasing, which was a disheartening outcome of his incessant labors and of the numerous laws which had been enacted in their behalf.[70] It is no wonder that in what was probably his last writing he foretold that the wrath of God would be visited on Spain for the wicked and impious treat-

---

[67] *Col. de Doc.*, LXXI, 386.—"Disputa con Sepúlveda," Princip. IV, *Conquista dell' Indie occidentali* (Venice, 1645), p. xi.

[68] *Ibid.*, p. 174.

[69] *Tratado sobre la materia de las Indias* (Venice, 1657).

[70] *Col. de Doc.*, LXXI, 369.

ment of the Indians, and that he bequeathed to the college of San Gregorio in Valladolid his collection of letters, descriptive of the cruelty practised on them, which he desired to be carefully preserved in order that if the Lord should hereafter destroy Spain the causes of his vengeance might be manifest.[71]

The encomiendas, as we have seen, had become too deeply rooted to be eradicated, and the kindly legislation which continued to be enacted was powerless to prevent the abuses inseparable from it—indeed, the repetition of prohibitions of overtaxing and maltreating the natives are only of worth as showing how vain was the effort to ameliorate the system and how inevitable were its evils under the lax and corrupt administration prevalent in the Spanish colonies. Philip II was constant and earnest in his efforts to protect his Indian subjects. In 1582 he ordered inspectors sent through all the provinces to reform abuses committed on them, and he instructed his viceroys and governors and judges constantly to report whatever seemed to them to require remedy; in 1595 he decreed that Spaniards who maltreated or injured Indians should be punished more severely than if the offence were committed on Spaniards; in 1596 he commanded all prelates to send detailed reports by every fleet as to the condition of the natives—whether they were well or ill treated, whether they were increasing or diminishing, whether the laws for their protection were observed or not—together with suggestions as to what could be done for their improvement.[72] A decree of Philip IV prohibited all forced labor and required satisfaction to be given to him and to the world for their ill-treatment, which is against God and himself and the total destruction of the empire.[73] As the Spanish conquests spread over South America, the most careful instructions were issued to preserve the liberty of the Indians, and when in 1629, the governor of Marañon sent some as slaves to other places, saying that they had been lawfully enslaved, Philip IV ordered their immediate release.[74] It was the same in the Philippines; in 1609 Philip III gave instructions that on all public works Chinese and Japanese should be hired; if they could not be had in adequate numbers the voluntary service of the natives might be accepted, but they were not to be compelled to labor unless the safety of the State was at stake, for their freedom was of greater moment than the convenience of the public or any saving to the treasury.[75] Charles II, by a decree of June 12, 1679, ordered all Indian slaves in Peru and New Spain to be set free; he had commanded this before, but the governor

[71] Fabié, *Vida* (*Col. de Doc.*, LXX, 235, 237).
[72] *Recopilación*, leyes 7, 8, 21, Tit. x, Lib. vi.
[73] *Ibid.*, ley 25, Tit. v; ley 2, Tit. x, Lib. vi.
[74] *Ibid.*, ley 4, Tit. ii, Lib. vi.
[75] *Ibid.*, ley 40, Tit. xii, Lib. vi.

of Chile had suspended it under various pretexts and he now makes the order peremptory, for it is of supreme importance that the Indians be treated lovingly and not be oppressed or molested.[76] There was an organization of officials known as Protectors of the Indians, whose function it was to see that their rights were preserved, and to enforce those rights by judicial action, and these protectors were instructed to keep the home government constantly advised as to any infringement on the privileges of the natives and as to whether the viceroys and courts did their duty in this respect.[77] The Sixth Book of the *Recopilación de las Leyes de las Indias* contains hundreds of decrees manifesting this constant and anxious care of the sovereigns for the welfare, temporal and spiritual, of the native race committed to their charge; and the spirit in which this compilation was made, in 1680, is revealed by the fact that in the section devoted to the good treatment of the Indians the first place is given to the earnest and touching codicil of Queen Isabella, which is ordered to be observed by all officials as of full legal and binding force.

The contrast between the kindliness which reigned in Madrid and the oppression which prevailed throughout the colonies illustrates the uselessness of legislation when its execution is committed to defective or corrupt administration.

[76] *Ibid.*, ley 16, Tit. ii, Lib. vi.
[77] *Ibid.*, Tit. vi, Lib. vii.

CONTEMPORARY (NINETEENTH CENTURY) CHURCH AFFAIRS

THE RELIGIOUS REFORM MOVEMENT IN ITALY*

[This article reflects the keen interest everywhere felt regarding the attitude of the Church in the years immediately preceding the final unification of Italy. In accordance with the usual custom of the period, it takes the form of a review of the following books:

Talmadge, William: *Letters from Florence on the Religious Reform Movements in Italy*, London, 1866; *L' Esaminatore: Foglio Periodico Settimanale*, Firenze, 1867, 1868; *L' Emancipatore Cattolico: Giornale della Società Nazionale Emancipatrice e di Mutuo Soccorso del Sacerdozio Italiano*, Napoli, 1867, 1868; *Programma e Statuto Fondamentale della Società Nazionale Emancipatrice del Sacerdozio Italiano*, Napoli, 1864; Prota, P. Luigi: *Il Matrimonio Civile e il Celibato del Clero Cattolico*, Napoli, 1864; Panzini, Paolo: *Pubblica Confessione di un Prigioniero dell' Inquisizione Romana ed Origine dei Mali della Chiesa Cattolica*, Torino, 1865; *Recueil des Allocutions Consistoriales, Encycliques, et autres Lettres Apostoliques des Souverains Pontifes Clément XII, Benoit XIX, Pie VI, Pie VII, Léon XII, Grégoire XVI, et Pie IX, citées dans l'Encyclique et le Syllabus du 8 Decembre, 1864*, 2nd ed. Paris, 1865.—H.]

*　　*　　*　　*　　*

WHEN M. Rouher pronounced in the *Corps Législatif* his emphatic "Jamais, jamais, jamais!" it is probable that he sealed the doom of that temporal power to which he was pledging the unqualified support of thirty-eight millions of Frenchmen. The promise which he then made, that under no circumstances would France permit the absorption of the papal territory by United Italy—a promise extorted from the Imperial cabinet by the sudden and unforeseen exigencies of debate—shows how difficult it is for the coolest and shrewdest despot to control his own policy under even the forms of constitutional government, and how all the cunning experience of diplomacy may come to naught when subjected to the pressure of popular clamor or fanaticism. Nothing could have been much more unwise, whether as regards the future of the Second Empire or of the papacy, than such a pledge given at such a time.

Italy can hardly as yet be considered a nation. The Tuscan and the Piedmontese, the Neapolitan and the Lombard, still look upon one another as strangers, and much is yet needed of common sufferings and dangers, of common humiliations and aspirations, to weld them into a compact and homogeneous nationality. The lines which have been drawn by segregation, under a thousand years of foreign domination, are too deep to be effaced in a single decade; nor is ruinous taxation, repaid only by the disasters of Custoza and Lissa, calculated to foster

* From the *North American Review*, CVII (1868), 51-76.

loyalty to the house of Savoy. Whatever, therefore, tends to excite community of feeling and to break down reverence for the past, whatever kindles the passions and hopes of the whole people, from Messina to Turin, making them throb in unison to hot desire or passionate revenge, is the surest means of destroying their separate provincialism, and of moulding them into a people one and indivisible. It would be difficult to say which has been the more successful in accomplishing this, Garibaldi at Mentana or Rouher in the Palais Bourbon.

In another aspect of the question, however, Rouher may be said to have been even more potential than Garibaldi. Difficult as it may be to fuse into one the dozen principalities into which Italy has been divided of old, impossible as may be the creation of an Italian nation so long as its natural capital is withheld from its grasp, yet the chief obstacle to success in the new order of things arises from the inevitable and implacable antagonism between Italian Catholicism and Italian nationality. Not that the pure dogmas of Latin Christianity have in them anything of itself incompatible with social or national development, but that the ecclesiastical structure reared upon them is necessarily involved in internecine strife with the Italy of the present and of the future, and one of the antagonists must inevitably succumb. Compromise is impossible, and it will eventually rest with the people to determine which shall be the victor, progress or reaction. The useless slaughter inflicted by the chassepot at Monte Rotondo was well fitted to lend strength to the party of progress, and their numbers must be swelled incalculably by the bitter humiliation felt at the insolent attitude now so gratuitously assumed by France.

The political future of Italy must be decided by its religion. If a majority of its people retain a blind and unreasoning reverence for the sacerdotalism under which they have been reared, all that has been accomplished will be undone. If, however, the shackles which they have been trained to wear can be thrown off, the rest will be comparatively easy, for the complications of European politics will sooner or later afford them the opportunity of occupying Rome. To attempt this before they are prepared for the inevitable changes which would alone render such occupation permanent and fruitful would only be to risk what has already been gained. Any speculations, therefore, which omit the religious complications under which Italy is laboring leave out of the problem its controlling element.

To comprehend the religious reformatory movement now in progress throughout the peninsula, it is necessary first to understand the guiding principles of the hierarchy against which that movement is directed. To do this it is not requisite to enter upon questions of religious belief, for the reformers profess entire devotion in all points of faith inculcated by the Church. Schism they may perhaps not shrink from, but heresy forms, as yet, no part of their recognized program, and they seem to have no intention of voluntarily withdrawing from communion with the visible head of the faith. It is the structure and policy of the Church which are the objects of their assaults, and while they reverence the pope as the legitimate successor of St. Peter, they desire him to be venerable in apostolic simplicity and holiness, and not a sovereign whose indefinite powers and undefinable pretensions render impossible any progress, moral or political, to which he does not lend his assent.

In this country we see the Catholic clergy adapting themselves without complaint to republican institutions, subjected to the laws of the land, enjoying no special immunities or privileges, busily devoted to the duties of the pastorate, propagating their faith by persuasiveness, earnestly engaged in the religious instruction and moral training of their flocks, and active in the charitable work of feeding the hungry and curing the sick. More than any other denomination throughout the populous North, their labors lie among the poor and humble, and their ceaseless ministrations accomplish results which could be reached by no other instrumentality. It is difficult to imagine these ardent and self-denying men as members of the same brotherhood, believers in the same faith, part of the same organization, as that which from the Vatican has armed the Antibes legion, and which proclaims eternal war against equality, freedom of conscience, liberal education, self-government, and, in short, all the forces which constitute progress and modern civilization.

While the ministers of the Church, under the pressure of circumstances, can adapt themselves to the necessities of their position in a free community like ours, it is the misfortune of the papacy that it is the exponent of an infallible Church, and that, acting under the immediate inspiration of St. Peter, the popes have always been and must always be infallible.[1] Infallibility is a heavy burden for poor humanity. It can confess no errors, it can rectify no blunders, it can offer no expiation for wrongs. To be consistent with itself, it must remain in one age what it was in another, under totally different conditions. The world moves on, while it is forced to lag behind, and it thus becomes an anachronism which has lost its usefulness, and can only exert its powers for evil rather than for good. Thus Mastai Ferretti, kind and benevolent as a man, finds himself as Pius IX charged with the tremendous task of perpetuating in the nineteenth century the theocratic autocracy which Hildebrand aimed to establish, and which Innocent III wielded with awful effect.

[1] Pius IX, Encyc. *Qui pluribus*, November 9, 1846.

Pius has not left us to gather this from his actions alone. In December 1864, he issued to all the prelates of the Church his famous Encyclical epistle, accompanied by a Syllabus of prevalent errors for condemnation by the faithful; and in this formal proclamation he condensed an emphatic declaration of the pretensions, the designs, and the policy of the Church. No claim of supremacy over princes and peoples, which made the mediæval Church the unquestioned master of Europe, is abandoned; and power unjustly withheld alone is wanting to restore the halcyon times when the successor of St. Peter regulated the conscience of Christendom, dethroned kings, commanded war and peace, and insured the purity of faith by an occasional *auto-da-fé*.

On one point, indeed, Pius advances a step beyond his predecessors. While the Church has always assumed infallibility in matters of faith, it has hitherto been held that on points of discipline she may err; but Pius, in the Encyclical, claims that papal decrees, whether they affect dogma or discipline, are equally binding on the consciences of the faithful, and that no dissidence in either case is admissible on the part of anyone pretending to belong to the communion of Rome.

Thus all the old extensions of ecclesiastical despotism, founded on the False Decretals and enforced throughout the darkness of the Middle Ages, are to be found condensed in the Encyclical and Syllabus, with a cynical contempt for modern intelligence. In claiming peremptorily that the Church should have unrestricted liberty to enforce her laws without limitation or hindrance,[2] it is not the free exercise of her religion that is demanded, but the power of persecution. That every man should be allowed to choose his religion according to the dictates of his own conscience is repeatedly denounced as a fatal error, a madness, and a liberty only of damnation.[3] Catholicism is declared to be the only religion which should be suffered to exist by the State,[4] and those nations which tolerate, even in strangers, the exercise of other forms of worship are specially condemned.[5] It is declared to be the duty of the State to punish all who wander from the true faith, and the Church itself is asserted to have the power of enforcing its decrees by temporal as well as by spiritual punishments.[6] That Protestantism should be considered as a form of Christianity is declared to be a pernicious error,[7] and the efforts of Bible societies to diffuse among the people a knowledge of the Scriptures are

---

[2] Syllab., Prop. 19; Alloc. *Multis gravibusque,* December 17, 1860; Alloc. *Maxima quidem,* June 9, 1862.

[3] Encyc., December 1864; Gregor. XVI, Encyc. *Mirari,* 1832; Syllab., Prop. 15, 16.

[4] Gregor., XVI, *op. cit.;* Syllab., Prop. 77.

[5] Syllab., Prop. 78.

[6] Syllab., Prop. 24.

[7] Syllab., Prop. 18.

condemned as tending to lead the flock astray.[8] What is especially shocking in all this is not merely its bigotry and intolerance, which are shared, unfortunately, by too many of the followers of Christ. When these are passive, they injure only the individual who indulges in them; but Pius proclaims the principles of active persecution for conscience' sake, which have repeatedly desolated Europe from end to end, and have done more to retard human progress than the wildest ambition of kings. How sedulously the people are trained to this unchristian duty is visible in the Roman breviary, which, in the office of May 5, is careful to recite that Pius V was enrolled among the saints of heaven to reward the inflexibility with which, as Inquisitor, he had pursued the enemies of the Church; and the lesson was emphatically repeated when, in June 1867, at the celebration of the centenary of St. Peter, Pedro Arbués, one of the bloodiest of the Inquisitors of Spain, was solemnly canonized. It is easy thus to understand why the Inquisition has been maintained in Rome after its expulsion from every other land, and how culpable are the Catholic sovereigns in not reinstating it with full power to repeat the exploits of Torquemada.

If freedom of conscience is thus to be sternly repressed, it is not surprising that freedom of education is also to be destroyed as a dangerous error of modern times. That the State should provide schools for its youth, independently of the Church, is denounced as an evil to be suppressed. It is formally declared that all public schools should be under the supervision and control of the ecclesiastical authorities; and as it is a mistake, according to the Syllabus, to consider the methods of the mediæval theologians as unsuited to modern progress in knowledge, we can readily fancy the application of these principles restoring to us the ages of faith, when the populations were steeped in ignorance dense enough for unquestioning credulity, and when subtle Schoolmen ranged themselves under the banners of Duns Scotus and Thomas Aquinas.[9] We are not, indeed, left entirely to conjecture as to the effect of thus placing the control of education in the hands of men trained in the principles of the Roman curia. This was done by the concordat with Austria, the result of which is described with homely vigor in the petition for its abolition lately presented by the Transylvanians to the *Reichsrath*:

At the annual examinations, the best children are able to give an account of how things look in heaven; they know the names of the principal angels, the number of the saints, and they know something about hell and purgatory.

[8] Syllab., § IV; Encyc. *Qui pluribus*.
[9] Syllab., Prop. 13, 45, 47.

But how things look in their own land, what it produces, what might be produced better and cheaper, what is exported and imported, etc., of all this they know nothing. If the children are able to repeat, like parrots, their catechism and Bible history, they get presents, the ceremony is over, and the old story is repeated in the old way. The municipality has nothing to do with the school beyond furnishing the building, fuel, and all other necessary or unnecessary expenses. It is no wonder that the greater part of the inhabitants of the Austrian monarchy believe that religion, faith, and Concordat form one indivisible trinity.[10]

In the Middle Ages, one of the most fruitful sources of oppression to the people, and of demoralization to the clergy, was the immunity enjoyed by every ecclesiastic from subjection to the law. The jurisdiction of the spiritual courts was not confined to spiritual cases, but extended its shield over all members of the Church, and the practical immunity thence afforded to clerical offences is evidenced by the "benefit of clergy" in the common law of England, which was virtually a free pardon for crime. The common sense of modern times has put an end to this absurdity, and the law, even in Catholic countries, recognizes in the ecclesiastic no superiority elevating him beyond its reach. But the Church has once claimed and enjoyed this privilege for its members, and its infallibility requires that the claim should not be abandoned. Accordingly, Pius demands that the cases of the clergy should not be tried by the secular tribunals, and for this claim he asserts a divine sanction.[11] The value of such a privilege, where religion and politics are so inextricably intermingled, can be estimated from the fact that, in 1862, the government of Italy was obliged to prosecute the bishops of Bologna and Fano for issuing circulars to their priests, instructing them to make use of the confessional for the purpose of stimulating desertion in the Italian army. The bishops assembled in Rome in June 1862, for the canonization of the Japanese martyrs, denounced this act of self-preservation as a violation of the imprescriptible rights of the Church, and

---

[10] To this plain speaking the Austrian bishops, in their address to the Kaiser, retort that "it is not better instruction that is wanted. What is desired is to attack religion and morality. It is wished to make the school serve to propagate unbelief; that is the chief thing." It would be difficult to estimate how much religion has suffered in all ages from the arrogant defenders who identify their own interests with those of Christ. The zealous churchman on the battlefield of Mentana could see the smile of heaven on the placid features of the papal Zouave who had fallen in defence of St. Peter, while those of the Garibaldino near him were distorted with the scowl of hell; and the same spirit leads the *Unità Cattolica*, the organ of the papal court, to declare that God, foreseeing the weakness of Francis Joseph, would not permit the beneficent concordat to render him fortunate, and that the disasters of Solferino and Sadowa were the punishments in advance (for to God the future is as the past) of his letter of October 15, 1867, to the cardinal archbishop of Vienna.

[11] Syllab., Prop. 30, 31.

bemoaned the hard fate of these worthy prelates thus persecuted for the discharge of their duty.[12]

With regard to the relations between the papacy and temporal sovereigns, the Encyclical and Syllabus are similarly indisposed to abandon one jot of the old assumptions of supremacy. When we see it formally asserted that the popes have never transcended the limits of their just authority,[13] we are driven to conclude that the opportunity, and not the will, is wanting for Pius to repeat the exhibitions of papal autocracy which in the Middle Ages rendered the successors of the humble fisherman of Galilee the arbiters of the destinies of Christendom. Indeed, the Roman breviary teaches us the same lesson in still reciting, on the festival of Gregory VII, May 27, that he was canonized for his courageous resistance to the Emperor Henry IV, in depriving him of his crown, and releasing his subjects from their allegiance. As the old traditions of ecclesiastical supremacy are thus carefully treasured, it need not surprise us to see that kings and princes are positively asserted to be subject to the jurisdiction of the Church, and that even the internal municipal laws of states are declared to be involved in the same subjection.[14] Separation between Church and State is denounced as a dangerous error, but this union is not to be a partnership, for, as the civil power is asserted not to be competent to define the limits of its own authority, the privileges claimed for the Church must necessarily render it paramount.[15]

Thus we find in this authoritative exposition of the papal pretensions and policy every principle requisite to the restoration of the Middle Ages in all their glory of credulous faith and spiritual despotism. Indeed, we are not left merely to guess at the aspirations of the Roman curia; for the Syllabus ends by boldly declaring the incompatibility of its system with the present order of things. Its Eightieth proposition positively condemns as a pernicious error the idea that the supreme head of the Church either can or ought to reconcile himself with progress and modern civilization—that "Romanus Pontifex potest ac debet cum progressu, cum liberalismo, et cum recenti civilitate sese reconciliare et componere."

It is melancholy to see an organization so powerful for good as the Catholic Church thus deliberately nullify its usefulness, and array itself against human liberty and intelligence. Yet at the same time we cannot but admire so striking an exhibition of moral intrepidity on the part of an old man on the verge of the grave, already shorn of half his domains,

[12] "Venerabiles Antistites ac Dei Sacerdotes exauctorantur, exulare coguntur, aut in carceres detruduntur; quinimo ante tribunalia civilia, pro constantia in sacro ministerio obenundo, contumeliose pertrahuntur."—Declarat. Episc., June 8, 1862.

[13] Syllab., Prop. 23.

[14] Syllab., Prop. 54, 57.

[15] Syllab., Prop. 55, 19.

and indebted solely to foreign bayonets for the support of his tottering throne and the unwilling submission of his few remaining subjects, while boldly proclaiming war upon all the principles of progress and of modern ideas, asserting all the prerogatives which enabled his predecessors to tread upon the necks of kings, and desperately but resolutely battling to hand down to his successors unimpaired the heritage which he has received; his sturdy faith never questioning whether that heritage was honestly acquired and worthily used, nor whether the good of mankind may not demand that he and all his machinery of obstruction and wrong should be incontinently hurried out of sight and buried forever beyond the possibility of resurrection.

The Italian reformers, however, to whom these claims are not mere theoretical opinions, but solid and most uncomfortable facts, have no admiration to waste on a fortitude which persists in endeavoring to treat them as Arnold of Brescia was treated by Adrian IV or Savonarola by Alexander VI. The papal supremacy and policy are to them the source of daily tribulation, and consequently have become the object of their strenuous and unremitting assaults. Beginning with a keen sense of the injuries inflicted on Church and people by the abuses of overpowering sacerdotalism, they have been gradually led to examine the foundation on which rests the structure that so long overshadowed Christendom; and as their minds have become freed from the incubus of established authority, they have seen that tradition and custom had no weight when opposed to Scripture and the authentic records of the primitive Church. Their object, therefore, has become the restoration of the Church to its condition in the earlier days, before wealth and power had subordinated its spiritual to its temporal interests. Devoutly believing all the points of faith inculcated by the council of Trent, and willing to accord to the bishop of Rome a primacy of honor, they strive to dissociate spiritual from temporal affairs, to throw off the autocratic and all-pervading authority which renders every man's conscience and actions subject to the supervision and direction of the Roman curia, to restore to the local churches the independence which they originally enjoyed, to relax various points of discipline which separate the priesthood into a class distinct from the laity, and generally so to liberalize the Church as to bring it within the influence of modern ideas, and to place it in accord with the progress of modern civilization.

As the active movers in this effort at reform are ecclesiastics, and as its success is to be assured by influencing the ecclesiastical body, the boldness of the task can be appreciated only by understanding how completely all members of the Church in Italy are at the mercy of the hierarchy, and how utterly the hierarchy are dependent upon the pope and the curia. In Italy the priesthood are drawn almost exclusively from the humbler classes. Educated in seminaries where seclusion from the world is rigidly enforced and passive obedience is taught as one of the first of duties, any native spirit of independence which may perchance exist is thoroughly eradicated. When admitted to holy orders, as their daily bread is dependent upon their daily ministrations, and as these may at any moment be suspended by their superiors, nature, training, and necessity conspire to hold the clergy in the most abject subordination. Their personal importance, moreover, is derived from the superstitious veneration of the people, who regard them as part of a splendid establishment, endowed with mysterious and undefinable power, so that every motive is brought to bear to render them the zealous champions of a system which holds them in perpetual slavery.

If the plebeian clergy are thus the passive instruments of their superiors, those superiors are equally held in subjection by the pope. The appointment to the episcopate is virtually in the hands of the Roman court, and zeal in its service is the surest avenue to promotion. The episcopal oath, which beyond the Alps has been modified to suit the exigencies of jealous monarchs, in Italy still binds the prelate as a vassal to the pope, without even an exception of the allegiance due to his sovereign, and forces him to oppose and persecute all heretics and rebels against the papal power.

The Church Militant being thus composed of such materials, and thus organized like an army on a war footing, the position of mutineers who seek to throw off the bonds of discipline can readily be imagined. The troubles of such men as Scipione dei Ricci, Rosmini, and Gioberti are well known, and with the increasing troubles of the Church its ruling spirits grow more vindictive. For urging some moderate reforms, Father Gioacchino Ventura was forced to fly from Italy. When Father Passaglia, in 1862, endeavored to array the priesthood against that temporal power which compromises all the higher interests of religion, adhesion to even the very temperate protest to which he procured thousands of priestly signatures was visited with exemplary chastisement. The signatories were promptly suspended from their functions, and deprived of subsistence until they humbly signed a recantation; and Passaglia, notwithstanding his eminent reputation, was excommunicated, and is still under deprivation. Cardinal D'Andrea, a prelate justly revered for his distinguished virtues, was suspended from all his functions, his offences being his known liberality of sentiment and his resignation of his office of prefect of the Congregation of the Index to avoid being made the instrument of oppression. Submitting without a murmur, he left Rome for his health, and resided privately at Naples, but the jealous fears of his colleagues were still unsatisfied. In December 1867, after the reactionists had been strengthened by the victory of Monte Rotondo, he was ordered back to Rome where he has been forced, by means which can only be guessed at, to sign a most humiliating retractation, and to withdraw the countenance which he had extended to the *Esaminatore*, the organ of the reforming Catholics at Florence. In 1854, Panzini, a learned Capuchin friar, conceived the idea that the evils under which the Church was laboring were principally the result of the enforced celibacy of its members. He privately addressed an anonymous memorial to Pius, praying for an investigation of the subject, and its submission to the prelates then assembled in Rome. This and several similar applications being disregarded, he finally, in 1859, prepared a voluminous essay on the subject, addressed to the Catholic bishops at large, and committed it to the press. The printer made haste to submit the manuscript to the ecclesiastical authorities; Panzini was at once imprisoned and handed over to the Inquisition, which, after six months spent in investigation, condemned him to twelve years' incarceration and perpetual degradation, notwithstanding his earnest protestations of belief in all the points of faith inculcated by the Church, and of his readiness to be convinced of any error into which he might have fallen as to the expediency of the rule in question. At the instance of the Italian ambassador, however, in 1862, he was released from prison, but not restored to his priestly functions, and in 1865, in the safe refuge of Turin, he published the essay, rewritten from memory, under the title of *Pubblica Confessione di un Prigioniero dell' Inquisizione Romana*. The work is well worthy the attention of the student of contemporary history and of human nature. The thesis is argued exclusively from a Catholic standpoint; the profoundest veneration is manifested for all the dogmas of the Church, outside of whose pale salvation is impossible; while the bitterest spirit of revolt is displayed against the grinding tyranny of the hierarchy, and the condition of ecclesiastical morality throughout Italy is described as terrible. We have it on good authority that a distinguished prelate exclaimed, on reading the volume, that if it had been cast in a more popular form it alone would have been sufficient to provoke a revolution in the bosom of the Church.

Of late the trials of the reformers have been sharpened. The Italian government at first protected them, but under the reactionary tendency of the recent cabinets of Florence, they have had much to suffer. Still clinging to the Church, and claiming a place among its ministers, they are exposed to many evils which they might escape if their consciences would allow them to renounce all allegiance to the power against whose abuses they gallantly struggle. In a letter now before us from the Reverend

Dr. Prota, the energetic leader of the movement in Naples, he touchingly alludes to the trials endured by him and his brethren for the cause which they have espoused:

Up to the present time we have suffered everything,—the desertion of friends, the calumny of enemies, the curses of our brethren of the priesthood, the enmity of the prejudiced and fanatical masses, and even the want of the necessaries of life. Yet have we borne all with resignation, and the mercy of our Lord and Saviour has never failed to comfort us in our trials, and to raise in the hearts of strangers sentiments of kindness and charity towards us.

The position of the Neapolitan reformers, in fact, has been of late one of peculiar hardship. The reactionary archbishop, Cardinal Riario Sporza, was one of the prelates exiled for his opposition to the new régime. In his absence much was accomplished. Dr. Prota founded the "Società Emancipatrice e di mutuo Soccorso del Sacerdozio Italiano," which soon enrolled in its membership three hundred priests. The royal chapels were placed in their charge, and money was appropriated by the government for their support. A year ago, however, the policy of Baron Ricasoli underwent a mysterious change. With the other reactionary bishops, Sporza was reinstated, and lost no time in visiting the reformers with his vengeance. They were forthwith suspended from their functions, and as at the same time the public subvention was withdrawn, all sources of support were cut off. Under this pressure the major part "reconciled" themselves to the Church by taking an oath dictated by Sporza, "which amounted not merely to a renunciation of the society and a recantation of every reforming principle, but even to an abjuration of their civil allegiance as Italian citizens."[16] A remnant of the band, however, stood firm, and have continued to maintain a gallant though unequal contest. One of their efforts has been the founding of an "Asilo di lavoro," under the guidance of Padre Ragghianti Salvadore, where a certain number of these persecuted ones unite their slender efforts at self-support by teaching and ministering the Gospel to the scanty flock which they have succeeded in collecting around them. Every Sunday they address a congregation of eighty or one hundred of the faithful, and through the week they hold day schools for children and night schools for adults, in each of which they number about thirty scholars.

[16] Report of Reverend W. C. Langdon, secretary of Italian Committee, American Episcopal Church. In an address to his brethren, under date of January 2, 1868, Dr. Prota bitterly alludes to these cruel trials, brought upon them by the shortsighted weakness of the government: "Nè valsero a scuotere la nostra fede politica le crudeli ed efferate persecuzione di certi uomini, che assunti al potere adoperarono ogni mezzo per aggiogare al carro della prepotenza straniera la patria loro. . . . E quanto più vile ed abietta fu la loro vendetta contro di noi sino a privarci di quei pochi mezzi di sussistenza che lo stesso governo nazionale a noi avea concesso in omaggio ai principi che abbiam propugnati."

The isolation of these men is indeed well fitted to test their thorough conscientiousness in the task which they have undertaken. Still Catholics in faith, they can neither ask nor expect active aid from the flourishing Protestantism of other countries. The laity which surrounds them is either superstitiously subjected to the Church, or else, with rare exceptions, perfectly indifferent to religion and impervious to religious influences. Their fellow-churchmen naturally regard them with horror as heretics in all but name, and as traitors and rebels of the worst sort. The prelates in general lose no opportunity of persecuting them with all the ingenuity of enemies armed with irresponsible powers of oppression. The very numbers of the ecclesiastical army,—in the Pontifical States, before the annexations of 1862, there was one churchman to every fifty-five inhabitants, and in Northern Italy the proportion is as one to one hundred and forty,—by subdividing the sources of revenue into the minutest portions, render them all dependent for their daily bread upon the daily stipend derived from their ministry, which is at the mercy of the irresponsible caprice of their superiors.

The training of the seminary not only carefully unfits the priest for the active duties of life, thus rendering him wholly dependent upon his profession, but it further makes him incapable of forming a correct estimate of the movements taking place around him, and precludes all sympathy between him and the people whose religious guidance is committed to his hands. With some, perhaps, a sense of patriotism may neutralize this to a certain extent; but, with the majority, class influences and early education destroy the sentiment of nationality, by rendering the Church the sole object of aspirations, and by making obedience to its behests paramount to all other duties. The priesthood is thus a nation within a nation, and the antagonism which is daily growing between the clergy and the people threatens results more disastrous to the pretensions of the Church, and perhaps in the end to religion itself, than all other causes combined. Under the Austrian rule in Lombardy, for instance, the Church establishment was molded and controlled in the interest of the secular tyranny; the priesthood came to be regarded as an efficient branch of the police system, and its spiritual influence over the laity was reduced almost to a nullity. Since then the conflict between the papacy and the new régime has not tended to harmonize matters, and the breach grows daily wider. What sympathy, indeed, can exist between a people eager to deprive the pope-king of his sovereignty, and a clergy which can exhibit, as was lately done in a Venetian sacristy, a picture representing on one side the symbolic triangle of the Father, the rays of which surrounded the legend "Ineffabilis Deus," while on the other side, to balance this, was the holy Dove with rays embracing the word

"Syllabus"? When that essence of spiritual and temporal tyranny can thus be deified by the priesthood, it is no wonder that Garibaldi, in a letter written on the last day of 1867 in answer to a friend pleading for the toleration of intolerance, is led to exclaim:

I know you say, "Liberty of worship, liberty of conscience, liberty for all opinion," and I repeat the cry; only it must be in the mouths of honest men. Does anybody believe in liberty for vipers, for crocodiles, for thieves and assassins? And what is the priest but the assassin of the free soul,—far more mischievous than the assassin of the body?

The result of this antagonism, as stated by an ecclesiastic in the *Esaminatore*, August 1867, is that the laity and clergy are separated into two camps, *umanamente irreconciliabili*; and by another, in the same journal of December 1, that a priest cannot appear in public in his sacerdotal habit without being exposed to insult—that the name of priest has become to the popular ear the synonym of rogue and impostor, and that the virtuous are enveloped indistinguishably in the evil reputation of the bad, to the destruction of the highest interests of religion, and to the neutralizing of all the good influences of the ecclesiastical body at large.

Unfortunately, the character and morals of the clergy in general are not such as to redeem them from odium, or to preserve for them the influence which they risk by their reactionary tendencies. The reformers unanimously attribute the notorious clerical licentiousness to the operation of the rule of compulsory celibacy, and look to its abrogation as the only efficient remedial measure; while the position occupied by the priesthood in public estimation is confessed by a writer who, in defending them from the assaults of the liberal press (*Esaminatore*, November 15, 1867), is reduced to the argument that they are not in reality worse than the laity, but that owing to their position their evil courses are more scandalous and attract more attention.

Such being the condition and relations of the Italian Church, it is evident that the attempt now making by the ecclesiastics who are endeavoring to rescue it from the demoralizing preponderance of its hierarchy, and also to defend it from the assaults of freethinking liberalism, may have results of the gravest importance. At the same time the position of the leaders is by no means a bed of roses. For the last five years they have fought their desperate battle with a gallantry which does them the highest honor. Adopting as their motto Cavour's celebrated aphorism, *"Libera chiesa in libero stato,"* they have on the one side to ward off the attacks of their infuriated brethren, and on the other to stay the sacrilegious hands which their only allies seek to lay on the holy of holies.

For a long while they flattered themselves that the panacea for all ecclesiastical woes was to be found in a general council, and for this they lustily called. At length Pius IX listened to their cry, and, with the bishops of Christendom assembled around him on the centenary of St. Peter, he had the opportunity of ascertaining whether such a dangerous expedient could be safely dared. Constance and Bâle were full of significant warning of the antagonisms which might arise between the Church universal and its visible head, when the one, acting under the direct inspiration of the Holy Ghost, might seek to exert its supremacy at the expense of the other. If the council of Trent—where the Holy Ghost was profanely said to be carried backwards and forwards in a dispatch box between the council room and the Vatican—was more reassuring, yet on the other hand there was the example of the assembly of Notables and the Three Estates, whose convocation ushered in the Revolution of '89. Apparently, however, the temper manifested by the episcopal pilgrims, who laid their tribute reverently at the foot of the papal throne, was satisfactory, and the great council, the first which the Church has held for three centuries, is appointed for November of the present year.

The reformers had so often demanded such an ecclesiastical parliament as the cure for the evils of which they complained that at first they could only express their satisfaction at the prospect of its assembling. Reflection, however, speedily caused a change of tone. It was in the highest degree improbable that a court so entirely reactionary as that of Rome would voluntarily call together in deliberation the representatives of the whole Church, if thereby there should be any chance of imperiling either its privileges or its policy; and the rumor soon spread that the real object of the projected council was to render, by an organic law, the autocracy of the Holy See as perfect in theory as it already is in fact,— to sanctify, by an article of faith, the supreme infallibility of the Pope, which is as yet only a matter of assumption. That the reformers should forthwith direct their bitterest attacks against the council is therefore scarcely a matter of surprise.

It would be difficult, indeed, to see what hopes they could reasonably entertain from the deliberations of such a body. In earlier times, when bishops were freely elected by their flocks and enjoyed local autonomy, their assembling to counsel together on the spiritual and temporal interests of the Church was not a mere form, and the result of their deliberations might well be looked for with hopeful solicitude by Christendom. The bishop of to-day is, however, a very different personage. Selected with a view to his probable usefulness to his superiors, at his consecration he takes an oath of feudal allegiance to the pope, which, with careful superfluity of verbiage, binds him to regard the temporal interests, privileges, and power of the papacy as superior to all other worldly considerations; to defend and advance those interests with all his power; to hold as rebels and enemies all who oppose them, and specially to take part in no councils where any attempt is made to diminish them; and, moreover, to use every effort to enforce the decrees and statutes of the Church.[17] Thus bound to absolute vassalage by the terms on which he has accepted his office, and subjected to the absolute and irresponsible authority of the curia, there is little danger of uncourtly opposition to the wishes of the supreme pontiff. To what depths of degradation and self-abasement, indeed, the assiduous enforcement of the teachings of the council of Trent have reduced the once independent representatives of the Apostles, may be gathered from the man-worship offered to Pius IX by the 275 bishops assembled in June 1862, for the canonization of the Japanese martyrs. Not one of them refused his signature to the declaration in which the Pope is addressed:

Thou art for us the master of sound doctrine, the centre of unity, the unfailing light prepared for the people by the wisdom of God. Thou art the stone and the foundation of the Church, and against Thee the gates of hell shall not prevail. When Thou speakest, we hear Peter; when Thou commandest, we obey Christ.

When men who proclaim such sentiments are called together by the object of their adoration, it can only be for the purpose of registering decrees drawn up in advance.

It is true that all these reverend prelates may not be personally in favor of arbitrary centralization. The Gallican Church has its traditions of self-government, and the free atmosphere of Great Britain and America cannot but have its effect on those who are trained under its bracing influence. Yet there is little to be dreaded from such possibilities. The archbishop of Cincinnati, who is regarded as one of the most enlightened

[17] "Ego N. electus ecclesiæ N. ab hac hora in antea fidelis et obediens ero beato Petro Apostolo sanctæque Romanæ Ecclesiæ et Domino N. Papa N. suisque successoribus canonice intrantibus. . . . Papatum Romanum et regalia sancti Petri adjutor eis ero ad retinendum et defendendum, salvo meo ordine, contra omnem hominem. . . . Jura, honores, privilegia et auctoritatem sanctæ Romanæ Ecclesiæ, Domini nostri Papæ, et successorum prædictorum conservare, defendere, augere, promovere curabo. Neque ero in consilio, vel facto, seu tractatu, in quibus contra ipsum Dominum nostrum, vel eandem Romanam Ecclesiam aliqua sinistra vel præjudicialia personarum, juris, honoris, status et potestatis eorum machinentur. Et si talia a quibuscunque tractari vel procurari novero, impediam hoc pro posse; et quanto citius potero, significabo eidem Domino nostro. . . . Rebelles eidem Domino nostro . . . pro posse persequar et impugnabo." As stated above, beyond the Alps Catholic sovereigns no longer allow their subjects to renounce their allegiance by this form of oath, and it has been modified accordingly. The Italian government has taken the same stand, but Rome has refused to yield, and some fifteen of the Italian sees are consequently vacant; as incumbents have died, no successors could be consecrated. In America the most obnoxious portions of the oath have likewise been omitted.

and liberal prelates in America, when he received the Encyclical of
December 1864 with its accompanying Syllabus, published a pastoral to
his flock, in which he declared: "We receive it implicitly, we bow to it
reverently, we embrace it cordially, we hail it gratefully. To us it is as
the voice of God on Sinai, on the Jordan, on Thebor." Of the Gallican
Church, which still affects to reverence the memory of Bossuet, there
were fifty-four prelates present at the assembly of June 1862, who abjured
all independence in signing the declaration just alluded to, and every
bishop in France subsequently followed their example. Even if these men
who thus proclaimed their helpless and hopeless degradation could be
aroused to assert their manhood, yet a glance at the statistics of the
Church will show how little they could effect by such an effort. There
are in all about 675 Catholic sees, of which, including one in Algeria,
nearly 570 are European, and a little more than one hundred are American, from Quebec to Valparaiso. Now, of the European sees, three hundred, or more than half, are Italian; and though some of these, in consequence of the rupture between the courts of Florence and Rome, are
vacant, still the latter can count upon no less than 280 Italian prelates
bound to implicit obedience by the oath of vassalage and by every motive
of self-interest. Even if this were not sufficient, there are moreover to
be summed up the bishops *in partibus infidelium,*—men who are consecrated to ancient sees, now in possession of the infidel. Nearly all of
these are hangers-on or attachés of the Roman court, and, having no individual or conflicting interests, they are to be relied on as a corps
devoted at all hazards to its master. Their number is not readily to be
ascertained, but we have met with a partial list amounting to 146. Adding these to the existing prelates of Italy, we have 426 within the
Alps, or more than half of all the Catholic hierarchy. Holding thus an
overwhelming majority close at hand and easily controlled, there would
seem to be little risk incurred from any possibly independent spirits
who may wearily journey to Rome from distant regions.

If the material to be collected together is thus plastic, the arrangements for molding it are none the less carefully contrived. Every precaution has been taken to prevent any voice from being raised in opposition to the preconceived designs of the curia. The pope has nominated
a *Congregazione Centrale* which is to decide, without appeal, as to the
matters to be submitted for discussion; and this body is exclusively
composed of cardinals who hold positions in the Inquisition. Under it
are five sub-committees, termed *consulte,* to regulate the details of their
respective departments, and each of these is presided over by one of the
cardinals of the Central Congregation. The results which are to be expected from their labors may be anticipated from the character of the

men selected to manage them. The less important ones are committed to prelates comparatively unknown: that on Oriental affairs is given in charge to Cardinal Barnabo, that on ecclesiastical diplomacy to Reisach, and that on the religious orders to Bozzari; while everything relating to dogma is directed by Cardinal Bilio, who is notorious as the compiler of the Syllabus; and the momentous questions involved in the canons and discipline are under the guiding hand of Caterini, whose whole career has been passed in the Inquisition, and who has already distinguished his new office by issuing to all the bishops of the Church a circular propounding seventeen questions for discussion. These questions carefully avoid all the subjects on which reform is vital, and confine themselves either to points of minor importance or to the endeavor to give practical effect to the principles of the Syllabus. As the reformers indignantly declare, Rome is busy in tithing the mint and cumin and anise, while the law and the faith are left to shift for themselves, and the laity is every day cherishing a sentiment of deeper contempt and hostility for the Church.

It is no wonder, then, that protests are being issued in advance. Instead of being a general assembly of the Church to devise remedies for the evils which pervade the whole body, it is declared to be an ingenious device to consolidate the power which is crushing out all self-sustaining vitality in the establishment, and the reformers naturally see their condemnation already drawn up and only awaiting a formal indorsement. They therefore declare that they recognize in no body of men convened under such conditions the authority to speak in the name of the Church at large; and the bolder spirits are already demanding that all sects of Christians shall be received as belonging to the same brotherhood in Christ; and that only by assembling delegates from all communions can a truly œcumenic council be held, whose decrees shall be binding as the emanation of the Holy Ghost.

In the existing condition of humanity, such a convocation is of course impracticable, and the call for it is interesting only as showing how rapidly Rome, as is her wont, is driving her disaffected children into open revolt. They are still struggling hard to persuade themselves that this is not inevitable, and that in a church which claims implicit obedience in everything, they can still retain their place while striving to alter its whole internal structure. Thus Dr. Prota, in his address of January 2, 1868, declares that he and his associates have not failed to advocate the ancient and wise institution of the papacy, and he repudiates with indignation the assertion that their opposition to the temporal power and to the usurped authority over the hierarchy is drawn from heterodox and Protestant sources. So Panzini, while attacking with ferocious energy the whole system of arbitrary regulations which render the ecclesiastical body the slaves of its visible head, is careful to declare in advance his belief that the Church is infallible and without taint in its faith and morals; and one of his strongest arguments for reform is, that the abuses which he condemns have insured the perdition of so many million souls by driving them into heresy.

Illogical as this may seem to us, it is the necessary pathway to freedom of conscience. Savonarola was a good Catholic, and his works have always been pronounced strictly orthodox, yet his hopeless contest with the papacy was rapidly ripening him into a heretic, when his career was cut short by the stake. Luther held to the faith for fully three years after he had committed himself to exposing the evils of the ecclesiastical system, and it was only his excommunication by Leo X that forced him to the conviction that disobedience was possible to him.

Yet the end is plain. An infallible church is of necessity immovable. *Nulla vestigia retrorsum,*—the way once entered must be pursued, and to all demands for the abolition of evil the only answer is *non possumus.* Men bred in the atmosphere of the Roman curia cannot but regard their privileges and authority as of divine origin and as part and parcel of religion itself. The dividing line between faith and discipline—between that which is immutable by its essence and that which, being the work of man, can be changed by man—is difficult to draw, when infallibility has prescribed and still enforces the rules of discipline. All which those in power desire to retain can thus be so inextricably entangled with points of faith, that no very ingenious casuistry is required to prove all efforts at reform heretical. Thus fortified, it is vain to expect that the Roman court will listen to demands for reconstruction. Its only answer must be a command of silent obedience, and, if this is refused, it can only respond by excommunication.

The reformers seek to reduce the papacy to a simple primacy of honor; to restore to the episcopate the independence which it enjoyed in the primitive Church, to the priesthood its due protection from arbitrary authority, and to the laity its proper share in the selection of its pastors and in the affairs of the Church. They ask that the Scriptures be no longer sealed in an unknown tongue, and that the ritual be translated into the vernacular; that compulsory celibacy and irrevocable vows be abolished; and that the long canonical hours of fasting and prayer be no longer obligatory, but be left to the conscience of the individual, as a voluntary oblation and sacrifice. Auricular confession—the most powerful source of priestly influence—is no longer to be imposed as a duty, but only to be encouraged as an incentive to virtue. Some of the reformers, indeed, have refused to adopt the new dogma of the Immaculate Conception, and have been duly excommunicated in consequence; but thus far they have all held fast to the ancient faith, and their efforts at reform have been directed to simple points of discipline; yet the program is wide enough to afford them ample work, as it is nothing less than the remodeling of the whole ecclesiastical structure. That structure has thus far resisted the shocks of centuries. Every breach that has been made in it has been carefully repaired and strengthened by new lines of circumvallation; and, however we may admire the gallantry of the forlorn hope now advancing to the assault, we can scarcely reckon upon their success. If the General Council be held as promised, their condemnation would seem to be inevitable, when some will probably retract and submit. The bolder spirits, however, will carry on the contest, no longer as schismatics engaged in a revolt, but as heretics in open war. Thus released, in spite of themselves, from the remaining links of the chain which fetters their conscience, the critical spirit which they have carried into the examination of the external history of Latin Christianity will be extended to its spiritual record, and a new reformed church will arise, to take its place among the countless denominations of those who reject Catholic unity.

Indications of this tendency, indeed, are already beginning to manifest themselves, under the pressure of recent events. In the same number of the *Emancipatore Cattolico*, in which Dr. Prota publishes his address recognizing the papacy as the center of Catholic unity, he admits two articles denouncing it for more than mere abuses of discipline. Thus Luigi Settembrini writes: "The Catholic faith must render itself more spiritual, must divest itself of the gross superstitions which are opposed to the Gospel, which ruin the faith, and which lead men, by confounding the true and the false, to reject all"; and Padre Cristofero Coppola does not hesitate to declare that "the religious common sense of the most pious and learned Italians recognizes that the apostate and illegitimate sovereign of Rome is Judaizing and imposing on the consciences of men a fictitious and injurious religion."

The extent and ultimate results of this reform movement, however, must be influenced largely by political events. If Savonarola had enjoyed, as did Luther, the puissant protection of a temporal sovereign, the Reformation might have dated from the fifteenth instead of the sixteenth century; if Luther had been abandoned to the unrestricted persecution of Leo X, his reformation might have been as short-lived as that of John Huss and Jerome of Prague; while if the temporal princes of Italy had imitated the elector of Saxony and the landgrave of Hesse, and had sustained Peter Martyr, Bernardino Ochino, and Aonio Paleario, all Europe might have been led to throw off the yoke. Thus far the aid which the Italian reformers have received has been rather passive than active, while the fluctuating policy of the government has frequently thrown obstacles in their path. The absorption of Rome, even though it might not alter theoretically the relations between the pope and his subordinates, would materially improve their condition. As the allies of the government against reaction, they would be efficiently protected against the petty persecution which now harasses them so effectually; and as the kingdom of Italy would have triumphed in its efforts to render the temporal interests of the Church subordinate to the State, many of the worst abuses of which they complain would die a natural death. With the extension of secular education, the diffusion of intelligence, and the training of the people in self-government, their sphere of action would enlarge, and Italy might in a generation be prepared to range herself in the van of modern progress and liberalism.

To bring about all this, the disasters of last November have largely contributed. The unification of the Italian nation has been greatly accelerated, while the pope-king has stood forth more prominently than ever as the obstacle to progress. As long as he protested his helplessness to resist, and declared his readiness to die rather than to abandon the sacred heritage confided to his feeble hands, even his enemies could not but entertain a feeling of respect for the fortitude which seemed to draw its strength from faith alone, and to preserve its consistency with the precepts of the Saviour. When, however, he showed to the world how perfectly the Church represents the ultimate development of feudalism —a lord paramount whose vassals of whatever degree are equally his serfs—and how utterly the spiritual sovereignty has been subordinated to the temporal; when men reflected that in the height of its mediæval power the Church always denied to itself the right to shed blood, and that even the fiercest Inquisitor always "relaxed" his victims by handing them over to the secular tribunals for punishment, they could not but shudder to see the Vicegerent of Christ recruiting soldiers in every corner of Catholic Europe, offering blessings and bounties with equal hand, signing death-warrants, sending his mercenaries to battle, and after killing his enemies, enjoying the additional satisfaction of consigning them to eternal damnation, and of ordering their friends to sing Te Deums over their graves. It is not every one whose heart is so hardened by religious zeal as to enjoy the pious joke of Bishop Dupanloup in rejoicing over the papal victory. "It was necessary," said he, "that blood should flow, *Transtulit illos per mare rubrum.*" This terrible commingling of the sacred and profane was aptly illustrated by the awkward enthusiasm of General de Failly, when he hastened to inform Louis Napoleon that at Mentana the new rifles had performed miracles; and it is no wonder that the reformers eagerly caught up the idea by suggesting that the new saint should be added to the calendar, and that a new invocation should be inserted in the Roman litany,—*Sancte Chassepot, ora pro nobis!*

These shocking incongruities have been made use of skilfully and vigorously, and their effect upon the popular mind cannot but be deep and lasting. More than ever the papacy has become the enemy of Italy and of civilization; and though the unfathomable mysteries of intriguing diplomacy may yet for a while preserve its secular authority over populations which detest its rule, yet the antagonism thus developed can hardly be assuaged. The opposing principles admit of no compromise; they are committed to inevitable strife and, unless the progress of the last three centuries be a mistake, it is the papacy that must ultimately be worsted. Under the guidance of Jesuits inflamed with the *rabbia sanfedistica*, it cannot bend; and, unless wiser counsels prevail among its rulers, it may come to be broken.

Meanwhile the apparent triumph of the reactionary movement is tempting it on to fresh assertions of power, and the present appearances are that the reformers will shortly be exposed to sharper persecutions than ever. By the enforced submission of Cardinal D'Andrea they have lost an efficient protector, and they are momentarily in expectation of measures of repression which will test their steadfastness to the utmost. It is the turning point of their fortunes. If they can hold their own through the contest of the next twelve months, the movement will assume a solidity and power that must lead to notable results, and in the trials thus near at hand they should have the sympathy of all friends of civilization and freedom throughout Christendom.

MONKS AND NUNS IN FRANCE*

[The material for this article was drawn from *Les Congrégations Religieuses—une Enquête* by Charles Sauvestre. Paris, 1867.—H.]

*   *   *   *   *

IT IS THE POPULAR BELIEF that the age of romance has long been past. We look back upon the strongly-marked individuality of character, the wild adventure, the selfish recklessness, the blind superstition, the intense devotion, the abounding faith which give prominence to so many stirring episodes of mediæval history and, contrasting them with the dull routine of everyday life around us, we imagine that such things are impossible in these later days. The world seems to us to have grown old and to have lost the fiery vivacity of youth. Abandoned to the lust of money-getting, that "good old-gentlemanly vice," it appears to have outlived or outworn its other passions and to be no longer capable of the splendid virtues and crimes of its younger age.

People who reason thus forget that there is in human nature a great deal of human nature. It may be smoothed over with a thin varnish of civilization which hides its inequalities, but for all its outward show of polished uniformity the original Adam is there, subject to the same impulses, glorying in the same strength and yielding to the same weakness as of old. Somewhat more of self-command there may be, of outward reticence and deference to higher standards of morality, but the man remains underneath and it requires but an exciting cause to render him capable of all that his ancestor of five hundred years ago would have done or dared to accomplish his object, whether of good or evil.

The believers in the advance of modern intelligence who thus think that the world has changed are apt to fancy, for instance, that monk-hood is one of the institutions of the past. They imagine that its remains are slowly dying out, and that a comparatively short time will see the end of that powerful organization which was one of the great vital forces of mediæval Christianity, and through which the loftiest aspirations and the meanest passions of our nature were so successfully turned to account by the skillful men who controlled it. The philosophers and sociologists who indulge in these anticipations know little of what is passing around them. It is true that the French Revolution secularized the immense monastic possessions of France and turned their whilom professors adrift, as Henry VIII, two hundred and fifty years before, had relentlessly done in England, and as, some seventy years later, a united Italy has recently ventured to do; yet monachism is a hydra which quietly and energetically seeks to replace each decapitated head with

* From *Putnam's Magazine*, IV, N.S. (1869), 265-74.

two new ones. As long as it continues to respond to a want in the human soul it will flourish, and the world will yet have to undergo a long course of education before that want will cease to be felt.

It is impossible to conceive of a more thorough uprooting than that which was inflicted on the religious congregations of France by the storms of the Terror. Their wealth sequestrated, their establishments broken up, their institutions prohibited, their persons subjected to every outrage, it seemed impossible that they should again take root in a soil over which so fierce a deluge had passed. Yet quietly and stealthily they have returned and step by step they have advanced until the old territory is reconquered. Re-admitted under sufferance and barely tolerated by the law, they have succeeded in forming an unwritten law which favors them and, in spite of the unyielding bureaucratic tendencies of French institutions, no one dares to make them conform to the written law. Conscious of the prejudices existing against them in the minds of a large portion of society, they carefully conceal their progress. That progress, however, has already been sufficient to render them virtually masters of the situation. In their schools more than half of the children of France are educated; by their confessors a large proportion of the faithful are ruled; through their charities countless thousands call them blessed. The present generation and the next are thus under their control, and the myriad sources of influence thus placed in their hands are used with consummate dexterity by men whose training teaches that whatever means they may employ are sanctified by the holy objects in view. It is a proverb that the arms of the revered fathers are long and that he who obstructs them is sure to rue it, sooner or later. Practical immunity thus is obtained which can only be overcome by a decided public opinion, and public opinion cannot be formed where the press is either partisan or muzzled. The tortuous policy of Napoleon III, his alliance with Rome, the influence of his empress, and his dread of provoking the opposition of a most powerful network of organizations ever on the verge of disaffection lead the government to bestow its favor on the religious congregations. Every forward step gives vantage ground for another advance; the power of attraction increases as with the mass and the growth of the monastic corporations is progressively rapid. So quietly has all this been managed and so carefully have results been concealed that few people are aware of the progress already made or of the danger to which liberal institutions are exposed by the reactionary tendencies of so vast a body controlling so many sources of influence, owning fealty to the papacy as its superior, and sworn to carry out the principles of the Encyclical and Syllabus. A recent writer, however, M. Charles Sauvestre, has had the patience to investigate the subject thoroughly, and the hardihood to publish the results in a deeply interesting volume, *Les Congrégations Religieuses—une Enquête,* where the heaviness of official documents is lightened by the sprightly good sense of the comments with which their significance is illustrated.

From the census of 1861 it appears that there were then in France, officially recognized, 108,119 persons of both sexes bound by religious vows and distributed among 14,032 houses; besides a large and indefinite number who had not yet obtained official recognition. In 1789 trustworthy statistics report that the monastic orders of France comprised but 52,000 men and women. It would thus appear that the ground lost in the Revolution has not only been regained, but has been enlarged twofold. How rapidly this growth is increasing is evident when we see that in the eighteen years of Louis Philippe but fourteen authorizations were granted for the founding of new congregations, while in the first eight years of the Second Empire, from 1852 to 1860, 982 were recognized, being an average of 109 new orders per annum.

This prodigious activity is the more impressive, since few of these orders are devoted as of old merely to religious contemplation and ascetic observances. The practical tendency of the age manifests itself in the vast proportion of those who enroll themselves as laborers in the tasks of charity and beneficence. Thus the numbers specified above may be divided as follows:

Devoted to education	71,728
Engaged in care of the sick and charity	20,681
In charge of houses of refuge and farm schools	3,569
Engrossed in religious duties alone	12,141
	108,119

Thus the Church, with its accustomed wisdom, accommodates itself to the new wants created by modern civilization and institutions, and acquires fresh influence by the vast good of which it renders itself the instrument. It recognizes how little human nature has changed and it calls to its support those influences which more progressive forms of Christianity blindly regard as obsolete, or conscientiously condemn as incompatible with a purer and more advanced state of moral responsibility. How surely the Church may rely upon its premises can readily be judged from two or three instances afforded by the recent history of monachism.

LES PETITES SŒURS DES PAUVRES

When we read how, amid the darkness which marked the opening of the thirteenth century, St. Francis of Assisi stripped himself naked and clothed himself in ragged garments compassionately thrown to him that he might possess nothing of his father's patrimony; and how he devoted himself to the tenderest nursing of lepers until his superhuman self-abnegation drew around him admiring imitators who rapidly multiplied into the powerful order that bears his honored name, and arrested the premature decay of the Church—when we read such a religious romance, we might pardonably regard the story as one that could have no modern parallel. Yet it may well be doubted whether, if we could strip the history of its legendary ornamentation, it would show more heroic exaltation or more perfect abandonment to the will of God than the career of the *Petites Sœurs des Pauvres*.

In 1840, at Saint-Servan in Britanny, two young peasant girls, the eldest one not yet eighteen, felt impelled towards a religious life. Their pastor, the Abbé le Pailleur, had long wished to found an order devoted to the care of the aged and infirm. He counseled patience and the performance of works of charity and piety to keep alive the zeal which animated them. Accordingly they undertook the care of an old blind woman, devoting to her comfort their scanty leisure and scantier wages. At length they were joined by two elderly women, Jeanne Jugan, a servant who had amassed some six hundred francs, and Fanchon Aubert, who likewise had some money. A garret was taken and furnished and then the ground floor of a tavern where twelve beds were established as a hospital for the poor and infirm, to be maintained by begging alms. These came in slowly, and the enterprise seemed desperate, when Jeanne conceived the idea of going around with a basket every morning to collect the refuse remnants of food rejected by the housekeepers of the little villages. This humble and self-denying zeal attracted attention and contributions became more frequent, yet many times the infant community seemed on the point of extinction. Yet the reliance of the four helpless women on divine succor never faltered, and in after times they loved to relate how often God had rescued them when human help seemed hopeless. Once their little stock of linen was exhausted. They appealed to the Virgin. On Assumption day they raised a tiny altar and spread before it the half dozen tattered chemises which formed the sole supply of the establishment, for sheets they had none. The spectacle touched the hearts of the charitable and the hour of distress passed away. Poor servant girls, who were penniless, took off their finger rings and hung them on the neck of the infant Christ who, seated on his Mother's knee in a group three inches high, presided over the little altar; while richer votaries made more substantial offerings which enabled them to keep the wolf from the door.

Ridicule and poverty, the scorn of their companions, and the pinching necessities of a life of beggary were alike powerless to turn these devoted souls from their vocation. Gradually their field of usefulness widened and the tavern-floor became too small. In 1842 they bought a large house for twenty-two thousand francs, having absolutely nothing wherewith to meet the purchase money. Their trust in Providence was answered. The Abbé le Pailleur sold his gold watch and the sacred plate of his chapel; the peasant girls redoubled their industry. At the end of the year the house was paid for.

In eighteen months more, this new establishment again was found too small, and the four heroic women had but a half franc in their little treasury. The coin was placed upon the altar of the Virgin, and they unfalteringly undertook the erection of a larger building. They bought a piece of ground and themselves set to work digging the cellars and laying the foundations. The example was contagious. Workmen flocked to labor for them, materials were given gratuitously, alms flowed in upon them, and a large and commodious asylum for their dependents soon rewarded their patient hopefulness.

The little hamlet of Saint-Servan was evidently too contracted a theatre for natures so nobly resolute. As their labors attracted attention, new sisters joined them. Missionaries were dispatched to the larger towns where they commenced as the founders had done and were more speedily successful. Rennes, Dinan, Tours were successively thus occupied, and in 1849 the order was extended to Paris. It now has fifty-five houses, numbers a thousand members, and owns more than twenty-five millions of francs invested in real estate. Yet the sisters have never abandoned the humble functions to which the order was consecrated in its infancy. Where an establishment is newly founded, the sister carries around every morning the basket in which she gathers the broken victuals of the rich for her poor invalids. If the establishment is on a greater scale, perhaps she may have a donkey with panniers; or, where the city is large and the rounds extensive, a little wagon with baskets and reservoirs for soups and coffee—but in all it is the same humble devotion to collect, by repulsive labor, the crumbs from the table of Dives to succor Lazarus.

ANNABELLA KOHRSCH

If the story of the *Petites Sœurs des Pauvres* shows that Christianity has lost nothing of its beneficent and self-sacrificing fervor in the lapse of ages, the case of Annabella Kohrsch proves that the fanaticism which kindled in the breasts of St. Dominic and Conrad of Marburg is still as active as of old. Fortunately the laws which some centuries ago permitted this fanaticism to find expression in the torture and the stake now force it to seek the salvation of souls in a manner less decided, but the spirit is there as fervent as ever, though it may perforce be limited in its manifestations. From the official record of the trial, which took place at Ghent in July 1860, as printed by M. Sauvestre, we condense a story that might have served Mrs. Ratcliff or Monk Lewis.

A family of Lutherans named Kohrsch consisting of a father, a son, and a daughter from Pillau in Prussia settled at Antwerp. The father dies and on his deathbed exacts from the son, Richard, a solemn promise to guard his sister's religion steadfastly in the faith of her ancestors. Richard is a young man earning a moderate livelihood as a clerk. Living in rooms from which his duties keep him absent throughout the whole day, it becomes evidently necessary for him to provide some more fitting home for a girl of seventeen and, as his means are straitened, he finally from motives of economy places her as a boarder with the Sisters of Charity of Melsele. Mindful of his promise to his dying father, however, he makes it a condition that no attempts at proselytism shall be made, and in July 1857 he receives from the superior of the convent a written declaration—

En égard aux craintes que vous venez de m'exposer, je vous garantis que mademoiselle n'est obligée à suivre aucun exercise religieux et jouit d'une entière liberté, quant aux prescriptions de sa propre croyance.

Within a month after this, Annabella is converted and secretly baptized in the Catholic faith, and a fortnight later is admitted to communion. So little connection do these fervent propagandists of the faith recognize between religion and morality that no resources of falsehood are spared to prevent the truth from being known. On the very day of her baptism Annabella received a visit from her brother, and the neophyte was trained to lie unblushingly in order to avert his suspicions.

At length Richard grew uneasy and in May 1859 he withdrew his sister from the convent. Her spiritual director, Pierre-Gérard Bogaerts, curé of St. Augustin in Antwerp, and the principal instrument of her conversion, counselled her to continue to conceal her religion and dispensed her from its observances. This necessary dissimulation, however, threatened too serious a risk to her salvation, and in company with a Jesuit father, Philippe-Jacques Schoofs, also deeply interested in her conversion, he plotted her abduction. Three days after her return home, three days of apparently uninterrupted affection, Annabella disappeared, leaving behind her a most loving letter in which she bewailed the necessity of separation. Richard, suspecting the religious intrigue that was at the bottom of the affair, applied to the Prussian consul who set the authorities actively at work in search of the missing girl; but for nine months all trace of her was lost.

Leaving her brother's lodgings at five in the morning of the eleventh of May, Annabella went to the house of Marie-Jeanne Lauterbaen, who had served as godmother at her baptism. There she was disguised as a servant girl and was then taken to Marie Vanderneolen, a dealer in embroideries. Meanwhile, Bogaerts and Schoofs had arranged to send her, under charge of Rosalie de Duve, a milliner, to Brussels, with a letter to obtain admission for her in the convent of Jette. A carriage was procured in which, to avoid pursuit, the two women were driven out of town to a way station on the railroad, and they reached Brussels without misadventure.

All this was a serious crime in the eyes of the law, for Annabella was yet a minor under her brother's guardianship. The nuns of Jette suspected that something was wrong and refused to receive the fugitive. Rosalie then, after much difficulty, succeeded in obtaining for her permission to remain for a few days in another convent. This proposed retreat having failed, Schoofs and Bogaerts then resolved to send their convert to Paris. Under the name of Eugenie de Marie, and with a false passport, Annabella was accordingly taken by Rosalie to the house of St. Joseph in Paris, and there she remained at the expense of Bogaerts until September. Rosalie was then sent to Paris to bring her back. At Mechlin they were met by Schoofs who conducted them to the house of the *Sœurs de l'Union au Sacré-Coeur* at Hougaerde where arrangements had been made for Annabella's reception. After three months of rest something occurred to render the reverend conspirators uneasy and Rosalie was sent to bring Annabella back to Antwerp where she was placed in the Carmelite convent. The superior of the Carmelites found that she had undertaken a venture which she dared not long undergo, and she applied to a house in Bruges to receive the fugitive. The risk was prudently declined, but a bolder spirit was found in the head of the Sisters of Charity at Eecloo. To Eecloo, therefore, two days before Christmas, was Rosalie despatched by Bogaerts, in charge of the luckless Annabella, to whom the name of Marie Toinez was given.

Thus far the plot had been successful, and if the object of these ceaseless cares had gratefully persevered in preferring heaven to earth as advised by her ghostly counselors, she might never more have been heard of among men. Unfortunately, she was human. Thoughts of the brother whom she had been led to desert and of the faith which she had been persuaded to abandon would intrude themselves and twice during her weary wanderings she had attempted to communicate with Richard, but fear of those around her had rendered her efforts nugatory. A third time she was bolder and more successful. On January 16, 1860, Richard received a letter, postmarked at Ghent, which over an unintelligible signature informed him that his lost Annabella was in the convent of Eecloo under the name of Marie Toinez, where she could be recognized on Sunday during mass behind the screen in the church.

The following Sunday, January 22, a witness was sent to the convent church where he recognized Annabella. On Monday Richard presented himself at the convent and claimed his sister. The lady superior solemnly denied any knowledge of Marie Toinez or Annabella Kohrsch, but as soon as Richard had left the house she hurried Annabella to the residence of Jean-Antoine van Peteghem, the spiritual director of the community. Her precaution was not useless, for Richard speedily returned with the police. His search was vain however, and to keep up the comedy the superior feigned to be touched with his grief, promised to aid him in tracing his sister and actually took his address so as to be able to send him news in case she could discover the hiding place of the missing girl.

By this time the affair had created considerable scandal and, as the pursuers were so nearly on the track of the precious convert, it had evidently become dangerous to afford her a refuge. Her soul was to be saved however at all costs, and the pious conspirators were not disposed to abandon the prize which had cost them so much risk and labor.

Accordingly, at midnight, Annabella was taken, carefully guarded, to a retired spot near the cemetery of Eecloo, where a carriage was in waiting for her. Before daylight she had been driven to Bruges and taken to a convent there. The superior, afraid to give her refuge, placed her with a trusty person named John Callaghan, who kept her until the evening of the twenty-sixth. Then by the night boat he conveyed her to Ghent, where, after one or two vain attempts to find a hiding place, he succeeded in lodging her with Jeannette van Hauwaert a former pupil of the convent of Melsele, which, it will be remembered, was the house where Annabella had been converted.

The quarry was now nearly brought to bay. The police had not been idle, and Callaghan's visit to Ghent was thought to have some connection with the flight of the fugitive. On a first examination he eluded the inquiry, and sent word to his colleagues at Ghent in order that their stories might accord with his own. The authorities, however, succeeded in proving its falsity, and at last he was obliged to confess the truth. Following up the clue which he had given, Richard at length recovered his long lost sister, January 28, in the house of a peasant at Gentbrugge.

If all this were not in evidence before a court of justice, one would hesitate to believe that such a fragment of the twelfth century could be transferred to the nineteenth. Nor, however guilty in the eyes of the law, are the actors in this strange history to blame, any more than those who might be concerned in a suttee or in driving the car of juggernaut, believing that they were thereby rendering an acceptable service to the Deity. It is the system which is accountable. Priests and nuns who had seen the abduction of the boy Mortara defiantly justified by the Vicegerent of Christ might well consider it their duty to labor for the salvation of the young Lutheran whom God seemed to have placed in their hands for that purpose, and if deceit, dissimulation, and mendacity became necessary to effect so holy an object, the fault was not with them but with the irreligious laws whose impious toleration guarantees to every human creature of mature age the right to seek salvation or damnation as his erring instincts may direct.

ADÈLE CHEVALIER

If, as we have seen, religious ardor still manifests itself as of old in the extremes of self-devotion and fanaticism, we need not be surprised to find it degenerate into superstition with equally persistent vitality. In some of its grosser forms this perhaps may be extinct; but a system of belief which teaches the constant interposition of God and his saints in the daily affairs of life, and which builds up its vast structure of sacerdotalism on the power of intercession between man and his Creator, makes superstition so near akin to theology that the subtlest casuist might well be puzzled to draw the boundary line. When the divine mission of Joan of Arc, and the reality of her conferences with the Virgin, are warmly maintained by learned men, it need therefore not surprise us to find enthusiasts who mistake their ecstasies for heavenly revelations or sharpers ready to speculate on the credulity of reverend prelates.

In 1854, Adèle Chevalier, aged about nineteen, a novice in the convent of Saint-Thomas de Villeneuve at Soissons, was attacked with cerebral congestion severe enough to cause blindness. Given over by her physicians, she was miraculously cured by the intercession of *Notre-Dame-Réconciliatrice de la Salette*. Monseigneur de Garsignies, bishop of Soissons and Laon, ordered an investigation into the authenticity of the miracle. An elaborate report by his vicar general, M. Guyard, dean of his cathedral chapter, pronounced that it was unmistakably the result of the supernatural intervention of the Mother of God, and measures were adopted to celebrate with becoming solemnity so auspicious an event.

Adèle Chevalier, thus brought into notice as the fortunate protégée of the Virgin, received still further manifestations of divine favor. She was frequently blessed with revelations from the same source, and of sixteen confessors who successively had charge of her conscience during her career all without exception confirmed her in the belief of the truth of her inspiration.

In 1856 her voices called her to La Salette, and the superior of her community obediently made haste to send her there. At La Salette they are accustomed to such manifestations. It was there that in 1846 Our Lady appeared to Maximin and Melanie, two children herding cows among the mountains, and warned them that she could not much longer restrain the anger of her Son, incensed against the people for their sins in blasphemy and Sabbathbreaking.[1] The experiences of Adèle coming thus within the round of their ordinary experience, the good fathers of La Salette were readily impressed by her and asked the bishop of Grenoble to place her under the direction of the Abbé Bouland. This gentleman was eminently fitted for such a charge. He was a doctor in theology, was the author of several books on canonical subjects, the founder and chief editor of the *Rosier de Marie*, and had been at one time superior of a monastery at Strasbourg. Bouland reported favorably as to the reality of Adèle's inspiration, and the community of la Salette sent him to Rome to lay the matter before Pius IX and the Sacred College.

What the result of his mission was does not clearly appear, but during his absence Adèle continued constantly to receive revelations from the Virgin Mary. Among these was one commanding her to found a new religious order, the *Œuvre de la Réparation des Âmes*, the rules for which she drew up under divine inspiration. She was endeavoring to induce her confessor, at that time a canon of Amiens, to undertake this labor with her when, after an interval of two years, Bouland sought her out and took upon himself the enterprise. As a preliminary they made together a pilgrimage to La Salette, to ask of the Virgin her final confirmation of the work which they had undertaken, and on this occasion their conduct towards each other was such as to lead to the suspicion that warmer bonds united them than merely mystic sympathies.

Bellevue, near Versailles, was selected as the seat of the new community. The bishop of the diocese prudently held aloof, but other prelates of high rank were found to lend it their countenance and many pious souls eagerly joined in the *Œuvre de la Réparation des Âmes*.

[1] This story is related as an unquestioned fact in a series of religious books for children, published by authority in Dublin, in 1864. Another number of the series recommends children always to keep a pot of holy water in their rooms in order to keep evil spirits out of the house.

It is from such works as these that one learns to realize the sources of influence which the Church exercises over her votaries, the results of which are beginning to form one of the political problems with which in this country we shall have to deal. The priest stands between God and man as the dispenser of salvation. Thus in treating of confession and absolution, it is the priest, not God, that is said to forgive the sin. Where such a training is thoroughly carried out, it is not easy to see how the faithful can escape being either an infidel or a man-worshipper.

After a while reports began to circulate that the practices of the sisters were hardly consistent with received ideas of religion and even of decency. The Abbé Bouland professed to cure diseases arising from demoniacal possession, and the processes which he adopted are unfit to be repeated. Still Adèle's communications with the Virgin were uninterrupted and the house became a sort of theological tribunal to which numbers resorted in order to have doubts resolved or delicate cases of conscience settled; while new orders frequently submitted to the oracle their proposed rules in order to secure for themselves the favor of the Mother of God.

Complaints gradually became numerous as to the scandals and immoralities perpetrated within the holy walls, but the ecclesiastical authorities prudently abstained from action. At length there was a direct charge of swindling brought against the inspired Adèle and her spiritual counselor, and the police irreverently seized them. It seems that a brotherhood of monks had quietly amassed from their alms a little treasure of twenty thousand francs. After many fruitless schemes for its employment, they finally determined to take the advice of the Virgin, and the superior applied to Adèle. She wrote to him to visit her. On his arrival, the Abbé Bouland ordered her to seek her accustomed monitress. She retired and in a few minutes returned with the information that the Virgin commanded the money to be lent to the *Œuvre de la Réparation des Âmes*, promising to reward obedience with blessings and to punish refusal with damnation.

The worthy prior returned to his brethren with the message and urged compliance. Some doubters there were, and they addressed the superior of La Trappe for his advice. He recommended acquiescence; and, sure of purchasing the favor of the Virgin, the community handed over the money. Notwithstanding the divine character of the transaction, however, to pacify some incredulous recalcitrants it had been agreed that the loan should be secured by a mortgage on the real estate of the *Réparation des Âmes*. The mortgage was not forthcoming, and after fruitless demands appeal was at length made to justice. Unfortunately for the defendants, their principal witness, the Virgin Mary, could not be reached with a subpoena, and the case went against them both in the lower court at Versailles and on their appeal to a higher jurisdiction in Paris. In July 1865 the final hearing took place and, after a patient investigation in which their whole career was thoroughly examined, the abbé and his inspired votaress were condemned for swindling, but to the last they both energetically maintained the divine character of their mission and the faith of many of their followers remained unshaken.

Perhaps, in all this curious case, the most significant fact is that stated by M. Sauvestre, that not a journal in Paris dared to publish a report of the trial.

Clever swindlers abound in all communities and are ever ready to prey upon the special weaknesses of their neighbors. A nation that has given birth to the fantastics of spiritualism has no right to be over-critical with the credulity of other races, and isolated examples of hypocritical duplicity of themselves prove nothing. Yet the facts which are illustrated by the above suggest many social problems worthy of more detailed examination than we can give them here. If in the glitter and reckless ambition which characterize the society of the Second Empire, when the International Labor Congress at Lausanne indignantly rebukes its president for attempting to open the proceedings with an allusion to Divine Providence, when those who think appear to be divided between indifferentism, positivism, and infidelity, and those who do not think seem to be wholly abandoned to the mad pursuit of riches—if, in such a community, the spirit of mystic fervor is advancing with strides so rapid, if constantly increasing thousands are detaching themselves from such a society and devoting themselves irrevocably to the beatitude of contemplation or to the hardest tasks of charity and beneficence, is it not a protest worth heeding as to the insufficiency of our modern civilization? Human institutions are more or less imperfect as they satisfy or obstruct the aspirations of immortal souls. The crude attempts of mediæval civilization could only result in either gross animalism or the superhuman refinements of mystic asceticism. Is it impossible for Latin Christianity to devise a system in which the demands of Nature and of Nature's God will harmonize without conflicting?

In the approaching great Oecumenical council, it will be interesting to observe how enormous will be the influence which the papal court will derive from the·numberless and unceasingly active adherents which it has so laboriously recruited and organized.

KEY NOTES FROM ROME*

AT THE LAY CONGRESS of the Roman Catholic Church of the United States held in Baltimore in November last,[1] the genial and gifted Mr. Daniel Dougherty complained that

We . . . American Roman Catholics . . . have silently submitted to wrongs and injustices in manifold shapes and from time immemorial. . . . The highest honors of the Republic are denied to us by a prejudice that has all the force of a constitutional amendment. . . . Political parties in the past have sought to deprive us of our constitutional rights, and we are branded as tools of a foreign potentate and unworthy to enjoy the name of Americans.

Perhaps the eloquent orator may obtain an inkling of the cause of this apparent injustice, if he will weigh the words of a speaker who followed him, Father Nugent, of Liverpool, who stated that the idea of the congress had originated with the cardinal archbishop of Westminster and the archbishop of St. Paul, and who added, in rhetoric slightly mixed: "But I hope now the keynote will be seized and bind us together in the great social questions of our people." Herein lies the trouble. The Catholic Church is not American or independent; it looks abroad and not at home for its guidance. When the third plenary council of Baltimore was convoked, in 1884, its proceedings had all to be arranged the year before in Rome with the Congregation of Propaganda; and when its sessions closed, they were sent to Leo XIII, who modified them at his pleasure. The bishops who rule the American church are all appointed by the Pope, for the transmission of three names by the provincial suffragans, when a vacancy occurs, is simply advisory and in no way limits the papal discretion of selection. Even so trivial a matter as the introduction of electric lighting in the churches, we are told, has to be referred to the decision of the Propaganda, which a recent traveler describes as containing no representative of the English-speaking peoples save a venerable Irish Benedictine. Thus the interest of "our people" in "great social questions" is apt not to be the same as that of the people at large, and the faithful are bound together with a "key note" which is sounded in Rome. If they are "branded as tools of a foreign potentate," the brand is self-inflicted; and if they are denied the highest honors of the Republic, it is not through an unreasoning prejudice, but through the instinctive popular perception that they own obedience to a higher law than that which binds their fellow citizens.

In saying this I would not not a moment call in question the good faith

* From the *Forum*, VIII (1890), 622-37.

[1] [This congress, made up of lay delegates appointed by the various bishops in this country, was held on November 11 and 12, 1889, in celebration of the hundredth anniversary of the establishment of the Catholic hierarchy in the United States in 1789.—H.]

or the patriotism of Mr. Dougherty, which no one who knows him will impugn. Nor do I forget the distinguished services of General Sheridan, whose elevation as the successor of Generals Grant and Sherman shows that no unworthy jealousy prevents the nation from entrusting with positions of high honor and responsibility Catholics who have deserved well of the Republic. Yet the questions raised by Mr. Dougherty are not to be dismissed with a reference to individuals. The principles involved underlie the whole social organization; in considering them we cannot disregard the lessons of the past and the warnings of the present, which fully justify what Mr. Dougherty complains of as an injustice.

In this no question of religious intolerance is involved. Not the least of the great political innovations reduced to practice by the fathers of the Republic was the severance of State and Church. Prior to their time it had been an accepted maxim of statecraft that religion and politics were so inextricably intermingled that the State must recognize some form of faith, must render it dominant, and must enter into alliance with it to control the souls as well as the bodies and purses of its subjects. The framers of the Constitution wisely disregarded all precedent. They assumed that the State had nothing to do with the faith of the citizen. Abstaining from all formulas, they reverted to the natural law which guarantees to every human being the enjoyment of his creed, whether Buddhist or Confucian, Islamite or Jewish, Catholic or Protestant, Spiritualist or Agnostic. Even this did not satisfy the scruples of the people, and, to prevent all future misunderstanding, by the First Amendment the power was expressly denied to Congress to establish or prohibit any religion.

As the State thus resigns all control over religion, so, reciprocally, religion must make no attempt to control the State. Not only must it engage in no overt acts in this direction, but, if its organization and tenets be such as to threaten interference, measures must be taken to avert the danger. The popular jealousy of which Mr. Dougherty complains is such a measure—not intolerance, but a wise precaution seeking to avert the necessity of intolerance. The Mormon question is a case in point. No one cares to interfere with belief in the Book of Mormon, but the constitution of the Mormon Church is a theocracy. Practically, if not literally, the Latter-day Saint owes obedience first to his ecclesiastical superiors, and secondly to the United States. There is no place in our system for such an *imperium in imperio*, and, in spite of the First Amendment, it is universally recognized that Mormons under their present organization cannot be admitted to full citizenship. Congress therefore has availed itself of one of the Mormon doctrines that happens to be incompatible with our present social order, and has thus endeavored indirectly to break up the Mormon Church. Yet, logically regarded, Senator Edmunds' law for the suppression of polygamy is an interference with religious belief. So were in India the stern and sanguinary measures requisite for the suppression of Thuggee, whose victims were immolated in honor of the awful goddess Kali. No church can claim exemption from the law of self-preservation, which is supreme in all social and political organizations.

These instances illustrate the difficulty of drawing a hard and fast line of demarkation between secular and spiritual affairs. There is a vast field of human activity which may be classed with either group according to custom or faith. We in the United States have reached a tolerably clear perception of what shall be held to lie on either side of the line, and we manage, without much friction, to preserve the distinction between matters concerning earth and those concerning heaven. Yet our definition is very different from that of Rome. The power of the papacy grew up in rude and uncivilized times, when the law of the strongest was dominant in secular concerns, and when the moral forces were feeble and scarce found expression save through the Church. Unquestionably the Church rendered great service to civilization in extending its influence throughout all the ramifications of civil society, and the able men who guided it claimed and obtained the right to control Latin Christendom in almost every relation of human life. Its head was the living representative of Christ on earth. He spoke in the name of God, and as God is infinitely superior to all mortal powers, so he was supreme over secular potentates and his decrees overrode all merely human laws. His jurisdiction extended everywhere, and any local legislation that interfered with it was simply null and void. He was the sole judge of his own authority, and Boniface VIII, in the bull *Unam Sanctam*, which still retains its place in the canon law, defined it to be an article of faith, necessary to salvation, that every human being is subjected to the Roman pontiff. Thus all distinction was virtually lost between the secular and the spiritual spheres. The papacy grew into a theocracy equally absolute over both, at least in theory, and the extent of its intrusion upon the functions of the secular ruler was limited only by the moderation of the occupant of the chair of St. Peter, or by the patience of the sovereign whose rights were invaded. The exercise of this vast and undefined power was further complicated by the position of the popes as Italian princes—temporal monarchs of a territory which they were at frequent intervals endeavoring to extend at the expense of their neighbors, with claims more or less shadowy over almost all Italy south of Lombardy; and the history of the papacy, from the time of Gregory VII, in the eleventh century, is a history of political intrigues and wars, in which every kingdom in turn was obliged to struggle to retain control over its internal affairs, and the interests of Christianity were too often held subordinate to those of the possessor of the patrimony of St. Peter.

All this cannot be dismissed as merely a matter of forgotten history, interesting only to the student. It is the misfortune of an infallible church that it can confess no errors. Whatever it has once formally claimed, becomes its imprescriptible right, which it cannot abandon without being recreant to the trust divinely confided to it. Circumstances, such as the triumph of the ungodly, may for a time render it unable to enforce its rights, but they still exist and are binding on the consciences of the faithful. Pius IX was careful to announce that no concession of principle had been or would be made on account of the altered condition of the modern world, when, in the Syllabus of December 1864,[2] he condemned as an error the assertion that the popes had ever exceeded the limits of their authority or had usurped the rights of princes. Not content with this, he condemned as another error the proposition[3] that the Roman pontiff can and ought to reconcile himself with progress, liberalism, and modern civilization—a declaration that recently found an unexpected echo on this side of the Atlantic in Cardinal Gibbons' unseemly harangue on the occasion of the monument dedicated to Giordano Bruno.

Thus the papacy of to-day is not simply a spiritual power but possesses, according to the received doctrines of the church, an indefinite jurisdiction over temporal affairs throughout Christendom, which can be enforced at pleasure. It is a political force, and as a political force it must be treated when considered in its relations with our institutions. But the pope is more than a mere political sovereign. Not only has he the right to intervene in the domestic concerns of any nation, and to abrogate its laws when he considers that the interests of the Church are at stake, but all citizens owe to him obedience in whatever he may command. St. Alfonso de Liguori only repeats a commonplace when he says[4] that all who have been admitted to Christianity by the waters of baptism, even though they may be heretics, are bound by the precepts of the Church; and if I quote him in preference to other authorities, it is because he was promoted, so recently as 1871, to the rare dignity of a doctor of the Church. As obedience to these precepts implies submission to the papal autocracy, which St. Alfonso had previously proved to be untrammeled even by the authority of general councils, it follows that all who claim to be Christians are bound to render implicit obedience to

[2] § 22.
[3] § 80.
[4] *Theologia Moralis*, Lib. 1, no. 154.

the Holy See, and that the pope is justified in making good his supremacy whenever the opportunity offers.

How complete is that supremacy, and how tenaciously it has been maintained, was shown in the question of the oath of allegiance under James I of England. When, in 1569, St. Pius V excommunicated Queen Elizabeth, deposed her, and released all her subjects from their allegiance, it became customary to question all Catholic missionary priests in England as to whether they considered the papal action binding, and whether the Pope had a right to incite subjects to rebellion. Finally, under James I, after the warning of the Gunpowder Plot, this took the shape of offering to them an oath of allegiance, in which they were required to swear that they would not regard any such bull, but would render true and honest obedience to the sovereign. All allusion to the royal supremacy over the Church of England was carefully omitted, and the obligation was confined simply to temporal duty. Of the two clauses that were peculiarly objected to at Rome, the first was:

And I do further swear, that I do from my heart abhor, detest, and abjure, as impious and heretical, this damnable doctrine and position, that princes who are excommunicated and deprived by the pope may be deposed or murdered by their subjects or any one whatsoever.

The second simply disclaimed belief in the papal power to absolve the juror from the oath. The first person to whom it was administered was George Blackwell, who for nine years had been archpriest and head of the Catholic mission in England, and he recommended all his brethren to follow his example. As soon as the news of this reached Rome, Cardinal Bellarmine wrote to Blackwell, sharply reproving him for taking an illicit oath derogatory to the primacy of the Holy See, in place of preferring the glory of martyrdom; and Paul V accompanied this with a brief addressed to all English Catholics, sternly forbidding them to yield. The oath, he said, could not be taken without infringing the Catholic faith, and he expected them rather to welcome torture and death. A year later, on learning that some of them doubted the genuineness of the brief, he wrote again to inform them that it had been framed after mature deliberation, and that it must be obeyed at whatever cost to them of property or life. King James sallied forth with an *Apology*, to justify his demand of the oath, and called the attention of all Christian princes to the slender tenure by which they held their thrones. Cardinal Bellarmine responded, and essayed to prove that kings held their thrones on condition of obedience to the Church. An Englishman named John Mole, who happened in Florence to show a copy of King James' *Apology* to an acquaintance, was seized by the Inquisition, and died in its prison after thirty years' incarceration; and Paul V looked serenely on while his missionaries in England suffered the penalties of high treason for refusal to take the oath. In all this, Pius IX tells us, the Church never exceeded its rightful authority.

So intolerable was the perpetual papal intrusion in the internal affairs of nations that, as the mediæval confusion between temporal and spiritual matters gradually cleared away, and the dissolution of the feudal system rendered the sovereign absolute, the most Catholic of monarchs could not endure it. Spain and France and Naples refused absolutely to allow papal bulls or letters of any kind to be published within their boundaries without preliminary examination by the secular authorities, and an *exequatur* granting permission was issued only for those considered unobjectionable. In 1508 Ferdinand the Catholic bitterly reproached the Count of Ribagorza, his viceroy of Naples, for not hanging, as an example, a papal messenger who had brought an obnoxious bull, and he ordered it still to be done if the man could be caught on Neapolitan territory. When efforts were made to introduce into Spain the bull *In Cœna Domini*, so destructive to the rights of princes, the authorities of Aragon in 1551 punished the printer who dared to print it, and in 1582 the pious Philip II unceremoniously expelled from Spain the papal nuncio who undertook to publish it. This supervision over papal utterances, so necessary to the peace of a well-ordered state, was carefully provided for by Napoleon when he restored Catholicism to France by the concordat of 1801. It is still found requisite; and when Professor Nuytz, of Turin, in a treatise on ecclesiastical law, defended the practice, Pius IX, in his letter *Ad Apostolicæ*, of August 22, 1851, condemned it as schismatic and heretical, and subversive of the government of the church—a condemnation which he embodied in the Syllabus of 1864.[5] Another measure which Catholic monarchs had found requisite for the protection of their subjects was also upheld by Professor Nuytz and similarly condemned by Pope Pius. This is what is known in France as the *appel comme d'abus*, and in Spain as the *recurso de fuerza*, by which abuses committed in the exercise of the papal jurisdiction within those kingdoms could be redressed by an appeal to the supreme secular tribunal. The effort to escape the evils of this papal jurisdiction produced constant wrangling, especially in Spain, where it was exercised by the nuncio and was a source of considerable revenue to the Holy See. When a new nuncio presented his credentials, they were returned to him with a warning as to the restrictions to be imposed on his powers; and if his commission specified authority in conflict with the laws of the land, a statement would be written on the back that the exercise of such powers

[5] § 41.

would not be permitted. Even with these precautions it would be difficult to exaggerate the abuses of the papal jurisdiction in Spain—its greed, its venality, and the misery with which it afflicted the people—as described in the memorials vainly addressed to the Holy See by Philip IV between 1630 and 1640.

All this is not merely a matter of historical interest. In the bull *Apostolicæ Sedis*, of October 12, 1869, Pius IX inflicts excommunication, *ipso facto* and removable only by the pope himself, on all who shall impede, directly or indirectly, ecclesiastical jurisdiction in either the *forum internum* or the *forum externum*, or shall procure an appeal to the secular courts, or in any way aid or abet such an attempt.

In this same bull a similar condemnation is pronounced against all who shall endeavor to subject ecclesiastics to the jurisdiction of the secular courts. Clerical immunity from secular law, during the Middle Ages, was an abuse which worked enormous injury to both Church and State. In spite of the remonstrances of the Catholic princes, the council of Trent emphatically refused to surrender the privilege; but it was gradually curtailed in one state after another, and the remnant was swept away in most countries by the Revolution, which did so much to render all men equal before the law. In Catholic eyes this is a full wrong. The ecclesiastic is a privileged being, under no obligation to obey the laws of the land and not amenable to them. When Napoleon negotiated the concordat of 1801, he provided by decree that an *appel comme d'abus* should lie to the Council of State for all contraventions of the law by ecclesiastics. Against this Pius VII energetically protested through his legate, Cardinal Caprara, pointing out that the laws might be in opposition to the faith, when the government could not expect priests to obey them. Many of the laws of every modern state are in opposition to the faith, as expounded by the Vatican, and are therefore not binding; while, if an ecclesiastic commits a crime and is subjected to a jury trial, it is an invasion of the rights of the Church, which submits because it is powerless in these evil days to enforce them. Pius IX, in the apostolical letter *Multiplices inter*, June 10, 1851, expressly declared that clerical immunity, both as to person and property, is an ordinance of God and in no way derived from civil law. As such, it must be an article of faith, which the Church has no power to abandon.

I have touched on only a few of the numerous points in which the domain of the Church, as defined by the Vatican, extends over what in modern political systems belongs exclusively to the secular power; but these will suffice to show what ample opportunity the papacy enjoys of intervening in the internal affairs of states. To what extent it will do this is simply a question of policy or of temperament. When, in May

1851, New Granada proclaimed religious toleration and subjected the clergy to the secular courts, Pius IX, in the allocution *Acerbissimum*, of September 27, 1852, pronounced the laws to be null and void, and threatened heavy ecclesiastical penalties on all who should dare to enforce them—a declaration which he repeated in the allocution *Incredibili*, of September 17, 1863. When, in 1855, Mexico adopted a constitution embodying the same principles, Pius, in the allocution *Nunquam fore*, December 15, 1856, annulled the constitution and forbade obedience to it. When, about the same time, Spain, made an effort in the same direction, the allocution *Nemo vestrum*, of July 24, 1855, similarly abrogated the obnoxious provisions. Even a powerful empire like that of Austria fared no better when, in December 1867, it decreed liberty of conscience and of the press, and in May 1868, adopted a law of civil marriage; for the allocution *Nunquam certe*, of June 22, 1868, denounced all these as atrocious laws, and declared them to be void and of no effect.

It is easy to smile at these outbursts as powerless exhibitions of obscurantism, scolding at the progress which it is impotent to stay; but none the less are they protests placed on record with a purpose; and none the less are they binding on the soul of every Catholic in whatever land he may dwell, for it is his duty to obey the voice of the Vicegerent of God in preference to the commands of earthly rulers. The Church, as Pius IX declared in the apostolic letter *Jam vos*, of September 13, 1868, wields an authority granted by God to govern human belief, and to regulate the actions of every man both in private life and social activity. As the theocratic ruler of the Church, it is the pope who decides how this universal authority shall be exercised. The oath embodied in the Catholic profession of faith is not as sensational as that taken to the prophets in the Endowment House at Salt Lake City, which recently has been judicially decided to render those who take it incapable of naturalization, but it is none the less binding on the conscience of the sincere believer:

"I acknowledge the Holy Catholic and Apostolic Roman Church as the mother and mistress of all churches; and I pledge and swear true obedience to the Roman pontiff, and vicar of Jesus Christ and successor of the blessed Peter, prince of the apostles."[6]

In this, it will be observed, there are no reserves; no exception is made of allegiance due to the State, and in the wide field of conflicting sovereignty the duty to obey the pope is absolute over the duty to obey the laws. Henry VIII might well complain to his parliament in 1532

[6] "Sanctam Catholicam et Apostolicam Romanam Ecclesiam omnium Ecclesiarum matrem et magistram agnosco; Romanoque Pontifici, beati Petri Apostolorum Principis successori ac Jesu Christi Vicario veram obedientiam spondeo ac juro." *Acta et Decreta Concilii Baltimorensis* III, liii. (Baltimore, 1886).

that the clergy were but half subjects to him in consequence of their oaths to the pope. The same is true to-day. It was only a few weeks ago that in the Bavarian Landtag the Catholic deputies were forced to admit that they did not regard their oath of office in the sense attached to it by the state. The conscientious Catholic, in fact, is of necessity but half a citizen; he can give but a secondary allegiance to the land of his birth or of his adoption. Is it our fault if, in the words of Mr. Dougherty, he is "branded as the tool of a foreign potentate"?

If American Catholics have not thus far been made to recognize the dilemma in which they are placed, that has been the result of chance or of expediency, and the occasion to make them realize it may come with any day. Elsewhere their fellow-believers are simply counters in the game, to be moved at will in the incessant political activity of the Vatican, for purposes of which they know nothing. But a few months since we listened to the indignation of the French bishops at a circular from M. Tirard reminding them of the laws that wisely prohibit their interference with elections. Since then Boulangism has disappeared, and we now hear from Paris that the nuncio has been instructed to favor the adhesion of Catholics to the Conservative Republican Party. The other day, when Brazil was suddenly converted into a republic, as soon as news reached Leo XIII he telegraphed to Monsignor Spolverini, at Rio de Janeiro, to instruct the Catholic bishops and clergy to abstain from meddling or participating in politics—admirable orders, but the right to issue them implies the right to issue others countermanding them, which may be done at any time, and certainly will not be long postponed if the proposed civil-marriage law is pushed. Everywhere the pope is a factor in the political situation. Bismarck boasted that he would never go to Canossa; but the time came when he needed the votes of the compact body of Catholic deputies to render him independent of the people by a seven years' grant of appropriations for the army. It required but a short negotiation with the Vatican, Herr Windthorst received his orders, the Liberals were defeated, and Bismarck humbly carried to Canossa the modification of the Falck laws. What price Lord Salisbury agreed to pay for the papal rescript against the Plan of Campaign, may perhaps never be known. The project failed under the intense enthusiasm of the Irish people, which threatened a schism; but nevertheless it shows how readily even a high-minded pontiff like Leo XIII will sell his influence for promised benefits wholly dissociated from the interests of those whom he attempts to coerce to pay for them. How advantage is taken of political ascendancy when acquired, is seen in the success of the claim of the Jesuits of Quebec to be reimbursed for property confiscated a century and a quarter ago, not from them or from their predecessors, but from a previous Society of Jesus, which was suppressed and disbanded for cause.[7] There is no statute of limitations against the Church.

We have not, like the French, laws against priestly or episcopal interference with elections; but they would be quite as reasonable and necessary as those which prohibit under heavy penalties employers from influencing the votes of employees, for the prelate or priest who wields the delegated power of the keys has quite as much opportunity of controlling the vote of the conscientious believer as the wage-payer has over the wage-receiver. Our institutions render us peculiarly liable to the domination of compact masses of voters that can be thrown at pleasure on either side. In the even balancing of parties, a comparatively small body of disciplined electors, controlled by a single head or influenced by a common sentiment, can command almost what terms it chooses. Possibly the extraordinary selection of Mr. Egan to represent this country in Chile may thus find its explanation. The dynamitards are said to be an insignificant fraction of the home rulers of the United States, and yet their possible influence has been advanced to explain the long postponement of an extradition treaty with Great Britain. In the degraded condition of politics, trading politicians are careless what they pay for temporary success. In such a market, leaders of the Church who boast that they have behind them a population of ten millions, can find tools enough to do their bidding. To the uninstructed eye it would seem that the position is already tacitly recognized when the contract labor law closes its meshes upon a pastor of Holy Trinity, an Episcopal church in New York, and opens them wide to admit the professors of the Catholic University. Even more significant is the opposition to the confirmation of an Indian commissioner by Catholics, on avowedly religious grounds, with a scarcely veiled threat of defeating the Republican party if the demand is not complied with, though in this case the cynical openness of the assault may perhaps lead to its defeat.

What we want in this land of ours is that our laws and our policy shall be regulated by ourselves for our own interests, and not by foreigners for interests in which we have no concern. We have suffered enough from the Irish vote, controlled by sympathies with which we

[7] To be convinced of the groundless nature of the Jesuit claim it is sufficient to consult the *Arrêts de Parlement* of April and August 1762, suppressing the Society of Jesus in France and the colonies, and converting to public uses such of its property as was not required for the support of its members. Also the bull *Dominus ac Redemptor* of Clement XIV, July 21, 1773, dissolving the society and making no protest against this; and the bulls of Pius VII, *Catholicæ*, March 7, 1801, *Per alias*, July 30, 1804, and *Sollicitudo*, August 7, 1814, founding it anew, in which no allusion is made as to conferring upon the new society any claim on the confiscated estates.

on this side of the Atlantic have nothing to do. As nearly as one can guess from the names of the prelates and theologians who attended the last plenary council of Baltimore, between eighty and ninety per cent were of foreign birth and training, which shows how the disciplined army of the Church is officered. It is quite true that Archbishop Ryan, in the opening sermon at the lay congress, eloquently declared that the atmosphere of liberty is most congenial to the Church, and urged his hearers to be cordially American. It is also true that the declaration of principles there adopted asserted that

We repudiate with equal earnestness the assertion that we need to lay aside any of our devotedness to our church to be true Americans; the insinuation that we need to abate any of our love for our country's principles and institutions to be faithful Catholics.

I would not call in question the sincerity of these utterances any more than that of the declaration recently made by Wilford Woodruff, president of the Mormon Church:

So far from any doctrine or teaching of the church being hostile to the United States government, members of the church are under divine command to revere the Constitution as a heaven-inspired instrument, and to obey as supreme all laws made in pursuance of its provisions.

Still, we have seen contingencies in which our Mormon brethren held a divided allegiance, and thought more of their duty to their church than of their duty to the United States. Such divided allegiance is always a dangerous factor in the body politic. Notwithstanding the care with which the founders of the Republic sought to determine the delimitations between the authority of the Union and of its component parts, four years of tremendous war were necessary to settle the elementary principle whether the citizen's allegiance to the state or to the nation was paramount. We can scarce hope that the time will not come when our Catholic fellow citizens will be put to the strain of electing between the allegiance due to the State and that due to the Church.

Such a strain, in fact, may come any day, in view of the ceaseless political activity of the Holy See. I select a possible case as an example, because it happens at the moment to be prominent in the mind of every Catholic—the condition of the so-called "prisoner of the Vatican"; and I venture to connect with it a gentleman who may be cited as the highest type of public-spirited American Catholic—Mr. Charles J. Bonaparte, who so worthily wears his historic name. No student of history or of politics will delude himself with the idea that the last word has been said as to the sovereignty of Rome. *Tout vient à qui sait attendre,* and the patient watchfulness of the papacy is matchless. While Cola di Rienzi's power appeared to be established, and, again, while Pius VII was a prisoner of Napoleon, the sovereignty of the Roman bishop seemed even more hopeless than it does at present. The political chessboard of Europe has infinite combinations, and, sooner or later, the time will come when there will be at least a prospect of ousting the Subalpine government and restoring to the pope the control of the Papal States. The heart of every true Catholic on earth will be fired, and every Catholic pulpit will resound with appeals to aid the holy cause with prayers and money and men. If then the political situation were such that the intervention of the United States would turn the scale, can we doubt that the most urgent commands would come from the Holy See to obedient American bishops, and that all true Catholics with fierce enthusiasm would labor to effect it? Can we doubt also that promises and threats would be freely used with political managers? Mr. Bonaparte does not leave us to guess where his sympathies would lie. In a paper on this subject read before the congress, he tells us: "We demand, not that he [the pope] be granted privileges as though he were a sovereign, but that, since he is and always must be a sovereign, his existing rights as a sovereign be respected." If, then, in such a conjuncture as I have suggested, Mr. Bonaparte were President or Secretary of State, could the country rely upon him for the unclouded intellect and unbiased judgment necessary to resist the clamor of ten millions, or perhaps by that time of twenty millions, of our people?

The policy of the Roman Curia is so subtle and far-reaching that one hesitates to assign reasons for its moves; but the persistent effort now on foot to persuade our government to accredit a minister to the Vatican is probably founded on the expectation that diplomatic relations might prove useful in the above contingency, especially if a mistaken sense of comity should induce us to appoint a Catholic to the post. Moreover, while awaiting such opportunity to turn our legation to account, the Curia would obtain an immense advantage by the mere fact of our recognizing the Vatican as entitled to diplomatic relations, including the maintenance of a nuncio at Washington. It would be virtually an official admission of the subjection of American Catholics to the Holy See and of the temporal authority of the pope over them, for our envoy could have no possible functions to perform with regard to their religious duties. It would be an acknowledgment of the papacy as a political power in our internal affairs, for with the political activity of the Holy See in other lands we have absolutely no concern. Nations that have state churches may be compelled to maintain relations with the Vatican; but we have none, and we can know the pope only as the claimant from our citizens of an allegiance which we are bound to deny. If we should fall into the trap thus cunningly set for us, it would not be the least of the successes of the Curia, so renowned for its diplomatic astuteness.

Yet I would not be supposed to believe that all, or even a majority, of our Catholic fellow citizens are consciously "tools of a foreign potentate." Outside of the priesthood, probably but few of them realize the extent of the reserved claim on their allegiance held by the Holy See. Even as the Catholic, Lord Howard of Effingham, commanded the fleet which in 1588 destroyed the Spanish Armada, twenty years after St. Pius V had deposed Queen Elizabeth, so on any supreme question a large portion of our Catholics would very likely range themselves on the side of patriotism against priestcraft, as did the Irish on the occasion of the papal rescript. But these supreme questions are of rare occurrence, while there are minor ones liable constantly to arise, on which plausible casuistry can mislead them into an attitude wholly antagonistic to the spirit of our institutions.

I can imagine, moreover, that in the surprises which time has in store for us, there may possibly lie the solution of the problem in a thoroughly American way. The triumph of ultramontanism in the church has been too thorough, the national churches have been too completely crushed out, and papal autocracy has been established too unreservedly. All this is so repugnant to the American habit of thought that already there are occasional symptoms of unconscious rebellion, which in time may ripen to overt revolution, resulting in the organization of a national American Catholic Church, faithful to all the dogmas of Catholicism save the central one of the supremacy of the so-called successor of St. Peter. Because Old Catholicism has not prevailed in Europe, it does not follow that it might not succeed in the less conservative and freer atmosphere of America.

CATHOLICISM AND POLITICS*

[The preceding essay, "Key Notes from Rome," drew a sharp rejoinder from an anonymous correspondent in the *Evening Post* of March 1, 1890, charging the author not only with prejudice, but with reliance on untrustworthy sources of information. Mr. Lea seldom replied to his critics or allowed himself to be drawn into controversies; but in this instance he made an exception and answered the attack in the following letter, which shows his ability to defend his views vigorously, especially when his historical knowledge was called into question.—H.]

* * * * *

To the Editor of the *Evening Post:*

Sir: The admission to your columns of Mr. "G. F. X. G.'s" criticism on my *Forum* article invests his remarks with a factitious importance which perhaps renders them worthy of brief notice.

When I wrote that article I anticipated that it would call forth disclaimers more or less energetic, but the opportune publication of the recent Encyclical of Leo XIII has so completely justified the position which I assumed that I have thus far escaped serious criticism. Rashly as your correspondent has ventured to discuss subjects of which he is profoundly ignorant, he has had discretion enough to leave unassailed all the main substance of the argument, and only calls in question two subsidiary matters. To undertake a defence of the Church after this fashion is virtually to abandon the case, and the Church may well pray to be delivered from such a champion.

One of the two points excepted to is my assertion that the Church still upholds as its indefeasible right the immunity of the clergy from the operation of secular law. When your correspondent humorously suggests that I get this assertion "out of the servants' hall," he hits the mark more nearly than he imagines, for it is derived from the utterance of the Servant of the Servants of God, as he would have found had he, before questioning its truth, been at the pains to refer to the authorities which I cited in its support. Of these a single one will suffice for his enlightenment. No more carefully considered decree has emanated from the Holy See within a century than the bull *Apostolicæ Sedis*, issued in 1869 to replace the older bulls *In Cœna Domini*. In this, among other offenders subjected to excommunication removable only by the Pope himself, are enumerated those who require lay judges to summon to their tribunal ecclesiastical persons in spite of the canonical provisions ("Cogentes sive directe sive indirecte judices laicos ad trahendum ad suum tribunal personas ecclesiasticas præter canonicas dispositiones").

* From the *New York Evening Post*, March 8, 1890.

313

If your correspondent desires to know what these canonical provisions are, he can find them tersely expressed in the authoritative *Prompta Bibliotheca* of Ferraris, under the head of "Immunitas ecclesiastica," Art. 4: "Ecclesiastical persons and all property belonging to ecclesiastical persons or to any church are free and exempt from the jurisdiction of any secular person or power"—all of which Ferraris assures us is of divine law, even as Pius IX has asserted it to be. The fact is that, if the recent Encyclical has been correctly reported in the journals, I might have broadened my assertion and have averred that not only the Catholic ecclesiastic, but also the Catholic layman, "is under no obligation to obey the laws of the land," for Leo XIII expressly says, "If the laws of the State are in open contradiction of the divine law, if they command anything prejudicial to the Church or hostile to the duties imposed by religion . . . then, indeed, it is a duty to resist them and a crime to obey them." Thus the obedience of the Catholic is due to a higher law enunciated by the Holy See; the laws of the land have per se no binding force on him, for their validity depends on what the Church may be pleased to think of them. Moreover, as clerical immunity is of divine law, it is the duty of a priest to resist a summons before a secular court, whether in a civil or criminal action, and it is a crime if he obeys it.

The other exception taken by your correspondent is to my passing allusion to the papal rescript against the plan of campaign. I share with all who know Mr. W. J. Stillman[1] the highest respect for that gentleman. I read with interest his letter on that subject which appeared[2] after my article had gone to press. I presumed that of course he represented truthfully the case as stated to him by the *monsignori*, but this did not seem to me to alter the aspect of the matter. "G. F. X. G." may, if so inclined, believe that the whole unlucky business was simply an affair of morals and not of politics, but if so, he will have to explain the papal recreancy in abandoning the defence of morals rather than risk the dangers of an Irish schism. Meanwhile, I confess my inability to understand by what process of reasoning he finds that I drew the details from Llorente and committed the offence of not warning the reader that Llorente is a "tainted witness." The books tell us that Llorente died in 1823, some sixty-six years before the papal rescript in question.

For his own sake I sincerely deplore that my article has prevented "G. F. X. G." from reading my *History of the Inquisition of the Middle Ages* (not *of Spain*), for I am sure that it would furnish him with knowledge of which he seems sorely in need. Of one thing he may be

[1] [Special correspondent of the London *Times*, residing in Rome from 1876 to 1898. —H.]

[2] [In *The Nation*, Jan. 16, 1890.—H.]

sure, that the "better understanding" desired by all reasonable men will not be furthered by those who require the plain facts of history to be suppressed or distorted to suit their fancies or convictions, or by those who cannot understand that when any religious organization oversteps its spiritual limits and descends into the arena of politics, it must be treated like any other political machine. To chatter about sectarianism and intolerance in such connection is self-deception or worse.

AN ANTI-MASONIC MYSTIFICATION*

WE ARE TOLD by a recent writer that when Anthony Sayer, George Payne, Dr. Desaguliers, and a few others, in 1717, organized in London the Masonic Order, their object was to procure the secession of all Catholic nations from Rome and to prepare the union of all the peoples of the earth under the dominion of Great Britain. If they entertained such far-reaching designs under their ostensible purpose of promoting toleration, good-fellowship, and benevolence, they must have felt themselves cruelly deceived, for their earliest extension on foreign soil was the founding at Saint-Germain of the Paris lodge, in 1725, under Lord Derwentwater, the Chevalier Maskelyne, Dr. Ramsay, and other Jacobites, who found the secrecy of the order an admirable cloak for Catholic plots against the house of Hanover, and its spread on the Continent was largely owing to the use made of it by the exiled Stuarts. It is therefore not easy to understand the antagonism manifested towards it, almost from the beginning, by the Holy See—an antagonism which has necessarily resulted in mutual hostility.

Outside of England and her colonies the development of Masonry was by no means rapid, but the Church early took the alarm, and, in 1738, Clement XII condemned it in his bull *In eminenti*. No reason for this was alleged except its secrecy and that under its rules men of all religions associate together, giving rise to suspicions of evil, wherefore all members incur excommunication removable only by the pope, and all bishops are instructed to prosecute and punish them as vehemently suspect of heresy. As the Parlement of Paris refused to register this bull, it could scarce accomplish much outside of the Papal States, except in Spain, but within them it was rendered effective by an edict of the cardinal secretary of state, January 14, 1739, pronouncing irremissible pain of death, not only on all members but on all who tempt others to join or favor the society in any way, such as leasing a house for its use. This was a declaration of war to the knife, although the only victim of the death penalty is said to have been the French author of a book on Masonry. In spite of the papal denunciation the grand-mastership in France was assumed, in 1742, by Louis de Bourbon, Count of Clermont, a prince of the blood royal, and the order continued to grow. In the jubilee of 1750 so many of the pilgrims flocking to Rome had to be relieved of excommunication incurred on this account that the attention of Benedict XIV was called to it and, May 18, 1751, he issued the constitution *Providas*, in which he renewed and confirmed the bull of Clement XII; he pointed out the injury to the faith arising from the association of men of different beliefs and he invoked the aid of all Catholic princes to enforce the mandates of the Holy See. After this Rome

* From *Lippincott's Magazine*, LX (1900), 948-60.

appears to have been quiescent until, in 1789, the arch-impostor Cagliostro had the audacity to attempt to found a lodge in the Holy City. Arrested December 27 of that year, his trial by the Inquisition lasted until April 7, 1791, although he freely confessed and recanted and offered to sign any declaration that might be drawn up for the purpose of disillusioning his disciples. It was probably to this that he owed his escape from execution, for his sentence recites that he had incurred the death penalty provided by the edict of 1739, but as a special mercy it was commuted to life imprisonment in a fortress; he was immured in the castle of San Leone where he is supposed to have died in 1795.

The upheaval of the French Revolution distracted the attention of the papacy from Masonry, and under Napoleon it was too valuable an instrument of his policy to be meddled with, but Pius VII was scarce more than reseated on his throne when he issued, August 15, 1814, the brief *Si antiqua*, and two edicts of his secretary of state were directed against it. Thus far Masonry, although so rudely attacked, had apparently done nothing to provoke hostility, but a real danger soon manifested itself in one of its offshoots, the secret society of the Carbonari—a distinct organization, with very decided political objects, but modeled on the Masonic pattern. As it claimed not to be included in the decrees of Clement and Benedict, Pius issued, September 13, 1821, his bull *Ecclesiam*, subjecting it to the same penalties and charging it, among other crimes, with allowing every man to enjoy his own religious opinions, than which scarce anything can be more pernicious. Then Leo XII, in his bull *Quæ graviora*, May 12, 1825, informs us that immediately on his accession he had diligently investigated these sects and had found that they were spreading and were threatening the peace of Europe, wherefore he reissues the decrees of his predecessors and impressively urges princes and prelates to be vigilant in repressing the evil. Pius VIII followed, May 21, 1829, with the encyclical *Traditi*, in which the former papal utterances were confirmed as against the secret societies from which, as from the depths of the abyss, have arisen the evils so destructive to religion and to the State. The encyclical *Mirari vos*, of Gregory XVI, August 15, 1832, is commonly quoted as directed against Masonry, but is, rather, a fierce objurgation of all modern progress and of the pestilent madness of so-called freedom of conscience, while the secret societies are only alluded to as sewers of sacrilege, wickedness, and blasphemy, and the chief source of the calamities of the times. It seems to have become customary for each new pontiff to signalize his accession by some outburst of the kind, and Pius IX, in his encyclical *Qui pluribus*, November 9, 1846, renewed against these clandestine bodies the anathema of his predecessors and ordered its strict enforcement. His bitter experiences during the next two decades explain the wrath against Masonry exhaled in the allocution *Multiplices inter*, September 25, 1865. To it are attributed the wars and seditions that have convulsed Europe and brought such evils on the Church; the utterances of the Holy See had been so unsuccessful that Masonry had spread everywhere, owing to the ignorant belief that it is innoxious and charitable and that religion has nothing to dread from it, wherefore he is compelled again to condemn it and to confirm the penalties set forth in previous papal constitutions. Naturally in the great bull *Apostolicæ Sedis,* October 12, 1869, the Masons, the Carbonari, and all similar societies are included in the excommunications *latæ sententiæ,* absolution for which is reserved to the Holy See. Finally, in the epistle *Scite profecto,* July 14, 1873, he set the example, which has proved so fruitful, of attributing Masonry to Satan, for he says it can only be the devil, the eternal adversary of God, who is responsible for it; he founded it and has contrived its development.

Subsequently to this the Grand Orient of Paris gave some color to such accusations by removing from its conditions of membership the belief in God and immortality, and substituting a declaration that it had nothing to do with metaphysical conceptions—an admission of infidelity which promptly brought from Albert Pike, as grand commander of the Scottish Rite in the United States, and from the Prince of Wales, as grand master of English Masonry, decrees sundering all relations with the French organization. Leo XIII took advantage of the opportunity, and in the long and elaborate encyclical *Humanum genus,* April 20, 1884, he undertook to examine the whole doctrine and methods and objects of Masonry, so that its maleficent pestilence might be understood and restrained. The result of this investigation is condensed in the opening sentence, that the human race is divided into two sections, of which one serves God and Christ while the other is the kingdom of Satan and wars against God. To the latter belongs the Masonic Order, for it seeks to overflow the Church of God and to restore the paganism of eighteen centuries ago, in which insane desire may be recognized the quenchless hate and thirst for revenge of Satan against God. In the most solemn manner the bishops throughout the Catholic world were commanded to tear off their masks from the Masons and to teach the people what they are in reality.

So formal and absolute a declaration from the infallible head of the Church could not fail to produce a profound impression upon the faithful. The necessary corollary was seen to be that Masonry is devil-worship, and honest fanaticism eagerly developed the theme. Father Joseph Müller, of Vienna, in his *Geheimnisse der Hölle,* or *Secrets of Hell,* proved that Masonry is organized Satan worship, and so did Jean Kostka in his *Lucifer démasqué.* Bishop Fava, of Grenoble, declared that it is nothing but the religion of Satan. Archbishop Meurin, S.J., in his exhaustive *La Franc-Maçonnerie Synagogue de Satan*, describes Charleston as the provisional Rome of the Satanic Synagogue, where Satan appears to his representative and issues his orders, for the grand master of the Supreme Council of Charleston is the pope, the vicar-general of Satan upon earth. The rites of this infernal cult are not reserved to the higher degrees, for the anonymous author of *La Loque Noire* tells us that the very apprentice, at his first initiation, is taught that Lucifer is the Good God, and in order to obliterate his Christian baptism he receives the baptism of fire, which is the baptism of Lucifer.

It was not, however, honest fanaticism alone which followed the impulsion given by the encyclical *Humanum genus*. The possibilities of the situation were quickly grasped by an individual who presents himself to us as a typical product of *fin-de-siècle* decadent civilization. Gabriel Jogand-Pagès, better known by his pseudonym of Léo Taxil, was born in Marseilles in 1854.[1] He received a good education, partly at the hands of the Jesuits, and while yet a youth betook himself to journalism, wherein he speedily won distinction by reckless contempt for religion and virulent personalities. To escape a sentence of eight years' imprisonment he fled to Geneva in 1876; an amnesty enabled him to return to France, and in 1879 he settled in Paris, where his attacks on the clergy brought him a series of prosecutions and condemnations, the heaviest of which was in the sum of sixty-five thousand francs for a scandalous work entitled *Les Amours secrètes de Pie IX*. He established an anti-clerical bookstore; his tireless pen produced a series of irreligious books, many of which had a very extended sale, and he issued a daily paper entitled *L'Anti-Clérical*, to promote an association of freethinkers which he founded and which before long numbered seventeen thousand members. Regardless of truth, fertile in imagination, and audacious in assertion, he won for himself the reputation of one of the most dangerous antagonists of the faith.

The reception throughout the Catholic world of the encyclical *Humanum genus* suggested to him that credulity might be a more profitable field to cultivate than incredulity. Light suddenly broke in upon his darkened soul in the early morning of April 24, 1885, and he was a converted and penitent sinner. He closed his anti-clerical bookshop and suppressed his irreligious writings. His conversion was regarded as a triumph of divine grace, and the papal nuncio in Paris, Monseigneur di Rende, condescended to absolve him from the numerous excommuni-

---

[1] [Part of the material concerning this disreputable character was obtained by Lea from Dr. J. Riek's *Leo XIII und der Satanskult* (Berlin, 1897); the remainder from Taxil's own writings and the writings of his associates.—H.]

cations which he had incurred. As a convert his ardor for the faith was even greater than had been his former antagonism, and the encyclical pointed out Masonry as the subject of attack. He had entered the order in 1881, but had soon afterwards left it, without advancing beyond the degree of apprentice, but ignorance of its secrets was to him no impediment in revealing its hidden villainies, and in 1885 and 1886 he published a series of works comprehended under the general title of *Révélations complètes sur la Franc-Maçonnerie* which had an enormous circulation. Their general purport was to prove that Masonry is Satan worship, based on the elder Manichæism and mediæval Catharism, and as regard for truth never restrained the activity of his invention, he was at no loss in proving his thesis with abundant documents and rituals and marvels well adapted to gratify popular curiosity. He devoted an entire volume to female Masons—who are nonexistent in regular Masonry— and his foul imagination reveled in describing the scenes which occur in "androgynous" lodges. Throughout Europe these works were received with great applause by the Catholic press, which pointed out that all this was the direct development of the Reformation, and Father Gruber, S.J., in his German translation, asserted that Masonry was thus only carrying out what Luther had begun.

The field proved too large and productive for a single laborer, and Taxil called around him several writers of the same stamp—notably a Dr. Hacks, who under the pseudonym of Dr. Bataille produced a work of nearly two thousand pages entitled *Le Diable au XIXe Siècle*, in which all Protestants were represented as in reality Luciferans. Another of the group was an Italian named Domenico Margiotta whose chief production was *Adriano Lemmi, chef suprême des Francs-Maçons*; of this a German translation was issued at Paderborn, for the right of which he demanded fifty thousand francs. The character of these books can be guessed from the fact that for repeating in the Papal sheet *Moniteur de Rome* a shocking account of the hideous and beastly practices of a lodge in Swiss Freiburg, Monseigneur Vöglein was prosecuted and condemned in two thousand five hundred francs. The fact is that the associates used to chuckle together over the limitless popular credulity which they were exploiting, and to rival each other in the extravagance of their inventions. They included Spiritualism as one of the forms of Masonry, and if one of them related how in a table-turning séance the table suddenly rose on two legs while the other two clutched the unlucky medium by the throat and strangled him to death, another one capped the story with a scene in which the table·floated to the ceiling and descended as a crocodile, which sat down at the piano and played for the delectation of the assemblage. Nothing was too absurd to be printed and the wildest fictions were devoutly accepted as truth. Margiotta received letters of thanks and recommendation from the bishops of Grenoble, Annecy, Pamiers, Montauban, Oran, and Tarentaise, and from the archbishop of Aix and the patriarch of Jerusalem, while Leo XIII recompensed him with the Order of the Holy Sepulchre. The pope, in fact, assisted the industry of Taxil and his collaborators with several stirring trumpet blasts to stimulate popular horror of Masonry. In the vernacular encyclical *Dall' Alto*, October 15, 1890, addressed to the clergy and people of Italy, he described it as pervaded with the spirit of Satan and burning like him with implacable hatred of Christ. Again, on December 8, 1892, he addressed to the Italians his letter *Custodi*, a dithyrambic exhortation conveying a fearful picture of the war waged by Masonry against both the heavenly and the earthly fatherland, against the religion of our fathers and civilization itself. On the same date the epistle *Inimica vis*, addressed to the Italian bishops, asserts that the diabolical spirit of all former sects is revived in Masonry which attacks everything sacred, while the public, lulled in false security, does not recognize the danger, for Christianity itself is at stake.

In the various productions of the Taxil workshop allusions were made to two matters which assumed especial importance in the development of the anti-Masonic movement. One of these was the so-called Palladium, or inner and higher Order of Masonry, of which Stevens, in his *Cyclopædia of Fraternities*, informs us that it claims to have been instituted in 1730 and to have been early introduced into Charleston, where it lay dormant until it was revived in 1886 as the new and reformed Palladium to impart new force to the traditions of high-grade Masonry, but that little is known of it, as its membership is very limited and its proceedings are strictly secret. Dr. Bataille, however, tells us that it was founded by Albert Pike on September 20, 1870, the day on which the Italian troops entered Rome and overthrew the temporal power. As, in the Taxilian scheme, Charleston, with its Sanctum Regnum, was, until the death of Albert Pike in 1891, the headquarters of Luciferan Masonry, the Palladium was eagerly seized upon and developed to its utmost terrifying capacity. Its "triangles" constitute the inner lodges in which the Satanic spirit of the order exhibits itself without disguise, and it is the real directing and governing body. Initiation to the third and highest degree of a triangle is always conducted by the demon in person, and, according to Archbishop Meurin, it is in these triangles that Satan appears to his worshipers and issues his orders. To render the story complete, a high priestess of the Luciferan cult was necessary, and one was found in the person of Miss Diana Vaughan.

The distinguished descent of this personage rendered her worthy of the honor. Thomas Vaughan, twin brother of Henry Vaughan the Silurist, was the head of the Rosicrucians whose object was the overthrow of the papacy. On March 25, 1645, he signed a compact with Satan assuring him thirty-three years of life for the propagation of Luciferism. In 1646 he came to America and domiciled himself with the Lenni-Lenape. While there he was visited by Venus-Astarte, who submitted herself to his embraces and in eleven days presented him with a daughter to whom he gave the name Diana and whom he left with the Indians when he returned to England in 1648. She married the greatest warrior of the tribe and gave birth to a boy who in 1675 was suddenly brought to his grandfather in Hamburg for a few hours, during which Vaughan had the gift of the Lenape tongue, and who then disappeared back to his Indian home. From him was Diana descended; her father was an earnest Palladist who founded the great triangle of the Eleven-Seven in Louisville, with its three thousand members; he carefully trained her in Palladism, and in 1884, after passing through the lower grades, she was initiated as a member of the Eleven-Seven. While yet a girl she had betrothed herself to the great daimon Asmodeus, and when twenty-five, on April 8, 1889, at the command of Lucifer, she was officially presented to the latter in the Sanctum Regnum of Charleston. There he appeared to her in majestic beauty seated on a throne of diamonds, and, amid wonders surpassing those of the Arabian Nights, he announced to Albert Pike that he consecrated her his high priestess and the organ of his wishes, to be everywhere held in highest respect, whereupon Pike signed a decree to that effect addressed to all the triangles.

There was, however, another high priestess, also of daimonic origin, named Sophia Walder, the putative daughter of Phileas Walder, a Protestant pastor of high grade in Masonry, but in reality the offspring of Lucifer by Walder's wife or mistress, Ida Jacobsen. It was foretold that in the summer of 1896 she would go to Jerusalem where, on September 29, she would give birth to a daughter by the daimon Bitru; the latter in thirty-three years will have a daughter by the daimon Decarabia, and she in thirty-three years more (1962) will give birth to Antichrist. As the destined great-grandam of Antichrist, Sophia was held in the highest reverence by the Palladists; she had been specially trained in Charleston by Albert Pike and was gifted with sundry supernatural powers, such as rendering her body fluid and passing through a stone wall. She and Diana quarrelled when the latter, March 25, 1885, sought, in the triangle Saint-Jacques of Paris, initiation to the highest degree of Maîtresse Chevalière Templière and refused to perform the ceremony of spitting upon and stabbing a consecrated host. Diana, after being worsted in the struggle, created a schism in the Palladium and organized the Independent Regenerated Luciferans—a body which should be purely Luciferan and not Satanic. The London "convent" of this Regenerated Palladium resolved on a public propaganda of the faith and entrusted its conduct to her. Accordingly, Taxil issued, March 21, 1895, the first number of a periodical entitled *Le Palladium régénéré et libre—Directrice Miss Diana Vaughan*. In a manner designedly offensive to Catholics it set forth the creed of the sect, which was a curious adaptation of the dualistic Catharism of the Albigenses. Lucifer, the Light-bringer, is the principle of intelligence and light; Adonai, of matter and death, and they have been in conflict since long before the creation of the worlds. The book *Apadno* gives the Bible history in its true shape, relating how Adonai created the animal man while Lucifer conferred on him intelligence and the power of reproduction. The soul is an emanation of Lucifer, which Adonai is always trying to win over. After death the saints of Lucifer are reunited to him in his kingdom of eternal fire; imperfect souls have a new trial through transmigration into animals or man; the saints of Adonai are cast into his kingdom of water, where they exist as spirits until the final victory of Lucifer, when they will be destroyed. At present humanity is everywhere emancipated from Adonai except on earth and in the planet Oolis. The angels of Lucifer, the Good God, are called daimons and are of both sexes; their chiefs are Moloch, Beelzebub, Baal, Asmodeus, Antichrist, Astarte, Leviathan, Behemoth, etc. The spirits of Adonai are unsexual and are known as maleakhs; their chiefs are deserters from Lucifer—Michael, Gabriel, Uriel, Raphael, etc. One of the worst and most powerful of them is known to Catholics as the Blessed Virgin; her name among Palladists is Mirzam in so far as relates to her human life, but spiritually she is the abominable Lilith. Jesus, the son of the maleakhs, Joseph and Mirzam, had good qualities derived from his ancestor Beelzebub, but pride wrought his fall; he betrayed the Good God when he signed the covenant of Mount Tabor, after which his work was evil. In 1995 Antichrist will reveal himself; the reigning pope, who will be a converted Jew, will abandon Catholicism and will embrace Lucifer worship. A year of war will ensue, during which the Catholics will be exterminated, and this will be followed by the heavenly struggle between the daimons of Lucifer and the maleakhs of Adonai, ending in the overthrow of the latter, who will be confined in Saturn under guard of the spirits of light, already visible there, as they form the rings encircling the planet.

Three monthly numbers of the *Palladium* appeared, horrifying the faithful with these blasphemies, whose suggestiveness was heightened with abundance of mysterious detail. All this, however, was merely the prelude to a dexterous comedy. The *Palladium* was discontinued, and with July 1 it was replaced with another monthly entitled *Miss Diana Vaughan*. *Mémoires d'une Ex-Palladiste,* which opened with a quarrel between Diana and the convent of London, her defiance of that body, and her conversion to Catholicism, with the resolution to devote her life to undoing the evil which she had so blindly wrought hitherto. This conversion was precipitated by a visit, June 6, from Beelzebub, Ashtaroth, Moloch, and Asmodeus, in their customary radiant beauty, but wroth against her because she had promised, out of consideration for Joan of Arc, not to speak of the Virgin Mary in terms of disrespect. To protect herself against them she invoked Joan of Arc, when they were transformed into their real shape of demons with horns and tail and disappeared howling. She sought the retreat of a convent, where her conversion was completed and she was admitted to the mysteries of religion. Her consecration to her new faith was to be manifested by writing her autobiography, to appear in the monthly issues of her periodical.

The Catholic world hailed with acclaim this new evidence of divine grace, akin to that of Taxil's conversion. But in Diana's case it was accompanied with the necessity of the strictest seclusion, for her life, it was asserted, would not have been worth an hour's purchase if the Palladists, maddened by her desertion and her revelations, should be able to reach her with the dagger or the bowl. Only a few friends of tried fidelity were to know the place of refuge whence month by month she poured forth her narrative and her descriptions of the fearful secrets of Masonry. It shows the inexhaustible imaginations of Taxil and his collaborators that after ten years of shocking disclosures they could still feed the insatiable appetite of public credulity with an endless flood of marvels of the most diverse character. We have, for instance, a melodramatic scene in which Albert Pike, disillusioned of his earlier paganism and wearied with hermetical researches after the Grand Arcanum, flees to a solitude where Korah, Dathan, and Abiram rise from the solid rock, convert him to Lucifer worship, and gratify him with some particles of the philosopher's stone. The grotesque is carried to its highest denomination in the account of Friar Francisco Barri and his spouse, the salamander Elkbamstar, and in that of the Magus Van Geer who used to divide his body into minute fragments, which when put into a sack reunited themselves. We hear of Brother Hubert, who has for protecting daimon Arkathapias, the terrible favorite of Moloch, and who possesses the faculty of bilocation—of being in several places at the same time. Audacity is pushed to the utmost in the account of miraculous proceedings in the triangle of Malta where various English officers are named as witnesses and we are told that Rear-Admiral Markham, who became grand master March 6, 1893, on reading the minutes of the meeting, expressed incredulity, when he was instantaneously transported to the Sanctum Regnum of Charleston, where the Baphomet asked him if he still doubted, and on his declaring his belief he was similarly conveyed back to Malta.

It is humiliating to modern intelligence that such a farrago of absurdities, poured forth month after month, should be unhesitatingly accepted by the devout, but so it was. As an evidence of her converted zeal Diana composed a little devotional work, *La Neuvaine Eucharistique*, and sent a copy of it, in November, 1895, to Leo XIII, by whose order Cardinal-Vicar Parocchi returned her a special papal benediction, adding his own and expressing his sympathy; her conversion is a magnificent triumph of grace, and he is reading her *Mémoires*, which he finds of palpitating interest. Diana also published in the summer of 1896 *Le 33ᵉ Crispi*, a heavy volume of five hundred pages, revealing all the secrets of Italian politics and Masonry. Monsigneur Vincenzo Sardi, one of the papal secretaries, in a letter of July 11, thanks her for a copy and urges her to continue to unmask the iniquitous sect; it was for this that Providence had so long permitted her to belong to it. He alludes, however, to calumnious reports denying her existence, which he regards as artifices of Masonry, and suggests that her disproval of them would be for the benefit of a multitude of souls. The fact is, there were too many in the secret of the imposture for it to be kept. About this time Margiotta and Dr. Hacks quarrelled with Taxil over the division of the profits and began to boast of their share in the business. Yet the leading organ of the Church, the *Civiltà Cattolica*, in an issue for September 1896, speaks of Miss Diana Vaughan, called from the depths of darkness to the light of God, prepared by divine Providence, armed with personal knowledge and experience, who turns to the service of the Church and seems to be inexhaustible in her precious publications, which have not their equal for exactitude and usefulness. Freemasonry in consternation, to escape her blows, denies her existence and treats her as a myth. In fact, an Italian translation of the *Mémoires* was published in Rome by the *Rivista Antimassonica*, the official organ of the Anti-Masonic Union of Italy.

Yet the crisis was approaching. Under the impulse of papal utterances and fabricated revelations a great Anti-Masonic Congress had been summoned to meet in Trent at the end of September. The gathering was enthusiastic and successful. The honorary president was the prince-bishop of Trent and the presiding officer was Prince Karl zu Löwenstein; the number of members was about a thousand, among whom were thirty-six bishops and the delegates of about fifty more; there was a great procession, reckoned at eighteen thousand strong; a telegram from Leo XIII conveyed his blessing on the assemblage; a crusade against Masonry was decreed, and the Congress unanimously declared that Masonry is the Synagogue of Satan and that Masons recognize Lucifer as God. Léo Taxil was the hero of the hour and was appointed on a commission to organize a universal anti-Masonic association, but there were four honest Germans hardy enough to express doubts as to the existence of Diana Vaughan, and on September 29 a special session was held to consider the question. Demand was made for the details of her conversion and for the names of her godparents and of the bishop who authorized her first communion. Taxil replied that he had the proofs in his pocket but could not produce them, as it would imperil her life; all he could do was to communicate privately to an ecclesiastic going to Rome the name of a bishop who should be summoned on some pretext to the curia and who would give to the pope himself the necessary assurances. Bishop Laz-zareschi was selected as the recipient of the confidence. Taxil met him in the evening at the episcopal palace. Some months later he declared that Taxil had refused, on a frivolous pretext, to give him the name of the bishop, whereupon Taxil gave him the lie direct, and his prolonged silence during the interval shows that he recognized the delicacy of the situation, involving the honor of the Church. In the congress, the Commendatore Alliata, president of the executive council of the Universal Anti-Masonic Union, had announced that it had a commission specially charged with everything concerning Diana Vaughan, and to that body the further investigation of the matter was tacitly abandoned.

The Catholic journals throughout Europe were beginning to realize the absurdity of the situation, and denounced Taxil as the creator of a myth, but Rome was committed and could not afford to admit the deception. On October 16, A. Villard, a domestic chaplain of the pope and secretary of Cardinal Parocchi, wrote to Diana to encourage her in the tempest of calumny which did not scruple to deny even her existence. He had the proofs, he said, material and psychologic, not only of her existence, but of the sincerity of her conversion, and he urged her to continue the writings which furnish weapons for the overthrow of the enemy of the human race. Meanwhile Alliata's commission was at work, and the public utterances of some of the members showed that it had soon come to the conclusion that the whole affair was a fraud, but orders from above delayed its report, and when this appeared, January 22, 1897, it bore evident signs of having been drawn up under compulsion. It said that the commission was not empowered to judge as to the revelations but only as to Diana, and that it had not been able to obtain any conclusive proof for or against her existence, her conversion, or the authenticity of her writings.

This cautious noncommittalism was not shared by the Catholic press, and Taxil, in the monthly issues of the *Mémoires*, had been bravely making head against torrents of obloquy and abuse, but the game was up. There were still a few who resolutely maintained the reality of Diana Vaughan and her experiences, such as Bishop Fava, of Grenoble, and Canon Mustel in his *Revue de Coutances*, but the journalistic hubbub grew louder and more exasperated, and Taxil recognized that the mystification must come to an end. In the number of the *Mémoires* for February 25, 1897, Diana therefore announced that she would make a public appearance on Easter Monday, April 19, in the hall of the Société de Géographie, where she would deliver an explanatory address, illustrated with numerous photographic lanternslides. It was to be reserved to journalists, and all the journals of Europe and the United States were invited to be present or to order their correspondents to be there. In subsequent numbers an elaborate abstract of the promised address was printed and an itinerary was given of a long series of appearances in the principal cities on both sides of the Atlantic. Characteristically the autobiography was continued up to the last, with its customary assortment of marvels. In the number for April 15, only four days before the meeting, Diana relates how, after escaping death in the triangle Saint-Jacques for refusing to desecrate the host, that triangle wrote to the Eleven-Seven of Louisville to expel her. She hurried to Louisville, where she was miraculously saved from expulsion. The most cherished object in the triangle was the tail of the lion of St. Mark, which Asmodeus had hewed off in battle and presented to it. This was kept locked in a box, but it sprang forth and wound itself affectionately around her neck; the tuft of hair at the end changed into the head of Asmodeus, who informed the triangle that she was under his special protection, and he further warned her never to marry, as he would strangle her husband. Then when she was chagrined because the triangle Saint-Jacques would not complete her initiation, Asmodeus, to distract her thoughts, carried her on a trip to Mars. Soon after this he made her float in the air as he respectfully presented her with a steel diadem. Her uncle, who was present, seized his kodak and photographed the group, and copies of this produced a great sensation when she distributed them among the mother lodges of the Lotus.

When April 19 came the hall was well filled with an audience who had been required to surrender their canes and umbrellas at the door. In place of Diana, Taxil appeared and made a speech unrivaled for cynical effrontery. He confessed himself guilty of child-murder, for

Palladism was dead and he, its father, had killed it. The only Diana Vaughan he knew of was his typewriting girl, to whom he paid one hundred and fifty francs a month. For twelve years his object had been to study intimately the Catholic Church through a series of mystifications that should expose the secrets of the minds and hearts of the hierarchy, and he had succeeded beyond his most sanguine anticipations. After his pretended conversion the obvious means for this was suggested by the fact that the Church sees in Freemasonry its most dangerous enemy, and that many Catholics, with the Pope at their head, believe that the devil is the real chief of this anti-clerical society. He asserted that in Rome the cardinals and the curia had in conscious bad faith favored the writings issued in his name and in those of Bataille and Diana Vaughan; they knew the fictitious character of the pretended revelations, but were glad to use them to keep the faithful in a belief advantageous and profitable to the Church. The bishop of Charleston, he said, had written to the pope that the stories about that city were false, but Leo XIII had imposed silence on him as well as on the apostolic vicar of Gibraltar, who had assured him that there were no caves there in which the Masons celebrated their foul mysteries, as asserted by Dr. Bataille. Thus Taxil went on imperturbably amid the howls and curses of the audience, who recognized too late why they had been deprived at the door of their possible weapons. At length they became uncontrollable; he escaped under protection of the police and quietly betook himself to a neighboring café.

For a time nothing was left for the anti-Masonic movement but to bind up its wounds. There were still a few whose steadfast souls refused to accept the unreality of Diana and who darkly hinted that Taxil had made way with her or had sold her for an enormous sum to the Palladists, but even these in time became silent. Canon Mustel in his palinode suggested that when hell shall swallow its filthy prey, Taxil, the damned will feel disgust and will bow their heads under the weight of a new degradation. He justified his belief in the marvelous revelations by pointing out that Taxil knew better than many well-instructed Catholics the facts and the teaching of the Church in the difficult and abstruse matter of supernatural manifestations, and he had succeeded in his fraudulent work only by resting it on this solid foundation. Was it a recognition of this or a consciousness of complicity that has kept the works of Taxil and his collaborators out of the Index of Prohibited Books? One may find there such works as Sabatier's sympathetic *Life of St. Francis* and Taine's *History of English Literature*, but the names of Taxil, Bataille, Margiotta, and Diana Vaughan are significantly conspicuous by their absence. The faithful are still at liberty to seek them for enlightenment on the mysteries of Freemasonry.

PUBLIC INTERESTS

BIBLE VIEW OF POLYGAMY*

[As an active member of the Union League of Philadelphia during the Civil War, Mr. Lea wrote many of the pamphlets issued by that body, among them this mock defense of polygamy as an answer to Bishop Hopkins' defense of slavery. In 1861 the Protestant Episcopal bishop of Vermont published an article condemning the view that slavery was a moral evil. By copious citations from Holy Writ he showed that the institution of slavery was accepted without question in both the Old and New Testaments and so must be considered as approved by God. To condemn it on moral grounds was blasphemy against the Almighty. His article was reprinted and widely circulated as a Democratic campaign document in the gubernatorial campaign of 1863 in Pennsylvania; but its effects were completely nullified by Lea's burlesque, in which he parodied all the good bishop's arguments in order to defend that other honored institution of antiquity, polygamy.—H.]

* * * * *

To the Right Reverend John Henry Hopkins,
     Bishop of the Diocese of Vermont.

Right Reverend Sir: I venture to dedicate to you these few pages, which derive their inspiration from your writings. An admirer, like yourself, of the institutions of old, I should hardly have dared to declare these truths to a perverse and self-glorifying generation, had I not been emboldened by the example of one who so worthily wears the highest honors of the Church. In constructing my argument, therefore, as I have done, with paragraph after paragraph of your very words, it has been because I felt it necessary to shield myself behind your authority from the charge, which ignorant presumption might else have brought, of irreverently travestying the Word of God. A race which can stigmatize as "twin relics of barbarism" two institutions such as slavery and polygamy, which are divinely sanctioned if not divinely ordained, is capable of any act of irreligious fanaticism. The Utah expedition failed to accomplish the destruction of the one; let us hope that the present abolition war will prove equally unsuccessful as to the other. To aid in the good work, then, let us bend our united energies to the task of forcing the light of truth through the accumulated darkness of our so-called modern civilization, in the hope that the time is not far distant when every citizen may have as many slaves as Abraham, and as many wives as Solomon.

Trusting that you will accept my coöperation in the spirit in which it is tendered, I beg leave to subscribe myself

Your humble admirer,
Mizpah.

*Union League pamphlet No. 62, November 1863.

Polygamy may be defined as the union for life of a man with two or more women. And this kind of union appears to have existed as an established institution in all the ages of our world, by the universal evidence of all history, whether sacred or profane.

This understood, I shall not oppose the prevalent idea that polygamy is an evil in itself. A *physical* evil it may be; but this does not satisfy the judgment of its more zealous adversaries, since they contend that it is a *moral* evil—a positive *sin* in a man to be married simultaneously to more than one woman.

Here, therefore, lies the true aspect of the controversy. And it is evident that it can only be settled by the Bible. For every Christian is bound to assent to the rule of the inspired Apostle, that "sin is the transgression of the law," namely, the law laid down in the Scriptures by the authority of God—the supreme "Lawgiver who is able to save and to destroy." From his Word there can be no appeal. No rebellion can be so atrocious in His sight as that which dares to rise against His government. No blasphemy can be more unpardonable than that which imputes sin or moral evil to the decrees of the eternal Judge, who is alone perfect in wisdom, in knowledge, and in love.

If it were a matter to be determined by my personal sympathies, I should be as ready as any man to condemn the institution of polygamy, for all my prejudices of education, habit, and social position stand opposed to it. But, as a Christian, I am solemnly warned not to be "wise in my own conceit," and not "to lean to my own understanding." As a Christian, I am compelled to submit my weak and erring intellect to the authority of the Almighty. For then only can I be safe in my conclusions, when I know that they are in accordance with the will of Him, before whose tribunal I must render a strict account at the last great day.

I proceed, accordingly, to the evidence of the sacred Scriptures, which, long ago, produced complete conviction in my own mind, and must, as I regard it, be equally conclusive to every candid and sincere inquirer.

The first appearance of polygamy in the Bible is in the case of Lamech, fifth in descent from Cain, whose two wives, Adah and Zillah (Genesis iv:19-23) are mentioned by the inspired writer without any expression of reprobation, or any allusion to the transaction being unusual or irregular. Introduced thus early, it may be regarded as among the primal principles of human society, though our knowledge of antediluvian times is too scanty to enable us rightly to determine its extension and prevalence. It is probable, however, that the great duration of existence might well render men cautious how they bound themselves for life to more than one partner whom incompatibility of temper might render distasteful after a few centuries.

For several generations after the Deluge, population was not sufficiently dense to render polygamy frequent. Accordingly the first who revived the time-honored custom appears to have been Esau, as might have been expected from his vigorous nature and ardent character. He seems to have contented himself with three wives, Judith, Bashemath, and Mahalath. (Genesis xxvi:34; xxviii:9; xxxvi:2, 3.)

If the descendants of Cain and Esau, however, be regarded as somewhat questionable sponsors for the custom, all doubt as to its righteousness is removed by the example of the patriarch Jacob, the blessed of Heaven. His union with Leah and Rachel is well known, as well as the amiable zeal with which his wives supplied him with supplementary consorts in the persons of their handmaidens, Bilhah and Zilpah (Genesis xxix, xxx); while the blessings subsequently promised to him and to his posterity show that his plurality of wives was sanctioned in the highest and most direct manner.

Polygamy being thus divinely approved, it became a recognized part of the domestic economy of the chosen people, as we learn from the direct rule established by the wisdom of God for Israel, on the very point in question.

If a man have two wives, one beloved, and another hated, and they have borne him children, both the beloved and the hated; and if the first-born son be hers that was hated;

Then shall it be when he maketh his sons to inherit that which he hath, that he shall not make the son of the beloved first-born before the son of the hated, which is indeed the first-born (Deut. xxi:15-17).

With this law before his eyes, what Christian can believe that the Almighty attached immorality or sin to the condition of polygamy, especially when one may look in vain through the Mosaic regulations of marriage (Leviticus xviii) for any limitations on the number of wives?

The blessings vouchsafed to those who took to themselves numerous consorts, and the lofty positions to which they arose show that in the eyes of God and man they were pure from sin and worthy of all honor.

It is recorded of two judges of Israel, Ibzan and Abdon, that the one had thirty sons and thirty daughters, while the other had forty sons, showing conclusively that their gynecea were abundantly peopled (Judg. xii:9, 13). That the Prophet Samuel—the asked of God—sprang from a father, Elkanah the Levite, who had two wives (I Sam. i), is sufficient reproof to those who impiously use the word bigamist as a term of contumely and reproach.

David, the man after God's own heart, before he was thirty-seven years of age, had taken to wife Michal, Ahinoam, Abigail, Maacah, Haggith,

Abital, and Eglah (II Sam. iii); while he was living with them all,
God prospered him and made him king over Israel and Judah, and
the prophet Nathan announced to him the favor of the Lord, to him
and to his generation. Even his indiscretion in adding Bathsheba to the
list was readily pardoned, and the union was blessed in the birth of
Solomon.

Solomon, wisest of men, "had seven hundred wives, princesses, and
three hundred concubines" (I Kings xi:3). In this, he sacrificed himself
to the vindication of the great principle of polygamy, for the tempter
easily found admittance among such a multitude, and seduced him to
follow strange gods—a warning to us all to be moderate, even in what
is right.

Such, then, is the institution of polygamy, laid down by the Lord God
of Israel for his chosen people, and continued for fifteen centuries, until
the new dispensation of the Gospel. What change did this produce?
I grant, of course, that we, as Christians, are bound by the precept and
example of the Saviour and his apostles. Let us now, therefore, proceed
to the all-important inquiry, whether we are authorized by these to
presume that the Mosaic system was done away.

First, then, we ask what the divine Redeemer said in reference to
polygamy. And the answer is perfectly undeniable: HE DID NOT ALLUDE
TO IT AT ALL. Not one word upon the subject is recorded by any of the
four Evangelists who gave His life and doctrines to the world, even
when He repealed the Mosaic law of divorce (Matt. xix, Mark x).
Yet polygamy was in full existence at the time throughout Judea, and
among the scattered Jews for centuries later, as we learn from Justin
Martyr (*Dial. cum Tryphone adv. Judæos*) and Theophylact (*Comment.
in I Epist. ad Timoth.*). Even as late as 393, Theodosius the Great, in
his ignorant zeal, endeavored to put an end to it, by a law which was
continued in force by Justinian in the sixth century (*Const. 7, Cod.,
Lib. I, Tit. ix*). How prosperous would be the present and how glori-
ous the future of Utah, if the eloquent and pertinacious declaimers
against polygamy had been willing to follow their Saviour's example!

But did not our Lord substantially repeal the old law by the mere fact
that he established a new dispensation? Certainly not, unless they were
incompatible. And, that he did not consider them incompatible is
clearly proved by his own express declaration. "Think not," saith he,
"that I am come to destroy the law or the prophets. I am not come to
destroy, but to fulfil" (Matt. v, 17). On that point, therefore, this single
passage is perfectly conclusive.

But the precepts and the conduct of St. Paul himself, the great Apostle
of the Gentiles, are all sufficient, because he meets the very point, and

settles the whole question. Not only do his admonitions concerning marriage (I Cor. vii) contain no prohibition of polygamy, but in his directions concerning the choice of bishops, priests, and deacons (I Tim. iii:2-12; Titus, i:6), he specially requires them to be men of one wife, thus tacitly, but fully, allowing a plurality of consorts to the laity of the faithful.

The evidence of the New Testament is thus complete, plainly proving that the institution of polygamy was not abolished by the Gospel. Compare now the course of the ultra reformer with that of Christ and his inspired apostle. The divine Redeemer openly rebukes the sanctimonious Pharisees. He spares not the infidel Sadducees. He denounces the hypocritical Scribes. He calls the royal Herod "that fox." He censures severely the Jewish practice of divorcing their wives for the slightest cause. He makes a scourge of small cords, and drives the buyers and sellers out of the Temple. Yet he lived in the midst of polygamy, maintained in accordance with the Mosaic law, and uttered not one word against it! What proof can be stronger than this, that he did not regard it as a sin or a moral evil? And what contrast can be more manifest than this example of Christ on the one hand, and the loud and bitter denunciations of our anti-polygamy preachers and politicians, *calling themselves Christians*, on the other? For they not only set themselves against the Word of God in this matter, but—strange to say—they do it in the very name of that Saviour whose whole line of conduct was the very opposite of their own!

Yet I do not mean to charge the numerous and respectable friends of this popular delusion with a wilful or conscious opposition to the truth. They are seduced, doubtless, in the great majority of cases, by the feelings of a false philanthropy, which palliates if it does not excuse, their dangerous error. Living far away from Utah, with no practical experience of the institution, and accustomed from childhood to attach an inordinate value to the individuality of the domestic relation, they are naturally disposed to compassionate the Utah wives, and to believe that they must be supremely wretched in their subdivision of a husband's affection. They are under no special inducement to "search the Scriptures" on this particular subject, nor are they in general, I am sorry to say, accustomed to study the Bible half as much as they read the newspaper, the novel, and the magazine.

Thus the mistaken bigotry of the community, acting through the time-serving pliancy of politicians, has disfigured our statute-books with laws which place a ban upon this patriarchal institution. Noble Christian souls in our midst, yearning to revert to the hallowed rites of old, are obliged to practise them covertly, and under the opprobrious name of bigamists are tracked and persecuted as felons, martyred like the primitive Christians under Decius and Diocletian. When some, bolder than the rest, founded on the banks of the Mississippi a community, which they fondly hoped by its happiness and purity might convert a stiff-necked generation, they were driven from their homes by uncontrolled fanaticism. When, after sufferings unspeakable, these martyrs of Scriptural faith at length found a refuge in the far distant desert, and their prosperity testified to their righteousness, still the persecutor was upon their heels, and the whole nation, as Mr. Floyd's acceptances will testify, poured forth its money like water for the pitiful pleasure of reforming their domestic observances.

Shall we boast that we are wiser, purer, better than the men who walked with God? Is it not time that we should confess our worldly wisdom to be ignorance, and lean with simple faith on the law that is written? Let the infidel and abolitionist prate of purity and domesticity; but let us imitate the noble example of our Southern brethren, who are ready to sacrifice all that the world holds dear in defence of patriarchal institutions. Returning to the principles ordained and sanctioned in the Book of Books, we may hope to see arise amongst us new Jacobs and Samuels, Davids and Solomons.

MUNICIPAL GOVERNMENT*

[A Municipal Commission was appointed by the governor of Pennsylvania in 1876 to consider a uniform code of city government for the state. During its deliberations Mr. Lea addressed an open letter to the Commission, analyzing the evils of the existing form of government in Philadelphia and suggesting certain fundamental changes to overcome these evils. The letter shows his interest in political reform and his grasp of local affairs, while some of his suggestions are an interesting anticipation of the city manager system of municipal government, a system not adopted by any American city before 1908.—H.]

* * * * *

ALL THOUGHTFUL CITIZENS of the Commonwealth who view with anxiety the practical failure of our institutions as applied to the government of large cities, must regard as an important step in advance the appointment of your commission, charged with the duty of investigating existing evils in our municipalities, and of suggesting such legislation as may seem fitted, in the language of the Governor's recent message, "to make impossible the extravagance and mismanagement that have characterized the last decade."

Unless some such change can be effected, it is evident that universal suffrage and popular government must be pronounced incompatible with municipal prosperity and good order. The conditions which suffice for agricultural regions, where public interests are simple, where the citizen has leisure to give them the attention requisite to comprehend them, and where the character of every candidate for local office is familiar to every voter, obviously will not apply to dense communities where the fevered struggle for existence absorbs almost every man in his private affairs, where the structure and administration of government are so complicated as to require special study and training for their bare comprehension, and where, with rare exceptions, the personal reputation of candidates can only be known in the limited circles of their own acquaintances. It is obvious, therefore, that the system which works well in the country is inapplicable to the city, where it is a moral and physical impossibility for the voter to acquire the knowledge requisite to the intelligent exercise of suffrage in the choice of the multitude of officials who have been made directly elective by the people. This has given rise to a class of professionals who make municipal politics the business of their lives, who understand the mysteries of party organization and management, and the intricate details of municipal administration. Such a profession rarely has attraction for the honest; its legitimate gains are

* Privately printed, Philadelphia, 1877.

moderate at the best, and are at all times uncertain. For the reckless and unprincipled, however, it has the fascination of the lottery and the gambling table, for its illicit prizes are splendid, and are won without steady and continuous labor. The professionals therefore, as a class, are men of easy conscience, who regard the public as their legitimate prey, while their special training gives them in election contests the advantage of veteran troops over unorganized and undisciplined militia.

As though to render absolute the control of these professionals in Philadelphia, our municipal government has become so complex and unwieldy that responsibility for malfeasance has been virtually lost. Some important officers, such as the mayor, the tax receiver, the treasurer, the controller, the city solicitor, members of councils, and school directors are elected by the people; others, of equal importance, such as the heads of the Gas, Water, Highway, and Survey departments, and the board of Health, are appointed by Councils; others, such as the board of Education, the board of City Trusts, the board of Revision of Taxes, and the Park Commission are appointed by the courts, and others again, as in the building Commission, are self-appointed. As chief executive, the mayor is really only a chief of police, but he shares in the legislative functions of councils by reason of a qualified veto power. The Select and Common councils are the municipal legislature. They levy taxes, borrow money, make all appropriations (except where commissions or boards of trust have been rendered independent of them), and generally are entrusted with the duty of supervising and regulating the infinite details of municipal administration; but their power is seriously crippled by their inability to summon witnesses and examine under oath, so that they are frequently unable to investigate corruption for which they are themselves directly or indirectly responsible. It is to a government so chaotic that are entrusted the peace, the health, the comfort, the education, and the prosperity of eight hundred thousand human beings living under the fierce competition of the nineteenth century. To show how completely, under such a system, all real responsibility is frittered away, even in the simplest necessities of municipal existence, it will be sufficient to allude to the fact that a few years since, when filthy and neglected streets were the subject of general complaint, those whose duty it was to repair them excused themselves on the ground that the accumulated dirt in the highways rendered repairs impossible, while those who should clean them retorted that cleaning was impracticable, owing to their lack of repair. It is the same in almost every detail. When money is wasted or stolen in paving, or culverts, or reservoirs, or bridges, or schoolhouses, and double prices are paid for imperfect work, responsibility is bandied about between councils and the various executive departments until the fault cannot be definitely traced to any one. The distinction between capacity and incapacity, honesty and roguery, is thus lost, and the administration of the second city in the Western hemisphere becomes a thieves' carnival, in which stealing is reduced to a science, a premium is set on corruption, and the helpless taxpayer feels his pockets emptied by invisible fingers.

These evils are the natural outgrowth of our system, and their continuance can be prevented only by a radical change in that system. Occasionally, when their magnitude reaches a point which threatens immediate bankruptcy, public attention may be excited sufficiently to produce a momentary check; but the professionals know that the excitement will be but temporary, that they can wait until the storm blows over, and can then resume their occupations with the same sense of security as before. It is useless to expect the inhabitants of a great city to zealously perform what are called their "political duties," when those duties require special training, close daily attention, an accurate knowledge of the details of municipal business, and an acquaintance with the character of every aspirant for nomination to candidacy. If taxpayers desire a reasonably efficient and economical government, they must surrender a part of their apparent privileges. They must have fewer candidates to vote for, so that they can more readily ascertain the character of those for whom they vote. Responsibility must be concentrated, so that when wrong is done the wrongdoer can be held accountable. Power must accompany responsibility, and when the latter is no longer divided the former must be similarly concentrated. Thus we reach the necessity of a chief magistrate, no longer merely the nominal head of the city, but clothed with real power to appoint and dismiss the heads of departments, responsible to the people for the honesty and capacity of his subordinates, and held to that responsibility by a moderate term of office, eligibility to re-election, and liability to impeachment by councils, while his veto power should be retained as a safeguard against hasty and improvident legislation. His position would thus be assimilated to that of the President of the United States, while our present system is as though the Cabinet were partly elected by the people and partly selected by Congress in joint convention of the two Houses, a comparison which sufficiently illustrates its absurd and clumsy inefficiency.

The anomalous mingling of legislative and executive functions now exercised by councils should cease. No matter how elaborate may be their machinery of committees, or how enduring may be the zeal of members, a cumbrous representative body must always be a conspicuous failure when it attempts to control executive details, and the history of our local legislature since Consolidation is no exception to this rule.

The ambition of public spirited citizens would find ample opportunity of development in purely legislative business, regulating taxation and appropriations, and framing such ordinances as may wisely provide for the peace, the health, the prosperity, and the development of the city; while the removal of the grosser temptations now incident to their executive duties would tend to purify the atmosphere of the chambers, and render membership attractive to those whose services would be most valuable to the community. By conferring upon councils authority to send for persons and papers, to administer oaths, and to invoke the power of the courts to commit for contempt, they would be enabled to check malfeasance in the executive departments, and the dignity of the chambers would be enhanced.

As an additional means of holding the executive departments to responsibility for the proper discharge of their duties, it might be well to empower taxpayers to examine into their affairs. Such a power ought to be surrounded with strict limitations to prevent its frivolous exercise, and these limitations your commission could readily devise. The affidavits, for instance, of five or ten citizens might be required, setting forth their belief in the existence of specified irregularities, and on the presentation of these affidavits to the courts, the bench might have discretion to order the investigation prayed for, selecting for the purpose three of the affiants, and requiring security from them to defray the necessary expenses of the proceedings in case the allegations proved to be frivolous and vexatious.

A system such as the above would render necessary the adoption of the civil service reform to which both political parties now stand pledged in national affairs, for a chief magistrate clothed with power such as I have suggested ought not to be able to perpetuate his rule by filling all public offices with political janizaries who would be devoted to his personal interests. It is computed to-day, by those who ought to know, that in Philadelphia fifteen thousand voters are dependent, directly or indirectly, on public employment, and can thus be relied upon to vote and work for the administration that is in power. No improvement that you can devise will be permanent that leaves untouched this vast and fruitful source of political corruption. By giving to all subordinates tenure of office during good behavior, and rendering them removable only for cause, placing both appointments and removals in the hands of independent boards, and prohibiting political assessments, you would do more than could be accomplished by any other single measure to render possible an efficient and economical administration of the city. Elections would be no longer a wild strife for office, in which thousands of incumbents are defending their daily bread against the assault of tens of thousands of hungry applicants. Public business would become an assured career in which men of industry and experience could engage with the knowledge that an honest discharge of duty would secure a provision for life. Relieved from political labors, the number of employees could be reduced by fully a third, and the prohibition of political assessments would enable their salaries to be cut down to the point at which similar labor is paid by private employers. The most degrading element and the most corrupting influence in our existing political system would be removed, and the business of the city would stand a chance of being carried on like that of a bank or of a mercantile house.

This reform would, of course, include the police department. It would be under the control of a chief appointed and removable by the mayor, but the men would hold office during good behavior. The force would speedily become non-partisan, its indifferent members would be weeded out, and in a few years we should have a body of trained and efficient policemen, who would no longer derive their chief importance from their real or assumed control over primaries and general elections.

The subject of the debts of municipalities is a vital one, which must necessarily engage the earnest attention of your commission. Everywhere throughout the country the alarming increase in the indebtedness of cities is becoming one of the worst symptoms of the time, revealing a weakness in our institutions which must lead, unless speedily checked, to the most deplorable consequences. The rapid growth and unwieldy aggregate of this local indebtedness are doubtless familiar to you, and show that it is not a trouble peculiar to us, or to the other cities of our Commonwealth. With regard to Philadelphia it is sufficient to advert to the fact that our debt to-day is nearly double that which within forty years was so serious a burden upon the whole State of Pennsylvania as to lead to default in the payment of interest, and that it is nearly as large as the debt of the United States before the war. The major part of this crushing weight is the work of the last fifteen years. The present constitution has imposed some check upon its nominal growth by diminishing the facility with which funded indebtedness was formerly created; but the principal result of this has been, not to check extravagance, but to swell the proportions of our floating debt until this latter has become too great to be longer carried. Possibly your wisdom may devise some means by which the restrictions of the constitution may be made more operative than they have hitherto been; and, if so, you will render us an essential service. The most effectual relief, however, is to be sought in diminishing the tendency to reckless and wasteful expenditure.

The changes suggested above would all conduce towards this result, but another one can be named that would be still more effectual. It would, moreover, be simply just; and though at first sight it may be called unrepublican, it would in reality be merely a logical application of the fundamental theories of our form of government. Our fathers held that taxation and representation should be correlative. In theory we have held to this, but in practice we have allowed representation to escape the limitation of taxation. The payment of taxes is nominally a condition precedent to the exercise of the elective franchise, but this has been reduced to an infinitesimal capitation tax, and, at least in Philadelphia, a very large portion of the voters do not personally pay it. The political organization which is out of power regularly purchases tax receipts, and furnishes them to its voters; while the party which has control of the tax office is universally believed to distribute them gratuitously, and the amount which reaches the public treasury from this source is insignificant. Thus, while recognizing the principle, we have virtually abandoned it in practice.

I would suggest to you the propriety of reviving this principle, and giving it an application that would render it a valuable safeguard against municipal extravagance. The present form of our local legislature in two chambers is fashioned after the state and national governments, and these, again, after the British Parliament. In England, and at Washington, this dual legislature has a real significance, the two houses having different origins and constituencies. In Philadelphia it is a delusion, the constituencies being the same, and the only use of a second chamber is to place some check upon improvident legislation by increasing its complexity, an advantage fully neutralized by the attendant diminution of responsibility. It is worthy of consideration whether the interest of the whole community would not be subserved by giving to the second chamber a different constituency, rendering it a representation not of population but of taxation, and restricting its functions to questions connected with taxation and expenditure originating in the other chamber. Such a plan would of course be open to numerous modifications of detail. The number of members of such a chamber might be limited to fifteen or twenty, to be elected on a general ticket, the qualification for eligibility being the payment of municipal taxes amounting to not less than five hundred dollars per annum. The electors might be citizens paying municipal taxes of not less than twenty-five dollars per annum, to be registered as such on the exhibition of their receipted bills.

In this there would be no infringement on the principle of manhood suffrage, for the chamber so constituted would be restricted to the consideration of financial questions, and would be merely an administrator of the moneys levied upon its constituents. At the same time the salutary influence of such a body upon the prosperity of the whole community must be self-evident.

The anomalous position of the Gas Trust of Philadelphia will undoubtedly attract your attention. As a compact and easily wielded center of political power its influence on our municipal affairs has been most unfortunate. The trustees, nominally appointed by councils, in reality have their subordinates and tools elected to councils, and in alliance with other departments maintain an irresponsible close corporation which defies all attempts to penetrate into its mysteries and management. If, by appropriate legislation, provision could be made for the due security of the holders of gas loans, and if the works could then be put up for sale to the highest bidder under restrictions that would protect the consumer, not only would considerable financial relief be afforded the city, but one of the most dangerous elements would be removed from our politics. The secret disbursement of over four million of dollars of public money per annum, virtually without accountability to any one, creates an *imperium in imperio* to which a parallel may vainly be sought elsewhere.

I have thus ventured briefly to make suggestions as to a few of the points which will naturally present themselves for your consideration. The evils which these suggestions are intended to remove are real and pressing, and threaten, unless checked, not only to destroy the prosperity of the great centers of population in our Commonwealth, but to shake confidence everywhere in the capacity of man for self-government. I have not sought to weary you with details illustrating our present condition, for the financial crisis which is impending over Philadelphia is notorious, and sufficiently proves the necessity of immediate and decided change if the gravest misfortunes are to be averted. To your commission our people are looking with the hope that its earnest and dispassionate labors may lead to such reforms as are necessary for our preservation.

INTERNATIONAL COPYRIGHT*

[The first international copyright law of the United States was enacted by Congress in 1891 after ten years of debate and discussion due to the conflicting interests of authors, publishers, and the reading public. Several unsatisfactory bills were introduced in congress, but the one finally passed (the Chace bill) reconciled most of the interests involved and was mainly written by Mr. Lea, who had taken a leading part in all discussions of the subject and on whose judgment Senator Chace fully relied. Among the many pamphlets and letters written by Lea in his effort to secure a satisfactory copyright law, this has been selected to illustrate his grasp of the subject and his recognition of the various aspects of the problem.—H.]

*   *   *   *   *

Sir: I respond with much pleasure to the invitation of the Committee on Patents, as communicated by Senator Mitchell, to lay before them, in print, my views on the bill creating International Copyright recently introduced by Senator Hawley. For forty years I was a book publisher, largely interested in valuable copyrights, and I have, moreover, always been a lover and collector as well as a writer of books. I think, therefore, that I can approach the subject, which is by no means a simple one, from every side and can give it, perhaps, a more impartial consideration than those whose interests or habits of thought confine them to but one aspect of the question.

I trust that by this time everyone will admit that the existing state of American law inflicts injustice on literary men on both sides of the Atlantic. The foreign author is deprived of his just dues when his works are reproduced in this country without his permission and without payment, and though it is the custom of all reputable American houses to compensate the writers whose works they reprint, still the absence of all legal rights necessarily limits such payments. The American author is subjected to an unfair and unnatural competition with the unprotected labor of the foreigner. His markets are limited by the excessive sales of works written abroad and made here at the lowest possible cost, and the prices at which his books can be sold, and his consequent remuneration, are reduced below what they would be in the absence of such competition.

If this were the only point to be considered; if abstract justice required the recognition of the rights of authorship as indefeasible and unlimited, then nothing could be said in opposition to Senator Hawley's

* Open letter to the Hon. O. H. Platt, Chairman of Senate Committee on Patents. Privately printed, Philadelphia, 1883.

bill, except, perhaps, that it does not go far enough and render copyright perpetual and universal, without requiring reciprocity.

In accepting limitation of duration, and in conditioning international copyright on reciprocal action by foreign nations, Senator Hawley's bill admits that the legislation by Congress is not to be governed by admitting an author's absolute ownership and exclusive control of his productions when he lays them before the public as a seller of words and calls upon the public to protect them against infringement. This admission, in fact, is a matter of course in all legislation. Society recognizes no absolute and unlimited ownership in any species of property. All that the individual makes, earns, or inherits is held under such limitations as society sees fit to impose in return for the protection which is afforded by the social compact and the value which is imparted to ownership by the aggregation of individuals in communities.

This limitation of ownership is especially applicable to so purely an artificial creation as copyright. I have alluded to the author in his commercial capacity as a seller of words, and such, under the legal construction of copyright, he simply is. There is no copyright in ideas, but only in the form in which they are clothed. The man of science, the philosopher, the historian, the investigator in any branch of human knowledge, may spend a lifetime in discovering principles which may profoundly affect the moral and material well-being of the race, or in discovering facts of the highest interest to the progress of mankind, and as soon as he divulges them to the world they become the common property of his fellow men. Any author may at once seize upon them and embody them in his essay or his textbook, without even an acknowledgment to the laborious originator or discoverer, and can then claim a copyright upon the dress in which he has clothed his borrowed ideas. The wisdom of society has decided that it is conducive to the progress and welfare of mankind that in books the verbal expression alone shall be the subject of monopoly and ownership, while the ideas shall be free to all, rewarding the inventor and discoverer, the thinker and investigator, with only the barren tribute of fame or the consciousness of service rendered to his fellow creatures; while it stimulates the compiler and the literary man with a certain limited monopoly in selling the form in which he may clothe ideas, whether original or borrowed. In the cognate subject of patents, the wisdom of society has arrived at a conclusion almost directly opposite. There the monopoly has been bestowed on the idea, as an incentive to inventiveness, and the material form in which that idea is clothed is regarded as indifferent. If a patentee makes a machine in one style, it cannot be reproduced in another, or even improved if the patented principle is retained. The subject of the patent is the idea; the subject of the copyright is the form.

Thus, by common consent, literary property, the creation of law, is peculiarly subject to the limitations which society may see fit to define for its own protection or advantage, when asked to grant and enforce a .monopoly. No natural exclusive rights ever have been or can be recognized, and it becomes simply a matter of expediency what conditions shall be imposed when the benefit of monopoly, heretofore restricted to our own citizens, is proposed to be extended to foreigners. Senator Hawley's bill accepts the conditions existing as to our own citizens, and merely adds the condition of reciprocity. In this he has consulted solely the interests of authors as he understands them, but the Congress of the United States, before it enacts the bill, must consider whether other interests are not involved, and must see whether in legislating for a particular class it is not inflicting unreasonable damage on other classes, and on the community at large.

To weigh these considerations properly, it must be borne in mind that the millions of readers in the United States have been accustomed for generations to procure books at the minimum cost.[1] Any form of copyright which shall convert into a monopoly the existing free competition in the reproduction of new foreign works will greatly raise the price of current literature. It will not be the mere addition of the sums paid to authors, but it will be the highest price which the business sagacity of the holders of the copyrights shall consider likely to bring in the largest profits. This is an axiom so self-evident that it need only be alluded to. Rightly or wrongly, the people who buy books will deem this a hardship, and any form of international copyright will excite widespread discontent. It is not the part of statesmanship to shut the eyes to this, but rather to legislate so as to minimize such discontent. It would be wise for the friends of authorship, also, to recognize this, for such popular discontent, if goaded too far, will inevitably result in an angry reaction which will undo the present work, will destroy all chances of international copyright for a generation to come, and may perchance question, more closely than will be agreeable, the grounds on which all copyrights

[1] It is not worth while to allude in more than a general way to novels, which are still published in England in three volumes at a guinea and a half, equivalent to $7.87, and are supplied to the public here at from 15 to 20 cents. Many books of more sterling value are issued in the same way. Thus the recent *Life of Lord Lytton* (Bulwer) costs in England, 32 shillings, or $8.00, while here it is 40 cents. Jeffreason's *The Real Lord Byron*, is 30 shillings ($7.50) in England, in America, 20 cents; Anthony Trollope's *Autobiography*, in England 21 shillings ($5.25), in America 20 cents. No one can say that this is a proper or healthy condition of affairs, but it has its advantages in the dissemination of culture and intelligence, and the reading public which has become accustomed to it will unquestionably revolt against too sudden and too severe a change.

are based. In connection with this, moreover, you cannot wholly disregard the important consideration of the spread of intelligence and diffusion of knowledge which is stimulated by cheap literature. The Government recognizes this when it carries in the mails books and periodicals at far lower rates than other merchandise, and authors who are directly, though incidentally, benefited by this, cannot object to the weight which must justly be assigned to this aspect of the matter by those who are legislating for the whole community.

There is another class of the population whose claims to be recognized in this legislation cannot be ignored. The book business in this country gives support to many thousands of industrious people of both sexes. There are few products in which labor forms so overwhelmingly large a percentage of the value as in books. The raw material of the most finished volume is a few rags or a billet of wood, a little lampblack and oil, and a handful of cotton fibre. The rest is labor, partly unskilled, but mostly skilled and requiring long apprenticeship. In every paper mill, printing office, and bindery in the United States the effect of this legislation will be felt. If it is so framed as to lead our markets to draw their supplies from abroad, diminished work must throw numbers out of employment, while those who are retained must be content with lower wages. In considering the expediency of the conditions to be imposed on foreign authors admitted to the benefits of American copyright, this is a consideration which legislators cannot overlook. Its neglect would, indeed, be suicidal, as there would be an additional and most powerful element of discontent created for the speedy overthrow of improvident and one-sided legislation. I am sure that what every one wants is that this question shall be settled with such wise and equitable adjustment of all contending claims that each shall be measurably satisfied, and that the present decision shall be a finality.

I have ventured thus to indicate the points which should be borne in mind in any legislation which grants international copyright. On turning to Senator Hawley's bill, it will be found that no consideration whatever is given to them. Under its operation the foreign author or his publisher will be entitled to an American copyright on the simple formality of registering the title before publication in this country, and paying the fee of fifty cents. Virtually all English books, at least, will thus be copyrighted and a monopoly of our market be secured. Few authors will make arrangements with American houses, but will naturally entrust their interests to their home publishers. Every English house will have its representative in New York, the larger ones their own agents, the smaller ones combining to support agencies. Printing and binding being much cheaper in England than in this country, and the facilities of invoicing between principal and agent being well understood, our supplies of current English literature will be made almost wholly abroad. The prices to consumers here will be on a level with the high rates customary in England, our own operatives and mechanics will be deprived of work, while our millions of readers will be debarred from their accustomed literature or be forced to depend upon the system of circulating libraries, endurable in the British Islands but totally unfitted for our wide-spread and sparsely populated continent. The blame of high prices will at first be laid upon the tariff, and the duty on books will be swept away. This will result in a large portion of our manufacture of domestic books being transferred to England, whence they can be freighted across the ocean at a trivial cost; and whatever relief this may afford to the book buyer will be offset by the additional distress inflicted on the producing classes. Can any sane man believe that such legislation would be permanent, that the indignant protests which would arise all over the land from both consumer and producer would not speedily enforce a reaction, in which the last state of our authors would be worse than the first? As an old bookseller, I assure you that such legislation to cure existing evils is mere midsummer madness.

It has been hinted that the gentlemen interested in Senator Hawley's bill designed it to present merely the author's side of the question, and that, to avert opposition, they would be willing to accept the insertion of what is known as the "manufacturing clause," under which the validity of an American copyright of a foreign book would be dependent upon its manufacture in this country. This "concession," however, would be almost impossible of legal definition, and would give rise to an infinity of lawsuits. If a piece of English muslin were used in the binding, would the copyright be forfeited thereby? This is but a sample of numerous similar questions which would arise, and which would have to be settled by the courts. Moreover, unless accompanied by an absolute prohibition of importation of copyrighted books, it could be easily evaded in the case of all works of extensive sale. The English publisher, through his American agent, could print a small edition, and thus secure the copyright, after which he would issue to himself a license to import and supply our markets from abroad.

The reciprocity clause in Senator Hawley's bill, limiting its effect to the authors of those countries which shall confer on American authors rights equal to those enjoyed by their own citizens is both objectionable and superfluous. Objectionable, because it introduces an unnecessary complication in a matter already sufficiently complex and renders our legislation, which should be independent, dependent on the action of foreign countries. Superfluous, because the only foreign market of importance is the English one, and American authors already enjoy there the same rights as British subjects. The only condition is first publication in Great Britain, which is perhaps sometimes onerous, and which would not be removed by the clause as it stands. The complaints which our authors naturally make that their works are reprinted in England without compensation, would not be remedied by this bill or by any other. The only cure for this evil is to be found in the growing recognition of American literature in England. Authors whose names are well known already find no difficulty in making arrangements with English houses and enjoying the proper compensation for their popularity. Authors not so widely known would not find themselves benefited in this respect by the bill. If a "pirated" English edition of a work proves a success, the author may be sure that his next book will be accepted on remunerative terms. Other than this there is no cure, and legislation is unavailing, for the trouble is inherent in the very nature of the business. I may add that there would seem to be no reason why through an English copyright an American author may not be entitled to copyright in all the countries with which Great Britain has copyright treaties, thus rendering it coextensive with the civilized world. Possibly hereafter the growth of the English colonies may require special legislation, but at present they offer no question of practical importance.

There are other points which might be discussed, but these I think sufficiently prove the improvident character of Senator Hawley's bill, and I will not weary you with further comment upon it. I take this opportunity, however, of calling your attention to another bill designed to accomplish the same objects, introduced by Senator Chace, which I think attains the desired result with much less injury to American interests. It secures the rights of authors as fully as Senator Hawley's bill, and will be as beneficial, both to those of the United States and of foreign countries. It insures the manufacture, by our own people, of all copyrighted books for our markets. Thus the interests of author, producer, and consumer will be guarded; the books made here will be in a style and at a price suited to our own wants, and though they will necessarily be higher than in the present state of free competition, they will be far cheaper than those customarily made for the English public.

The prohibition of importation provided for in the bill is an absolute necessity. It is an invariable rule in all countries where copyright exists, and the provisions of the bill designed to make it effective would long ago have been an essential feature in our copyright legislation had it not been that hitherto the introduction into this country of foreign editions of American books have been too infrequent to lead to any adequate regulations for their prevention. So unused are we to such infractions of the law that when, some years since, copies of a Canadian edition of Stanley's *Through the Dark Continent* were sent into the United States, I am informed that Messrs. Harper & Brothers, on asking the Treasury Department to issue orders for their seizure, were told that it was not the business of the customhouses to prevent the entry of such books, and they were reduced to the inefficient and costly process of tracing them up on the shelves of dealers. Subsequently Messrs. Houghton Mifflin & Co., of Boston, after a long struggle, prevailed upon the department to issue a general order to enforce the law; but, in the absence of any arrangement for keeping the customs officers advised of what books are copyrighted, it is virtually ineffective. The extensive use of the mails for the international transmission of books renders necessary the extension of the system to the post office. The provisions of the bill are founded on the existing English law, and it is believed that the precautions taken to render it self-supporting will be effectual, so that no outlay will be imposed on the Government.

The prohibition of importation will naturally be objected to by a few gentlemen who collect handsome libraries, and who will deem it a hardship that they are debarred from procuring the expensive original editions. I have myself collected a library of some magnitude, and can sympathize with the dilettantism that delights in large type and wide margins, but I cannot conceive that the tastes of a class so comparatively small should be allowed to weigh against the vital interests affecting the vast multitudes of consumers and producers.

You will probably be told that no harm could arise if, to meet the wishes of collectors and amateurs, importation should be permitted on license issued by the author or proprietor of the copyright. Yet this apparently harmless concession would overthrow the whole design and purport of this bill. The American agent of the English publisher would take out the American copyright, and receive from his principal, or issue to himself or a subordinate, a license to import. The whole business would thus be in the hands of the foreign houses; the books would not be made here, and our market would be as absolutely dependent upon foreign supplies as under Senator Hawley's bill. As respects translations from foreign languages, the wants of scholars are provided for by relaxing the prohibition and allowing the importation of the original works.

You will observe that a limit of fifteen days after publication abroad is provided within which the copyright is to be entered here. There would in reality be no hardship in requiring the entry to be made here prior to publication in the country of the author, for, in almost all cases, arrangements are made in advance, and with the adoption of international copyright such will become the universal rule. The foreign author will arrange simultaneously with his home publisher and with the American. On the other hand, prolongation of the time would lead to the practice of supplying our market from abroad during the interval in which the book would be shielded by an expected copyright. In the case of many books no American copyright would then be taken out, and no American edition would be published, as the market would be spoiled, to the manifest disadvantage of the foreign author and of American consumers and producers. To guard further against such practices, the American copyright is made dependent upon the deposit of a copy of an American edition within three months of the date of entering the copyright. This, I may add, will throw no obstacles in the way of bona fide transactions between foreign authors and American publishers.

The clause which renders void a copyright of which the publication is abandoned by the American manufacturer is designed to obviate cases in which a book might not be kept in the market, and which otherwise could not be obtained from abroad. This would be an unjustifiable hardship on the student; if the American publisher abandons the publication, there should be no hindrance to importation.

The bill of Senator Chace has received the support of those whose employment is dependent upon the book manufacture of the United States, for they recognize that under its provisions their labor will be suitably guarded. I am confident that when it is carefully examined by those who represent the literary interests of the country it will be regarded with equal favor, for it will work as effectually as Senator Hawley's in protecting them from the unjust competition of which they reasonably complain. It is perfectly fair to the foreign author, as it places him in this country on an equal footing with his American brethren. In fact, I have not been willing to admit that there is any real antagonism between the different classes. There is solidarity of interests between them all. No one of them can be injured without the others suffering; no one can be benefited without the others sharing in the benefit. It is a short-sighted and limited view of their relations which regards them as hostile, and I am confident that if Senator Chace's bill shall be enacted, as soon as its working is understood all those who are directly interested will unite in regarding it as a satisfactory solution of the problem which has been so variously debated for the past fifty years.

THE POLICY OF INSURANCE*

THE FACT that insurance has been the gradual growth of the last seven
or eight hundred years shows that it has been in some degree a factor
in the wonderful development of the industrial age of civilization. But
for its meeting a want in the progress of humanity, it could never have
attained its present importance. Commencing with an occasional application to merchandise in transportation, it has been extended to cover risks
of the most varied description, and human ingenuity is constantly at
work to discover new fields to which it may be applied. Its theory is
faultless: by association, losses which would be crushing to the individual
are subdivided so that the burden becomes trivial to each. The command
of St. Paul, "Bear ye one another's burdens," by the alchemy of modern
enterprise is transmuted from a barren effort of charity to a profitable
business in which both the succorer and the succored find their account.
Credit is facilitated and commerce is stimulated; the widow and the
orphan are protected from poverty.

Such is the theory of insurance; and yet, in spite of the experience
of so many centuries, it may be questioned whether the evils inseparable
from the modern development of the system have not grown to out-
weigh its advantages. The fact that a thing has been long practised in
many lands raises of itself only a faint presumption in its favor. Strongly
akin to insurance in the aleatory character common to both is the lottery,
which for centuries after its invention, or rediscovery, by Benedetto
Gentile was favored by every government in Christendom, and has only
within little more than a generation been forbidden by a portion of them
as contrary to public policy. Even the legal prohibition of the lottery is
insufficient for its suppression, and contraband speculation in its chances
is still one of the commonest of offences.

It would seem worth the while of our legislators to consider whether
the prohibition of the lottery should not be followed by the suppression
of insurance. The evil of the lottery is the temptation with which it
lures the people to risk sums which they cannot prudently afford in the
hope of securing gain without labor; its benefit, when conducted by
governments, is that it affords a liberal source of revenue willingly
contributed by the taxables. The benefit of insurance I have already
described; and as this is greater than that of the lottery, so are the correlative evils greater. The fact that insurance can be obtained upon almost
any risk, thus relieving the individual from responsibility for his own
laches or recklessness, exercises a moral influence on the community
even worse than the gambling spirit fostered by the lottery. More than
this, it is a direct incentive to crime. Underwriters have told me that it is

* From *Lippincott's Magazine*, XXXIX (1887), 469-71.

a received axiom in insurance circles that from twenty to thirty per cent of fires are incendiary, purposely set for the purpose of gaining the amount insured. Even more serious is the case of marine risks, where life as well as property is sacrificed. To say nothing of absolute barratry, can anyone imagine that without insurance such legislation as that of Mr. Plimsoll would be requisite?—that merchants would deliberately send forth unseaworthy ships, overloaded and undermanned, taking the chance of making a sale of vessel and cargo to the underwriters? On every ocean "Plimsoll's line" is a standing advertisement of the effort required to abate in some degree the wrongs arising from insurance. Any system which can stimulate the perpetration of a crime like that of Thomassen at Bremerhaven must involve possibilities of evil well worthy the thoughtful consideration of the publicist.

When New Hampshire not long ago enacted the valued policy law which induced all the insurance agencies to withdraw from the state, there was a general chorus of ridicule and a confident prediction that a twelvemonth would see the obnoxious law repealed and the insurance companies supplicated to return. Yet New Hampshire is thoroughly well satisfied with the position, and has no desire to invite the underwriters back. Since they expelled themselves and deprived the state of the benefits of their presence, losses by fire have diminished by about thirty per cent. Take the tremendous aggregate of annual loss on the continent, which for 1886 is estimated at $116,600,000, and assume that this would be reduced even one-quarter by the abolition of insurance, and we will see how much property, how much of the result of human labor, would be saved, and how much richer the community would be. The saving, moreover, would grow as the years rolled on; for not only would each individual be rendered more watchful and more careful, but a safer style of building would prevail, more substantial structures would be imperatively demanded, and the "defective flue" and other deathtraps would in time become things of the past. A minor but yet highly important consideration is the fact that under modern methods the rates charged for insurance are absurdly greater than the risk. The statistics of the last five years show that more than half the fire-insurance companies of the United States have paid out for expenses and dividends as much as they have for losses, thus forcing the assured to pay for protection double the value of the real risks assumed. At the same time, no one can afford not to insure, for his property is at the mercy of his neighbors or of his tenants, rendered reckless or possibly criminal by the temptations of insurance.

The same reasoning applies to marine insurance. Deprived of it, the shipowner would be compelled to see that his vessel was stanch, fully found, safely loaded, well manned, and ably commanded. He would do this not only for the sake of the bottom, but because shippers would not otherwise intrust him with their freights. The list of maritime casualties would diminish, including the frightful aggregate of the loss of human life by sea.

There is another class of insurance against those casualties which may be described as acts of God, against which human prudence is virtually unavailing,—such as the cyclone insurance so rapidly growing in this country, and the insurance against hail common in Southern Europe. Of this class, the only one of magnitude sufficient to render it of public concern is life insurance, and in this the evils are not, at least as yet, so great as in fire and marine underwriting. Cases of murder or suicide for the insurance money are, happily, rare, and speculative "graveyard insurance" is not practised to any great extent. Yet there can be no question that, looked upon in the light of a savings bank, life insurance is a very costly depository for the accumulations of thrift, and that it could scarce flourish but for the attractions of its aleatory or gambling character. In the reckless effort to create business the commissions granted to agents are so large that a charge for premiums becomes necessary greatly in excess of what is justified by the expectation of life. The insured is practically contributing a notable portion of his premium, not for insurance, but for the support of a horde of canvassers traversing the land and pursuing an unproductive industry of no value to the community. A system of post-office savings banks would furnish a vastly cheaper and more wholesome incentive for small economies. The rich can take care of their own accumulations.

For these reasons it seems to me a question well worthy the attention of the sociologist whether public policy does not require that insurance should follow the lottery in being subjected to legal prohibition. The favor shown by underwriters to what are known as coinsurance policies, in which the assured participates in the risk, is in itself an admission that the whole existing system is a vicious one. It points, moreover, to the adoption of the strictly mutual plan, so successful in the case of what are known as the "Factory Mutuals," by which in fire underwriting the evils are reduced to a minimum. If insurance should not be wholly abrogated, it might at least be restricted, as regards fire, to this basis.

FETICHISM IN POLITICS*

THE RECENT EXPOSURE of abuses flourishing under Tammany rule in New York, naturally calls renewed attention to the most serious problem in the development of American institutions—the application of universal suffrage to municipal government. This problem is becoming more serious year by year. The urban population increases disproportionately, through the tendency of modern civilization to stimulate the gregarious instinct by the facilities which it affords for supplying the needs of huge masses of men, by the higher degree of comfort or luxury which applied science puts within the reach of wealthy communities, and by the craving for excitement which is constantly becoming a more marked feature of average human nature. Professor A. B. Hart tells us that the growth of the urban population has been from 3.9 per cent of the nation in 1800, to 22.5 per cent in 1880. The process is continuing with accelerating force, and the cities probably now contain a full fourth of the inhabitants of the land. In the older states, any growth which the approaching census may show will be seen to be due to the cities, for the rural districts are fortunate if they hold their own. Not only are our towns thus absorbing yearly a larger proportion of the population, but a modern municipality is a much more complicated machine than the city of a hundred, or even of fifty, years ago. New wants have sprung up, requiring new instrumentalities for their satisfaction; and the socialistic tendency, which is becoming so strong, leads ever more and more to multiplying the functions and enlarging the operations of the public authorities. Thus the question as to the wise and efficient administration of large cities grows more intricate as it grows more important. It cannot be shirked, and on its proper solution will depend in great measure the verdict of mankind as to the success or failure of the grand American experiment of self-government.

It is not that municipal troubles are the symptoms of a special disease or the outgrowth of special causes; it is simply that great cities are the weak spots, where functional and constitutional disorders manifest themselves soonest and in their worst forms. The cure is not to be sought in local applications which, at most, even when valuable in themselves, are merely palliatives. To be efficacious, the remedy must be constitutional; it must be directed to the causes of which the visible effects are only the indications. These causes are manifold, but the most potent of them may be traced to a habit of mind which, for want of a better appellation, we may call fetichism.

One development of this fetichism ascribes to political institutions a sort of supernatural power. This has infected the speculations of almost all philosophers since the time of Plato, and perhaps has never been so

* From the *Forum*, IX (1890), 430-36.

strong or so widely diffused as it is to-day, especially among the believers in popular government. It seems to be thought that if a constitution theoretically perfect can be framed, it may be suffered to run itself; that it will have an inherent virtue to suppress the wicked and to elevate the good; that if evils occur they are attributable to some defect in institutions, and that they can be remedied with a few strokes of the pen when they become sufficiently onerous to arouse the attention of the majority. Far be it from me to deny the power of institutions in molding human character and in affecting human happiness, or the benefit which may be derived from well-devised reforms; far be it from me to decry popular government, in which I am a firm believer; but nevertheless we must remember that there is a partial truth, which we are apt to disregard, in the couplet—

> For forms of government let fools contest;
> Whate'er is best administered is best.

An enlightened despotism, the ideal of the so-called philosophy of the Carlyle school, would undoubtedly be the best, if the limitations of human nature did not always prevent the despot from being sufficiently enlightened for the proper discharge of his unlimited responsibilities. Self-government, by dividing and decentralizing responsibility, affords a fairer opportunity for good government; and the admirable structure of our Constitution, with the scope which it allows to the individual citizen to make his influence felt in both local and general matters, unquestionably presents, with the possible exception of the Swiss Federation, the nearest approach to an ideal government that human wisdom has yet devised; but, for all that, its working will be good or evil as it is administered well or ill. The trite phrase, that eternal vigilance is the price of liberty, has a significance beyond what is usually attributed to it, for liberty imposes on the citizen duties which he can discharge only by incessant attention to the common weal.

Human nature is the same under all institutions. The ambitious and the unprincipled adapt themselves to their environment, and find means for the attainment of their ends. The favorite and his minions under a despotism, become bosses under a republic—men who learn how to lay hold of the secret springs of power, whether these lie in the favor of princes or in the manipulation of caucuses, and who plunder the public to keep it enslaved. What creates the peculiar class of the American boss and gives him his influence, is the careless indifference of one portion of the community, largely due to the fetichism of which I have spoken, and the blind partisanship of another portion. Here we encounter another form of fetichism. Government by parties would seem to be indispensable in the existing stage of political development. Parties are

undoubtedly admirable things in their proper character of instruments
to an end, but unfortunately party organization has become, in the eyes
of a large portion of the community, an end in itself—a fetich which is
worshiped irrespective of the objects for which the party was ostensibly
organized. When the fetich-worshiper succeeds in establishing his special
idol in the national shrine, he expects it in some supernatural way to
shower blessings over the land; if he is defeated, he regards the elevation
of the rival fetich as the triumph of a demon whose malignity in some
occult manner will blight the national prosperity and ruin the national
morals. Such being his frame of mind, the men whom he votes into
office, and the means whereby success may be secured, become to him
matters of comparative indifference. He is thus material suited exactly
to the requirements of the boss, for he is no longer a freeman exercising
intelligently the priceless right of suffrage, but a slave to party, driven
to the polls to vote as his masters may dictate. Those masters are the
bosses, who could not exist without him, yet who naturally regard him
with the contempt which he deserves. They are under no illusions; they
know how worthless is the fetich which he worships, and of which they
are the priests, and they despise him for the blind credulity with which
he submits to their orders when speaking in its name.

These two varieties of fetishism are the main causes of our political
troubles. The results are visible throughout the land, but they make
themselves more apparent in the municipalities, for many self-evident
reasons. In the eager struggle and excitement of city life, the citizen
more readily yields to the temptation of neglecting his political duties,
and comforts himself with the assurance that our institutions can take
care of themselves. He is only one molecule in so large a mass that his
influence and his vote seem of infinitesimal importance. The complexity
of municipal machinery is such that to exercise the franchise intelligently,
and still more to attend primary meetings and understand their intrigues,
would require more time and thought than he could conveniently bestow.
If inert, he consequently stays at home; if a partisan, he goes to the polls
and votes the regular ticket with the proud consciousness of discharging
a public duty. On the other hand, the boss finds in the city a field eminently suited to his peculiar gifts. The prizes are greater, and the dangers
of detection less, than in the rural districts. The flock of sheep to be
shorn is larger, and more helpless in proportion to its size. The political
machine is so intricate that only a professional can comprehend and
manipulate it. Thus, in the survival of the fittest, the shrewdest and
most audacious bosses are developed in the cities or are attracted to
them, and the evils of their rule are greatest; yet none the less the causes
of mischief are general and not local, and if a cure is to be found, it
must, as I have said, be constitutional and not topical. Amendments to

city charters and modifications of municipal regulations, are often but doubtful expedients, and at best give relief only until the bosses devise means to circumvent them. The foundations of pure government rest on public virtue, and if that is lacking the superstructure must needs totter.

Yet I, for one, do not believe in the decay of public virtue. I believe that the world at large is constantly, though slowly, growing wiser and better, and I see no reason to think that our land is an exception. We are apt to be prophets of evil because we feel acutely the abuses existing around us, while forgetting those of the past; and we are thus led to imagine that public life is becoming more debased and corrupt. This is wholesome if it nerves us to stronger effort to promote righteousness; but it is more apt to lead to apathy and hopelessness, and the average man will struggle with more energy when convinced that he is on the winning side. Confidence in the ultimate triumph of right over wrong is therefore a frame of mind which it is wise to cultivate, and I see no reason for doubting it. The Civil War, though glorified by a splendid outburst of patriotism, left behind it many evils, as all great wars must do. Not only was there the inevitable corruption attendant upon gigantic expenditures hastily made, but the overmastering passions of the time naturally erected a false standard of public opinion. Everything might be permitted to him who was sound on the main question, for all else was insignificant in comparison. It was hard for us to outgrow this fierce partisanship, and some of us have never done so; but it is rapidly declining, and the younger generation of voters has happily escaped its influence. To the conscienceless politician, who trades on the passions and prejudices of the public, no opportunity could be more tempting than that afforded by the war, and he made the most of it. Bosses had existed before, but now they came to the front with a boldness previously unknown. They have had their day, but it is waning. Every year sees an increase in the mass of intelligent, independent voters who cast their ballots according to their convictions and not at the dictation of the political machines. When parties are nearly equal, the independent voter holds the balance of power and must be reckoned with. He strikes down a candidate of conspicuous unfitness, and the lesson is not forgotten; he demands a measure which will aid him in future struggles, and his demand is complied with after more or less resistance. Every step he advances gives him a vantage ground for the next conquest. The future of the Republic is with the independent voter.

To descend from generalities to particulars, there are at present four measures for which the independent voter should strive with unremitting ardor, each of which is fitted to diminish some of our existing evils. These are civil-service reform, the Australian ballot, the restriction of the liquor traffic, and the regulation of immigration, with modification of our naturalization laws. The beneficial effects of these measures would be felt everywhere, but chiefly in the cities, where they would do much to facilitate the introduction of purer and more efficient administration. But these, like all other laws, are merely instruments. They are not automatic; to be efficient they must be used, and used properly, and such use can be made only by unceasingly vigilant public opinion, manifesting itself in constant action.

Of these measures, civil service reform is the most urgent and the most efficient for good. To deprive the bosses of the control of "patronage" and of their consequent ability to maintain their henchmen and heelers at the public expense is the readiest method of destroying the political machines and of restoring politics to its true function of wisely administering the affairs of the people, instead of being as at present, for the most part, a selfish struggle for office. Yet the virus of the spoils system has so thoroughly infected our national life that it will yield only to heroic treatment. The reformer must resolutely determine to regard the question as the controlling one, and must strike unflinchingly at all candidates, whether Democratic or Republican, who cannot be trusted to enforce existing laws and to be guided by their spirit in dealing with the unclassified service. Party managers will not surrender control over the spoils until they recognize that the people are thoroughly in earnest, and this conviction can be impressed on them only by successive defeats. Usually the party in power is the one to be struck at as it is, for the moment, the offender to be punished.

Yet all these, and all other devices, will be neutralized unless a check be put on the tendency, now so visible, to experiment with state socialism. This is in the air, and schemers and dreamers of every degree of irrationality are busy with their nostrums for the cure of all political and economic evils. Government ownership of telegraphs and railroads, government loans on farm lands, and government advances on farm produce are proposed on the one hand and, on the other, municipalities are expected, or are urged, to supply light and heat and water and locomotion and other public wants. Jeffersonian Democracy was right in seeking to restrict and simplify as much as possible the functions of government. More or less corruption there always has been in the management of public affairs, and always must be so long as human nature remains unregenerate. Government itself is an evil—a necessary evil incident to human imperfection—and the less of it we can get along with the better, for thus only can we reduce its accompanying abuses to a minimum. Every added function introduces additional corruption and renders detection and purification more difficult. The paradise of the boss would be a community organized on the Bellamy pattern.

THE INCREASE OF CRIME, AND POSITIVIST
CRIMINOLOGY*

THE TWO great scourges of humanity are disease and crime, and man's struggle against them forms a notable portion of the history of the race. The advance of science within the last generation has greatly modified and improved the practice of medicine, and it is natural that earnest sociologists should be incited to the endeavor to reduce into something like scientific method the hopelessly empirical and haphazard treatment of crime.

The necessity for improvement is admitted on all hands. In 1826 France commenced to collect and publish statistics on the subject; in 1835 England followed the example; and at intervals the other Continental nations have, one by one, done the same. Thus there has gradually been accumulated a vast body of materials for scientific study and, although comparative criminal statistics are notoriously apt to mislead, the figures show undeniably that, with the exception of the British Empire, society has been worsted in the conflict with its criminals, and that crime has been increasing in spite of perfected police organization and the anxious labor of the tribunals. In France, for instance, from 1826 to 1880, the population grew only from 31,000,000 to 37,000,000, yet the trials for adultery multiplied ninefold, rape committed on children increased from 136 per annum to 809, assassinations from 197 to 239, arson from 71 to 150, infanticide from 102 to 219. The aggregate criminality of Christendom to-day is hideous to contemplate, demonstrating the insufficiency of the existing means of repression and the crying necessity for a change. If we take, for example, homicide, we are told that in the seven years 1881-87, the annual average in some of the leading states of Europe has been:

Austria.......	689	Germany......	577	England.......	318
Hungary......	1,231	France........	847	Scotland......	60
Spain.........	1,584	Belgium.......	132	Ireland........	129
Italy..........	3,606	Holland.......	35		

—amounting in all to 9,208 yearly; and that, if to this be added the homicides in Russia, Sweden, Norway, Denmark, Portugal, Roumania, Servia, Montenegro, Bulgaria, and Greece, the total would be about 15,000. Accurate statistics for the United States are not accessible, but the usual estimate of 3,000 is probably below the truth; and, if we include Canada, Australia, and the Spanish republics of Central and South America, the homicidal aggregate of states professing the Christian faith must be between 20,000 and 25,000 annually. The most deplorable feature, moreover, of this swelling tide of crime is that the increase is specially mani-

* From the *Forum*, XVII (1894), 666-75.

fested in the class of habitual criminals, for the convictions for repeated offences multiply more rapidly than those for first offences. In France they grew, for misdemeanors, from 21 per cent of the whole in 1851 to 44 per cent in 1882, and for crimes from 33 to 52 per cent. In Italy they were but 10½ per cent in 1876, while in 1885 they were 34¾. Yet these official figures are greatly too low, for, as relapses are visited with increased penalties, the offender naturally conceals the fact as far as he can, and the means of ascertaining it are necessarily imperfect. Ferri says that by personal investigation among 346 persons condemned to hard labor he found 37 per cent to be old offenders, and among 363 condemned to prison 60 per cent, though the official returns make out only 14 per cent of the former and 33 per cent of the latter.

The causes at work to produce these disheartening results are not far to seek. One of them unquestionably is the marked increase in the consumption of intoxicating liquors which is shown by the statistics of almost every nation. Tolstoy may perhaps exaggerate when he asserts that alcohol is accountable for 90 per cent of crime, and that of women who go astray one-half yield to temptation when under its influence; but the best-informed criminologists ascribe to it a large share not only in stimulating to crime and in blunting the moral perceptions, but also in producing the peculiarly dangerous class of born criminals who are hopelessly incorrigible. Marro found by investigation among convicts that 41 per cent of them were children of drunken parents, and the incalculable extent to which such hereditary criminality will infect society is amply shown in Dugdale's remarkable study of the Jukes family.

The immense development in recent times of the urban population is another fruitful source of increasing crime, for cities, through their temptations and contaminating associations, are hotbeds of vice. The increase of wealth among all classes is to be reckoned as another cause, for, contrary to the popular opinion, poverty is not an incentive to crime. Morrison tells us that every rise in the rate of wages is followed by an increase of offenders, and that the prisons are never so full as in a period of general prosperity and abundant work.

Yet still more efficient than all these causes has been the humanitarian movement which is so marked a feature of the present century. The reaction against the barbarism bequeathed to us by the Middle Ages— a reaction led by Beccaria in criminal jurisprudence and procedure and by Howard in prison discipline—has not been without its serious drawbacks. Punishments have been mitigated, while methods of procedure have been adopted which, in their effort to avoid injustice to the innocent, afford impunity to the guilty, or so protract the trial that the deterrent influence of speedy justice is lost. Garofalo, indeed, does not hesitate to assert that to the popular mind the courts seem devised and conducted so as rather to protect the criminal against society than to protect society against the criminal.

Trial by jury, introduced into France by the Revolution of 1789, has spread everywhere for non-political criminal cases. It is a clumsy device at the best among races trained to its use, and is utterly unfitted to peoples whose sympathies are apt to be rather with the wrongdoer than with his victims, who are easily led away by the rhetoric of the advocate and who, if we may believe the criminologist, are frequently open to the seduction of bribery or liable to intimidation by the friends of the accused. This induces extra caution on the part of prosecuting officers, who hesitate to try offenders unless they feel a reasonable certainty of overcoming the scruples or the fears of the juryman. Thus in France in 1887, out of 459,319 complaints, 239,061, or more than half, were pigeonholed. Unlike the English, the Continental jury is not required to be unanimous; its decisions are reached by secret ballot, in which a tie acquits and a blank or illegible ballot is counted for acquittal. When, under these difficulties, a conviction is obtained, if the offence is a capital one, the diseased sentimentalism of the age steps in to preserve the worthless life of the criminal. In Italy, no execution, save in the army, has taken place since 1876, and the death penalty was finally abolished as useless in 1891, as it has likewise been in Holland, Portugal, Roumania, and practically in Belgium and Switzerland. In the other states the following curious table, quoted by Professor Ferri from the Howard Association, shows how tender are the Continental nations in the judicial shedding of blood:

Country	Period	Condemnations	Executions	Country	Period	Condemnations	Executions
Austria.....	1870–79	806	16	North Germany....	1869–78	484	1
France......	1870–79	198	93	England...........	1860–79	665	372
Spain.......	1868–77	291	126	Ireland...........	1860–79	66	36
Sweden.....	1869–78	32	3	Scotland..........	1860–79	40	15
Denmark...	1868–77	94	1	Australia and New			
Bavaria.....	1870–79	249	7	Zealand.........	1870–79	453	123

British severity, as illustrated by these figures, may perhaps explain how England has held crime in check better than Garofalo's suggestion of the purification of the race by the wholesale slaughter of vagabonds under the Tudors, and by the deportation of convicts to the American colonies in the eighteenth century and to New South Wales in the nineteenth.

This virtual abandonment of the death penalty leaves to the legislator no resource for the repression of crime but imprisonment in its various forms, and it is employed for all offences, great and small. In Italy, in the ten years 1880-89, the sentences to jail amounted to 1,112,079; in France, for the decade 1879-88, those by the lower courts alone were 1,675,000, of which 113,000 were for terms of less than six days. The prisons thus become nurseries of crime, where trivial offenders are trained to evil courses and are let loose with the taint and disgrace of the punishment clinging to them. At the same time they have lost their former terror for the hardened criminal, for the humanitarian instincts of the age have rendered them abodes far more endurable than the cabin of the peasant or the garret of the workman, to say nothing of the relief from the care of the morrow which oppresses the man who depends on his labor for his daily bread. Even the *bagne* and the so-called galleys are managed on benevolent principles and are regarded by the dangerous classes rather as a refuge in time of need than as a punishment to be dreaded. Coupling all this with the larger gains to be made in a society where the increase of wealth offers such opportunities to the spoiler, we can well appreciate the assertion of M. Tarde that the profession of a criminal offers greater profits and smaller risks than any other career open to the indolent poor.

That some change in the treatment of the criminal classes is a vital necessity admits of no question, and, with the scientific and materialistic tendencies of the time, it is no wonder that the attempt should be made to solve the problem scientifically—or at least with the appearance of scientific method. So long ago as 1848 Quételet pointed out the fact that crime is hereditary in some families as scrofula and phthisis are in others, and that the majority of criminals spring from these families, which should be isolated like persons suspected of bearing the germs of contagion. Maudsley in England and Despine in France did good service in defining the more obvious characteristics of the criminal diathesis, but it was reserved for Lombroso to make an exhaustive study of the subject and endeavor to reduce it to scientific accuracy.

Lombroso's *Delinquent Man*, of which the first edition appeared in 1876, may be regarded as the foundation of what is known as positivist criminology. By the personal examination of innumerable criminals he identified certain physical peculiarities and anomalies, which he claims to be diagnostic of the born criminal—the man who is by nature irreclaimable and who may be regarded from the start as hopelessly incorrigible. Of these the chief are lack of symmetry of skull or face, certain peculiarities of ears, hands, and feet, scantiness or absence of beard, nervous contractions of the face, prognathism, inequalities of the iris, twisting of the nose or absence of the bridge, retreating forehead, excessive length of face, prominence of cheek-bones, dark color of hair and eyes, while white hair and baldness are rare. He lays great stress, moreover, on tattooing—a practice which he regards as exceedingly symptomatic of criminal tendencies; and from these various external characteristics it is claimed that three types of criminals may be distinguished, the murderous, the violent, and the thieving. For all this there may well be some foundation of truth, but far less than is asserted by the discoverer and his disciples.

In fact, the character of Lombroso's mind is the reverse of scientific: he is imaginative and enthusiastic; and his definitions are so elastic that in one book he classes Charlotte Corday with Ravaillac, Guiteau, and the regicides as an example of hereditary degeneration, while in another he groups her with Paoli, Garibaldi, Gambetta, Marx, Lasalle, and the Christian martyrs. Yet, when divested of the extravagances incidental to overzealous propagandism, there can be little question that in the hands of cautious experts valuable indications may occasionally be had by the physical examination of those suspected of crime. Ferri tells us that the sphygmograph, by which internal emotion can be detected under external impassibility, has served to prove that one accused of robbery was innocent of the alleged offence, but guilty of another of which he was not suspected; and that in another case it determined the innocence of a man condemned for life, by revealing a grave judicial error. Yet in looking for practical results we can scarcely feel confidence in the realization of the glowing anticipations of the criminologists as to the benefits to accrue from their science, when justice, as they assure us, will have the aid of surer methods of detecting the criminal by the observation of tattooing, anthropometry, physiognomy, the physio-psychic conditions, the data as to sensitiveness, reflex activity, vaso-motor reactions, the extent of the field of vision, etc.; nor can we reasonably hope that the credibility of witnesses can be absolutely determined, as we are promised, by scientific applications of psychology and psychopathology. At all events, thus far the main service rendered by Lombroso and his school has been to call increased attention to the class of incorrigibles, the hopelessness of their reform and the necessity of their "elimination" for the protection of society.

Positivist criminology, however, by no means limits itself to the humble function of detecting and classifying criminals. It aims at a complete reconstruction of the whole theory of crime and punishment. It holds that there is no such thing as absolute crime, no acts that are in themselves prohibited by natural or divine law. What we call crimes are simply infractions of the rules which a given social organization at a given period has established for its convenience or self-preservation; and, as social organization changes with the development of civilization, these rules change, so that what is a laudable action at one period becomes criminal at another; there are no crimes on the statute-book to-day which have not been or perhaps now are permissible under social conditions of a lower type, and vice versa. M. Tarde points out that of the ten offences which, in the Hebrew legislation, were punished with lapidation, nine are no longer to be found in the penal codes of Europe, and if the tenth one is there it is on account of an entirely different motive. Garofalo even argues that chastity is an artificial and conventional virtue.

Virtue and vice being thus merely the expression of what is useful or hurtful to society in its existing condition, the question of morality disappears. The responsibility of the criminal also is removed by the absolute denial of free will. What a man does he does inevitably, according to the composition and resolution of the various influences acting upon him at a given moment; all living organisms are subject to the same laws, and their actions are governed in the same way. From the protozoön or amœba to man, the only difference is that, as we rise in the scale of being, the motives and impulses grow more complex, and man is as much the instrument of the forces acting upon his physical and psychical nature as is the protozoön in its simpler organization. Moral responsibility is thus an idle phrase, and to speak of punishment as retribution or expiation is merely to reëcho an outworn superstition. The conception embodied in the word "guilt" should have no influence on the framing or administration of the law. An involuntary homicide is on precisely the same moral plane as one committed through cupidity or hate, and if society sees fit to visit it with a lighter penalty this should be simply because negligence is less threatening to social order than violent and unrestrained passions. The insane murderer is in the same category and is to be dealt with in the manner that will best preserve the State from further injury by him. Thus, under these theories, society is left free to deal with every individual offender in the mode best fitted to subserve its interests and promote the well-being of its members as a whole; and the boast of the positivist criminologists is that, while heretofore penal codes have regarded the crime rather than the criminal, in the new order it will be the criminal who will be considered, and not the crime.

When we reach the practical measures proposed to give expression to these theories, we find valuable suggestions mingled with others that are visionary. That habitual criminals—the incorrigibles or born criminals of Lombroso—who are and always will be at war with society, should be "eliminated" by death or perpetual confinement and thus be prevented from propagating their kind, is a proposition which will probably be assented to by all save ultra-humanitarians. Yet Ferri hesitates to recommend the death penalty for them and suggests agricultural colonies in which they can be confined for life, with the further proposal that they be set to work to reclaim malarious districts in place of employing honest peasants in that deadly labor. Agricultural colonies, in fact, are the main reliance of the Italian school to avoid the acknowledged evils of prisons, and in place of fixed terms they propose indeterminate sentences under which all prisoners are to be examined from time to time by experts in psychopathology and criminal anthropology, and are not to be released until there is satisfactory evidence of their readaptability to society. Garofalo makes a fruitful suggestion in pointing out that in the existing penal codes the interests of the victim of a crime are wholly overlooked, while reparatory damages payable to him ought to be a feature of all sentences: if the offender has property it should be seized; if he has none he should be required to work it out, the state paying the sufferer and putting the convict to hard labor till his wages suffice to refund the amount. Such fines or damages would be a wholesome substitute for the innumerable short-term sentences to prison which now exert so evil an influence in recruiting the criminal army and converting casual into habitual offenders. Prisons, moreover, should be made really penal in character, and be no longer, as at present, comfortable abodes, while special asylums should be provided for the confinement of insane criminals.

Much of this is reform in the right direction, though the advantage to be expected from it scarcely responds to the exultant promises held out by the new school. They claim, however, that by the application of their principles penal codes can be reduced to extreme simplicity, for the degree of punishment will depend on the character of the criminal and not on that of the crime. The whole administration of criminal justice will resolve itself into determining, according to the rules of science, first, the guilt of the accused, and, second, his adaptability to the social environment. In the words of Professor Ferri:

When the repressive social function assumes simply the character of a defensive force, by excluding the ethical notion of retributive punishment of crime, the penal judgment can no longer busy itself with apportioning carefully the penalty to the moral responsibility or culpability of the criminal. Its only object will be to prove that the accused committed the offence, and then to determine to what anthropological category he belongs, and thereby what degree of anti-social perversity or social readaptiveness is presented by his physio-psychical personality.

To this end judges and police are to be carefully trained in all these matters, and every prosecutor's office is to have a staff of experts in criminal anthropology. Students are no longer to trouble themselves with the intricacies of criminal jurisprudence, or to cultivate the eloquence so seductive to juries, but are to be drilled in psychopathology and anthropometry, and are to attend, under their instructors, clinics in the prisons as their medical brethren do in the hospitals.

Such, in brief outline, are the leading tenets of the positivist school, whose views, if we may judge from the immense accumulation of literature on the subject during the past twenty years, are exciting no little attention throughout Europe and are doubtless destined to contribute a share to the changes in criminal law and practice which are inevitable if the rising tide of crime is to be checked. Although some of these philosophic daydreams may provoke a smile, yet the thoughtful publicist cannot but be grateful for any honest and resolute effort to lift the administration of criminal jurisprudence from the perilous routine into which it has fallen. In this, we of the Western world have as large an interest as our cousins of the older hemisphere. While the boundless resources of our territory and our more scattered population have hitherto rendered these problems less immediately pressing for us than they are for the crowded nations of Europe, and while the easygoing optimism of our people has disposed us to the belief that they will solve themselves in time, symptoms are not lacking of a serious character to show that we must bestir ourselves if we are to avert most threatening evils. The growth of the urban population is becoming even more disproportionate here than it is abroad. The increase of vagabondage, encouraged by the thoughtless good nature or timidity of the rural districts, promises to breed for us a large and dangerous class of born criminals whom it will be hopeless to reclaim to honest labor, while the development of Coxeyism shows us how readily the ranks of these shiftless tramps can be recruited, and how reckless they become of the rights of others. The interminable delays and evasions through which legal ingenuity is allowed to defeat the ends of justice are directly responsible for the alarming increase of the practice of lynching, which is the natural expression of a deplorable popular loss of confidence in the courts; while on the other hand there is a maudlin sentimentality ever on the watch to sympathize with the convicted assassin and to urge in his behalf the abusive exercise of the pardoning power. Immigration of late years has cast upon our shores vast hordes of the most degraded and lawless races of Europe; and though we have been accustomed to flatter ourselves that our native population contributes less than its share to the criminal classes, the researches of Professor Falkner have recently shown that when the statistics are applied—as they should be—to adults alone, the percentage of native offenders is larger than that of foreign.[1]

Already the class of habitual culprits is as large with us as in Europe, where it is estimated to constitute between forty and fifty per cent of convicts, for in the penal institutions reporting to the Bureau of Education in 1892, ten per cent of the inmates are set down as incorrigibles, and thirty-five per cent as returning to a life of crime. Homicide has increased to such degree that, except in cases of peculiar atrocity, it is popularly regarded almost with indifference, till, as Dr. Andrew D. White happily observes, the only taking of life that Americans object to seems to be that which is done by judicial process. The general diffusion of education from which, a generation ago, so much was expected, has utterly failed; for statistics show that literates contribute a larger percentage of their class to the criminal ranks than do the illiterates. In spite of the enormous expenditure of sixty million dollars per annum on police, judiciary, and prisons, the class which lives by preying upon society increases, and all discussion is to be welcomed which will attract popular attention to the magnitude of the evil and excite thoughtful consideration as to the measures best adapted to work a much-needed reform.

The foregoing subject may be pursued by consulting the works here named, but recent literature on criminology has become so vast that only a brief selection of typical works can be enumerated: Lombroso, *L'uomo delinquente,* Turin, 1889, 2 vols. with atlas (it has been translated into French, German, and Russian); Ferri, *La Sociologie Criminelle* (author's translation from the 3d Italian edition), 1 vol. Paris: Rousseau, 1893; Garofalo, *La Criminologie,* 1 vol. Paris: Alcan, 1892; Tarde, *La Criminalité Comparée,* 1 vol. Paris: Alcan, 1890; Falkner, *Prison Statistics of the United States,* Philadelphia, 1889; Morrison, *Crime and Its Causes,* 1 vol. London: Swan, Sonnenschein & Co., 1891; Köbner, *Die Methode einer wissenschaftlichen Rückfallstatistik,* 1 vol. Berlin, 1893; Von Oettingen, *Die Moralstatistik in ihrer Bedeutung für eine Socialethik,* 1 vol. Erlangen: Deichert.

[1] Possibly, if we include children born in this country of foreign parents, Professor Falkner's conclusions may be subject to modification. The statistics of the last census show that of 82,329 prisoners in 1890, 25.55 per cent were white natives, 29.49 per cent were negroes, 34.66 per cent were foreign-born or with both parents foreign, 9.40 per cent were unknown or with one foreign parent, and .09 per cent were Indians, Chinese, etc.

BOOK REVIEWS

BOOK REVIEWS

[Of the many reviews of learned works written by Mr. Lea, a few have been selected to illustrate his method of reviewing and the scholarly care with which he dealt with the work of other men.—H.]

* * * * *

Du Cange: *Glossarium Mediae et Infimæ Latinitatis, cum Supplementis . . . Aliorum, suisque digessit*. G. A. L. Henschel. 7 vols., Paris, 1840-1850.*

No STUDENT of modern history can pronounce the name of Du Cange without a feeling of affectionate veneration. The rare combination of qualities requisite to lexicography—patient industry, critical acumen, exhaustless learning—so seldom vouchsafed to a single individual, render those who succeed in perfecting their self-imposed and repellent tasks benefactors of no common order. When, in addition to the ordinary difficulties surrounding such labor, the attempt is made in a new and almost unexplored province, which by its vast extent and intricate recesses seems beyond the capacity of one finite mind to grasp, success would appear hopeless, and even failure not undeserving of praise. Such was the endeavor of Du Cange, and his generous self-confidence was not deceived; the fullest triumph crowned his gigantic labors, and the scholars of succeeding ages look up to him as their master and their guide. A simple glossary of bastard Latin—a vocabulary of the barbarous words which had crept into the language used after the destruction of the Roman Empire—such is the modest form of his undertaking; but to accomplish it on his plan required him to present all the details of mediæval life, civil and military, legal and political, commercial and ecclesiastical, technical and artistic, public and domestic. Each word gives rise to an essay in which the subject is examined on all sides with an exhaustive erudition that seems almost superhuman. Sparing of his own remarks, which are terse and to the point, he cites contemporary authorities with a profusion of research that leaves little to be asked for; while by his skilful apposition and comparison of doubtful allusions obscure points become clear, and that which before was inexplicable is brought within the domain of positive knowledge. In this Du Cange had but little assistance to expect from his predecessors. The glossaries and notes appended by Lindenbruck, Pithou, Bignon, and others, to their editions of ancient laws and formulæ, had, it is true, assembled together a certain amount of material; the *Glossary* of Spelman, a more ambitious attempt, and highly creditable to that learned and accurate archæologist, was more

* From the *North American Review*, LXXXIX (1859), 32-98.

to the purpose, and contained the results of much curious and profitable research; but these were as nothing, in plan or in execution, to the vast conception of that enterprise which Du Cange alone could dare and accomplish.

In 1678, three folio volumes conveyed to the public this stupendous work, which was at once received with acclamation by the learned throughout Europe, and was acknowledged as indispensable to the apparatus of all scholars. Diligent critics calculated that the number of extracts embodied in its pages amounted to one hundred and forty thousand, derived from six thousand different sources, printed or manuscript; while the immense range of topics discussed was rendered manifest by forty-five indexes or catalogues of words, each representing a special class, for the benefit of those who might desire to follow up particular subjects throughout the work. The very assistance afforded by the Glossary to antiquarian studies contributed, however, in the course of time, to render it imperfect, and caused deficiencies to be felt which had not previously existed. The renewed zeal of the learned gave to the world vast masses of mediæval manuscripts, which had lain concealed in dark corners of provincial libraries and ecclesiastical establishments, and the accumulation of fresh material rendered necessary an enlargement of the only work which could be referred to for its elucidation. A new edition was at length resolved on by the Benedictines, and when it appeared, in 1733-36, the original three volumes had expanded to six. This was no more a finality than its predecessor. The untiring efforts of Bouquet, Sécousse, Muratori, and their collaborators, to say nothing of the never-ending labors of the Bollandists, continued to collect additional matter, and in 1766 a Supplement of four more folios was published by Dom Carpentier, who had assisted his brethren in the preparation of the second edition. This huge and overgrown bulk of course placed the rich treasury of erudition beyond the reach of ordinary students, and the whole speedily became scarce and high-priced, notwithstanding various reprints of the Benedictine edition in Switzerland and Italy. At length, in our own day, the Didots of Paris, with a liberality more nearly allied to the professional pride of the early printers than to the practical money-making ideas of the present age, undertook to reconstruct this magnificent monument of their country's learning, and the result is before us. By the resources of modern typography, seven royal quarto volumes, with more than six thousand triple-columned pages, present the contents of the ten folios of the last century, augmented by much valuable matter. M. Henschel, the editor, has not only incorporated throughout the Supplement of Dom Carpentier, but, from the labors of Adelung, Haltaus, and other German lexicographers, together with his own researches, he has also remedied to a considerable extent the deficiencies formerly existing with respect to the Teutonic writers and history.

Prodigally as Du Cange lavished his intellectual wealth on this immense repository, we must not imagine that it exhausted his resources. A similar key was required to the Greek authors of the Lower Empire, and this, long vainly desired by scholars, was supplied by him in two folios, overflowing with the same abundant learning. Other works, illustrative of Byzantine and French history, any one of which would be sufficient to establish an ordinary reputation, were given to the public with equal facility; and the piles of manuscripts left behind him show that these were for him only the prolegomena of designs yet more vast and comprehensive. These labors, which without exaggeration may well be termed gigantic, were accomplished by steady and unremitting application. During a long life, fourteen hours a day were allotted regularly to study, and he yet found time for the domestic duties of a husband and father, and for the faithful performance of the functions of a public office. So intense was his mental activity, that his marriage-day only found him willing to reduce his allowance to six or seven hours. Looking round at the learned of our own day, and marking their skill in beating out their intellectual minimum of gold, we feel abashed in presence of the simple and single-minded scholar, with his unfathomable erudition.

If History be indeed "Philosophy teaching by example," then her text should not be merely the scandalous intrigues of a court, or the desolating achievements of an army. The inner life of the people affords the most instructive lessons, and he who would attempt to study or to teach, must seek to penetrate into these recesses. The fact which to the mere chronicler is a result, to him should be only material which, in combination with other facts, may enable him to deduce a principle. It is from this consideration that the work before us derives its special and incomparable importance. Scattered amid masses of documents, printed and manuscript, accessible to few inquirers, lie the treasures from which the history of Europe and of modern civilization is yet to be constructed. Careless allusions to forgotten customs, hints of matters which the contemporary annalist or scrivener takes for granted, when rightly understood often throw a flood of light on the character and manners of a period; and yet who, aspiring to more than the simple collection of materials, can undertake the hopeless task of traversing public libraries, or of penetrating carefully guarded archives, guided only by the instinct that there must be something lying concealed, yet scarcely knowing what to look for, and happy if he recognize it when found? Such efforts necessarily circumscribe the sphere of research to the narrowest possible bounds, and no enlarged results can be deduced from them. Even should

the student be fortunate enough to have at his command the interminable bulk which has already been committed to print, the span of a
single life is barely sufficient for the examination of his materials. To
such investigations the assistance of Du Cange is inestimable; not that he
supplies all we may want, but that, used merely as an index, his work
spares us endless, useless labor, by guiding us to the fields which yield
the fullest return, while from his own inexhaustible stores he does much
to make good our deficiencies. In the following attempt to group together
some of the peculiarities of human progress as developed in the institution of the ORDEAL, we pay the best practical tribute to the utility of this
opus magnum. The frequency of our citations will show the assistance
derived from its richly stored pages.

[There follows, as was common in serious reviews of the period, an
essay of 63 pp. on "Judicial Ordeals." This later formed Chapter 3 of his
studies in medieval legal history entitled *Superstition and Force* (Philadelphia, 1866). In the fourth, revised edition of this work (Philadelphia,
1892) this chapter was expanded to 180 pages.—H.]

*   *   *   *   *

Güterbock, Carl: *Bracton and His Relation to the Roman Law. A Contribution to the History of the Roman Law in the Middle Ages.* Translated by Brinton Coxe, Philadelphia, 1866.*

THE KÖNIGSBERG professor and his Philadelphia translator deserve the
thanks of all students of English history on two accounts. Firstly, for
bringing before them a very curious and hitherto imperfectly known
aspect of the influence of the Roman jurisprudence upon the institutions of England; and secondly, because it is not impossible that such
a work from the depths of Germany may shame Englishmen into something like an earnest and rational cultivation of the materials at their
hands for a proper understanding of their own history.

Had any other nation of Europe boasted of a thirteenth-century writer
like Bracton, what a wealth of critical acumen and erudition would have
been lavished upon him! He would have been carefully edited by profound and patient scholars; the most painful collation of manuscripts
would have rendered a perfect text accessible; the influences of the age
upon him would have been studied; his influence upon succeeding ages
would have been carefully traced; and many obscure problems in the
development of the institutions of England would doubtless have been
elucidated.

---

* From the *North American Review*, CIII (1866), 284-86.

As it is, the contrast is somewhat humiliating. No nation in Europe possesses a work so important to the right understanding of its existing jurisprudence as England has in Bracton's treatise *De Legibus et Consuetudinibus Angliæ*, and yet but two editions of it have been printed—one in 1569 and the other in 1640[1]—both without editorship and simply as a legal textbook for practitioners. In Bracton's time, all Europe was waking up to the revisal and systematizing of the law. Frederic II had just completed his *Constitutiones Sicularum*. Germany was engaged upon the *Sachsenspiegel*, the *Schwabenspiegel*, the *Kayser-Recht*, and the *Richstich Land-Recht* and *Lehn-Recht*. Alphonso the Wise was bestowing upon the unwilling Castilians the *Siete Partidas*. Hako Hakonsen was performing with the *Jarnsida* the same office for Norway and Iceland. Waldemar II of Denmark was giving to his subjects their first written code. St. Louis was issuing the *ordonnances* which were soon afterwards collected under the title of the *Établissements*, and the school of legists whom he trained, such as De Fontaines and Beaumanoir, were writing the treatises which give us a clearer view of the France of that day than all the annals and chronicles that have been preserved to us.

All these Continental codes and books of practice have become utterly obsolete, while Bracton is still an inseparable part and parcel of English law. Yet the Continental works have been printed and reprinted; everything that could throw light upon them has been thoroughly ransacked, and nothing has been left undone to extract from them every fraction of information attainable. The contrast between this and the neglectful treatment of Glanville, Bracton, Britton, and the Fleta is discreditable to English industry and learning.

Few questions more interesting can be presented to the student than the influence of the Roman law upon the customs and jurisprudence of modern Christendom. In Italy, it was perhaps never entirely extinct, though long overridden and almost smothered by the Lombarda. In Spain it was preserved as a national code by its thorough interpenetration throughout the Wisigothic laws and the Fuero Juzgo. In France, it gave form and shape to the efforts by which St. Louis and his successors broke down the decentralization of the feudal system and achieved their victory over the canon law. The constitution of the Germanic Empire presented greater obstacles to its reception, but it gradually won its way and undermined all opposing forces. Ample materials have been collected for the elucidation of all these stages of its history, and laborious scholars have traced them step by step. England remained a problem. The Conquest

---

[1] [The 1640 edition was merely a reprint of that of 1569.—H.]

had given to her institutions a completeness as a whole which was lacking in other countries, parcelled out into chartered towns and provinces, each with its special code. Her feudal system was more vigorous and compact than that of any other nation, and her judicial machinery far more uniform and effective. She was therefore prepared to resist the invasion of the civil law, and she manifested for it a jealous repugnance, composed of mingled fear and contempt.

That the civil law, nevertheless, exercised some influence upon the common law has long been understood; but the exact nature and extent of that influence have been a question with even the best-informed English jurists, whose distinguishing characteristics are not those of patient research and accurate familiarity with the Digest and Code. Accordingly, it has been left for Dr. Güterbock to make a thorough comparison of Bracton's treatise, as the principal source and authority of English jurisprudence, with the foreign sources from which he could have drawn materials to modify and reduce to system the practice of his day. The result is the compact volume before us, of which the size bears no proportion to the labor it has cost, or to its value to all who would have a clear idea of the formation of our legal institutions.

Those who believe that the common law of England is an independent creation will be surprised to see how much Bracton has borrowed from abroad. He was thoroughly familiar, not only with the Institutes, the Digest, and the Code, but also with the writings of the principal commentators of the Italian schools. Azo of Bologna, a celebrated glossator of the thirteenth century, seems to have been his principal authority; and the *Summa* of Azo furnished him much, not only as to arrangement and principles, but even as to details. All this is carefully traced out by Dr. Güterbock, who traverses the entire treatise of Bracton, and by references and parallel passages shows how much of Roman law was incorporated by Bracton, either to supply deficiencies or to modify what was defective in the customs of the land.

Mr. Coxe, in his preface, remarks that, while the author intended his work to be a contribution to the history of the Roman law, the translation is presented as an aid to the study of the English law. That it is a valuable one, no one will deny; but it might have been more valuable, if not to professional, at all events to unprofessional readers. We gather from a note that Mr. Coxe originally intended to follow up the subject, and to trace the development to the extinction of the various principles and details adopted by Bracton from the Roman law. We greatly regret that he did not carry out this purpose. Judging from the notes which he has added, we should presume him to be eminently fitted for such a task by familiarity with the subject and by habits of a close reasoning and laborious investigation.

We would hope that the intention may not be abandoned, but only postponed, to ripen hereafter into an independent volume, in which the sources and development of the English law may be traced from the earliest times to the present day. The materials for such a work exist in a richness and continuity that no other nation possesses, and they should long since have been turned to account. Mr. Coxe, apparently, has both the taste and the ability to supply the void, and the task is one well worthy of his ambition.

* * * * *

Lagrèze, G. B. de: *Histoire du Droit dans les Pyrénées* (*Comté de Bigorre*). Paris, 1867.*

WHATEVER MAY be the political sins of Louis Napoleon, he at all events deserves the thanks of students for his enlightened encouragement of all learning that is not dangerous to Cæsarism. It is true that the classical attainments of Professor Rogeard, as displayed in the *Propos de Labiénus*, met with no very flattering reception at the hands of the imperial police, but these little eccentricities must be pardoned in the founders of dynasties; and when research into the past is not animated simply by the desire to excite discontent with the present, it finds in the Second Empire an intelligent patron, whose example more liberal communities would do well to imitate. Under the stimulus thus afforded, France is gradually rendering accessible an amount of historical material which must eventually prove of the utmost value to all who seek to trace the development of European civilization.

One of the latest productions of the imperial press is the volume named above. M. de Lagrèze has already done good service in both juridical and historical literature; and his labors were well worthy the seal of approbation bestowed on them in the selection of this work for publication by the government. Fully impressed with the truth that the laws and customs of a race are the surest guides to a knowledge of its condition, revealing all that is best worth knowing in its history, he has with unflagging zeal sought to reconstruct for us the past of feudal noble and peasant in the secluded valleys of Bigorre. This is no easy task for a period and region where every village and almost every glen had its separate code of laws and charter of liberties; but his industry has been equal to the labor. From every available source, printed and manuscript, he has gathered his materials together, and by intelligent arrangement and commentary has succeeded in presenting us with a faithful delineation of society, as it existed among his native mountains, from the commencement of the feudal era until the general unification of France under the Bourbons, which prepared the nation for the cataclysm of 1789.

In many respects the subject which M. de Lagrèze has so successfully treated is a unique one. Without entangling ourselves in the interminable ethnological quarrels as to the origin of the Basques, it is not to be denied that they are a peculiar race, which has maintained its individuality under the domination of Celt and Roman, Wisigoth and Frank. This individuality continually displays itself throughout the institutions reconstructed by M. de Lagrèze; and his wide acquaintance with the legislation of other races enables him constantly to point out notable contrasts. We have not space for the discussion of the numerous questions, historical, legal, and social, which suggest themselves on almost every page, but we may group together a few particulars concerning a problem which possesses as much interest in the present as in the past.

One of the peculiarities which distinguished the customs of Bigorre would have delighted Gail Hamilton and Mrs. Elizabeth Cady Stanton. The equality of the sexes was almost complete. In those ages of class privileges, the only suffrage permitted to the people was that of the *vesiau*, or vicinage, which, under the charters granted by the seigneurs, was competent to assemble and deliberate upon the interests of the commune. In these assemblages the women were included, as well as the men; they participated in the deliberations and shared in the vote. That they should have enjoyed these political rights is not, however, a matter of surprise, when we find that, in an age of feudality and strict primogeniture, the eldest born without distinction of sex inherited the estate, whether noble or *roturier*. An elder sister thus excluded her brothers. She was the head of the family, and the other children were placed under her protection, were legally designated as her *esclaus*, or slaves, were unable to abandon the ancestral roof without her permission, and were compelled to labor for her, while she was bound to support them. If the heiress married, her husband assumed her name and came to live with her; while her brothers were to be married to heiresses of other families, where their identity and origin were similarly lost.

Perhaps our advocates for woman's equality may be disgusted to learn that, while the weaker sex was thus intrusted with all the privileges which we have been taught to regard as exclusively masculine, the gallantry of the Bigorrais went farther and invested their women with special rights which were a tribute rather to their weakness than their strength. Thus, when a man was slain in war, his widow was exempted from all legal process until either she should remarry or her sons attain the age for bearing arms. Still more romantically chivalrous was the provision which invested the person of woman with the sacredness of an asylum. In her presence, as at the altar of God, the fugitive criminal could not be seized; his personal safety was assured, and he was only to be held liable to the legal fine for his offence. *"Omni tempore pax teneatur dominabus, ... ita quod si quis ad dominam confugerit, restituto damno quod fecerit, persona salvetur."* In an age which esteemed the right of private vengeance as one of the dearest of privileges, the sense of respect for women must have been profound indeed, when that vengeance could thus be stayed.

Yet, with all this, there occasionally rises to the surface a remnant of the wild aboriginal estimation of woman as the slave and plaything of man. It may have been a Basque tradition, or a reminiscence of Roman license—it assuredly was not of Teutonic or Gothic origin—that led to the institution of *massipia,* or recognized concubines, bound under notarial contracts to serve their paramours for a definite number of years, upon certain specified conditions. Thus, M. de Lagrèze gives the text of a formal agreement in writing, made in 1462, between Augé de Carassus, de Beaucens, on the one part, and Augé d'Abadie, de Visos in Barèges, on the other, by which the former delivers to the latter his daughter Gailhardine for four years, with a stipulation, that, if she should not bear children to him, he was to give her at the end of the term eight florins and a furnished bed, according to the customs of Barèges; while, if children were born, they were to be provided for, according to the same customs. If, moreover, the wife of D'Abadie should die during the term of concubinage—which God forbid, *"loque no placia a Diu,"* as the contract piously exclaims—then D'Abadie was bound to marry Gailhardine, and to institute her as his universal legatee. When women were thus bought and sold, and the marriage sacrament was thus lightly treated, it is questionable whether the political and legal privileges accorded to them made them much happier than they are to-day, though exposed to the crying injustice of taxation without representation. It is evident that the franchise did not cure all social evils.

Somewhat akin in its contempt for womanly modesty is a curious feudal tenure quoted by M. de Lagrèze from a charter of 1330. When the seigneur de Sadirac married, his vassal, the seigneur de Bordeu, was bound to meet the bride at the boundary of his lands, accompanied by all his tenants. There he was to dismount from his horse, to salute the lady, assist her to alight, kiss her, and strip her of all her clothes, to the chemise, keeping them as his perquisite. If he politely vouch-

safed to lend her the garments until she reached her home, the ceremony of disrobing her might be postponed until then, but the spoils still
belonged to him.

M. de Lagrèze's work covers the whole structure and organization
of society, and arranges methodically a vast amount of information,
gathered from all sources accessible to a zealous archæologist, concerning
the institutions of the Middle Ages, military, political, judicial, and social.
He has, however, a keen eye for the picturesque, and can find room,
amid disquisitions on *ceysaux, questaux, francaux,* and *cagots,* for many
a curious incident illustrative of customs and manners. We may conclude
our imperfect sketch of his very interesting volume with one of these,
which reveals some of the peculiarities of human nature in Bigorre.

About the year 1709, Charles Maumus, of Saint-Ours, an old soldier,
was condemned to the galleys for the indiscretion of extorting, with
the aid of a loaded musket, a signature from his brother-in-law. The
marquis of Castelbajac took an interest in the criminal and had him
released, cautioning him to abandon his habit of carrying fire-arms and
of hunting. Maumus gratefully pledged himself to respect the wishes
of his protector; but, as he was the keenest of sportsmen, he soon forgot
his promises and, in spite of warnings and remonstrances, his fowling-
piece again became his inseparable companion. Somewhat irritated at
this breach of faith, M. de Castelbajac finally summoned him to appear,
and condemned him to a few days' imprisonment in the castle dungeon
—for the marquis was a *haut-justicier,* enjoying the right of pit and
gallows—*furca et fossa.* Maumus made no resistance, but meekly asked
to be shown the way to his prison, and the noble condescended to play
turnkey for his involuntary guest. No sooner had they reached the place
of confinement than Maumus seized his host, thrust him within, double-
locked the door, and quietly went home, leaving the keys on a table
in the corridor. The unaccountable disappearance of Castelbajac soon
alarmed his people, and they vainly searched for him in every direction.
He might have perished of starvation in his own dungeon, had not a
tailor's apprentice chanced to remark that he had seen him going with
a stranger towards the prison; and this trace being followed up, he was
at length released, after passing a most uncomfortable night. Strange
to say, in place of being incensed at the scurvy trick thus played upon
him, he took it in good part. The horrors of the dungeon so impressed
him, that he resolved never to entomb a fellow creature there again. He
complimented Maumus on the strength and dexterity which he had
displayed and, to manifest his consideration for him, promised to act as
godfather to his next child. Accordingly, the curé of Montastruc records
the appearance, July 1, 1709, of Messire Godefroy Joseph de Durfort de

Duras, marquis de Castelbajac, seigneur de Montastruc, etc., and of Mlle Jeanne de Castelbajac, his sister, as godfather and godmother, at the baptism of Godefroy Joseph Maumus. Even in the eighteenth century life in Bigorre must have retained much of its primitive wild individuality.

* * * * *

Schottmüller, K.: *Der Untergang des Templer-Ordens*. 2 vols. Berlin, 1887.*

PROFESSOR SCHOTTMÜLLER has given us a valuable contribution to the already extensive Templar literature. In two visits to the Vatican library, made in 1880 and 1886, he found and transcribed some hitherto unpublished documents which, together with a brief abstract of some records in the archives of Marseilles, form the second volume of the work which he has laid before the public.

The first of these documents he entitled "Processus Pictavensis" (II, 13-71). It contains the examinations of thirty-three out of the seventy-two Templars brought before the papal court at Poitiers in June 1308. It is interesting as partly filling a gap in the series of documentary evidence, but throws little new light on the affair, except as illustrating incidentally the perfunctory character of the whole performance at Poitiers, and as affording to Professor Schottmüller fair grounds for discrediting the currently accepted statement that Molay in 1306 brought with him to France an immense amount of treasure.

Then follows "Deminutio laboris examinantium processus contra ordinem Templi in Anglia" (II, 78-102). If this be, as the author is probably correct in assuming, an abstract of the English evidence, officially prepared at Clement's command for use at the council of Vienne, it is important as a proof of the unscrupulous manner in which the testimony was garbled for the purpose of misleading those who were to sit in judgment. All the favorable evidence is suppressed, and the childish gossip of women and monks is seriously presented as though authentic. Even making allowance for the weight ascribed to popular rumor in medieval trials for heresy, the deliberate purpose manifested throughout this paper throws a fresh and sinister light on the management deemed requisite to effect the predetermined object.

The bulky "Processus Cypricus" (II, 143-400) is of value, although the unfortunate omission of some of the formalities of the proceedings prevents us from estimating accurately their precise purport. The testimony of the non-Templar witnesses shows a higher estimate of the

* From the *English Historical Review*, III (1888), 149-54.

Order among those to whom it was best known and who, moreover, were not friendly to it, than has been generally supposed. The interrogatories of the seventy-six Templars examined are, however, by no means deserving of the importance attached to them as a proof of innocence by Dr. Schottmüller (I, 484-93). It was a matter of course that where torture was not used they should assert their purity and orthodoxy, and evidence in their favor must be sought from other sources.

The "Processus in Patrimonio Petri" (II, 405-19) has importance as manifesting the real design of the commissioners sent out in 1310 by Clement V, ostensibly for the purpose of affording the order an opportunity of making a defense before the council of Vienne, but in reality with the object of collecting evidence for its condemnation. Thus when imprisoned Templars declined the invitation to appear and defend the order they were forced to come forward and testify against it. The extracts from the archives of Marseilles (II, 423-34) would doubtless have been of greater value had not the author unfortunately been prevented by illness from transcribing them in extenso. A secret order of Charles the Lame of Naples to his seneschal not to deliver the sequestrated property to the papal agents illustrates the scramble which was going on for the spoils.

Had Professor Schottmüller confined himself to the publication of these documents with illustrative and explanatory notes, there could have been nothing but praise for the acuteness which enabled him to recognise them under deceptive inscriptions and for the painstaking labor with which he has deciphered the mouldy and battered parchments. Unfortunately, however, he has deemed it necessary to accompany them with a diffuse and confused history of the whole affair, occupying nearly seven hundred and fifty octavo pages. With true German assiduity he has ransacked all the authorities within his reach; he has studied all the official documents with microscopic minuteness; many of his observations on them are shrewd, and occasionally his comparison and confrontation of the evidence throws a new and valuable side light on certain points; but he lacks the impartiality of the historian, he is a special pleader rather than a judge, he has framed a theory of the whole affair, and his book is an elaborate *plaidoyer* in its defense.

The work thus becomes a misleading one, for the author is so profoundly convinced of the truth of his speculations that he confounds his conjectures with his facts, and presents both with equal positiveness so that the reader often cannot distinguish between them. The groundwork of his whole hypothesis is an imaginary alliance between Clement V and Molay to protect the former from the arrogant domination of Philippe le Bel and thus save him from sharing the fate of his predecessor

Boniface VIII. The growth of this myth illustrates the idiosyncrasy of the author's method. First it comes before us (I, 80) as a suggested explanation of Philippe's attack on the Order. Then we are told (p. 91) that Clement's summons in 1306 to the masters of the Temple and the Hospital was for the purpose of obtaining their support; then (p. 101) that it is uncertain whether Clement and Molay were arranging an armed assault on Philippe. Gradually the idea assumes in the author's mind the consistency of absolute fact; we are assured (p. 115) that Philippe recognised that Molay's presence had encouraged Clement to resist his demands; and finally (p. 120) it is positively asserted that Philippe's whole expectations of advantage from the transfer of the papal court to France had been shattered by the protection given by the Templars to the pope. Thus it becomes assumed as an historical fact (p. 564) that the chiefs of the order had promised security and protection to Clement, an assertion for which there is not a particle of evidence. This would perhaps matter little were it not that it places the sequel of the story on a thoroughly false basis, forcing the author to represent Clement as bravely defending the Order until obliged to abandon it to its fate by Philippe's visit to Poitiers in May and June, 1308. To make this apparently credible, the bull *Pastoralis praeeminentiae* of November 22, 1307, which virtually settled the fate of the order, is dismissed with a brief allusion wholly inadequate to its supreme importance, and the author practically ignores the controlling fact that during those fateful six months in which his theory requires Clement to be staunchly maintaining the cause of the Order, it was being broken up at his instance and under his express authority in England, Spain, Italy, Cyprus, and such parts of Germany as he could induce to take action. This sufficiently shows that the temporary suspension by Clement of the powers of the inquisitors and bishops of France, on which Dr. Schottmüller dwells with so much insistence, was mere skirmishing for position, to be abandoned as soon as Clement had secured his terms.

This tendency to assume facts which sustain the author's theory pervades the whole work and renders it untrustworthy in spite of his evident desire to be accurate in the minutest particulars. We repeatedly meet with positive assertions for which there is no authority. We are thus told over and over again that the initial proceedings under the authority of the inquisitor Guillaume de Paris were declared to be invalid (pp. 140, 231, 287, 407); in fact (p. 244), that these examinations were made by the royal officials and were therefore illegal, when, on the contrary, Philippe had been especially careful to shield himself behind the authority of the Inquisition and his officials were ostensibly only lending their aid as required by law to the inquisitors commissioned for the purpose by Frère Guillaume, who deputed all Dominican priors, sub-priors, and lectors to act in that capacity. Possibly in some cases official zeal may have outrun discretion, but the whole proceedings were covered with a cloak of strict legality, and any indiscretions were condoned in the bull of November 22. So (p. 140) we have a wholly unsatisfactory argument to prove that Molay's letter to his brethren advising them to confess was forged or falsified; and then a few pages later (p. 143) there is an illusion to Molay's falsified letter as if the falsification was a recognised historical fact. We are told (p. 670) that Molay and the master of Normandy were burnt against the will of the cardinal judges, when there is no evidence either for or against it, and the probabilities are that the cardinals were delighted to be relieved of the responsibility, which they could not otherwise have escaped, of handing the prisoners over to the secular arm for burning. In like fashion the author positively asserts (p. 558) that the non-appearance of Renaud de Provins before the papal commission as a witness after being sworn was because he was so broken by torture that he was unfit to give evidence— an assumption for which there is no warrant. In writing history after this imaginative fashion a good memory is requisite to avoid occasional self-contradiction, as when (p. 128) a visit of Hugues de Peraud to Poitiers just before the arrest is described as an effort to save himself from the blow which he is assumed to know was impending, and is subsequently (p. 243) alluded to as evidence that Clement was commencing an investigation himself—a most important feature of the case if only it were true, in place of being a bald supposition.

This unfortunate tendency is rendered still more serious by the author's lack of familiarity with the ecclesiastical jurisprudence of the period, leading him to frequent assertions and arguments for which there is no justification. Thus (p. 124) we are told that Philippe lured Molay and his brethren to Paris from Poitiers as a necessary preliminary to their arrest, and we are treated to an elaborate disquisition on the limitations of jurisdiction, ignorance of which, he says, has led all previous writers into blunders—the fact being that all the arrests were made under the authority of the Inquisition of Paris, whose jurisdiction in such matters at the time was supreme from the Atlantic Ocean to Geneva, and there was no more occasion to entice Molay to Paris for the purpose than the rest of the brethren, who were seized everywhere throughout the kingdom. Equally groundless is the assertion that the arrest was in violation of all recognised law of the period, and that the Inquisition exceeded its powers in prosecuting Templars whose immunities rendered them justiciable only by the pope (pp. 126, 251, 640). The facts are that even before the Inquisition was founded Lucius III abrogated all immunities in accusations of heresy; that suspected heretics had practically no legal rights, and their capture was the highest duty of all secular officials; that, moreover, the Inquisition exercised authority directly delegated by the pope; and that even the mendicant orders, whose immunities were quite as great as those of the Templars, when they endeavored to escape the jurisdiction of the Inquisition were rudely remanded to it by Innocent IV in 1254. It follows that the author is completely in error when he says (p. 149) that Philippe had subverted the foundation-law of medieval society whereby ecclesiastics were subjected exclusively to spiritual jurisdiction. Similar ignorance is manifested in the argument (p. 203) that the absolution given at Chinon in August 1308 to Molay and the preceptors shows that they could not have confessed any heresy worthy of death; for no heresy confessed and abjured was at that time punished by death, except in cases of relapse, and it was a universal rule that even relapsed heretics were entitled to absolution if they asked for it, although they were to be burned immediately thereafter, for the bosom of the Church was never closed to the repentant sinner. Equally erroneous is the assertion (p. 231) that at that time torture could not be legally employed against witnesses, for it was habitually so employed in both the inquisitorial and episcopal courts. More serious is the ignorance displayed in the effort to show (pp. 298, 663) that Clement, as late as August 1309, was still endeavoring to protect the Templars against Philippe by his bull ordering the bishops to follow the law and not introduce new methods, which the author regards as a prohibition of the use of torture, in place of being, as it was, an order for its employment under a decent veil of reserve—a reserve thrown off a few months later when the necessity of incriminating evidence became pressing, and Clement reprehended those who had not had recourse to torture, the employment of which, he told them, was customary in such cases. Twice (pp. 619 and 627) the author manifests complete confusion between witnesses and compurgators, whose functions, under medieval customs, had no relations with each other; and he even seems to think (p. 320) that the Templars might have cleared themselves by compurgation but for Philippe's violent measures, apparently not knowing that it rested wholly with the inquisitor to determine whether the accused should be admitted to this method of proving his innocence. When he says (p. 573) that the burning of Molay and the master of Normandy was an act of violence in open scorn of all spiritual law, he seems unaware of the fact that the canons ordered relapsed heretics (and the victims were technically relapsed by reason of revoking their confessions) to be abandoned without a hearing to the secular arm for burning, and that Philippe only took for granted what would have been a mere formality on the part of the cardinal judges. All this may seem minute criticism, yet these errors are important, as they serve to prevent the recognition of what is really the most weighty lesson taught by the whole dreadful tragedy—that it was merely an exhibition on a more conspicuous stage of the atrocities habitually perpetrated for centuries throughout nearly all Christendom, in the effort to secure the supreme blessing of uniformity of faith. Had not the author been blinded by the strength of his convictions, it would surely have occurred to him that Philippe, to whose great capacity he does ample justice, was far too shrewd to commit such violations of law as are here imputed to him, and that Clement would have been a far less able man than he is here represented if he had not taken full advantage of such blunders on the part of his assumed antagonist.

Professor Schottmüller loses no opportunity of pointing out the errors of his predecessors in a manner implying his own infallibility. Unfortunately, he is as liable to inaccuracy as the rest of us. Thus, in his desire to show that Philippe failed to secure popular belief in his charges against the Templars, he gives (p. 139) the answer of the University of Paris to his inquiries, as though it were rendered in October 1307 and proved that the University was incredulous, when in reality it was only a decision on certain legal points and could not have been other than it was; then (p. 167) the date is stated to be May 25, 1308; and it is not until we reach the chronological summary (p. 656) that the correct date of March 25 is given. When (p. 414) we are told that the archbishops of Sens and Reims burned "hundreds" of Templars for revoking their confessions, the exaggeration of the real number of sixty-seven, instead of increasing our sense of the enormity only diminishes our confidence in the accuracy and impartiality of the historian. Twice (pp. 195, 649) the confusion as to the commencement of Clement's regnal year is said to have been only recently cleared up; and in the latter passage it is alluded to as illustrating the ignorance hitherto prevailing as to the order of events, when in reality the difficulty was explained by Dom Vaissette a century and a half ago. We are told (p. 447) that in Italy not a single knight was examined: had the author consulted the sole authority for the proceedings in Romagnuola (Rubeus, *Hist. Ravennat.* [ed. 1589], p. 525) he would have found the names of seven knights—*Templarii ordinis equites*—examined by the council of Ravenna in 1311. Similarly, had he referred to Allart's researches, his exceedingly imperfect account of events in the kingdoms of Majorca and Aragon would have been fuller and more exact; but even the authorities whom he cites should have preserved him from the repeated misstatement (pp. 551, 560, 639) that in Aragon the Templars passed into other orders and that the Temple continued in existence *mit kleinen Abänderungen*. On page 585 it is suggested that previous liberalities of Molay's family may have entitled him to gratuitous entrance into the order, apparently in ignorance of the fact that by the statutes payment for admission was severely punishable, although in the later corruption of the order it was sometimes winked at. Equal unfamiliarity with the statutes is manifested in a matter to which, by his repeated allusions (I, 187, 264; II, 12), he seems to attach singular importance. In the protocol of the examinations at Poitiers, the applicant for admission is reported sometimes as asking for *fraternitas ordinis* and sometimes for *fraternitas domus*. The author regards this variation as of special significance as indicating the "subjectivity" of the reporter and as showing how little he knew about the order when he thus describes a postulant as seeking admission into a single house. It happens that the two expressions mean precisely the same thing and can be used indifferently, for "house" is the official synonym for the order in the statutes of the Temple. The blunder is the more incomprehensible since the author quotes (I, 294) the initial words of the statute-book offered in evidence by the brethren of Mas Deu: *Quan alcum proom requer la compaya de la Mayso.*

It is scarce worth while to pursue this examination further. The original documents printed in the second volume render the work a necessity to all students of the Templar catastrophe; but the first volume, despite the immense labor bestowed on it, and the ingenuity which it frequently displays, must take its place in the long series of works on the subject which a fondness for theorising, combined with imperfect knowledge, render unsafe guides for the inquirer.

* * * * *

Gmelin, J.: *Schuld oder Unschuld des Templerordens: kritischer Versuch zur Lösung der Frage.* Stuttgart, 1893.*

THE FATE of the Templars seems destined to be the source of endless dispute. As M. Langlois acutely observes, the highest triumph of the agents of Philippe le Bel in the coarse and impossible series of accusations which they framed is not that they succeeded in imposing on the credulity of the fourteenth century, but on the scientific skepticism of the nineteenth. There would be little significance in the attitude of Catholic apologists who are bound to rehabilitate the memory of Clement V, but when independent reasoners like Wilcke, Hammer-Purgstall, Michelet, Henri Martin, Loiseleur, and Prutz still exhaust their ingenuity in framing and applying oriental mysteries to explain the heresies imputed to the Templars, the question cannot be considered closed, in spite of the new documentary evidence which the labors of scholars have exhumed during the last half-century. In fact, within a few years there seems to have been

* From the *English Historical Review*, IX (1894), 365-68.

a revival of interest and recrudescence of debate. In 1887 Konrad Schottmüller printed a large amount of new and valuable material, accompanied by a ponderous volume, of which I gave a brief account in these pages. In 1888 Professor Hans Prutz responded with a work of much learning (*Entwicklung und Untergang des Tempelherrenordens*) in which he mercilessly exposed the shortcomings of Schottmüller and maintained the heresy of the Templars, though in a less incisive fashion than in his previous essay, *Geheimlehre und Geheimstatuten des Tempelherrenordens*. Schottmüller unfortunately died last June without responding to the assaults upon his position, but his place is taken by another most laborious German scholar who, after years devoted to the minute study of all the documents, has produced a valuable contribution to the discussion, as he not only goes over the whole ground with thorough knowledge, but affords to others the opportunity of testing his conclusions in a manner which no previous writer has attempted.

Perhaps I am too firmly convinced of the false and fraudulent character of the main charges on which the Templars were convicted to be an impartial judge of a work which so ably defends the same side of the argument, and hence I would only remark in general terms that Dr. Gmelin appears to me to have reached a correct judgment as to the springs of action in the affair, and as to the deductions to be drawn from the course of the trials, which he follows minutely and accurately, step by step. His characterisation of the two leading actors, Philippe le Bel and Clement V, and of the Inquisition, which served as their indispensable instrument, is skilfully presented from all accessible sources, and is not unduly severe. In fact, to him who has studied the details as presented in the authentic records of the time, nothing can exceed the horrors of what Henri Martin has well stigmatised as *"l'épisode le plus hideux de cette hideuse époque, si digne d'inspirer les sublimes indignations du chantre de 'l'Enfer.'"* I confess that I could have wished something less of acerbity in the controversial portion of Dr. Gmelin's book—the *polemisch-kritischer Teil*—extending to page 221, in which he pays his respects to Professor Prutz—the "proto-Prutz" and the "deutero-Prutz" —and meets him at every point; but unfortunately we are too much accustomed to the polemical style in which our German friends are apt to conduct their discussions. The feature of the work, however, which will be of special value and comfort to future students is the *Mappe*—a series of twenty extensive tables, folded and enclosed in a separate envelope. In these Dr. Gmelin, with almost incredible patience, has given us tabulated analyses of the leading points in each of the 138 examinations by the Inquisition of Paris in 1307, of the 33 yet extant from the hearing before the cardinals at Poitiers in 1308, and of the 232 recorded in the protocol of the papal commission in 1309-11. These constitute the bulk of the evidence remaining to us from the confessions made by the inculpated Templars, and it is a real service to the student to have the details thus presented in a form susceptible of easy reference and comparison—a service, perhaps, scarce to be rightly estimated save by those who have painfully labored through the mass of material in the endeavor to construct some working hypothesis from its confused and contradictory elements. In performing this arduous labor Dr. Gmelin seems to me to have settled for the future the long debate, for he has thus enabled everyone to see for himself the worthlessness of the testimony on which the Templars were convicted.

A few trifling inaccuracies may be noted, if only to show that the critic has performed his duty. On page 386 Dr. Gmelin alludes to Roussillon as politically united with Aragon, and as therefore independent of French influence, while on page 476 he more correctly describes it as a portion of the little kingdom of Mallorca, and as therefore obliged to respect the wishes of Philippe de Bel. On page 473 he speaks of Ximenes de Luna as archbishop of Saragossa, though that see was not raised to an archiepiscopate until 1318, under Pedro Lopez de Luna, the successor of Ximenes. The three daughters-in-law of Philippe le Bel were not all daughters of a duke of Burgundy, nor were they all convicted of adultery, as stated on page 504, for Jeanne, wife of Philippe le Long and daughter of Otho IV, count of Burgundy, escaped, although accused. In the account of the Tuscan proceedings (page 450) some reference should have been made to a council held at Pisa, September 20-October 23, 1308, in which the Templars are said to have confessed all the crimes laid to their charge.[1]

To these I may be allowed to add a little reclamation of my own. Dr. Gmelin informs me (page 478) that I am in error in having stated (*History of the Inquisition*, III, 316) that in Castile "no action seems to have been taken until the bull *Faciens misericordiam*, of August 12, 1308, was sent to the prelates," and that, on the contrary, Fernando IV lost no time in arresting the Templars on receiving Philippe le Bel's letters of October 16, 1307. For this assertion he quotes Havemann and Schottmüller, who in fact make it, but cite no authority for it, for the very good reason that no authority for it can be cited. The Spanish writers, including Campomanes and Benavides, know of no official action of any kind prior to the citation issued April 27, 1310, by the archbishops of Toledo, Plasencia, and Lisbon.[2] Other direct documentary evidence of the period is wanting, wherefore I abstained from an absolute asser-

---

[1] The authority for this is Bzovius, who states that the proceedings are to be found in a Vatican manuscript, *Nat. Alexand. Hist. Eccles. Saec. xiii-xiv.* Diss. 10, q. ii, Art. 1, n. 8; Campomanes, *Dissertaciones de los Templarios*, p. 93.

[2] Campomanes, *op. cit.*, p. 105; Benavides, *Memorias de Fernando el IV*, II, 738.

tion, but to any one in the slightest degree familiar with the condition of Castile under Fernando el Emplaçado such energetic action as is attributed to him will appear manifestly impossible. The crown was weak, the Templars were relatively strong; they were constantly rendering essential service in the sempiternal struggle with the Saracens, which endeared them to the popular mind, and they were recruited from the noblest families of the land. Until the reign of Ferdinand and Isabella the national military orders were among the most powerful political factors of the kingdom, and it was not the least sagacious act of Ferdinand when he incorporated with the crown the masterships of Santiago, Alcántara, and Calatrava. Under Fernando IV, moreover, there was no Inquisition in Castile to furnish impulsion or machinery for the destruction of the Templars. There was, therefore, everything to make him hesitate and nothing to cause him to take hasty action. Benavides,[3] indeed, quotes though without putting much faith in it from the somewhat dubious authority of Garibay's manuscripts, that the first act of Fernando was to send his cousin and *alferez mayor*, Don Lopez Diaz de Haro, as a special envoy to Clement V, to represent to him the unblemished reputation and distinguished services of the Castilian Templars.

Connected with this is a curious passage in a nearly contemporary authority which appears to have escaped the attention of all writers on the Templar catastrophe. It throws so much light on the course which affairs took with the Templars, and incidentally on the internal condition of the Castilian monarchy, that I may be pardoned for introducing it here. The "Crónica del Rey Don Fernando Cuarto" (cc. xv., xvi.)[4] informs us that when King Fernando summoned Rodrigo Yañez, the master of Castile, to surrender the Templar castles, the latter in place of obeying went to the queen dowager, Doña María de Molina, and offered to surrender them to her. She consulted Fernando and with his consent agreed to receive them. Yañez appointed a time for the delivery, but in place of keeping his promise negotiated with the Infante Felipe, the king's brother, who was in Galicia in a rebellious frame of mind, and delivered to him the four castles of Ponferrada, Alcañices, San Pedro de la Tarce, and Haro, near Coruña, on condition that Felipe should offer to the king, in the name of the order, that if a regular trial before the bishops should be accorded to them all the castles should be surrendered within fifteen days; but if this were refused then Felipe and the order should make common cause in defence. The royal power in Castile had been hopelessly abased by the troubles of Fernando's minor-

[3] *Memorias*, I, 626.

[4] Rosell, *Crónicas de los Reyes de Castilla*, I, 159-60.

ity; rebellions were frequent, and the Templars, under the protection of a prince of the blood, might not unreasonably hope to maintain themselves, at least until they could make terms. After some delay Doña María went to Leon where Felipe came to meet her; she showed him the papal letters ordering the imprisonment of the Templars and the seizure of their property, and convinced him of his mistake in assuming the protection of excommunicates who were accused of heresy. At the same time she promised that his word should be held good and that Fernando would give them a hearing before the prelates of the realm. Yañez was sent for, and finding himself abandoned empowered Felipe to deliver the four castles, and agreed to surrender the rest. Thus in the absence of the Inquisition the Templars secured a fair trial before the bishops, which resulted in a declaration of their innocence by the council of Salamanca in 1310.[5] Evidently Fernando could not have arrested the Templars in 1307.

It is to be hoped that we may hear further from Dr. Gmelin, and that his thoroughness and assiduity may serve to elucidate many more historical problems.

* * * * *

Reusch, F. Heinrich: *Der Index der verbotenen Bücher. Ein Beitrag zur Kirchen-und Literaturgeschichte.* 2 vols. Bonn, 1883, 1885.
Die Indices Librorum Prohibitorum des sechzehnten Jahrhunderts. Tübingen, 1886.
` Index Librorum Prohibitorum gedruckt zu Parma, 1580, herausgegeben und erläutert.` Bonn, 1889.*

IN THESE days of copious research and still more copious writing it might seem that no positive want of the scholar had been left unfilled and no aid unsupplied. The Roman censorship is an affair of common

---

[5] There is an evident error in the date of a document printed by Benavides (II, 607) in which Fernando grants to the order of Santiago the *derecho de Luctuosa* (certain forfeitures on the death of a vassal) "asi como lo avian fasta aqui el maestro é los freires le la Orden del Temple, por razon que el papa dió sentencia contra los freires del Temple que fuese desecha su orden por merecimiento de cosas muy malas é muy desguisadas que facien contra Dios, en que fueron fallados en culpa. . . . Dada en Burgos, 20 dias de Julio, era de 1346 años" (1308). In July 1308 it is manifestly impossible that Fernando can have spoken of the order as dissolved and its members as found guilty, and can have been distributing its property. As Fernando died September 17, 1312, the grant must have been made in July of that year, after the action of the council of Vienne. In contrast with this is the precaution exhibited in a grant of July 15, 1309, by which Fernando sold to the order of Alcántara certain Templar possessions for one hundred and sixty thousand maravedís; this charter contains a proviso that if the Order of the Temple is restored, or if the pope will not grant its property to the king, the purchase money must be returned before the lands can be reclaimed (Benavides, II, 667).

* From the *English Historical Review*, IV (1889), 781-86.

knowledge, and everyone speaks of the Index as a matter of course. That it contains mines of fabulous wealth to reward investigation, and that its treatment in a thorough and scientific manner would give to students of modern civilisation assistance of the most valuable character, seems to have occurred to no one until Dr. Reusch produced the results of his arduous and well-directed labors.

It would be difficult to exaggerate the worth of these volumes to all who may desire at any moment to trace the details of any of the countless movements which have agitated the spiritual and intellectual life of Europe since the beginning of the sixteenth century—since the uniformity of the Middle Ages was broken by the Lutheran revolt, and the conservatives found themselves obliged to construct dikes to keep out the advancing floods of innovation. It is not that Dr. Reusch has found a store of inedited documents throwing new and unexpected light on the mental development of the last four centuries. It is that with unwearied diligence he has sought in all quarters for everything which elucidates his enormously wide subject, that he has digested his materials compactly, grouped them systematically so that each fact stands in due relation to the rest, and has so arranged them that the inquirer into any episode of religious or literary history coming within its scope finds at once the minute details for which he might otherwise spend months of perhaps fruitless labor. To accomplish such a task as this is to be a benefactor deserving of no common gratitude.

The first work on the list, comprising nearly 1,900 closely printed pages, is the *opus magnum*, to which the others are confirmatory appendixes. These latter give the student the opportunity of verifying for himself the censorship of the sixteenth century, when it developed the principles which have since guided it, and they are valuable to those who desire to recur to the original sources, for the indexes here reprinted are among the rarest of books. The former is indispensable to all students of the interior life of modern Christendom. It is not only the warfare of creeds as represented by Lutherans and Calvinists that is here detailed, but also the perpetually recurring movements in the bosom of the Latin Church itself, and the strife which attended the development of philosophy and science and popular liberties. The first volume of *Der Index* is devoted to the sixteenth century and presents the numerous successive attempts to frame a catalogue of forbidden books from the tentative English list of 1526 to the systematised Indexes of the Congregation of the Index and of the Spanish Inquisition. In this the author is obliged to trace the fate of various pre-Reformation writers—Raymond Lully, Nicholas de Clémanges, Savonarola, Geiler von Kaiserspurg, and others, as well as the curious vicissitudes of Erasmus—and then to treat of the various episodes of the period, such as the prosecution of Carranza, the Italian reformers, Protestant censorship, and many other interesting topics. In the second volume, after a condensed account of the later indexes issued in all Catholic countries, he considers the condemnations and suspensions of books in groups of subjects. These are too numerous to be recapitulated, but the mention of a few will indicate the wide scope of the work and the method of its treatment. We have, for instance, the different schools of Protestant theology, the Protestant jurists, the various phases of the Jewish question, poetry and facetiae, philosophy and science, magic and astrology, history, lives of the saints and Mariology, forgeries, the interminable quarrels of the Jesuits and their downfall, the casuists, the Gallican school, the regalistae, the controversies over moral theology, the Jansenists, Quietism and Fénelon, the strife kindled by the bull *Unigenitus*, the Bible in the vernacular, communists and socialists, animal magnetism and Spiritualism, the Freemasons, and countless others, for the Index touched on all spheres of human activity, and little that was new escaped its condemnation. In the treatment of themes so numerous and so diverse the reader is impressed with the firm grasp which Dr. Reusch has of his subjects in their minutest details, and his faculty of presenting lucidly and concisely the results of his multifarious researches in every field of literature.

If I venture to add a few notes of points which have suggested themselves to me in frequent consultations of the work, it is partly because it is the duty of every student to contribute to the completeness of a book which must long remain the leading authority on its topic, and partly because the triviality of the criticism will serve to show how little there is to criticise.

For the account of the Jesuit father, Juan Bautista Poza (II, 434) and his lifelong struggle with the Roman censorship, Dr. Reusch could have found some interesting material in the "Cartas de Jesuitas," printed in the *Memorial Histórico Español*, volumes XIII-XVIII. The same correspondence would have furnished details for an interesting paragraph on Dr. Juan de Espino, the ex-Carmelite, Poza's chief antagonist, and the untiring enemy of the Jesuits. His fifteen imprisonments by the Inquisition, in punishment of his dauntless succession of pamphlets against Poza and the Society of Jesus, merit more than the passing allusions to him in II, 281, 435. The saintly bishop, Juan de Palafox, says, in 1647 (*Obras*, 1762, XI, 213), that to Espino was chiefly owing the final condemnation in Spain of Poza and the burning of his works; but then Palafox missed his canonisation through the hostility of the society.

We are told (I, 488) that only in the Lisbon Index was Leo Abarbanel's *Dialoghi d'Amore* prohibited *donec corrigatur*, and there is no allusion to the Spanish translations. Yet the Spanish Index of Sotomayor in 1640 prohibits a version of the work with the date of Saragossa 1593, and includes all translations in Castilian and other modern tongues. Small as is the importance of the work, I should be glad to see its bibliography straightened, which Ticknor has rather confused. I have a copy of the first Spanish version by "Guedalla Yahia" (Venice, 1568), dedicated to Philip II, which appears to have escaped notice. According to Ticknor, the translation by Garcilasso Inca de la Vega appeared in Madrid in 1590, and was speedily placed on the Index; but Sotomayor only alludes to the Saragossa edition of 1593, possibly a pirated reprint, for the Castilian *privilegio* did not extend over the dominions of the crowns of Aragon and Navarre. The crime of the book is alleged to be its judaising and Platonising tendency; but its learned dullness might well have saved it.

There appears to be no reference to Francisco de Quevedo, whose works furnish an interesting bit of literary history. In Sotomayor's Index of 1640 (Geneva ed., p. 425) there is a curious entry, permitting his works of edification and suppressing all the rest—the *Sueños*, the *Buscon*, the *Discurso de todos los Diablos*, the *Casa de Locos de Amor*, etc., by which he is best known to modern readers—and this in pursuance of his own request, *no reconociendolos por propios*, probably the only case of the kind in the annals of the Indexes. Yet this prohibition disappears in the *Indice Ultimo* of 1790 (p. 221), where the only entry is his posthumous *Parnaso Español*, to be corrected according to the "Expurgatorio" of 1747.

The reluctance of the censorship to retract any decision once published becomes noteworthy when political or other changes reversed its policy. Such an occasion was the downfall of the Jesuits. The first step leading to the catastrophe was the appointment by Benedict XIV of the Cardinal de Saldanha as *visitador* of the society in Portugal in response to the complaints of King Joseph as to their trading operations. The *visitador* speedily pronounced the complaints justified and suspended the Portuguese Jesuits from preaching and hearing confessions. Hereupon the general, Ricci, addressed, July 31, 1758, a memorial to Clement XIII, complaining of the injustice done to the society: this was referred to the appropriate congregation, and its report, coldly and cruelly justifying the action of Saldanha, was virtually the death knell of the order. In Portugal soon followed the arrest of the unfortunate Malagrida and the expulsion of his brethren. Both the memorial and the report were speedily translated into Spanish and issued in Madrid, where Jesuit influence was still all-powerful. By a decree of the Inquisition, May 13,

1759, their suppression was ordered with such rigor that even those who held licenses to read prohibited books were forbidden to read or possess them. Thus far Dr. Reusch gives us a brief account of the matter; but he omits to notice that after the Jesuits were expelled in 1767, in 1768 the forbidden memorial was again printed in Madrid with a long adverse commentary. This was never placed on the Index, but when the *Indice Ultimo* appeared in 1790 it duly repeated the decree of 1759 with its stern prohibition of the document. In the rapidly shifting scenes of history it was impossible always to be consistent. Thus, in his exceedingly interesting account of the condemnation of the Copernican system, Dr. Reusch might have pointed out a still more unfortunate inconsistency —that Pius VII, in his Index of 1819, continued the prohibition of Galileo's *Dialoghi* (p. 124) and Kepler's *Epitome* (p. 163) only three years before the controversy over the licensing of Settele's *Optics and Astronomy*, in 1822, compelled the curia to permit the teaching of the motion of the earth. Another indication of the same conservatism is the retention in the latest Index (Leo XIII, 1887) of the old general prohibition of all books accusing of heresy or impiety those who deny the Immaculate Conception (*Index*, Innocent XI, 1681, p. 173), although a preliminary note is careful to inform us that the Immaculate Conception was made a dogma of faith by the definition of December 8, 1854.

In connection with the mandate of Leo XII, March 26, 1825, calling the attention of all bishops to the necessity of preserving their flocks from evil books, and authorising them to suppress all such, as their number rendered it impossible to enumerate them all in the Index, Dr. Reusch (II, 882) might have added a reference to Leo's remarkable and urgent instructions, in the constitution *Exultamus*, § 12, December 25, of the same year (*Bullar. Roman. Contin.*, VII, 362), in which he promises the bishops the active sympathy of all Christian monarchs.

To the lists of editions of the Index of Clement VIII (I, 543, II, 23) might be added two now before me—Urbino, 1596, and Piacenza, 1617 —a matter of no moment except for the sake of completeness. In the account (II, 24, nn. 3, 8) of Capiferrea's *Elenchus* of 1632 and the addenda accompanying it, it is described from a copy of Oxford, and is spoken of as "apparently a reprint of the Roman edition"; while the addenda, consisting of the Index of Clement VIII and subsequent decrees up to 1629, are described as to all appearance printed at the same time, and a bad reproduction of the Roman edition. The volume is rather a puzzle, but from an examination of my copy, which tallies precisely with the description of the Oxford one, I have no doubt that the *Elenchus* is the genuine Roman edition, and that the addenda have been merely bound up with it. Had they been printed together, the register would have been continuous, whereas the *Elenchus* ends with a sheet of eight pages, in place of the customary twenty-four, and the Index of Clement VIII commences not only a new paging but a new register. Besides, the watermarks of the two portions, though similar in general design, differ in details.

One subject seems to me to have received inadequate treatment— the issue of licenses to read prohibited books. Numerous scattered allusions to it are to be found, but a comprehensive sketch is lacking, which the exhaustive learning of Dr. Reusch would have rendered exceedingly interesting. The papal policy varied continually in the granting of these licenses, and at intervals all outstanding ones were revoked. At one time all bishops and inquisitors were authorised to issue them, as in the Tridentine rules, iv, vi; then at another we find it specified as a peculiar and limited privilege of the Congregation of the Index that it can grant to its examiners the right to read forbidden books in the strict line of their duty; and then again unlimited right is vested in the Congregation. If all these and other variations had been noted and compared, possibly some explanation might have been deduced from them. Possibly also some light might be thrown on the subject by the sudden and repeated revocations of all licenses such as those by Gregory XV in 1622 and Urban VIII in 1631 (*Bullar. Roman.* [ed. Luxemb.], III, 493, V, 220[1]) which Dr. Reusch does not mention. The latter has interest because it gave occasion to the Spanish Inquisition to assert its independence by solemnly decreeing that the licenses issued by the inquisitor general were not affected, although Urban had expressly excepted only those granted personally by himself. A good deal of matter on the subject is to be gathered from Catalani's book *De Secretario Sacrae Congregationis Indicis*, and possibly the wavering papal policy may only be an indication of the greed of the officials, for these licenses were worth money, and Father Curci tells us (Reusch, II, 1169) that at present a few lire and a certificate from a confessor will procure permission to read all prohibited books, present and future, with the exception of two or three especially obnoxious works.

Probably some error of reference has led Dr. Reusch to speak (I, 72) of the bull *Apostolatus* of Urban IV in 1364 (*Bullar.*, I, 261) as furnishing the model for the earlier forms of the bull *In Coena Domini*, for it is not a bull of anathema, but simply an enlargement of the jurisdiction of the papal chamberlain. The origin of the curses in *In coena Domini*

---

[1] I may here note a typographical error in section 2 of the bull of 1631 as printed in the *Bullarium*, V, 220, col. 2, l. 9 from top, where, on collating it with an original broadside copy of the bull, it appears that *judicibus* has been printed for *indicibus*.

I think may be traced to the Verona decree of Lucius III in 1184 (Lucius III, *Epist.* 171), growing, through general excommunications uttered by Innocent III and Honorius III (Innocent III, *Regest.,* II, 228; Raynald., Annal., ann. 1220, No. 23), to a bull by Gregory IX in 1229 (Raynald., ann. 1229, Nos. 37-41), perfected by Nicholas III in 1280 (*Bullar.,* I, 156), which, allowing for the special grievances of the thirteenth century, would seem to be the progenitor of the famous subsequent anathemas. The synod of Worms in 1610, alluded to in this connexion (I, 77, n. 3), I think ought to be of Ermeland (Warmiensis), and the reference to Hartzheim should be "IX, 384" and not "VIII." Absolute typographical accuracy we all know to be a matter not to be hoped for, however earnestly desired, and while these volumes are surprisingly correct, in view of their multitude of names and dates and citations, the inevitable slips sometimes occur.[2]

All this is microscopic criticism only to be justified by the eminent merits and permanent importance of Dr. Reusch's labors, for it is not too much to say that to the student of culture and civilisation since the Reformation no books will prove more serviceable than these; there are none on his shelves to which he will find himself referring more frequently or with so large a measure of satisfaction.

It were greatly to be wished that Dr. Reusch would supplement his works with one of the same thorough character on the secular censorship of the press—the efforts and devices of governments to limit the freedom of thought and expression. Such a book, written with the exactness and impartiality of his present volumes, would present much curious detail and would teach many valuable lessons. To some extent he has already trenched upon this field when rulers have issued lists of forbidden books, more or less in conjunction with the Roman Index. Censorship, in fact, could only be thoroughly successful when Church and State went hand in hand, and there was an inquisition in working order to enforce effectually their decrees. Great as the influence of the Roman Index has been, its results have been infinitesimal in comparison with what they would have been had the spiritual and secular forces been everywhere conjoined, as they were in Spain and in parts of Italy, to resist the march of ideas and to preserve the faithful from contamination. As it was, in spite of unrelaxing effort, the Holy See was incessantly deploring the constant increase of the pestilence of evil

---

[2] Such errata as have occurred to me are: Vol. I, 368, l. 5 from bottom, "15" should be "25"; p. 596. l. 10 from top, "1439" should be "1539"; p. 615, the reference to Illescas should be p. 593; Vol. II, 247, l. 27 from top, "1651" should be "1652." In the Index to Vol. I, under Carranza, there should be a reference to p. 455. In the Index to Vol. II, p. 1251, there should be a reference to Mercier, p. 917; and on p. 1264, to Fr. de Vargas, p. 196.

books, which multiplied like the heads of the Lernæan hydra, and remained immortal in spite of the anathema. Could the censorship have had its way unchecked, European literature would have been a very different thing from what it is. From Rabelais and Montaigne, from the *Religio Medici* of Sir Thomas Browne and the *Essay on the Understanding* of John Locke, to Voltaire and Rosmini, the list of condemned writers is full of illustrious names of every kind, whose influence has triumphed over the obscurantism that sought to bury them in oblivion. Machiavelli was placed in the first class of authors by the Tridentine Index—those of whom all the works, present and future, are prohibited —and he is still kept there in the 1887 Index of Leo XIII; Urban VIII in 1631 specified him and Charles Dumoulin as the two writers for whom no licenses to read should ever be granted; yet in 1782 a complete edition of his works was issued in Florence, and I presume that few intelligent Catholics at the present day would hesitate to consult them, even though the bull *Apostolicae sedis* of 1869 revived in full vigor the penalties of the obsolete bull *In coena Domini* for all who read forbidden books.

YOUTHFUL SCIENTIFIC WRITINGS

REMARKS UPON AN EXAMINATION OF THE PEROXIDE OF MANGANESE*

[Due to his surroundings, Lea's earliest intellectual interests were in science. His father was the best known malacologist of his day while his brother, M. Carey Lea, two years his senior, later enjoyed an international reputation in the field of photochemistry. In 1839 the two boys were placed in the private student laboratory of Booth and Boyé in Philadelphia to study chemistry, and the younger one's first published work was this analysis of the peroxide of manganese, undertaken at the suggestion of Dr. Booth. The *American Journal of Science and Arts*, in which it appeared, was the leading scientific periodical of the country. At the time of publication the author was only sixteen years old, but already some of his later characteristics as an historian may be seen— his insistence on dealing with original sources of information, his reliance on the results of his own investigations rather than on the conclusions of others, and the urge to put in written form the results of his researches.—H.]

*   *   *   *   *

IT IS OF GREAT IMPORTANCE, both to the practical and theoretical chemist, to have the combinations which the different metals form with the acids, investigated, in order that the proper degree of confidence may be reposed in the various theories which have been formed from time to time by so many celebrated chemists. It is with this view alone that I consider these examinations as worthy of being published, as I unfortunately had not time to pursue them far enough to afford any very definite result. They may however serve to point the way to some one who has sufficient zeal for the science, to carry them out to some more useful end than I could hope to attain. I must here make my acknowledgments to Professor Booth, in whose laboratory, and with whose assistance, these examinations were made.

The peroxide of manganese has never been investigated, as its existence has until lately been questioned by some of the first chemists in Europe, and the tendency of its salts to convert themselves into protosalts, contributed to render it problematical whether it was not merely the protoxide disguised. It can be obtained in various ways, but the most convenient is to calcine the proto-nitrate gently until the nitrous acid ceases to be given off. A less troublesome method is to heat the common black or deutoxide, until part of its oxygen is given off, but this method is uncertain, as too great a heat converts it into the manganoso-

* From the *American Journal of Science and Arts* (Silliman's *Journal*), XLII (1841), 81-87.

manganic oxide, and it is almost impossible to obtain the black oxide free from admixture with iron. When obtained by calcining, its color is of a deep black, and sometimes shining; but when precipitated from a liquid, as the permanganate of potassa, it is of a dark brown. It has sometimes been found native, and is then known to mineralogists under the name of Braunite. It unites with water and forms the hydrate, which may be readily produced by precipitating the hydrated protoxide from a proto-salt, and exposing it to the action of the atmosphere. Obtained in this manner it appears under the form of a brown powder, but, when found native, it is black and crystallizes sometimes in acicular crystals, and sometimes in octahedra, resembling in this state the deut-oxide. The peroxide is composed, according to the calculations of Berzelius, of 43.37 of oxygen to 100 of manganese.

With the different acids it has very various actions; with some it is converted into protoxide, forming proto-salts; while with others it immediately forms per-salts, which seem to have no regular color, some being red, while others are nearly white, brown, or yellowish; a dirty white is however the most usual appearance. I have found it to be the case, that most vegetable acids which convert the peroxide into protoxide by giving off oxygen, when acting upon the deutoxide, will form per-salts by the loss of oxygen. They all contain a very great excess of acid, without the presence of which the peroxide seems incapable of forming any salt. The best test I have met with for distinguishing them from the soluble proto-salts, to which they in appearance bear a great similarity, is the yellow prussiate of potash. With the per-salts it gives a greyish green precipitate, while with the protoxide solutions the precipitate formed is white or whitish pink. The hydrochlorate of platina is also a good test for them, as with them it forms a yellowish precipitate, but with those of the protoxide, it forms none.

Sulphuretted hydrogen.—When this gas is passed over the peroxide placed in a tube, which at the same time is heated, the gas is decomposed, sulphur and water are given off, and the oxide is converted into a sulphuret of a light green color. The gas must be passed over until the tube becomes cool, for if the sulphuret be exposed to the air while hot, it inflames, acting the part of a pyrophorus. When digested in fuming nitric acid, a violent action takes place, the sulphuret is decomposed and converted into a proto-salt, and all the sulphur is precipitated. Analyzed in this manner, it gave 9.6 per cent of sulphur, and when heated in the open air until the sulphur was burnt out and the oxide converted into manganoso-manganic oxide, it yielded 100 per cent of manganoso-manganic oxide, which contains 72.178 per cent of metallic manganese. Now 9.6 of sulphur will combine with 16.51 of manganese, which makes

26.11 per cent of sulphuret. There then remains 55.67 per cent of manganese, which, if considered as manganoso-manganic oxide, would form an oxy-sulphuret, containing

Sulphuret of manganese,   26.110
Manganoso-manganic oxide, 71.893
_____
98.003

Thus in the operation, both the oxide and sulphuretted hydrogen are decomposed. The oxide is partly reduced to manganoso-manganic oxide, and partly to metallic manganese. The sulphur from the sulphuretted hydrogen is mostly driven off, but some of it combines with that part of the oxide which has been converted into the metal, while the oxygen from the oxide, and the hydrogen from the gas, unite and pass off under the form of steam. This oxy-sulphuret very much resembles the substance formed by gently calcining the red sulphuret in a close vessel, (during which operation sulphuretted hydrogen is given off,) but it upon analysis gave but 92.857 per cent of manganoso-manganic oxide, while the first forms 100.

Cyanogen.—When cyanuret of potassium is added to a solution of a per-salt of manganese, the cyanuret is precipitated under the form of an extremely fine greyish green powder, which remains suspended in the liquid for some time.

Sulphuric acid.—The persulphate may be formed by digesting the black oxide in sulphuric acid for several days in the cold, or when peroxide is placed in dilute acid, it is formed in a few hours, but when the peroxide is used, there is a greater excess of acid. This solution is of a beautiful carmine red, but if the oxide be that precipitated from the permanganate of potassa, the solution has somewhat of a violet tinge. It has so great a tendency to convert itself into protosulphate, that it can neither be evaporated nor crystallized, and it cannot be kept for any time, as it is decomposed in the course of two or three weeks. This change may be accelerated by the addition of alcohol.

Sulphate of manganese and potassa.—This salt, which is the manganese-alum, may be formed, according to Mitscherlich, by adding a concentrated solution of sulphate of potassa to one of persulphate of manganese. It crystallizes of a violet brown color, and is decomposed by the addition of water.

If bisulphate of potassa be digested upon deutoxide of manganese, there is a strong action, which results in the formation of a double salt, which, upon evaporating, remains under the form of a somewhat crystalline mass of a dirty white color, and a pleasant acid taste; it reddens litmus paper, and shows the reaction of the peroxide with yellow prussiate of potassa, and does not seem to be decomposed by water; but it is most likely the manganese-alum of Mitscherlich.

Nitric acid.—When nitric acid is digested upon peroxide of manganese, it does not form a per-salt, but the nitrate may be made by adding nitrate of lead to the persulphate of manganese, until they are both neutralized.

Hydrochloric acid.—If this acid be digested upon per or deutoxide of manganese, there is a perchloride formed of a dark brown color, and which decomposes immediately by the application of heat, or in a week or two, in the cold. There then remains protochloride, while chlorine is evolved. When evaporated to dryness, we obtain crystals of protochloride of a fine pink. Dr. John passed chlorine through a solution of three hundred grains of protochloride, dissolved in 12 oz. water, cooled to 41°. The liquid gradually congealed as the operation proceeded, and produced a yellowish crystalline mass, which melted at a temperature a little above 41°. It was decomposed by evaporation.[1] This may only have been the perchloride, surrounded by liquid chlorine, for when I repeated this experiment, at a temperature above 41°, I obtained a yellowish crystalline mass, which, however, on being placed between blotting paper to dry it, proved that a yellow liquid imparted that color to the salt, which itself was pink. I did not however observe that it was decomposed by evaporation.

Sulphurous acid.—This acid has no action upon the peroxide, even when passed over it in a heated tube; and with the deutoxide it forms proto-hypo-sulphate. I do not think that the persulphite can be formed unless by double decomposition with some other salt.

Carbonic acid.—It has no action upon the peroxide, and, as far as I have observed, it cannot be made to combine with it. The brown substance mentioned by Thomson (*Chem. Inor. Bodies*, Vol. II), and formed by decomposing the persulphate of manganese by carbonate of potassa, is most probably an hydrate of one of the oxides.

Phosphoric acid.—When digested upon peroxide, this acid forms a pink solution, giving the per reaction with tests, and which upon evaporation leaves an uncrystallizable pasty mass, of a pink or violet color, which becomes colorless in a short time, most probably by decomposition.

Boracic acid.—The borate can be readily formed by dissolving the peroxide in boracic acid. The solution thus formed by evaporation leaves a whitish crystalline mass, soluble both in nitric and muriatic acid.

[1] Berzelius, *Traité de Chimie*, IV, 170.

Arsenious acid.—When peroxide is digested in arsenious acid, they unite and form a soluble pinkish white salt.

If bi-arsenite of potassa be digested upon peroxide of manganese, it forms a double salt, being arsenite of manganese and potassa.

Chromic acid.—Chromic acid seems to have no action upon the peroxide, but a chromate may be formed by digesting the peroxalate in chromic acid. The solution is of a dark chestnut brown, but it cannot be evaporated or crystallized, as it is decomposed by the application of heat.

Bichromate of potassa has no action upon the deutoxide of manganese.

Oxalic acid.—This acid has a violent effect upon the peroxide. Oxygen is given off, the insoluble protoxalate is precipitated, while a soluble peroxalate remains in solution. By careful evaporation it may be crystallized, but it is very apt to be decomposed, forming an insoluble salt, most probably the protoxalate. It dissolves in muriatic and nitric acid. It was analyzed by dissolving and precipitating the oxalic acid by chloride of calcium; while another portion was calcined and converted into manganoso-manganic oxide. Treated in this manner it showed 27.4348 per cent of oxalic acid, and 8.5 of manganoso-manganic oxide = 11.73 of peroxide. This leaves a very large percentage for water of crystallization. Thus

Oxalic acid,	27.4348
Peroxide of manganese,	11.7300
Water and loss,	60.8352
	————
	100.0000

The 11.73 of oxide requires very nearly 16.0 of oxalic acid; which leaves 11.4348 of free acid, so that this salt, in common with the others, possesses a great excess of acid.

If binoxalate of potassa be digested upon the deutoxide of manganese, in the cold, a pink colored solution is formed, which by standing becomes yellow, letting fall a pink powder. If the solution of the binoxalate be hot, the action is very violent, and the resulting solution is yellow. By evaporation it leaves a crystalline, almost tasteless mass, partly white and partly green, and which is readily dissolved in water.

Acetic acid.—Glacial acetic acid does not form a per-salt when digested on peroxide of manganese.

Tartaric acid.—If this acid be digested upon peroxide, oxygen is given off and the prototartrate is formed. But if we dissolve deutoxide instead of peroxide, a pertartrate results, which on being evaporated leaves the salt of a light yellow or straw color.

Bitartrate of potassa, particularly if warm, dissolves the deutoxide of manganese with considerable energy, at the same time evolving oxygen and forming a tartrate of manganese and potassa, which is a highly crystalline brownish mass, of hardly any flavor, and soluble both in nitric and hydrochloric acids.

Benzoic acid.—When benzoic acid is boiled with peroxide of manganese, there is a benzoate formed, slightly soluble in water. Thus obtained, it is a dirty white substance, of a crystalline appearance.

Succinic acid.—This acid forms a protosuccinate when digested upon peroxide, but with the deutoxide, it, like tartaric acid, forms a per-salt, which is soluble in water, of a whitish color, crystalline and very acid.

Racemic acid.—This like the last forms a per-salt with the deutoxide, and a proto-salt with the peroxide. The resulting solution, by evaporation, leaves the salt somewhat crystalline, whitish brown, and quite acid.

Citric acid.—With citric acid, both the per and deutoxide act as towards the last. The percitrate obtained from the deutoxide is a brown, gummy, seemingly uncrystallizable mass, of a pleasant acid taste, slightly deliquescent, and is soluble, although not very readily, in both nitric and muriatic acids.

Gallic acid.—The pergallate of manganese may be obtained by dissolving the peroxide in gallic acid. The solution thus obtained is of a deep brown color, and the salt obtained by evaporation is nearly black. It does not appear to crystallize.

These are all the acids, of which I have been able to note the action with the per or deutoxide of manganese. I have followed Berzelius in calling peroxide, that one which might perhaps be more correctly termed sesquioxide, as its formula is Mn, but as it is very similar to the analogous oxide of iron, also termed peroxide, and as it is the highest oxide of manganese which forms combinations with acids, it seems best to apply the term of peroxide to this, and super or binoxide to the black oxide of commerce.

If time should favor me, I propose to pursue the above subject, as it is probable that much remains to be determined, concerning the compounds of manganese, before we can say with propriety that we are acquainted with the metal.

DESCRIPTION OF SOME NEW SPECIES OF MARINE SHELLS INHABITING THE COAST OF THE UNITED STATES*

[Between the ages of sixteen and twenty-three Lea devoted his spare time to the study of conchology, and during that time published seven papers in scientific journals in which he identified and described two new genera and 133 new species of mollusks. An eighth paper, prepared in collaboration with his father and in which one new genus and fifty-one new species of fresh water shells were identified, was published in the *Proceedings of the London Zoological Society* in 1850. For the next few years ill-health forced him to confine his working hours to the publishing business, in which he became a junior partner in 1851. As a relaxation from business, however, he spent his evenings reading the medieval French chronicles and the interest thus aroused turned his attention permanently from science to history.—H.]

*   *   *   *   *

Pholas Semicostata

P. testâ sub-triangulari, posticè productâ et acutâ, anticè obliquè truncatâ, tenui, albidâ, diaphanâ, anticè inflatâ et costatâ; costis transversalibus, muricatis, magnis, crebris, posticè obsoletis; sulco uno longitudinali, a natibus decurrente; margine basali curvato; margine dorsali vix recto; natibus valde inflatis; laminâ dorsali parvâ; cochleâ ligulatâ, acutissimâ, incurvâ. Long. .17. Lat. .32. Diam. .16 poll.

Hab. South Carolina.

Remarks. The transverse ribs are rather large, very regular, and distant from each other about their own width. They are muricate, or covered with small, arched scales, from the anterior margin to the longitudinal sulcus, when they suddenly become smooth, and soon after disappear. The rest of the shell has a few small, transverse lines of growth scattered irregularly over its surface. The outline of the shell is somewhat that of an acute-angled triangle, having the anterior margin for the base, and the posterior end for the apex. The beaks are very much inflated and incurved; the dorsal plate is very small, and formed by the bending back of a portion of the dorsal margin, with no cells underneath. The cochlea is ligulate, with the axis perpendicular, appearing very acute when viewed from above. About one-half of the area of the shell, extending from the beak nearly to the basal margin, and from the anterior margin a little more than one-half to the posterior end, is

* From the *Boston Journal of Natural History*, V (1845-47), 285-90. Abstract published in its *Proceedings*, I (1844), 204-05.

somewhat incrassated, and raised above the surrounding surface. To this part are confined the costæ and sulcus, and it presents the appearance of a secondary shell. Anteriorly, its margin is sinuous, which causes a similar bending of the ribs. The rest of the shell is nearly smooth, very thin, and diaphanous.

This curious little species I found among some shells sent to my father many years since, from South Carolina. It has not the most distant relationship to any of its congeners as yet described in this country. Although it might seem to be an immature shell, from its small size and extreme thinness, yet, from the peculiarity of its growth, being centrally incrassated from the outside, I am inclined to think that it had reached its full period.

Bulla Biplicata

B. testâ cylindricâ, sub-quadratâ, crassâ, albidâ, politâ, eburneâ; spirâ occultâ; anfractu ultimo supernè calloso, infernè striis transversis parvis; aperturâ supernè arctatâ, infernè ovatâ; columellâ plico magno et parvo. Long. .15. Lat. .07 poll.

Hab. Shore of New Jersey, near Cape May.

Remarks. The striæ on the base are small and insignificant. The columella has a large oblique fold, about one-fourth the length of the shell from the base; below this, it takes an undulation, scarcely deserving the name of a fold, and descends suddenly to join the outer lip. The columella is continuous posteriorly, and, above, it widens out into a callus at the region of the spire, where it turns round, and is produced into the outer lip. The substance of the shell is thick, smooth, and ivory-like.

There is no danger of confounding this little shell with any of the genus in the United States. The two folds at once distinguish it, and it is the only species with an occulted spire and plicate columella.

Littorina Lunata

L. testâ quadrangulari, imperforatâ, crassâ, costatâ, lutescente vel brunneâ; spirâ elevatâ, conicâ, acutâ; suturis inconspicuis; anfractibus quatuor, planis, costis transversis magnis, crebris; anfractu ultimo angulato, usque ad basim costato; aperturâ obliquè ellipticâ; labio acuto, undulato; columellâ infernè latissimâ, planâ. Long. .07. Lat. .05 poll.

Hab. Coast of New Jersey, near Cape May.

Remarks. The general outline of the shell is remarkably quadrilateral, almost rhomboidal. The whorls are flat, and covered with numerous revolving costæ, which are much smaller on the base of the last whorl. The outer lip is very sharp, and with a waved edge caused by the exterior costæ. For a short distance inside, there are sulci, corresponding to the ribs. The thickening of the columella commences about halfway from the top of the mouth, and continues round the base towards the outer lip, forming a broad, crescent-shaped area, which is very remarkable. The substance of the shell is exceedingly thick. The color is mostly brown, turning to yellowish where the thinning of the outer lip commences.

I met with a number of these pretty little shells among the interstices of a stone overrun with *Serpulæ*, found at Cape May. I was at first tempted to suppose it the young of some other species; but it has all the characteristics of a mature shell, in the thickness of the substance, number of whorls, broad columella, etc. I know of no species with which it could be confounded.

Cingula Robusta

C. testâ ovato-acuminatâ, perforatâ, lævi, crassâ, albâ; spirâ brevi, subacutâ; suturis impressis; anfractibus quinque, ad suturam superiorem subangulatis; anfractu ultimo rotundo; basi lævi; perforatione arctatâ; profundâ; aperturâ ovatâ, magnâ. Long. .10. Lat. .07 poll.

Hab. Cape May, N. J.

Remarks. The substance of this little shell is quite thick and stout. The surface is occasionally slightly wrinkled by minute lines of growth. The whorls are five in number, increase rapidly in size, and have a small angle, or shoulder, immediately at the superior suture, which has thence the appearance of being deeper than it is in reality. The mouth is large, ovate, acute above, and rounded below, with a sharp outer lip, and continuous posteriorly. The inner lip, indeed, is almost separated from the last whorl by the umbilicus, which is long, narrow, and profound.

This little shell I found on the beach at Cape May, and though I obtained but a single specimen, yet I feel no hesitation in pronouncing it distinct from any species hitherto described. In outline it is not unlike immature specimens of the C. *minuta*, (Turbo *minutus*, Totten) but differs from it entirely in the thicker substance, more robust form, and the separation of the columella from the preceding whorl. In color, too, they are essentially different.

C. Modesta

C. testâ ovatâ, imperforatâ, lævi, tenui, diaphanâ, virido-corneâ; spirâ brevi, ovatâ, haud acutâ; suturis parvis; anfractibus quatuor, planulatis; anfractu ultimo rotundato; basi lævi; aperturâ ovatâ, supernè acutâ, infernè rotundatâ. Long. .12. Lat. .05 poll.

Hab. Long Island, near Brooklyn.

Remarks. The spire varies somewhat as to length in different specimens. The whole shell is of a uniform dark greenish horn-color. There is a slight depression about the umbilical region, but in no specimens that I have examined does it amount to a perforation. The whorls are but slightly convex, and the sutures small, which gives the shell a very regular appearance. The margins of the mouth are united over the last whorl by a very thin plate of calcareous matter, which in some specimens is almost obsolete.

This little shell appears to be quite common on the shores of Long Island, just below Brooklyn, where I found it clinging to the under surface of stones below high water mark. It approaches the C. *minuta*, but is easily distinguished by the absence of the umbilicus, and by its dark color, besides the flatter whorls and regular spire.

C. Turriculus

C. testâ elevato-conicâ, perforatâ, lævi, crassâ, fulvâ; spirâ valdè exsertâ, conicâ, obtusâ; suturis parvis; anfractibus sex, convexis; anfractu ultimo subbullato; perforatione parvâ, arctatâ, lunatâ; aperturâ ovatâ; columellâ crassâ, anfractu ultimo pene disjunctâ. Long. .12. Lat. .05 poll.

Hab. South Carolina.

Remarks. The substance of the shell is very thick and calcareous. Color, a light yellowish tawny, sometimes approaching to white. The surface is occasionally somewhat wrinkled with lines of growth. The spire is elevated, and composed of about six convex whorls. The columella is thick, and somewhat raised above the surface of the last whorl.

This shell I obtained, together with the *Pholas semicostata*. It differs essentially from all its congeners on this coast. Perhaps the *Cingula aculeus*, Gould, is its nearest analogue, but there can be no danger of their being confounded.

LIST OF ARTICLES

LIST OF ARTICLES LATER INCORPORATED IN LEA'S HISTORICAL WORKS

CANONICAL COMPURGATION AND THE WAGER OF BATTLE

The North American Review, LXXXVIII (1859), 1-51 (in the form of a review of L. J. Königswarter's *Études historiques sur le développement de la société humaine*). See *Superstition and Force* (Philadelphia, 1866), chaps. i and ii.

JUDICIAL ORDEALS

The North American Review, LXXXIX (1859), 32-98 (in the form of a review of Du Cange's *Glossarium Mediae et Infimae Latinitatis*). See *Superstition and Force*, chap. iii.

TEMPORAL POWER OF THE CHURCH

The North American Review, XCII (1861), 416-65 (in the form of a review of Milman's *History of Latin Christianity*). See *Studies in Church History* (Philadelphia, 1869), essay 1, "The Rise of the Temporal Power."

THE EARLY CHURCH AND SLAVERY

The North American Review, C (1865), 21-53 (in the form of a review of J. P. Thompson's *Christianity and Emancipation* and J. Yanoski's *De l'abolition de l'esclavage ancien au moyen âge*). See *Studies in Church History* (2d ed., Philadelphia, 1885), essay 4, "The Early Church and Slavery."

CONFISCATION FOR HERESY

English Historical Review, II (1887), 235-89. See *History of the Inquisition of the Middle Ages* (New York, 1888), I, chap. xiii.

THE MARTYRDOM OF SAN PEDRO ARBUÉS

Papers of the American Historical Association, III (1889), 435-53. See *History of the Inquisition of Spain* (New York, 1906), I, 243-58.

BRIANDA DE BARDAXÍ

Atlantic Monthly, LXIII (1889), 261-67. See *Chapters from the Religious History of Spain* (Philadelphia, 1890), 469-79.

EL SANTO NIÑO DE LA GUARDIA

English Historical Review, IV (1889), 229-50. See *Chapters from the Religious History of Spain*, 437-68.

INDULGENCES IN SPAIN

Papers of the American Society of Church History, I (1889), 129-71.

See *History of Auricular Confession and Indulgences* (Philadelphia, 1896), III, 412-36.

THE ENDEMONIADAS OF QUERÉTARO

Journal of American Folk Lore, III (1890), 33-38. See *Chapters from the Religious History of Spain*, 423-36.

A COLONIAL INQUISITOR

Atlantic Monthly, LXVIII (1891), 186-90. See *The Inquisition in the Spanish Dependencies* (New York, 1908), 491-99.

PHILOSOPHICAL SIN

International Journal of Ethics, V (1895), 324-39. See *History of Auricular Confession and Indulgences*, II, 254-58.

THE FIRST CASTILIAN INQUISITOR

American Historical Review, I (1895-96), 46-50. See *History of the Inquisition of Spain*, I, 145-54.

FERRAND MARTÍNEZ AND THE MASSACRE OF 1391

American Historical Review, I (1895-96), 209-25. See *History of the Inquisition of Spain*, I, 101-10.

LUCERO THE INQUISITOR

American Historical Review, II (1896-97), 611-26. See *History of the Inquisition of Spain*, I, 189-211.

HIDALGO AND MORELOS

American Historical Review, IV (1898-99), 636-51. See *Inquisition in the Spanish Dependencies*, 276-97.

MOLINOS AND THE ITALIAN MYSTICS

American Historical Review, XI (1905-06), 243-62. See *History of the Inquisition of Spain*, IV, 42-62.

FINIS